Dedication

To all who insist on understanding

—not perfectly, but better

THE
HUMAN
AGENDA

INTERNATIONAL COLLEGE
19 70
IN VESTIGIIS INSTITUTORUM ANTIQUORUM

The Guild of Tutors Press
LOS ANGELES

How To Be

at Home

in the Universe-

without Magic

—Roderic Gorney, M.D., Ph.D.

PRINTING HISTORY:
Simon & Schuster edition published April 1972
Psychology Today, Book-of-the-Month Club edition
published October 1972
POPULAR PSYCHOLOGY *Magazine edition published November 1972*
Bantam edition published April 1973
Guild of Tutors edition published March 1979

ISBN 0-89615-014-3
Library of Congress Catalog Card Number: 78-75233
Manufactured in the United States of America

Thanks are due the following for permission to include certain excerpts:

Academic Press, Inc., New York: from *Cognitive Consistency, Motivational Antecedents and Behavioral Consequence*, Dr. Aronson.

American Anthropological Association, Washington, D.C.: from "Synergy: Some Notes of Ruth Benedict" by J. Honigmann and A. Maslow, in *American Anthropologist*, Vol. 72, No. 2, 1970.

Atheneum Publishers, Inc., New York: from *Human Aggression* by Anthony Storr, copyright © 1968 by Anthony Storr.

Doubleday & Company, Inc., New York: from "What Is Real" in *The Velveteen Rabbit* by Margery Williams.

Holt, Rinehart and Winston, Inc., New York: from *The Effect of Unemployment upon the Status of the Man in 59 Families* by the Institute for Social Research.

Journal of Individual Psychology, Vermont: from "Synergy in the Society and in the Individual" by Abraham Maslow, 1964.

The Macmillan Company, New York: from *The Control of Human Heredity and Evolution* by J. Sonneborn; and "For Anne Gregory," from *Collected Poems* by William Butler Yeats, copyright 1933 by Macmillan, renewed 1961 by Bertha G. Yeats.

Routledge & Kegan Paul Ltd., London: from *The Origins of Love and Hate* by Ian D. Suttie.

Charles Scribner's Sons, New York: from *This Side of Paradise* by F. Scott Fitzgerald.

Foreword

This book fulfills a vital function. Some books abstractly discuss only the future of the universe, the solar system, the earth, life, and humankind. *The Human Agenda* boldy attempts also to integrate the experiences of daily life in a way that is helpful to the reader in sorting out many of today's bewildering complexities. And it does this without reliance on anything mystical.

This accomplishment is especially precious in a time when bizarre and malignant fanaticisms are embraced everywhere as a substitute for thought. It is precisely in showing with good will and wit how we can survive humanely, without the support of such paralyzing dogmas, that Gorney has answered a key need of our time.

It is in this spirit that I welcome this third edition of *The Human Agenda*.

Alvin Toffler

Preface to 1979 Edition

Seven years after publication, this book has gone out of print in both hardcover and mass paperback editions (Simon & Schuster, Inc., 1972; Bantam Books, Inc., 1973). Meanwhile, demand for copies from teachers and students in schools, colleges, and universities (as well as from general readers) has continued to spread. Hence this high-quality but low-cost new edition.

I had hoped to completely update the book, but there just hasn't been time. It remains true, however, that much of the detail offered here is intended mainly as illustration of a way to tie divergent threads of daily experience into a coherent strand of understanding. For that purpose, exactitude in detail is irrelevant. The general direction of evolution is discernible despite minor blurrings of its image.

Nevertheless, there are a few points which must be made.

First, the word "abundance" has proved to be a stumbling block. I meant by it not the dripping luxury it connotes to many people but merely the opposite of scarcity. Therefore, please read "abundance" as more like "sufficiency."

The word "mankind" I would now replace with "humankind," for obvious reasons. I regret that the importance of such a subtle substitution was not clear to me when the book was set in type.

Finally, though the text of the present edition is a facsimile of the original hardcover version, the book bears a new subtitle. It was suggested by a thirteen-year-old boy soon after the book first came out. He called me on a phone-in TV program.

"You're telling people the wrong thing about your book," he said.

"What should I tell them?"

"Tell them that *The Human Agenda* is a manual on how to be at home in the universe without magic."

I wish I'd thought of that.

Roderic Gorney
January, 1979

Prologue

Thought is born of failure.

—LANCELOT LAW WHYTE[1]

The development of this thought world is in a certain sense a continuous flight from wonder.

—ALBERT EINSTEIN[2]

1)

This is the most marvelous moment of man in which to be alive.

Neither blindness nor optimism underlies this judgment. For the first time in our two million or more years we have the possibility of enough to go around. Although destitution still torments us, scarcity *could* be replaced at last by abundance as the central condition of human life.

The new condition promises more than a sufficiency of *things*. Although we may shortsightedly reject the opportunity, for the first time the future promises that all human beings may look forward to a fully human life, the right to explore, to be, and to become potentially whatever they desire.

Yet everywhere there is spreading fear that man cannot survive the *by-products* of abundance. I believe that this blight of hope springs from two seemingly contradictory causes:

1) Concern that we do not have the material resources or cooperativeness to neutralize in time such hazards as war, overpopulation, poverty, pollution, and injustice;

2) Concern that we *do* have these capabilities and will use them, and will therefore soon find ourselves living in a world in which our preferences, plans, and goals, which grow out of scarcity—in effect, our values—will have become obsolete.

Whereas we are conscious of our fear of annihilation, most of us as yet are *unconscious* of our *fear that we may survive*. This anxiety I believe to be the major obstacle to resolution of the threats that imperil us. Powerful people among us are so terrorized unconsciously at finding themselves cast adrift in paradise without a map, without the guiding star of scarcity to tell them what is right or wrong, good or bad, worthwhile or worth nothing, that they—again unconsciously—would prefer extinction. Dedicated to preserving yesterday, they are tempted to wipe out the experiment of man and throw away the victory that belongs to us all.

But while their power to destroy remains strong, their power to persuade or coerce others to a suicidal course is waning. Each passing day sows realization that misery is becoming optional and survival a matter of choice.*

Cooperation is the law of life. Appearing first as the tendency of individual cells to thrive in clusters, and later to revitalize one another by exchanging genetic material, cooperation has been elaborated by higher species, through a series of intervening steps, into love.

Cooperation is also the most deeply rooted theme running through the success of man. This is demonstrated by the enormous adaptive strength in adulthood we derive from prolonged dependent weakness during infancy and childhood. This is demonstrated by the confidence with which we eat food prepared by total strangers, accelerate without looking when the light turns green, and relax trustingly beneath the knife of a surgeon we may barely have met. This is demonstrated by our efficient collaboration in control of epidemics and disasters, supervision of peaceful commerce, and a beginning of arms control.

Despite assertions that man is hereditarily programmed for murder, even in our highly competitive, violent, crowded, industrialized society which fosters accident, crime, and war, almost all two hundred million of us live out our pressured lives without becoming the victims or the perpetrators of serious physical injury. Our ultimate safety depends only upon enlarging the circles of helpful cooperation one last step to encompass our largest units, the nations.

Man's specific tool for adaptation and survival is, in my view, the evolution of values. That which works in helping us survive becomes a "value." Values gradually are integrated into complex adaptations we call value systems. Value systems develop momentum of their own and then enhance or impair our ability to adapt to new conditions.

Up to now the rate of change in our lives has been slow enough to permit the processes of evolution of values to remain automatic and therefore largely unconscious. Today the rate of change we now produce in the conditions of our lives is too swift for the processes of spontaneous evolution of values to keep up. For the first time in two million years we

---

* This of course refers not to control by one individual over his own circumstances, but to a choice by mankind as a whole. And of course, while providing enough for everyone, we must learn to stop exhausting our common resources in order to survive as a species.

must learn to exercise a new freedom—the option to *choose* our values *consciously*.

But no one today is equipped for such responsibility. There was at least one Aristotle. There was at least one Leonardo. Although being a universal mind was of little practical importance, in classical Greece and Renaissance Italy a single exceptional mind could span the wisdom then accumulated.

Today it has become impossible for any mind to encompass the available knowledge, while ironically it is becoming indispensable for every mind to do so. The time when we could leave our survival to specialists is past. The responsibilities of citizenship in a democracy, which soon will include voting on genetic manipulation, weather control, and interplanetary relations, require us all to be competent generalists. In writing this book I may have carried to extremes he never intended a favorite teacher's idea that the psychiatrist is the true general practitioner.

2)

I am a physician, a psychiatrist, and a psychoanalyst. Ten years ago puzzlement over failure of ordinary theory to account fully for some motivations of patients started me wondering about the broader significance of *values*. And it was apparently unrelated incidents from my practice, such as the three that follow, that started me thinking about the *adaptive implications* of values.

"It's immoral!" Thus a middle-aged industrialist refused a union demand for a thirty-hour week. He preferred to automate his plant "rather than turn my employees into a bunch of lazy bums." Warned of the economic and emotional dislocation of a whole community that would result from sudden massive disemployment he replied, "That's no concern of mine."

There was a ghastly fascination in his total unawareness of any moral problem in causing the destitution of the same thousands he felt obligated to protect from the depravity of the six-hour day. Connected in some way then obscure to me was his righteous insistence that we should atom-bomb the Russians and Chinese even if it meant the whole world's incineration.

A young man "humiliated" by seeing his psychiatrist drive an old car inquired why I did so.
"Because I enjoy it."
"You enjoy it! What difference does *that* make!"

My uncommon self-revelation proved useful. It helped us clarify how, for him, in emulation of his mother, "things" had lost their primary meaning as sources of satisfaction and had become merely magic amulets for winning the approval of others.

A patient preoccupied with making money told me an ancient but pertinent joke. Crates of imported herring are passed along in a series of transactions from one friend to another, each time at a profit. The last man eats some. The next day he phones his supplier.

"Hey, what did you do to me? That herring tastes like cardboard!"

"You didn't *eat* that herring, Ed!"

"Yes, of course I ate it. Why?"

"Ed, that herring is not for *eating*. It's for *buying* and *selling!*"

What determines attitudes toward new automation and old cars? What determines attitudes toward herring as food versus herring as commodity? In each instance it must be the circumstances, psychological and otherwise, that instruct us as to their use and worth in a particular society.

What I was observing here was one aspect of the process of evolution and transmission of values among individuals. Because an industrialist and his father before him had found it necessary to work twice as long, permitting employees to work a thirty-hour week was immoral, although throwing them out of work altogether was not. Because a young man had been carefully taught that his personal worth resided in his possessions, he was robbed of the capacity to enjoy things for themselves. Because scarcity has for so long transformed the significance of food in most societies from sustenance to profit, cardboard herring is "valuable." I began to see that the psychiatrist is forced to consider his patient's values because they embody not only the residue of the patient's early experience, but the direction given his behavior by realities and judgments common to his *culture*.

Thus concern about individual patients and their values led to questions about people in groups, communities, and nations, and how they survive or die. And so I was led to restudy the evolution of man, then that of his closest animal relatives, and finally the long chain of living creatures and inanimate events that preceded them. Because I am not a professional naturalist, biologist, evolutionist, astronomer, or historian, it has been necessary to explore intensively. Darwin, Spencer, Hubble, Hegel, McLuhan, Feuerbach, Marx, Suttie, Teilhard de Chardin, Lorenz, Montagu, Fromm, Ellul, Rieff, Lifton, and Marcuse are but a few of the thinkers I tried to comprehend and relate to one another and to my observations, all in the hope of understanding better the adaptations that make man what he is, including the cultural values that make him *who* he is.

Malcolm Muggeridge, after being elaborately introduced to an audience, once remarked, "Now that I know who I am, I can hardly wait to hear what I'm going to say."[3] It seems to me that this book was written partly because I wanted to find out who I am. And in contrast to Muggeridge, I've learned that there is no way to know fully who I am *until* I hear what I'm going to say.

As a busy person learns the customs of his culture, the facts taught in his schools, the skills needed in his profession, he may grow into adult responsibility knowing almost nothing about himself. He can learn something about those elements of his early individual emotional development we designate as "unconscious" through a personal psychoanalysis. For example, he can learn how, in terms of his own individual development, it can become a moral issue whether or not to reduce drudgery below seven hours a day, and a moral irrelevancy to eliminate it entirely.

However, he may also have learned nothing about the origins of even his *conscious* mind. Upon investigation he may not only find unsuspected intellectual forefathers (in my case the Talmud, Omar Khayyam, and—on the eve of publication—R. Buckminster Fuller), but also be astonished that ideas he thought general are considered by colleagues to be original with him.

More fundamentally, he may remain unacquainted with the implications of the long procession of events and creatures from whom he, and all of us, acquired our bodies and minds, our right- and left-sidedness, upright stance, dextrous hand, binocular vision, and ability to remember and respond. He may never know or understand the significance of the fact that during his womb sleep he once had rudiments of gills of remote fish predecessors. He may never consider what it means to be a member of the only species capable of highly developed imaginative fantasy and critical judgment. He may never know the import of the wish for love that shadows him from birth to earth.

In sum, especially if he is like me, and not that rare genius who somehow without strain can draw into his mind and synthesize the volumes most of us never even read, he may never come to know himself in any wider perspective than as an individual person. If he does devote himself to learning more about himself, to finding out what he thinks and why he thinks it, he may be astounded to encounter his antecedents in evolutionary principle gracing the galaxies, his genetic forebears scattered throughout the geologic layers, and his intellectual ancestors strewn across the many cultures which sprouted great minds to loose new sparks into old darkness.

Shaken by the bewildering rapidity of changes in our world and lives to which we must somehow adapt, we all suffer from some degree of what Toffler calls "future shock."[4] Like everyone else, I've been troubled about where we are going. By reconnoitering, at first tentatively and then purposefully, the range of human wisdom, I tried to grasp thereby what is on "the human agenda."

An agenda is a plan that organizes a series of matters to be dealt with in sequence later. As I heard myself using the metaphor, it became plain that it implies no necessary conscious or unconscious *intent*, but only that earlier events predispose to others later. A child's terror at a narrow escape from drowning may enter upon the agenda of his middle age a permanent dread of closely approaching any large body of water.

The metaphor applies to widening circles beyond the individual human being. The upright posture of early man entered a hernia operation on the agenda of many a modern person's later years. One might also think of similar agendas of life, and of the larger inanimate bodies. Clumping of nerve cells into the head end of worms placed the complex brain on the agenda of mammals. Incandescence of the sun helped inscribe earthly life on a later page of the agenda of the solar system, and so on.

3)

The Human Agenda, then, is an exploration of the evolution of values which examines the relationship of the long past to problems of the present, and to the challenge of finding a viable way into the future. It is divided into four major sections. The first traces evolution in general, out of which human evolution in particular has arisen, mostly amid conditions of scarcity. In the second the characteristics of human love, work, and play up to the present are examined, and projected into the future as they may be transformed by conditions of abundance. The third appraises a number of alternative themes for value systems of the future and illustrates them out of trends presently observable. And the fourth section sums up some implications of this panorama.

As well as examining the processes that have produced the universe, the book traces man's quest for understanding of them, and in particular one person's struggle to synthesize from a rational view of evolution a concept of the direction in which values must be guided to assure man's survival. In attempting such a task I am reminded of Churchill's appraisal of Clement Attlee, "He is a very modest man. And with reason."[5]

Although I have tried to harmonize and relate its various themes, the record of such an exploration cannot be reduced to a completely consistent and simple linear explanation without doing violence both to objective truth and to the story of the pilgrimage. Therefore my camera traverses the same ground more than once from different angles, in order to disclose a new perspective with each pass.

The Human Agenda is more of a spiral staircase than a fireman's ladder, more a poetic evocation of reality than a college outline depicting it. To see what I have seen, the reader will sometimes have to shift lenses with me, review an intriguing point with me, and occasionally look past me at the landscape when my own image becomes a distraction.

Traditionally the specialist, and the professor in particular, has confined his public pronouncements to his specialized field. I have presumed to trespass far beyond the boundaries of my academic credential. Although I regret any errors or omissions, exactitude in detail for its own sake is irrelevant. The general direction of evolution is discernible despite minor blurrings of its image. Sometimes "facts get in the way of truth." And on the human agenda there are no truths, let alone facts, that are complete, final, and unassailable.

I am satisfied if this book indicates a way of looking at things from many points on their circumference, and of using all one's resources in understanding them.

As abundance and cooperation become transcendent, we must focus on the current items on the human agenda, attainment of international peace, as well as cures for injustice, poverty, pollution, and overpopulation.

But simultaneously we must consider the item *after* next on the human agenda—*how to live without panic in the world of peace and plenty,* bereft of the firm guidelines of traditional values which, under the weight of new conditions to which they are not adaptive, are already sinking into functional obsolescence. This feat demands that we use our new freedom promptly to devise new values pertinent to new realities. It was in the hope of fostering this development that this book was written.

Well may we wonder at the failure of our values, and take flight into thought. For if thought is born of wonder and failure, it likewise gives birth to understanding—and success.

Acknowledgments

The content and implications of thought become conscious only as they are unearthed in words. While writing I've often had an experience sculptors report, the feeling of excavating a preformed object rather than creating it as the work proceeds. First appreciation must go to my parents and their friends, who during my childhood ignited an enduring romance with language. I must mention also a few of the many others whose influence is represented in what has been laid bare verbally in these pages.

Our family physician, Dr. A. L. Goldwater, first exemplified for me the physician as individual and social healer. Decades later he shared his office and the pleasure of my first practice with me.

Barney Girden, a summer camp director, introduced his charges to an endless array of fascinations, from hypnosis and polarization of light to the effects on the abdominal wall of man's upright posture. As we lolled on pine needles, firelight dwindled, and stars hung in branches, he would conclude an explanation of the massive mysteries of the universe with the correct prediction, "Let these sights, sounds, smells, and thoughts way into your minds, and you'll always have them in memory." And as we struggled sleepily to bed he somehow managed to convince us of the possibility and necessity of carrying on "stronger at the finish" despite exhaustion. Forty years later he dismisses his impact upon me with the diffident surmise that he probably had a chance to influence young kids when they were most impressionable.

Later came my own agemates, with whom I treasured the American Museum of Natural History, explored Death Valley, and learned to relish being young in Los Angeles. Along the way came more good experiences with grownups, some complete strangers, such as the eighty-four-year-old man who one day at a soda fountain gave me his prize-winning pigeons. Then there was Miss Phillips, the sixth-grade teacher from whom I learned to make clay tablets, papyrus paper, and parchment scrolls, and Mr. Gram, the carpenter who helped me build a replica of Gutenberg's movable-type printing press. There was Charles Wright, who taught me to speak publicly in English, and Victor Seine, from whom I learned to think privately in Spanish. There was Dr. Lowell Frost, the former psychiatrist who surmounted a brain injury to become my high school's favorite biology teacher. And Leona and Ernst Wolff, both physicians, who during my youth encouraged my intellectual interests and made their family my supplementary parents and siblings. In particular I must mention all those who contributed to my medical education, which marvelous stimulus to curiosity for me turns every garden snail, every technical innovation, every value judgment, and every day into an adventure.

From hundreds of patients, acquaintances, and strangers have come some of the most worthwhile clues to unfamiliar pages of the human agenda. All of these have made me one of the most fortunate of human beings.

During the years of writing many students and colleagues have helped through critical reviews of chapters. Foremost among the latter are Professors Elof Carlson and Ashley Montagu, who read critically the entire manuscript, as did also Professors Barrows Dunham, Martin Grotjahn, and Judd Marmor. Professors Andrea Tyree and Thomas Wolff contributed valuable information and suggestions.

Financial assistance in completing the manuscript was provided by anonymous donors to the Human Agenda Research Fund. Participants in the UCLA Faculty Lecture Series entitled "The Human Agenda: Biological Prospects and Human Values," which I organized and moderated in the spring of 1966, are due my special thanks for valuable ideas (credited in the footnotes), as are the staff of the *UCLA Law Review*, wherein appeared an earlier version of "The New Biology and the Future of Man." Much appreciated is the generous assistance of the editor and staff of the *American Journal of Psychiatry*, which published a portion of chapter 4 under the title "Interpersonal Intensity, Competition, and Synergy: Determinants of Achievement, Aggression, and Mental Illness" (October, 1971). Also due my thanks for their sympathetic encouragement are members of the UCLA School of Medicine's Department of Psychiatry (particularly its chairman, Dr. Louis Jolyon West) and of the UCLA School of Social Welfare.

Over the years I have had the good fortune of help by a series of excellent research assistants: Kathryn Miller, Day Dobbert, Bruce Williams, Scott Kaufer, John McDonald, George Garrett, and Gary Steele, who has not only brought the bibliography, footnotes, and index to final completion, but during two arduous years has contributed many valuable ideas to the text. Sherri Butterfield devotedly copy-edited the entire book. Amelia Girden helped edit the final text. Jean Anderson provided invaluable aid in preparing the manuscript.—R. G.

Contents

SECTION THREE: MASTERY OF THE FUTURE

Part I: Ways to Go

Part II: The Quest for Blondness: An Example Explored

SECTION FOUR: CONCLUSIONS — 555

SECTION ONE

EVOLUTIONARY
PERSPECTIVES

Part I

Man in Evolution/ Evolution in Man

1 Universe and God

Thirteen billion years ago thermonuclear blast vaporized the original ball of matter. Fiery gases spewed in all directions at the temperature of atomic fusion. The universe was born. Time began. And with it, the cosmic agenda.[1]

Within the first half hour were formed the myriad miniature universes of the atomic elements. After a quarter million years of expansion and cooling, the tugging cords of mutual magnetic attraction at last overcame the declining energy that had maintained the particles' even dispersion.

In some places the now chilled particles drew together into turbulent clouds of gas and dust, thus emptying others. Cooling and condensing, solidifying and impacting, they fell together into larger and heavier masses. Evolving through billions of light-years of black space, the clouds clustered into billions of isolated spinning galaxies, including our Milky Way.

Ten billion years ago, as the particles in its larger clouds crushed inward with sufficient gravitational force to reignite nuclear combustion, the Milky Way began forming more than one hundred and fifty billion stars. Thereafter the universe was lighted and warmed again near each radiant sphere. From then on gravity was helped to sweep even distant particles into larger masses by the frail force of faraway starlight.

In this fashion, five billion years ago the center of a whirling disk-shaped cloud at the edge of the Milky Way contracted into an incandescent hub, a medium-sized star we call the sun. Smaller clusters circling in the web of its gravity condensed into the planets. One became our earth, mother of life, midwife of the human agenda.

The universe goes on expanding, its galaxies still rushing apart at enormous speeds. If the velocities imparted to matter at the moment of the initial explosion were sufficient to cause the galaxies to escape the backward pull upon them, the expansion will continue forever. If not, eventually the elastic bands of gravity will tug with a force equal to and then in excess of centrifugal force. The huge systems will slow and come to a halt. Then, dragged back toward each other at increasing speeds, the galaxies eventually will crash again into the original ball. And, until next time, time will end.

Some see it differently. The outer galaxies are rushing apart, but not as the aftermath of an explosion. They are driven by the force of new matter entering already occupied space. Between galaxies new hydrogen atoms are always being made out of nothing. Floating in space the new atoms coalesce by stages into new galaxies, replacing those displaced. The universe never had a "big bang" birth. It will go on being created eternally. So we cannot date its birth and need not anticipate its death.

In this century we take for granted that rival theories of the origin and structure of the entire universe can be debated in peaceful good fellowship. Only a little yesterday ago they could not.

Even as to the behavior of the animals, plants, rocks, and streams in his immediate vicinity, early man was too vulnerable for objectivity. His survival depended upon divining the right explanation of means to command their spirits, and then enforcing conformity within a little band of his own kind to the required rituals and taboos.

When he came to ponder the more awesome problem of the relationship between earth and sun, man was no better prepared for detached reflection. For even in the earliest times, long before astronomy became a science, observations of the celestial bodies were of critical importance to human survival. Daily the movements of the sun brought the fluctuating safety and danger of its light and heat. Monthly the new moon piled up the flood tide on which the coastal fisherman might float or founder. Motions of the stars could forewarn the canny of the hunger of frozen snows and the thirst of parched summers. They taught the patient planter to foresee nurturing spring rains, and sow his hoarded seed in time for reaping in the fall. They guided the wise wanderer in his pursuit of caribou and climate. And they abandoned the dull-witted to extinction.

Achieving safety on earth under conditions of severe scarcity has almost always been at the top of the human agenda. Rarely was there enough food, shelter, or knowledge to go around. Beginning perhaps two million years ago, man gazed aloft and thought in order to understand. If only he could have stopped there!

But in his desperate helplessness he also *bowed* and *worshiped* in order to *control*.

Man invented stories to explain the changes he could observe but not comprehend. Then, based on these fancies, he devised complex schemes with which to convince himself he was master of what he could not fathom.

But why did he waste his feeble efforts coaxing the skies when he was in constant peril from dangers below?

It was precisely his powerlessness against threats on the ground that made him invent powerful friends in the sky. While man could never be certain of help from above, it was often certain that there was none to be had on earth. And it was to be thousands of thousands of years before some human beings could begin to accept that there are phenomena, even lethal ones, which at the time they cannot grasp or govern. Such acceptance of reality is born of an outer and inner security still denied to millions.

Terrified early man dreaded the danger of nighttime darkness. So when shopping for a god, naturally he selected the sun. Drawing on the lessons of his infancy, he treated the sun as a superpowerful parent in the hope of learning how to induce it to supply the sustenance he needed. Because, like his human counterpart, the sun-father was often out of earshot, the suppliant shifted from the magic of crying to that of conjuring. His panicky concern with survival drove him out of babyhood dependence on mother into childhood devotion to father. And into the comforting conclusion that father sun-god had little to do but rush endlessly about him and his earth, rewarding and punishing him for his goodness and badness.

Because the sun, and his court of moon and stars, seemed to revolve around his platform, it was reassuring for the boy-man to decide that he and the flat earth stood still at the center of all. Thus his constant jeopardy and insignificance on earth were compensated for by his secure and eternal consequence on high.

As man moved into the light of civilizations no more than ten thousand years ago, he probed more deeply into the heavenly mysteries. Ancient Mesopotamian priests recorded the celestial movements and roughly foretold the lunar eclipses they could not grasp. About the same time the ancient Chinese did the same, and in the New World the Mayas devised a calendar superior in some ways to our own.

Not all the faiths that developed kept the sun as the main god, but dominant religions everywhere needed to believe, and therefore taught as established truth, that earth and man were the hub of the heavens. Ancient priests defended belief in their mechanically rigged stone idols (that moved and talked to awe people) no more rigorously than they did the doctrine of the earth's centrality. Both kinds of beliefs were felt to be essential to securing man's precarious livelihood, as well as to keeping the faithful in line and maintaining the flow of offerings.

Ceaseless toil remained the price of a full stomach and a warm bed. So man's nose was kept to the grindstone, and his mind to the "godstone," by the nearly universal conditions of scarcity.

Although man cannot think objectively in the midst of emergency, to discover truth, including truth about the solar system, had been on the human agenda from the beginning. After a few thousand more years, improved technique and good luck gradually brought abundance to a few places. Here and there it created tiny islands of leisure in the sea of drudgery. One such was the small community of full-time thinkers in Greece during the fifth century B.C.

It is no accident that the first minds to find essential pieces of the truth about the solar system did so among Greece's favored olive trees. For in addition to abundance they possessed the crucial tool: geometry. In 600 B.C. Thales taught that the earth was round. Two centuries later the followers of Pythagoras declared it was spherical, and even that it was not fixed but moved through space. But such was their persisting need for mystic security that they had to invent an invisible "anti-earth" to increase to the "perfect" number, ten, the nine circularly moving bodies of which they knew.

In his youth Plato had imagined the sun as a divine fiery chariot driven across the skies as required by priestly dogma. As secure decades of study brought him more information, he decided, instructed by the curved shape of the earth's shadow on the moon during a lunar eclipse, that the earth was not flat but round.

Although he maintained the earth's fixed centrality, other evidence eventually convinced Plato that the earth both rotates on an axis and revolves in an orbit. And toward the end of his life he had become so emancipated from self-deceptions that, according to Plutarch, he even regretted locating the earth at the center of the universe since that place should be reserved for "something more worthy." Having concurred with Plato's earlier advances, Aristotle rejected his brilliant intellectual swan song. A century later, for teaching such ideas as Plato's, Aristarchus incurred the hostility of contemporaries. They grumblingly suggested that he be censured for impiety, an offense that was at times punishable by blinding with hot irons. Thus has the man of vision often been dealt with when people are threatened by his investigation of the next step on the human agenda.

But from his misty beginnings, the pondering primate pushed ahead to understand and master whatever there was to know. Driven as much by his evolutionary inheritance as by his dependence, never was he long dissuaded from the search.

In the last few thousand years, man has learned how to protect himself from most dangers on earth with knowledge instead of magic. Supernatural help in daily life has been needed less as man's power has increased. But he has continued to dread death and the erasure of his identity. Thus the main focus of religion gradually has shifted from achieving temporary survival in this world to ensuring permanent salvation in the next, from the here and now to the hereafter. However, even in creating this new assurance of man's importance, religion had to build on his concrete old insistence that he is central in the universe.

The emotionally precious view of earth's centrality in a fixed, unchanging universe was crystallized by Ptolemy in the second century A.D., and then taken over by the Christian church. What had been ancient pagan punishments for contradicting pagan theology became orthodox Christian punishments for questioning orthodox Christian dogma. Despite man's continued secret probing, fourteen centuries brought no serious challenge.

Ironically, it was a Catholic priest who next had the leisure and inclination to unravel this solar security blanket. In 1543 at the end of his life Copernicus hesitantly published his view, which concurred with Plato's as to the earth's movement and also located the sun at the center of the solar system. In 1600 Giordano Bruno taught Copernicus' theory, and was burned alive for his temerity.

In 1604 Galileo used the appearance of a new star in the constellation Serpentarious to show that the universe changes. A few years later his telescopes brought evidence confirming the Copernican theory. Panic-stricken churchmen brought Galileo before the Inquisition with the dreaded epithets "atheist" and "heretic." Ill and alone at seventy, imprisoned and probably under the threat of torture, Galileo kneeled and publicly recanted. Thus ended his attempts to bring to the parliament of the mind a matter too long tabled by the terrified.

Lest this all seem remote, consider that it was not until the time of Newton that even Protestants openly accepted the sun's centrality. It was not until 1835 that Popes ceased to dignify with their "infallibility" the dogma that the earth is the center of the solar system. Only in 1870, a century ago, was infallibility restricted to matters of faith and morals so that future Popes would not be tempted to forbid the earth to move or the universe to go about any of the rest of its regular business. And it is only now, some four hundred years after his brilliant mind ceased to be troubled by truth or tormentors, that the shamefaced inheritors of the

institution that condemned Galileo have preposterously considered re-
trying and "exonerating" him, thus belatedly bringing authority into conformity with fact.[2]

How could a different idea concerning celestial movement have so
threatened defenders of the faith? The Inquisition's inferno of words
clarified its devotion to flames: "If earth is a planet, and only one among
several planets, it cannot be that any such great things have been done
specially for it as Christian doctrine teaches. If there are other planets,
since God makes nothing in vain, they must be inhabited; but how can
their inhabitants be descended from Adam? How can they trace their
origin to Noah's ark? How can they have been redeemed by the Saviour?"
The astronomer's "pretended discovery vitiates the whole Christian plan
of salvation" and "casts suspicion on the doctrine of incarnation; in short
it upsets the whole basis of theology." Incredible though it seems, the
doctrine of the sun's central position was denounced as "of all heresies
the most abominable, the most pernicious, the most scandalous" (H. Smith,
pp. 312–313).

The reaction of churchmen sprang from the same danger as has faced
all authoritarians before or since, that the workings of the human mind
will show their doctrines to be false. If a priest (or king) does not really
represent God, if a dictator is not the instrument of mystic destiny, he is
apt to be overwhelmed by despair from within if not overthrown by
rebellion from without. Moreover, the whole way of thinking and living,
actually the pattern of adaptation for survival of an entire society, is in
danger of being swept away in the tide of new understanding.

In an oversimplified way, one could say that the whole sequence we have
examined here came about and continues in other areas because of *man's
panicky need for certainty*. We need to feel certain of understanding a
problem so that we can take action to avert catastrophe. So we spin hypotheses into dogmas under pressure of emergency. The perception of the
problem, as well as its proposed resolution, may be truly irrelevant to our
current real needs. Even worse, they may be arrived at so prematurely
that they freeze the thought of later generations for whom the problem
may have real relevance and possibility of solution.

For example, let us imagine how primitive man shivered and cowered
in the cold dark nights in the wilds. He needed a nighttime substitute for
the cheering sun, a replacement for its warmth and its protection from the
occasional prowling predator willing to attack sleeping man under cover
of darkness. Often he must have felt the glow of flames kindled in the
forest by lightning during the fearsome nights. Often he must have seen
the most ferocious animals retreat in terror from the hot glare. He needed
to learn to command the power of the fire within his reach. But how many

generations must he have invested instead in fruitless efforts to cajole the remote sun?

We can only guess how much time early man may have wasted devising fantasies to explain the sun's inconvenient daily disappearances, to compel its return, and to bolster his shaky but reassuring belief in his own importance. But it seems plain that beyond forcing him to spend lifetimes needlessly in chilled wretchedness, these fictions based on maladaptive value judgments set a booby trap for his remote descendants.

For example, by the time long-range ships and navigation were developed, their use was impeded by fixed erroneous ideas about the sun's rotation around a central flat earth, off the edge of which man could sail into an abyss. Had primitive man decided earlier simply to master fire and to leave cosmology to later generations equipped to study it, subsequent history could have been much different. Without the burden of prying off layers of venerable superstition, his successors might have recognized earth's roundness, rotation on its axis, and revolution about the sun thousands of years sooner. And with earlier mastery over the aspects of light and dark that specifically complicated his life, man might have avoided making the related irrelevant value judgment, which causes such trouble today, of tenaciously associating light with "good" and dark with "bad" in general.

It is too much to ask that early man should have been able to foresee this sort of thing. *But is it too much to ask that we do so?*

At the threshold of space travel, it is paradoxical but true that today it is urgent for us to understand the mechanics of the universe and yet we feel relaxed about it. How astonishing it is that in these few centuries we have become so strong! Not only have we been able to give up the dogma of earth's centrality, but we have permitted Albert Einstein, in safety if not instant popularity, to overthrow the rational gospel according to Newton as well as the scripture of common sense. Four hundred years ago it was worth your life to say the earth revolves about the sun. Today you can claim that matter and energy are two forms of the same thing, that space is curved and, together with time, comprises a four-dimensional continuum, that the shortest distance between two points is not necessarily a straight line, that when transported at high speeds a yardstick shortens and a clock slows.

Why wasn't Einstein burned? Because, for one thing, progress is so much more rapid now than in Copernicus' day that the practical uses of Einstein's ideas became evident quickly. But there is a more important reason. Our attitude toward the value of "progress," and its role in our lives, is fundamentally changed. In the past, although human beings struggled desperately to achieve it, progress toward abundance was considered irrelevant to the soul, which was considered the essence of man. Now that we at least behave as though we regarded the essence of man to be his earthly potential, progress toward abundance is considered indispens- able. Because people have been so delighted with the increasing power progress has brought them in the past century, fewer and fewer of them have been preoccupied with their power hereafter.

Through the successes of new science and technology, powerful leaders today are better able to protect themselves against all dangers than were the despots of long ago. They can preserve their privileges better by inducing cooperation with their *economy* in this life than their counter- parts in the past could be enforcing submission to their *theology* concern- ing the next. Einstein's work furthered this change by laying the basis for placing in their already potent hands a new tool of undreamed-of force, nuclear energy, with its mastery of the power of the sun.

With nuclear energy, one can create without end or destroy without limit. With this tool leaders feel they can really dominate their reality, even including all other people. In this fashion, largely forsaking man's intervening central preoccupation with eternity, we have ironically re- turned to something resembling early man's absorption with daily life. With such magic at your command, what need have you for Newton's physics, or common sense, or even the hereafter?

What need have you for a sun god, or even a son of God, if you have become God of the sun?

Apparently plenty. Because when it comes to *values*, to deciding in which ways the new tools are to be used, so many people still revert to their old patterns. They show the same old disdain for observation and thinking. In the face of anxiety about the uncertain future, people every- where still hunger for proof by revelation or authoritarian pronouncement. Whether an argument concerns what to do about capitalism, communism, social upheaval, drugs, love, sex, or adolescents, there is too often evident on every side the same stifling demand for premature certainty as formerly was concentrated on disputes over genesis.

We must learn that, despite out newfound nuclear brawn,* often we still cannot satisfy our old wish for instant certainty with unambiguous and reliable answers to our questions. Until evidence is complete, the uni- verse, like the Oracle of Delphi, may respond only with a flat "maybe." That would have been its reply five billion years ago to a query as to whether or not among its fellows in our solar system planet Earth would someday be in a unique position to contribute something new to evolution.

But four and a half billion years ago its testimony became an emphatic "yes."

*[Third Edition, 1979] Obviously, nothing said here about nuclear energy is meant as an endorsement of the *wisdom* or *safety* of the use of nuclear energy.

2 Earth and Life

The Solar System

The turbulent spinning cloud on the outskirts of the Milky Way destined to become the sun and planets carried more than the material stuff of our solar system.[1] In the drift of each atom, in the collision of every particle, came a compelling inheritance. For eight billion years, the galaxies had swirled away from each other in its grasp. This inheritance was bequeathed also to our sun and its planets. All, including earth, home of our hopes, have developed within the imperative of our cosmic legacy, *evolutionary change*.

At some critical moment within the evolving, churning cloud, the substance at the center began to collapse inward upon itself. Perhaps the first particle collections were pushed together by the pressure of invisible faint light from a distant star. Then gravity drew in more and more, and became the dominant force.

Meanwhile, bits of matter circling in the outer layers of the cloud were stuck together by the same forces to form the planets. Ninety-nine percent of the cloud's mass was swept into the sun, and 1 percent into the revolving planets tethered to it. Like its parent cloud, the sun rotated counterclockwise and revolved in a counterclockwise orbit. So did the earth and most of the planets. Like a spinning skater pulling in her arms, most whirled faster on their axes as their mass condensed.

And so the enormous amount of work of condensing a cloud into sun and planets, and then settling them into orbits, was performed with the expenditure of energy long present in the universe. Once sounded, the music of the spheres would play on over nearly infinite reaches of time without further work.

All this took place in darkness.

Then within the sun and its planets, heavier elements sank to form

their cores. Compression raised their temperatures, and all began to radiate. The greater mass of the sun drove its temperature still higher until
at a threshold point it became incandescent. It shone still brighter as
nuclear fusion reactions ignited, bathing the solar system in radiated
light. Streams of ions evaporated from the sun's surface, scouring earth
and the other inner planets free of their helium and hydrogen gas envelopes. Over several hundred million years, radiant heat also boiled away
into space most of their solid mass, leaving the warm but barren inner
planets, including earth, encircled by the gas-enclosed outer planets.

The Earth

As it spun through more hundreds of millions of years, the earth steadily
became hotter. Only a part of its increasing temperature was due to energy
from the sun. The rest of the heat was generated by gravity through the
compression of its substance, and by decomposition of its radioactive elements. Scattered iron and nickel deposits sank into the central core. The
lighter mantle layer, composed mainly of olive green silicates, was laid
down, enveloping the core. On top of the mantle eventually floated the
crust, the surface of our familiar world. Today, the core and mantle each
comprise about half the earth's 8,000-mile diameter, while the crust which
precariously sustains our lives varies in thickness from thirty miles to only
a few thousand feet.

In growing its clothing crust and atmosphere, the naked early earth
over millions of years passed through complex processes as yet incompletely understood. Trapped gases escaped through cracks in the mantle,
while upwelling convections of heat exploded as volcanoes, and spewed
gases, steam, water, and molten lava over its outer layer. As the surface
cooled, water vapor clouds precipitated as windy torrents of rain. Rivers
ran off the new-formed lava, joining volcanic water in hollows as the beginnings of oceans, and starting the process of erosion which to this day
chews away the mountains into fertile valleys, often then dissolving their
rich soil and our poor dreams in the seas. Huge land masses formed, accumulated from lava above and churnings, warpings, crumblings, and
heapings below. Their great weight caused some to sink deeper into the
supporting mantle while others rose. Great ice caps grew at the poles,
advanced and retreated in waves, alternately sinking and releasing the
bouyant crust beneath them. Glaciers plowed and pulverized the surfaces
they traversed. Oceans came to cover nearly three-fourths of the crust,
separating continents which communicated intermittently by land
bridges, and probably have meandered away from their birthplaces.

Having only one-eightieth of the earth's mass, the moon could not generate as much of the inner heat and upheaval that would so many times completely transform its dominant neighbor. For the same reason, it could not release or retain an atmosphere. No water vapor could cling to cloud its sky, fill its "seas," or ice its poles. No oxygen could moderate the sun's radiation and the 250-degree centigrade temperature swings from day to night. No climate or weather changes could bring rain, wind, or glacier to erode its surface.

In contrast with the busy earth, the moon has circled through its billions of years almost unchanged, recording little more in its craters than the impact of countless meteors. As a result of the earth's gravity, the one face the moon shows us bulges toward us massively. But the protrusion is disproportionately large. Why? The excess curvature measures the greater force exerted by the earth when the two bodies were warmer, softer, and closer. Because of the earth's rotation, the moon's tidal pull raises and drops our oceans and continents every day. But the tidal pull of the earth on the moon was frozen into a static contour as it cooled and hardened long ago. Since then it has been receding from us at the rate of four inches every new moon.

Earth and moon impart an extra wobble to one another's course as they orbit the sun tied together like a lopsided dumbbell. But they do more than this. They mutely herald the difference in fate determined by a difference at birth. They proclaim the degree to which the futures of even inanimate bodies moving in space are limited by the unfolding of the provisions of their advance agendas.

Earth became, for its volume, the heaviest planet, placing portentous possibilities on the geologic agenda. For one, its relatively great mass and gravity allowed the earth to capture and retain the moon as by far the largest planetary satellite in our system (relative to the size of its companion).

Thus earth acquired nightly moonlight. But more crucial even than the light atmosphere of love, earth's gravity guaranteed the abundant accumulation over time of the heavy atmosphere of life.

Evolution

Nonlife

At the threshold of a new epoch, let us pause to take stock. As we traced in compressed outline the development of the universe, the solar system, and the earth, we followed at successive levels the imperative of the cosmos, evolutionary change. Although in different directions and at different rates, everything everywhere must change. And it must change within limits determined in advance by preceding stages of a kind of program that we can think of as an agenda. Without inventing an explanation of "who" inscribed it or "why," within the limits of our present knowledge we can discern the direction and pace of the changes to be expected.

So far, we have focused on the inorganic life of celestial bodies floating in space. Whether it be an atom, a planet, a star, or a galaxy, each has a birth, an evolving life span, and a death, and each may leave relics that linger as fossils. The microuniverse of a radioactive atom, wrenched apart, may give up energy as well as orbiting particles, its inactive remnant thereafter being as quiescent as a mummy. The "dead" planet is another example. Mars may be dying only in the limited sense that the life that may once have flourished on it may be on its way to extinction. A planet may also be dead in the sense that it has hit a dead end in its evolution. For instance, Mercury, unlike earth, appears to be both too close to the sun and too small to retain an atmosphere productive of weather, climate, and erosion, and so may be incapable of an extended life of change. Our own middle-aged sun in hundreds of billions of years will have become a shrunken cinder, as inert as the corpse of uranium we call lead.

Within any phase of its existence, the fate of any body may be altered by events originating outside itself. The external forces that molded the planets and bowled them into different orbits around the sun created *spontaneous variations* among them, thus inscribing into their agendas crucial differences determining their individual lives and longevities. Some became warmer and some cooler. Some retained a hydrogen atmosphere while others did not. One developed diffuse rings while others acquired discrete moons and still others no satellites at all. The asteroid belt may be a planet that never coalesced, dying before birth without achieving individual identity, or it may be the remnants of a planet that was drawn and quartered by gravitational force from Jupiter, or one that was dispatched in youth by collision with another planet or a comet, which scattered its bones in the sea of space. In the course of evolutionary change, these variations were operated upon by *natural selection* to bring about planetary survival or extinction.

What justification have we for projecting outward upon the "inanimate" universe ideas that Darwin and Wallace intended a century ago only as an explanation of the evolution of living things?

The principles of evolutionary change through natural selection among spontaneous variations describe how some living things survive while others do not. External factors result in individuals with a wide range of different characteristics. Some of these prove advantageous or "adaptive" and therefore enhance probabilities for survival. Other variations prove disadvantageous for survival, or even lethal. The question of which is which is answered through interaction with the environment.

Doesn't the same hold true for everything from atoms to stars to galaxies? By colliding with a fellow, any of these may lose its identity. On the other hand, provided that its velocity is sufficient, an atom, star, or galaxy that falls into the gravitational field of another may circle away unscathed, surviving an otherwise fatal encounter. Thus we have glimpsed how—although in distinctly different orders of time, magnitude, and mechanism—*life* is linked into continuity with everything above and below it in the universe by the unifying principle of evolutionary change.

Admittedly, halfway between atom and star, there is something wondrous added to the process of evolution by the entity we call life. This new factor both speeds the process of change and deflects the emphasis of survival from the *individual* to the *kind*. It also superimposes upon earlier modes of adaptation to inorganic change in the surroundings a *new* dimension of evolution through natural selection. We must focus upon it.

Life

The gases belched into the sky by earth's early volcanoes consisted primarily of water vapor. Small quantities of nitrogen, carbon dioxide, chlorine, hydrogen sulfide, carbon monoxide, methane, and ammonia were present, as were traces of other gases, but no oxygen. This steamy atmospheric mixture coated the primitive crust and irregular bodies of water.

The various gases accumulated in shallow pools dissolved in the rains that filled them from above and in the hot springs that fed and warmed them from within the earth. Cosmic rays, intense sunlight, electrical storms, streams of electrons from the decay of radioactive material, and volcanic heat all bombarded the primitive landscape. These energies, acting upon the gases, synthesized amino acids and other complex molecules. From the amino acids were formed the basic building blocks of all life, the organic proteins. Other molecules were transformed into nucleotides. Nucleotides became the components of the special molecules of *living cellular inheritance*, DNA (deoxyribose nucleic acid) and RNA (ribose nucleic acid). Somewhere in a warm tidepool, in the presence of an extra influence as yet unknown, these chemicals wrapped themselves in a membrane envelope and sent a chain letter to the future.

Earth was now a billion years old. It had taken that long to form and stock the warm lagoons with rich concentrations of amino acids, sugars, and other compounds. Molecules of these substances could be formed near the surface of the water under the influence of ultraviolet light. But the same wavelengths would have destroyed the nucleic acids and proteins of actual living substance then constructed of these building blocks. So, after formation, the amino acids and sugars would have had to sink to safer depths. Thirty or forty feet below the surface, their integration into the nucleic acids and proteins of life could be accomplished where only nonlethal energies penetrate. At this level, sometime during a brief few millions of years, intense but noninjurious radiant energy assembled the raw ingredients into a coherent whole, the first living cell.

The conditions of all the steps toward life are fairly well known, except this last one. For all but the final synthesis have been reproduced by electrical apparatus acting upon liquids in the glass containers of our laboratories. Some nutrient chemicals have even been observed to form and enclose themselves in cell-like membranes in the presence of heat alone.

The Cell and Reproduction

The first living cell—what were its characteristics? Although much simpler, it could perform all the most fundamental functions of today's cells. It was "irritable," or responsive to stimuli, it could perform work by extracting and transforming energy from an external source, and it could make copies of itself. It could form a membrane of fat and protein separating its internal and external environments, but selectively permeable to outgoing wastes and incoming nutrients. Because the waters of its birth were so much more nutritious than any since, our primal microbic ancestor could live more simply than its descendants. It had no need to manufacture many of the essential compounds living creatures today must synthesize for themselves. It could absorb not only sugars and amino acids, but also adenosine triphosphate, the source of energy for building nutrients into its own larger molecules.

However, within its own delicate skin it would produce the more complex substances required to build and sustain its body, such as proteins, fats, and enzymes. Yet in the absence of free oxygen, energy for the cell's use could be released from these materials only by the inefficient process of fermentation, with the attendant production of waste carbon dioxide and alcohols.

After reaching a certain size it must then have performed for the first time the most crucial function of life: *reproduction.* By dividing itself into two daughter cells, the first cell began a sequence of events that added a new dimension to natural selection and to evolution.

Still it is difficult for us to articulate what specifically had been added. After all, some atoms, planets, stars, and galaxies may grow by incorporating material from the environment, and even break up into smaller different fragments. But they do not regularly reach a certain size, and then reproduce a new generation that will in turn grow to maturity and do the same. Moreover, unless interfered with (or in rare instances exploded from within), they continue to follow the movements imparted to them from without, and experience passively any changes later imposed upon them. They do not initiate new movements *in adaptation to or anticipation of* collisions or other external catastrophes. Besides, the distribution of bodies in the universe is sparse compared with the distribution of living creatures on earth. Therefore the chances of one celestial body having to "compete" with another for *Lebensraum* are several hundred thousand times smaller.

Then too, certain lifeless crystals sometimes will reproduce themselves. Crystals of salt dropped into a heated saturated solution of sodium chloride will propagate identical crystals throughout the solution. Somehow, the crystal acts as a model that the molecules in solution imitate. Because the characteristics of the parent are always copied identically in the daughter crystals, there is no evolutionary change in successive generations. In living organisms, evolutionary change depends upon "genetic" reproduction, in which *slight errors* occur in the copying of parental hereditary information into the offspring. These changes are the "mutations" that produce spontaneous variations between generations of living organisms. It is upon these slight inheritable differences that natural selection operates to bring about survival or extinction of a particular line.

No one knew the cause of these variations at the time of the investigations by Darwin and Wallace. They nevertheless made the invaluable discovery that the bewildering profusion of complex living forms could be accounted for as a progressive evolution from simpler forms based upon the "survival value" of these variations. Over enormous reaches of time and numbers of generations, some of the variations proved to be helpful in adapting to constantly changing environmental conditions, while others did not. Those individual organisms that had the beneficial variations were more often able to reproduce than those that did not.

Viruses present a borderline case. Composed only of proteins, in their dormant state they do not seem to be alive in that they do not need a source of energy to survive, do not metabolically release energy by decomposing complex substances into simpler ones, and do not grow or reproduce. Yet they will spring to life when in contact with suitable living cells, invading through their host's cell membranes to destroy first the cell nuclei. In the process, they reproduce themselves in astronomic numbers, apparently by changing the code of the host's protein to match their own, thus turning the cell's own substance into enemies that attack from within. In this process, radiation or other influences may cause changes in the virus protein structure which sometimes result in major alterations in its characteristics that are transmitted to later generations.

What was the crucial invention of genetic reproduction? It was the development of the chemical DNA, which contains the code whereby a cell produces offspring like itself, including any mutations it has sustained. The cell can and does reproduce *without* invading the membrane of a host or calling upon the host's living machinery in the process. Of course, a dividing cell might require the substances produced by another cell, and might even kill the other cell in order to metabolize its components. But it duplicates its DNA code independently *within its own boundary,* giving to each daughter cell a copy of the manual that guided the thousands of chemical transformations of its metabolic processes. In this fashion each daughter cell and all its descendants are modeled after the original.

Survival, Species, Genes, and Values

Thus life transformed evolution. For the first time, what mainly counted in survival was not the future of a single entity, but that of its *offspring.* Survival now hung not on the fate of the fragile individual, but on the durability of his *species.* Whether the withering dandelion casting its seeds on the breeze, the senile salmon straining toward its ancestral spawning grounds to breed and die, or the wounded mother bear risking her life to defend her cubs from man—all of the million species that have contended on earth have struggled to survive by passing the special freight of their spark to progeny.

The essentials of this process, which began within that simple bacteria-like first cell, continue in every reproducing cell today. Packed into its central nucleus (in man) are forty-six chromosomes. Each is a package containing a compressed spiral chain of DNA hundreds of times the length of the cell. Along this chain are arranged the genes, the DNA molecules that set the hereditary limits within which environment determines the individual's actual characteristics. Enzyme molecules skim along the chains of genes, transcribing their codes at 30,000 messages a second into

RNA molecules. These RNA messengers rush the information to the outer portions of the cell where newly arrived amino acids and other molecules are waiting to be built into the cell as proteins. Some of these proteins, in the form of enzymes, in turn help form other cell components such as fats and carbohydrates.

These raw materials are hustled to various parts of the cell, some to the nucleus where the DNA thread is splitting lengthwise. There other molecules hook into proper sequences the nucleotides needed to make two perfect replicas of the DNA thread. But not *exactly* perfect.

X-rays and cosmic rays knife constantly through the cell, like the magician's swords that ordinarily do not harm his assistant inside the box. Once every 100,000 gene copies, however, a vagrant ray may deflect the genetic pen, and the code message is changed by this accident. Each such change in the message brings about at least a minute change, or mutation, in the hereditary characteristics of the offspring. For, as the cell membrane pinches inward between them, the two intertwined spirals of DNA are winched apart and deposited in each of the two daughter cells.

In thus arranging reproduction so long ago, life borrowed and transmitted to us three principles from the legacy of the inorganic universe:

1) The tendency to continue to exist and move through a preprogrammed life cycle, which appears in living creatures as the struggle for survival;
2) The tendency to conserve established patterns, which appears in living creatures as the hereditary transmission of most of the characteristics of previous generations to their offspring;
3) The tendency to innovative change through spontaneous variation, which appears in living creatures as the inventions brought about by inheritable mutations.

Even more, in thus arranging reproductions so long ago, life laid down the kernel of its _central values_. These might be expressed as: *survival, through preservation of the wisdom of the past, amid constant revolutionary whittling away at its roots.*

Evolution of Metabolism

Fermentation

In the quiet depths of the warm pools 3.5 billion years ago, the primitive single-celled creatures reproduced rapidly but evolved slowly. Their inefficient metabolic process depended on fermentation of nutrients absorbed from the water. It produced so little energy that larger or more vigorous organisms could not have survived. Just what adaptations these pioneer microbes developed in the course of life's agenda we may never know, for their bodies were so fragile as to have mostly disappeared without a trace.

It is essential to recognize that at this initial stage *cooperation* became life's crucial survival technique, thereafter outdistancing competition in survival significance everywhere and always. Until we return to this topic later, one example must suffice: one-celled plants or animals co-operate by providing one another favorable conditions, so that they grow and reproduce more rapidly when their population reaches a certain optimum density than when only a few organisms are present.

The numbers of organisms using energy finally exceeded the pace at which spontaneous chemical reactions could replenish their usual nourishment. Some weakened and disappeared, while others became equipped by chance mutations over many generations to utilize different organic substances. Some cells learned to attach themselves to others that had died and became the first scavengers. Others consumed cells that were still living and became the first parasites. Like many bacteria and fungi today, they functioned to decompose the chemical constituents of life and keep them from pooling wastefully in dead bodies.

All the while the cells' fermentations were producing useless carbon dioxide, a gas which faintly soured the seas as carbonic acid and accumulated in the gaseous atmosphere. Carbon dioxide absorbs the sun's energy and converts it into heat. As it increased from 1 to 3 percent of the earth's atmosphere, it thus markedly raised the temperature of the earth's surface. More water vaporized into clouds, reducing the amount of light available to replace already dwindling food supplies.

At some point the conditions for the spontaneous synthesis of life disappeared in the teeming pools. From then on all living things arose only from preexisting cells whose adaptation was becoming outmoded.

Almost a billion years had passed since the first cells flickered into life. Now life was in jeopardy.

Photosynthesis

Suddenly, somewhere in an acid, bubbling pool, life's lease was renewed. Even if we never find its remains, we know the nature of the originality of the new cell. Its crucial invention, probably achieved over relatively few generations, produced the first molecules of *chlorophyll*, the green pigment in plants which now blankets the globe. With chlorophyll those first green microbes in a stifling, starving world found how to capture the energy of sunlight to make food.

With this discovery of "photosynthesis," processes were initiated that two billion years later led to the fulfillment of potentialities long on life's agenda: the evolution of large as well as small forms adapted not only to shallow pools but to conditions nearly everywhere on earth.

For these first green cells, carbon dioxide became a *utilizable raw material* instead of a waste. And they produced a new waste, *oxygen*, that was to transform the surface of the earth as well as life. Green plant cells combined carbon dioxide produced by fermentation into complex carbon-containing substances in their own bodies, in the process releasing free oxygen. Other cells decomposed plant bodies again into carbon dioxide and water. Thus a sequence was established which vastly accelerated the cycling of organic materials through living organisms, thereby increasing the speed of evolution.

Still more critical was the accumulation of oxygen. Hydrogen, methane, and carbon monoxide are gases turned into water and carbon dioxide by oxygen which readily combines with them. Oxygen makes less soluble salts of iron and phosphorus out of more soluble ones, causing all living organisms to pursue difficult detours to obtain necessary iron and phosphorus. And oxygen breaks down organic nutrients in water, thus extinguishing forms of life dependent on absorbing them.

Respiration

The most momentous result of increasing quantities of free oxygen, however, was the freeing of life from the cumbersome burden of obtaining energy from fermentation. Not only was the formation of toxic alcohol avoided, but organisms that could release energy by *respiration,* employing oxygen, were given an enormous advantage. Fermentation can release only a small amount of the energy contained in sugar; but with oxygen, organisms can release 100 percent, an efficiency increase of about twenty times. With the modest energy resources of fermentation, single cells could do little more work than was required to maintain their basic metabolism and reproduction.

Pasteur found that modern yeasts will switch from fermentation to respiration when the amount of oxygen in their environment reaches 1 percent of that in our modern atmosphere. When it reached this proportion in the distant past, oxygen respiration became the dominant fueling system for the work of life. That unheralded moment silently signaled the beginning of a new era for animal life, all of which depends upon respiration. First of all, cells restricted to a sedentary or passive existence by the scarcity of energy available through fermentation could now develop vastly increased active mobility. With this abundance, at least in the means of energy extraction, came vastly increased capacity to accomplish the work of survival in a world of increasing food scarcity. But more important, in going about the work of surviving, *they could now afford to cooperate fully.*

When energy sources were limited to fermentation, despite the benefits of proximity, adjacent cells had to remain mechanically separate in order to keep their entire surface area free to absorb nutrients and excrete wastes. With the development of respiration, however, conditions were created in which *elaborate* and *intimate* cooperation would become a crucial survival benefit. Cells could join together, gradually becoming specialized for particular functions, although at the cost of losing their capacity to perform all functions equally well. Cells and eventually organs specialized for digestion, circulation, movement, message transmission, and reproduction, became feasible. Modern one-celled animals called paramecia illustrate one way in which this cooperation between two cells might have begun.

Sexual Reproduction and Love

The process of reproduction described above involves one cell dividing into two cells. After reproducing by dividing in this "asexual" manner for a number of generations, any strain of one-celled animals may age and become relatively less vital and vigorous. The more primitive roughly globular intermittently flowing amoebas may die off unless revitalized by some environmental change. But the later-evolved paramecia, in addition to acquiring a stable cigar shape with front and back ends, as well as tiny oars called cilia, developed a unique new method of rejuvenation employing cooperation.* Two paramecia approach and adhere to one another. At the point of contact their cell membranes open and their nuclei draw close to each other. Then a remarkable collaboration occurs. *The nuclei exchange half of their genetic material.* This process innovates the essence of "sexual" reproduction, which predominates in higher animals and which involves combination of genetic material from two separate cells. The two paramecia then separate, revitalized to continue dividing asexually through many more generations.

* Professor Alfred Emerson, University of Chicago zoologist, says that the actual innovator was probably a flagellate rather than a paramecium.

In these minute creatures we find not only the essentials of sex, but also, out of the simple chemical cooperation of primitive colonial bacterial cells, the elaboration of the first animal beginnings of *love*. In man, love has been defined by Ashley Montagu as the conferring of developmental and survival benefits upon another in a creatively enlarging manner. And here, between lowly paramecia, we glimpse the easy melding of the rudiments of sex and love which is so problematic an achievement between two human beings.*

Life Moves Upward

Although most of these early one-celled plants and animals left us no record, some learned to build themselves rigid frameworks or enclosures out of silica or lime from the sea. When their living protoplasm died and disappeared, these minute skeletons sedimented into heavy layers, later raised by earth movements into crumbly grayish masses such as those we know as the chalk cliffs at Dover.

Oxygen

Oxygen atoms secreted by green plant cells unite to form ozone, which joins a layer around the earth that absorbs the lethal ultraviolet rays in proportion to its thickness. At 1 percent of the present-day concentration of atmospheric oxygen, the ozone layer would have made safe for life all but the first foot or so of water. Green plant cells and the one-celled animals that fed on them, previously confined to the depths by murderous ultraviolet rays, could begin to inhabit vast areas of ocean formerly off limits to them because of the risk of being swept to the dangerous surface by waves and tides. Surface plants could also adapt gradually to using the more plentiful newly filtered light for photosynthesis. And they could substitute efficient oxygen respiration for the nightly fermentation that in their more primitive ancestors had alternated with photosynthesis. Thus they could contribute further to the constantly increasing concentrations of oxygen and ozone in the atmosphere. With this boost to their metabolism, plants too could eventually grow larger and contribute still further to oxygenation. All the oxygen needed by life is still produced by plants.

---

* Another result is rapid formation of many new combinations of the characteristics of the two parents, upon which natural selection then operates. Man exploits this feature of sexual reproduction for the improvement of everything from roses to horses.

About 70 percent of it comes from the microscopic plants that float in the ocean and are so jeopardized nowadays by pollutants.

During the two billion years in which green plant cells had brought about these changes they had made the surface of water and land, and the air above, habitable for living beings. Due to the great increase in available oxygen all was now in readiness for the realization of the next step on life's agenda.

Multicellularity

Until only 600 million years ago the fossil record is unequivocal: life existed only in single-celled forms. Then at the beginning of the Paleozoic era the story of an evolutionary frenzy is written in rock with the remains of *multicellular* forms which suddenly began to flourish. Within a few million years, life had branched out into the seas and even rivers and lakes in such profusion of varieties as to establish the early lineage of all current species. Now the fossil record becomes more complete. But their living descendants are so similar in fundamentals that we can also trace through them the characteristics of their ancestors. Unable to explain this startling proliferation because of his lack of understanding of its relationship to increased concentrations of oxygen, Darwin postponed for a time publishing his theory of evolution, finally assuming that there must have been a long slow evolution from unicellular life of which we can find no vestige.

The earliest multicellular animals were the sponges, which were much like those we know today. Some of their cells are specialized for passing oxygen or food into an interior cavity. Others, called wandering cells, feed those that are fixed, and also cooperate to secrete the skeleton of lime needles, glassy silica, or a protein called spongin which we recognize, once the living cells have been removed, as the common bath sponge. Still others become reproductive cells, both eggs and sperms. Not only can sponges regenerate themselves from fragments, even from little piles of cells that have been completely separated and disorganized by being strained through a fine screen, but all the cell types retain the ability to transform into the others.

From here on, as animals become more specialized, this "omnipotentiality" of cells is progressively lost. Although the simplest adult animals such as sponges can regrow entire organisms when injured, "higher" creatures like the adult lobster can regenerate only lost limbs. By the time it reaches man, the capacity for regeneration has so declined that although we can heal a cut we cannot regrow even a finger. In general, the more complex the form, the more the capacity is lost for cells to transform into other cell kinds or to regrow missing tissues, and the earlier in life it is lost. Take the adult frog for example, a considerably higher animal than the lobster. It cannot regrow a lost leg. However, its *immature* form, the tadpole, can do so, but only if the leg is removed early enough.

In man damage to the limb bud of even a young embryo will lead to irreparable injury of the leg. As evolution advances, the adult sponge cell's ability to transform into other cell types finally is confined to the few cells of the tiniest embryo, or just to the fertilized egg itself. But research has shown that the *code for making the changes* remains in the DNA of every cell, and that under some circumstances the ability lost during evolution of the group or maturation of the individual can be restored.

After the sponges came the group that includes the round drifting jellyfish and sedentary sea anemones, which acquired a central gut cavity with a single opening. Next up the ladder are the flatworms, including parasitic tapeworms and free-living forms. They innovated several crucial changes. In the first place, they are not round but *bilaterally symmetrical,* having two sides, each one a mirror image of the other. They have a head, with sense organs and beginnings of nerves concentrated in the rudiments of a brain. At the other end is a tail with reproductive organs and forerunners of excretory organs. Employing primitive muscles, they move—· headfirst.

Still higher are the roundworms, such as the hookworm, which acquired an elementary circulatory system that brings nutrients and oxygen to all their cells and removes their wastes. In addition, they possess a hollow gut with a mouth at the head for entry of food, and an anus at the tail for emitting wastes.

Next in complexity came the lamp shells which gave special emphasis to *top and bottom surfaces,* evolving heavy protective calcium carbonate shells attached to each, in contrast to the other group, the clams and oysters, whose shells originate from right and left sides.

Further up the line are the segmented worms, such as the earthworm, which introduced the segmented body plan followed by all higher animals. Each segment has its own nerves, muscles, blood vessels, and waste tubules. The superiority in coordination and efficiency this design afforded is demonstrated by the fact that all the most successful animal species are segmented.

The arthropods, represented by lobsters, insects, and spiders, brought the next advances. Not only were they segmented, but unlike the vulnerable roundworms, they were provided with an external armor. Their protection was a great improvement over that of the shellfish, however, in that it was made of the light tough polysaccharide called chitin rather than cumbersome limestone. Moreover, it too was segmented, over both extremities and body, thus affording mobility as well as support and safety. Three quarters of all animal species are arthropods, which attests to the success of this group.

The peculiar echinoderms are distinguished by having five-sided radial symmetry, as in the starfish and sea urchin, although in early life on the way to maturity they pass through a stage of bilateral symmetry.

Life on Land

To better capture the power of sunlight, as their oxygen by-product gradually added to the absorptive ozone layer, a few hardy multicellular plants began to grow their tops above the water's surface, and then took root on dry land. They left their spores as fossils to record their claim as the first living forms to sparsely populate a barren landscape, and they instituted the "value" of life ashore.

Then, when atmospheric oxygen reached 10 percent of the present-day level, 400 million years ago, another explosion of life invaded the shore. Within 30 million years most of the land surface was coated with intense plant growth, including many trees, accelerating the accumulation of oxygen and protective ozone. Thirty million years later the land became hospitable for the first multicellular animals, ancestors of modern crabs, molluscs, and worms. Insects became the first land animals with much mobility, thanks to wings which loosed the leash of gravity that tied other animals to a tedious crawl.

Death Becomes a Law of Life

One-celled animals could go on dividing indefinitely. Barring unfavorable external conditions, individuals did not have to die. But along the road from sponge to sea urchin, paralleling a development in plants, multicellularity stealthily introduced a sombre revolution into life among animals. For the first time *death* of the organism became a *normal event* in the life cycle. Now only the reproductive cells could survive in progeny. Other types of general body cells gave up, along with their omnipotentiality, the indefinite lifespan that had once belonged to all cells.

This general sacrifice was necessary to improve the chances for survival of the few that became sperms and eggs specialized for immortality.

Simple Animals and Complex Values

So these simple, undramatic animals pioneered cell differentiation and body structure that have written crucial provisions into the agenda of life and shaped the futures of all larger land-dwelling animals, including man. What we call our minds are organized about concepts that derive from this bodily plan. We revere the head where are located not only the mouth but the special senses and the organ of thought, and denigrate the nether end from which issue wastes. Hundreds of millions of years of evolution express themselves in figures of speech: we resolutely stiffen our backbones, meet difficulties head on or face to face, present our fronts to the world (united or divided), and feel ashamed if we turn our less sensitive backs on a problem or a friend. When faced with injury, we cover up our more vulnerable fronts and try to take the blow on our less fragile backs, as though we too had the armor of an arthropod. Yet we fear being stabbed in the back, a direction from which our senses offer us less protective warning. We tend to think of things dualistically, as either this on the one hand or that on the other. Had we been built irregular like sponges or round like hydras, or if like sea urchins we had matured into a form in which our mouths faced downward beneath a radially symmetrical five-sided body, how different might our minds and values have become?

Moreover, we take it as a matter of course that so many of us invest enormous effort in begetting and nurturing children to outlive us. And that we so often nervously measure our accomplishments against the time left us to live. Most of us even accept without question that, for so long, a major investment of human energy should have been made in efforts to prove by authority rather than by evidence the still unverifiable prejudgment that individual personality survives after death.

We can see that it was out of the sacrifices of cell-specialization that both the big brain and mandatory death of higher forms were born. But because until recently no one knew the biological origins and implications of cell specialization, this understanding was not available to help man do without creating and crediting endless fictions that deny its consequences.

Judging from past events, it seems unlikely that new information alone even now will terminate this panicky preoccupation. Ironically, the result is that man may nevertheless continue for a time to engage one of these legacies, the resourceful brain of which he is so proud, in asserting wishfully that death, its dire companion, is but an illusion.

Birth of Backbone

About 450 million years ago the group to which we are direct heirs appeared, the chordates. They introduced an *internal skeleton* to support bilaterally symmetrical, head-oriented bodies. They became ancestral to the bony fishes 350 million years ago, who in turn developed two pairs of fins. But the land was to wait another 50 million years for fulfillment of the promise entered into life's agenda when these four extremities were added to the vertebrate pattern.

Some fish migrated to the ocean deeps, like the coelacanth, a supposedly extinct form which astonished biologists recently by being caught alive. Others stayed in coastal waters, gradually adapting to tidal shallows where food was plentiful. There those that could survive occasional marooning outbred the rest, and were able to push gradually onto land in pursuit of the food being generated there, the females always returning to lay their thousands of eggs in quiet water where the male could effectively spray them with sperm.

Lungs and Limbs

From the swim bladder, an air-containing organ regulating buoyancy while swimming, some of these fishes developed a new mechanism for bringing in oxygen and expelling carbon dioxide. It was the crossopterygians, the fish that brought vertebrate life ashore, that in this way invented a lung. Some became modified into "lungfishes," varieties of which still live in Australia and Africa. There they survive stagnation and drought which in summer dries out their puddles, a stress that would kill other fish. By 300 million years ago some of the primitive crossopterygians, equipped with gills as well as with imperfect lungs, were propelling themselves clumsily across land on their four incompletely adapted fin-legs. It was they who, 160 million years ago, gave rise to true amphibians.

Like fish, amphibians were born in water as tadpoles equipped with tails and gills. But they became transformed during early life, losing tail and gills completely, growing air-breathing lungs and true legs, and becoming as dependent as we are upon air for survival on dry land. Like our modern frogs and toads, eventually some amphibians became so terrestrial that they could live for long periods away from water, but their reproduction and the survival of their species depends to this day upon return to a pond or stream.

There in the water the male of some species squeezes hundreds of eggs out of the female into the ancestral womb of water, fertilizing and sometimes anchoring them to plants as they emerge.

Home Ashore and Internal Fertilization

The earth continued to evolve, as it does today. The oxygen percentage of the atmosphere may have exceeded modern levels 300 million years ago when the huge layers of dead vegetation that became our coalfields were buried and compressed by sedimentation on top of them. Reduction in atmospheric carbon dioxide could have cooled the earth sufficiently to produce the extensive ice ages that in turn reduced the growth of vegetation 200 million years ago. The advance and retreat of glaciers carved the earth's surface and loosed torrents to carry away their whittlings as sediment to be deposited below.

Now the land was inhabited by vertebrates, but as with Frost's Americans, the land was theirs before they were the land's. None could truly call it home.

Then 250 million years ago out of amphibian ancestry, emerged the first true *natives* of land, and the age of reptiles began. The group to which snakes, lizards, turtles, and the extinct dinosaurs and flying pterodactyls belong innovated means of conducting their *entire lives* away from water. To do so they had to evolve ways to protect their delicate eggs from drying out during their transformation into new individuals. And so those species survived that developed the ability to encase their eggs in tough shells which could protect them during gestation resting in a nest or buried in sand. But these eggs had to be fertilized before the impenetrable cover sealed out the sperm. So reptiles perfected the innovation of an amphibian ancestor, the males depositing their sperm, by sexual intercourse, inside the female, where her secretions could substitute for open water in preserving them until they could penetrate the developing eggs. Notice that here we find independent duplication of the rudiment of love innovated by paramecia over two billion years earlier. Again, survival benefits are conferred through the physical conjugation of two individuals. A measure of the enormously increased efficiency of such reproduction is that in the course of its development the numbers of eggs had been reduced from many thousands to a few dozen.

New Warmth and Old History

The most profound revolution in reproduction was yet to come. Both of the two new groups that evolved from reptiles made the greatest improvement in metabolism since the introduction of oxygen respiration. Reptiles, like all their forerunners, are at the mercy of their surrounding temperature. When the weather is cold they tend to slow down, and in near-freezing temperatures even spend months in a coma-like state of hibernation. But both birds and mammals, which emerged from reptilian forebears about 60 to 80 million years ago, found means of becoming "warm-blooded," controlling their body temperatures within a narrow range suitable for year-round full activity. Feathers and hair provided insulation.

By then the thin film of life that imperfectly enveloped the globe was pushing into nearly every clime and crevice. With each of its endless succession of generations, in a seed or an egg was transmitted an abridged and annotated copy of all the stages of evolution that had gone before. And, particularly among animals, a careful reading of the development of the embryo discloses that it goes through stages showing traces of the structures of simpler ancestors. For example, just as tadpoles have fish gills, so the embryos of mammals go through an early and brief transitional phase of having gill slits. At that age the human embryo also has a tail resembling that of a fish, and is difficult to distinguish from the embryo of a pig or a puma, which also recalls the common heritage.

Birds retained and improved the egg-laying pattern, creating better egg shells and taking better care of the hatchlings, and usually reducing the number of eggs laid to but a handful. While birds only improved the reptile reproductive scheme, mammals innovated a pattern that was truly different: internal development of offspring and nourishment of them from the maternal body after birth.

Mama

The most primitive mammals alive today disclose their ancestry with astonishing clarity. So improbable is the duckbill platypus that it was considered by zoologists to be a clumsy fraud when in the nineteenth century they were shown a preserved specimen. However, its birdlike webbed feet, bill, and *egg-laying* behavior, like its mammalian hair, are genuine parts of the same animal. Moreover, after hatching, its young are *fed by milk from its mammary glands*. And its close relationship to reptiles is

revealed by its imperfect warm-bloodedness, which allows body temperature fluctuations of as much as 10 degrees centigrade. When the eggs of
such a mammal are laid, they are fairly well developed and hatch soon
after.

On the other hand, the young of the marsupial mammals, such as opos-
sums and kangaroos, although born "alive" without a shell, arrive in
an extremely immature condition. They must reach the mother's pouch
promptly and be nourished at the nipples within it for many months if
they are to survive.

The largest and most familiar group of mammals, to which man belongs, are those that have developed a special reproductive organ, the
placenta. It is created in the womb during pregnancy. Composed of tissues from both mother and infant, the placenta effectively utilizes the
mother's bloodstream to bring nourishment to the baby and to carry
away its wastes.

Invention of the placenta brought revolutionary changes into the lives
of mammals. Protective growth within the womb could be extended
as long as nine months in man and up to nearly two years in elephants,
greatly increasing the proportion of young who survived. Therefore the
number of offspring produced at one time could be reduced again, often to
fewer than a handful. Whereas armadillos regularly have quadruplets, the
usual human pregnancy yields only one baby. The gradual increase in
relative brain size and complexity from fish to amphibian to reptile to
mammal permitted acquired *learning* to increasingly displace inherited
instinct in the control of adaptive behavior. Even eating and sex patterns,
rather completely programmed in bats and rabbits, are dependent upon
learning in ourselves and our closest relatives among the higher primates,
the apes and monkeys. With fewer to look after, the parents of mammals,
whether mouse, mastodon, or monkey, could take advantage of their off-
springs' greater braininess, giving each more help in learning their species'
techniques of survival.

Because the mammal mother fed her infants with milk from her
own body after birth, the nourishment and survival of mammalian young
became closely dependent upon maternal care and love. Out of this extended, concentrated period of loving and learning grew a new exuberance of freedom expressed in the unique and many-faceted behavior of
mammals we call *play*. In the service of survival, play combines learning
with zestful involvement with life. As mammals grow more complex,
play becomes more prevalent and extends longer into maturity. Play not
only emerges from the milieu of love in infancy, but remains closely associated with it later in life.

So in mammals love attained heightened importance. In fact, in most species *mother love* in particular, the cornerstone of human personal and interpersonal relationships, became indispensable to life. Thus, long before man was invented, long before he turned love into an abstract value, mammals raised love to an essential survival value.

Evolution and Anxiety

Early Science

Imagine how different would have been the history of human thought about the shape of the earth and the nature of its movements had the moon turned to man the full circle of its faces. Early man could have watched with his naked eye the recurrent parade of landmarks on its obviously spherical surface, and perhaps have realized sooner that his own world, whose alternating days and nights had so perplexed him, might also rotate and be spherical. Perhaps he might have been able to accept sooner the pivotal position of the sun with reference to Earth and the other planets. Perhaps he might even have avoided centuries of trying to cram down the throats of his wiser fellows the comforting but erroneous commonsense conviction that the heavens circle about man and Earth.

Perhaps. But not necessarily. For better information would not have alleviated the insecurity *motivating* his impassioned ignorance.

The history of man's thought about the evolution of life is another good illustration of this paralysis of learning in the presence of fear. Even within the confines of the knowledge available to ancient Greece it would have been difficult to avoid the notion that life had evolved slowly from the simplest forms to the most complex. Beginning with Aristotle, various teachers had proposed such explanations. But building on the same pitiable need to aggrandize man as had motivated the old pagan religions, monotheism set man again in the center of celestial concern, insisting that God had created all species of life at one instant, fixed and unchanging, with man separate from and preeminent over the rest. With the rise of Christianity, Moses' ancient rationalization of the need to feel special and safe gained new and fanatical support. Gospel was taken as gospel literally.

Renaissance Science

The increasing success of the Copernican-Galilean challenges to belief in Earth's centrality only inflamed the defenders of the separate creation of immutable species to more frenzied efforts to defend their precariously rooted and, by this time, painfully abraded self-esteem. Nevertheless scientists continued to make observations and to weave them into theories that salted the wound. Like the ancients, later students of the earth suggested that fossils of seashells found on mountaintops indicated huge elevations of the sea floor and other enormous changes in earth contour over vast reaches of time. Geology was attacked as "a dark art," "infernal artillery," and as "calculated to tear up in the public mind every remaining attachment to Christianity." The familiar epithets of "infidel," "atheist," "heretic," and "assailant of the volume of God" were flung at its proponents as they have been at nearly every fundamentally creative thinker since the second century. Bruno could have developed the concept of evolution had he not already been burned for his equally heinous affront to churchly dogma. Descartes, chastened by Bruno's death, as well as by the fate of Galileo and his own repeated condemnations, refrained from applying the evolutionary conceptions with which he had explained the solar system to the changes in living organisms. The eminent Buffon, Leibniz, and De Maillet were also forced by church pressure to curtail their study and communication in this field.

Modern Science

By 1700 the conclusions of earlier students were supplemented by calculations of the age of successive strata of rock, making plain the impossibility of earth's history extending backward no further than Bishop Ussher's Bible-based speculation of October 23, 4004 B.C. But all this, and the appearance of fossils of species no longer living, were dismissed by the desperate as deliberate deceptions by the Devil. Even Linnaeus, the great naturalist of the eighteenth century who created the system still used to classify related organisms, held to the Old Testament view of separate origin of species. For a long time, of course, it had been realized that an organism of one species generally reproduces only its own kind, and does not crossbreed with others.

As the nineteenth century approached, paleontologists had shown that fossils of increasingly primitive species occurred in progressively older layers of rock. And in 1801, Cuvier himself, despite his unrelenting adherence to the biblical account of genesis, showed that the remains of an extinct flying animal, the pterodactyl, were clearly those of a reptile related to modern lizards and turtles. Later a fossil of a primitive bird was found that, in addition to feathered wings and a feathered lizard-like tail, had reptilian teeth. Archeopteryx was thus as clearly transitional from reptile to bird as the duckbill platypus is from reptile to mammal.

Also in 1801, Lamarck tried to explain the increasingly evident variations among animals as a result of the transmission to descendants of changes individuals produced in themselves by constant effort. He thus explained the giraffe's long neck as the result of the stretching efforts made by many generations to reach leaves on tall trees. Had he been correct, Jews today should surely have no reason to continue circumcising their male babies. His erroneous theory, which won him denunciation by Cuvier and the orthodox, had the virtue at least of making a place for the evidence of evolution of species.

At the end of the eighteenth century, the spread of democratic revolutions from France and the newborn United States of America was imminent. It so threatened people of power elsewhere that they renewed a relentless campaign to defend the letter of scripture, which they perceived as a lonely bulwark against loss of their property and privilege. But revolution was also erupting elsewhere. The discovery of the human egg in 1828 by Karl Ernst von Baer seemed to many to close the gap between animal and man. The advance of science, always sensed as a danger, became a source of panic as evidence of the continuity of evolution of the universe, life, and man increased from a trickle to a torrent; however, the final inundation was yet to come.

The Theory of Evolution

In the mid-nineteenth century Darwin and Wallace came to the conclusion that evolution advanced over enormous numbers of generations by "natural selection" among variations that occurred not as a result of effort but *spontaneously*. Their studies were so comprehensive and convincing that they spelled the beginning of the end of efforts to defend the biblical theory, although it was not until the development of modern genetics during the twentieth century. that the previously mentioned mechanism of *mutation* underlying spontaneous variation was discovered.

Darwin in 1831 began a five-year voyage on the *Beagle,* collecting the observations that led to his monumental work on evolution, *On the Origin of Species by Means of Natural Selection,* published finally after much soul-searching in 1859. On the Galapagos Islands he discovered fourteen species of finches which had descended from a single South American mainland species. He observed that three of the Galapagos species still fed on seeds, as did the mainland bird, but varied tremendously in size corresponding to the different kinds of seeds they ate. Two other species lived on cacti, and most of the others consumed insects.

For years Darwin puzzled over possible explanations for these facts, and eventually found a clue in the writing of an earlier scientist. Malthus had used the phrase "the struggle for existence" in theorizing that a species tends to outgrow its food supply, until scarcity reduces its numbers through starvation, disease, or war. It was Herbert Spencer who coined the additional phrase "survival of the fittest," another that Darwin's work eventually validated. Darwin recognized that once the finch population outran the seed supply, competition for scarce food would favor individuals who happened to possess variations that made them more efficient. Those who were stronger, had bills that permitted them to eat larger or tougher seeds, or switch to cacti or insects, were the "fittest" in the sense that they would outbreed the others. Whereas each new adaptation found an empty "niche" in the previously birdless Galapagos environment, on the mainland competitors already filled all the niches, confining finches to their ancestral food and preventing them from differentiating into new species.

This view, which Wallace reached independently after similar experiences, explained innumerable other observations. The giraffe's long neck is of obvious survival value in enabling its possessor to reach new food; therefore, any mutations causing it to grow still longer would tend to be reproduced whereas the opposite would tend to die out. But the giraffe's spots, which Lamarck would have difficulty in accounting for as a result of the animal's efforts, can be understood as an adaptation readily achieved through natural selection, and one that is of great survival value in the giraffe's sun-spotted leafy habitat as camouflage against attack by a predator. This concept indicated also that evolution is a *gradual continuing* process, making comprehensible not only extinct transitional species, but the occasional instances of living species, such as the lion and the tiger, that are still close enough to crossbreed.

Evolution Theory Established

While the precise mechanism of the *origin* of life remains obscure, a century of investigation and sharpening since Darwin has brought the theory of evolution of life, once established, to nearly undisputed acceptance as fact. The inheritance of mutations brought about in fruit flies by deliberate man-made X-radiation in the laboratory permits one to observe the process of evolution taking place before his very eyes.[2]

Further corroboration comes from every quarter, most recently from the field of biochemistry. The close relationship of all currently living forms is demonstrated by the finding that all are composed of the same amino acids. And recent analyses of protein remnants in 300-million-year-old fossils have shown that they too contain the identical amino acids, as well as traces of the same carbohydrates, fats, cellulose, and porphyrins. Comparison of the physiology and biochemistry of the major groups of animals provides further substantiation, if more is needed.[3]

Evolution of Work, Love, and Play

Before moving on to explore life's subsequent ventures, including man, let us turn our eyes back over the long path across which evolutionary change has led us, noting where each innovation of our legacy takes up the march. They are work, love, and play.

The first inheritance, which life shares with all nonliving matter, is *work*. The energy expended to accelerate or slow an inanimate body bears a direct relationship to the work performed by a wolf in bringing down a deer. No new work, however, is needed to maintain unchanged the existence and orbital movements of the planets and sun. In fact, at the inorganic level work can only produce change and perhaps individual destruction, as for example the sun's constant combustion and radiation which eventually will transform it and the busily eroding earth into still serenely orbiting embers. In contrast, at the level of living creatures work must be performed *just to maintain existence and individual movements,* as well as to produce change.

Nonliving forms can "work" in only a few ways, all of which involve *motion* but not *motivation*. This fact has enabled us to discern physical "laws" that predict the behavior of nonliving things. For example, should a new comet invade the solar system, scientists could predict its orbit and foretell whether it would survive its encounter with the sun.

The simplest living forms are also quite predictable, but the biological "laws" governing their workings do not permit nearly the same degree of certainty. Although single-celled animals seem to react to stimuli automatically, they have a much larger repertoire of response than nonliving things. However, because they have but one cell with which to accomplish all of life's functions, the variations between species are sharply limited. While general knowledge of the behavior of one species therefore often allows considerable prediction of the behavior of unfamiliar species, there are unforeseeable exceptions. For example, while most species will turn toward light and move toward moderate warmth, unexpectedly others will not. Although work is still performed in the course of these motions, a new determining factor has intruded itself into behavior. Motivation, the highly variable new element, does play a role. The cell's motions are motivated perhaps by the rudiments of hunger, pain, and even pleasure.

As we move up the scale, the behavior of individual multicellular organisms quickly becomes so complex that prediction is increasingly chancy, unless the characteristics of the *particular* species and even the *strain* are well known to the observer. For example, from knowledge of the scavenging behavior of a lobster, one would be able to predict little about the feeding behavior of a lamprey and even less about that of a lizard.

By the time we reach mammals, possible actions have become so numerous that no one can predict with certainty even within a particular species and strain. On the basis of general knowledge of a certain breed, a trainer could not predict whether individual dogs he had not observed previously would be friendly, hostile, or indifferent in unfamiliar surroundings.

What we are following here in the decline of predictability is actually the increase in range of *freedom* afforded successively more complex animals by their more complex nervous systems. When we consider mammals such as dogs, we see that something about the *individual* and his experience determines a large part of his behavior, rather than its being determined by the general characteristics of his major group, species, or strain. We tend to say that he "decides" to do this instead of that, a notion of freedom of choice which would seem dubious applied to a snake and preposterous applied to a starfish.

The increasing scope of individual freedom is directly related to increasing capacity for *learning* and *intelligent behavior*. These are accompanied by progressively *heightened levels of consciousness,* as can be inferred from the seemingly thoughtless reflex actions of sharks as compared with the innovative and ingenious behavior of dolphins. And it is the gradual increase in size and complexity of the nervous system, particularly of the forebrain, which permits the heightening of consciousness. The resulting increase in the complexities of motivation makes it much more difficult to formulate psychological "laws" that will predict individual higher mammal behavior.

Each creature in his own way, within various ranges of freedom determined by his species' characteristics, more or less diligently works for a living. While we can trace work to roots in the physical world, comparisons between *love* and physical forces, such as the gravitational attraction between celestial bodies, are of course no more than analogies. Love, however, goes way back. Its seeds were planted by the primitive organisms that outmoded the hermit existence. Spontaneously some acquired the mutations that transformed the proximity of newly divided daughter cells from a side effect to a survival value. The fruit of this primeval good-neighbor policy was the collaboration between cells that led to multicellular animals; and its remote descendant, passed through the cool crucible of fish, amphibia, and reptiles, was *love*.

Amphibia and reptiles had raised physical closeness to a new intimacy with the invention of internal fertilization. Mammals, with their addition of placenta and mammary gland, completed the transformation. What had been *colonial cooperation,* useful for perpetuation of the group, now became *individual love,* indispensable to survival of the young. The power of this bond is attested to by the willingness of many mammals, such as dogs and cats, to suckle and succor the young of other species, even those of so-called "natural enemies."

Now was introduced the third inheritance, the recent innovation of play. The prolonged period of dependency of the offspring of early mammals provided them freedom from having to work for a living during the period in which the young mammal was most able to learn. And so the possibility arose for *learning* to replace the rigid determination of behavior by *heredity.* And with it came the possibility of replacing the unrelieved seriousness of fish, amphibia, and reptiles, which seem to us so "cold-blooded," with the smile, the laugh, the "joy of learning," and the delight of "let's pretend."

The more closely the characteristics of the mammal studied approach those of man, the larger proportion of its lifespan is spent in dependence and playfulness, and the longer is retained the capacity for playful joy. It is the magnetism and infectiousness of this mammal interaction between love and play that glues our noses to pet shop windows where cavort the nonserious puppies or kittens that entrance us.

Here let us notice that in tracing evolutionary change we encounter *dis*continuity as well as continuity in both function and structure. What is new grows out of what is older, but it is different unpredictably from what came before.

While it is necessary to understand the fish from which the frog evolved, it is not *sufficient* to understand the earlier creature if one wants to comprehend fully the later. How, on the basis of familiarity with fish alone, could one anticipate the development of lungs and legs, let alone fathom the extraordinary implications of breathing air and walking on land? How could one appreciate the intricacies of the flight of a robin from observing the slithering of a rattler? Plainly the properties of one level cannot be predicted solely from those of another. This limitation applies equally to function and to structure. Thus, differentiation into dissimilar species and individuals adds complexity to motivation. Despite all the continuities between them, one man does not behave the same as another man, let alone another mammal.

And so in the course of evolutionary change, life's recipe for mastering reality employed the values of increasing intelligence and heightened levels of consciousness, under conditions of expanding freedom and joy. In so doing it appropriated work from the cosmos, added love, and just recently stirred in a pinch of play.

3 Animal and Man

Primate Evolution

Scurrying Shrew

Man and his closest relatives, the monkeys and apes, are "primates," a group of mammals mostly distinguished by adaptations to living in trees. The small mammal that evolved into our first primate progenitor arose, as is always true of a major new group, from a primitive rather than a specialized ancestor. For it is the primitive form that by relatively modest changes can take advantage of a new environmental opportunity. Hence we began as ground dwellers, retaining four limbs for walking like a lizard, rather than crawling like a snake (which lost its legs in the course of evolution) or flying like a bird (which traded its forelimbs for specialized wings).

Of living mammals, the tiny mouselike shrew is closest to this common mammal ancestor.[1] Three inches long, tense, frenziedly active, and fiercely combative when competition for food or mate becomes intense, the shrew rushes jerkily along the ground through its fifteen months of life.[2] Devouring its own weight of insects, worms, and any meat it can get every three hours, it supplements this diet with berries, nuts, and seeds. No other creature must work so furiously and relentlessly to keep its flame alive as the tiny shrew. Punctuated by a few reproductions, and terminated by the swoop of an owl or a sudden senility, its brief lifespan is guided primarily by a well-developed moist snout and sense of smell. Like most largely nocturnal vertebrates, it has color-blind vision of poor acuity, but its large outwardly directed eyes rove independently and give a panoramic report of movement, of special consequence to the minute predator and prey.[3]

It was from this unpromising start 60 million years ago that our remote ancestor lifted himself into the third dimension, and onto the path to manhood, by *climbing a tree*.[4] Life on the ground keeps the limbs in bondage to locomotion, the senses enslaved to the immediate, and the mind cramped into the moment. The *adaptations to living in trees*, which characterize all higher primates including man, liberate the limbs for exploration, the senses for perceiving the distant, and the mind for anticipating the future.

Grasping Tarsier: Vision over Smell

Foremost among these adaptations of our faraway forebear was the *ability to climb by grasping*, which afforded not only security and agility to enlarging animals, but the potentiality for manipulation. This pioneer "prosimian" primate has his modern five-fingered, five-toed counterpart, the tiny tarsier that can sit upright in your palm. He is the first mammal who can regard you in depth with his synchronized forward-directed eyes. His snout is diminutive, leaving his small dry-nosed face almost as flat as man's. These changes, which added acute binocular vision to the primate scheme, also simultaneously subtracted acuity and importance from the sense of smell, the olfactory part of his generally larger brain being reduced as much as the visual part was expanded.[5] These modifications made for a creature adapted to looking, and judging distance, before it used strengthened hind legs, acquired later, to leap.

Such talents fitted it for life spent increasingly in the by then flourishing and newly diversifying trees. Here in this three-dimensional world, as yet unpopulated by mammals, food was plentiful and best located by sight. And here, in contrast to life on the hunting ground of so many predators below, the main danger was the impersonal and impartial force of gravity. Visual depth perception became much more the means of survival than smell or panoramic vision. Restriction of fighting with fellow tarsiers, and further increases in cooperation between mates, became necessary for survival at hazardous heights. And further reduction in the number of offspring became possible and valuable. Improved maternal care of the fewer babies that clung to a mother's body during aerial leaps of up to six feet intensified the love bond between mother and baby innovated by ground-bound mammal forerunners long before.

Manipulating Monkey: Brain over Body

More was needed to adapt fully to the arboreal life, and it was among creatures similar to the tarsiers that the crucial inventions of the monkey arose. They were increasingly *opposable thumbs and toes* on hands and feet equipped also with *separately movable* fingers, which enabled monkeys to seize things at arm's length and draw them to the eyes for inspection. Thus came about the mechanism for manipulation and intensified curiosity, which early monkeys passed on to early man. And along with probing eye and prehensile hand came the physical basis for all man's comforts as well as conflicts over looking and touching.

Monkeys grew larger, for reasons we will consider later. Increased size and weight afforded some species better defense capability and demanded the extra security provided by progressively more powerful grasp. Safety of such an enlarged body required an enlarged sense of balance, which once attained in turn permitted vast increases in acrobatic agility with leaps exceeding thirty feet. No longer did these animals scuttle along led by a sensitive wet nose; instead, they moved erect, guided by the literal foresight of binocular vision.

All these changes were of survival value, and so the spontaneous variations that produced them were passed on as the favored monkeys who possessed them progressed through the primate agenda. Of preeminent importance was the larger monkey brain, which by now had reached a volume of 100 cubic centimeters. While a ten-pound monkey is 40 times heavier than a shrew, his proportionately much larger brain is 120 times heavier.[6]

Mind and Sight

The nocturnal mammal mind, previously confined to the shadowy vista of the forest base and thicket, when hoisted by a shrewlike forebear into the brilliant sunlit arboreal realm brought with it only the monochromatic vision of its predecessors. But monkeys, who had a loftier habitat, could benefit from the widened perception of reality. They were the first mammals to acquire the mutations for color vision which treated their minds to the riotous hues of the daytime treetop world. Again the crucial visual brain expanded, and the disemployed smell brain shrank.[7]

The monkey's three-dimensional depth perception in color laid the groundwork for the selection of the ancestors of modern man. Early man's descendants became men of vision, capable eventually of *hind*sight sufficient to perceive with their expanded minds the long path of kinship with their treetop clambering cousins, and all that lay far behind them. Some modern men also became capable of *in*sight sufficient to grasp their human *differences* from animals, and many fewer are today developing the abstract *fore*sight to do something about preserving them.

Modern man still perceives the world in the basic pattern perfected 25 million years ago by the monkey. The more complex human brain, on the average about a dozen times larger, has gained mainly in those areas devoted to abstractions—associative thought, memory, and speech—which are the physical basis of man's distinctive concepts, symbols, and ethics. Among the 200 living primate species, these are fully developed only in man.

Instinct: Lower Animals versus Primates

What behavior patterns does an infant monkey, ape, or man bring with him at birth?

We know that "lower" animals such as fish and birds as they develop will show complex fighting, courting, nest building, fertilizing, or copulating behavior without ever having had an opportunity to observe another member of their species.[8] Without knowing exactly what is going on in the nervous system to make possible such complex and apparently largely unlearned activity, we speak of it as "instinctual." At the usual age and season, the male chaffinch, without a model to imitate, will produce a song with characteristic chaffinch rhythm, although it will never learn to sing the chaffinch song "right" unless it hears an experienced male.[9] The red patch on the bill of its herring gull mother makes the chick peck at it, which in turn causes her to disgorge food for it.[10] Ducklings are born with an innate tendency to follow the first moving objects they see, be they birds or other animals or men, but if they are not "imprinted" with the image of a particular leader within a certain critical period of life they will never do so.[11] Certain fish and birds, if deprived of foreign members of their species onto whom to discharge spontaneously upwelling aggressive urge, will attack and kill their mates.

It is important to note that the *expression* of even such behaviors as these, which we can legitimately call instinctual, is dependent upon interaction with environment.[12] A pertinent example is the presumably "instinctual" cannibalism of bass fish. It turns out that eating the smaller members of their own kind is a survival behavior dependent upon specific environmental conditions. When their ponds contain weeds, the larger fish become separated from one another and do not develop social groups.

Also, the vegetation prevents them from seeing food thrown into the pond. The simple removal of the weeds beforehand enables fish introduced into the pond to see one another and the food thrown in. As a result they form large social groups which eat together peaceably and do not prey upon one another. In some ponds merely adding as role models fish that have learned elsewhere to be dependent upon food offered by the fishery attendants will terminate the cannibalism.[13] So the conclusion is inescapable that expression of even supposedly instinctual aggressive behavior in a so-called lower animal may be far from obligatory, and may in fact be controlled by learning. This fact should be borne in mind when we come to consider aggression in man.

Instinct consists of three parts:

1) An innate, spontaneous motivating *impulse,* urge, or drive, to perform a certain behavior;
2) An innately determined *signal,* or stimulus, which releases the behavior;
3) An innate *action pattern,* or complex sequence of activities, for carrying out the behavior.[14]

In lower animals, all three elements are clearly present, as may be seen in the spawning behavior of salmon, or the hive-building behavior of bees. In higher animals, such as the dog, the releasing signal is *learned,* that is, *which* tree is to be urinated on and *which* stranger is to be threatened. But the impulse (territorial defense) and action pattern (leg-lifting and barking) for delimiting a territory and warning off trespassers remain innate and difficult to modify.

In still higher animals, such as the primates, including man, not only the *signal* but also the *action pattern* for carrying out an impulse is learned. Only the impulse, urge, or drive is innate and spontaneous. Unfortunately, the German word *Triebe,* which Freud used for such an impulse, often has been translated into English as "instinct" instead of the more correct "drive." Thus many people have been misled into thinking that Freud believed human beings have, in addition to innately determined impulses, innately determined action patterns and releasing signals. No matter how he is translated, Freud was referring only to impulses.[15]

However, in many instances of human behavior, also the *impulse itself* is learned. For example, in human beings there is no good evidence of an innate impulse to defend territory. So a person must learn the *releasing signal,* the *boundaries* of a territory to be defended, the *action pattern* to be employed (i.e., firing a gun at intruders or asking to see I.D. cards), and also whatever *territorial impulse,* if any, is characteristic of his culture.

Whereas in Beverly Hills, California, you are defined as a trepasser if you merely vault a neighbor's backyard fence, among the Eskimos unauthorized entry into a neighbor's igloo may transform you into an honored guest.[16] A further example is the fact that in all higher primates thus far studied, including man, although various pleasure-seeking erotic impulses we could call "lust" seem to be innate, neither the *impulse to copulate* nor the knowledge of the *technique of sexual intercourse* are instinctual, copulation being a learned behavior.[17]

Basic Needs and Urges

The higher primates in general come into the world with many of the same *basic needs* as other animals, such as those for oxygen, water, nourishment, rest, elimination, security, and stimulation. But these are *expressed* in ways commensurate with their differences from other animals. These needs are rooted in bodily biochemical and physiological processes, and give rise to basic *impulses, urges,* or *drives,* such as the urge to breathe, drink, eat, sleep, urinate and defecate, move, hold and be held, have pleasurable sensations, have companionship of one's own kind, and so on. All higher primates will show reflex actions that tend to satisfy these urges or drives, such as sucking, eliminating, clinging, crying, eye blinking, yawning, and startling at noises or loss of support, particularly if the environment provides the right resources.

The human baby within a few weeks adds the weeping of tears and the smile which is our species' unique greeting behavior. In monkeys, apes, and man during the juvenile period there also develops what are apparently pleasure-seeking impulses for genital stimulation. And at puberty, a heightening of intensity of this drive is noted, varying somewhat with the sexual cycle, which in monkey and ape females produces much more marked physical and behavioral changes than in human females.[18]

It is important to emphasize that the more or less interchangeable words "impulse," "drive," and "urge" are used generally to indicate only the *motivation* for behavior, and do not refer to the signal that releases or to the action pattern that guides the carrying out of the behavior. Also, it should be remembered that a *reflex* is only a simple innate motor reaction to a stimulus, such as a knee jerk, and not a complex train of coordinated behavior involving goals which we could describe as either instinctual or learned. A true instinct *must* include as innate, unlearned, and spontaneous factors, all the elements of *impulse, signal,* and *action pattern* integrated into purposeful behavior.

As Dunlap, Bernard, and others showed two generations ago, there is no evidence in man or his closest relatives of any instincts whatever in this sense.[19] The overwhelming preponderance of information now available suggests that the innate signals and action patterns found in lower animals have disappeared, and the impulses, urges (or drives), and reflexes are *all that is left in the higher primates of the elaborate instinctual endowment of our remote forebears.*[20] It is especially important to underscore that these innate reflexes are only *simple* reactions, not complex sequences of activities such as, for example, unlearned complicated courting or nesting behavior in birds. (For further discussion of basic needs and drives in man see Chapter 11, subsection: The Newborn Human Baby.)

Are there then no inherited factors differentiating primate behavior? Do monkey, ape, and man all enter the world with the same equipment and become behaviorally different only as a result of learning? Of course not.

At birth, as the result of long processes of selection, a member of any of these species brings with him, along with inherited differences in body and brain, inherited differences in propensities and aptitudes for certain behaviors, which will predispose him to learn or not learn those behaviors under appropriate environmental stimulation. These predispositions vary not only among species, but also among individuals of the same species.

However, all these are variations in the inherited *options open* to the individual, not in the *compulsions commanding* him. To jump ahead for a moment, given the same learning experiences, a baboon would be much more likely to develop ferocious defense of his position in a dominance hierarchy, and an arboreal monkey to casually shift his allegiance to a new band. Given the same learning experiences, a chimpanzee would be much more likely to develop agility in swinging from the arms, and a human to communicate in words. But without the appropriate learning experiences, none of these behaviors will appear *spontaneously*, as will the basic song of the chaffinch or the attack of the cichlid fish. Therefore, unlike the latter behaviors, they are not instinctual.

Monkey, Ape, Man

To follow our still incompletely understood ancestry a bit further, we must back down the genealogical tree to about 30 million years ago. Somewhere in the forests that then reached uninterruptedly from Africa to Asia, apelike animals began to differentiate from monkey stock. Altogether, they evolved to reach physical characteristics much closer to those of man than monkey.

Monkeys have the long, narrow, deep, and flexible trunks of other mammals, with arms and legs suspended so that they move mostly backward and forward. Apes have short, wide, shallow, inflexible trunks and long arms that move freely in all directions like man's. Unlike monkeys, who generally run on top of branches, apes swing along gracefully suspended beneath them, employing the method of locomotion called "brachiation." Especially when young, we human beings too can brachiate from our apelike arms.

But the ape's pelvis and lower limbs are as different from man's as his torso and arms are from the monkey's. The ape's hips cannot be fully extended, so that when he supports his weight on his lower limbs he cannot rise to his full height. The ape remains crouched, his knees likewise flexed, a position requiring constant muscular effort to maintain. Hence he welcomes and uses the support of the backs of his hands which are suspended from arms that reach the ground because they are longer than his legs. Although like some monkeys he can shuffle awkwardly and run clumsily on two legs for short distances, on the ground the ape is really quadrupedal. Only man can fully extend the hip and knee joints of his greatly lengthened lower limbs. Only man has a foot fully adapted for locomotion on ground. So only he can truly walk erect. Only man has the large gluteal muscle to power the hip, and the ability to lock the knee by slightly overstraightening it so that the fully erect position can be maintained and his full height enjoyed without constant strain. As Weston LaBarre has put it, "Man stands alone because he alone stands."[21]

Bare facts such as these can outline but not fully depict the transformation of shrew into man. They are the skeleton. To flesh the bones of this most astonishing of stories, we must perform the most characteristic human job of relating facts to one another. We must interpret their significance. Yet to grasp and describe the interplay of hand, eye, brain, stance, posture, mind, arm, food, society, reproduction, curiosity, hip, foot, and many more that comprise an avalanche of separate and dissimilar factors is a bewildering task. That is why it took so many minds to ferret out and articulate even the partial understanding now available. One way I have found to grapple with the task, although not to make it simple, is to trace the metamorphoses the long journey brought about in work, love, and play. Because all the factors affect all three basic activities of living organisms, it is of course impossible to sharply demarcate one topic from the others. But in a rough sort of way, I will group together and discuss first those that seem to have most to do with work, leaving love and play for later (beginning p. 97).

Primate Work: Size, Leisure, Imagination

The tiny shrew, with its sensitive, constantly wet nose kept to the grindstone, could never live through the same season more than twice. Its intense metabolic processes could barely be fired by frantic constant gobbling of food, and, worse yet, they burned out its diminutive cells and organs in little more than one whirl around the sun. To become a man a shrew would have to live much longer. It would have to have time to learn, leisure to reflect, and opportunity to teach. But longer life could be achieved in only two ways, either by drastically turning down the thermostat and sacrificing activity or by *growing much larger*. In general, increase in size is accompanied by lengthened lifespan with only moderate reduction in metabolic rate and activity. The larger animal has more reserves of food stored in its body and its larger organs do not have to work as hard to perform their vital functions. Then, too, because the ratio between the volume of its heat-producing cells and the area of its heat-losing surface is so much greater, it takes proportionately much less fuel to keep it warm. And of course the bigger you are the harder you are to swallow whole.

And so with each leap from shrew to tarsier to monkey to ape to man there was progressive increase in size as well as in longevity. An average man may weigh 600 times as much as a shrew and live 60 times longer. And with each increase in size came a reduction in the frenzied concentration on the work of feeding needed to maintain life, and a proportional increase in the amount of time and attention that could be shifted to wider horizons of perceiving, reflecting, and thinking.

Here we must recollect that it was not a *modern* shrew that became modified into a tarsier, or a *modern* monkey that gave rise to the ape, or a *modern* ape that gave rise to man. In each instance it was a primitive, unspecialized early *ancestor* of these modern forms that evolved gradually over countless generations into the next variety. So it was a shrew*like* forebear who became modified into a tarsier*like* descendant and so on up the line until an ape*like* forerunner became transfigured into a man.[22]

At last the buried books of the earth have disclosed in their layered pages enough transitional forms that there is no longer any doubt about the general course of evolution from a tiny ground-dwelling shrew to man. In particular, the discoveries of the last four decades have filled in the general course of transformation of primitive ape to modern man, so that the last uncertainties about the fact of continuity of descent between animal and human life have been erased.[23]

With larger size, greater strength, and longer life came the mechanism for benefiting from the unique opportunities of arboreal life. Here a monkey could learn to stoke his dampened fire in three dimensions, primarily on a plentiful vegetarian diet, supplemented by small birds, eggs, and insects. Here his environment placed a premium on both the capacity to perceive at a distance and the capacity to reach out to pluck and pull close what was wanted, rather than to shove the lowered head and jaws at it. Thus was fostered not only the ability of a hand to grasp and do fine manipulation, but the dawning ability of a mind to grapple with what lies beyond a grasp: the space and therefore the little fragment of future time which unfolds in front of the face. And thus simultaneously the mouth was freed from gripping, long in advance of the invention of the distinctive human communications of smile and speech.

Through victory in reducing the work of making a living, the monkey earned from the forest a precursor to the greatly expanded opportunity for thoughtful wonder that man is beginning to enjoy in his urban jungle through his industrially generated abundance and leisure. And so it happened that enlargement of parts of the brain that underlie memory and planning as well as vision acquired survival value. Perhaps this is how it came about that a monkey or ape can make a split-second assessment of his lightning course through the branches of a half dozen trees, and then pass a contented quarter hour in still contemplation of a sunset.

Apes and Anticipation: Tools

The early apes, having acquired the grasping hands and feet, the binocular vision, the beginnings of erect posture, and the more complex brain of the monkey, now added in a paradoxical way to the emerging freedom embodied in this scheme. By acquiring arms able to move in all directions at the wrists and shoulder, and the skill of moving through trees while swinging from them, they simultaneously almost freed the lower limbs from the burden of locomotion while recondemning the skillfully manipulative upper extremities to being predominantly a means of locomotion, a prison in which it had languished for so long on the forest floor. But at the same time the generally increased weight and strength of apes, like that of the larger monkeys such as macaques and baboons, had gradually restricted their suitability for life aloft and increased their security on the ground.[24] Although they continued to retreat from predators into trees, the fine twigs could no longer provide them the safe haven afforded a small monkey. All these larger animals, over thousands of generations, came gradually to pass most of their lives moving about on the ground, returning to trees rarely for any purpose but to sleep. The baboon and macaque repatriates to earth added little to the monkey pattern but a revived and modified version of the shrew's long-forgotten ferocity, which we will consider presently.

However, the apes came up with something truly new. With their imperfect legs planted clumsily on terra firma many hours a day, the apes diverted their free-swinging arms to innovate joyously the most momentous advance in the technique of work achieved by animals until the seventeenth century: the anticipatory making of tools.

It is not so widely known that the "lower" forms also employ tools. For example the burrowing wasp uses a pebble to hammer the soil down about its eggs. One of the Galapagos finches described by Darwin uses a cactus spine to pick insects out of bark crevices. The southern sea otter when swimming brings a stone along upon which to crack the shellfish on which it feeds. The "firehawk" of the Northern Territory of Australia has even mastered a use of fire. Grasping burning twigs it finds in a spontaneous brush fire, it flies over a grassy patch dropping them from its claws, and then pounces on animals fleeing the fire.[25] It is significant that whatever combination of genes and learning is responsible for transmitting this tool-using ability, it never includes techniques for *making* tools. The pebble, spine, stone, and faggot are simply naturally occurring objects that readily come to pincers, claw, or paw and are used *unmodified*. How is it that in all the millions of years these highly specialized animals have had in which to learn the manufacture of tools they have not done so?

There are several reasons. One cannot manufacture anything without the *manus* (Latin for "hand"), which only the higher primates possess. But will not a pincer, claw, or paw do? In animals, apparently not.

We know, however, that unfortunate human beings who either lose their hands, or suffer the tragedy of being born without hands, are not thereby deprived of the tool sense characteristic of human beings. Equipped with an artificial mechanism resembling a pincer or claw, or at least a paw (or employing the mouth or a foot), such persons are able to learn to use tools most skillfully, and *even to make them*, provided only that the mechanism *controlling* such a substitute is intact. It is not because he has bird *claws* that the firehawk cannot learn to make fire, but because he has a bird *brain*. So the crucial distinction today between animal and man as to tools lies not in the manus but in the *mind*.

The great apes under wild conditions employ simple tools. Chimpanzees may throw branches or stones at any creature that frightens them in order to drive it away, and in the presence of a termite hill, they may actually *create* a tool. After first picking a twig and stripping the leaves from it, the animal pokes his probe into the central hole in the hill, withdrawing it carefully and licking off the clinging termite tidbits.[26]

The mind of man has added an extra dimension to toolmaking which vastly outreaches the work capability of apes. A chimpanzee can make a probe when confronted by a termite hill, or fit a jointed stick together with which to pull fruit lying outside its cage into immediate reach. It can make a tool to deal with an immediate reality. It can even make a tool in response to an *anticipated* reality, as for example termite hills or bananas beyond the next rise. The expansion of its visual perception and even its elementary problem-solving capacity make it equal to present and upcoming challenges that would defeat a bird or otter. So man is not alone in being able to anticipate the *proximate* future. The chimpanzee's hindbrain is every bit as developed as man's. What he lacks is man's enormous enlargement of the forebrain. As a consequence, while a simple solution of a simple problem is something the ape can see and even foresee a bit in advance, he cannot anticipate the *remote* future nor can he think ahead in complex and abstract sequences. He cannot strip twigs and build a bridge *now* with which to cross the river to hunt termites *next week*.

All the complexities of man's life today depend on the ability to anticipate and plan far ahead. The work of man's world is rehearsed in advance in his head. How did man acquire this faculty?

Return to Earth

Although they had already begun to return to earth, the apes remained tree dwellers, and so were largely spared the assaults of predators who preferred to hunt in the open.[27] The group that went on to become the modern apes remained specialized for swinging through trees, in their wanderings keeping within the gradually receding forests. They retained the old arboreal limbs, the arboreal posture and habits, and the ancestral arboreal mind. By now they were nearly instinctless, as were the monkeys, but they were not challenged to develop the new behaviors that lay within their limited genetic potential, nor was there much premium placed on chance mutations that might have enlarged it. So they became specialized at the dead end of apedom. Never very numerous, all the apes today are in danger of extinction by man, who does not hesitate to invade their sanctuary with weapons against which they are helpless.

It was about 15 to 20 million years ago that a new environmental stress was placed on apes. As the result of widespread drought, the forests began to retreat more rapidly. The group of apes that became terrestrial, and ancestral to man, did not so much leave the trees as they were left by them in open grasslands, scattered with trees and brush, which are called savannas. The new conditions of life on the ground favored the survival of those apes whose chance mutations better fitted them for rapid running on two legs, distant vision, and sharp thought. One group named Proconsul had an apelike skull and teeth, a quadrupedal gait, and a small brain probably not over 200 cubic centimeters. His height could not have exceeded three feet. He shows us what an unspecialized ape was like.[28]

Barely two million years later in what is now Kenya lived an ape (*Australopithecus wickeri*) known to us only through a few upper jaw and tooth fragments.[29] The teeth are more manlike, and the jawbone shows evidence of muscle connections not present in apes but found in early and modern man which provide lip mobility useful in speech. This change was a "preadaptation" and does not signify that he spoke, for his brain was certainly altogether too small for such talent. But it does disclose that modifications in the direction of man have been in process for much longer than previously supposed.

In northern Italy has been discovered another fossil ape (*Oreopithecus bambolii*) which dates to ten million years ago.[30] Although he is an offshoot rather than in the line of man's descent, and although his long arms show he remained a tree-swinger, his shorter, flatter face, his larger lumbar vertebrae, and finally his pelvis with modifications that indicate he was capable of bipedal locomotion all demonstrate that considerable advance toward human physical characteristics had already occurred among various apes.[31]

While we cannot designate precisely which of several varieties of manlike apes may have progressed into apelike men, it is certain that somewhere among the extinct forms now known or to be discovered are the transitional species that during eight million years bridged the gap.[32] They had retained their primitive unspecialized malleability so that they were able to make new adaptations to the drought conditions that had evicted them from their ancestral abode in trees.

Uprightness

By this time *bipedal* gait was accompanied by *increasingly erect posture*. These accomplishments, once fully attained, had momentous importance for the ability to anticipate and plan ahead. For one thing, the eyes could see farther, thus stimulating whatever capacity to foresee mentally had been vouchsafed by one's genes. For another, one could *walk* as well as run on uniquely modified feet, allowing not only the traversing of great distances without undue fatigue, but also the quiet approach to unwary creatures. Over hundreds of thousands of years these abilities were selected and preserved because they conferred enormous survival benefits in the overriding task of all animals: securing food.

The carnivorous shrew *supplemented* its diet with seeds and berries. Its herbivorous monkey descendants *supplemented* their diets with bird eggs, insects, and lizards, while their ape cousins did the same with occasional birds and small animals. But with the return to the long-forsaken ancestral earth, the manlike apes pioneered a change in work unique not only among primates but also in the larger groups of mammals: they became *omnivorous*. That is, they made a *regular* rather than an occasional practice of eating both plant and animal food.

Cultural Guidance of Evolution

At first bipedal apes gathered only the slower moving animals and birds, especially the young. With increasing skill at walking and stalking quietly, some must have begun to *hunt,* or to attack as predators the more agile adults, at first using their bare hands. Perhaps one day a hunter was given a momentous new idea by a falling rock which by chance crushed an escaping rabbit. However it came about, at some moment the old habit of throwing stones at intruders in defense was suddenly employed instead by a hungry man-ape to fell an escaping prey. Perhaps this first use of tools for hunting a regular rather than incidental part of his diet inaugurated the first technological revolution. From there, hunting larger and more dangerous animals, the new method of work led not only to the challenges and rewards of slaying the larger animals, but it brought about a decisive guidance of man's further evolution. At some point the hunter also would have the experience of throwing a pebble that accidentally splintered on contact with a boulder, creating a sharpedged scraper or knife. This is the sort of tool that man alone is capable of using skillfully by virtue of his unique fully opposable thumb that permits thumb and index fingers to cooperate in the "precision grip." Over thousands of years and many generations this sort of accident must have been transformed into deliberate toolmaking by individuals with minute additional genetic improvements, who passed it on in exploding numbers to become the distinguishing features of the new animal, man. For it is man who in doing his work can turn *accident* into *invention* by *imagining* its possibilities, *foreseeing* and *remembering* its remote consequences, *anticipating* its uses, and *planning* how to exploit them. Thus the ingenuity and selection pressure evoked by hunting for his omnivorous diet made the final transformation from brachiating ape to cerebrating man. The factor determining these abilities is the genetically circumscribed but culturally elicited faculty of human intelligence.

Those who chanced to have the genes for improved brains could better learn the use of tools, and thereby gain the chance to pass their inherited genes and acquired skills on to progeny. The most intelligent among them in turn would be best able to learn the rudimentary tool culture, improve it with experience, and pass it on best to their more intelligent offspring. And thus it was that man began, albeit unknowingly, the cultural direction of his biological evolution.

In the process a major evolutionary discontinuity was created, the sharp declivity between an animal who exists in the narrow present between short tufts of past and future, and a human being with the potentiality to live mentally in the expanse of space-time between the big bang and the death of the sun.

Early Man

By about two or three million years ago the ape brain must have reached 400 to 500 cubic centimeters, approximately the size of those of modern chimpanzees and gorillas, man's closest living relatives.[33] The first definitely human fossils, like those of many transitional types, have been found in South Africa, and are about that old.[34] Once it was thought that the brain had enlarged to near-modern human proportions before the transformation of ape into man, and that therefore the distinction between them was a matter only of brain size. But it now appears that once the 400-to-500-cubic-centimeter level is reached, the genetic changes that allow a brain to integrate its owner's life at a level we recognize as human are *qualitative* rather than quantitative.[35]

And so it is that the extinct "Apes of the South," or Australopithecines, first discovered in fossil form by Raymond Dart in 1925, although they have brains of only 450 to 500 cubic centimeters, are nevertheless human, despite their owners' fascinating mixture of ape and human characteristics.[36] The height of these primitive men was under five feet. Their faces were large. Their small brains were encased in skulls much like those of apes, but nevertheless produced a modest but distinctively human forehead bulge, and more to the point, the means for conceptualizing the human implements and way of life that no ape can achieve. The teeth in the apish skull are decidedly human, even the canines being reduced in size, and the opening at the base of the skull is shifted forward, disclosing that it was carried much more erectly than that of its definitely nonhuman forebears. Pelvic and leg bones confirm that these small ape-men habitually employed the *fully* erect bipedal gait. Nevertheless, because of their small brains some anthropologists were reluctant to accord them true human status. The humerus bones of antelope found in the same locations, and the presence of baboon and their own skulls showing crushing injuries, were interpreted as evidence of the use of bone tools.

But the absence of definitely *modified* tools among the fossils did nothing to contradict the notion that these creatures had not made the conceptual leap to manhood.[37]

Then in 1959 the Leakeys made the most momentous discovery yet unearthed by students of human evolution. At Olduvai Gorge in East Africa they uncovered the remains of a closely related but different primitive man-ape (*Australopithecus boisei*), *surrounded by his tools,* dating to 1,750,000 years ago.[38] These included choppers, hammers, stone flakes, and unworked stones. These were clearly modified tools. But more than that, since the embedding about his remains consisted only of clay, the evidence was clear that this toolmaker had thought his plans out well in advance.[39] He had *anticipated* his needs and deeds *over an extended course of time,* and had brought his materials *over an extended course of space.* And in leaving his bones and artifacts together he had provided the proof that creatures such as himself and Australopithecines, with brains of only 530 cubic centimeters, could be fully human.

Moreover, the remains of his food, consisting of baby pigs and antelope, small reptiles, birds, and fish, disclosed that his hunting techniques had so far yielded only those animals accessible to bare hands or thrown stones. He had not yet learned to devise the advanced tools and collaboration required to bring down the giant adult pigs, sheep, and cattle that surrounded him, so the bulk of his waking hours had to be spent in the enslaving labor of just feeding himself and his family.

This was the ape-man who also confirmed that both erect bipedalism, with all its advantages for seeing and stalking game, and true anticipatory toolmaking were achieved *before the brain had enlarged* much beyond ape dimensions.[40] Furthermore, this early man's apelike skull showed that formerly massive canine and incisor teeth, evolved originally by arboreal predecessors for shredding the tough husks of vegetable food, were now markedly reduced in size.[41] This change was the result of a long slow evolution made possible by the substitution of hunting for foraging, and the gradual substitution of tools for teeth during the preceding half million years.

But most of all, this first definite ape-man demonstrates that it is *functional* rather than physical characteristics that define humanity.

Fascinating further physical changes of skull and enlargement of brain are revealed in the continuing parade of new finds of extinct early forms of man, but I will refer to them only in passing, as they relate less critically to the center of our interest.

A half million years ago, man's brain had reached 1,000 cubic centimeters, and his remains show that at last he had learned to control fire.[42] He had long since discovered how to kill and eat large animals, thus reducing to four or five hours per day the chewing and swallowing time required to stay alive. Now mastery of fire not only provided warmth and visibility at night, but a means of softening tough animal and vegetable fibers so that eating time could be further reduced to two or three hours daily, and time for problem solving, love, and play proportionately increased.

Forty thousand to one hundred thousand years ago the first "modern" man (*Homo sapiens*) appeared, with a brain of about 1,400 cubic centimeters. Since that time there have been practically no significant further biological changes.[43] The earliest cave paintings of about 18,000 years ago were created by the same species that created "Mona Lisa" and "The Thinker."

Modern man on the average has added about a foot to his height, about 50 percent to his weight, and has nearly tripled his brain volume. Since mental capacity above the basic human level is related to increasing brain size, there has been substantial increase in human intelligence, now made possible by brains that contain about twelve billion brain cells. But in two million years the remade arboreal ape mind which has spun the poetry of Shakespeare and hurled astronauts to the moon as yet has been unable to feed, let alone control, pyramiding expansion of its 35,000 times larger population of three and a half billion people. Man, unlike any other animal known, has become the only serious threat to his own survival, a menace that can be overcome only through his extraordinary capacity for abstract thought and communication. So we must now look more closely at this capability.

The Symbol

What distinguishes man from other creatures? Carlyle noted that man is a tool-using animal, but we have seen that he is not the only one. Adam Smith characteristically viewed man as an animal that makes bargains, but so do other animals. Whoever said that man is the animal who cooks seems to have emphasized a unique trait, if not the most important. William Whitehead underscored a factor of endless import when he noted that the only laughing animal is man.[44]

But the functional capacity that truly separates man from ape and all other animals is that of using *complex symbols*. So crucial is this difference that, in his illuminating *Essay on Man*, Ernst Cassirer has urged that man be regarded not as the *animal rationale,* as Aristotle called him, but as the *animal symbolicum.*[45]

All animals have a sensory receptor system and a motor effector system. It is on the basis of the information brought to the animal by the receptor system that—controlled by reflexes, innate action patterns (in lower animals), and/or learning—his effector system reacts. Between the receptor and effector systems, man has interposed something new, the *symbolic system,* which permits him to *respond* rather than merely to react. And it is the symbolic system that, in delaying and multiplying the possibilities of response by channeling it through the byways of *thought,* has brought into human life a new means of adaptation to reality.[46]

What is a symbol? Put most simply it is something that stands for something else, something that signifies or represents something else. Something becomes a symbol, is endowed with symbolic significance, *as the consequence of a psychological act.* Tool-using, and especially tool-making, are manifestations of the symbolic process. The chimpanzee's twig probe stands for or represents his desire to eat termites as well as the work process of securing them. In the same way the cowboy's chaps and the miner's pick symbolize their desire to eat other things and the work process of securing them. So at an elementary level the ape mind is capable of symbolizing. But this capacity stops with representation of the simple wish or process. It remains in this way close to the concrete experiences of appetite and termites.

In contrast, to a human being the cowboy's chaps can symbolize *remote* and *highly abstract* things, such as the idea of the freedom of outdoor life, whereas the miner's pick can symbolize the idea of the confinement of drudgery. Moreover, a man can be profoundly affected in his functioning by the mere *representation* of a symbol, say a photograph or drawing of chaps or a pick, something generally beyond the capability of an ape.

Human symbolic process extends even further. A representation of a hammer and sickle may stir up an avalanche of emotion-laden responses, ranging from fearful suspicion and outrage to prideful solidarity and confidence. The same spectrum of response is forthcoming from a representation of a totally abstract figure of lines and colors that does not depict tools or anything literal at all, but is recognized as an American flag.

In this multiple layering we humans have hopelessly outdistanced apes in the invention we are employing in written form at this moment, the symbol that can represent the banner that signifies the nation that stands for a host of other symbols. The boundary beyond which, so far as we know, no other living creature has ever passed unaided by man is the *word.*

Do not apes and other animals have language? Of course they do. They communicate by posture, gesture, even grimace and vocalization, but their language is confined to the communication of their subjective emotional states.[47] It is limited to *signals* or *signs* of their inner reactions to internal or external events. It does not represent or symbolize the event itself. Animals may send one another messages that convey "I am afraid" or "I am content." But they never convey "There is a lion" or "What delicious bananas!" For that you need words. Even if it should be shown eventually that the large and complex brains of dolphins are capable of conceptualizing and using words, it will remain true that no other creature but man has built his life and survival upon them. Whatever there was in the beginning of the universe, in the genesis of man there most certainly was the word.

Let us be clear. Although animals do not learn words in the wild state, of course apes and even dogs can be taught by man to react to a few words. And apes in captivity can be taught to mimic the sounds of a few spoken words. Since their vocal and mouth structures are adequate to produce the necessary sounds, no doubt apes could learn to "speak" in this imitative manner, just as they can imitate much other human behavior— if their brains contained speech-integrating mechanisms to program the movements needed for speech. However, they do not.

Moreover, even with such speech equipment they might still not be able to use *language* in the truly human way, which requires not just reproduction of another's utterances, but the *recombination of the word-elements of language into original statements.*

Is it possible that the apes may have this sort of human symbolic language ability which remains hidden due to the lack of speech centers with which to demonstrate it? Recently a young female chimpanzee named Washoe was taught the hand-sign language employed by the deaf, and she learned to use signs for both nouns and verbs abstractly to convey original messages! For example, after learning the sign for "dog" she used it upon hearing the bark of an unseen dog, and when someone drew her a caricature of a dog. Also, when taught the word "open" in relation to a door, she eventually generalized it to express her request that a water faucet or pop bottle be opened. So apparently apes can learn to use words, at least with human help.[48]

Although of course we continue to employ subjective emotional language as well, words are the units of human objective communication. To understand their origin we must return to the complex of interacting factors that shaped the evolution of the earliest men.

In the long process of coming down from the trees to the forest floor and then out of the jungle onto the surrounding grasslands or savannas, adaptation to continual environmental change required of man's forebears increasing behavioral flexibility. Most needed was freedom from the rigidity of the preprogrammed behavioral responses that characterize more specialized and static species. Accordingly, what slight remnants of instinctually determined behaviors persisted in the early monkeys became a survival hazard, and were virtually extinguished over thousands of generations of ground apes ancestral to man.

Earliest man, therefore, was both untutored and unencumbered by instincts. A mass of experimental and field observations indicates also that modern monkeys, apes, and men, while retaining the basic impulses, urges, or drives and reflexes referred to earlier, exhibit no trace of the elaborate instinctual signals or action patterns found in fish and birds.

These observations, and their implications for the study of such human behavior as aggression, are discussed in more detail later. Here the important point is that *early man had to* <u>*learn*</u> *his responses from moment to moment.* This learning he could accumulate from his own experience, or from that of other men. One hunter saw another down a rabbit with a stone, and imitated him. Such a learned behavior could become the common property of a whole tribe, and thus the rudiment of a culture.

This sort of learning, although not involving tools, can be done by monkeys. One group of macaques acquired the habit of washing chunks of potato before eating them, while a group of baboons learned to flee automobiles after a single episode in which a car disgorged a rifleman who felled two of their members.[49]

The human erect posture that elevated the eyes to become still longer-distance receptors, and the bipedal gait that permitted both sustained quiet walking and sudden rapid running, equipped man for a great expansion in his repertoire of response. And quick adjustment to the constantly changing conditions encountered in the hunt demanded the utmost degree of spontaneous ingenuity.

Perhaps a hunter in the stress of the chase emitted the grunts and cries of which his prehuman ancestors had been capable. No doubt a companion at a distance could soon learn to distinguish a sound that meant danger from the one signifying success. But at first there could have been no way to transmit to someone out of sight *two different* messages involving danger, to which opposite responses are required, such as the difference between "forest fire—run away!" and "lion—come and help!" But at some moment a chance sound emitted by a respected hunter when he encountered a big fire was adopted by others to designate the same threat. Now they could communicate at a distance, not just danger, but the presence of a danger against which the only defense is flight. It would then have been easier to add a second commonly accepted sound to signify lion which when uttered urgently would have the enormous advantage of bringing your friends on the run to help drive off a powerful predator in order to steal his prey. And this simple but epochal feat of differential communication is one that, so far as we know for certain, no animal has ever been able to master on its own.

Out of such humble beginnings evolved over thousands of years must have come selection pressures that further perfected the function of the brain. Somewhere men were born who, when the day's hunting was terminated by nightfall, were able to employ the word for fire or lion afterward in recalling and recounting their struggles. Thus the word became a tool for infinitely sharpening and strengthening memory. After a while a few men must have used these words the next morning in anticipating the hunting of the coming day.

Somewhere men emerged who learned to tame fire for cooking, warmth, and protection, rather than simply to run from it like animals. But even more crucial, by naming it with their word for fire, or a variation, they learned to tame it for *thinking* and *communication*. Thus the word became the building block of improved planning for the future, and the vehicle of imagination.

The signals of wild animals which convey their subjective emotional states do not give information about the environment. More important, they are not composed of elements that can be broken down and recombined to convey other messages according to an *order* characteristic for a particular language, the grammatical rules regulating use of subject, predicate, and object. Now, although Washoe learned to recombine word-symbols into original messages, apparently these have not, at least so far, been organized in conformity with the structure of the English language in which she was taught the symbols, or even of any personal system of her own. For example, the signs for *you, me,* and *tickle* have been used indiscriminately in all possible sequences to indicate the same situation. Requesting someone to tickle her, she signed *you tickle* and *tickle you.* And again, she signed *me tickle* for someone tickling her, and also *me tickle* to indicate she would tickle someone.[50] Thus, in and of themselves, her messages were often ambiguous. Although apes progress faster in general development, children of the same age (three years) already show clear beginning evidence in their own speech of the conventions of sentence structure which make meaning clear and precise.

So the somewhat tattered self-esteem of many may yet be bolstered by a biological distinction from other species, the reassuring new Rubicon of *grammar,* across which the nonhuman mind may not be able to sail even aboard the ferry of human instruction.

What we have been tracing here is the emergence of human out of animal language. Improved communication in speech made possible intensification of the ability to *cooperate,* a survival technique inherited from the earliest life and brought to a new level of consciousness, complexity, and joy in the relations between men. Improved cooperation, building on the basic amiability of apes, and employing the potency of the symbol, made of the word a transmission belt for conveying to the young the compressed wisdom of the old. And so there came into being the distinctive new adaptation required by instinctless free creatures for the further advance that we know as *human culture*.

The word "culture" is often misunderstood nowadays as referring only to nonessential artistic activity. To those who so restrict its definition it will seem strange to trace not only the spoken word but culture in general to primitive man's strenuous efforts expended in the work of obtaining food. But it seems likely from studies of both ancient cave art and modern nonliterate societies that even creative activities such as painting, dance, and pantomime were devised originally as earnest if magical efforts to influence the hunt.[51]

Social Relations: Territoriality and Dominance, Aggression and Survival, Love and Play

Now we must focus on the part of the primate agenda that has to do with relationships between individuals. Consideration of social relationships requires bringing into view the other two basic activities of mammals, love and play.

In addition to our fundamental physical and perceptual equipment, we have inherited also from the early tree-dwelling monkeys our fundamental emotional and psychological propensities. We will evaluate some of their permutations in recapping the long adventure from shrewhood to humandom.

Let us recall how the shrews, their tiny bodies burning furiously, were forced to consume food in the vicinity of eight times their own weight during each of their five hundred days. Their young, suckled in a nest reachable between frantic foragings, all too soon were grown competitors contributing to the scarcity that drove their desperation. In their struggle to make a living the strongest, who could devour the most, and drive away rivals for food and mate, survived and reproduced in greater numbers.

Thus arose the most intense "territoriality" found among mammals.[52] Territoriality refers to the defense of a feeding and breeding ground against members of the same species. Ethologists, or students of animal behavior, have found that animals with strong social organization show relatively little territorial defense and vice versa.[53] In many fish and birds, such as the brilliantly colored cichlid fighting fish and the black-tailed godwit, patterns of laying claim to and defending a territory are prominent and are apparently transmitted genetically as "instincts."[54] This means that the animal seems not to need any experience with others of his kind in order to manifest the behavior characteristic of his species. Territoriality functions to disperse the members of a species over the available feeding and breeding ground in a density conducive to maximum survival.

Among mammals in general, territoriality is not very well developed.[55] But for shrews, with their high energy requirements and diminutive reserves, the possession and defense of a territory from which an adequate food supply could be gobbled became a survival issue. In the absence of an alternative, fighting to the death would become for male shrews a way of life.

Nature, however, has provided an alternative to fatal fights for shrews and all animals who struggle over food or mates: after various threatening sounds and movements, the loser gives a signal of surrender and abandons his claim, or simply runs away. To this day, while one of two male tree shrews will kill the other *if confined in a cage where neither can escape*, it is extremely rare under wild conditions for a victorious shrew to kill another even in the grim frenzy to live. It was more economical of precious energy and time, as well as of life, if a rival could be disposed of by threat and intimidation rather than by injurious combat. So those ravenous warriors who could scream, grimace, and gnash most fearsomely and convincingly, or who could run away when overmatched, came to have greater survival potential than those who could only kill or be killed.

What happened to this pattern in the ascent to the trees? Along with the remnants of other instincts, individual territorial defense faded out in monkeys where it was no longer of survival value in an environment that now provided an *abundance* of food. Combativeness also tended to fade out in an environment relatively safe from predators. Protection against the occasional cat, snake, or bird was much better achieved by the ability to escape into fragile branches and leafy concealment. There a pursuer either could not follow or could not see his prey, or at least would cause a warning sag that would alert a monkey even if it were sleeping. There ferocity (and the sort of body adaptations that go with it) would have been a liability, while timorousness and lithe agility were of great survival value. Thus it came about that arboreal monkeys of all varieties tend to be generally timid and unferocious.[56]

Animals that have little to fear from one another tend to live in groups, and thus acquire both the advantages and disadvantages of social life. The advantages of which monkeys avail themselves include the multiplication of eyes and ears so that even infrequent danger is more readily averted.[57] Monkeys, especially those who spend time on the ground, make good use of this collective defense in their alarmed chattering, which not only serves to alert all members of the group, but sometimes to frighten off an attacker. Another advantage is the ready availability of sexually receptive mates at all times, and monkeys generally copulate with whatever partners are accessible. Then there is the possibility of a loving accumulation and transmission from generation to generation of a rudimentary culture. This includes, in addition to the basic skills of monkeyhood, familiarity with the particular trees, water holes, and so on that comprise a troop's home, or knowledge of special feeding habits such as the washing of sweet potatoes mentioned earlier. And there arises the possibility, realized by some monkey species, of continuing into adult life the frolicsome friendships that arise during the uproarious play of the juvenile period, and with it the potentiality for enduring close relatedness between individuals.

When individuals live together throughout life in groups of ten to one hundred, some means must be found for avoiding total chaos. Whether they are arboreal monkeys or terrestrial men, the method developed by group-living primates is formation of a *social dominance hierarchy*. In the case of monkeys, each member of a troop finds his niche, so that he knows those to whom he is superior and inferior. Among monkeys such as the langur, the dominance order is established by the skirmishes of juvenile play, and maintained among adults mostly by bluff, since they almost never get into physical conflict.[58] A langur may shove its inferiors away from a preferred food, sleeping spot, or receptive female, but in general the hierarchic structure is somewhat flexible and the social organization it imposes is a benevolent one. On balance, the advantages of some variety of social dominance hierarchy among monkeys, apes, and men in providing a reliable framework to guide behavior from moment to moment, are overwhelming. In fact, it is doubtful if their survival adaptations, particularly those serving to educate the young, would have been possible at all without the stabilizing effect of some sort of social dominance system.

Nevertheless, two aspects of the social dominance hierarchy constitute the main *disadvantages* in primate group living, the unachieved solutions to which are high on the human agenda at present. The first is *social rigidity*, and the second is *fear*.

Social Rigidity

In some species, such as the ground-dwelling baboons (and macaques) whom we shall consider in a moment, the structure can be so *rigid* and *stultifying* that some highly qualified individuals simply cannot ever fully develop their capabilities. What is worse for the species, as we shall consider later, is that these individuals may also be unable to pass on their superior characteristics to be amplified in progeny. This can happen, whatever their other attributes may be, if they are lacking in the qualities required for social dominance to the degree that they may be shouldered away from every opportunity, including that for mating.

Like the ape line that led to man, baboons are higher primates that returned to living predominantly on the ground. But it must be borne in mind that they are *monkeys* and not apes, and are therefore far removed genetically from the ancestors of man.

Although baboons return to trees to sleep or escape danger, their way of life differs in many ways from that of arboreal monkeys. It has evolved out of the need for defense against dangerous savanna predators such as cheetahs, hyenas, and lions, which timid arboreal monkeys (and forest-dwelling apes) ordinarily do not have to face. As a consequence, where arboreal monkeys are light and fragile, baboons are heavily muscled and rugged. The large canine teeth, which all monkeys and apes developed, not for combat but as shredders for the tough coverings of plant food, in baboons have further enlarged into fearsome weapons, while the jaws have elongated like a dog's to accommodate them.[59] The males, who may weigh up to one hundred pounds, are powerful adversaries for any attacker smaller than a lion, and look even more dangerous because of the ruff of hair about the shoulders which makes them seem larger.[60] And the fierce belligerence they have developed to propel this aggressive endowment makes them truly effective fighters.

Baboons, in contrast to arboreal monkeys, live in extremely rigid dominance hierarchies and frequently engage in violent fights to maintain or advance their rank. While even among such a combative species fatal fights are rare, it is not at all uncommon for one or both contestants to be badly injured. The net effect of these behaviors is to assure protection of the troop from external danger by establishing clear and instant compliance with the authority of those most formidable fighters brought to leadership through dominance struggles.

Although some baboons learn to supplement with small animals (such as hares and the young of gazelles) the herbivorous diet with which they came down from the trees, unlike the ape line that led to man, they never became true omnivores or habitual hunters. *Their remarkable aggressive ferocity therefore could not have been the consequence of the need to kill prey.*[61] It is important to keep this fact in mind when thinking about man because it indicates clearly that "intraspecific" aggression (see p. 107) in higher primates may arise from adaptive pressures completely unrelated to hunting, in this instance to those having to do with group defense. Clearly, no matter how crucial hunting was in human development, man's violent aggression *toward his own kind* need *not*, as often alleged, be an outgrowth of his having been a hunter. In fact, the evidence suggests that it *was* not. Those animals, such as lions and tigers, in whom hunting behaviors are best developed, unlike baboons, show little aggression toward their own kind. And since they are safer living alone or in mated pairs with young, they do not depend for survival upon a large group organized according to a dominance hierarchy.

Despite these differences in origin and function of the structure, intraspecific aggression in both baboon and man derives from the need to maintain or acquire the *power and privilege belonging to a particular niche in a social dominance hierarchy.* It is intended to defend the individual against what he rightly or wrongly conceives to be a danger, often more to his prerogatives than to his person. The utility for survival of such adaptive patterns depends upon the continued presence of the external danger. If the enemy disappeared, whether carnivores for baboons or scarcity for man, over a sufficient number of generations such behaviors might become maladaptive, and eventually be extinguished. This possibility, at least for man, is explored in Part II.

Both baboons and man evolved prominent social dominance hierarchies which clearly function as *group defenses against outside dangers.* But similarity of function now must not be mistaken for identicality of function or origin long ago.

Before exploring further, it is well to underscore several points. Since no one was around to give eyewitness reports of early baboon or human behavior, anyone's reconstructions made today are hypothetical. Some hypotheses, however, accord better than others with the sparse fossil records, and with the lives of modern animals and man we *can* observe. Both sources suggest that the general tendency of animal behavior to evolve along many different lines in separated groups was even more pronounced in man, because genetic mechanisms of behavior transmission had been replaced in him by the much more flexible social and cultural devices. No doubt many behavioral patterns became extinct as reality conditions changed. The adaptations we observe today survived the challenges of the past, but may not prove adaptive to conditions of the future.

Baboons and man, although only distant relatives, *seemingly* faced the same dangers in emerging from forests onto open grasslands. And since both developed social dominance hierarchies, it is easy to suppose that they also evolved the same defenses. But this hypothesis is based on a misconception. The dangers they faced were *not really* the same; therefore, their defenses could not really have been the same either.

When early baboons came out onto the grasslands they brought with them only the monkey endowment.[62] They had no more than a rudiment of erect posture or bipedal gait, little practice in anticipating the future, and no ability to use, let alone make, tools. On the ground waiting for them were dangerous rapidly evolving predators, against whom they had defended themselves in the past only by retreat and alarum. The male specializations for combat and the rigid dominance hierarchy—almost military in character—evolved by those who survived, must have served them, as they plainly do today, to defend the troop against its carnivorous enemies.

As herbivores who foraged singly, they found plentiful food[63] without special effort, although its relatively low nutritive value required almost continuous eating during waking hours.

For the *prehuman apes,* however, who millions of years later moved onto the same terrain, the circumstances must have been quite the reverse. For they brought with them the *ape* endowment. This by now included an almost completely erect posture and a fully bipedal gait with which to exploit the much more significant capacity of apes for thinking ahead, and for using and making tools. It seems probable that even at this stage predators would have found our forebears awesome. Indirect confirmation is offered by the fact that, although an occasional modern predator will venture into the forest to carry off a chimpanzee or gorilla infant, ordinarily it will be unwilling to assault an adult ape even when on the ground. Partly this reflects fear of the great strength of brachiating arms. Partly it results from dread of the screaming aggressive displays of upright, frightened, branch-wielding, stone-throwing chimpanzee males, or breast-thumping gorilla males. But largely it reflects the fact that the great predators, by the time apes evolved, had already become highly specialized for hunting a very different prey, and simply did not associate the newcomers with food.

By the time the earliest *man* had emerged on the savanna, all these attributes, now greatly heightened, must have made him a creature to be treated with the combination of disinterest and fearful respect generally accorded modern man by all wild animals, who in addition apparently find our flavor and even our odor offensive. Although an exceptional tiger or other carnivore will learn to prey upon unprotected children or isolated adults, especially when they are asleep, as a rule not even the largest and most fearsome predators will dare or even care to hunt man. This fact is attested to by the widespread lack of fear of predators on the part of nonliterate peoples living in Africa, who know that even one person alone can usually drive them away by beating the ground with a stick, shouting imprecations, or throwing stones. It might be tempting to dismiss the predators' fear of modern man as the result of a million years of experience with (and selection by) wit and weapons not possessed by earliest man. But that does not dispose of the modern predators' common fear of chimpanzees and gorillas.[64] It is not too likely that modern arboreal apes have learned much about repelling predators that their remote ancestors did not know.

So primordial man was not in the same danger as baboons. But whereas baboons lived in an abundant economy of plentiful but bulky herbivorous food, human beings, because they evolved a new requirement for the time-saving concentrated diet of meat, lived in a *scarcity* economy of fleet-footed prey. What is more, whereas the baboons were heavily furred and so required no extra protection from the weather, naked early man also needed hard-to-get tools, shelter, and clothing. Therefore, while the well-armed baboons had little to do but defend themselves against predators, human beings in contrast were threatened by *starvation* and *the elements*. And that is why the dominance hierarchies of baboons and man are basically different in origin and function. They were adaptations to different stresses, in baboons to the threat of attack, and in man to the threat of scarcity. In baboons the structure functioned for defense, in man for organizing the primal hunting group to make a living. For baboons, hard work could never become a "value." For man, military talent eventually did. Secondarily, with the advent of warfare only a few thousands of years ago the group defense function of the human dominance hierarchy became preponderant in some places. But even so, the resemblance to baboon society is only superficial since, as far as we know, baboons in the wild, the most intraspecifically aggressive of all primates, have never organized to defend themselves against (let alone attack) other groups of *baboons*.

Fear

Here we must underscore a feature of mammal life not previously emphasized, the role played in it by fear. From the squirrel fleeing in terror at the slam of a window to my neighbor's chow snarling at the garbage-man across the street, and more particularly to most free-living wild animals excepting the large carnivorous predators, a great part of all animal life is spent in a state of fearful alertness. Especially is this true of the primates, such as adult arboreal monkeys screeching or mute with panic at the approach of an intruder, or the majestic dominant male baboons apprehensively checking the savanna for lions every ten seconds. Their fear is comprehensible in terms of possible physical peril against which they are on guard. But it is not so easy to explain why a monkey reacts even to an unfamiliar member of its *own species* with fear and defensive aggression.

With this behavior, we should pair the common human reaction of fearful suspiciousness of and aggression toward foreigners. We should also ask ourselves why monkeys, like men, so commonly tend to remain in their accustomed communities even when their social status dooms them to permanent misery. Or why, freed from the bondage of individual territoriality and in the midst of abundance, monkey troops, like many men, will voluntarily confine themselves for life to a diminutive familiar home range, varying from one half to fifteen square miles.[65] Or why, in the midst of abundance, they will apprehensively and aggressively warn others not to trespass on the few hundredths of a square mile they may defend as a tiny group territory.[66]

Despite all their revolutionary innovations, there is a *deeply conservative tendency* in primates which seems to be *based on fear*. That fear is as much a reaction to *unfamiliarity* and *uncertainty* as it is to danger. It is easy to understand how early man's helplessness in the face of most dangers led him to find protective gods as symbolic magnified parents. But one cannot account satisfactorily on this basis alone for the later terror of churchmen over challenges to religious doctrine from science. The fear that put the torch to Bruno for teaching a hypothesis (solar centrality) at variance with established doctrines grew not out of imminent physical danger but out of the threat of the unfamiliar, out of uncertainty about the *impact of the new idea upon the established social dominance hierarchy*. And while fear of "crime in the streets" can largely be attributed to potential external danger, is it not obvious that the terror evoked by "atheistic communism" or "reactionary revisionism" is less the result of any physical danger they entail than it is the threat they pose to established social dominance structures?

It appears that man shares the conservative primate tendency to preserve the status quo out of fear of the unfamiliar or uncertainty about its effect upon established authority. But we must ask ourselves why this is so, both for individuals and for species.

The reason is immediately clear in the case of an individual or a small group with common interests. Whether we are thinking of a dominant male baboon and the ruling clique of four or five to which he belongs or a human financier and his associates, it is evident that the individual and group try to defend those elements of the status quo from which they feel they derive the power and privilege they value. On the other hand, the subordinate baboon who feels he has a chance tries to *upset* the status quo, and win for himself the pick of food, sleeping rock, and mate, by challenging and dethroning his superior.[67] And it is the millionaire automobile manufacturer living in the country who is most likely to aggressively defend his right to produce unshielded internal combustion auto motors rather than the smog-breathing Los Angeles psychiatrist, who would be more inclined to curtail it.

In terms of a primate *species,* what can be the survival value of a trend in evolution that brings to such a pinnacle the tendency to cling to one's group that, for the vast majority of monkeys and men, the worst fate that can befall an individual is to be deprived of association with his group? What is it that accounts for the individual monkey's meek acceptance of an arbitrary limit on living space, or the urban physician's resignation to living in a city where he will have to breathe poison should his protests prove ineffective?

As we will see shortly, it is easy to offer explanations based on instinctual lower animal behavior and attribute these remarkable acquiescences to "territoriality." Such extrapolations to higher animals and man are founded on errors of fact and logic. Generally an *individual* animal defends a territory against *members of his own species* as his private source of food and locale for reproduction.[68] A howler monkey stays within his *group's* communal one-half square mile, *putting up with* rivals for not only food but mates as well,[69] and a doctor remains in Los Angeles although his chances of eating well and raising healthy children are demonstrably greater in many other accessible spots. These primate decisions have *nothing* to do with territoriality and *everything* to do with clinging to the security of membership in a familiar group and to elements in a social dominance hierarchy felt to be advantageous.

Mothers and Peers

Instinctless primates in general, and man in particular, cling because they have evolved in a way that makes membership in a group, including filling a niche in a dominance hierarchy, absolutely indispensable for attaining or maintaining the *full identity characteristics* of their species. To become a healthy monkey, ape, or human requires social relationships with both an adequate mother and adequate age-mates.

Dr. Harry Harlow's experiments with infant rhesus macaque monkeys beautifully demonstrate the details.[70] Infant monkeys raised without any contact with others grow up severely damaged. Some stare fixedly at nothing, while others hug themselves and rock interminably. Some suck fingers or thumbs, and others react to the approach of people by chewing or scratching bleeding holes in their skin. When later brought together with other monkeys they are never able to make adequate relationships. They show no sign of friendliness, play, or copulation, and may strike out indiscriminately with arms and teeth in apparent terror at the unfamiliar stimulation. Under natural conditions, they would surely die. If artificially inseminated, a female so raised is unable even to give her baby, when it arrives, any mothering affection or attention, stepping on it absently or even deliberately shoving it away and injuring it severely. Such disturbances confirm the judgment that *monkeys are devoid of instinct even for fundamental copulation and mothering behaviors.*

The same conclusion applies to the other higher primates. For the same dependence of social, maternal, and sexual behavior upon learning is found in apes, and especially in man, where pathetic instances of isolation and neglect have produced clinical psychotic pictures highly reminiscent of those seen in deprived monkeys.

If infant monkeys are raised separately with only their own mothers for company, all the psychosis-like reactions are prevented. They seem to be more or less normal baby monkeys. But when brought together with age-mates several months later, they show no capacity whatever for social or sexual relationships. So good mothering, although essential for healthy survival, is not *enough* to bring about the interactions with peers that eventually teach a monkey to copulate, to mother, and most important, that guide it through play into membership in the group's social dominance hierarchy.

Harlow found that a terrycloth-covered wire dummy used as a substitute for a real mother could also prevent the worst (but not all) of the psychosis-like results of mother-deprivation. If infants raised separately with such artificial mothers are brought together for twenty minutes a day, after initial hesitancy they play with all the rollicking vigor of normal monkeys. Before the end of a year all adopt their ordinary sexual roles, the males showing dominance and the females submission, indicating that normal copulation will soon follow. What is more, the playmates begin to form a recognizable social dominance order. These results, corroborating the observations of child psychologists as well as ethologists, suggest that normally it is through the *play relationship with peers* that the primate newcomer not only imitates his elders and rehearses the skills for individual adaptation to his world, but also finds his place in the group both socially and reproductively.

Incidentally, although these patterns appear to be the result of learning, as yet we do not know for certain whether any higher primate carries an *innate* predisposition to develop hierarchical behavior independent of learning. To test this question a most impractical experiment would be required. A group of newborn baboons, for example, would have to be raised in a large natural area and fed only by humans, in the absence of close confinement, adult baboons, and predators. Of course, such an experiment would be impossible to perform with man. But such instances as can be drawn from the natural experiments of widely diverse human societies suggest that if there is any genetic predisposition in man to form dominance hierarchies, its expression is extremely variable, ranging all the way from the rigid structure of classical Chinese antiquity to the relatively informal organization characteristic of small Eskimo bands.

Clinging and Loving

As the evolutionary distance from the shrew widens and proximity to man increases, the proportion of the total personality which must be created through socialization enlarges. So individuals cling to their sometimes oppressive group and dominance hierarchies because these social arrangements are the only means by which monkeys and men *can become and remain fully themselves*. In man, socialization implies the distinctive acquisitions of abstract thought, language, and culture, without which man may be an animal but not human. And these characteristics are born in the love relationships between the baby and his family, the first and most elemental social order he experiences.

Later we will trace the development of the human baby within the family structure. Here we must underscore the implications of the frequency with which the word "cling" recurs in this discussion. To grasp its significance we must look back to primate evolution. It can be no accident that even the words I am driven unconsciously to select all relate to the hand. *Understand* means to *comprehend* or to *take hold of*, to grasp. The prehensile or grasping hand (and foot) of monkeys permitted them to cling to and thereby master the trees. Moreover, a truly arboreal life demands ability to cling at birth to a maternal body as it flies through the trees. Through its grasp on its mother's body an early ancestor of man clung also to its first social relationship, and to the first representative of its social order. As it clung tightly it was accepting gladly the subordinate position that sustained its life, and the introduction to lifelong dependence on the social group to which, no matter what rank it would eventually attain in the dominance hierarchy, in a crucial sense it would remain subordinate for the rest of its life. Incidentally, baboon society is even more rigidly structured than is human society. A subordinate female at the lower end of the hierarchy is usually more nervous, smaller, and less confident than the others. Her offspring is likely also to become nervous and unconfident, and when grown is almost certain also to remain at the lower end of the social order.[71] Among baboons social status may be destiny as much as is heredity.

The tenacity with which primates cling to their social dominance patterns is nowhere more eloquently illustrated than in the following incident observed in the wild. A male baboon, apparently wounded in a fight, under unknown circumstances had either chosen or been forced to separate from his troop, as occasionally occurs. A female had left with him, which is practically unheard-of behavior. The two baboons joined a troop of langur monkeys, a completely different species, and of course, although hopelessly outnumbered, established immediate and unquestioned dominance over the timorous smaller animals. Like a tiny garrison of soldiers that tyrannizes a peaceful human community, their authority was so absolute that they were able to enforce on the langurs the characteristic baboon intolerance for foreigners. When a lone langur male from a different group tried to join their band, the baboons forced the langurs to drive him away unmercifully, although under ordinary circumstances eventually the langurs probably would have accepted the newcomer of their own species.[72]

The monkey's grasping hands and feet are the means by which it clings to mother's body and becomes initiated into its social order. But *why* does it cling? Again, Dr. Harlow's ingenious research has shown us the answer.[73]

For a long time animal psychologists studying monkeys, like many who studied humans, had assumed that the infant's attachment to its mother derives from the oral satisfaction of nursing. Dr. Harlow tested this idea by giving his monkey babies two substitute dummy mothers, one consisting of a bare cylindrical wire frame, and the other of the same skeleton covered by terrycloth. Both had wooden heads and artificial breasts. For half the babies milk flowed from the wire mother's breasts, while for the other half milk came through the terrycloth mother's breasts. The infants could have reacted to neither dummy mother. Or they could have shown an attachment only to the dummy that gave milk, whether bare wire or terrycloth, a result that would corroborate the assumption that suckling leads to emotional attachment.

What actually occurred was that all the infants became attached to the *terrycloth mothers, whether or not they gave milk.* The infants would spend hours clinging to them for the pleasure of the physical contact alone. Those whose wire mother had the milk would visit her only long enough to satisfy their hunger, and then scamper right back to the comforting terrycloth mother. Those whose wire mother had neither milk nor terrycloth ignored her altogether.

In the wild, the infant who clings closely to the mother will be both better fed and better protected. With her close by he feels secure enough to venture away for longer and longer intervals during which he explores his world, only to scurry back to her for reassurance at the slightest alarm. The question arises as to how the infant acquires this feeling of safety. For example, is it a result of the experience of being protected?

Dr. Harlow found that infant monkeys are terrified by a toy teddy bear that walks while beating a drum. Some crouch with hands over their heads and others lie face down screaming inconsolably. If now the terrycloth mother is placed in the room, the infants will stop crying and dash to her, clinging desperately and burying their heads. Within a few moments they are reassured by the loving contact and will peek at the cause of their recent terror. Soon they are leaving mother to explore and then even play with a previously dreaded object, often bringing it back to her side during periodic returns to her for comfort and reassurance. Moreover, if the terrycloth mother is only *visible* beyond a glass screen, the infant is reassured without even being able to touch her. So apparently the experience with a living protective mother is *not* necessary to elicit the reassurance she provides. It is evoked by just the image of the comforting texture of an inanimate body, to which the infant has clung for many a contented hour.

So for a monkey as for a man, love is built in layers of memory, is cued by vision, and made by hand.

Maturation

Brain Calendars

Of course the human infant cannot grasp well enough to sustain its weight. Like all the rest of its biochemical as well as physiological functions, a human baby's grasp is extremely immature at birth relative to those of an infant monkey or ape.

It is interesting to compare the maturation schedules of higher primate species.[74]

	GESTATION (MONTHS)	INFANT DEPENDENCY (YEARS)	PUBERTY/SEX MATURITY (YEARS)	AVERAGE LIFESPAN (YEARS)
Rhesus monkey	5.5	1	3	14
Chimpanzee	7.9	3	8–9	35
Man	9.0	8	14.0	70

You will notice that all the phases of life in man are markedly elongated with the exception of that of gestation. Because the gestation period of chimpanzees relative to lifespan is about *twice as long* as man's, they are much better developed at birth. Thus apes are able to complete proportionally more of their growth within the womb *because their heads will never enlarge to the degree that man's does.* A human baby must be born while still extremely immature in order for his head to be able to pass through the mother's pelvis. Soon after birth an ape can crawl on all fours, whereas it takes a human infant about another nine months to reach this stage, a period requiring especially intensive womblike care which Montagu calls "extra-uterine gestation."[75]

Whereas the ape is born with about a 200-cubic-centimeter brain, which will reach its full size of about 500 cubic centimeters within two years, a human baby is born with about a 400-cubic-centimeter brain which will reach 750 cubic centimeters by the end of the first year, having achieved by then only half its adult size. By the end of the third year, it will have reached 960 cubic centimeters, or about three quarters of its full size, adding the balance over the next seventeen years to reach about 1200 to 1400 cubic centimeters *at age twenty.*[76]

It is plain that so rapidly expanding a brain must be gotten through the birth canal early, and out into the world where it can begin learning in infancy all the things that its startling expansion makes possible, and the complexity of human life makes necessary, especially the language and other symbols of its culture.

Neoteny

Aside from the amazing brain growth, human development proceeds at a quite leisurely pace and in some ways never reaches the level of complete differentiation found in apes. This is part of a fascinating process called neoteny which signifies the tendency to retain early developmental features throughout life. The developmental features retained are not only those of its own embryonal stages, but also those of the immature stages of the *remote ancestors of its species.*

Various "lower" animals begin as eggs that hatch into immature forms known as larvae. A larva then becomes transformed through intermediate stages into the adult, say a fish, a frog, or a salamander. The eggs of many species are so nearly alike that they cannot be distinguished in appearance except by the most painstaking examination. The larval forms that emerge from the eggs also bear a great deal of similarity to one another, so that only an expert can discriminate one, for instance, that will become a salamander from one that will become a frog. The later developmental stages become progressively more "differentiated," that is, changed not only from one another, but also from the common characteristics their egg and larval stages shared. The specialized adult forms that then result are markedly differentiated and therefore easily and immediately recognizable by anyone. From study of fossils we can also see that the *immature* stages of certain modern animals resemble the *immature* stages of ancestral extinct animals much more closely than the adult modern forms resemble the adult extinct forms.[77]

Now suppose that through various mutations a particular animal became adapted to live its entire lifespan, and even to reproduce, while arrested in an immature form, say the larva stage. Then its potential to become a specialized differentiated adult would never be realized. Such is actually true of Proteus, one of a group of modern salamanders living in deep, cold water, which normally retains its gills, remaining and reproducing in the larval stage throughout its life.[78] The existence of its adult stage was unknown to investigators until by chance the larvae were exposed to warm water which activated their previously dormant thyroid glands, causing them to metamorphose unexpectedly into the mature adult form. By the neotenic process an animal thus retains throughout life its immature nonspecialized characteristics which, as in Proteus, may be of more survival value in stressful circumstances than adult ones. As would be expected, larval Proteus resembles extinct salamander forebears more closely than adult Proteus does.[79]

More important, as we have seen in the last chapter, such immature nonspecialized characteristics are the ones that *maintain an animal's potential for giving rise through mutation to a major new group that will succeed it.* The nonspecialized early ape line that gave rise to the modern specialized apes on the one hand and to man on the other is a good example. The modern apes have lost too much of their immature nonspecialization to evolve basically new adaptations, let alone give rise to a new species. But modern man, the example par excellence of neotenic retention of immature or "embryonal" characteristics, is capable of evolving not only adaptations to every circumstance and clime from outer space to ocean depths, but also of giving rise as did his early ancestors to a *new and more successful species.*

The components of man's skull, teeth, brain, and mind are the best examples of neoteny in our species (see Figure 1, p. 96).

In the embryo of all vertebrates there is a frontward bend at the head end which points the part that will become the jaws, nose, and eyes

FIGURE 1

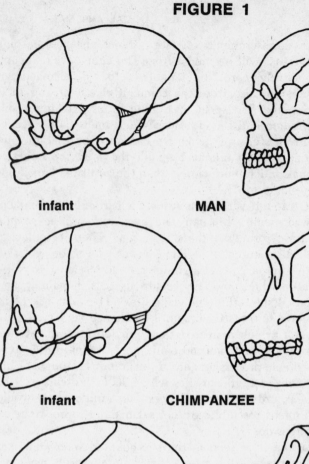

infant   **MAN**   adult

infant   **CHIMPANZEE**   adult

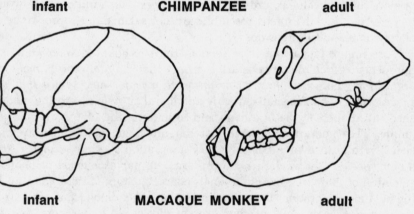

infant   **MACAQUE MONKEY**   adult

NOTE: Drawn to approximately the same size, not to scale.

The infant skulls at left are quite similar to one another. The adult human skull at right is much more similar to the infant form than are the adult skulls of the chimpanzee or macaque. In other words, the adult human skull is "neotenous"; it retains its infantile characteristics. (After Ashley Montagu, The Human Revolution. *New York: Bantam, 1967, p. 133. Courtesy of A. A. Abbie and the Royal Society of South Australia.)*

down toward the portion that will become the feet. Thus the part that will be the brain bends and therefore lies at the extreme front tip of the body.[80]

In every species from frog to alligator to dog and shrew this bend is secondarily *straightened out* by the time maturity is reached, so that the jaws and *nose* wind up at the extreme front tip of the body, followed by the eyes and then the brain, making a straight continuous line with the horizontal body. Man is the only vertebrate that *retains* the original bend in adulthood, so that in his erect posture his jaws and nose are still largely directed downward toward his feet, making almost a 180-degree angle curving back upon his vertical body, while his eyes look horizontally and his brain is at the top.[81]

In contrast, the adult chimpanzee shows an arrangement of both body and head that is halfway between the condition in dog and that in man. His body is not erect but it is carried obliquely, and his head accordingly shows a partial straightening out, with the jaw jutting out ahead while the nose, eyes, and brain follow in sequence up a slanting plane.[82]

The most intriguing aspect of this evolution is that in the *young* chimpanzee the head and body *are* carried erect, the jaws do not protrude, and the face is vertical, thus strikingly resembling those of an adult human. So the adult human retains arrangements that the juvenile chimpanzee has to start with, but loses as he matures (see Figure 2, p. 98). What is more, the juvenile chimpanzee, much more closely than the adult, resembles the nonspecialized apes that evolved into both modern apes and man, particularly their immature forms.[83]

So, in the sense that we never develop the slanted body and head posture and jutting jaws of adult chimpanzees, we could be considered, like the Proteus salamander, as creatures that never reach full maturity.

The same principles apply to our teeth. Our permanent teeth resemble the milk teeth of apes more closely than the permanent teeth of apes. Likewise the permanent teeth of modern man more closely resemble the milk teeth than the permanent teeth of Austalopithecines.[84] The long-delayed eruption of both milk and permanent teeth is also a neotenous prolongation of the toothless state of the unborn baby.

But the most critical manifestation of human neoteny lies in the realm of brain and the extraordinary mind it supports. Whereas in apes brain growth is completed by the end of the second year, in man it continues until the end of the second *decade*.[85]

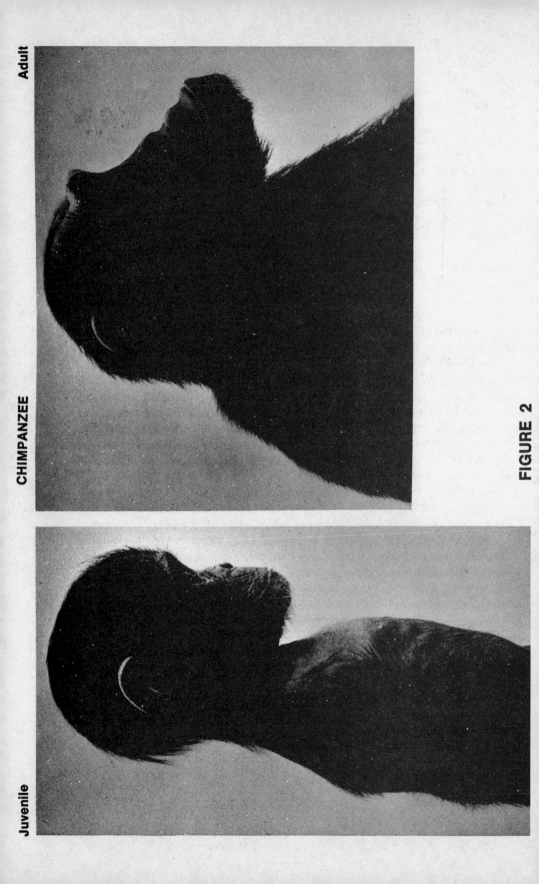

FIGURE 2

Primate Love and Play: Nurture, Educability, Humor

The monkeys, through emancipation from instinct (and from the ground), achieved markedly increased plasticity of behavior and ability to learn. Love became the bond that assured that the infant, once produced, would be not only nurtured until it could fend for itself in terms of finding food, but also be taught the skills that make for survival in an (albeit loosely) dominance-ordered society.

Play became the vehicle of that learning. By the end of a year most monkeys are pretty much freed from the intense attachments to mother, although they maintain some proximity for another year or more, and by the age of three their juvenile playfulness and ability to learn have begun to decline. Apes retain their intense love attachments to mother for three to four years, and remain somewhat close into adult life. And although their learning ability and involvement in play decline after sexual maturity at six, chimpanzees in particular retain for many years a degree of zestful curiosity, manifested especially in the exuberance of relationships with peers.[86]

Enlarging on these foundations, man has built *educability* into his central species characteristic, capacity for which he *retains throughout life*. His love attachments to both parents may persist lifelong and are supplemented by bonds to friends, spouse, and children. His playfulness likewise may be retained for life.

Furthermore, under favorable conditions a grown man's ability to learn does not remain dependent for its momentum on parental love bonds. His play, likewise no longer required to be the vehicle for learning his "place" or for adaptation to a basically unchanging society, can be focused instead on pleasurable expansion of his identity and on *prospecting for adaptations suitable to a very different future*. The rigidity of some human dominance hierarchies is thus more likely to prove an increasing hindrance than a help to successful adaptation. As a person's phases of life follow one another, both his learning and play shift increasingly to the distinctively human realm of language.

Our intellect and imagination are crucial new human survival adaptations. But man's mind owes much to neoteny. The neotenic retention of the capacity for *love* throughout life creates for a person the possibility of using these resources to extend to all people in the world the protective caring that preserves human life from its individual beginning. Equally important is the neotenic human capacity to retain *play* into advanced old age, for playfulness is the seedbed of humor. And human life without the perspective and relief of humor is scarcely human. Notice that the playful puppy becomes the sombre, dignified but unamused and un-amusing old dog. In the same way our closest relative, the chimpanzee, is transformed by age from a brash, playful clown into a dour sourpuss. Of all species, only neotenic man can retain the playful sparkle of humor that makes a delight to everyone of Bernard Shaw's, Pablo Picasso's, or Charlie Chaplin's old age.

Cooperation: Voluntary and Compulsory

The lengthy paths of animal evolution underline several trends that are of critical importance to us in understanding human beings. We must consider the nature of communication, of cooperation, of "instinct," of learning, and of aggression.

First, it is clear that from the time of the earliest one-celled animals to the present, animal survival has depended upon a high degree of coop-eration between individuals. Simple proximity of many individuals of the same kind of amoebas leads to accumulation of chemicals favoring their asexual reproduction.[87] Simple proximity of many paramecia leads to conjugation and sexual reproduction.[88] The flocking of birds results in their being mutually stimulated by their feeding movements so that they eat much more than they would separately.[89] The congregation in social groups of monkeys and apes leads to increase in the individuality, power, and subtlety of interpersonal relationships, with accentuation of the op-portunity to learn and to teach.

In fact, if one makes an exhaustive compilation of cooperative relation-ships among animals, including those between *different* species, one is driven to the conclusion Piotr A. Kropotkin expounded in his pioneer work, *Mutual Aid: A Factor of Evolution,* that the element of cooperation in animal life certainly is equally or even more impressive than that of competition.[90] Such a list would have to include the endless variety of parasitic relationships, the symbiotic relationships where two species make common cause for mutual benefit, and even relationships in which one species serves another as food and is in turn eugenically improved by the predator's success. Incidentally, for several days after a lion has made a kill, the wildebeest or antelope herd on which he preys are not even jittery in his presence because experience has taught them that only hunger and not bloodlust or "aggression" will cause him to hunt them again, and meanwhile with him in their vicinity, smaller predators are likely to look elsewhere. When not actually being chased by wolves, caribou linger near wolf dens when they could be moving to a safer distance, perhaps for the same reason.[91]

Kropotkin recounts how little lapwings protect other aquatic birds from a preying buzzard, kite, crow, or eagle,[92] and how various species will not abandon a wounded comrade until certain it is dead and they cannot restore it to life.[93] Carrighar relates that an elephant who finds a small, helpless animal on the trail will gently pick it up and lay it to one side.[94] Baboons and gazelles spend safe days together, recognizing each other's alerting barks; pooling the keen baboon vision and the exquisite gazelle hearing and smell, they jointly possess an almost infallible early warning defense against predators. Impalas have been observed to stand by nervously, but without stampeding, while their baboon companions drove away three cheetahs.[95] And in the laboratory so-called natural enemies such as cat and rat have learned readily to collaborate in simultaneously pushing levers to obtain food.[96]

Writing of ants, the innovators of division of labor, Kropotkin suggests that

> . . . we already might safely conclude that mutual aid (which leads to mutual confidence, the first condition for courage) and individual initiative (the first condition for intellectual progress) are two factors infinitely more important than mutual struggle in the evolution of the animal kingdom.[97]

And later:

> . . . we find, at the top of each class of animals, the ants, the parrots, and the monkey, all combining the greatest sociability with the highest development of intelligence. The fittest are thus the most sociable animals, and *sociability appears as the chief factor of evolution* [italics added], both directly, by securing the well-being of the species while diminishing the waste of energy and indirectly, by favoring the growth of intelligence. . . . Happily enough, competition is not the rule either in the animal world or in mankind. . . . Better conditions are created by the *elimination of competition* by means of mutual aid and support. In the great struggle for life— for the greatest possible fullness and intensity of life with the least waste of energy—natural selection eventually seeks out the ways precisely for avoiding competition as much as possible . . .[98]

Man, with his highly developed social hierarchy, has carried cooperation to new heights. Of course the evidence of competition between people is everywhere and cannot be dismissed, but whether expressed in the daily care of infants, the sick, or the elderly, the "women and children first" ethic of passengers on a sinking ship, the flow of automobile traffic through crowded streets, the millions given away every year by philanthropic foundations, or the rallying behind a Roosevelt, Churchill, Hirohito, Stalin, or Ho in times of national crisis, any objective appraisal of modern man will disclose that in the overwhelming preponderance of human interactions cooperation *completely overshadows* competition.

The ubiquitous sociability of living creatures required means of communication so that individuals could cooperate. Animal communication, as we have seen, consists of systems of signals, organized at increasing levels of complexity as independence, initiative, and intelligence become better developed.

The work, love, and play of the animal world, however, is conducted without the *word*, the crucial symbol added to language and embedded in a grammar, that makes it human. Although we now know that the brain operates as a whole, and that localizations of function are not as precise as older investigators believed, it remains true that somewhere in the greatly enlarged cerebral cortex are the structures that invent words, as well as all the complex tools and culture that raised human consciousness and power to levels never achieved before. To comprehend the significance of the *discontinuity* between this new addition, which primarily mediates intellect, and older parts of the brain, which primarily mediate emotion, we must again look backward to the monkeys and apes, only this time to the evolution of their social lives which became the forerunner of man's.

The relatively loose but enduring social structure of arboreal monkeys is the critical survival means which has allowed many species to survive relatively unchanged for twenty million years. At the top of the pyramid is an older dominant male whose guidance is followed willingly by the troop, especially when it comes to moving in search of food, taking flight from predators, or warning other monkey troops away from the home range. The females are almost as large as the males and generally just as powerful and agile.[99] They have full responsibility for the care of the young, shared between the mother and others, while the males generally play no part whatever in the feeding, care, instruction, or protection of the young. Each adult monkey is on his own in foraging for food and in avoiding danger, which usually involves flight. Aside from vocal warnings of infrequent danger, the males do not provide even protection for the females, who must scamper to safety on their own, their infants either clinging to them tightly during tumultuous escapes or falling prey to marauders or gravity.[100]

When the baboons (and macaques) became readapted to living on the ground, profound changes occurred in monkey society as well as body. As we have seen, although these animals are not ancestral to man, their adaptations are illuminating in tracing superficially parallel but deeply contrasting human development in similar circumstances.

Because, unlike the generally safe arboreal monkeys, *baboons were in constant danger* from predators on the savannas, their need for protection led to the first restoration of combativeness among primates since the ancestral shrews. This resulted in a new *division of labor between males and females,* with marked accentuation of specialization of both body and social role.

Over many generations, baboon males became nearly twice as large and heavy as the females, with massive powerful muscles, bigger teeth, and aggressive temperaments.[101] Whereas the minor bickering of arboreal monkeys and apes practically never leads to physical conflict, let alone injury, the fierce male baboons will back their threatening stare, stiffening mane, and slapping of the ground with sudden chase and attack. Ordinarily the swift punishment is limited to pinning the loser to the ground and biting him on the loose skin of the neck without breaking the skin, perhaps followed by the ceremony of sexually mounting the cowering subordinate who presents his hind end as would a submissive female.[102] Like the surrender signals of all fighting species, this behavior has the effect of stopping the attacker, thus usually preventing significant injury. If the opponents are both large dominant males seriously contesting for dominance, until the surrender signal is given the struggle can include serious bites and even grievous or fatal wounds.[103] The touchy combativeness of baboons results not simply from their desire to enjoy the pick of sleeping rocks, food, and females, but from the dire necessity for maintaining order and discipline in a social group that amounts to a wandering garrison surrounded by dangerous enemies against whom they are armed for moment-by-moment survival only with the weapons of their bodies and their cohesive social cooperation.

Our carnivorous shrewlike forebears lived short lives, evenly dispersed over an area, each male solitarily defending a territory as a source of relatively scarce food, while relying on small size, agility, and cover for protection against larger predators. In contrast, herbivorous baboons pass their entire lengthened lives living on abundant food in an interdependent *group* organized for defense. Arboreal monkeys ordinarily stay together out of the comfort of familiarity with well-known companions, but occasionally change groups without too much ado.[104] Apes do the same, except that their groups will mingle and individuals change groups quite readily. Not only that, but since they are not in much danger, males not uncommonly will go off *alone* for days or weeks at a time, behavior in-conceivable among baboons who are fiercely loyal to their group and will not leave unless physically driven away.[105] Baboon troops may peacefully share a water hole, but unlike arboreal monkeys and apes they will not mingle.

Whereas an individual chimpanzee may withdraw from danger without giving so much as a warning call, male baboons are certain to bark a warning to the group and then undertake its defense, offering special protection to females and infants. The young males move at the periphery of the group as scouts, while the dominant males march at the center, guarding the females and young.[106] At a sign or signal of danger, all the males will organize into protective ranks, placing themselves between the predator and their females and young. Safety depends on certainty as to authority and the responsible performance of duty by every indi-vidual. The constant threats and rare fights among baboons serve to suppress the petty squabbles so common among arboreal monkeys and apes, thus maintaining clear and rigid authority within the group for the serious job of repelling the attacks of outside enemies.[107]

In order to motivate the males to carry out such protective functions, the usual male monkey indifference to the young and to the females (ex-cept for mating behavior) had to be replaced during evolution with inter-est and concern. Accordingly the males, including the most dominant, have evolved so that the young are extremely attractive to them and, along with their mothers, are entitled to special consideration. They will seek out opportunities to play with infants first demonstrating friendly intent to the mothers by their manner of approach. Later they take an active part in disciplining the young when juvenile play or squabbling be-comes too rambunctious, thus initiating them with gentle neck-bite chas-tisement into the lower rungs of the dominance hierarchy.[108]

But as is true of any threatened human military community, the price for security is not only eternal vigilance but *inflexible subordination of the individual and his idiosyncrasies to the needs of the group.* Suppose mutation should give rise among baboons to a smaller and less aggressive male who happens also to acquire a brain capable of inventing a tool, perhaps the use of a stick to make easier the digging up of roots baboons prize as food. Because he would not be powerful in the ways ordinarily selected for among baboons, he would be at the bottom of the dominance hierarchy.

Imagine the frustration of a life in which every detail of communal behavior is rigidly dictated by your superiors. No desirable piece of fruit can be eaten, no comfortable sleeping rock may be occupied, no appealing infant can be played with until any superiors present have given permission. Each in turn must specifically show first that he is not hungry, does not want to sleep, or has no wish to play, and then by mounting the next inferior below him demonstrate conclusively that relinquishing the desirable object does not signify yielding his dominance. Then, and only then, may the subordinate act. Most painful of all to the individual, as well as injurious to the species, is the fact that such a subordinate but ingenious baboon might never be able to pass on his superior brain because such males are often kept at the periphery of the group and are never permitted access to the females.[109] Although such rigidity admirably serves the individual and group need to survive by emphasizing the old pattern, in this way the highly specialized baboon has come to a dead end in its evolution. Maintenance of excellent but limited baboon adaptation tends to *prevent innovation even of advantageous changes,* a fate to which human communities also are all too susceptible. But then baboons, in contrast to men, survive in a world thronged with dangerous attackers of other species whom they cannot eliminate. Pogo could never say on their behalf, as he did on ours, "We have met the enemy, and he is us."

Touching

In this somewhat grimly structured society, baboons have developed a loophole that permits pleasant interaction among all individuals. In the arboreal monkeys and apes, *social grooming,* the mutual removing of parasites and debris from the fur and skin, is a comforting service that any two individuals may perform for one another, but it is essentially a lazy, low-key, hygienic activity which occupies only a few minutes at a time and is usually confined to the hair the individual cannot reach for himself.[110]

For baboons social grooming has become a device that cuts across otherwise rigid hierarchical lines. They gather in grooming groups as humans do for conversation, and spend hours grooming one another all over and obviously as much for physical and social pleasure as for cleanliness. They assume a posture of languorous contentment, like people in a barber's chair or on a massage table. Subordinates give more than they receive, especially the females. But even the most dominant males will spend a half minute in reciprocal grooming of the female.[111]

Baboons can relax into this enjoyment without concern because at a moment's notice a cry of alarm will restore effective hierarchical discipline, as with soldiers on bivouac who leap up to grasp arms at the first crack of an enemy rifle. But human beings never have the baboons' degree of certainty about hierarchical relationships. Therefore, even when far from possible battle they are so insecure that officers and enlisted men's social clubs are segregated in order to prevent even social "touching" between superiors and subordinates which might undermine hierarchical discipline.

This fear of undermining hierarchical discipline is probably the reason there tend to be in human society generally strong inhibitions regulating who may touch whom. At first glance these might seem to derive primarily from sexual prohibitions. But I believe that more careful scrutiny will reveal in every instance that the ultimate purpose of the restriction is *maintenance of a dominance order* that among humans might collapse under the impact of touching intimacy. An example is the Plains Indian group among whom the highest status was achieved by touching but not killing the enemy in battle.[112] Another is the taboo in our own culture against the sexes and the races touching one another. A white woman doctor at a Christmas party at our hospital one year would not willingly be kissed under the mistletoe by a black janitor. This might at first sight be mistaken for miscegenation taboo. However, a black psychologist was not only bolder, but welcome. Neither sex nor race had anything to do with it. The embrace of a fellow professional was not as much a threat to her social dominance status as that of a blue-collar worker would have been. The implications for human "encounter groups" which encourage touching between strangers, supposedly avoided only because of erotic overtones or neurotic isolation, should be obvious.

Primate Behavior: Spontaneous versus Provoked, Aggressive versus Violent

One must realize three things about the list presented earlier of innately determined elements of primate behavior. First, that in primates as in other animals, the basic impulses, urges, or drives themselves, to breathe, drink, eat, sleep, and so on, *do* periodically well up from within spontaneously, as well as awaken when stimulated from without. For most of them corresponding elements have been found in the brain which give rise to the impulse or inhibit it in response to changes in the body. Thus a decline in blood sugar stimulates the structures that initiate eating, whereas a full stomach stimulates structures that stop it. Electric stimulation by wires placed in these brain areas can bring about much the same result.

Second, although aggression can be provoked by stimuli from within or without, and brain areas related to its *expression* have been found in monkeys, apes, and man, there is *no observed tendency for aggressive fighting behavior to well up spontaneously*. Although a cichlid fighting fish in the absence of another male will threaten and even attack a stick or pebble in its territory, a dominant male baboon, like a human child or adult, can live quietly for long intervals without showing any threatening or combative behavior whatsoever provided he is not challenged by another animal or stimulated otherwise, as for example by an electrode in his brain.

And, third, in relation to sexual behavior (which has at least a demonstrable spontaneous drive component), and in relation to aggression (which has not), the *signals* that release the behavior and the *action patterns* for fully carrying out the behavior are *entirely learned*. This means that grown monkeys, apes, and men can indulge neither in sexual intercourse nor coordinated fighting without learning when and how to do so.

Therefore in man love and hate may be made by hand, *but only if learned by mind*.

How then can we account for the undeniable profusion of fighting behaviors found among human beings? Human freedom must lead to instability of social dominance arrangements. And, just as in baboons, one of the consequences of resultant uncertainty *may* be violent aggression. But among higher primates, this reaction is *learned*. For example, when the "old man" of a gorilla band is killed by hunters, his females may react to the uncertainty of leaderlessness with total *passivity*.[113] Then human hunters can rush in and beat such a group of animals into insensibility, one of whom, properly conditioned, could dispatch their tormentors with a few well-placed flicks of the wrist.

What do we mean by aggression?[114] This is not as easy a question as it appears. We are used to speaking impressionistically of an aggressive hunter, boxer, salesman, lover, or baby. Obviously the same word cannot be used with precision to designate so many different behaviors.

First, we must separate off predatory or hunting behavior from aggression. Everyone agrees that the motivation of an animal hunting food is unrelated to that of the same animal engaged in a fight with another of his own species. The difference in the inner motivation is clearly revealed in expressive movements. Growling, hackle-raising, and laying back the ears are not shown by a hunting animal unless he is much afraid of a fiercely defending prey, and then only slightly. Instead, a dog, for example, shows the same sort of happy excitement when pursuing a rabbit as when he is about to be fed.

Konrad Lorenz, renowned Austrian student of animal behavior, has defined aggression as "the fighting instinct in beast and man which is directed against members of the same species."[115] He recognizes that this fighting behavior may consist of nothing more than threats at a distance, and is intended only to drive an intruder away from the defender's territory, food, or mate, or to establish a superior position in a social dominance hierarchy. If the fight progresses to combat, the intention is the same. Should injury occur, it is generally the result of accident, so compellingly are the signals of submission given and received.[116]

In contrast, that which in human beings is most universally regarded as aggression is behavior that *is* intended to injure or destroy a person or object. This intention establishes it as *qualitatively distinct from animal aggression.* Such human behavior is designated by Judd Marmor as *violence,* a term useful in distinguishing it from animal aggression.[117]

Lorenz

Despite the weight of evidence of the instinctlessness of higher primates, Lorenz claims that man, too, has an aggressive instinct which makes him fight his own kind. He further claims that man has the same weak inhibitions against doing so with which the relatively unarmed apes are also equipped. He asserts that the reason man is now in danger of self-extermination is that neither his inhibitions against killing his fellow humans nor his ability to *ritualize* aggression are strong enough to prevent him from using the massively lethal weapons his ingenuity has invented, especially since they are capable of inflicting suffering and death so far out of sight that the submission signals of victims are not even perceived. He assumes "militant enthusiasm" in man is an instinct genetically inherited from anthropoid ancestors.[118] And he argues for intensified efforts to deflect aggression into athletic and cultural competition.

The trouble with Lorenz's earnest suggestions is that they are erroneous.[119] He knows very well that one cannot even judge the behavior of geese by observing closely related ducks. Yet, employing a method he would reject as unscientific within his own area, without considering studies of man himself in the process, he extrapolates directly from fish and birds to man. *There is simply no evidence in man or any of his closest relatives of the spontaneous upwelling of aggression admittedly seen in the lower animals.*[120] Furthermore, even when men fight hand to hand there unfortunately seems to be no evidence of even a weak *instinctual* inhibition against killing fellow human beings. Like homicide, the sparing of human life is a *learned* behavior. As Montagu says, arguments from fish and birds are strictly for them.[121]

Ardrey and Dart

Robert Ardrey, a talented American dramatist, has exploited the conclusions of Lorenz and Professor Raymond Dart, a South African anatomist, in several popular but seriously misleading books.[122] On the basis of Australopithecine remains Dart insists that man at his inception was not only a hunter, and killer of his own kind, but a *habitual murderer* and a *cannibal.*

> The blood-bespattered, slaughter-gutted archives of human history from the earliest Egyptian and Sumerian records to the most recent atrocities of the Second World War accord with early universal cannibalism, with animal and human sacrificial practices or their substitutes in formalized religions and with the world wide scalping, head-hunting, body-mutilating and necrophiliac practices of mankind in proclaiming this common blood-lust differentiator, this predaceous habit, this mark of Cain that separates man dietetically from his anthropoidal relatives and allies him rather with the deadliest of carnivora.[123]

One must wonder at the motivation for such a gratuitous calumny against carnivores who, whatever may be their other shortcomings, have never before to my knowledge been accused of harboring cannibalistic, scalping, or necrophiliac impulses.

Furthermore, Dart does not mention that these finds, from which he concludes that Australopithecine was a "habitual" murderer, include only a single shattered adolescent jaw and several crushed animal and human skulls.[124] As Montagu points out, even if inflicted by another Australopithecine, this damage could have been accidentally sustained during a hunt. With our infinitely more accurate firearms we modern men accidentally kill thousands of fellow citizens every year. Either ritual cannibalism or the eating of corpses during periods of starvation may also be the explanation, since they have occurred even in recent times and among advanced people.[125] Dart's findings, as well as those of others, indicate that cannibalism of *any* sort was relatively uncommon.

All three authors appear to neglect evidence incompatible with favored theory about aggression. Without exception our nearest relatives, the chimpanzee, orangutan, and gorilla, in their natural habitats are generally amiable and peaceable to their own kind, scuffling occasionally but rarely injuring one another seriously.[126] This fact is especially notable in view of the fact that the ape arm has many times the strength of a human arm and, even without a rock or branch weapon to supplement it, can easily dispatch a fellow ape with one blow. It is extraordinarily improbable that the small roving bands of early men could have so suddenly acquired such new ferocity toward one another as to outdistance not only that of more primitive baboons, with their million-year head start on man in returning to ferocious life on the ground, but even that of our ancient shrewlike forebears. Especially is this true because man indubitably inherited the *amicable sociability of apes* and added *educability* as his central species characteristic, making him incalculably more dependent for survival than even apes were on cooperation and instruction by scarce fellows. Habitual killing of their own kind by either apes or men would surely have extinguished their species.

Yet Dart maintains that among the very first uses to which these unaccountably bloodthirsty ape-men put their new tools was the intentional killing of each other for food. Lorenz himself points out that cannibalism is almost unknown among mammals because they do not like the taste of their own species.[127] Nevertheless he joins Dart in alleging that early man was a murdering cannibal, on the basis that among the traces of the first use of fire a half million years ago are found the cracked and sometimes charred bones of Peking man himself. That these also may have been remains of individuals who died and then were eaten during a famine is not considered. Not mentioned is that cremation may have been then as now a means of disposing of the dead. Also not mentioned is that there is no evidence whatever anywhere among prehistoric or living peoples of any group that *habitually* killed human beings in order to eat them. With one or two exceptions, infrequent ritual cannibalism is the *only* kind known to occur regularly among men.[128] And of course they do not cite the overwhelming evidence that ancient man, like his ape ancestors, was peaceful and cooperative.

War

All three authors assume, as Lorenz explicitly states, that groups of early men constantly discharged their aggression by attacks on hostile "neighboring hordes." Aside from the fact that groups of early men rarely exceeded tens or hundreds, there is again no evidence whatever that the relations between groups were any less amicable than they are between groups of food-gatherers and hunters today. Even where intermittent ritual attacks are found, they rarely result in a carnage remotely suggestive of the mass slaughter conjured by "war." Indeed, there is no basis whatever in evidence even for suggesting that intergroup conflicts were ever of much consequence in human affairs *until the development of settled agricultural communities about 12,000 years ago.*[129]

In general, warfare among nonliterate peoples consisted of minor raids in which only a few were captured, injured, or killed. Quincy Wright, in his monumental study of war, concluded that generally the more complex human organization became, the more likely it was to be warlike.[130] Also, while no tribes had been adequately described which would not fight under certain circumstances, more primitive peoples seemed to conduct war only after they had picked up the habit from their more "civilized" neighbors.[131]

And Peter Farb more recently notes that warfare is virtually *absent* among the most primitive of men, as for example the Great Basin Shoshone of North America, or among those peoples living at close to the maximum potential of their environment, such as the Eskimo. It was those Indian tribes that were more culturally complex, and particularly those that had had contact with whites, that tended to conduct organized warfare, not only against whites, but among themselves.[132] "Thus the Iroquois, much admired by Americans for their primitive democracy, were among the most warlike of tribes," while the Aztecs developed both the highest level of civilization and most bloodthirsty warfaring habits on the continent.[133]

Human Territory, Property, Dominance

It was only when complex settled communities developed that the *learned* need to defend real estate introduced into human concerns anything remotely resembling animal territoriality. Ardrey's unsubstantiated assertions to the contrary, there is simply no evidence for his reincarnation of the conviction that man has an "Instinct of Property" which, along with the social Darwinism of which it was a part, has been rejected by scientists for the self-seeking rationalization of the status quo it was.

Earlier I suggested that human "aggressiveness," like that of baboons, stems from the higher-primate need to maintain a social-dominance hierarchy and the individual's position within it (ultimately in the service of group survival). That this is truly the overriding concern among humans is illustrated by violence among Eskimos. Wresting a living from one of the most inhospitable environments on the planet, they of necessity are profoundly interdependent. Each person's contribution to the group is so precious that war is too expensive a folly for them. But individual homicide does occur, and almost invariably as a result of adultery. One might be tempted to jump to the conclusion that such killing is "natural," provoked by violation of an "innate" or at least acquired sexual possessiveness. However, the well-documented Eskimo custom of wife lending dashes any such explanation. Rather, the potentially fatal insult occurs when a man has sexual relations with another man's wife *without first obtaining the husband's permission,* which of course is a direct threat to the husband's position in the all-important social- dominance order.[134]

Import of Biological View of Human Violence

One could continue at length correcting the misinterpretations underlying this gloomy view. Here we must turn instead to a brief sketch of what reliable evidence tells us man actually did with his endowment. It is pertinent, however, first to conjecture for a moment about the possible psychological significance of such conclusions in the lives of their authors, as well as their function in society at large.

All three have come from parts of the world in which individuals in recent decades had more than the usual opportunity to be impressed with the ubiquity of man's aggressive destructiveness toward his own species. The cruelties of apartheid in South Africa, of Nazism in Austria, and of the remunerative American obsession with violence reveal humans as more bestial and savage than ever were the maligned apes and ape-men. Such conditions might well drive sensitive and gifted men to specious convictions as to the innateness of human aggression.

Even more crucial is the role such convictions play in *moderating the guilt* any decent man must have at being the beneficiary of institutions that needlessly inflict agony on so many of one's fellow creatures. What better exculpation than to decide that the suffering is *not* needless, but is in fact obligatory? If one can believe that his own and everyone's meanness is enforced by the inexorable hand of immutable instinct, then *it is not our fault* that we create and maintain conditions which continue to shatter millions of human beings.

From such explanations it is but a gentle step to justifications. And justification was indeed the use the British Empire made in the last century of such social Darwinesque slogans as "the white man's burden," in subjugating Indians and so many other militarily weaker peoples. In the past many churches have sanctified resignation to every hideous but profitable consequence of learned human aggression, from the Crusades to slavery, with the admonition "It is God's will." Today, for those no longer susceptible to ecclesiastic tranquilization, this function is largely taken over by distorters of biology who chant what Montagu has so penetratingly designated "the new litany of the innate depravity of man."[135]

It is unfortunate that proponents of the instinctual theory of human aggression seem rarely to respond to the *substance* of critiques of their work,

Instead they usually confine themselves to imputing discreditable motives to their critics, and then attacking them on those spurious grounds.

A sad example is Lorenz himself. He asserted recently that his opponents believe in what he says Philip Wylie calls the "pseudodemocratic doctrine" which denies that individual differences are biologically determined, and holds that "If all men had the same possibilities to develop themselves all men would be equal."[136]

Not only is the doctrine itself erroneous, but its attribution by Lorenz to any responsible critic of his theory is preposterous. Obviously there are gross biologically determined differences between people in height, skin color, vocal timbre, athletic ability, and so on. And there are more subtle biologically determined differences in everything from longevity and allergies to temperament and special talents. But again, our recognition of biological influence in all such factors is based upon *evidence,* not inference. And the conviction that human aggression is instinctual is based entirely upon inference, while it substantially contradicts evidence.

Lorenz has a peculiar propensity for citing irrelevant authority to bolster his unprovable theory: "Lao-tze has said, I believe, that all of the animal is still in man."[137] While I too sometimes find value in the intuitive grasp of reality of a creative mind, in this instance not only the pertinence but the significance escapes me. Surely Lorenz does not mean to assert that unmodified adult human beings can reproduce by being cut in half, or can breathe underwater because our remote ancestors did so. Since vestiges of ancient *physical* structures do not confer the full capability of these structures, why assume that vestiges of *behavioral* structures do so?

Another example of Lorenz's ignoring of the evidence, wrongly ascribing discreditable ideas to his critics, and citing irrelevant authority comes from the testy introduction to his book *Studies in Animal and Human Behavior.*

> . . . I seem to have incurred the fanatical hostility of all those doctrinaires whose political ideology has tabooed the recognition of this fact [human instincts] . . . as Philip Wylie has pointed out, the very cause of this hostility is instinctual. He writes: "No other force could account even for the fury with which men hold to their beliefs, against all evidence and all reason . . ."
>
> Indeed, the deep emotional disturbance so clearly apparent in many adversaries of ethological theory is far more intense than that ever elicited in one scientist by the errors of another. . . . Religious fervor like this is only aroused in men who sense the explosion of a long cherished dogma.[138]

I suppose, in view of my presumption in making an ethological analysis of ethologists, that I must accept gracefully the turnabout of Lorenz's right to make a psychiatric diagnosis of me. But to do our jobs properly each of us must address himself primarily to the formulations rather than the foibles of the other. On the page from which the above quote is taken, Lorenz finds it useful to refer to Wylie approvingly no less than three times. Judging from the high regard in which he holds this American literary Hobbes-goblin, and from Lorenz's dyspeptic view of humanity, one might wonder if Wylie is the only human being he has ever studied.

Does Lorenz seriously mean to advance a novelist's unsubstantiated opinion to counter the opinions of scores of experienced scientists, not to mention extensive evidence? It would be refreshing to read, instead of such pejoratives and references to unqualified authority, a reasoned reply in detail to evidence cited. For the rest, I must leave it to the reader to decide who in this controversy is motivated by doctrinaire political ideology, religious fervor, or cherished dogma, and affirm on my own behalf only that any aggression revealed in these paragraphs of mine was not only learned, but taught.

Tangled Roots of Human Culture

Although they protected their females and young, the prehuman apes and earliest ape-men did not evolve primarily into fighters as did the baboons, as is shown by the gradual general *reduction* in the size of their jaws and teeth.[139] Instead they extended the cooperative sociability of the apes. But *why* did they progress in so different a direction?

Possessing the upright posture and arms free to move in all directions, in addition to greater intelligence, they were able to employ their superior brains to invent *tools,* including words, and then use them for hunting food or producing clothing and shelter. This crucial interplay between brain and body could not have been accomplished by the dolphin, for example, whose great brain is imprisoned in a body at a dead end of specialization for life in water. Possessing tools for hunting, and words for communicating, early man progressed from gathering vegetable and small-animal foods to true hunting of the larger animals. In the course of the constant novelty of the hunt, and the rapid flexible adaptiveness it demanded, ape-man became human. As always in the development of a new species, *the way the new creature did the work of getting its food helped shape its life, including its love and play life.*

Food-Sharing and Division of Labor

The relations between male and female were changed profoundly. A new type of *division of labor* between the sexes brought about a considerable differentiation between them physically. Men, being the hunters, had to be somewhat larger and stronger than women, but since both sexes relied upon cleverness, upright stance, and odor for protection against predators rather than upon teeth and other body specializations, the enormous disparity in body size observed in baboons did not occur. Women became specialized for staying near home to care for babies and children who would constitute impediments to, or be in danger during, the hunt. So it fell to woman's lot to gather and prepare the vegetable foods, as well as to perfect the other homemaking arts, while their men hunted meat. After the hunt, men needed a home base to return to for rest and food, carrying meat they shared with women and children. So *the rudiment of food-sharing found in apes was developed into the spine of human family organization.*[140]

Love and Sex: Dependence, Possessiveness, Dominance

Food-sharing with family made necessary an emotional tie to women and children which would bring the man home to them with his kill. He had to be *attached* to them in a way that would transcend the rudimentary protectiveness and inconstant sexual interests of apes, and even the baboon male's greater protectiveness and enjoyment of playing with infants.

Evolution found a way by transforming the human female from one who is sexually receptive only a few times a year at the fertile periods, as are baboons and apes, into one who is *sexually receptive at all times.* Thus, whereas the perennially active monkey or ape male must shift from one female to another as each becomes receptive in turn, the way was cleared for a man to focus his sexual needs year-round on *one* woman. The rigors of supplying a woman and her children with food were probably such that it was the rare early hunter who could take care of more than one wife and brood at a time. So probably very early it became a common pattern for one man and one woman to devote themselves to each other.[141] It was in this way, some two to three million years ago, that the conditions were created for both parents to give the educable human baby, child, and youth the sustained care that transmitted to him the human innovation of culture. And that is when play took on the function of "self" development, our species' unique preparation for manhood. And thus it was that in primates for the first time love became linked with problematic sexual monogamy.[142]

The cooperative proximity of cells that was built up into love over eons of evolution has become the source of taboo, inhibition, and conflict precisely *because* it is so vital to man's survival. The pale shadow of necessity hovers over the "possessive" love between a man and a woman, even today, when for most of us as adults, no matter how intensely we feel "I can't live without you," the love of any particular individual is in fact an enrichment and not a preservation of life.

But to the *primitive hunter* the woman who in the true sense "cared" for him at home meant the difference between life and death every day, as he did for her, and of course for the children. In fact, from birth to death, the survival of each individual, like that of Eskimos and other peoples who still live at the edge of starvation, hung by the thread of devotion of the few who loved him.

So this human mutual life-and-death dependence lasted a much longer time in early man than it did in other higher primates. And it persists in modern man as a symbolic *psychic* dependence and possessiveness. For example, the infant langur monkey may slap resentfully at the male who mounts the mother on whom his life depends, and he cries piteously when at ten months she shoves him away from her breasts to wean him.[143] But by the end of a year he is fully self-sufficient, at least as to survival, paying no particular further attention to mother's activities, and needing from then on only playmates and companions, not nurturers and protectors.[144]

By comparison, whereas the growing langur monkey soon forgets not only his attachment to his mother but also his rivalry with the grown male who stimulated his jealousy by mounting her in his presence, a human child in the same circumstance, dependent on mother so much longer, may remember and carry a grudge. And nowadays a human child in Western culture of even five, six, or sixteen years who witnesses his mother's intercourse may suffer a "psychic trauma" with injurious consequences that persist for a lifetime. And even a human adult, with or without similar prior experience, may be made uncomfortable by such a scene.

Among apes the progress toward full independence as to survival comes along more slowly than in monkeys, and there is a tendency for a special affection between mother and child to persist into adulthood. The situation otherwise closely resembles that among monkeys in that the adult is virtually independent of the group or any particular individuals for nurture and protection. While the baboons all their lives remain dependent for *protection* upon the group, because each baboon forages for itself, dependence in adulthood is *not upon particular individuals*. Therefore baboons' attachments remain loose, and individuals are interchangeable.

In contrast, since throughout his life man remains dependent for *nurture* as well as protection upon *specific* individuals within his group, his love relationships take on a lifelong neotenic possessiveness. What had been largely a temporary means of assuring the monkey or ape infant's *physical safety* has thus in man been elaborated into a permanent means of achieving adult *emotional security*. Such reflections raise troublesome questions. For example, does the current decline in exclusivity and stability of sexual relationships, manifested with special clarity in the accelerating divorce rate as well as in organized "wife swapping" and so on, reflect the increasing ability of women to "forage" for themselves? If it does, should we human beings therefore regard the adoption of baboon-like relationships between the sexes as an imminent step on the human agenda?

There are already increasing numbers of authorities who claim that marriage is obsolete and will disappear as a social institution in future decades because its economic foundation is evaporating. Others make such epigrammatic recommendations as "every woman should be married, and no man," by which they draw attention to the apparently greater persisting need of women as compared to men to hang onto at least a vestige of the possessive dependency of the past. Still others insist that the human organism and the future of the human enterprise in general will continue to depend on the enduring stability of attachments between men and women. As Montagu points out, it is well to remember that authorities are people who should know.

The matter is made superficially more confusing but profoundly more plain by the fact that it is precisely among Eskimos that we find one of the most ancient traditions of what might seem to be a related behavior, that of wife lending. If sexual division of labor in provision of scarce food is an important factor in the evolution of sexual possessiveness, Eskimos should have been the last people in the world willing to share their mates. But in their world, where the terrain yielded so little food that friends from separate tribes could seldom afford to be close neighbors, the rare visit of a guest was so precious that everything possible had to be done to make his stay pleasant, including provision as a matter of pride of all the sexual comforts of home. Yes, a man might enjoy "laughing with" his host's wife, as these perceptive people are said to have called sexual intercourse,[145] provided the husband first *asserted his social dominance* by giving permission, in which case no threat to either the husband's economic or psychological security was created.[146] It seems that his unrelenting struggle for survival required the Eskimo to find a way to organize his social dominance order so that prized infrequent contacts with fellow humans from other groups could be kept maximally sociable, whereas in our affluent and overpopulated world we have not been forced in general to value amicable relations with others over simple exclusive sexual possession of a woman as a symbol of security. We must note also that unlike our wife *swapping*, the context of the Eskimo's wife *lending* was the respectful offering and obligatory acceptance of hospitality, rather than the frenzied and frustrating pursuit of fun.

Cooperative Sociability and Taboo

As they grew up together generation after generation, early men had to levise regulations of their interactions that would make possible their continued close cooperative relationships. Because human beings, unlike baboons, became dependent for survival on enduring loving attachments to *specific individuals,* the main activities sustaining such relationships had to be controlled. Accordingly, the obtaining and eating of food became carefully regulated by social custom, progressing into taboo and law, sometimes more stringent than those relating to sex. In some nonliterate cultures a man and woman may have sexual intercourse without entering into any extended commitment to one another, but cannot eat together unless they marry. However, although sex might be looked upon tolerantly as a part of play with peers during childhood, most human groups carefully regulated it, too, after adolescence.

One of the most widespread regulations was the taboo against incest, for then as now inbreeding must sometimes have led to plainly disadvantageous results reproductively, and even more so socially. Sexual rivalries and conflicts between members of a tiny family or clan living at the edge of starvation could be catastrophic. So all human groups learned to define forbidden incest according to one scheme or another, and to deflect the sexual needs of children toward members of other bands in accordance with requirements enforced by the parental dominance hierarchy. Small human groups needed one another to provide mates for their offspring. Because it was more often these loving impulses that were diverted onto the outsiders, rather than the hostile ones found by Lorenz and others among birds and fish, neighboring groups generally remained friendly.[147]

Complicated taboos were evolved that served to reduce the sexual temptations within the family and clan, the most widespread of these eventually being the wearing of bodily covering even when climate or activity did not require it. With but less than a handful of exceptions, all human societies described require that at least the directly genital mucous membrane be clothed after adolescence.

By forcing the dependent child to give up the attachments of infancy and replace them with others, early man learned to encourage him to grow into individual adult responsibility. There is also a broader and deeper human social need for control of impulse, of which sexual restraints are only one manifestation. It is only as a consequence of living by sets of morals or ethics that crystallize these restraints that man can *turn impulse to elaborate social purpose.* For example, while incestual urge is transformed into mating and marriage, hunger pangs may give rise to provident plowing and planting, and abject cowardice be reversed into courage.

We are touched emotionally by those who touch us physically, which fact has also contributed to the restrictions among men we considered earlier of impulses that are organized as indiscriminate grooming among baboons.

After all, love and its various components had become too crucial to survival to be bandied about by adults promiscuously. And even today, when daily individual safety no longer depends on *individual* love, the survival of our species so completely depends on love in the broader sense that adults cannot afford to allow it to degenerate into the empty slogan it has become for many.

In order to avoid forbidden touching, it may be best to avoid touching with the eyes, or *looking* at, a taboo person or the taboo part of his body, and perhaps even to avoid using his name. Accordingly, complex avoidances of endless varieties in different cultures have arisen which restrict looking and naming. Nonliterate peoples know the power of vision and of name words. That is why among the Zulu a man may not see his mother-in-law's uncovered breasts, and why among the Eastern Bantu a man may not speak his mother-in-law's name.[148]

One of the most interesting of these behaviors has to do with the personal body space or buffer zone surrounding the individual. A bright green and blue parrot fish swims languorously near a skin diver, but darts swiftly away if approached closer than five feet. The moray eel rarely bites a hand unless it approaches within his three-foot body buffer zone. Except during the breeding season some birds will not allow themselves to be approached within touching distance even by members of their own species. Among arboreal monkeys the buffer zone is nonexistent or very small. But the dominant male baboon jealously guards as much as ten feet about himself which is invaded without permission at his peril by a subordinate, whose personal body space is correspondingly smaller.[149]

Among human beings the personal body space varies widely, having to do with dominance relationships. Within the realm of consciousness lies the edict that a commoner may not too closely approach a king. These differences, even when brought about by largely unconscious cultural influence, can also exert profound effects on the relationships of peers. E. T. Hall points out that Latin Americans stand very close by our standards when conversing.[150] Consequently, North Americans talking with them frequently back away to a distance they find comfortable, resenting the intrusiveness of "pushy" foreigners, and at the same time conveying an impression of coldness or unfriendliness. Neither party may be clearly aware of this culturally conditioned "silent language," which can bring the best-intentioned foreigner a response of puzzling mistrust or even enmity.

Baboons confined with strangers will fight constantly and fatally over such slights to their status. Often such combative behavior in *captivity*, which forms the basis for many commonsense but mistaken impressions of primate "instinctual" aggression, is intensified (as it is among ordinarily peaceable rats) by overcrowding.[151] Human beings may do the same in their wider zoos, loading space with many more complicated and private implications that lead to lethal fighting. It is a tribute to the greater power of human social cooperativeness that the crowded conditions in our cities, and especially the inhumane compression of people in our slums, do not create virtual *abattoirs*.

Even within one culture, wide differences exist in the meaning of personal space. One woman may resent her husband's "smothering" tendency to stay at her side all evening at a cocktail party. Another, whose husband circulates freely, is infuriated by her husband's "abandonment."

The personal body space, and the larger fixed areas outside it, which human beings have learned to value in terms of comfort, privacy, and control are complexly linked into social dominance systems. A woman resents the "invasion" of her kitchen by her mother-in-law. A man's children are gloweringly informed that they must "never put foot in my workshop." A psychotic man goes about angrily elbowing people on a sparsely populated street in order to "make myself a place to breathe." An equally delusional idea not many years ago sent panzer divisions in quest of "lebensraum."

Man and Values

Out of his animal beginnings, sociable, cooperative man thus learned to do the *work* of staying alive within a social dominance hierarchy consisting at first only of his family and clan. And in the complex hugeness to which his social order has grown, man often still yearns for the manageable intimacy of his primordial tribe.

For man, *love* became at least an equally crucial survival force, while *play* became a lengthening opportunity to try out, to expand, and to rehearse the learned as well as the innate wisdom of the past, in order to build a self that could better enjoy and expand it in the future.

Neotenic man thus became a creature of more or less stable mores handed down from generation to generation, and eventually of *values*.

But having evolved to relative biological stability, man's unspecialized physique and endlessly curious mind endow him permanently with the childlike powers of discovery and innovation. For biological change man substituted nimble cultural evolution as his specific adaptation to reality.

In so doing, he also took command of much around him, creating the accelerating changes to which he then had to adapt. In hewing stones into knives and axes he could grasp and wield, and molding emotional cries into denotative words he could comprehend over distance in space and time, he simultaneously transformed them into the first symbols, and himself from ape-man to man. Slowly, over millennia, man created and compiled myriads of cultural objects. Judging by the most primitive peoples of our own times, the first modern man, Cro-Magnon, probably had two thousand or so cultural objects. Twentieth-century man has tens of thousands of things just within his own home, culled from a choice of millions. Most have been invented within the last one hundred, and made during the last twenty, of man's two million years.

But to really understand ourselves, and to master continuously the threats to our survival without dogmatic fancies, we must maintain perspective on all the *billions* of years of adaptation that produced us. For that long past still lives in various ways in man and his values.

Our line of descent traverses fiery clouds of cosmic gases which adapted to energy loss by condensing into solids, a planet that adapted to condensation by rotating faster, mountain crags that adapted to wind and rain by eroding, atoms that adapted to concentration by forming simple molecules, simple molecules that adapted to ultraviolet light by forming complex amino acids, which in turn adapted to further radiation by combining into proteins, viruses, and the first self-reproducing cells. Our lineage continued through genes that adapted to X-radiation by mutating, cells that adapted to scarcity by clustering, specializing, and cooperating to form myriad plants and animals, fish that adapted to entrapment in drying tidepools by learning to breathe air, and reptiles that adapted to cold by becoming warm-blooded mammals.

Our heritage veered sharply when primates adapted to scarcity by climbing trees, developing binocular vision and grasping limbs, and exchanging the remnants of innate for acquired knowledge; it accelerated greatly when apes adapted to the retreat of trees by returning to the ground, specializing their hands and minds for tool-using, and intensifying their sociable cooperativeness; and it came into precise focus as man adapted to scarcity by becoming a fully erect, omnivorous, highly cooperative, hunter-forager, symbol-maker, culture-transmitter, and future anticipator.

Modern man, spreading over the globe in the largest numbers ever reached by a primate, continues adapting to scarcity by devising social orders based on elaborate divisions of labor, as well as by revolutions of values involving agricultural, technical, scientific, industrial, commercial, political, social, and other innovations.

This last grotesquely oversimplified statement will have to take the place of a comprehensive tracing of the bewildering saga of man's migrations outward in all directions from his African birthplace to penetrate every sector of the globe. Limitations of space and time also restrict me from attempting to present any sequential account of the roiling eddies of humanity that have hatched the numberless cultural variations and successions that comprise what we call history. In their place I will focus on the *human agenda,* and the *human mind.* Man's mind both inscribes items into future pages of the human agenda and devises means of managing those on the page open before us. The human agenda is a plan, and the human mind is that aspect of man's total personality that both contrives and follows it.

The human agenda, thus extending the progression of the cosmos, takes up from the agenda of life the task of mastering reality through increasing intelligence and heightened levels of consciousness, within conditions of expanding freedom and joy.

But the byways of that adventure constitute a separate chapter.

4 Adaptation and the Human Agenda

The Human Agenda

Introduction

A man may fling a stone and predict with fair accuracy both its arc and its landing place. But if he should toss a dove into the air, the living creature may fly in any direction and come to rest anywhere within a circle of two hundred miles. Its range of freedom is so much wider than the stone's as to confound human prediction.

The forces that set our sun and its planets into their stately minuet so long ago are regular. Barring external accident, our solar system's death and chill interment in darkened space billions of years hence could be predicted now with some accuracy. But no one today, let alone long ago when first was lofted from ape loins, could predict accurately his trajectory or remote destination. The best we can do, while dealing with the current items on the human agenda, is to try to plan for the item *after* next in such a way as to preserve man's *freedom to choose* his path of flight when he gets to it. Because phases in the past development of matter, life, and man follow one another in an understandable pattern, we have some assurance that the future will be characterized by an understandable and at least partially predictable sequence of *new* phases.

Evolution of everything in the universe proceeds through the cosmic, biologic, and human agendas according to these universal themes: constant order, constant change, constant conservation, constant innovation, constant predictability within an area of uncertainty, and constant heightening of consciousness.

Reading these lines one could suppose that I am attributing all events

123

to a first mover or god who arranged whatever has happened. Anyone who has read the earlier chapters will realize that this is precisely the opposite of my intention. It is not anxiously postulated primal causes but resolutely investigated *proximate* causes that we need to pursue. And the important characteristic of an agenda is not who made the paper on which it is written, or even by whom and why the earliest entries were made, but rather how the items already taken up have shaped the alternatives posed by the items before us, and those ahead. *The panicky search for ultimate truth is the biggest stumbling block in the way of finding the pieces of truth needed for survival and advance now.*

One of the aspects of the human agenda that it is most urgent for man to become aware of is just how minute are the pitiful crumbs of time that so far have been allotted to accomplishing so much in the human experiment. Man's entire existence as an identifiable animal is compressed into the final one twenty-five-hundredth of the earth's existence. All of civilization has been achieved in the past 1 percent of human existence. But man, through these instants of time, has awesomely extended the central theme of biological evolution: *the bringing to conscious decision aspects of adaptation previously arranged as nonconscious and often instinctual compulsions.*

The most momentous contribution with unforeseen consequences for our present reality was the introduction of agriculture and animal husbandry only some twelve to fifteen thousand years ago. For it was then that the hunting-foraging way of life which had shaped ape into man began to give way to life in settled communities, which in turn made possible all the blessings and afflictions of civilization. With his first deliberate sowings and reapings prehistoric man unknowingly entered into a far-off chapter of the human agenda the first possibility in the history of all life of generating *controllable abundance of food.*

The inventor of the wheel unknowingly entered the automobile into a remote page of the agenda for future consideration. Development of the tribal council entered into a distant future page an elected legislature. The work of Marie and Pierre Curie entered the cyclotron into the page for the 1940s. Louis Pasteur's studies entered into the page for the 1950s Salk's immunization against polio.

Failure consciously to plan for upcoming items is becoming increasingly dangerous. The scarcity that impelled the spread of agriculture also brought about the bitter irony of surpluses rotting amid starvation. Unpleasant but unimportant auto exhaust fumes of 1915 entered upon the human agenda the smog menace of the 1960s. Limited debauchery of the naïve hot jazz age entered the joyless promiscuity of the "sophisticated" cool age. Alamogordo of 1945 may have entered Armageddon of the 1970s.

It has always been up to each generation of man to master current challenges on the human agenda. From now on every generation will have a
new responsibility. Since the establishment of human culture it has been
man himself who has been making a large part of the most crucial entries,
although they have been largely compiled unconsciously. The most significant change in current human evolution is that now this process of making
agenda entries is being brought under *conscious* control, so that the item
after next on the human agenda can be chosen consciously and anticipated
in time for us to adapt. In Part II we will consider how conscious control
is being extended even over our own biological evolution.

Another aspect of the human agenda it is urgent for us to become aware
of is the nature of the special discontinuity between otherwise continuous
animal and human evolution. In the animal series from protozoa to man,
most crucial adaptations have depended mainly upon structural bodily
change. However, as we have seen, adaptation through association in
groups also begins with the simplest unicellular organism, and increases
in importance in the progressively more complex organisms.

While body structure in man has reached an evolutionary plateau on a
nonspecialized, vertebrate, mammalian, primate pattern, changing *psychosocial* adaptations have become the primary apparatus conveying human evolution toward increased consciousness, thereby making possible
advance adjustment to upcoming items on the human agenda. The aspect
of the human personality that contrives these psychosocial inventions we
call the mind. And the human mind is therefore the organ of human
adaptation.

Darwin: Opposed and Embraced

Before examining the mind more closely, we must consider the crucial
implications for man's future of the contributions of Charles Darwin,
touched on briefly in Chapter 3. For it is through an understanding of
his work that we are able to clarify the critical *differences* as well as
similarities between the evolution of animals and of man.

But his findings often have been distorted to bolster the position of one
or another special interest group, and thus *obscure* either the similarities
or the differences. The first notable outcry was from religionists offended
by inclusion of man in the general scheme of biological evolution on the
basis of his similarities to other animals. The response of outrage was of
the dimension one would expect from the previous history of the conflict
between science and religion. Some came from fellow scientists such as
Sedgwick who feared that Darwin's theory would "sink the human race

into a lower grade of degradation than any into which it has fallen since its written records tell us of its history."[1] But as always the clergy were the most vociferous. The sense of their attacks can be summed up in the declaration that "the principle of natural selection is absolutely incompatible with the word of God."[2]

Despite the attacks of powerful and articulate orthodox enemies ranging from Benjamin Disraeli and Bishop Wilberforce to Pope Leo XIII and William Jennings Bryan, it has prevailed. Foremost among its defenders was renowned biologist Thomas Henry Huxley, who was always ready to uphold Darwin's epochal discoveries with wit and wisdom, in print or from the podium, a task of which their shy and unaggressive author was not capable himself. Moreover, in *Man's Place in Nature* he applied them, as Darwin had not at the time, to the human species.[3] The panicky fulminations of opponents were fruitless against not only Darwin's original defenders but also the avalanche of subsequent corroboration.

When Clarence Darrow failed to win acquittal for John T. Scopes in 1925 on the charge of breaking the state law of Tennessee by teaching Darwinism, the antievolutionists won their last hollow victory. The overturning of his conviction on a technicality by the Tennessee Supreme Court was followed by decades in the United States in which it has been hardly possible to mount any successful assault whatever against the theory of evolution. In fact, its fundamentalist enemies have been unable even to prevent the wiping out of the last few state laws forbidding the teaching of evolution. This picture has been clouded but not obliterated recently by partial victories of antievolutionists in forcing schools to teach the theory of special creation of man as an alternative to evolution.[4]

Of course what had so exercised the fundamentalists was not just the challenge Darwin's theory presented to the biblical concept of the origin of all plant and nonhuman animal species, but its prompt application to man. Had Darwin and his supporters been willing to draw an artificial line between man and the rest of life, no doubt accommodation to the scientific view would have come much sooner. But they were rigorous and successful in pointing out the evidence that man too is the result of evolution from simpler forms.

Then began a continuing trend in which similarities were *embraced* by religion so as to achieve what opposition had failed to accomplish. Nowadays there are those who try to recoup the loss by helping religion swallow science. They claim that the whole controversy between the Darwinists and fundamentalists was based merely on a misunderstanding of the Bible, which when properly interpreted reveals evolution to have been God's will all along. We are even sometimes treated to assertions by scientists that the entire controversy between science and scripture was just a mistake since they are merely different ways of coming to the same conclusions! We must be wary of such glib efforts to blur the distinctions between basically different human endeavors.

The approach of religion usually is to establish by authority the foreordained conclusion that man is significant in some way beyond what can ever be known of him in his temporal life. Its constant effort is not to discover new truth, but rather to confirm the thesis that man matters to and is observed by some ineffable power beyond himself, that he is thereby rewarded and punished, loved and protected—especially the individuals who most closely resemble the affirmer. Without making the unscientific blunder of arguing the negative, we must assert that any science worthy of the name cannot begin this way, but must instead always rest on scrupulous efforts to exclude this and any other bias from the process of objective observation and thinking, regardless of the palatability of the conclusions reached.

By the time of Darwin, science had convincingly displaced man from the center of the universe, severely shaking his faith in ecclesiastic authority. His priests were still smarting from the resultant diminution in respect in which they felt held by both God above and their flock below. They, and all the conservative forces of society which looked to them for rationalization of the status quo, were not prepared to permit man's further reduction from angel to animal, with the inevitable further sharp decline in both the prestige of the clergy and popular acquiescence to "divine will." But there was nothing they could do to prevent it. Whether or not man is the special concern of a God, it was soon widely apparent that there was no longer any plausible basis for insistence that either man or his abode on earth, in the solar system, or in the galaxy, had been created *separately* and *specially* to receive a deity's devotion. Even more important, our species' progress toward material security and abundance was by now so great that for the first time large numbers of men could bear to *acknowledge* this demotion.

The dropping away of these shackles of terror would seem to have presaged a new era for man, one in which recognition of man's continuity with the universe and all life might be matched by comprehension of the possibilities inherent in the propensity for loving cooperation built into all protoplasm. But the time was not yet ripe. Epochal as were Darwin's findings, the momentum of society and the grip of its values on the mass mind were so powerful as to be rocked only slightly in the wake of his ideas. The power structure of the land of its birth seized upon his theory of evolution through natural selection of the fittest to survive by *out-reproducing* others and distorted it into artificial selection of the fittest to survive by *out-exploiting* others. In a tour de force of the engulfment and perversion of science, they installed it in the niche then vacated by Genesis as the new scripture of commerce and imperialism later called "social Darwinism."

Social Darwinism

The essence of the web of social Darwinism was that all its confusing strands argued for the intrinsic rightness of whatever circumstances existed. No matter how hideous were the conditions of slavery, starvation, or warfare, not to mention the lesser evils in society, we were urged to rest content because all operated to *eliminate the unfit*. German General Friedrich von Bernhardi even wrote shortly before World War I that "War is a biological necessity of the first importance . . . without war, inferior or decaying races would easily choke the growth of healthy budding elements, and a universal decadence would follow."[5]

Conversely, anyone who tried to ameliorate the sufferings of the poor, the sick, or the weak was opposing the "law of nature" by preserving the unfit. This view, if carried to its logical next step, would lead to the conclusion that any aid rendered a fellow human being would sabotage natural selection. This is like saying that if one discovered a modern Mozart suffering from dietary deficiency and rickets, as did the original, treating him with vitamin D would be encouraging deterioraton in the next generation. Quite the opposite is true, for the simple truth is that while musical genius may have a genetic element, rickets is purely an *acquired* disease.

Progress, as Leonard Hobhouse points out, was defined as "the process wherein the fittest survived . . . it is always the fittest who survive, because the fact of the survival proves their fitness."[6] This sort of empty circular thinking discards not only all human values but erases the crucial distinction made by Darwin that the struggle for survival under conditions of natural selection resulted from success in *reproduction*, which entails enormous cooperation, rather than success in besting or killing one's fellows, which does not. There is no species, in fact, which has evolved by killing off its own weakest members.

Darwin himself understood that while natural selection produced man's intelligence, it was man's intelligence and not natural selection that had produced language, complex cooperative social life, tools, control of fire, and all that we call culture.[7] Thus man early began removing himself from the control of natural selection. And Darwin plainly stated that the human invention of war operated always to promote survival of the *unfit*.

The bravest men, who were always willing to come to the front in war and who freely risked their lives for others, would on the average perish in larger numbers than other men.[8] . . . In every country in which a standing army is kept up, the fairest young men are taken to the conscription camp, or are enlisted. They are thus exposed to early death during war . . . and are prevented from marrying . . . the shorter and feebler men with poor constitutions are left at home and consequently have a much better chance of marrying and propagating their kind.[9]

Social Darwinists distorted and capitalized upon man's previously despised similarities to animals while denying his important differences from them. In the evolution of species other than man, killing is almost completely restricted to the process of hunting for food, the prey generally being confined to members of other species. As we have seen, fighting between individuals of the same species almost never results in serious injury or death because this would be biologically disadvantageous. Instead, competition between members of one species centers almost exclusively on securing the means of individual and procreative survival. Even where territoriality or social dominance hierarchy is best developed, *the net effect of the maintenance of personal privilege is the protection of the reproductive issue.* Competition between members of the same species is never, as in man, over capital or real estate or the power they confer, *as ends in themselves.*

They also ignored the plain fact that it is often the wealthiest and most powerful tyrants who (as a consequence of illness or accident) are least fitted to survive reproductively or in other ways, and that it is often the poor and helpless who are not only the most fertile, but the most fitted to survive in *human culture* by the capacity to love, or to creatively confer survival benefits upon others.

So while the religious antievolutionists succumbed, those defenders of special privilege who were able to capture the new understanding were able to prosper as social Darwinists. As often happens in military conflicts, he that is vanquished then wins in defeat what he could not gain in battle. And the victorious army of evolutionists *for the time being* was and is traduced by the fraternization of the former foe. But there will come another day, for in the long run reason survives subversion as well as victory. As Max Planck put it: "Truth never prevails, but her adversaries always perish in the end."[10]

Aggression in Higher Animals: Evidence, Fantasy, Theory

Social Darwinism, never endorsed by its namesake, was soon recognized as a dangerous myth, and was finally exploded in the early decades of this century.[11] But it appears that some mistakes are written into the human agenda over and over again. We saw in the last chapter how man's systematic extermination of his own kind, far from being an outgrowth of his biological evolution, is really an evolutionary perversion of recent social origin. We saw how Lorenz failed to take into account the enormous evidence that in higher animals and man destructive violence toward fellows is a result of *training* or the *breakdown of social organization* and not the consequence of the firing off of innate action patterns. Acquired action patterns are taught by society, whether peaceful or destructive. A crucial current issue on the human agenda is to demonstrate the validity of the conclusion that the individual must *learn* to be peaceful or violent.

Laboratory and Field Studies

This empirical finding must be differentiated from any romantic biases. I am not asserting that "man is innately good," or that the solution to all our problems is substitution of permissiveness for frustration. The conclusion that aggression is not innate is based rather on solid laboratory and clinical evidence.

Dr. John P. Scott, a zoologist and biopsychologist, has been studying animal aggression since the 1940s. He states, "There seems to be no internally arising drive that has to find an outlet." There must always be some outside cause to provoke attack even when an animal has been made very irritable by surgical modification of the brain. Unprovoked attack can only be produced by *training*. In his experiments with mice, the trainee is subjected to attack by a mouse placed in his cage which is experienced in fighting. When he fights back the attacker is removed from his cage. The following day the trainee is provoked by a mouse only dangled in his cage by the tail. As soon as he attacks the intruder is removed. On the third day a noncombative mouse is placed in his cage which the trainee pursues and quickly intimidates. Within one or two days of easy victories the trainee will attack any mouse, even a female or young one, something that never occurs otherwise. Not innate action patterns, nor frustration, but *success in fighting* makes this mouse fight.

Inhibition of fighting in a mouse is produced by fixing the fight in the opposite direction, by arranging that he is always defeated by a trained fighter. Another method is to *prevent him from ever being attacked*. In both cases the experimenter controls what action pattern the animal acquires by *altering its social experience*.

Such unequivocal results are doubly obvious among higher animals who are more dependent on social structure than mice. Dr. Scott found that with dogs social dominance arrangements serve to inhibit aggression almost completely. To prevent attack by a former winner, a puppy has only to roll on his back and yelp. Social control of aggression *between species* was demonstrated in another of his studies. Only gentle restraint without punishment was used. Yet in raising 500 puppies Dr. Scott was nipped only once, when a mother resented his handling her newborn offspring.[12]

With primates the picture is even more clear. Sir Solly Zuckerman at the London Zoo found that in a group of male and female baboons restricted within a space about the size of a city lot the males fought viciously for possession of the females. Sometimes the females were torn to pieces, and during three years of observation but one infant survived.[13] Some have concluded from such evidence that this must be a model of man's nature unrestrained by civilization.

But the free-ranging baboon troops of the African plains show none of this brutal behavior. In their social organization the males have a well-established dominance order and avoid one another. Females and young are never attacked as in the socially disorganized zoo group, and are in fact protected from predators within a circle of cooperating males. A juvenile baboon who so much as makes an infant cry is repelled by its mother and may be punished by a dominant male. Frequently the males even wait for a female in heat to select a mate, sometimes several in sequence. As a result serious fighting is rare. And one should add that, in contrast to the behavior of cichlid fish, there is no evidence in baboons of unrest or tension due to pent-up aggression.[14]

Baboons develop peaceful habits through the enforcement of peaceful behavior on the young by older members of the troop.[15] So it is not even baboon "nature" that results in destructive aggression. Rather it is the *prevention of its full expression in social organization.*

These research results, added to evidence discussed earlier concerning man, should dispel any remnants of conviction left by the early social Darwinists that an instinct for collective warfare as well as individual aggression is part of man's primate inheritance. It should also clear some of the fog generated by the latter-day social Darwinists such as Lorenz and Ardrey. It should even relieve the gloom cast over man's future by the epochal mind of the founder of psychoanalysis. Freud decided that aggression is an instinctual drive. Moreover, he felt that the restraints of impulse and sacrifices of gratification imposed by society must increasingly exceed what man can bear. Therefore, he believed that most of man's suffering is imposed by his need for a social organization itself.[16] Had he been convinced that human aggression is not spontaneous but must be provoked, and that it is either disintegration of social organization or training that transforms his provoked aggression into violent destructiveness, his conclusions might have been more hopeful.

Newer "Biologizers" of Human Aggression

One might suppose that now such tidings would be widely disseminated before man is turned into an optionally aggressive mouse. Unfortunately, instead of being encouraged by the important new evidence that man may be able to be both peaceful and healthy, from all sides people are rushing to join in what could be called a revival of social Darwinism. Here are three brief examples of such distortions of evolutionary thought.

Bigelow

Robert Bigelow, a zoologist, correctly identifies man as the most cooperative of all animals. But he then adds the preposterous propositions that his ability to cooperate is inseparable from his ability to make war, and that his brain has trebled in size because of the interaction of these two talents.[17] He thus ignores the evidence that cooperation has been characteristic of life for three and a half billion years, and that cooperation and enlarging brains have been characteristic of man for at least two million years, whereas war was born at the outside not more than 12,000 years ago.

Morris

Desmond Morris, another zoologist, attempts to sweep even the erotic life of man into the aggressive camp.[18]

In a long series of intentionally shocking and often undocumented assertions, Morris employs Lorenz's practice of citing analogies between behavior of lower animals and man, and by implication leaving the lay reader with the impression that these are *homologies* indicating a direct hereditary relationship.

On the other hand, Morris tends to evaluate human success in the most provincial manner. He refers several times to small societies which he regards as unsuccessful, in fact "stultified," because they have not developed large numbers, great territorial hegemony, and technological advance. He dismisses their experience and behavior as not relevant to the fundamental nature of man, which apparently is to be found revealed only in the ways of Western industrial society. He does not explain how presumably biological factors of our species could fail to appear in the other groups, leaving one with a vague suspicion that he supposes these "backward" peoples to have become genetically defective, an assumption geneticists do not support. He pays no attention whatever to the fact that some such societies have learned to maintain a nondestructive ecological balance, have learned how to raise their children to be emotionally well suited to their culture without being plagued by psychological and psychosomatic illness, and that some have learned to control their population numbers and live at peace with their neighbors.[19] These facts, which should qualify as evidence of human biological *success,* are rejected because they do not coincide with his prejudgment that such societies are unsuccessful.

Morris's ethnocentrism is revealed with particular clarity in his explanation of the spherical-shaped human breast. Man is the only primate that has spherical buttocks, these having evolved in connection with the larger muscles required to maintain the erect posture.[20] Morris draws attention to the indubitable fact that in copulating from the rear our earliest male ancestors were treated to an especially favorable view of the female buttocks. From there he moves to the spherical shape of the human female breast, also unique among primates. He concludes, in a piece of teleological reasoning astounding in a modern biologist, that the human female needed to produce upon her front an attractant equal to that on her back, and did so through a process of "self-mimicry." Thus, equipped with spherical breasts, she could lure her front-mounting mate as powerfully as before.[21]

Parenthetically, the fact that many men have as esthetically rounded buttocks as women is not accounted for by Morris. Would he assert that men are thus imitating women? It would be difficult to explain the male buttocks as a kind of erotic mimicry, unless one postulated that males were thereby keeping open the option of homosexuality in case they might someday rather switch than fight.

Getting back to the breast, Morris not only manages to shift attention away from the primary postural function of the buttock, but also to obscure the primary infant-nurturing function of the breast. But the more important point is that thereby both buttock and breast take on a significance more congenial for Morris's view of man, the more "aggressive" function of seduction. He ignores the troublesome details that prior to the evolution of either round buttock or breast, there must have been something about flat-breasted and flat-buttocked ape females which sufficiently attracted males, and that in many human societies today neither buttock nor breast have any pronounced erotic appeal.[22] In fact, no known human societies, except our highly technological one, regard the breast as serving primarily an erotic function.[23]

Ashley Montagu has given an explanation of the evolution of the human spherical breast which is more in keeping with the primary function. The chief influence on the development of the breast was the form of the suckling infant's face. As the jaws of the infant of early man became smaller the female breast would have become larger, for an infant with retracted jaws would have considerable difficulty in suckling at an undeveloped breast.[24]

It is in keeping with his general approach that Morris has explained the evolution of the human breast in terms of its advantages in sexual rivalry rather than in terms of nurturant function. Yet it is this latter function which such thinkers as not only Montagu but many psychoanalysts and other observers have seen as the origin and archetype of the especially human capacity for loving, survival-assuring cooperation.[25] Ignoring this, Morris ends by urging that our best chance of survival lies in "submitting" to our biological urges which he erroneously characterizes as predominantly aggressive.[26]

The danger of following such advice, which ignores not only the findings of behavioral research, but also newly emerging direct biological controls of behavior, is that under the guise of science it can provide both a rationale and a map for converting the abundant future into an age of pansadism.

Far from expressing concern about the amount of cruelty still countenanced in human behavior, Morris leaves us with the impression that a man fighting a bull is really no different from a cat playing with a mouse. Morris ignores psychological differences. First, the cat is simply responding to a stimulus with an innately predisposed behavior that has been prepared by some prior learning. The cat does not *plan* with foresight to selectively breed and nurture its victim for its climactic agony. And it does not carry out the performance with elaborate ritual for the delectation of not only itself but thousands of its fellows. Most important of all, the cat cannot be enjoying cruelty because it cannot *empathize* with the mouse. In a human being there is also no sadism until a child has attained awareness that the creature whom it mistreats has a life and sensibilities in some way akin to its own. Before that stage the child who pulls wings from a fly is manifesting nothing more than the exploratory curiosity which equally leads the child to dismantle an alarm clock to find out what makes it tick.

Consequently, it is only the developing or mature human being who is capable of sadism and only he who is capable of restraint. And consequently, it is only the human being who bears the special responsibility of *selecting* which of his hurtful impulses to enact or restrain, on the basis of an ethics that is not limited to, but includes, their survival value for his species.

These are matters on which psychiatrists and psychoanalysts are particularly qualified to speak. It is perplexing and disturbing to find not only that they so often remain silent about their special knowledge, but that on occasion they too seem to be guided rather by the pseudoinsights of analogies between animal and man. A particularly bizarre example was the occasion recently at an international meeting where psychiatrists permitted themselves to be seduced into a bullring to learn matador technique, and be knocked by irritated cows and calves onto their highly evolved posteriors.

Storr

Another instance of this sort of ethologizing is personally more distressing to me than some of the others because it comes from a psychoanalyst, Anthony Storr. His book, *Human Aggression,* is largely inspired by Konrad Lorenz, to whom it is dedicated, and from whom it receives a panegyric reproduced on the dust cover.[27] Unlike Lorenz, he recognizes the virtual absence of instinctual action patterns in man. But he does assert that there are spontaneous instinctual *motivations,* and that aggression is one of them. Storr criticizes Freud for not having decided that aggression is an instinct until near the end of his life. He also disputes Freud's opinion that the aggressive instinct arises as a force directed inward against the person himself, only secondarily being diverted onto other individuals. His theme seems to be that aggression is the instinctual basis of *all human attempts to master reality,* and as such is indispensable to human survival.

Storr particularly chides Americans for their "perennial optimism" which "makes it hard for them to believe that there is anything unpleasant . . . in human nature which cannot be 'fixed.' "[28] Apparently he sides with that form of perennial pessimism which seizes upon the study of animal behavior to prove that what exists in human behavior must be inevitable, and therefore right.

Storr then goes on to give an account of the neurophysiological mechanism underlying aggression and properly asks:

> But need the trigger be pulled? What has not been decided is whether there is any pressing need for the mechanism to be brought into use.[29]

He even cites the important passage from *Aggression,* by J. P. Scott, which says:

There is no physiological evidence of any spontaneous stimulation for fighting arising within the body. This means that there is no need for fighting . . . apart from what happens in the external environment. We may conclude that a person who is fortunate enough to exist in an environment which is without stimulation to fight will not suffer physiological or nervous damage because he never fights. This is a quite different situation from the physiology of eating, where the internal processes of metabolism lead to definite physiological changes which eventually produce hunger and stimulation to eat, without any change in the external environment.

We can also conclude that there is no such thing as a simple "instinct" for fighting, in the sense of an internal driving force which has to be satisfied. There is, however, an internal physiological mechanism which has only to be stimulated to produce fighting. This distinction . . . leads to a hopeful conclusion regarding the control of aggression. The internal physiological mechanism is dangerous, but it can be kept under control by external means.[30]

Storr then proceeds to what seems a puzzling illogicality to sustain his own position. He cites Eibl-Eibesfeldt's finding that a rat raised in isolation will attack another of the same species just as will an experienced animal.[31] He seems not to notice that this experiment demonstrates nothing more than the existence of an innate action pattern for fighting which is fired off *by the appropriate external stimulus.* And it demonstrates this only in the rat. Likewise, he concludes that, because electrical stimulation of the brain of cocks can elicit seeking of objects upon which to discharge aggression or courtship behavior, "it looks as though aggression is as much an innate drive as sexuality."[32] He does not explain how one can regard an electrical shock to the brain as "innate," let alone what these avian results show about man. Then comes this remarkable passage:

It is true that aggressive tension cannot yet be portrayed in physiological terms as we might describe hunger; that is, as a state of deprivation which drives the animal to take action to relieve it. But the same is actually true of the sexual instinct; and most people, rightly or wrongly, accept the idea that sex "is an internal driving force which has to be satisfied."[33]

We are left with the peevish recommendation that since people are willing to be wrong about sex, the least they can do is to be equally wrong about aggression. Then he proceeds to quote, and attempts to refute, Berkowitz:

Since "spontaneous" animal aggression is a relatively rare occurrence in nature (and there is the possibility that even these infrequent cases may be accounted for by frustrations or prior learning of the utility of hostile behavior), many ethologists and experimental biologists rule out the possibility of a self-stimulating aggressive system in animals. One important lesson to be derived from these studies is that there is no instinctive drive toward war within man. Theoretically, at least, it is possible to lessen the likelihood of interpersonal conflict by decreasing the occurrence of frustrations and minimizing the gains to be won through aggression.

. . . .

Authors such as Berkowitz and Scott never suggest that the sexual impulse could be abolished or seriously modified by learning or by decreasing the rewards of sexual satisfaction, for, in their minds, sex carries a positive sign, whereas aggression is negatively labeled.[34]

Whether or not ethologists or laboratory researchers make the suggestion about animals, the clinical experience of a psychoanalyst should convince him that in regard to man, he must make not a suggestion but an assertion. In contrast to the impulse to eat, for example, in patients the sexual impulse is indeed seriously modified if not actually abolished by learning, at least as betrayed by any particular behavior readily recognized as sexual without analytic translation. Without this assumption we cannot account for the multifarious and shifting vagaries of the sexual impulse, from prolonged apparent disappearance in celibacy to excess frequency in satyriasis, let alone the changes in the character of the sexual impulse itself brought about by psychoanalysis.

It is in his chapter "Aggression in Social Structure" that Storr reveals fully the premises that condition the preceding treatment of his subject. He quotes and then comments upon a passage by Schjelderup-Ebbe concerning "pecking order" in hens:

In human society the equivalent to this last bird would be a member of some pariah caste such as the untouchables of India, which . . . serve a valuable function in human communities for the discharge of aggressive tension. The creation of a scapegoat cannot be considered the main reason . . . many animals form hierarchies based on dominance. Washburn and De Vore, writing of baboons, state that "Although dominance depends ultimately on force, it leads to peace, order and popularity. . . . In earlier or more primitive forms of [human] society . . . the aggressive drive may well have had the same function . . . that of creating a stable society based on dominance. . . . Aristocratic societies have a firmly established rank order . . . each man knows his place; and the more he is content to regard his lot as ordained by fate, the more stable is the structure of the whole. The aggressive potential of the group is disposed hierarchically in such a way that each man dominates the next below him in rank until the lowliest peasant is reached—and it may be assumed that his aggression is fully engaged in wresting a meagre existence from the land which he is compelled to cultivate.

> Modern democracies have moved some way from this more primitive pattern. . . . In doing so, they have set themselves a problem in the disposal of aggression.[35]

While it might not be fair to assume that Storr endorses continuation of these arrangements, it is certain that he sees no viable alternative. He seems to regard as inevitable that human beings must continue, as they have done for so long, to arrange their lives to be as much as possible like those of barnyard fowl.

Earlier I have noted that peaceful social stability is brought about and maintained among even our closer relatives, monkeys, baboons, and apes, by varying degrees of aggression manifested in the service of a social dominance hierarchy. Lest these facts be misunderstood as substantiating Storr's conclusions, let me reiterate that their aggression is *never* spontaneous, always being a response to outside stimulation. Also to be recalled is that among baboons aggression rarely results in grave injury, *unless outside forces have seriously disrupted the social order*.[36] Above all, Storr's description of aggression as creating a continuous "disposal" problem, representing it as a sort of free-flowing psychological sewage, is clearly from the realm of fantasy.

In his absorption with *discharge* of aggression, Storr seems to be trying to draw conclusions about human social relations from considerations that may appropriately circumscribe the reality of lower animals. At the same time he appears unconcerned about the aggression among humans which such hierarchical systems *provoke*. Missing such an essential point threatens not only psychoanalysis but our entire social organization with attack and destruction under the charge of irrelevancy.

Here we encounter again an instance of the recurrent implication that an analogy between animal and human behavior is really a *homology*, and a desirable one at that since it produces "stability." This language is uncomfortably reminiscent of the "law and order" refrain of ultra-right-wing political spokesmen—in this case an analogy which I very much fear is not so much of an homology as it is a direct translation. The crises in our large city ghettos stem directly from the fact that the "scapegoat" at the bottom of the "pecking order" is no longer willing to expend his provoked aggression in submissively "wresting a meager existence" from the land or elsewhere. Instead he is turning it outward against his oppressors. It is this variety of instability which authorities most detest and fear, and with which naïve analogies to animal behavior will not help us to deal. Unlike animals, human beings are motivated by urges for *justice, freedom,* and *opportunity*. The contents of such abstractions, although acquired and not innate, spring from the fundamental brain and mind characteristics of man with such regularity as to confound and enrage those who would stamp them out. Rather than recognizing the impossibility and undesirability of suppressing human aspirations, those desperate to do so will seize upon arguments such as Storr's to distort what they see welling up before them into a spontaneous and *generalized* aggressiveness. By this maneuver they can simultaneously shift attention from the *substance* of human strivings onto the purportedly instinctual *means* by which the objectives are pursued. Thus the problem of managing aggression becomes transformed from the complex challenge of satisfying subtle and profound human needs to the simple matter of getting rid of contentless animal tension.

It is not surprising, in view of Storr's remarks on social organization, that his view of women is a conservative if not reactionary one:

> . . . it is highly probable that the undoubted superiority of the male sex in intellectual and creative achievement is related to their greater endowment of aggression. . . . there have been no women of genius comparable to Michelangelo, Beethoven, or Goethe.[37]

Storr bolsters his assertions by noting that "In the relation between the sexes, the spermatozoon swims actively whilst the ovum passively awaits its penetration."[38] He here offers an analogy so misleading that it would seem extreme even for an ideologist of innate human aggression. If the relationship between ovum and spermatozoon determines the relationship between the human sexes as adults, we could also confidently expect that the female would be hundreds of times larger than her more active and aggressive partner.

Despite Storr's protestation that a woman's activities in the kitchen or nursery are as important as a man's in a spaceship or a Sistine Chapel, his aggressive condescension toward women seems as apparent as his denials of antifeminism seem unconvincing:

> This is not *necessarily* a plea for a return of a Victorian type marriage in which the female is totally subservient. The emancipation of women is an inescapable fact which will not be altered by artificial attempts to put the clock back [italics added].[39]

It is quite clear from his tone of unhappy resignation that he regards efforts to repeal the emancipation of women not as theoretically undesirable, but only as practically impossible.

In addition to Storr's treatment of instinct and society, his assumption that all *self-assertion* or attempts at *mastery* are manifestations of aggression must be challenged. This assumption is an extremely common one among American psychoanalysts, one of whom at a recent symposium on violence maintained with Storr that "the very fact that the baby breathes is a sign of his aggression." Except where the individual is competing for air in a sunken submarine, it is difficult to imagine how the assertion of inhaling is, as Lorenz defines aggression, *against* anyone.

Why should we derive all attempts at mastering the environment from redirected aggression? It would be observationally more sound to maintain that aggression is a *form* of effort to master the environment. Rather than maintaining such injurious confusions, would it not be appropriate for analysts to set themselves the task of fostering a capacity for environmental mastery and self-assertion which makes aggression unnecessary?

On the other hand, making aggression the generic category of all behavior leads to an attitude of resignation to its inevitability and even desirability. Not only clinical mistakes and personal unhappiness may be the result, but also callousness in the face of human suffering and injustice which is dangerous for human survival.

Suttie: Aggression and Thwarted Dependency

Other psychoanalytic views should be considered. Some suffer from a shallow attribution of aggression to frustration imposed from without by a variety of purely social factors. They do not take into account that, in the face of urgent needs, man's biological helplessness at birth and for a time thereafter makes a certain amount of frustration implicit in the human condition. They may even ignore the additional biologically imposed frustration of having to choose between simultaneous but incompatible urges. For example, think of the exhausted and hungry baby who keeps falling asleep while sucking only to be awakened repeatedly by hunger pains.

In 1935 Ian Suttie, a Scottish psychoanalyst, presented in his little-known book, *The Origins of Love and Hate,* a thorough discussion of human aggression which sets in appropriate perspective both its biological and social determinants.[40]

Suttie starts from the supposition that

> the child is born with a mind and instincts adapted to infancy;[41] . . . it is born with a simple attachment-to-mother who is the sole source of food and protection . . . the infant mind . . . is dominated from the beginning by the need to retain the mother—a need which, if thwarted, must produce the utmost extreme of terror and rage, since the loss of mother is, under natural conditions, but the precursor of death itself.[42]

Suttie argues that human beings are predisposed to be not individualistic and competitive but social and cooperative. This is a view endorsed by the majority of students of human social biology and evolution.

Anger is then aimed, not at the direct removal of frustration or attainment of the goal of the moment, still less at her destruction, but *at inducing* the *mother to accomplish these wishes for the child.* Instead of being the most desperate effort at *self-help* it has become the most insistent demand *upon the help of others*—the most emphatic plea which cannot be overlooked.[43]

This anger of the infant is the prototype for all human anger and aggression. Suttie goes on to maintain that the anxiety of the child in response to separation from his mother is the source of all human neurosis.

Suttie clearly stated at this early date that it is the child's earliest dependent relationship with its mother that is of primary importance in the development of mental health and illness. He denies that incestual sexual wishes are crucial factors in neurosis. Instead he singles out the wishes for dependency, tenderness, and nurture which are part of the primordial attachment to mother. Rather than indicting repression of incestual striving under the influence of *fear of father* as does Freud, he attributes most neurosis (including extreme childhood conflicts over incestual wishes) to insufficient earlier renunciation of the dependency wishes ordinarily gently effected in the child by *mother.*

The mother's will and capacity to enforce the renunciation ("psychic weaning") will vary directly with (a) the quality of her own character and personality and (b) with her own domestic status and dignity in the child's eyes and inversely with (c) the importance of the *child* in her own emotional life relative to other attachment and interests (i.e. her dependency on the child).

Any social factors therefore which stunt the character-development of women, contract her interests, or lower her prestige with her children will interfere with her functions of promoting the maturation of her children and their independence of herself.[44]

Among such social factors are the multitudinous daily consequences of denigrating attitudes of men, including some psychoanalysts, toward women. Suttie suggests that men have systematically ignored and misunderstood the cultural contribution of women and undermined their status as a defense against their own dependency wishes. He indicates that in the process men have lost sight of the fact that much of their vaunted creativity is brought to fruition largely through the emancipating love of women rather than the tyrannizing intimidation of men. The total effect of his book is to place aggression in a distinctly subsidiary role in human affairs as compared to love.

While all theoretical viewpoints in this field must still be regarded as tentative and unproven, Suttie's ideas offer a carefully considered alternative to the concept of instinctual aggression. It has the advantage of taking into account not only the mother-worshiping cults of Western antiquity, but the experience of nonliterate and non-Western people which Freud largely ignored, and which so often seriously contradicts the instinctual theory of aggression.

Consciousness, Scarcity, Abundance

All such misinterpretations of man as Bigelow's, Morris's, and Storr's fail to take into account the essential differences between other animals and man, not only man's lack of instinctually determined behavior, but his enormously increased consciousness. As Teilhard de Chardin suggested, it may be difficult to decide just where consciousness emerges in the evolutionary ascent to man.[45] But even were the dire ethological pronouncements concerning instinctual aggression in human beings accurate, it is incontestable that consciousness has reached in man a pinnacle that fundamentally alters not only his relation to the biological past but also to his evolutionary future. In fact, man's heightening consciousness places squarely in his own hands power as well as responsibility for directing all aspects of that future evolution.

Because I must do so in order to examine the item *after* next on the human agenda, I will assume that we will resolve the critical threats to survival now jeopardizing man's future through increasingly rational conscious control of human evolution. That accomplishment will bring us face to face with the most momentous revolution in human history: the *extermination of scarcity*. Through technology already devised or possible we will soon begin to actualize in earnest the transformation already under way of this central condition of most past human life into its welcome but potentially disruptive opposite, *abundance*.

Values and Volition

With the demand from people everywhere for a share in abundance comes a nearly universal lack of understanding and planning for the *consequences* of being released from the age-old bonds of necessity. Ominous examples of such premature power from the realm of new biological technique, involving artificial gestation, genetic alteration, life suspension, and so on, are explored in Part II of this section, and the impact of general *economic* abundance is examined in Section Two. In view of the perils of such progress to our current lives and values, as well as the uncertainty of requirements for life in the remote future, it behooves us to preserve the maximum range of adaptive potentiality by avoiding restrictive specializations.

In following the human agenda we will find that this principle applies as much to the realm of thought as to body structure. Fixed dogma becomes an obstruction to survival when it prevents comprehension or control of new reality. We must learn to prefer the partial security of clinging to gradual expansion of our higher-primate understanding over illusions of having a full grasp of ultimate truth. We must relinquish magic and, like the rest of the universe, learn to live with uncertainty.

Such an achievement requires changed values. Adaptation through changing values represents the most distinctive contribution of culture to evolution, and is considered further in Chapter 13. Groups of interrelated individual values, or "value systems" are formulated unconsciously in part as adaptations to a specific set of realities, and must evolve with them to remain relevant. For example, the value of rugged individualism begins to pale with the waning of the frontier, as does the value of marrying the boss's daughter with the waxing of general abundance.

Realities now change too rapidly for the old unconscious mechanisms of value development to keep up. Soon to come up on the human agenda is raising evolution to higher levels of consciousness through innovative *conscious* mechanisms of value development. Such a change will put man in direct and deliberate control of his own social organization.

Origin of Interpersonal Bonds: Aggression versus Cooperation*

Lorenz reports that among species of fish, birds, or animals which do not form individual bonds but associate in an anonymous crowd there seems to be very little interaction of any sort between individuals, let alone fighting. On the other hand he found that among lower animals, especially fish and birds, it is those species whose social organization includes a definite bond between individual friends or mates which also show the greatest hostility and combativeness toward one another. He states, "A personal bond . . . is found only in animals with highly developed intraspecific aggression; in fact this bond is the firmer, the more aggressive the particular animal species is."[46] He explains that most of the hostile combative element in the behavior of such pairs is displaced onto an outsider in terms of actual or symbolic threat.[47] The rest is *transformed* into the various *rituals* shared by the bonded friends or

* Much of the material appearing from here to "The Human Mind" is included in Gorney, "Interpersonal Intensity . . ."

mates, such as the "triumph ceremony" of geese performed after outsiders have been threatened or driven away, and he concludes that it is actually this "ritualized aggression" that forms and maintains the bond.[48] He also shows that a mated male cichlid fish cannot maintain the peaceful bond to his female unless that portion of his spontaneous aggression which cannot be ritualized into mating behavior can be discharged upon an outsider. If this "scapegoat" fish is removed from the aquarium the male is likely to turn upon and kill his mate.

On the basis of such information about lower animals, and a series of analogies to man, he concludes that the *human* bond (love) that unites individuals also is formed out of "phylogenetically programmed"[49] spontaneous aggression.[50]

We have already seen how dubious are such extrapolations from a distantly related species. But here the gravity of the error is particularly evident. Whatever may be the origin of the bond between goose and gander, it is plain that among primates the bond between individuals derives not from ritualized aggression *but from the early experiences of comforting interaction during infancy.* And the capacity to experience affectional bonds in adulthood depends upon having had such experience during the formative period. These conclusions, so persuasively supported by the findings of psychoanalytic and psychiatric study of man, are convincingly substantiated by the results reviewed earlier of Harlow's laboratory studies of monkeys. Furthermore, while a monkey's potential for developing affectional bonds may be permanently stifled by social deprivation in early life, merely removing a sociable adult monkey from the objects of his aggression does *not* by itself disrupt the peaceful amicability of his affectional bonds to other monkeys.

Comparison of various primates under natural conditions further corroborates these judgments. Arboreal monkeys show little individual bonding and little fighting, while (some) human beings show much individual bonding and much fighting. These observations would seem to accord well enough with Lorenz's formulation. But data on other primates would not. Baboons, who show very little more individual bonding than arboreal monkeys, show an enormous amount more of fighting. And apes, contrariwise, show much *more* individual bonding and much *less* fighting. So whatever may be true for lower animals, it does not appear possible to account for the intensity of primate interpersonal bonding by the level of intraspecific aggression.

However, I have found another factor which correlates well with intensity of affectional bonding in primates. It might be expressed as *the percentage of the lifespan passed in the state of marked closeness characteristic of the period of infant dependency on mother.*[51]

	END OF INFANT DEPENDENCY (YEARS)	AVERAGE LIFE-SPAN (YEARS)	PERCENT OF LIFESPAN PASSED IN INFANT DEPENDENCY
Rhesus monkey	1	15	6.7
Baboon	1.13	15	7.5
Chimpanzee/gorilla	3	35	8.6
Man	8	70	11.4

Furthermore, when more satisfactory data become available concerning the time required for various primates to reach full maturity, the correlation between intensity of affectional bonding and portion of lifespan spent in gradually decreasing dependency likely will become even more convincing.

Human Aggression and Love, Freud and Lorenz, Interpersonal Intensity

Because the human being is so much more helpless at birth, the character of his later affectional bonds is even more dependent than those of other primates on the subtle quality of the earliest interaction with members of his own species, which for him must include much more protracted experience with a loving mothering person. Accordingly, human interpersonal relationships, elaborating on the old primate pattern, have become much more intense in general.

Even so, the human being too can maintain established affectional bonds for long periods without discharging aggression onto others. The experiences of numerous couples who live amicably in isolated mountain cabins or fire observation towers are as convincing on this point as are accounts of small groups of Indians and other nonliterate peoples whose contacts with others were as uniformly peaceable as they were infrequent.

Freud's discouraging view of aggression was that it welled up from within spontaneously. Directed inward primarily against the self, it could be deflected outward upon other people or things. It would act to the detriment of the self or its external objects unless under special circumstances it could be blended artfully with, and diluted by, the person's loving impulses. These loving impulses arose from a separate source, were beneficial to the self or object, and were in fact indispensable protections from the destructive effects of undiluted aggression, the damage from which, however, they were never quite powerful enough to overcome completely.[52] This formulation at least allowed for the possibility that if somehow one could shut off aggression (and violence) at the source, love would still exist.

Lorenz's supposition carries the instinctual conception of aggression a dismal step further toward hopelessness. Because love is to him nothing but made-over aggression, *elimination of aggression would also eradicate love.*

In comparing human social organizations with one another I have been struck by a different and, to me, more penetrating relationship than that described by Lorenz in certain animal organizations, and herewith propose it in the form of three hypotheses. It seems that:

1) In just those societies that give rise to the most intense interpersonal relationships people often display not only the highest level of general cultural achievement, but also of intrapsychic conflict.
2) Excessively high intensity of interpersonal relationships is a *cause* of both the high level of achievement and high level of intrapsychic conflict.
3) Violent aggression and mental disorder in man are the results of intrapsychic conflict largely so engendered which exceed the individual's power to resolve conflict in better ways.

What I am suggesting, in other words, is that rather than high intensity of aggression being a prerequisite for interpersonal bonding, it is the other way around: *high-intensity interpersonal bonding may be a prerequisite for various human behaviors, one of which is aggression.*

Before examining some implications of the hypotheses themselves, it is necessary that we understand the significance and relationships of these terms.

We have seen how *love* arises as the joint product of the basic drives and the interpersonal relationships in which they must be expressed.

Unless the drives are thwarted, no matter how intense they may be, *no serious amount of intrapsychic conflict will result.* But since some frustration is inevitable in every life, every person must experience some intrapsychic conflict. Therefore, if my hypotheses prove correct, it behooves us to assure that the level of intrapsychic conflict does not exceed that which the individual can master through sublimation into achievement, without overflow into aggression or mental disorder. One obvious way to stay below the tolerable level might be the reduction of interpersonal intensity.

Interpersonal intensity in man derives from two principal factors. One is *urgency,* the degree to which the fire of the drives is fanned or dampened by the patterns of emotional conditioning prevalent within the culture. The other is *exclusivity,* the degree to which the drives are focused upon one or a very few persons.

As I use it, "interpersonal intensity" denotes a sort of cultural style which seems to regulate the *impact* of the communication transmitted in interpersonal relationships while leaving the *content* relatively unaffected. For example, feeding a child is ordinarily a loving act of conferring survival benefits. The *content*, but not the impact, of the communication may be the same whether the child is offered a variety of natural foods, by any of a group of responsible adults in his life (low intensity), or is given only heavily sweetened or otherwise overly tempting foods, which the mother insists must be presented only by herself (high intensity). By thus *heightening drive urgency* and *concentrating dependency exclusively* upon herself, the mother could be laying the groundwork for severe intrapsychic conflict in the child in the event that her early death or other circumstance should necessitate substitution of plain foods and a foster mother.

Likewise, there is a momentous difference between the *impacts* of the communication of the same hostile content when a handful of .22 cartridges is irritably flung at a group of one's noisy companions during target practice (low intensity), and when a pistol is turned and one bullet fired into one man's chest (high intensity).

In practice, in a way difficult to put into words, it appears that love, in terms of conferring survival benefits, can be satisfactorily transmitted and aroused through interpersonal relationships of a wide range of intensity. And of course, intensity is only one of many factors influencing the behavioral consequences of interpersonal relationships. In addition to the factors of duration and variability over time, profound effects will also be exerted by genetic endowment, cultural tradition, and reality opportunities.

If correct, the above hypotheses would lead to more hopeful conclusions. First, contrary to Lorenz, *we could afford to diminish aggression without jeopardizing love*. Second, contrary to Freud, we may conclude that aggression has a *stimulated* rather than a spontaneous origin. We could afford, therefore, to *reduce interpersonal intensity* because, while retaining any protective effects of love, we would thus be minimizing aggression.

While we have become aware of the nature of general cultural achievement, aggression, and mental disorder, to my knowledge no one has suggested that interpersonal intensity might be one *controllable determinant* of the incidence of all three.

Interpersonal Intensity: Cultures and Conflicts Compared *

Obviously the formulation of a series of hypotheses does not substantiate them, and so we do not know whether they or conclusions derived

* Much of this chapter appeared in different form in the October, 1971, issue of the *American Jouranl of Psychiatry*; a report of a study of 58 cultures that confirms many of its assumptions will appear in 1979 in the *Archives of Psychiatry*.

from them are correct. We must consult data for verification or refutation. And that is always a problem.

Particularly difficult is finding reliable data on human beings. We cannot subject them to such experimental variations in infant care as those carried out by Harlow on monkeys. But perhaps some hints could be obtained from the natural experiments in techniques of child raising which diverse human cultures constitute.

We need a culture that generates *high-intensity interpersonal relationships* to compare with one that generates *low-intensity interpersonal relationships*. Ideally all other factors should be the same in both cultures so that we would be sure our results reflected just this one difference. But human societies do not oblige us by evolving as controlled laboratory experiments. So we must make use of what crude information they do provide, and take care to interpret the results judiciously.

The cultures of the United States and of the Pacific islands in general, particularly that of Tahitians,* illustrate these two extremes in interpersonal relationships, although imperfectly. I am indebted to my friend and psychiatric colleague, Dr. Robert Levy, for first bringing this circumstance to my attention. It is upon his views that my basic assumption rests. Specializing in anthropological studies of Pacific island peoples, Dr. Levy has reviewed the extensive relevant literature, to which he has himself made some of the most fundamental and revealing contributions, and has come to the conclusion that these societies *do* tend to generate low-intensity interpersonal relationships. Dr. Levy does not concur with some details of my account taken from the work of others, and of course is not responsible for the theoretical use to which I have put his data.

It is problematic enough to depict accurately the predominant cultural patterns even of the American milieu that immediately surrounds us. But to do the same for the cultural patterns of Tahiti or other Pacific islands peoples is a formidable challenge. Hard as it is to understand your own culture, it is nearly impossible to understand someone else's from the outside. The task becomes especially difficult when one is forced to rely on the diaries of unscholarly sailors, missionaries, and painters for his grasp of the past, and on the tentative formulations of Western specialists for his picture of the present. But our careening advance through the human agenda does not wait for hard data, and even a momentary glimpse of Pacific island peoples viewed as a mosaic in the passing landscape is better than none in steering our course. With patience, discretion, and some luck we might be able to extract from the welter of published fragments and personal reports a picture that contains some hints useful in deciding

---

* As used here, "Tahitian" refers to the Society Islands in general.

which patterns of child raising would be preferable for a future in which we select our values deliberately.

The Family Romance: American versus Tahitian

We are all aware how in general the patterns of current American family life, descended largely from various European antecedents, include highly intense interpersonal relationships between spouses and between parents and children. However, we do not often think consciously of the consequences of such social arrangements, which are disclosed when they are studied in detail, as during psychoanalysis. Freud referred to the series of intense emotional attachments between a child and his parents as the "family romance."[53] The hostile rivalry between a five-year-old boy and his father, the tender attachment of a six-year-old boy to his mother and girl to her father, the bitter competition between siblings for parental attention, the possessive jealousy of a mother toward her growing son, the pouting dependency of a father neglected by his wife in favor of the children—all are familiar nursery-grown equivalents of the passionate "adult" romances that characterize so much of the rest of our lives.

These family romances, as well as their later progeny, are outgrowths of the particular patterns of family living and child nurture prevalent in our culture. In American cities we tend to isolate families from their close relatives who may live hundreds or thousands of miles away. Even next-door neighbors often remain strangers for years. Within these separated families the intense attachments, dependencies, and rivalries, which infants everywhere tend to develop, are *fanned into infernos* and *focused sharply only upon immediate family members*. In our society we cause the baby's psychological transition from infancy into childhood to proceed at an extremely *gradual* pace. As the scope of his independence widens at three to six years, his inflamed emotional attachments at home are allowed to continue into childhood, as well as to become the new models for relationships with others. So, added to the family romance, we find "best" friends, crushes on teachers, and eventually passionate infatuations during adolescence, all of which we accept as normal. Thus a pattern becomes fixed which persists throughout life of maximum emotional intensity in interpersonal relationships. The effort of today's adolescents to be "cool" seems largely an attempt to deny or conceal these inner fires, since it is too late to either prevent or extinguish them.

A consequence of such a culture which we have come to value is that the child's intense relationships provide the means whereby he is induced to incorporate into his personality the exacting standards of self-discipline, sacrifice, and attachment which he (rightly or wrongly) attributes to his beloved parents. Thus he "identifies" even today with adult subscription to residual elements of the Puritan ethic such as hard work, thrift, frugality, and so on.

Of particular significance is a further demand we make upon the child. He must continue to contend throughout childhood and adolescence with unrelenting family emotional closeness. And at the same time he must *stifle within himself* rather than act upon the most insistent sexual, hostile, or dependent urges thus stirred up in him. The consequences for his personality are often critical. For once the child's inner restraints have begun to collaborate with those exerted upon him from the outside, the pressure may be such that he renounces not only *expression* of his most urgent but unacceptable feelings and impulses, but also *awareness* of them as well. As parents we require that the child deflect and sublimate such feelings and impulses into the achievement and "success" on which our society places a premium. When any unmanageable excess of such energies in a child bursts out in the disguised compromise of intrapsychic conflict which we call a neurosis, psychosis, or behavior disorder, we promptly undertake to "cure" the symptomatic disturbance in one way or another. Then we send him right back to his intense family closeness, hoping naïvely—and often vainly—that this time the cauldron will sit calmly on the flame without allowing the steam to blow its lid.

Particularly illustrative of this pattern is our reaction to the child's immature sexual impulses, which inevitably focus first on those who nurture him and thus become the object of all his wishes. Of course, the incest taboos we considered earlier persist because they are still needed, and they still firmly block the child from the gratifications toward which our culture's extreme family closeness constantly entices him. And while sex education may provide him with information, it no more does away with sexual *urges* (however rudimentary) than a course in gourmet cooking does away with hunger. Even though some few "modern" parents may permit sexual impulses to be expressed in private play with other children, in general such outlets too are forbidden in our culture.

Considering the exaggerated dependencies and conflicts which our intense family relationships engender, it is no wonder that in our society the death of a parent, child, or spouse, or the breakup of a marriage or love affair, constitutes emotional catastrophe which can blight the rest of a person's life.

Building on these foundations, our society adds further provocations and frustrations to adult life quite sufficient to account for the cataracts of violence and emotional illness which inundate us.[54]

Whereas we seem in general to do whatever possible to heat up interpersonal relations, the Tahitians, at least those living closer to the old style, do a great deal to cool them down.

It would be marvelous for our inquiry if Tahitians arranged their lives to be simple opposites to ours in all ways bearing upon interpersonal intensity. Were that true, their families would live jointly instead of separately, in villages of perhaps fifty people so that everyone could be on familiar terms with everyone else. Instead of being totally dependent upon one set of parents, their children would be raised communally, having several other mothers and fathers in addition to their own on whom to depend for all sorts of satisfactions from food to affection, and onto whom could be diffused the hostile and loving impulses that here are concentrated on only one of each. Then if one mother were irritable or busy, an infant or child would not be forced to remain in a painful state of tension. There would be several others to come to his aid or to whom he could run for comfort. Room would be allowed for a child with a temperament different from his mother's to select and live predominantly with a substitute mother who might find his personality more compatible. Accompanying all this would be a general climate of more relaxed and low-key interpersonal relationships which would not stimulate *intense* dependence, jealousy, or hostility, which would not demand much accomplishment, and which would permit children to follow freely their sexual and other curiosities and impulses.

Although the contrast obviously cannot be so neat, Tahiti comes close enough to these conditions to be informative, and in some ways has evolved patterns that are even more illuminating for our purpose.

Whereas in our large cities and towns Americans may scarcely know anyone outside their families, Tahitians, although occupying separate households, tend to live in villages of no more than a few hundred people, all of whom are at least acquainted with each other. As in very small communities elsewhere, this circumstance by itself prevents isolation of families, and so tends to diffuse rather than concentrate emotional attachments. Operating in the same direction is the stable kinship system which maintains various ties between relatives outside the immediate family. For example, land is owned and worked jointly by related families. And children visit back and forth between related households much more readily than here.[55]

Most important for the development of character is the different way a Tahitian child is treated within its family circle. For the first two or three years the infant is indulged affectionately by its mother and everyone. Practically its every whim is gratified. Then a *sudden* transition to childhood is forced upon it, as the mother decides abruptly that the time has come to "cool" the child (in Tahiti the word does not signify a denial or pretense).* From that early moment on, its demands, its cries, and particularly its rage, are effectively discouraged. For example, a child might be allowed to cry vociferously when hungry, only to be fed when it slacks off. Urgent demands are increasingly ignored, ridiculed, or punished, and the child is given what he wants only when his wish is expressed mildly and moderately. Exclusive attachments of any kind, whether to persons, things, or activities, are also discouraged. In this way the child is systematically conditioned to be casual and never again become too involved or passionate about anyone or anything. Hostile aggression, whether in terms of feeling or of action, is particularly discouraged. Fighting ordinarily involves nothing but shouted imprecations between widely separated opponents, and very rarely includes anything more physical than a shove.

Whereas an American child or adolescent is constantly *stimulated to go on having* intense wishes and attachments, which he *himself* then must sublimate or stifle, a Tahitian child is decisively trained *by adults* to minimize the intensity of both permanently.

Easy mobility between families, particularly for the large group of adopted children, provides an extra parental reservoir to lean on. Moreover, the Tahitian child has a big circle of other children with whom he spends most of his time and to whom he can run at least for companionship, if not solace, when adults ignore his demands. The benign environment further favors low-intensity relationships by obviating the need for constant adult protection. Whereas our world is dangerous to a child without adult supervision, in the nonperilous surroundings of rural Tahiti a child may roam about safely on his own or in the company only of children. Most of his supervision outside the home will be carried out by newly cooled brothers and sisters, or aunts, cousins, and so on, which further helps dilute the intensity of his resentment against no-longer indulgent parents.

What the child learns about emotional intensity and how to be a Tahitian is described by Dr. Levy:

> One should not care enough, or be engaged enough to be vulnerable if anything goes wrong. . . . the message that relationships . . . must not be taken too seriously . . . is repeated in many ways. Children, from the age of four or five, are pushed by parents into sibling and peer group relationships and out of close parent-child dependency relationships; children's possessive attachments to objects are systematically shamed and interfered with; adolescent romantic love relationships are vigorously attacked by other members of the adolescent peer group; magic beliefs hold that mourning and intense desires are dangerous in that they attract dan-

* Compare discussion of Suttie, pages 140–142.

gerous spirits, which lose their power if one is casual enough . . . loneliness and feelings of deprivation involving broken intense relationships are interpreted as illness, or supernatural uncanny states.[56]

But perhaps the most significant institution that favors reduced interpersonal intensity is the Tahitian style of adoption of children, a social form widely distributed throughout the Pacific islands. Whereas in the United States only about 2½ percent of children are adopted, in a Tahitian village the rate may be as high as 40 percent.[57] Some parents wish to give their children in adoption, particularly those who are not married, are very young, or who have too many other children already. But a very large proportion of adopted children are given to foster parents who demand them *against the wishes of the biological parents,* particularly the mother.[58] Just as it discourages any behavior that indicates intense interpersonal involvement or attachment, the community exerts strong pressure against a parent's desire to keep his own child. And therefore a child someone has asked to adopt is generally yielded.

In all Tahitian adoptions, unlike ours, the degree of transfer is not complete, and may vary from the child having mere knowledge of the identity of his original parents to a continuing warm relationship with them. The adopted child may actually be taken back by the biological parents if he is badly mistreated or if his foster parents die.[59] And on his own initiative an adopted child may return to live with his biological parents following punishment or disturbance in the adoptive home.[60] Although it is more usual nowadays for a fostered child to make this shift, on occasion a child living in his biological home may still follow the old custom and go to live with another relative if he feels mistreated.[61] Altogether, the differences in experiences of adoptive and biological children seem minor.

As Dr. Levy cogently points out, these social patterns constitute a message to all members of the society which has profound impact. It reads, ". . . 'relationships between all parents and children are fragile and conditional.'"[62]

Thus the Tahitian society scarcely satisfies any romantic fantasies we may have of a culture which provides the child with multiple, intimately warm, stable, affectionate parents on whom he can rely consistently throughout development and after whom he can model himself into a nurturant parent to his own children. On the other hand, in addition to its firm direct suppression of interpersonal intensity, Tahitian culture does offer a number of other elements useful for our comparison.

If a Tahitian child's biological mother dies or goes off with another man, leaving her husband or children behind, there are a number of other women who will stand in for her. We might note here that in Hawaiian, the language of a related Pacific island people, the words "father" and "mother" are sometimes used to refer to all the women and men in the generation of a child's biological parents.[63] If his real mother returns a year later, she may be welcomed back with a casual shrug, even by the husband if he still wants her. If a young woman's husband leaves her and she sheds more than a cursory tear or two, she is chided by her friends who tell her that since men are plentiful and are all pretty much alike, no one man is worth making a fuss about.

Before the missionary invasion there was little secrecy or constraint about sex. In old Tahiti, and perhaps in other Pacific island societies, children were given instruction in sexual intercourse and possibly even explicit adult demonstration. The objective seems to have been suppression of the personal aspect of sex, in Levy's words, the transformation of sex "from a passion into a craft." Especially foreign was any notion of guilt in connection with sex. For example, the Tahitian Vahines thought it amusing that English sailors should want to go off to hide in the bushes when it was so pleasant to make love out in the open.[64] And even today, despite two hundred years of Western influence, in the villages the ordinary (and nonincestual) sexual curiosity and activities of children among themselves are generally considered by adults to be natural and of no particular concern.

Altogether, in this sort of world, the child grows up with fewer inner and outer restraints against casual pleasure seeking, and considerably less intense interpersonal relationships. The adult personality thus carved accords well with the island environment in which a basic livelihood is easily come by. Energetic striving of any sort is unnecessary in Tahitian culture and is in fact considered dangerous to the harmony and balance of man and nature. The emphasis in his extended family is on getting along with rather than ahead of everyone, on living harmoniously rather than accomplishing devotedly, on enjoying mildly rather than stifling righteously.

GENERAL CULTURAL ACHIEVEMENT.—Other non-Western societies, such as those of the Incas, Aztecs, India, China, and Japan, were found by their first European visitors to have developed various relatively complex cultural achievements. But when first observed by Captain Cook two hundred years ago the admirable adaptation of Tahitians to a generous clime did not include a written language, extensive development of arts, an elaborately organized religion, or an imposing political structure. Their idyllic life developed in an economy characterized by pretechnological abundance so luxuriant that there was practically no goad of scarcity to push them into preoccupation with material wealth. The productive virtues that were codified elsewhere as the Puritan ethic were not emphasized until the European invasion. For the Tahitians there was never a wolf at the door until the missionaries and mercenaries imported him in mercantile sheep's clothing. Given their already crystallized predilection for nonintense interpersonal relationships, one can readily grasp how it was that they did not evolve either a highly "productive" way of life or the personality characteristics that make up "ambition." Various studies reveal, furthermore, that the personalities of modern Tahitians, like those of other Pacific island peoples, show marked limitations also of the related characteristics of spontaneity and creativity.[65]

It is easy to see how such upbringing and personality patterns may produce adults who may seem by our standards "irresponsible." For example, if a man gets tired of his job, I am told, he is likely just not to show up for a day, a month, or ever. If asked why, he may reply without further explanation that he is *fiu*, a Tahitian word roughly meaning "fed up." He is likely to be astonished at the assumption that he has broken a promise or other obligation to which he committed himself, or that his employer would consider his own inconvenience of any consequence to an employee.

So it seems we can reasonably infer an association in Tahiti between the low levels of interpersonal intensity and low levels of general cultural achievement.

AGGRESSION.—The evidence seems equally suggestive as to aggression. Early descriptions of Tahitians depict a people in general remarkably peaceable and gentle to all living creatures. Here are a few examples of what was said of their human relationships. Based on his two years in Tahiti, Morrison wrote:

> . . . their behavior to strangers is such as to declare at first sight their humane disposition, and their courteous, affable and friendly behaviour to each other shows that they have no tincture of barbarity, cruelty, suspicion or revenge. They are of an unruffled temper, slow to anger and soon appeased . . .[66]

Naturalist John Forster, with Cook on his second voyage, wrote similarly:

> . . . their character is as amiable as that of any nation . . . The natives of these isles are generally of an open, easy, benevolent character.[67]

His son, George, a fellow voyager, described

> . . . their gentleness, their generosity, their affectionate friendship, their tenderness, their pity . . .[68]

These impressions were not dimmed by the apparent contradictions in the common Arioi practice of infanticide at birth, the stone-throwing attack made upon Cook's expedition five days after its arrival, or the desultory indigenous warfare. It seems to have been implicitly recognized by early observers that a technique of population control, an attempt to subdue a foreign invader, or occurrence of largely ceremonial feuds between rival upper castes were but incidental exceptions to fundamental Tahitian nonaggressiveness. An illustration of this trait was their response to Cook's punishment by flogging of an Englishman who had threatened a Tahitian woman with a knife. Quite unable to hold a grudge, they were so empathetic with suffering that they wept copiously after the first blow and begged Cook to halt the punishment.

What have been called the "tribal wars" which the explorers encountered were generally fought over such matters as insults between neighboring chiefs and their families, and usually consisted of months or years of lusty preparation followed by ritual battles in which killings ordinarily were sparse. Even at that time myths of a "golden age" of peace were present, which probably referred to a period several hundred years earlier. Before the population pressures of expansion within a fixed geographic area led to small-scale feudalism, with all its petty rivalries, neighboring Tahitian groups were probably as unaggressive and peaceful as are most nonliterate peoples.

As might be expected, two centuries of Western intrusion has modified much in Tahitian culture and personality patterns. For example, while children are still treated gently (aside from the rigors of being "cooled"), in some instances animals are not. Nevertheless, there appear to be enough remnants both to corroborate reports of the past and to bolster my hypothesis. What is of special concern to us here is that even today the Tahitian style of child raising results in adult personalities lacking in any troublesome amount of aggression.

Suicide and homicide rates are generally accepted as measures of aggression. In literate industrial societies, usually when one is low the other is high. This inverse relationship has been interpreted as indicating that aggression, whatever its source, must be discharged into killing others, if not oneself. But among Tahitians, the rates of both suicide and homicide are low. It is interesting that the suicide rate among Chinese living in Tahiti is considerably higher.[69]

Among Hawaiians also, both suicide and homicide rates are low. Furthermore, whereas suicide rates among Hawaiians after age thirty-five remain constant, among Chinese and Japanese living in Hawaii, they climb steadily with advancing age, as among most peoples.[70] It is notable that the Chinese and Japanese living in Hawaii are more like European Americans in interpersonal intensity, much higher achievers than the Hawaiians, and, according to some local observers, exhibit much more psychological suffering and emotional illness.

MENTAL DISORDER.—This brings us to the last of my three presumed out-growths of marked interpersonal intensity: mental disorder. Nowhere are the difficulties of cultural comparison more bewildering. First, there are the different significances attached to such behaviors as working hard, which in our world is a manifestation of health and in the Tahitian's of some sort of disorder. Then how can we determine the incidence in Tahiti of depression or hysterical paralysis when these "illnesses" are re-garded and treated as the result of supernatural influence? Finally, to whom would you go to determine the incidence in our society of posses-sion by spirits of the dead? One is reduced to using the statistics or intuitive impressions of Western observers who have bothered to write them down, and on balance it often seems that the latter are more in-formative.[71]

Early accounts indicate that even before the European invasion there were Tahitian words for shy, strange, morose, or otherwise disordered behavior, and there were shamans who undertook to exorcise the intru-sive spirits assumed to be the cause.[72] These devices indicate that pre-European Tahitians experienced some of what we would regard as ordinary psychological disturbances in living, and that, then as now, the culture provided means for relieving and disguising them quite in keeping with its requirement that interpersonal relationships be kept cool.

Nevertheless, these accounts agree that the early Tahitians by and large were extraordinarily healthy and even content and happy people. Ob-servers who have lived in Tahiti maintain that true *neuroses* were virtually unknown in each of several areas until explorers, and particularly mis-sionaries, reached them with their guilt-edged insecurities. Mental dis-orders seemed to follow in the wake of such reforms as insistence that Tahi-tians wear "modest" clothes and strictly circumscribe their sexual behavior. Europeans also did a great deal to intensify interpersonal relationships, stressing the overriding importance of devotion, fidelity, duty, and family closeness. Although anecdotes are not proof, it is striking how many stories are told of formerly well-adjusted adults (or their offspring) re-sponding to these new pressures with a variety of emotional disturbances.

Although we know that rapid cultural change enforced from the outside disrupts psychological functioning in various other ways also, I find it reasonable to surmise from these reports that there may be some causal relationship between the increased interpersonal intensity so generated and the increased amount of frank mental disorder now found in Tahiti. (Of course, this need not be true for all varieties of mental illness. The incidence of schizophrenia in Tahiti, as in other areas, apparently remains constant at about one per hundred population.)[73]

When one widens his perspective to a comparison with the avalanches of psychopathology in our own society, the impression is strengthened that elements in the Tahitian culture even today may generate less mental disorder.

Therefore I believe we are justified in concluding tentatively and provisionally that:

> It may be possible to *reduce* the likelihood of intrapsychic conflict, as well as its expression in violent aggression and mental illness, by reducing the intensity of interpersonal relationships in childhood and throughout life. But the catch is that the price may be a decrease in devotion to the persons and beliefs of the parents, as well as to much-prized general cultural achievement.

At minimum, it would be fair to say that these possibilities merit careful detailed study.

Some further factors influencing the effects of interpersonal intensity are explored in the next subsection.

Economy, Competition, and Intrasocial Aggression

In the course of following this account, the reader must have found questions forming in his mind which have also insistently pressed forward in mine. Since interpersonal relationships are the vehicle of the love so crucial to human beings, aside from anxiety over exaggerated dependence, *why* should high intensity in these relationships seem to be associated with undesirable consequences? *Does some other element in human life render toxic what otherwise is tonic?*

After pondering this problem, and the reservoir of information and opinion bearing upon it, I now must make an addition to the previous hypotheses, for elucidation of which I am grateful to my teacher and colleague, Dr. Judd Marmor.

We must begin here by remembering that interpersonal relationships are also the vehicles for *hostile* human attitudes and emotions. On the grounds of clinical evidence, it seems that high interpersonal intensity within even an American family does not often become destructive unless these relationships tend also to be excessively *competitive, controlling, or exploitative*.[74]

What cross-illumination of this idea can we derive from the broader panorama of anthropology? Certainly interpersonal relationships in our society, in addition to being intense, are often extremely competitive, controlling, and exploitative, whereas those in Tahiti, in addition to being cool, are much less frequently so. Without deciding which is chicken or egg, it is plain that what happens within the family is to some degree a reflection of conditions in the larger society of which it is a part. It is plain also that in this way, and others still not fully understood, any culture must generate personalities adapted to the requirements of its realities.

The foremost reality factor families must prepare children to deal with is that of economic structures. We have already considered some consequences of such differences between the United States and Tahiti.

The ambitious striving so prominent in the United States and so inconspicuous in Tahiti are parts of basic personality structures that fit their possessors for economic survival in their respective cultures. Since competition, control, and exploitation are hallmarks of American economy, but rarities in Tahitian economy, it is easy to understand the function of the differences in personality traits inculcated on the average by families in the two societies.

It is immediately apparent that a long interval of scarcity would endow ambitious striving with survival value in the United States, whereas the same interval of pretechnological abundance in Tahiti would not. But we must not succumb to the simplistic illusion that basic personality structure is determined *solely* by scarcity-abundance. For example, among the Zuñi and the Kwakiutl, subsistence, if not always truly abundant, is readily available to all. Yet one culture is characterized by virtual absence and the other by exaggeration of ambitious striving of the competitive, controlling, and exploitative sort. Likewise, the Chuckchee and the Eskimos both live in severe subsistence scarcity, yet the former manifest these traits in extreme degree while the latter do not.[75]

We are far from being able to explain through any of these considerations "why" a society adapts to its economic reality in one way or the other. But we are able to comprehend from these facts that economic adaptation includes more than just acquiring subsistence. It includes also acquiring the *prestige, esteem,* and *status* valued in the particular culture. These latter, sometimes called the *security systems* of a culture, tend to be related to the subsistence systems, but the connection is far from rigid. What stands out is that whether we are considering societies with subsistence *abundance* or subsistence *scarcity,* in every mentioned instance where interpersonal relationships tend to be competitive, controlling, or exploitative, the economy is characterized by the emergence of *have* and *have-not* groups. And although the data do not always tell us whether or not in such societies one can regularly find intense interpersonal relationships, it is evident that their basic personality structures tend to show marked ambitious striving and associated intrapsychic conflict manifested as aggression and mental disorder. Moreover, different as they are in terms of subsistence availability, the basic personality structures of Tahitians, Zuñi, and Eskimos, who do not prominently develop "have" and "have-not" groups, tend to be cooperative, noncontrolling, and nonexploitative, whereas those of Americans, Kwakiutl, and Chuckchee, who *do* prominently develop such groups, tend to be extremely competitive, controlling, and exploitative.[76]

A striking instance of the transformation of one sort of society into the other has been given by anthropologist Ralph Linton, and analyzed in terms of some of these features by Judd Marmor.[77]

The *Tanala* and the *Betsileo* are two neighboring tribes of Madagascar.* At the time of Linton's study both were wet rice cultivators, but the Tanala had shifted gradually from dry to wet rice cultivation during the preceding two centuries, whereas the Betsileo had been wet rice cultivators for a much longer time and had brought the technique to a much more efficient level by introducing terrace systems, transplantation, and fertilizers. Concomitantly, the Tanala had not yet experienced fully the psychocultural derivatives of wet rice economy which long since had crystallized among the Betsileo. Linton says, ". . . we can regard Betsileo as the Tanala culture, after all the changes consequent upon wet rice had become consolidated, organized, and institutionalized. We are therefore observing an important experiment in the dynamics of social change."[78]

Dry rice cultivation requires regular shifts to new fertile land, with resultant moves of the village in which its workers live. Wet rice cultivation, because the crop can grow almost continuously on the same terrace, makes a permanent village feasible and, what is more, makes individual permanent ownership of land near it valuable for the first time. With a dry rice economy, Tanala had been a transient, classless, democratic society in which recurrently abandoned land was owned communally by the village and worked jointly by family groups that, in the event of bad luck one year, were given an advantage the next, so that all remained more or less equal in wealth.[79]

It is particularly significant that in both Betsileo and Tanala-in-transition the *family organization* and *basic disciplines* remained similar to those of old Tanala, comprising a pattern likely to generate relatively high levels of interpersonal intensity.[80]

Like Betsileo, Tanala developed a landowning caste with the eventual establishment of a hereditary nobility and king! Linton saw that resultant changes in its culture already included replacement of tribal democracy by feudalism, development of complex upkeep and warfare in defense of the village, and evolution of economic importance in the institution of slavery.[81] Clearly Tanala was en route to the more exaggerated changes found in Betsileo: establishment of great differences in wealth, rank, and deference (including absolute power of the king over everyone's life,

---

* Now the Malagasy Republic.

property, and status); belief in retaliation for aggression; more common possession by evil spirits; suspicion that everyone was a malignant sorcerer; more apprehension expressed in dreams, omens, and superstitions; and increased crime, such as stealing and murder. Particularly impressive were fears of retaliatory misfortune, such as reluctance to announce the birth of a child, and the idea that a man who dies at the moment of a good harvest has been killed by his wealth—a reflection of the dread of the hostile envy of others.[82] All of these may be regarded as measures of increased tension within the society of a sort that tends to restrict the healthy development of the individual.

The conclusions described above square well with the impression of most social scientists that in general intrasocial aggression is greater in societies in which the structure of the economy depends on intrasocial competition. In contrast, those societies whose economies and institutions require cooperative living are much less apt to manifest intrasocial aggression. Marmor cites the Kwakiutl and the Zuñi as examples of the former and latter, respectively.[83]

The evolution of Tanala into Betsileo demonstrates a marked increase in aggression and mental illness in the *absence* of any evident change in the level of interpersonal intensity. This increase can be attributed to the great increase within the economic system of competition, control, and exploitation.*

So perhaps our tentative formulation of page 158 should be modified to include something like this:

If the level of interpersonal intensity in a society is high, the level of intrapsychic conflict (manifested as aggression and mental illness) will be directly related to the degree of competition within the security or subsistence sector of the economy.

This addition allows for the possibility that by reducing the amount of institutionalized intrasocial competition, a cultural factor within our control, we can perhaps *create conditions* in which (1) relatively high interpersonal intensity need *not* lead to undesirable results, and in which (2) relatively high interpersonal intensity can safely be maintained to foster general cultural achievement.

In the United States especially we need to know whether this possibility

* Not all individuals in one complex society have the same background as to interpersonal intensity, particularly those from widely divergent ethnic groups. A possible further test of the hypothesis might be to compare (for cultural achievement, aggression, and mental disorder) ethnic groups living in the United States who, although they have equivalent opportunities, have experienced different levels of interpersonal intensity, as for example Jews or Italians versus WASPs.

can be realized, for in both the subsistence and security sectors of the economy we engage in severe intrasocial competition. One has only to think of the intense competitiveness and high interpersonal intensity found among ghetto dwellers to realize how urgently we need to know if we can reduce the former while maintaining the possibly redeeming effects of the latter.

Synergy and Intrasocial Aggression

Here we must cast a thoughtful glance at the primate past. So far as we know, among neither the baboons nor apes was there ever the possibility of accumulating things such as land, food, or tools. Hence there could not emerge "have" and "have-not" distinctions between individuals or groups in terms of "wealth." But of course individuals of both groups developed marked differences in prestige, esteem, and status as they took their places in their respective social dominance hierarchies.

We must note that, in contrast to the effect in many human communities, such distinctions of prestige, esteem, and status between individuals generally contributed much more to relaxation than tension within the band. As I suggested earlier, the tyranny associated with these baboon equivalents of security systems could have squelched whatever mentally gifted but nondominant individuals might have come along. But in daily reality, the rigid discipline far more frequently *relieved* the individual from strain, such as that of being perpetually on guard alone against the stealthy lethal predator. The chimpanzees on the other hand, as an example of the apes, were almost never endangered by predators (see p. 86). It seems that their much looser hierarchical structure served mainly as a sort of etiquette lubricating the contact points between individuals, so that they could enjoy companionship and opportunity to learn from others without running afoul of excitable and occasionally irritable members of the band. In short, in these two quite different species, social dominance orders *simultaneously served* far more than they frustrated the needs of both the individual and group.

As one contemplates this happy circumstance, the question arises whether and to what degree the same simultaneity of individual and group need-satisfaction exists in human social dominance orders. And immediately we think of the many situations in which both the individual and his group benefit equally from his enterprise and labor, such as that of the successful small businessman or skilled construction worker. But with equal alacrity there leap to mind opposite instances in which a group benefits at the *expense* of individuals, such as the practice among some nonliterate peoples of enforced sale of oneself into semistarved slavery to pay debts, or the collection of gold dental inlays in Nazi concentration camps. In such examples it is plain that the needs of the individual run directly and gravely counter to those of the group.

One wonders what makes it possible for human social dominance orders to be so different in this respect from those of other primates. Several answers readily appear. First, as we have seen, among other primates social dominance orders cannot seriously jeopardize the individual's nutrition since each forages for his own subsistence amid ample vegetation. Second, no individual benefits from another's work. And third, the group does not benefit by the death of any of its members. Finally, with respect to other than survival needs, nonhuman primate individuals simply do not have the enormous potential of human individuals, and so there is in them neither as much to stifle nor to cultivate.

Having arrived at this perspective, I sought for clarification of its relation to human interpersonal relationships and had the good fortune to come upon a brilliant concept of anthropologist Ruth Benedict, and its elaboration by psychologist Abraham H. Maslow.[84]

Maslow explains that, following publication in 1934 of her popular classic *Patterns of Culture,* Benedict was irritated to be identified incorrectly with the doctrine of "cultural relativity." This view of man leads to the conclusion that each culture is a unique phenomenon, different from all the rest, about which scientific generalizations which relate it to others cannot be made. Maslow does not mention that it also was exploited to foster resignation to whatever cultural reality prevailed. Under the pessimistic judgment that no broad principles of cultural difference or change may be discerned, some argued that it will not ever be possible to guide human societies deliberately to more fulfilling patterns, any modifications introduced intentionally being as likely to hinder as help human well-being.

Accordingly, Benedict strove to develop a comparative sociology that would account for the differences in societies which she grasped intuitively and which, as I read her, she felt but did not explicitly state were related to the overall human fulfillment they could afford their inhabitants. She was a poetess published under a pseudonym, and as Maslow put it,

> she kept struggling with words which she did not dare to say in public in her capacity as a scientist, because they were . . . involved rather than cool, words that could be said over a martini but not in print.[85]

Perhaps that scientific objectivity accounts for her diffidence in publishing her ideas in this area which, because the complete manuscript was lost, reached print only in fragments and not until twenty-two years after her death in 1948. Ironically, it may turn out that her most important scientific contribution, like that of so many others, grew out of that very intuition against which she guarded.

Maslow describes how on huge sheets of newsprint Benedict summarized four pairs of cultures. One of each pair she felt was anxious, surly, and nasty, and showed low morale, much hatred, and much aggression. These people she did not like, and she spoke of their cultures as "insecure." The people of the contrasting other four cultures, whom she liked, were "nice," showed affection, and seemed to come from "secure" cultures. Says Maslow:

> The good ones, the secure ones, those she liked, felt drawn to, were the Zuñi, the Arapesh, the Dakota and one of the Eskimo groups. . . . The nasty, surly ones, that she would shiver a little about and shudder over were the Chuckchee, the Ojibwa, the Dobu, and the Kwakiutl.[86]

When I reached this point in Benedict's account, I was struck by the resemblance between her lists and those I presented earlier (p. 159) of societies that do or do not develop "have" and "have-not" groups, with their associated distinguishing characteristics as to competitive, controlling, and exploitative interpersonal relations.

Benedict tried all the standard generalizations then available as to race, geography, climate, size, wealth, and complexity in her attempt to find the distinctive features separating her two groups of cultures. But all failed. None were common to all four secure ones and absent in all four insecure ones. Then she compared the cultures for the presence or absence of certain behaviors, such as suicide, polygamy, matrilineality, and size of houses. Again, none of these classification principles worked.

What finally *did* work was what Maslow calls

> the function of behavior rather than the overt behavior itself. . . . It is this jump which I think was a revolution in the theory of anthropology and of society, laying the basis for a comparative sociology, a technique for . . . [placing societies] on a continuum instead of regarding each as unique . . .[87]

The concept Benedict finally formulated was that of "synergy," a term taken from medicine which is capable of more objective definition than her others. It signifies the combined action of separate factors which work in the same direction, such as the effects of two medicines given together, for example, aspirin and codeine, which thereby mutually strengthen one another's pain-relieving effects.

Taking aggression as a manifestation of social strain, one which could perhaps be regarded as the symptom to be relieved, she asks,

> Is there any sociological condition that correlates with strong aggression and any that correlates with low aggression? . . . From all comparative

material the conclusion that emerges is that *societies where non-aggression is conspicuous have social orders in which the individual by the same act and at the same time serves his own advantage and that of the group* [italics added]. . . . Non-aggression occurs not because people are unselfish and put social obligations above personal desires but because social arrangements make these two identical. . . .

I shall speak of cultures with low synergy, where the social structure provides for acts that are mutually opposed and counteractive, and of cultures with high synergy, where it provides for acts that are mutually reinforcing.

There is no problem about which we need more enlightenment than about concrete ways in which synergy is set up in societies . . .[88]

Through this concept, Benedict has also provided a way to understand the relationship to man of nonhuman primate societies. There synergy prevails, as I showed earlier, although it is established by *biological* rather than cultural means.

Benedict goes on to indicate that human societies with low synergy so arrange their relationships that "the advantage of one individual becomes a victory over another," whereas in societies with high synergy the advantage of one individual becomes a victory also for the group. She shows that

. . . raising yams is a general benefit, and if no man-made institution distorts the fact that every harvest . . . adds to the village food supply, a man can be a good gardener and be also a social benefactor. He is advantaged, and his fellows are advantaged.[89]

Benedict indicates that the absolute amount of wealth in a society is not the determining factor in the flavor or quality of life it affords, a conclusion also reached earlier from a somewhat different viewpoint (p. 159). She shows that what counts is whether the economic system, in both its subsistence and security sectors, tends to *concentrate a society's riches among a contracting "have" group, or to disperse them widely to all.* In the former sort of society, with low synergy

. . . no man can reach a security from which he cannot be dislodged. . . . He is insecure. His only security lies in having not merely much property but more property than his neighbor.

He is driven into rivalry with his peers and he must outdo them, better yet, if he can, undo them. He is driven into rivalry not because he is a bad man or because he is an ungenerous man but impersonally because the system works that way.[90]

In contrast, in the latter sort of society, with high synergy

. . . Since everyone is provided for . . . poverty is not a word to fear, and anxiety, which develops so luxuriantly in . . . [the type of society which concentrates wealth] is absent to a degree that seems to us incredible. These are preeminently the societies of good will, where murder and suicide are rare or actually unknown. If such societies have periods of great scarcity, all members of the community cooperate to get through these periods as best they can. . . .

. . . [A man from such a culture] sees life as an area of mutual advantages where by joint activity he attains his own personal desires. . . . His achievements are the boast of his group, and his group's prestige is his boast . . . fear of desertion, fear of humiliation, are only deterrents to improper behavior; and desertion and humiliation will not fall to his lot unless he defaults; he does not live in a threatening universe, and he does not have to snatch and grab to maintain himself.[91]

Although they sound pertinent to our own industrialized society, it is important to remind ourselves that in these passages Benedict had reference not to us but to an assortment of so-called primitive societies, some of which seem benign paradises in comparison with ours, and some of which included inhumanities so malignant as to cast ours by contrast in a rosy utopian glow.

As Benedict goes on to show, other aspects of a culture reflect the degree of synergy in its economic order. For example, in the secure or high synergy societies the gods, ghosts, or magic tend to be benevolent and helpful, whereas in the low synergy societies the gods, ghosts, or magic tend to be cruel and hurtful. The transformation of Tanala into Betsileo considered previously is amply illustrative.

So now I must add to my modified formulation of page 161 one more idea:

The level of intrasocial competition in a society is determined inversely by the degree of synergy between acts required to benefit the individual and acts required to benefit the group. Therefore, in order to create conditions in which the benefits to human well-being of intense interpersonal relationships can be maintained and the hazards avoided, the degree of synergy fostered by the institutions of a society must be increased.

Soviet Union and Israel

A bit of corroborative evidence comes from the experience of the Soviet Union and Israel in recent years. In both countries some children have been raised in groups largely by experts rather than individually by their parents. Observers have told me that when such children reached their teens and twenties, a small proportion showed a remarkable lack of interest in or dedication to the ideals of the collective farm or kibbutz on which they were raised, and which were of such moment to their parents, wandering away idly to languish in big cities rather than remaining as the stalwart, energetic pioneers it was hoped they would become. In effect these youngsters were precociously *fiu*, an effect regarded as undesirable by both peoples. As a result, according to reliable personal reports, the more extreme forms of separation of children from parents have been moderated in both countries. On the other hand, among adults raised on a kibbutz, a culture characterized by high synergy and modest individual creativity, interpersonal relationships tend generally to be quite cool, but also highly cooperative. Little aggression is shown, and neuroses and perversions are extremely rare.[92]

Conclusions

What use can we make of this perspective? We will be warned, for example, that an unreconstructed German businessman may face emotional stress to the point of distraction if he attempts to set up an enterprise with local help in an outlying village in Tahiti. Likewise, those who injudiciously bring Tahitian women to work as domestics in American homes are in for a shocking disappointment if (as has happened already) their babysitter should become *fiu* and disappear on the eve of the parents' departure on a long-planned vacation.

We can also use such comparisons more broadly. I assume, should my hypotheses prove correct, that the values the majority of mankind selects consciously and undogmatically to guide our future evolution will reconcile us neither to indefinite increase in intrapsychic conflict, aggression, and mental disorders, nor to adopting a lifestyle as relatively simple, static, and nonachieving as that of Tahitians. No doubt there is some room for compromise between the two cultural patterns, with some lessening of intensity in our parent-child relationships and some increase in closeness between our families. Providing we simultaneously reduce intrasocial competition and increase synergy, we might thereby be able to minimize aggression and mental disturbance without impairing the zestful investment of self in the learning and doing that makes life an adventure.

We might also anticipate and avoid the disastrous consequences of haphazardly transplanting bits and pieces from one culture to another. Take sexuality, for example. We need guidance in making the value choices required for healthy reintegration of sexuality into our more abundant lives. One proposal is that our children should not only live in a sexually permissive atmosphere, but should also receive the instruction in sexual intercourse reportedly given to some Pacific island children. So long as we maintain the exclusive, and I believe excessive, intensity of relationships of children to parents characteristic of our culture, such an innovation could have ruinous effects. Already overheated and erotically tinged attachments likely would boil over much more frequently into socially destructive behavior or emotional disturbance. Detergents disrupting our sewage-disposal systems, DDT accumulating to toxic levels in fish used for food, gonorrhea microbes learning to live with penicillin are examples from the simpler and more easily understood world of biochemistry of the dangers in upsetting the ecological balance by introduction of just one new, insufficiently understood factor. Changes in patterns of sexuality have at least as complex and unpredictable results. I remember well the "emancipated" couple I warned futilely against enforcing communal nude family swims over the objections of two of their five children. One of the girls developed a troublesome eye-blink tic and one of the boys a tenacious homosexual propensity that in later psychotherapy were found to be related to conflicts over feelings stirred up by being confronted with their parents' genitals three times weekly at a time in their lives when such intimacy was not a part of the culture, but was particularly stimulating to them erotically. The injurious results of the misconception that all our sexual troubles spring from Victorian taboos is considered in Chapter 9. It is important here to interject a few thoughts about the role of sexual intercourse in present human life.

It is evident that human sexual intercourse has become largely independent of, and has acquired crucial functions other than, reproduction. Foremost among these is to strengthen and stabilize the relationships between adults in a way that is favorable and in most societies even necessary for human well-being, especially for the well-being of children. Marriage everywhere has been the social outgrowth of the most elemental ties between men and women. Now that women are becoming as capable as men of "bringing home the bacon," food-sharing cannot create the bond between the sexes that it did when men only were the hunters. And because in Western culture we have almost eliminated parentally arranged marriages, the erotic function of sexual intercourse has become a necessary factor to the self-selection of mates among the young. Without it, economic, educational, professional, and certain emotional needs which often militate against marriage might much more frequently prevent it. Moreover, now that marriage bonds are less supported by economic pressure and parental or extended family ties, spouses turn increasingly to sex to preserve what is ever more prominently a tentative relationship. Perhaps marriage is a waning human institution, as many assert,[93] in which case different arrangements for child nurture will eventually have to be devised. But at present and for some time to come, it will still be important to preserve the family solidarity so vital in our culture for the healthy emotional growth of children.

There is a further function of adult sexual relations having to do with renewal and reinforcement of personality. Adult personality arises largely out of the matrix of interpersonal relationships the individual enjoys in early life. The quality of these interpersonal relationships is substantially determined in the course of events tinged with infantile sexual feelings, using that term in the broadest sense to include all the pleasurable experiences of holding, clinging, fondling, rocking, warming, bathing, diapering, feeding, eliminating, and so on. These early interactions, and responses to them, are gradually built into the person's identity structure and so become the spine of personality throughout life. During adulthood the erotic function of sexual intercourse takes over and continues this process, contributing powerfully to the ongoing maturation of interpersonal relationships and identity.

Of course, sexual intercourse periodically discharges accumulated erotic tensions. But what is not understood by everyone is that most people also seem at times to release through sexual intercourse other tensions which are not essentially erotic in origin or kind. The man who is anxiously awaiting word about a promotion at work may be much better able to bear the stress if his psyche is so organized and his wife so disposed as to permit him to discharge the tension in lovemaking. In this way, sexual intercourse functions to maintain psychobiological balance until appropriate nonerotic discharge can be achieved.

The major influence directing human evolution in the last few thousand years, including biological change, has been evolving human culture (see Chapter 6). Man's cultural ways of life have endowed certain psychological strivings for accomplishment with survival value.

I am driven to conclude that: (1) Intense interpersonal relationships between individuals are hazardous, but are necessary not only for full human creativity but also for human survival in the ever-changing world ahead. The question then becomes how to enjoy their benefits without suffering the associated drawbacks. (2) By taking charge of the process of values evolution, we should be able to affect not only various specific elements in man's personality but also the characteristics of human life in general. In time this influence will expand into control.

As we progress through the pages of the human agenda, just what is it that will wield this awesome influence? The answer, of course, is the human mind.

The Human Mind

. . . if the fertility of a planet is life, and the fruit of life is mind, then the human species becomes the first sign of real wakefulness in the solar system.

—N. J. BERRILL

Introduction

Outside the window a pair of finches chirrup over their little blue eggs in the nest they built in my warm front door light. Across the canyon neighbor children shout and splash in their pool. In between, my puppy bays at a butterfly, the pretty girl next door digs in her garden, and someone in the kitchen tries clumsily to unjam the garbage disposal. I recoil from the blank sheet in front of me into eavesdropping on these slivers of life during the eternities between typewriter clicks. I wrestle with the mind, struggling to pin to the page this elusive adversary I've chased through a thousand books. But he is invisible and intangible, and mightier than the word.

A shower of distractions entices me away from the hard work of compressing bounding ideas into understandable paragraphs. I would like to look again at the blue egglets and I wonder what the gardener is doing now, and you know I have a way with the disposal. Guiltily I drag my attention back to the task at which my mind boggles. The psychiatrist is willing, but the psyche is weak.

What is this wondrous weave we call mind, that can simultaneously record and then remember all these temptations, decide to resist them, drive itself back to a difficult but optional task, experience despair at roadblocks, and when a sentence is successful, can experience delight deeper than that which comes even from peeking at finch eggs?

Mind is the gossamer reality that controls behavior. As such, mind is the essence of man. We all sense that intuitively. My everyday round confirms it. I've spent most of my working life trying to help people resolve conflicts within their minds. It should be easy for me to formulate thoughts about so central a subject as compared with others in this far-flung inquiry.

And yet it is easier for me to deal with the foreign universe than the familiar mind. Is it easier to write about other realms just because I know so much less about them? Or is it that the mind is just too complex for me? To both questions the answer is probably yes.

But the greatest difficulty in understanding and discussing the mind seems to come not from the complexity of the subject matter or from my individual shortcomings, but rather from the shortcomings of mind itself, especially as a tool for studying itself.

In order to understand mind we will first look at some of these shortcomings in terms of the history of mind. Then we will consider man's mind as it exists today, and some of its specific limitations. We will next pick out five crucial aspects of mind and try to understand how they develop sequentially in the individual man. Because these five factors originated before our species, we will follow their long journey through the innovations of evolution to man, relating them particularly to consciousness. Finally we will try to grasp the significance for the future of a few current trends in the evolution of man's largely man-made mind.

Mind: Consciousness, Limitations, Values

The story of mind is of a trek toward *consciousness* in the control of behavior. While the pinnacle of fully conscious and complete control is still far off, the peak of consciousness attained so far is the mind of man. All across time, groups of our ancestors left the climb and settled in the valleys below, where their descendants remain today as monuments to advance scouts who, after reconnoitering new terrain, were left behind on side roads as new explorers surged past them. Electron and atom, molecule and virus, amoeba and anemone, lobster and llama, monkey and man are all forward scouts whom new waves of migrants toward still higher levels of consciousness did or might someday outdistance.

Mind and consciousness certainly did not originate with man. Precisely where they were born in the progression from particle to person is a matter of arbitrary definition. But wherever they began, mind and consciousness need not *terminate* with man who may well turn out to be, like other species, only the guardian, vehicle, and courier who passes them on to a pioneering new creature who will carry them to still higher levels.

Man's mind in particular has become the device for the increasingly conscious control of life. Now we must confront the sobering truth that the situation is comparable to that of the maybe not-so-far-off compleat computer which, in addition to performing its regular tasks, will design, manufacture, and repair itself and its self-reproducing successors. What is not comparable is that it is the present limited mind of man that must assume deliberate control of itself, and it must do so *today*.

Here I am not thinking of the mind's control of the brain, which despite its special status as the immediate house in which mind lives, is still part of the body. Rather I am referring to that part of a person which is psychological rather than physical, but which is nevertheless one of the organ systems making up the individual. Like the circulatory or digestive systems, the mind is composed of many parts, has its own structure and function, its own origin, its own past and future, its own health and pathology. Despite its intangibility, like other organ systems, it affects and is affected by all other parts of the person.

Mind cannot be separated from history. Or from biology, say the state of the liver and the level of blood sugar. And least of all can it be understood in isolation from brain. All these limit the mind's adaptive flexibility. But the critical flaw of mind is its stubborn aversion to standing back far enough for objectivity from the comforting familiarity of immediate troublesome concerns. Yet only by achieving such broadened perspective can it get past the obstacles to embracing whole the enthralling but disquieting future.

The mind has several such intrinsic characteristics which thus limit its objectivity and so constitute serious obstacles to fulfillment of its specific and irreplaceable function of coordinating all our resources in the service of adaptation. What are these obstacles?

First, there is the difficulty created by the split between conscious and unconscious mental functioning which has such momentous importance for human mental health and illness. Because mental development begins in infancy long before consciousness is well crystallized, much of mind remains permanently outside awareness. This is of little importance in animals, where consciousness is at best a dimly flickering spark, and where therefore the power it affords the animal over its own destiny is minimal. A dog, for example, without the subtle mental variations dependent upon higher consciousness, providing it has been well nurtured, develops about the same powers no matter where or by whom it has been raised. It will be able to communicate instantly and equally with all others of its kind no matter where they grew up. But its powers, and theirs, will forever remain so modest that it matters little to the survival of its species whether or not they can ever understand fully their own or one another's impulses.

However, the consequences for diversely acculturated human beings of the split between conscious and unconscious mental functioning are momentous. For the power over our own destiny, derived from the brilliant beacon of our extended consciousness, has become enormous in recent decades. The magnitude of its force makes potentially lethal any failure to communicate readily with our fellows, or to be aware moment by moment of impulses motivating its use. So damaging are the effects of this inaccessibility to consciousness of much of mind that the split has been considered an evolutionary defect. It may be more useful to regard it instead as an *imbalance* brought about by the changed relationships between various parts, something like the role of man's erect posture in causation of sagging belly and even hernia. It is not that the abdominal wall has become defective in the course of evolution, for if we still walked on all fours it would do quite well in supporting the viscera, but rather that it has not yet been *strengthened* proportionally to meet the new stresses imposed. So it is with the bridges between conscious and unconscious mental functioning. We will consider in Chapters 5 through 9 what may be done in the future to ameliorate such imbalances.

Next, we should focus on the tyranny of our emotional conflicts, our fears and anxieties, and especially our long-standing *hopes* and *wishes* that often interfere with the easy flow of thought of which ordinarily we are capable. For instance, I may be more concerned about the reaction of psychiatrists to this chapter than about the reactions of historians, biologists, or anthropologists to others. This wish to succeed in the eyes of colleagues, especially if I am unaware of it, can operate as more of an obstruction than a spur to good thinking and writing. Particularly is this true if my need to be "right" rests on unconscious conviction that to be "wrong" is to be worthless, and that therefore it is better to be "blank."

Second, marvelous as they are, all human minds are hemmed in by the structure of the language in which they grew. Most thinking exists as a flow of language, just as most electric current exists as a flow of electrons through a conductor. While some thought can proceed through mental pictures rather than words, and electrical energy can sometimes spark across a gap, in general it is as difficult for thought to flow across a language obstacle as for electric current to flow across a break in a wire. Every language smuggles into thought its historical freight of assumptions which together make up its "common sense." But as Einstein put it, common sense is only a deposit of prejudices laid down in the mind prior to the age of eighteen.[94] Each language locks us in a different prison, determining the ways in which we can think and understand, even the ways in which we believe. Because of language we are more likely to see what we believe than vice versa.

A friend tells me that the Eskimos have forty words for our one word "house" but none for our one word "love." If this is so, other things being equal, they should be able to think a wider variety of thoughts about houses and we a wider variety of thoughts about love.

Hopi Indians will say "a water" where we are constrained by our language to specify "a glass of water."[95] Here is a linguistic remnant of man's early observation that water does not have a shape unless contained. It is no more "reasonable" to tack it onto a designation of water than it would be to also add a reference to the fact that at low temperature water becomes a solid and retains its shape.

Westerners are sometimes frustrated in dealing with Orientals. For example, Chinese may not give straight "yes" and "no" answers because in their language and way of thinking there are no equivalents for simple yes and no.[96]

The reality a people understands is thus tailored by the thought its language allows. Does this mean that "there are many different realities" as mystics often claim? We will come back to this problem again. But for now let us keep a firm grasp on elementary facts. The water you and a Hopi drink is known by both of you to have the same objective properties, no matter how differently your languages may require you to speak of it. Affirmative and negative exist for Chinese even without what we think of as the convenience of plain words for them. And of course thoughts are not deeds for Eskimos any more than for Americans. It may well be that our indisputable superiority in building more kinds of houses is matched by their building more real love in practice, even if Eskimos do not have our one word for thinking about it.

What I am suggesting is that in a most crucial way reality exists "out there" and is not created by thought. The limitations of language and of thought, like the limitations of our sense organs, may restrict or distort our *knowledge* of reality, but not *determine* reality itself. X-rays existed before we had developed means for sensing their effects or words for thinking about them.

A third major limitation of our minds brings us back to our very practical concept of time. We divide the flow of events into a long past and future separated by a shorter and vaguely defined present. When looked at closely the present disappears instantly into the seeming eternity ahead or behind. We cling to this scheme because it gives us the illusion of allowing us to plot accurately any sequence of events, and to decide whether other events occurred earlier or later. And in this way the time concept helps us to grasp the scale of reaches of the past so enormous they are difficult to imagine. We could not have managed without this technique to reconstruct the story of evolution. For instance, in order to follow our line of descent, among many other things we need to know that bats had been lacing the skies with their tangled flight for twenty million years when man's primate ancestors emerged from the mammalian line forty million years ago.

When we leave the earth, however, our idea of time begins to falter. In terms of 24-hour days it takes Venus 230 days to rotate on its axis and 225 days to orbit the sun. Therefore on Venus a day is slightly longer than a year. And when we explore outside the solar system our terrestrial standards of time lose meaning altogether. On earth, events occurring anywhere can properly be considered as earlier or later than, or simultaneous with, other events, regardless of what time of day it may be in relation to the sun. You may properly regard both halves of a shortwave talk with a friend as being spoken and heard at the same time, although it is morning in your zone and night in his, if only you allow for the one-fourteenth of a second it takes for radio waves to encompass the globe. Without the sun as a common reference for time, for many people even the idea of simultaneity slips its moorings. If your friend were on the star Arcturus, which is 38 light-years away, you would have to wait that long to receive his message. Thus we cannot know what is happening on Arcturus at the present moment. The very image of Arcturus we have at this instance results from light waves that left it 38 years ago.[97] If somehow without our knowledge earth and Arcturus suddenly began to move apart at the speed of light, exactly 38 years later the image of the star and any radio messages would just disappear from our receivers. We might conclude that Arcturus had ceased to exist. We could not know for sure since no more information would reach us.

It is uncomfortable to realize that in such a universe in practice even the universal "right now" is a fiction, as are measurements of elapsed time made by observers moving with relation to each other. For example, when transported at 85 percent of the speed of light, the speed of a clock and the processes it measures will slow by half.[98] The odd consequence of this is that someday an astronaut could return after a long space voyage only fifteen years older while his friends who remained at home have been duly transformed by three full terrestrial decades into gray old men. At least such will be the case if Einstein's improbable truths continue to be confirmed by progress in physics.

Like many minds, mine is unable really to comprehend relativity of time. The wonder is that a few people can. The further wonder is that, despite our limitations, when such space-age aging begins to occur, the majority of minds, including those of children in school, will shortly be able to understand and even explain the pertinent principles of relativity.

Within a few years after Magellan sailed around the earth, proving it not flat, children were drawing globe maps and understood the long-taboo fact that the earth was spherical. It was not too long after Newton formulated his concepts that children began to explain matter-of-factly in terms of gravitation how it is possible for Chinese to walk around upside down on the underside of the earth. And today there are children who speak with confidence about the "unconscious" and its telltale signs in dreams and slips of the tongue only a little more than half a century after Freud's revelations were ridiculed. So it really should not surprise us when they begin to master relativity.

We do not yet know how to account for such enormous leaps in understanding in a "short time" by an occasional genius, and then by the general population. Nor can we really explain in the face of such progress in getting along with the universe that human ability to get along with one another, expressed particularly in ethics and politics, has remained nearly unchanged for such a "long time" as several thousand years.

A fourth limitation of the mind is its need to break a whole into parts in order to comprehend it. In earliest times apparently all knowledge was treated as an indivisible lake which individuals grasped as a whole. But then the accumulation outstripped the mind's ability to drink it in all at once. Aristotle was the first great categorizer. He subdivided knowledge and wrote the first textbooks in many areas. Ever since, people have been separating what became a river of thought into unnaturally isolated trickles. A disadvantage has been that specialists have often become so absorbed in details their eyedroppers disclosed they could not comprehend the broad stream.

Yet even in deliberately seeking out the wide view I find myself unable to avoid the same splitting of the whole into artificial categories. We have glanced over the evolution of the universe, earth, life, and man in sequence. In Chapters 5 through 9 we will look at various new prospects of man's controlling his biological future from the viewpoint of the impact of these new powers on his values. In order to grasp and focus on a manageable mindful of this infinite unity, you and I are forced to confine our thoughts temporarily to one corner at a time. We must proceed as though agriculture can be studied separately from aggression. Or God from genetics. Or even more absurd, as though brain and mind can be considered apart.

Nowhere is this limitation of mind more apparent than when we turn the mind's attention to understanding its marvelous self. Like the brain, the mind operates as a totality which defies our habitual need to break it into pieces convenient for study. Everything in the universe adapts to change. What we now designate as mind is the most complex and subtle sort of adaptation, charged with integrating all the wisdom accumulating on the human agenda. As such it is obvious that the indivisibility of the mind is even greater than that of its physical machine, the brain.

So as we focus down on mind let us keep in view all we have learned of adaptation earlier:

Cosmic gases adapting to heat loss by condensing and contracting into solids.

Atoms building molecules, molecules combining into amino acids, self-reproducing viruses, and cells, under the influence of ultraviolet rays.
Cells surviving dangers by specializing, cooperating, and clustering.
Gene modifications producing variations that led to fish, amphibia, reptiles, mammals, primates and man.
Now that his biology has become stabilized, man innovating adaptation by psychosocial processes rather than biological modification, guided by evolving values.

The mind makes choices. As its range of selection enlarges from worm to writer the process of "deciding" becomes progressively more complex. As it guides my typing and is assailed by distractions, my mind chooses whether to stay indoors and pursue the satisfaction of my own creation or to go out in the sun and enjoy nature's. This choice is made on the basis of my judgment at the moment as to which is more valuable. The scope of the control exerted by this value judgment and its fellows enlarges astronomically as our new technology offers you and me increasing power to select whatever reality we like. Our minds are required to make more choices than ever before.

These value judgments become the bricks stacked by our minds into the walls of value systems. We build these value systems into the social structures in which our ongoing psychosocial adaptation takes place. They both facilitate and confine our progress.

How does the mind go about making the bricks of value judgment, and laying out the walls of the social structures they are to become?

In attempting to answer this question we must keep before us the long way mind has come to perch behind our expanded foreheads. To comprehend the mind of man we need to retrace that route in imagination through the minds of the simpler creatures that preceded us across the three and a half billion years the journey required. How will we know which of the infinite number of impressions we receive are the most significant? How can we bring them home for future study and use? Once again we are forced to fall back upon *words* which with all their deficiencies remain the best device we humans have for extracting and perserving the essence of our experience.

But this procedure places us in danger. By trying to find evidence in the past of aspects of man's mind in the present we may trap ourselves into discovering what did not exist or is irrelevant. Those who debated the number of angels who could dance on the head of a pin made a bigger mistake than what many today would regard as the unwarranted assumption that angels existed in the first place. For nowadays even those who believe in angels regard it as ludicrous to project them into the concrete man-made world of pins where their dancing slippers may be measured and counted. It will help us guard against this pitfall if we recognize in advance that we are broadening the application and perhaps the definition of words now in common usage.

The apparatus of mind is too complex to be modeled fully, and many who have tried to reduce it to a comprehensible diagram have given up. Let us be brave enough to try to grasp at least its oversimplified outlines.

Individual Development of Human Mind: Five Crucial Aspects

Suppose we made a map of mind. I would indicate five main areas on the map within each of which we could locate details of the terrain. They are *intellect, character, mastery of reality, freedom,* and *joy.*

Intellect

When we say of someone "he has a good mind," generally we are speaking of his intellect. We mean that he understands and learns quickly, he remembers accurately, he reasons logically and has a freshness in his mental processes that may show as humor, originality, or imagination.

Character

But mind includes more than intellect. When we say of someone, "he is a good person," we refer usually to *character.* We mean by character *how* the person uses his particular intelligence, how he typically responds to the opportunities and stresses that rain into his life, how he reacts in general to life year after year. As everyone knows who has watched good intellect go down the drain, these elements which we lump together as character are equally or more important than intellect for a person's mind and life. As a result we tend to think of intellect as something a person "has," whereas character is something a person "is."

Mastery of Reality

Now let us consider intellect and character as they affect *mastering reality.* Within you and me there are certain realities with which we must deal. As you read my words, you may be hungry or worried about a convalescent child or bored with my ideas, or maybe all three. If your reality includes awareness of being overanxious, overfed, and underread, you may decide to remind yourself that your child's temperature has remained normal all day, to recall that you have resolved to deny yourself food, and to admonish yourself that you usually tend to give up too readily on a book, in which case you will plow doggedly ahead with protecting your child from your anxiety, losing weight, and continuing your reading, all (I hope) by sharing more of my adventure. Or you may rationalize that it has been two hours since dinner, that one cannot nurse the sick or concentrate with low blood sugar, and that it is convenient to look in on the little girl anyway on the way to the refrigerator. It depends on your character. So does most of what you get out of your resources and your life.

On the other hand, you may have a child restless with high fever, you may be underweight, and you may be reading a book that is really dull. If so you would be mastering reality by dropping *The Human Agenda* and heading for the child's bedroom and the kitchen, leaving me to decide whether to start rationalizing or rewriting.

That we are suddenly again talking about me and my reality may mean that I am like the self-centered writer who, trying considerately but fruitlessly to turn the conversation onto one of his fans, remarked, "But let's talk about you now. What did *you* think of my new book?"

Or it may mean that our realities overlap, that I must be concerned with your waistline and you with my tempting finch eggs. For we are all part of the same big enterprise, the same reality which we must master in different ways. We all affect each other through the taxes we pay for health and howitzers, the autos we drive for convenience despite their exhaust, the marriages and children we make for better or for worse, the votes we cast for lesser evils, even the repulsions and attractions we exert upon one another.

Of course there are many other components of reality in our individual lives which we must master in one way or another, such as love, work, and play which we will explore later. But after developing to the fullest your individual resources or mine, we need to experience vividly our collective roles in the human family, our continuity with the rest of the thin costume of life that gloves our globe, our obeisance to an upstaged sun in a fourth-rate galaxy with a cast of millions, our unmistakably off-Broadway corner in the extravaganza of an expanding universe.

Mastery of *this* dimension of reality is for the future the only reliable source of the serenity our grandparents were provided by their now-splintered creeds when horizons were close and comforting.

For clarity I've been pretending that intellect and character and mastery of reality are simple ideas and that we can carve fairly simple and stable definitions for them. But we cannot fool ourselves that *freedom* or *joy* are simple ideas. They slip through the fingers that try to tie them to a definition. Although the inner experience of fulfillment and delight they bring stays much the same throughout our lives, freedom and joy arise from such different conditions at each stage of development that they really mean different things at different times.

Your new baby is forced out of his warm bath into our noisy world at a time in his progress when he consists of a bundle of untried reflexes under no organized command. His "self" is not yet made. Nor is his "mind." Each reflex is set into motion without his "will" by the goads that surround him. His head and face are pushed upward over the rim of mother's body into the light his eyes are built to react to but have never seen. His shoulders and arms come next one by one, hands grasping automatically at whatever they touch, usually closing on his thumbs. His body and umbilical cord then appear, carrying the support systems that sustained him in his long weightlessness like a tiny naked astronaut. The air his skin was made to withstand cools the adventurer for the first time, starting the chain of response for his first breath and cry. Nerves lying in wait beneath the surface carry impulses from startled skin and jostled muscle to and from his sleepy brain and spinal cord. His lungs and larynx first suck in and then blow out the air they were constructed to move but have never before encountered, and he squawks his greeting to earthly life.

Freedom

For this new baby, freedom includes moving his arms and legs, urinating, defecating, nursing, sleeping, and waking reflexively—all without deliberate intention. His freedom also includes being relieved of hunger, cold, and excreted urine and feces through the deliberate actions of another person.

If we look in on the child a few years later we find him much changed. The child's freedom will still include moving his arms and legs, urinating, defecating, eating, sleeping, and waking. But now playing and speaking will be included, and all will be done according to an organized pattern, under the deliberate control of his shiny new mind, with decreasing interference from you, his parent.

A decade or two after this your baby's freedom will include all this, and the additions of specific use of his genitals, establishing his own family and life style, and submitting to a minimum of control by you or anyone else. In later life, perhaps after you are gone, his freedom may be modified again into emancipation from work and dependent children, so that he can give attention to other matters.

Joy

Joy for your baby at first results from unrestrained functioning of his reflexes in response to "all over" stimulation of his senses. He feels it as pleasurable oneness with the world. As his mind begins to crystallize, he sees that you are separate from him, and learns to crave your approval. As he grows into childhood his joy becomes focused into manifestations of the curiosity man appropriated from apish ancestors. His own body and the outside world are explored delightedly. Out of these adventures, and his developing sense of separate identity, come his first masterings of reality. These include pleasurable sensations in his genitals which further bolster the sense of separate identity. Soon are added the excitement of specifically erotic feelings.

For the young adult, joy shifts largely to the ecstasy of merging this painstakingly constructed separate identity in love and sexual pleasure with another person. As he becomes older still, joy may evolve into more and more productive mergings with family, community, and humankind.

Incomplete as such a compressed sketch must be, I think it can illumine a dark place for us. Today all but a few people would agree on the supreme worth of freedom and joy as values. But they disagree on their definitions. What we need to understand to reach useful agreement is that the nature of freedom and joy *changes* during a person's development.

Because he was so biologically unformed at birth your baby in a crucial way remained one with you. His freedom consisted largely of the automatic firing off of reflexes as they reached their ready state. His joy consisted of his pleasurable reaction to the general stimulation you provided and release from discomforts your kindly intervention brought about. He exercised no control or choice because the controlling, choosing element in him had not yet emerged.

Then as infancy gave way to childhood a remarkable change occurred. Your child gradually grew a *self*. And at a certain moment he began to speak of himself as wanting or doing something, probably beginning with "Johnny wants . . ." But soon the third person gave way to "I want." With his change from object to subject, his dawning identity had expressed itself in *language,* and was thereby confirmed and extended. Now he decided, he chose, he controlled. And he discovered yes and no. His freedom and joy were now centrally involved with his *separateness* rather than his oneness with you.

Only *after* going through the process of becoming a separate adult did he find freedom and joy again in merging his identity with that of others.

Much disagreement over definitions of freedom and joy disappears if we assess carefully the freedom and joy attained against the person's calendar reality. We all know of pathetic babies in old bodies who are still operating automatically as babies do, and expecting that some outside influence is going to come along to relieve their discomforts as needed. Naturally they are frequently disappointed. No one wants constantly to indulge a grown person as a baby. Sooner or later we snap irritably "do it yourself." Furthermore, through all the generations of man we adults have thrown misguided, wishful backward glances at the supposedly blissful and passive state of infancy.

Even at its best there are severe frustrations in this baby condition. Once you achieve the slightest awareness of dependence on others, you cannot feel completely secure in your own powers to satisfy a need. Also you gradually become aware that sometimes you have two needs at once. And that it is difficult to satisfy both at the same time but painful not to do so. While eagerly sucking your bottle to relieve hunger you may feel the pricking of an open diaper pin. If you go on drinking the pinpricking will continue. If you stop to yell for help to remove the pin the hunger pains will continue. It is partly out of such unhappy quandaries that the early sense of reality is built up (see also pp. 336–340).

Through need to reduce the likelihood of such dilemmas, the early yearning for power and independence arises. Some people never manage to renounce their primitive dependence and its primitive satisfactions, no matter how old they become. *Often it is these arrested developers who clamor the loudest for their freedom while achieving it the least.* One common expression of this petulant demand is the eager seizing upon every fad that comes along for inducing joy as a way of reducing awareness of dependency and helplessness in the face of painful tension. Within the last one hundred years, these have fallen into two main groups, the use of chemicals and the use of group rationalizations for withdrawing from reality.

In the mid-nineteenth century "laughing gas" was the rage at chic parties before its use as an anesthetic became known. Ether was similarly used. There were also the various patent medicines which secretly employed alcohol or opium for the same purpose.

Then came the frequent prophets who led their flocks up trees and mountains to await (and survive) the end of the world. And in the great migration westward, often the weak in character were taught that they need not be concerned with mastering the infant within while surmounting the challenges of the frontier without.

Today we have the revived furor for mystical melding with the infinite, the frenzy for marijuana, LSD, and other psychedelics, and the waves of social dropouts successively self-labeled as beatniks, hippies and so on. Properly included in this group are some of the more mystical offshoots of group treatment that specialize either in the grope therapy of clasping one's humble fellow seekers in the nude, or realizing oneself through grappling with the awesome almighty clothed in the stuff of the universe.

But we are drifting into side streets. The important point to be made here once again is that adult freedom and joy can involve merging the identity once more with the outside world *only after the individual has achieved his childhood separateness.*

The person who tries to jump from the dependent oneness of his babyhood directly into the adult forms of merging is likely to achieve only an imitation of adult freedom and joy because he skips learning how to use intellect and character for the mastery of reality. One example is the hippie proposition that love for everyone is all that matters. Its followers attempt to produce merging before individuals are sufficiently well formed to add much to the mix. They usually disdain education and books, and thinking, because all such intellectual activities require words. They cite the mental limitations imposed by language as justification for avoiding words as far as possible. They revere only nonverbal symbols such as auditory and visual images, thereby reducing the human mind to the kind of tools available to the animal mind.

Here we must be careful to avoid the unconscious arrogance of "the establishment" and its tendency to lump all dissent together. The "square" community uses marriage as an acceptable sort of merging even though the partners are often not developed individually first. And it is only fair to acknowledge that the square stampede into immature romantically distorted marriage, which has brought such agony to millions with or without divorce, is probably the most widespread example of the kind of psychological leapfrogging we are considering.

We should realize that a person might choose on a mature basis a way of living that to many others seems an evasion of maturity. You might be as impressed as I by the twenty-one-year-old son of old friends of mine. A cheerful, tanned young man, he came to see me out of consideration for his troubled parents, although he believes they are really the ones who need help.

"They say I'm throwing my future away. They think I'm not living up to the responsibility to use my opportunities to the fullest and am 'running away from reality' because I dropped out of graduate school and I live with a girl who isn't my wife.

"I work in a gas station from eight to twelve five nights a week. On my $38.00 take-home pay I support the two of us and our cat and our Honda, and I contribute a little to our Digger fund. That's the money a group of us put aside to feed any hungry hippies we meet, including us if we should ever need it.

"I don't think my parents are as healthy psychologically as I am. Dad is a systems analyst who hates his work but stays at it to pay for his house, his tennis club, and a wife he has nothing to say to. I enjoy my job and I choose to live modestly on what it pays me. I don't ask my parents to put me through graduate school, as he did, so I can get a job I despise and live with a wife who bores me. My parents belong to the United Nations Association and the American Civil Liberties Union. I organize peace and civil rights demonstrations. I don't agree with them that I 'have to be practical' by going into the Army. To me it's more practical to refuse to kill or be killed.

"Marsha is eighteen. We don't know whether we'll still want to be together in five years so we don't marry and don't have children. Her doctor told her it isn't yet certain the pills are safe, so I remind her to use her diaphragm.

"As for the rest, I'd prefer to relax in the privacy of my home smoking pot and feeling fine the next day rather than drinking booze in a bar and getting a hangover like Mother. But I don't want to go to jail so I won't use pot until it's legal. Dad puts down my 'mechanical' music. I play an electric guitar instead of his electric organ.

"I don't know everything about what is right and wrong and I don't think they do. Anyway, my mind is open to new ideas. Meanwhile I try to live what I feel. I try to be loving and not hurt myself or others. I only ask that they stop trying to tell me what to do and let me enjoy my freedom."

This young man uses intellect and character to master reality with ingenuity. In the process he experiences considerable joy. He wants to be free to follow his own values which certainly are different from those of his parents. But I could not find a fraction of the psychopathology in their son that one can uncover in an average graduate student. When his mother and father phoned I had to tell them so.

Evolution of Mind: Instinct, Learning, Consciousness, and Freedom

Alexander Pope said that the proper study of mankind is man. Sadly, most of man's effort has been devoted to learning about everything else. As his most crucial feature, you would suppose man's mind would receive the most attention from those few who did study man, but even they mostly studied everything else about him. In the last four generations, a small proportion of scientists turned their energies to understanding man's mind. Considering the long neglect, it is not surprising that despite an avalanche of new reports little is known.

Even if one resists the comfortable habit of dividing the whole into more manageable parts, it is not too difficult to see in broad outline how man's mind came to be. As we have observed earlier, in contrast to those of the nonliving world, one of the major characteristics of life is that in any set of conditions it may adapt to change in *several* ways, the selection and control of which is exerted in some fashion by the living organism itself.

As we move to more complicated life-forms the degree of freedom of the organism from external compulsion enlarges, and so does the degree of its control over its own adaptive behavior in the interests of survival.

A planet must cool when its sun burns out. Animals adapt to cold in various ingenious ways not available to planets. Cold-blooded types become sluggish and may adapt mainly by hiding in a safe place until warmer weather. Warm-blooded birds and mammals have a variety of adaptations. Birds migrate, bears turn down their thermostats and hibernate, and deer and dogs grow thicker fur. Some warm-blooded creatures, including geese and men, are able to assimilate larger quantities of food during winter, some deposited as a heat-conserving fat layer beneath the skin and the rest burned at a higher rate to maintain usual body temperature. Unable to grow his own external insulation, man long ago decided to appropriate the skins and furs of animals for this purpose.

At what point should we consider the behavior controlled by the organism under the control of its mind? Can we regard a lizard's entering his mud burrow or the "instinctually" timed departure of birds as mentally controlled? Must we look upon the growing of winter fur and fat layers as mentally determined? Or wait until we reach the level of man's deliberate use of animal skins for heat conservation before we consider such behavior as a manifestation of *mind*?

The seal is one of several lines of mammals which have evolved as though nostalgia for our watery past had directed their gradual evolution back into the sea. They have not progressed in this regression so far as the dolphins and whales who live entirely in the ocean, but we all have seen how a bumbling clownish seal on land is transformed into a glorious athlete in water.

Like dogs, these intelligent creatures have the ability to engage themselves with man to the extent of learning tricks we teach them, and some we had not intended that they learn. A seal ordinarily dives for a period of from a few seconds to three or four minutes. If conditions are right, however, he is able to stay submerged for almost an hour. This is accomplished by markedly reducing all body functions, including pulse, oxygen utilization, kidney function, and so forth, all of which quickly return to normal after he comes back to the surface.[99] Physiologists, of course, were interested in learning how this change is accomplished and so devised a technique. While instruments are attached, a seal relaxes in a tub of water, breathing comfortably. A researcher then submerges the seal's head. Sometimes the seal reduces his metabolism and sometimes he does not. If he does not, he begins to struggle to reach the surface after a few minutes. On other trials he will turn down his controls and remain comfortably submerged for forty-five minutes. Apparently the reduction of vital functions depends on whether or not the seal *believes* the experimenter intends to keep him underwater for a long time.

But are we to conclude that the seal *decides* to slow down his metabolism? We are beginning to learn how under special circumstances human beings can develop conscious control over "involuntary" activities, such as pulse rate, blood pressure, and urine secretion.[100] But even assuming the seal had acquired this talent, it would be difficult to understand why he could not produce the slowdown when he discovers that the experimenter in fact intends to keep him underwater for more than a few minutes. It appears that this profound physiological change depends upon a *psychological* process to initiate it, including advance perception of the experimenter and judgment as to his intent.[101] Therefore the physiological change is controlled by mind. However, we must conclude that although the control is mental, it is *not conscious*. And of course this brings us face to face with unconscious mental activity.

Although we commonly use the words nowadays, it is difficult to really grasp the idea of mental activity being unconscious because we are used to the dictionary definition of mind as "the total of the conscious states of an individual." Unconscious mind seems to be a contradiction in terms. But is it? We have seen how consciousness emerges gradually during the evolution of mind. And we know that a person's mental content at any moment is *relatively more or less* conscious, not absolutely one or the other.

It should be easier for us to enlarge our idea of mind if we think of the familiar behavior of my eleven-month-old pup. Val knows he will get a bone after his human companions finish dinner if he has been quiet. In that case he begins to drip saliva as soon as I push back my chair. If he has pestered me during dinner his lips stay dry. Clearly this is a reaction initiated psychologically. We can readily imagine that, to the degree dogs are conscious, he is conscious of wanting that bone, and even that he is conscious that he will or will not get it this time. We do not assume that he turns on or withholds the flow of saliva consciously. That is an unconscious response conditioned by experience to accompany my movements if he has behaved in a certain way, but it is evident that both conscious and unconscious reactions are "psychological," and therefore mentally controlled.

When Val hears footsteps in the driveway he growls and then barks unless he hears a familiar voice or whistle as a password. He is in control of this reaction and can prevent it entirely if I say "Quiet!" But even though he suppresses his growl and bark, his hackles rise and his mouth curls into a snarl for fifteen or twenty seconds. While he seems to control his growling and barking responses voluntarily and therefore consciously, the bristling and snarling are unconscious, or at least involuntary reactions. All these behaviors are truly mentally controlled, for none of them is elicited by the sounds of cats, squirrels, children, bicycles, or autos.

So the behaviors that are controlled mentally are partially conscious and voluntary, and partially unconscious and involuntary. Therefore we must *define mind* as: the collection of complex conscious and unconscious perceptions, judgments, memories, emotions, and so on which are built into complex chains of behavior controls. These controls, set in motion by various internal and external stimuli, are mediated by the brain. In the human mind the vast preponderance of behavior control is learned.

Where does that leave the *un*learned complex behaviors we called "instinctual"? Birds can learn complex behavior but are also born with some innate knowledge of when and how to build nests, how to sing, mate, raise young, and migrate. Are we to exclude these unlearned behaviors from the "mind" of birds?

Obviously we are faced here with the difficulties of concepts such as mind in relation to creatures so different from ourselves that they do not seem to apply. Again, this is a trap of definition we need not fall into. We need to understand that mind is a way of designating the controls of behavior from within, the continuously enlarging evolution of which we have been scanning in these four chapters. What we consider as mind in higher animals and man gives them increasing complexity of response to inner and outer conditions. As we ascend the scale toward man, unlearned, innate, automatic, and compulsory elements of response are gradually replaced by others which are learned, permitting the individual greater and greater degrees of freedom to choose among a greater variety of responses. From the nonliving realm of the cooling planet whose fate may be regarded as determined totally by outside forces, to the few reactions controlled by the amoeba, the greater number of responses available to the paramecium, lizard, bird, bear, seal, dog, and man, the story has one theme: liberation from foreordained compulsion and increasing freedom of *self*-determination in the service of adaptation.

In general this evolution of life and mind has been toward higher levels of consciousness as one kind of increased freedom. Yet there are still many situations for man in which greater freedom requires freedom *from* consciousness. For instance, you or I would probably be terrified consciously to swim toward a waterfall and would avoid doing so. However, if a beloved child were drifting toward the brink we might plunge into the water and be totally free of fear for ourselves until after we had pulled the youngster to safety.

In conformity with a limitation of mind, we have thus far for clarity regarded mental components as though they were *either* conscious or unconscious. But of course that is not so. Mental activities are *more or less* conscious depending on their nature and surrounding circumstances, and fortunately so, as we shall see.

Of what survival value is it to be "unconscious" of a large portion of the contents and processes of one's own mind? In Chapter 9 we will consider the momentous importance of the split between conscious and unconscious mind for human mental health and illness. Here we must try to grasp how such a puzzling division came about, and to understand its general adaptational significance.

Consciousness was added onto the mind *gradually* in the course of evolution, just as it is added onto the mind gradually in the course of development of each new individual. In both instances, consciousness is a kind of extension of the usual strata of mind into a new realm, but one with different conditions. Imagine that consciousness is like the peak of a volcanic island that projects out of the surface of the ocean, bathed in the light above sea level. Down below the surface, the successive layers of lava (or mind) upon which the peak rests would be of the same composition, but invisible due to their submergence in darkness. Consequently, consciousness could no more know the content of unconscious mind than the peak of the island, were it animate, could see its hidden pedestal.

Adaptational processes lay hold of this circumstance and, as happens so often in evolution, put a preexisting fact to a new survival use. Consider the *self-amputations* performed by animals to save their lives. Certain lizards, exploiting their preexisting capacity to regenerate, will wrench themselves free when caught from the rear, leaving in the disappointed predator's jaws several inches of tail which will be regrown later. Likewise, when threatened by a waterfall with loss of progeny, we can *self-amputate our paralyzing terror* while rescuing our child by thrusting the perception of danger into the conveniently preexisting state of un-consciousness, perhaps to be experienced consciously later.[102]

Evolution of Expression of Joy

Over the millions of years of evolution there arose a marvelous emo-tional accompaniment to the exercise of freedom. From a vague and shapeless seed planted somewhere between virus and viceroy, out of such elements as the practical delight of finches learning to nest in the warmth of my front door light, or my pup's delirium over his deserved bone, or out of the jubilation of flying bats or running horses, in other words, out of learning and use of capabilites for both organized mastery of reality and wild play, was born a new thread to be woven into the mesh of our lives. We call it *joy*.

How do we identify joy? Leaving aside for a moment all the inverte-brates whose life seems so different from our own, let us think just of those creatures who, like ourselves, have a jointed vertebral column, two symmetrical sides, two pairs of extremities, and a brain located up front with the special sense organs and mouth.

Take a sunfish. We watch it swim over the sandy lake bottom in which it has fanned out a hollow for its eggs. We drop a worm in its path. It ap-proaches warily and then rushes to seize and swallow it. Does it show any joy at its unexpected good fortune? We do not find the slightest indication of any "emotional" response. But what would we regard as a revealing signal?

Suppose we climb higher to look at the amphibians or the reptiles. What reaction would we look for to indicate joy? A frog strikes us as maybe bet-ter equipped. We impute a single emotional meaning to the monotonous sounds he makes, identifying his croaks with courtship yearning and his silence with fear if danger approaches. But joy? Somehow it doesn't quite fit. Whatever it may feel inwardly, the thought of a snake experiencing joy seems almost ludicrous despite its being a somewhat higher animal. It doesn't even croak.

In all this we are forced to admit that we are extrapolating backward from human behavior what we have learned to associate with our own individual inner emotional experience. We have no way of knowing for sure what a sunfish or frog or snake does or doesn't feel. But we have no alternative since at present we can make no direct assessment of the sub-jective emotional state of another species. In fact, the same problem exists even when one human being wants to understand the inner emotional state of another. He is forced to rely on behavioral signals which he *assumes* mean the same coming from someone else as they do from himself. And ordinarily, as a rough measure *within one culture*, this procedure works quite well.

Our empathetic puzzlement begins to wane when we look at mammals, evaporating progressively as we move up the scale. And when we reach my pup, who grabs a forbidden sock and rushes into the garden with it, yipping shrilly, we feel rightly or wrongly that all doubt is gone that we are in the presence of joy! Like the frog, he makes sounds, but his are very different depending on the circumstances. His shrill invitation to be chased contrasts delightfully with the incongruous bass bark he emits at the mailman, frightening both of them equally. Even when he is silent we can discern his joy. He prances with the sock. He crouches his shoulders to the ground while his rear end and tail tickle the sky. Most of all—allowing our anthropomorphic projection free rein—we can even fancy that turning his head slightly away, he looks at me out of the corner of his eye and *grins*. Peering across his long nose with that mischievous expression he at least *looks* as joyous as Jimmy Durante doing the same routine.

Val's smarter cousins all the way up the line convey joy by increasingly subtle use of the same means, primarily vocal and facial expression, supplemented by general body posture and movement. We feel more empathy with the baboon's joy than with the dog's. We are especially stirred by the gibbon's joyous singing of the halftone scale with which he greets the treetop dawn in the forests of Thailand. The delight and despair that radiate from the face of an infant rhesus monkey or chimpanzee travel in vocal and facial messages that resemble those of adult neotenic human beings even more than they do those of adult apes. And as Berrill says, "When I look at a monkey I don't know whether to laugh or cry."[103]

If we look downward we discover that facial means of conveying joy dwindle away even more quickly than vocal and general muscular means. The much-beloved dolphin lives behind a mask with a frozen smile, although no one who hears his ecstatic sounds or sees his exuberant play can fail to receive his joyous message. Armadillos also have completely immobile faces and not much vocal or postural expressiveness, either.

When we drop to the cold-blooded animals all but a few conceal what joy they may feel behind expressionless faces and only the most rudimentary voices. The sunfish we began with has not only a rigid face but lacks even the air-containing lungs that make possible a frog's croak or a crocodile's sigh. We are reduced to guesses about the meaning of his graceful slices through water in pursuit of food or mate, which by stretching the imagination we can interpret as joyous. Moving down to the invertebrate world we are still more adrift. Lobsters and crabs have no facial or vocal expressiveness. Even their leggy clambering or scuttling movements are so foreign to us that we are likely to feel nothing or a twinge of horror at the emotional blankness of a being who, despite profound differences from us, has at least a bilaterally symmetrical body with a head and brain, and jointed, paired limbs. When we reach the world of the sea urchin and hydra (and still simpler creatures) we are completely lost. If there is a way to read joy in the demeanor of an animal with a five-sided or radial body structure and no head or paired limbs, its discovery has not yet come up on the human agenda.

Notice that as a compensation for limitations of mind you and I have once again employed the convenient fiction of "higher" and "lower" animals. We must remain aware that it is only the relative complexity of structure and function of animals which we rank this way. And it is increase in complexity of structure and function *while generalized adaptability is preserved* that puts animals on the path to man's position, which we modestly regard as the highest. But it is plain that the body adaptation of birds for flying or porpoises for swimming is every bit as advanced in terms of evolution as is our adaptation for civilization of a big brain in a relatively nonspecialized body.

Notice also that we have been considering where in animal evolution the capacity for *conveying* joy arises, not for *experiencing* it. We cannot know for certain which other animals feel joy. But our empathic responses give us some reason to guess that joy is a relatively late arrival in the chain of evolution of emotions. For most of these animals, although unable to convey joy, can eloquently communicate its opposite. The agonized cries of a rabbit caught by the leg in a trap are unmistakable. The mute fruitless flapping of the hooked sunfish, the desperate struggle of the lobster to wrench itself loose from its main claw when it is caught, even the motionless spasm of the unshelled abalone, are emotionally overpowering messages of unjoy. That man has so often chosen to ignore these poignant signals of his fellow nonhuman beings' suffering is worth some musing.

In Conclusion: Evolution and Control of Joy

In barest outline this is the picture of the origin and development of mind. Nonliving substance has but one way of responding to a set of external conditions. The earliest living forms acquired more than one way of responding to the same circumstances. Choice between several responses gave the organism a measure of control and necessitated *decision*. Over time, *intellect* became the apparatus for decision. The weight of decisions made, and their consequences for survival, inscribed on every organism a style of response and adaptation which became its species' character, within which boundaries there could develop the variations of individual character. Intellect and character became the mental tools for *mastery of reality*. Man added the unique adaptive device of cultural transmission of knowledge, led by the guidebook of *values*.

At some phase the number of alternatives available to animals became so numerous, and the machinery for selecting among them so complex, that a new dimension we now would call *freedom* entered life. As the degree of freedom exercised by living creatures increased, their minds somehow sprouted the rootlets of that most recent expansion of freedom which has blossomed into what we now call *consciousness*. One of the components of consciousness, the pleasurable awareness of exercising faculties, eventually acquired the specific emotional quality we call *joy*.

For Freud, the goal of all behavior was to reduce the impulse or drive tension generated within the mind by bodily biochemical and physiological processes (see p. 65).[104] Sometimes, however, animals deliberately *increase* their tension by pursuing prey or a sexual partner. This heightening would be seen, according to Freudian theory, as a temporary device for concentrating and eventually discharging the tension of hunger or sex drive through eating or copulating.[105]

However, it is difficult to account for some other behavior under this premise. It is a common observation that dogs will stop eating to play. We cannot really account for this behavior as a means of reducing drive tension, unless we assume a specific separate drive on a par with the drive to eat.

But whether or not play is regarded as a separate drive, it would appear at least that the nonutilitarian *joy* of play can take precedence over the joy of gratifying the very plainly utilitarian drive to eat. And this means that joy *for its own sake* may sometimes be substituted in higher animals for joy achieved in the course of mastering reality.

The point is even more clear if we look at the behavior of a dolphin into whose brain has been implanted an electrode that stimulates his "pleasure center."[106] We can confront the animal with two levers, one of which when pressed will release his favorite food, while the other administers a stimulus to the pleasure center. For a while he will switch back and forth between the two levers, and devour the food delivered. But after a time the dolphin forgets all about the food lever even though he becomes physically hungry. He will continue pressing the pleasure lever indefinitely and may continue to do so with such singleness of purpose as to put himself in danger of starvation. The same may occur with a goat or a pig, and might with a man.

We are used to observing that man often puts pleasure ahead of business, and assume that this is a human foible. But here we can see that the tendency to be dominated by pursuit of joy begins with our forebears.

For them in their natural habitat there may be no problem. Except for play, *they do not often encounter sources of joy unrelated to activities that directly master reality.* Besides, their reality is relatively uncomplicated to master.

But for man there is a problem. Your reality and mine are extremely complex. We often find the task of mastering it distressing or beyond us. We need all our energy and ingenuity to find our way through the booby traps of the reality of our future. Moreover, the most exquisite experiences of joy for man come from the skillful exercise of his intellect and other resources in mastering reality. But as is shown by our tendency to become addicted to narcotics, or the potentiality we will examine later to become seduced away from assertive engagement with life by other chemical or electronic wizardry, we are as much endangered as the dolphin by techniques that artificially drench us with joy.

Just what and how much on the human agenda is at stake for man is as yet uncertain. But plainly, in adapting this way people would have much more of value to lose than dolphins.

Part II

The New Biology and the Future of Man

Introduction

A technical revolution is in process in every realm of human knowledge. My background best equips me to understand and interpret that under way in biology; this discussion will stand in lieu of a consideration of all.

Artificial gestation, genetic engineering, suspended animation—all of these and other biological innovations are on the human agenda, some to come up for consideration sooner and some later. They are not just more of the familiar kind of technical change. Taken together they constitute an arresting new phase in human life and its control. *For there is a qualitative change to "progress" when man learns to create himself.*

This new phase accelerates our leave-taking from the era of scarcity, to which we were at least poorly adapted, and our rude plummeting into the era of abundance, for which most of us are mentally unprepared. For our appropriate guidance in this new era, a reworking of values is required, which will take into account the new facts, and which will be as rapid and effective as is the new technique. Our reward for succeeding in this effort may well be the fuller liberation of mankind, and our failure may well be punished by the ultimate deterioration of all that human beings now treasure. In particular, though probably of crucial continuing importance for humane life in the future, high regard for the dignity of the individual may prove difficult to maintain when new biologic technique blurs his very identity.

Can we foresee now the values needed to govern our management of the new biology? With eyes tightly closed, we now invest tremendous effort in not looking—as the new biology resolutely hands us the wheel with which to steer directly the future evolution of man.

5 Gestation

Background

When mutation invented the first womb, more was born than an internal cradle to substitute for the heaving seas. The million years of tinkering that constructed that momentous mammal simultaneously devised the physical basis of what for man has been far more crucial, the *personal relationship*.

A fish could spawn its millions of eggs into the ocean, and swim away not even concerned whether they would be sprayed with sperm by the male. After a male frog had squeezed thousands of eggs out of the female into the shallow eddies of a lilied brook and had fertilized them, the two could swim away and never miss either their progeny or one another again. A female turtle needed the male only long enough to fertilize her dozens of eggs internally, and then she could deposit them in the sand and leave them forever to hatch alone. Even the warm-blooded female bird, who warmed her four or six eggs with her own body until they hatched in a nest she built for that purpose, and who fed the fledglings' gaping beaks from her own until they could fly, might push them out of the nest in a few weeks, and fly away never to see her mate or offspring again. In this gradual evolution of anatomy toward greater intimacy with the young, the final achievement was yet to come.

Only a mammal, who carries her fertilized egg inside her body until it is ready to be born, and who then must nourish the baby with milk from her body until it can feed itself, could have evolved into the personal mother, one who maintains a long-continued close relationship with her specific child after it is born. Only the personal mother could transmit to the baby clinging to her body the elementary learning of the prehuman society. Only such a mother-child mechanism and tradition, that sometimes included decades of continuing mother-child-father relatedness, could have been ready for the explosive revolution through which culture replaced instinct when, during a brief few hundred thousand years, an enlarging brain transformed a primitive anthropoid into a neurotically conflicted man.

It is true that a rudimentary kind of flock culture with occasional life-long monogamy is found among some birds,[1] but the period in which the young bird learns the ways of his society is brief. And in some subprimate mammals, such as the elephant and deer, the parent-child relationship is perpetuated throughout life because they remain members of the same herd. However, in neither group are individuals long burdened with conflicting subtle variations in parent-child attachments.

Only in man, and perhaps his immediate primate ancestors and relatives, is the parent-child relationship of sufficient intensity and duration to give rise to intense and prolonged conflict between the wish to grow up and the desire to remain a dependent child. That ambivalence underlies the endless variety of lifelong attachments between parents and children, the personal relationships characteristic of no other creature but man.

Gestation means carrying the embryo in the uterus through pregnancy to delivery. Gestation in that portentous pouch initiates not only physical closeness, but the rudiments of *psychic intimacy*, the indispensable condition for healthy human work, love, and play.

The sexual ties and mysterious reproductive processes that allow our species to survive have been part of the taboo-ridden core around which every human community has been organized. Now the new biology is placing in the previously helpless hand of man definitive control over reproduction to replace the feeble magic of the past.

Because of the welter of superstitions, old wives' tales, religious dogmas, and so on, the study of gestation has only recently been placed on a scientific footing. Unprecedented moral and legal dilemmas surround the use of each new piece of knowledge.

As our hesitant fingers close about the new instrument, deeply irrational emotional conflicts are generated. Will our mana be powerful enough to guide us safely through the jungle of taboos to the correct decisions?

Innovations

A team of investigators from Columbia Presbyterian Hospital in New York and the University of Vermont College of Medicine have shown that baby monkeys may be removed from their mother's wombs for medical or surgical procedures and replaced to grow uneventfully until delivered normally at the usual time.[2]

New techniques for not only ascertaining, but also *determining* the sex of the unborn child are just now being introduced.[3] Already concern is mounting that such measures might result in unbalancing sex ratios in our population. In the past five years, it has become possible to perform a number of medical procedures and surgical operations on the human baby in the uterus without affecting the course of gestation.[4] For example, blood transfusion into the abdominal cavity of the baby is given by injection through the abdominal wall of the mother. And already the uterus has been opened surgically to operate on the unborn child.

These successes foreshadow fantastic possibilities with humans in the not too distant future. Little objection will be raised when an unborn child is removed from the womb temporarily so that a congenital defect, say a cleft palate or an incomplete heart septum, may be repaired at the most favorable time. But such easily accepted measures will shade gradually into others that are dubious or downright objectionable to the average person today. Suppose in a few years it is decided to subject a baby to the risk of surgery to make genetic manipulations to change its color or alter its sex? Since the techniques to accomplish such unprecedented feats are in the works, there is grave risk they may arrive before sufficient thought and planning have been given to their proper regulation.

Soon it will be possible to stop release of eggs by the ovaries for a year or more by new drugs administered in a single injection or pellets implanted under the skin.[5] For many women, one result of elimination of the periods would be cessation of monthly "witchiness" and the widespread increase in other disturbances that accompany it.

But all responses may not be favorable. Leaving aside the possibility of serious physical reactions, there might be undesirable effects on emotional and social life. One concern is that the hormone might simultaneously affect the pituitary and the brain structures which control erotic behavior and might thereby interfere with the woman's sex life. Another concern is for those women who are especially dependent upon monthly bleeding and discomfort for reassurance that they are women. Having no periods for a year might threaten them emotionally.

The special considerations often extended to women in industry, school, and even in the courts, where menstrual difficulties are often invoked as mitigating circumstances in criminal defense, could lead to question or change of these privileges. And any such changes would contribute further to the already rapid rate at which social customs distinguishing the boys from the girls are disappearing.[6]

People want children. If they don't have them the ordinary way, they welcome unusual help. Therapeutic insemination has already achieved widespread acceptance, about one million babies having been produced by this means already.[7] But nevertheless there are many difficulties.[8]

Because the parents would prefer the child to be their own genetically on both sides, the doctor often mixes the fertile donor semen with the father's probably infertile semen, leaving open the possibility that the child is really the father's. Probably this lingering concern accounts in part for the occasional situation in which the father disavows the child and seeks to have it declared legally not his responsibility or heir, while the divorced mother seeks to disallow the ex-husband's right to visitation.[9]

Unlike the Tahitians, Westerners have long tried to conceal adoption of children. But our newer values now favor unsentimental disclosure to adopted children of the facts of their adoption in the hope of preventing their learning about it in unrealistic or unfriendly circumstances.[10] Children produced by therapeutic insemination face the same emotional hurdles we associate with adopted children.[11] But the idea of revealing the same sort of information to produced children is more shocking to us because of the weight of taboos associated with reproduction. Parents worry that the child will want to seek out his biological father, which does in fact happen. This desire might prove disturbing to the child first, because usually, with just such a possibility in mind, no records are kept. Second, assuming somehow he does locate the source of his parental heredity, what will have become of the fresh young medical student of his imagination? He is likely to have been transformed into a harried, middle-aged, balding practitioner, who may disclose in an unmistakable and painful way that he has even less time or energy for the fruit of his long-forgotten clinical donation than he has for his several offspring conceived later in more congenial if less remunerative circumstances.

The ease and anonymity of therapeutic insemination increase the risk that children unknowingly born of the same father will marry and reproduce, with all the possibilities of increasing genetic assets and defects that go with inbreeding. We may some day be forced to disclose paternity to the child, or perhaps encourage the wearing and mutual checking of coded dogtags on first dates. At present, it is up to the doctor performing the insemination to carefully check the donor's family and individual genetic history. Ordinarily no positive eugenic technique is feasible, other than the economical device of selecting a student. The procedure may include a careful interview to exclude a donor with a strong predisposition to allergies, diabetes, or lethal genetic disease. Or it may be confined to evaluation of height and general coloring. But at present, where it would be quite possible and acceptable to give at least all produced children the benefit of negative eugenics, there is no uniform minimum standard of practice required upon which prospective parent and community can rely. This could prove a serious catastrophe if a single donor inadvertently were permitted several times to seed unseen and unborn families with hidden genetic defects.

Dr. Edward T. Tyler of the University of California, Los Angeles, has said that with present methods, sperm have been capable of producing healthy babies one to three years after preservation by freezing. Eventually techniques will be developed which will allow virtually indefinite preservation. Then a prospective mother could select a father dead for centuries whose entire biography might be the basis for her choice.[12] This would not only serve a eugenic purpose but simplify the problem of what book to buy the child for Christmas.

Sometimes parents cannot conceive for want of an egg, or ovum, rather than a sperm. New techniques may soon make it possible in humans to supply an ovum when needed, just as it is in several animals.[13] Dr. James L. Burks of the University of Chicago has successfully fertilized human ova, kept in frozen storage and later thawed, in the laboratory. He suggests a number of clinical uses for his techniques.

Suppose a woman who wants a child suffers from the common obstruction of the fallopian tubes that prevents her egg from meeting the sperm and reaching the uterus. With the new method of therapeutic inovulation it will be possible to remove an ovum from her ovary through a small abdominal incision and insert it into the womb through the vagina. It could be fertilized by her husband either before or after insertion. She would then conceive and bear her own child as she might have without the obstruction.[14] There seem on the surface to be few value problems here. But wait.

Suppose her ovary is unable to supply the egg. A donor ovum could be supplied, perhaps one preserved for the occasion by freezing.[15] The child would be conceived and born as usual. But suppose the child should ask who is its mother? Would you answer with the name of the woman who carried and delivered the child, or the one who donated the egg? For a series of obvious reasons it may prove advantageous once again to resort to the Christmas book which would inform the child that mother was a medical student who died two centuries earlier.

So far we have considered techniques which supply a missing male or female sex cell. What about the whole embryo?

Recently it has been reported that the initial stages of fertilization and development of a human embryo have been achieved in glass substitutes for the tubes and uterus. Religious objections and even threats of legal prosecution have followed.[16] Although in some places this research thus has been hampered, the few days that human embryos have been sustained alive soon will suffice for their implantation into a uterus. The owner of that womb might then deliver a child genetically unrelated to either legal parent.

Moral and religious objections are bound to be fierce at first, and strengthened by personal bias. As a patient once told me, "There are some things a girl likes to do for herself."

But one day a young wife dying of leukemia will not have that option and will want to leave her husband a child, accepting her sister's offer to gestate it for her. Faced by such a choice, won't she and her husband be inclined to find an accommodation of old values to new realities?

Even more likely to be acceptable in the near future is such a situation in which the wife is already pregnant and wants the child to be saved although she herself is doomed.

Something similar has already been accomplished in sheep. The embryos of an English breed have been transplanted from ewes' uteri to the uteri of rabbits. The rabbits were then flown to Africa where the sheep were needed. Ten days later the embryos were transplanted to the uteri of a strain of African sheep who then went on to give birth to their aristocratic cousins.[17]

There is no theoretical reason why what can be done in one mammal cannot be accomplished in another. A similar scheme might be undertaken for human reproduction utilizing the specially bred apes some have suggested as a replacement for dwindling ranks of domestic workers. Then as she went about her cleaning, shopping, or chauffering the older children, the female chimpanzee housekeeper might also be gestating a new baby for the lady of the house. A likely occasion for such a technique in humans may arise when the child would be imperiled by a uterine tumor or weakness of the uterine wall caused by the scars of earlier deliveries by Caesarian section. In such instances a woman might need a womb with nothing to do for the rest of the year to gestate her child to term and deliver it healthy.

Even if its owner were human, complications could be distressing. Providing the volunteer's husband is willing, there would seem to be relatively little moral outrage attached to such a situation, especially if it all works well. But imagine the cries that could arise. Suppose the child is injured in transit and is born deformed or dead? Or suppose the volunteer changes her mind and wants to give the embryo back before delivery? Or just suppose that this embryo-sitter has become attached to the child and doesn't want to give it back to the genetic mother at all. What if foster-wombing becomes a profession? As Norman Corwin suggested, "We can look forward to surrogate mothers . . . banding together to form the first labor union worthy of the name."[18]

What is the effect of foster-wombing on the emotional health of mother and child? And who would be responsible for damages—the genetic parents, the hospital, the doctor?

Sometimes parents would like to have several children at once. With new techniques it will be possible to arrange that several ova are present to be fertilized at the same time, producing nonidentical twins. Dr. E. S. E. Hafez at Washington State University has already shown that it is possible in the cow to induce one ovum to divide in its early development in such a way as to give rise to identical multiple offspring.[19] It is difficult to foresee what effects this procedure would have on family life, on emotional health of parents and children, on human genetic goals and so on. But it is easy to see that there might be a great advantage to a couple who would like several children to be able to have all of them at once. Then when retirement came along in the late thirties, mother and father would be free to enjoy it, since the whole brood by then would be on their own.

But this prospect should be balanced by concern for the emotional health of the children. It is more difficult for children of multiple births to develop their own separate identities, since they are so much like one another and tend to be treated that way. This effect can be minimized if the children are nonidentical, both boys and girls, and if attention is devoted to finding and developing the unique qualities of each. And there is something to be said for the advantages to personality of being part of a group of siblings of the same age, with whom one must share the parents and from whom one receives support in establishing independence from them. Reduced intensity of interpersonal relationships might be one advantage.

For a long time it has been known that a pinprick through the wall of a frog's egg will start the process of cell division, and growth into a tadpole and frog, without fertilization by a frog sperm.[20] This fatherless reproduction technique is called parthenogenesis.

In recent years it has become possible to induce rabbits, who are mammals, to reproduce by subjecting an ovum to cooling at a particular stage in its maturation.[21] Under such circumstances the offspring have no fathers, only mothers. They are all female, but not identical with the mother. Their characteristics represent various combinations of hers.[22]

What can be done in one mammal is likely to be duplicated in time with another, even man. While offhand it may not seem likely to appeal to many women, this technique has a prefabricated clientele waiting for it to reach the *Reader's Digest*. Such a woman somehow avoids getting into that kind of proximity to a man which might lead to an ordinary pregnancy, either because she doesn't like or is afraid of males, or both. Think what it could mean if women could decide to have children on their own, without fathers even of the anonymous donor variety, and be certain that the offspring would all be girls!

There might be dangerous genetic consequences connected with prevention of the normal dilution of genes which comes about through sexual fertilization. For instance, normally a mother whose skin is so fair it cannot tolerate sunlight will likely have offspring whose skin color is darker than hers, since pigmentation is determined by the mixture of male and female genes. But a child parthenogenetically born to such a woman is likely to have skin color close to that of her mother.

The emotional consequences alone are cause enough for concern. What happens to the already flagging self-esteem of men when they are further deflated by also being made genetically superfluous?

Then there is the question whether women so born and raised would establish relationships with men when they grew up. In the past it didn't much affect the community if some women elected to avoid men. Traditional reproductive arrangements saw to it that each generation of women (and men) who didn't relate to the opposite sex at least enough to somehow bring a viable sperm and egg together were left without progeny. But through parthenogenesis women with this makeup would be quite able to reproduce and pass on to their daughters an ever-mounting disdain for men that in several generations could lead to establishment of matriarchy, with eventual demand for separate statehood.

A last thought on this matter. We might wonder what would be the total effect on man if the virgin birth ceased to be a matter of faith as to one disputed incident in the remote past and became a fact to millions in the immediate present.

Transplanted organs tend to be rejected and destroyed in time by the recipient through antibody reactions. Now that techniques are becoming available to prevent or at least delay rejection of foreign tissue,[23] it seems likely that the kidney and heart transplants of today may one day be followed by the surgically much simpler and safer transplantation of the uterus.

Some women have functioning ovaries but have had their uteri removed because of disease. Transplantation might allow a previously sterile woman to gestate a child from her own egg within her own body, albeit in a transplanted womb. Suppose the new womb aborted the child at the end of four months. Who would be responsible? The donor? The surgeon?

We ought not to leave this subject without mentioning a brand new prospect in gestation, a market for which can be foreseen by anyone with knowledge of the unconscious. The ordinarily rudimentary mammary glands of men can develop and even produce milk under the proper stimulation.[24] There are reports of Chinese men functioning in past centuries as wet nurses.[25] Theoretically, there seems to be no reason, with proper preparation, a pregnancy could not be gestated in a man's abdomen and thrive to term, in a transplanted uterus or other suitable spot, thereupon being delivered by Caesarian section into the affectionate arms of a nursing father.

Some women who now envy men will respond with resentment to this new usurpation of their functions by men. One woman angrily told me at a lecture, "Between your womb bottles and womb transplants we women won't have anything unique left."

Nature has made some experiments with minor variations in the locale of gestation even in the female since developing the mammal. Occasionally a pregnancy will settle down and grow in the tube before reaching the uterus. Less commonly a pregnancy is found growing on the ovary where an especially vigorous sperm penetrated an ovum prematurely. And very rarely a pregnancy that may have started in the vicinity of the ovary floats loose into the abdominal cavity, where it may settle and grow into the smooth peritoneal covering of the abdominal wall or a loop of intestine. Any place where the burrowing placenta can find a blood supply will do as a spot to grow for the tiny parasite called an embryo. And it will continue to develop normally so long as the available blood supply, space, support, and so on are adequate. But adequate conditions require extremely precise regulation of dozens of factors such as temperature, water loss, hormone, salt, glucose, and amino acid concentrations. Maintaining the exact levels is much more complicated than creating an environment to sustain astronauts in space.

No matter what experiments nature has made, it has never tried to set the clock back for man by doing away with the personal relationship and returning him to impersonal gestators such as those employed by fish, frog, and turtle. *But that is exactly what would result if man should succeed in growing babies in bottles.* Artificial insemination and inovulation, embryo and uterus transplantation, multiple birthing and parthenogenesis all interfere with a part of the physical antecedent of the personal relationship. Gestation under glass does away with it entirely.

So far, no mammal babies have been raised entirely in bottles, although as mentioned earlier fertilization under glass has been accomplished. But in the next few decades, given adequate study, it may be possible to develop successful ways of artificially duplicating womb conditions. Drs. Howard P. Taylor, Amarenda SenGupta, and others at the Cleveland Clinic Foundation's Department of Artificial Organs have published relevant studies, and Dr. Robert Goodlin of the Stanford University School of

Medicine has devised an apparatus in which to gestate prematurely born babies of less than 24 weeks. So far none has lived more than 48 hours.[26] The first artificial wombs might suffice at least for the final three to four months of gestation. Eventually machines will be perfected so that the entire process can be carried through outside the body.[27]

Most likely such devices will be employed at first to save unborn children whose mothers die during pregnancy. As in the case of embryo transplantation to a foster-womb, there probably will not be much difficulty in adjusting our values to accommodate such lifesaving innovations. But sooner or later a patient will request and get artificial gestation for her baby just because she is tired of the restrictions of pregnancy and wants to take a round-the-world tour or go skiing. The frightening ramifications of producing babies without parents and personal relationships in the ordinary sense have so far been best explored by Aldous Huxley in *Brave New World.* Without rehearsing his inspired account, it is worthwhile to touch on some psychological risks of gestation under glass.

After such a gestation the mother may be unable to feel close to and love this bottle-born baby, jeopardizing its emotional health. She may be subjected to injurious social disapproval of her lack of so-called mothering instinct. Such a child might be less responsive to personal relationships throughout life as a direct and indirect consequence of the artificial gestation.

Are the prospects all ominous?

Certainly there is value in the power to release women from the inconvenience and time loss of pregnancy, particularly where the mother is disabled. But are there any other optimistic prospects for artificial gestation?

There are, and they may lie first of all in the realm of expanding our understanding of earliest human development and then applying it to training and education.

The last decade of investigation has taught us that the potentialities of many ordinary people are much greater than we thought. For example, ordinary adults can learn to increase their reading rates from hundreds to thousands of words a minute. Bright normal children learn this skill even better. Also, at age ten such children have been able to engage in academic study ordinarily undertaken only by graduate students.[28] There seems to be some hope that very young children with brain injury can compensate for impairments of perception, locomotion, or speech if proper training is started early enough.[29] And all this involves only proper application of ordinary teaching methods after the organism is fully formed.

Suppose we could learn new teaching methods and apply them to new human beings from the moment of conception onward, so that by the time of birth they had already had nine months of experience, carefully controlled so as to bring about the best possible functioning. Perhaps in time we could not only eliminate various impairments early but even discover and accentuate the positive potentialities of a particular new individual.

For example, beginning about the middle of gestation, the unborn baby makes movements which swimming instructors tell us are well enough developed at birth to enable him to swim underwater without special training. If the baby could go on getting oxygen from his umbilical cord after birth, presumably he could continue to perfect his swimming right through to the period of adulthood. But after birth he must breathe air, which he cannot do underwater. Nor is he yet strong enough to bring his head to the surface regularly. The early ability to swim, then, goes unused, and by the end of infancy has disappeared. So most small children must be retaught the prenatal swimming skill they presumably lost at birth, and must "unlearn" their fears of water which may have developed in the interim.

But suppose we could conduct gestation in a tank large enough to enable the unborn baby to swim freely within the radius of his umbilical cord. After birth his swimming ability, heightened by the extra freedom of movement and exercise during gestation, might survive until breath control was acquired. The result might be not only improved final swimming ability, but also accelerated and fear-free learning of other motor skills throughout life.

There is much concerning ordinary movement we do not yet know anything about, including dance, athletics and so on. Then there is the obscure area of special talents for art, mathematics, and science, the very nature of which are unknown, let alone effective methods for detecting and enhancing them early.

Study of newborn babies is enlarging our information daily. Study of *unborn* babies in artificial gestators from the instant the two cells combine to create a unique new human being might add an imponderable dimension.

Might we discover means for regulating and controlling the quality of human relatedness that would help prevent mental illness, or in malevolent hands, help prevent formation of the links of loyalty that love forges?

It is evident that in devising these new techniques that modify the forerunner of the personal relationship and psychic intimacy, we are simultaneously gestating challenges, opportunities, and perils as yet barely imagined.

6 *Genetics*

Background

Three billion years ago an intricate message was written in a tepid tide pool. Carried in endless marathon, it ran off numberless copies of itself. Each was imperfect, marred here or there by vagrant radiation which changed a letter or word. Some of the changes made the message stronger, some weaker, some just different. Most versions disappeared. But a few survived to reach us.

Recently we have begun to learn a little about the message and its spontaneous changes. Soon our new knowledge will be put into action in making some changes of our own in the message of life.

And, oh yes—we hope in a few decades to finish deciphering it.

Analogies must not be pursued too far, especially ones about language, or we find that tedium is the message. But condensed to its essence, the above is our situation as research hands us the tools to commence controlling our further genetic evolution deliberately. That the changes we contemplate could be urgent, sometimes even crucial, does not alter the fact that, like so many of our interventions in nature, they will be undertaken before their implications can be fully understood.

Directing our own evolution deliberately is new. But directing it inadvertently is not new. We began that two million years ago when we learned to make tools.

Another example of how human culture has controlled evolution is the inherited defect of the hemoglobin called sickle-cell trait. The name is based on the tendency of red blood cells containing such hemoglobin to change from a round shape to an abnormal "sickle" shape when deprived of oxygen. The molecular nature of this defect was revealed by the now classical research of Dr. Linus Pauling.

It happens that malaria parasites cannot live as easily in red blood cells containing the abnormal hemoglobin as they do in red blood cells of a normal person. If a child inherits this trait from both parents, although resistant to malaria, he is likely to die of anemia before reproductive age. If he inherits it from neither parent, he is likely to die of malaria before reproductive age. But if he inherits the trait from *one* parent, he will not suffer from anemia but will have greater resistance to malaria, and so will have the best chance of surviving to reproductive age—and passing on the sickle-cell trait.

By chance the sickle-cell trait occurred among people in Saudi Arabia. The people who live in settled agricultural communities around a valley oasis create stagnant pools where malaria-transmitting mosquitoes breed. Sickle-cell trait has become widespread in this population. But in nearby mountain areas, where the conditions for malaria do not exist and are not created by man, sickle-cell trait is of no survival value, and so is not found among the nomadic tribesmen who live there.[1]

Then there is the evolutionary influence of the staggering shift we have brought about in the diseases from which we die.[2] Take infectious diseases as an example. In 1900 a person had one chance in three of dying of an infectious disease, frequently before reproductive maturity. Largely because of acceptance of better public health and medical measures, today the odds are one in fifteen.[3] The result is that many of the weaker among us who would have died of infections before reproducing now live to pass on their inherited susceptibilities of all kinds. These include lethal genetic diseases such as Huntington's chorea, which usually kills *after* reproductive maturity has been achieved, malformations and milder conditions such as predispositions to feeblemindedness, diabetes, allergies, possibly heart disease, cancer, and schizophrenia.

These are examples of man directing his own evolution, but only through indirect influence of his culture. They were side effects. They were not deliberate.

For the first time our culture is beginning to provide the means for man consciously and directly to control his genetic inheritance. As Julian Huxley remarked, man "finds himself in the unexpected position of business manager for the cosmic process of evolution."[4]

It will help us to get a sense of the reality of the dizzy world toward which genetics is leading if we review a few fundamentals. All living tissues are composed of cells. Microscopic in size, each cell is a complete living organism. It consists of a gelatinous material called cytoplasm enclosed in an outer membrane. Floating in this substance is the nucleus, a spherical cluster of controlling elements. Among these are the chromosomes which contain the genes. The cells are the living building blocks of which our tissues are made. Our organs consist of combinations of tissues. And our bodies consist of systems of organs, such as digestive, circulatory, or reproductive systems.

The way life works is transmitted through a kind of language. Its language is the genetic code, which imparts to each new generation the biological characteristics of its parents. The message is carried by genes, which are units of heredity, just as words are units of language. Each gene, usually operating in combination with others, establishes limits for a characteristic of the organism, say eye color or height or quality of temperament. Within these limits the environment accentuates or minimizes the feature. For example, genes establish broadly the shade of a person's skin. But he will be light or dark within those limits depending on how much sun reaches his skin.

Genes have the remarkable capacity to synthesize proteins, including those known as enzymes. And it is enzymes that regulate every activity of living substance, whether it be the building of a tissue out of other protein, or the synthesis of a hormone, vitamin, fat, or of sugar out of water, carbon dioxide, minerals and sunlight. The information in the DNA of genes is carried to the cytoplasm body of the cell by another chemical, abbreviated RNA. This "messenger" RNA, in concert with other types of RNA dissolved in the cytoplasm, permits alignment of amino acids to assemble correctly the proteins which in turn will manufacture the countless ingredients a cell requires.[5]

Spontaneous changes in genes resulting from radiation, chemical influences, or other unknown factors are called mutations. Once the gene is changed, the change is accurately reproduced whenever the gene is copied. And any resulting differences in the organism's enzymes or proteins are preserved along with it. These spontaneous changes have produced the variation in living creatures upon which natural selection has operated to bring about gradual evolution. A useful change is reproduced and survives. A harmful one dies out. But it is excessively rare that a genetic mutation is of any benefit. The vast majority of such changes are harmful to the organism.

Professor Elof Carlson, a geneticist at the State University of New York at Stony Brook, graphically points out that a gene's structure is delicate and may be compared to the mechanism of a watch. If we strike a watch several times on a hard surface, it is extremely unlikely that any resulting change in the machinery would improve its function.[6]

Genes are arranged in a long twisted strand of DNA which is packed into a microscopic envelope called a chromosome. Normally there are forty-six chromosomes in each human cell. Geneticists have been able to map the location of some but not all human genes. The mapping locates a gene in a specific chromosome as well as its approximate position on the DNA strand. Other things being equal, genes that lie in the same chromosome, expecially if near each other, are more likely to be affected by a passing X-ray or other cause of mutation than are genes in different chromosomes.

At each normal human conception twenty-three chromosomes containing about 50,000 genes from the sperm pair up with the same number of chromosomes and genes from the egg. The combined 100,000 make up, in pairs of genes that control the same characteristic, the unique design of the person's heredity.

This process results in transmission to the new individual of a nearly exact copy of the genes that have been received from each parent. Because about one error per 100,000 gene copies occurs, each individual has about one more defective or mutant gene than his parents.

If a paired gene received from one parent is normal, it keeps an abnormal gene "recessive" in that person, which means he does not show the defect. But even when kept recessive by a normal paired gene, *nearly all such gene changes result in a partially lost function,* a hidden impairment of maybe 1 or 2 percent per gene in what might be thought of as general vigor and vitality. If the paired gene received from the other parent is also abnormal, the result may be disabling or lethal. At present in the United States one in twenty babies is born with a discernible genetic defect. And it has been estimated that the number of such people alive worldwide is 150 million.[7]

Each of us carries in our genes about eight such "covered" mutation defects, our "genetic load."[8] Thus, the cumulative impairment is about 12 percent if an average of 1.5 percent impairment per gene is used. With four or five generations born per century, *our genetic load should double in two centuries,* because of the new mutations arising spontaneously each generation. Thus the average hidden impairment will be increased from its present level of approximately 12 percent to about 24 percent.[9] In practice, this means that such individuals will show about double the need for medical care for illness of various kinds. For example, if one or two members of a family of four today will require surgery, all four members of a comparable family then will have to be operated on at some time during their lifetimes.

Since this process has been going on for millions of years, why are we still alive and able to cause ourselves more trouble? Genetic defects might have overpowered us over the millennia if so-called natural selection had not carried off the weaker individuals before they could reproduce. Although we have been whittling away at natural selection for two million years—our brains and hands having devised tools and other means to keep us from being drowned by floods, frozen by blizzards, or starved to death by famines, and so on—there were always the infections to stop those with the heaviest genetic loads from reproducing. Victory over these enemies in the twentieth century has subjected us to a critical extra degree of man-made "unnatural" selection which at last threatens to permit marked increases in our genetic load.

We all want our children to live, so neither infectious disease nor starvation nor all the other features of so-called natural selection are going to be brought back deliberately. Our only choice is whether the new selection conditions shall be allowed to continue chaotic or be brought under some sort of planned control.

What are likely to be the consequences if the genetic load is permitted to go on increasing? We don't know the maximum genetic load compatible with life. But we do know that there is an upper limit. Some people are born with an extra chromosome, and are then burdened through gene overdosage with the equivalent of several hundred defective genes. The best-known condition in which this occurs is Down's disease, or Mongoloid idiocy. Most of its victims have multiple malformations which impair their function so seriously that they must be hospitalized permanently. They are extremely susceptible to disease, rarely surviving to reproductive age. A few years ago in Quebec a measles epidemic in such an institution killed thirty such children.[10]

Doubling or tripling our present genetic load might not produce serious results for our society, although it might mean, according to Carlson, that during his lifespan nearly everyone would need major surgery, dietary supplements, medicines, and artificial devices to stay alive. This would result in a major drain on our human and economic resources,[11] not to mention the fact that life would become more of a treatment than a treat.

When it comes to widespread disabling conditions such as birth defects of the heart or brain, or precocious heart attacks, strokes, and cancer, there is no question that people eventually will insist on preventive measures, even at the expense of some loss of freedom, just as we have in relation to infectious disease.

What becomes of the genetic load today? A part of it is eliminated spontaneously. About 10 percent of couples are infertile due to genetic defect. And about 20 percent of defective conceptions are lost through miscarriage. A few more percent are lost before maturity through conditions in which both parents contribute a defective gene, such as cystic fibrosis, muscular dystrophy, and childhood diabetes. The greater part, however, causes impairments in later life and is thus carried as a genetic burden to the older individual and to his progeny.[12]

But to prevent these tragedies, as well as the others caused by genetic load, deliberate intervention by man will be essential. Two kinds have been proposed.

Eugenics

The more conservative in terms of current values is called "negative eugenics."[13] It involves trying just to prevent defective conceptions. This can be done at present by persuading those who have a high likelihood of transmitting genetic defect not to reproduce. But that is difficult. A few years ago I consulted with a young mother who had watched her first child die slowly at the age of two from a genetic brain disease called amaurotic idiocy. The chance of another child sharing the same fate was estimated by a geneticist at one in four. After much conflict she decided to reject his counsel against having another child. She went all through the pregnancy, and the first year and a half of the new child's life, in dread that he too would begin to become ill when nearing two years. But she was lucky. He did not, and is well at age six, which means he does not have the dreaded defect. However, the chance of his being an unaffected carrier of the trait is 67 percent.[14] You would think her gratitude and relief at having a normal child would make her resolve strongly not to take another chance, especially in view of the continued risk to grandchildren. But now she is debating whether to have a third child.

Defects can be transmitted by both sperm and egg. If the defect is from the father, he can avoid passing it on by not fertilizing his wife himself. Today the couple may still have a child by means of therapeutic insemination performed by a doctor using sperm from a donor. As yet, however, there are no reports of human offspring being produced by the reverse procedure of therapeutic inovulation of a donor egg, although this technique has proved successful in other mammals.[15]

Negative eugenics could now be practiced with a minimum restriction of freedom by uniformly ruling out sperm donors with a history of genetic defect. It is likely that the community will step into the arena of genetic regulation by establishing required procedures at least for therapeutic insemination to protect parents and children produced by this technique. But eventually computerized techniques could give a complete record of each marriage license applicant's genetic code. Then, depending on this genetic load, he could be counseled or coerced to reproduce only through therapeutic means.

The more radical method of genetic intervention is called "positive eugenics."[16] This is a more ambitious and controversial proposal, championed, among others, by the late Herman Muller, who said:

> For any group of people who have a rational attitude toward matters of reproduction, and who also have a genuine sense of their own responsibility to the next and subsequent generations, the means exist right now of achieving a much greater, speedier, and more significant genetic improvement of the population, by the use of selection, than could be effected by the most sophisticated methods of treatment of the genetic material that might be available in the twenty-first century.[17]

He proposes by selective breeding not only to eliminate the defects we encounter now by reducing the present genetic load, but also to increase the number of people with "superior" qualities. One way to accomplish this would be to establish sperm (and eventually egg) banks in which the reproductive cells of individuals with exceptional health, intelligence, or special talent could be preserved. These could then be used by people who want to produce children with better endowment than would result from their own genes. Some have objected that people would not willingly agree to substitute the sex cells and characteristics of others for their own. Muller rejects "the stultifying assumption that people would have to be forced, rather than inspired, to engage in any effective kind of genetic betterment." He points out that

> if the opportunity of germinal choice were opened, a gradually increasing number of seemingly "normal" couples, in addition to a large proportion of those afflicted with seminal inadequacy or obvious genetic defect, would elect to use this means of having at least a part of their family. Moreover, as the saying goes, "nothing succeeds like success," and the obvious successes achieved by this method would within a generation win it still more adherents. It would constitute a major extension of human freedom in a quite new direction.[18]

But naturally, such a program poses a potential threat to our values more fundamentally than does negative eugenics. It opens the door to the frightening abuses of compulsion outlined in Aldous Huxley's *Brave New World*, such as the creation of special classes best fitted to be servants to others who are rulers. With good reason we might fear the consequences of such a system conducted according to the mad assumptions of racists.

And there is the very serious problem of determining which human qualities are desirable, especially for future generations who will live in profoundly different circumstances.

But these sobering considerations will not prevent the introduction of both negative and positive eugenic measures as both knowledge of techniques and general demand for genetic improvement increase. In fact, at least in regard to negative eugenics, the process is already under way.

In 1965, two thousand Danes were compulsorily sterilized under laws which make that the price for mentally retarded individuals and certain criminals and psychotics to live in the general community. It is noteworthy that in a country of four and a half million people, this is four times the number similarly sterilized in the United States during the same interval.[19] I am not recommending that we increase our use of sterilization, but that we increase our awareness of the implications for values of both genetic defect and measures for its control now characteristic of smaller countries. Included in such considerations should be the fact that compulsory sterilization is not effective because it only involves those *showing* the defect. For every defective person detected there are 100 carriers who pass for "normal" and pass on the defective genes.[20]

Here we should note that the ancient dread and loathing of mental illness allows its victims to be compulsorily sterilized in the hope of reducing their undesirable traits, even though the genetic nature of such conditions is often dubious. But there is as yet no comparable enthusiasm for compulsory sterilization of sufferers from severe inherited *physical* illness, although its genetic basis is certain. We tend to respond nowadays at least to disease of the body with sympathy instead of irrational fear and hate.

In England, active discussion is going on over an original, if unconventional, project which might be expected to adapt their society to the future with the usual British attention to tradition. It has been proposed that Parliament enact an "aristogenics" bill which would grant to the aristocracy of blood and mind certain eugenical privileges. According to a recent provocative account:

> The members of the House of Lords would under this scheme be allowed polygamous marriages, while knights would be asked to provide semen to a bank of superior genotypes. Women (married women, for the time being) will presumably be urged to use the bank by drawing freely on the account of their choice.[21]

To the above measures will soon be added means for selecting sex cells more precisely. For example, it may be possible to create a special vaginal diaphragm which would be capable of filtering out those sperm that bear certain damaged chromosomes or even genes. While such negative eugenic use should create little stir, use of a similar diaphragm which would allow parents to screen sperm so as to determine the sex of their child could lead to problems if it resulted in numerical imbalance. For example, although it is difficult to find published corroboration, several independent authorities have told me that just such a situation exists in one small nation. They claim that largely as the result of several wars, the male population of reproductive age is several times smaller than the female, that as a consequence women have been forced into desperate and often fruitless competition for men, while men have become an immature, arrogant, and indolent minority that insists upon being supported by women. Should these circumstances and conclusions be verified, it would seem that marked inequality in numbers of men and women has already played a critical role in inducing drastic social changes in at least one country.

All these techniques that depend upon selection are made potentially more powerful by the new methods for preserving and storing sex cells mentioned earlier. But modern genetics is moving far beyond these obvious primitive measures.

"Neo-Eugenics"

Gradually the chemistry of nucleic acids is being mastered, giving us control over the substance of which genes are made and the code in which their message is written.[22] Within the next few decades, methods will likely be worked out for using computers[23] in conjunction with biochemical data so that the three-dimensional arrangement of the chemical groups making up genes, enzymes, and other proteins will be understood. Then it should be possible to find out how their structure determines their function.

The first benefits are likely to be techniques for synthesizing artificial vitamins, hormones,[24] and antibiotics, and even for creating artificial photosynthesis so that an expanding population may have a food supply independent of living plant cells.

Eventually the chemists and computers will succeed in transplanting genes, or even in creating artificial genes and enzyme systems to repair or replace damaged natural ones in human reproductive cells. Techniques are already available by which the proper substance, once it is available, could be inserted into the sperm or egg to prevent a genetic defect.[25] Eventually, it should be possible by these means to eliminate all genetic defects, including serious conditions such as hemophilia (the excessive tendency to bleed) or albinism (total lack of skin pigment). As these words are written, news reaches me that Dr. Elena Otto Lenghi-Nightingale has succeeded in making the first successful gene conversion in mammals. She has caused the pigment-lacking cells of albino mice to produce melanin pigment by injecting the DNA from a strain of black mice.[26] No sooner is this sentence completed than word comes that Dr. H. Gobind Khorana has created the first artificial gene from simple organic chemicals, Dr. James Danielli of the State University of New York at Buffalo reports the "first artificial synthesis" of a living cell, and twenty scientists are meeting at Ames Research Center to discuss the proposal of the National Aeronautics and Space Administration to seed the planet Mars with artificially created life forms![27]

There is also the possibility of producing beneficial, hereditarily transmissible changes. The appendix might be eliminated, or tissues strengthened to prevent hernias or intervertebral disc disease. Perhaps it would be good to grow extra sets of teeth or more hair, or to arrange different rhythms for heartbeat, sleep-wake, and menstrual cycles. Intelligence, artistic ability, or cooperativeness might be increased.[28]

Or, since the characteristics of every body cell are maintained by its genes throughout its life, eventually it should be possible to change the genetic constitution of a fully grown individual. No longer would the phrase "it's constitutional" be the signal for despair, for our constitutions would be easier to amend than the by-laws of a Kiwanis Club. An appropriate substance might be introduced to cure any genetic defect present, or to modify any normal characteristic, such as those mentioned above.

Or, for another example, someday a color-blind adult might be treated so that he could perceive color normally. Perhaps a society which is supersensitive about color, and which has learned to welcome this improvement as well as the darkening of an albino, will have learned by then to be equally accepting if a normally light person should decide to darken his skin, or vice versa.

As our control over gene structure expands, more remote possibilities are raised. We cannot afford, as some have, to scoff at the likelihood of new techniques of gene tampering being used. For as Rollin D. Hotchkiss of Rockefeller Institute writes:

> The pathway will, like that leading to all man's enterprises and mischief, be built from a combination of altruism, private profit and ignorance. . . . In a country where, during every waking moment, one is being told to acquire and enjoy the products of industrial ingenuity, we can well expect that one will be told he owes it to himself to improve his own genes, as well as his neighbor's.[29]

All cells retain in their genes the code for the individual's entire development, from the fertilized egg through all the differentiation into eye, skin, bone, brain, and so on. So if one could restore to an adult body cell the embryonic nonspecialization possessed by its fertilized egg ancestor, it would then be possible for it to develop into an identical copy of any adult cell, tissue, organ, organ system, or body.

Hermaphroditism

During embryonic life, each baby normally has the rudiments of the sex organs of both sexes. One set ordinarily is suppressed in favor of the other, and appears in the adult as a small vestige of an undeveloped potentiality. It might be possible, perhaps by modifying genes, to cause those cells in an adult to return to their infantile power, resuming and completing the arrested development. Or maybe it would be easier to arrange that both male and female organs develop in the embryo in the first place. But in either case, the result would be a person who produced both sperm and eggs, a hermaphrodite.[30]

Recent studies of the currently unfortunate group known as "intersexes" have shown that various degrees of hermaphroditism occur spontaneously.[31] Although none is ever capable of producing both sperm and egg, there may be such well-developed fragments of both testes and ovaries, and the other external and internal organs, as to make determination of sex doubtful or even completely erroneous. A child thought to be, and raised as, an ordinary girl may unexpectedly develop at puberty the deep voice, facial hair, and body contours of the male, or vice versa. And a while ago a newscast contained an item about a Canadian researcher who claimed that genetic controls now being developed could lead to the possibility of deliberately creating adult human beings who have simultaneously the fully functional sexual organs of both male and female. If so, it appears likely that a relentlessly exploring mind somewhere will press on until the potentiality becomes a reality.

Leaving aside what such an innovation would do to the sense of identity or the structure of the family, it would add a whole new dimension to the significance of narcissism. And imagine the complications, providing such relationships still existed, if the lady you introduced as your wife were equally qualified as another woman's husband. Just consider the poignant quality of rivalry between a sibling who is the product of the ordinary union of sex cells from separate mates and another whose sole hermaphrodite parent obviously showed greater love by her-himself furnishing egg and sperm, as well as womb in which to gestate its very, very own child!

Before leaving this ambiguous subject, we must pause to reflect for a moment on what would happen to the English language if a certain vulgar expression of hostility were to be transformed by human hermaphroditism into invitation to a real possibility.

Regression and Regeneration

The same principle might be applied to man in another way. At one stage of development, human embryos also show, in common with many others, primitive structures which in fish would have gone on to produce functioning gills. In air-breathing animals they are transformed into other organs. But with the proper conditions it might be possible to cause some of the cells to regress and generate the gills they would have become in an ancestral fish. This sort of "genetic engineering" would then result in a subspecies of human who could respire underwater without complex machinery. Although this prospect may not appeal to all of us, we should remember that millions are spent each year on expensive diving equipment in man's accelerating stampede to follow the dolphin back into the ocean. *

Primitive salamanders retain the ability to regenerate limbs, while more advanced frogs ordinarily do not. But under laboratory conditions, a frog's cells can be made to regress to their early versatility and regenerate an entire new limb identical to a lost one. These chemical means for causing cells to regress and for turning gene behavior on and off will make it possible one day for a human amputee to grow a new leg. The same sort of technique will be applied to stopping cancer growth which, whatever else it turns out to be, is also a manifestation of the loss of gene control over the growth process of cells so that they reproduce wildly. Such applications ought to cause little conflict.

Twins and Clones

But beyond this frontier lies yet another. Reactions will be a different matter when a complete copy of a living human brain, or even a whole new individual, is produced.

But according to Dr. Joshua Lederberg, a Nobel Laureate in medicine, such problems will have to be faced. Sexual reproduction results in a mixture of genes from both parents. The assortment of genes contributed by egg and sperm is always unique, even in successive conceptions of the same parents. Therefore, the genetic recipe of each child is unique. The

---

* See Gorney, "Of Divers Things: Preliminary Note on the Dynamics of Scuba Diving."

consequence is that no child is genetically exactly like either parent, or any of its brothers and sisters.

The one exception is the identical twin. Here two babies, or more, result from a single conception, and so are genetically identical to one another but not to their parents. Dr. Lederberg points out that identical twins are

> notoriously sympathetic, easily able to interpret one another's minimal gestures and brief words . . . I will assume that genetic identity eases communication. This . . . might be singularly useful in stressed occupations—say a pair of astronauts, or a deep-sea diver and pump tender, or a surgical team. It would be relatively more important in the discourse between generations . . .[32]

But, as we have just seen, there is no possibility of narrowing the generation gap this way because there is no possibility of genetic identity between parents and sexually reproduced children. And what other kinds are there?

In my garden there is a dwarf peach tree which bears a metal tag which reads "Asexual Reproduction Forbidden." This is not an attempt by horticultural Victorians to restrict a new sector of the private life of the vegetable world. It is a hardheaded commercial acknowledgment of the ownership rights of the developer of a plant under the Plant Patent Act. We are not permitted to steal his formula by exploiting the well-known talent of plants for reproducing themselves from a small twig or cutting. Such reproduction is called asexual because the new individual grows from adult body cells which have resumed their early versatility rather than from the joining of male and female sex cells. An asexually produced individual is called a clone,[33] and is an exact genetic copy of the parent.

Under laboratory conditions plants such as the carrot have been induced to reproduce themselves from adult body cells. Many primitive animals can reproduce both sexually and asexually. But as evolution in animals proceeded, the sexual method gradually became exclusive. The ability to reproduce asexually has been lost by the mammals. Its one spontaneous expression in these higher animals is the tendency for an occasional fertilized ovum to produce two or more individuals. An identical twin is actually a clone, the result of an early division asexually of one conception into separate individuals. By dropping an early mammal embryo into special solutions, the cells could be separated, as can the cells of sea urchin embryos at present. And if implanted into a womb theoretically each could develop into a complete individual. One might obtain five or ten or a hundred identical twins in this way.[34]

And, similarly, some lower vertebrates, such as the frogs, have been induced to reproduce not only a leg but a whole new frog from *adult* body cells.[35] It is only a matter of time and more work until mammals and man can likewise reproduce from adult body cells. And the value of such clones, whether dwarf peach or man, is that they have exactly the same genetic characteristics as their single parent.

As Dr. Lederberg asks, "If a superior individual . . . is identified, why not copy it directly rather than suffer all the risks of recombinational disruption, including those of sex? . . . Leave sexual reproduction for experimental purposes; when a suitable type is ascertained, take care to maintain it by clonal propagation."[36] So the communication gap between generations may indeed be narrowed someday when human beings exercise a newfound option to produce identical children clonally.

The single adult could decide to have a clonal child without bothering at all with the opposite sex. Of course, the offspring could only be of the same sex as the parent, but perhaps this limitation would be compensated by the unique opportunity to relive one's childhood with an identical copy of oneself, unencumbered by the clumsy interference of a spouse with different genes and ideas.

Through cloning we could also find out whether a new Thomas A. Edison would excel the first—or a third. We could produce teams of identical Joe Namath football players, or a chorus of Carusos, or a young, vigorous Franklin Delano Roosevelt every four terms.

The ominous possibilities are more obvious. On the international level, an army of Sergeant Yorks in our behalf, employed, of course, only for our uniformly moral and righteous purposes, could find itself opposed by a superior force of clonally produced, doggedly determined Chinese guerrillas.

Diversity among people seems to be valuable for cultural advance. And genetic variation among individuals and groups provides a fundamental diversity. Not only is a larger pool of inherited possibilities supplied, but also a degree of novelty in human characteristics which gives an esthetic lift to life. Of course, judgments here depend on underlying values. But it will be necessary for all groups to agree on regulating and limiting clonal reproduction of people so as not to have the world taken over by any one fanatic clone clique.

Then there is the question of identity, of "who" such individuals are. Will they be accepted as human, with all the usual rights? Will they be regarded as a child of the parent, or as a separate person? Or might they be treated rather as the *same* person?

The question of identity of clones is likely to become particularly vexing when they begin to be propagated as farms for human spare parts.[37]

Suppose several years from now, after several heart attacks, you need a replacement heart. Just as with the fuel pump of your car, the best substitute is a new unit identical to the worn-out first one. Although a slightly different fuel pump or heart can be made to do the work by adapting its mechanical fittings, there is an additional serious problem for the living person that cannot arise in an automobile. A nonidentical heart has slightly different proteins than the person in whom it is installed, and his other tissues react to the "foreign protein" by manufacturing antibodies that damage or kill the heart in time.[38]

But identical hearts, like identical kidneys, can be found only for those few people who happen to be identical twins. And even for them, since there is only one heart per person, it would be an excessively rare situation where one could use the heart of one twin to keep another alive.

But a clonally produced identical twin could provide completely interchangeable and biologically compatible spare parts for every person. Perhaps we will one day grow a clone for each baby born so that it would be available and at the right stage of development at all times if needed. But what would you do with the clone until it was called upon to make its Aztechian sacrifice? In order for its organs, such as the heart, to achieve their proper development, the clone would have to live a life similar to the original's in terms of exercise, nutrition, and so on. In order to have such experiences it would have to be raised as a person, if not an identical brother. At which point might not any human society worthy of the name encounter the same ethical objection to destroying the clone copy as we would to destroying a natural identical twin?

Perhaps this difficulty can be gotten around by devising means whereby the clone can be permitted to grow up in a kind of unconscious storage so that it never develops human identity in the first place. But from the viewpoint of values is that any better?

Of course, the problem will be less bothersome when we learn how to accelerate the growth of a clone so that one could be generated in a day or two as need arose, or even better, when new cell-culture techniques lead one day to methods for clonally reproducing just the heart or whatever organ is needed.

About the time children begin to receive do-it-yourself cloning kits for their birthdays I suspect there may be strong pressure to stamp each human being "Asexual Reproduction Forbidden."

However, blanket prohibition of human cloning could be as much of a tragedy as its haphazard use. For it offers us a chance not only to have extra copies of superior people while they are alive, but also decades and centuries after their deaths. A few skin or blood cells can be preserved right now by freezing, which could be activated whenever needed in the future. Suppose we had cells from which to grow a new Socrates. Or a new Jesus, Shakespeare, or Lincoln.[39] Of course, they would bring to their times only the genetic potential of the original, *not his acquired knowledge*. But that is quite a lot. The value for positive eugenics of such delayed cloning far outdistances the usefulness of preserving sperm and eggs of the great, since sexual reproduction can produce only nonidentical children, not identical copies.

Of course, in view of the damage to all human heredity that could be caused by radiation from nuclear warfare, both sex cells and general body cells should be safely preserved starting now. We could thus safeguard the outstanding instances of genetic excellence attained by man for the future, when not only the techniques for revitalizing them have been perfected, but also the values have been consciously developed to guide us in using the techniques judiciously. Consider what a loss it is that such cells were not taken from our recent late greats such as Churchill, Shaw, Freud, and Einstein.

In some instances the loss will someday be reparable. When a body is buried it is usually embalmed. In the millions of mummified cells are millions of more or less well-preserved copies of the person's genes. Someday a combination of chemistry and computers will be able to map his genetic structure so that it can be rebuilt in the laboratory, according to Dr. Carlson.[40] The process would parallel the method whereby today we can rebuild Watt's steam engine or Leonardo's flying machine from drawings. Whom we would choose to recreate, and for what purpose, again would be a function of our values. We might be able to learn a great deal from a reconstituted Cro-Magnon man, or King Tut, or Galileo, in the event that any of their adequately preserved cells should turn up. Perhaps we could learn even more from a Ghengis Khan, a Torquemada, or even an Eichmann. Or, from a different viewpoint, from a Helen of Troy, a Cleopatra, or a Marilyn Monroe. But our values of necessity would set limits, especially on the nurture of such resurrected natures.

Chimeras

Whatever conflicts are generated by clones, they are elementary when compared to the tangles that will arise from the hybridization of genes from different species to create what are called "chimeras." Dr. Kimball Atwood, chairman of the Department of Microbiology at the University of

Illinois, suggests that future technical mastery could produce directly combinations of characteristics that would never have resulted from stepwise
evolution. "We could, for example, produce an organism that combines the
happy qualities of animals and plants, such as one with a large brain so
that it can indulge in philosophy and also a photosynthetic area on its back
so that it would not have to eat."[41] Would we be prepared to accord such
a "humanoid" the legal status of a human being?

On a more personal level, perhaps by then we will all have become so
emancipated as not to be disturbed by the new facet of the color problem
such a creature would introduce when he wanted to buy a house in our
neighborhood. But how would you feel about his wanting to marry your
daughter?

Dr. Lederberg points out that relevant experiments are now under way
in cell cultures. "Before long we are bound to hear of tests of the effect of
dosage of the human twenty-first chromosome on the development of the
brain of the mouse or the gorilla." He adds that the extension to man of
experiments already successful in plants and fruit flies requires only a
small advance in cell biology.[42] There has been enthusiastic talk about a
new species of ape that could be trained to do domestic work. But what are
we going to say of a gorilla whose brain has acquired a speech center
through the admixture of human genes? Or, rather, what will we say *to*
such a creature when it applies to enter the university?

The core of our best values depends, if not on Schweitzer's reverence for
all life, at least on respect for the sanctity of human life. But even using
just the mechanistic concept of life which is the basis of all scientific progress in biology, and omitting any consideration of undemonstrable "soul,"
how are we to decide where in the welter of living cells, tissues, organs,
and whole bodies the human being begins and ends? How much more
obscure will be the borderline when these are mixed and blended in various hybridizations with the same elements of animals!

Some researchers now have qualms about subjecting even an animal as
distant from us as the chimpanzee to experimental procedures which they
perform on lower animals without hesitation. We might reasonably be concerned about the effects on researchers of the psychic trauma of dealing
with experimental animals which have become human enough to acquire,
for example, true human speech. Memory of Nazi doctors experimenting
on concentration camp inmates should make us even more concerned
about a researcher who could go about his work on such hybrid creatures
completely unruffled. Medical ethics, sometimes in danger of disdain even
by the law, are crucial safeguards worthy of protection and further development.

Variation, Uniformity, and Values

Leaving aside these immediate consequences, we must all be concerned about the remote implications of such alloys for our species' future.

Value judgments have generally, though not always, deprecated frank deformities. Today, at any rate, we would have little hesitation declaring and doing something about our opposition to clubfoot, color blindness, or Huntington's chorea. But there are signs that along with soap and the hot shower, some growing groups have begun to reject the ordinary esthetic and health standards of our society. Sometimes they value instead the grotesque and even the frankly sick. Some hippies prize a lumpy or fracture-bent nose, or the gaping hole left by a missing front tooth. I once knew a Viennese writer who rhapsodized one day about his taste in emaciated, pale, languid women who coughed delicately: "I like a girl what has a little bit TB!"

By the extension of this trend, malformations could become beauty marks. But perhaps this drift of taste is only fashion, in which case we are protected because, in the realm of fashion especially, the one certainty is change.

But when it comes to normal variations in height, skin pigmentation, sex, and so on, decisions must be made almost entirely on the basis of personal taste. There are but few objective indications of what genetic emphasis is likely to prove of positive survival value. We know that in general people who have at least moderate, if not dark, skin pigmentation are more resistant to sunburn, skin cancer, and Vitamin D overproduction than very fair-skinned people.[43]

As to height, Dr. V. Elving Anderson believes "if we are heading toward an era of expanding population with growing food requirements, then small stature may be an advantage. Meanwhile, there is some evidence that intermediate height is associated with optimum survival." He found that infants neither too large nor too small seemed more likely to survive than those whose sizes were at either extreme.[44]

But in the West generally there has been a gradual increase in height over the past few hundred years. A striking illustration is that the most powerful warriors of all medieval Europe were enclosed in suits of armor that were rarely much more than five feet tall. And a similar enormous increase in height is observable among Americans of Oriental descent in the last one or two generations, as well as in the people of prosperous Oriental countries such as Japan. All these changes may be largely the result of better conditions of life, particularly better nutrition. This is a type of influence Dr. Lederberg would term "euphenics," since it influences the expression of genes during an individual's own life rather than making changes in genes that will be passed on to his progeny. Because euphenics includes all useful influences on development, such as medical care, nutrition, and so on but does not tamper with the gene pool, it can be employed now without jeopardizing future generations.

Two conclusions emerge. First, through our prized better conditions of life we may be producing inadvertently an enlargement of our physical dimensions that could prove detrimental for survival in the future.[45] Second, since we do not know in detail the kind of world in which our descendants will have to live, it seems possible that it might be wise to influence height, color, and so on toward the middle ranges rather than the extremes. But what sort of influence could be used? Certainly we must begin with education, in the conviction that understanding leads to persuasion. In this phase of human social evolution it is apparent that any effort to guide inheritance of stature, or especially of skin color, by force of law might provoke possibly catastrophic social upheavals.

Besides, many people find that an assortment of tall and small stature, as well as very fair and very dark complexion, is much more interesting than groups of people who are average. I recall seeing a generally stoic friend shed a shocked tear over a news account about a girl who had her femurs shortened surgically. The operations brought her height down to a socially more acceptable six feet. "How could she do that! What could be more beautiful than a girl six feet, four inches tall?" For him most definitely the median is not the message.

It may be important for us to try to design the future so that wide variations in all normal characteristics need not reduce anyone's chances of surviving.

Some extra urgency here arises from the phenomenon of the intermingling now in progress of human groups formerly widely separated. We know, for example, that as a consequence of their isolation from one another, and many generations of inbreeding, Chinese and Pygmy individuals are in general much more similar to their own group than to any other. But today the isolation is crumbling. And since all human beings belong to the same species and can interbreed freely, it is only a matter of time until racial differences between such subgroups become blurred, if not erased. Without our intent, humanity is becoming homogenized.

So enormous are the genetic streams thus being mingled that some geneticists conclude the process dooms any eugenic program to futility. The jet plane, they say, will make inapplicable to man the selective breeding techniques that have proved so effective in isolated groups of domestic animals.

However, in the process, blendings of characteristics occur which not only show extraordinary beauty but have the familiar increase in vitality and adaptability we have learned to expect of hybrids. But diversity, the advantages of which we mentioned earlier, would be undermined in the long run. Of course, the jeopardy to human society of such loss of diversity would be less serious than that brought about by cloning. At least, the gene pool would not be altered irrevocably and no identical dynasties created.

Population control is under consideration everywhere, but it is presently being exercised much more effectively where talk is backed up by money, education, and values. Reproductive rates differ widely, so there is bound to be an evolutionary effect through the differing contributions to the worldwide genetic melting pot. For example, if unchecked, the population of South America may be expected to double itself every thirty years. On the other hand, the North American population is growing at only one-third that rate. Tunisia's annual population increase is approximately 3.3 percent, while Sweden's is 0.3 percent. Costa Rica's rate is 4.2 percent, while Japan's is 0.9 percent.[46] Who is to say which race or nationality is best suited to contribute a disproportionate share to the world's culture in terms of intellect, morality, and artistry, let alone to the gene pool out of which those who must adapt to the unforeseeable future will be assembled?

Even on the local level, how can the decisions best be made?

Suppose a mother wants her sons to be tall and dark and her daughters to be practically albino. Is this a choice we can safely leave to her to make, relying on differences of taste to preserve genetic diversity? Or is it a choice that any presently organized system of values could assist her to make?

Should a parent have the right to order a likely college football player, or a likely scientific intellectual at will? Or would such specifications constitute unwarranted interference with the right of the individual to turn out as chromosome and luck would have it?

When it comes to choices between talents, the problem becomes impossibly complex. Aside from social factors, there are the difficulties of biological technique. Remember that because of their proximity within the chromosome, efforts to alter one gene may unintentionally affect others. Assuming some mutual incompatibility should be found, how can one decide whether to accentuate abstract thinking or artistic talent?

Present trends suggest that we will leave mostly to the individual those decisions that have to do with which sperm or egg to select. But won't our attitude be different when it comes to engineering changes in genes? If we decide here to limit individual freedom, should laws be enacted, or a do-nothing policy followed until inevitable crises have led to precedents in the courts?

I cannot leave this discussion without drawing into it a few more thoughts about the possibly dismal results in terms of values of efforts to improve man genetically. First, there are the losses that we might sustain as side effects of eliminating the conditions it seems so evident we should eliminate.

At a state hospital it was found that deprived psychotic children could benefit markedly from close individual attention many hours a day. But an ordinary adult may find such attention too wearing to supply. Mentally retarded women, however, proved ideally suited both to provide and to benefit from being mother-substitutes. With the disappearance of the mentally retarded go the particularly valuable devotion and simplicity characteristic of so many.[47] Certainly we would not want people in the future to suffer the disability, and scorn of self, inflicted by dwarfism. But would we be as willing, should that somehow prove to be the price, to get rid forever of a sort of poetic wit and mirth which in past centuries often made dwarfs the most sought after of court jesters? Surely we would spare unborn generations the torture of schizophrenia. But, should there prove to be some genetic connection, can they afford the loss of the special perceptive empathy some schizophrenics possess, not to mention the virtuosity of such probably schizophrenics as Newton, Nietzsche, Strindberg, or Van Gogh? In the words of Dr. John W. Crenshaw, Jr., "Many of the great contributions to human welfare in science, art and elsewhere have come from men and women with genetic fitness of zero."[48]

What if someday people want these conditions back, or at least their desirable attributes? Well, since they will have learned to manage heredity so neatly, genes for the lost variations can be reintroduced.

But suppose during the intervening period, as a result of genetic and environmental management, we lose the capacity either to *remember or to appreciate* their special worth? People living then may not any longer be able to miss the vanished treasure which from our vantage point in time we trust they will still need.

Suppose Hitler had won the war. We would now be well into a world in which everyone accepted his preposterous racial ideas as fact. In one or two generations of genetic and environmental manipulation it might have been made true, or at least universally believed, that all Negroes are stupid savages and all Jews avaricious cowards. Then it would no longer be possible for anyone living to be certain that his pronouncements were not factual when first fulminated.

So we decide to make genetic changes at our peril. For while reversal of a genetic change may be a possibility, men cannot realize a possibility for which they have lost the capacity to wish.

Consider the problem of the differences between the sexes and the changing meanings of male-female and masculine-feminine. Much discussion is devoted to proving that our culture is male oriented and that in order to get along in it women are being seduced or forced to become more like men. An equal avalanche of opinion holds that, on the contrary, it is men who are being feminized. In any event, it does seem that the characteristics and customs that traditionally distinguish the sexes are losing ground. Indistinguishable grooming and clothing, asthenic figures, casual sexual indulgence, and so on increasingly characterize not only the reality of young people but also the ideal they strive for.

This change must represent the underlying fact that division of labor and role between the sexes is of decreasing survival value. And the emancipation of women from the burdens of gestation, discussed in Chapter 5, may cut the last biological link to the value of physical differences between the sexes. It could turn out that the baby bottle which technologically displaced the female breast will be outdone by its later cousin which will do the same for the womb. And without the need for launching a baby, the wider and deeper female pelvis becomes like the appendix, functionally vestigial. Suppose by genetically engineering out of males their angular muscularity and broader shoulders, and out of females their softer curves and broader hips, people decide to speed up the trend toward unisex. Along with these distinctions, and the identifying if inconsistent personality demands on men and women, could go much of the charm of human life.

From there it may be but one disconsolate step to accepting hermaphroditism. Of the people I know, including the small minority who want to become the *opposite* sex, hardly any would regard this advance as progress. Yet which of us is doing anything to put a new functional basis under the biological distinction between the sexes? As Dr. Lederberg puts it, "To shout 'Vive la différence' and then ignore it is hypocrisy."

There are several influential groups in our culture, some artists, some hippies, and some others, who would have us ignore not only these differences and the words designating them, but the accepted meanings of words in general. They claim that words are often misused deliberately as disguises of meaning and so interfere with, rather than expedite, transmission of a message. They say with justice that "peacemaker" is used to camouflage one who actually is a "warrior." Therefore we are urged by some to discard word definitions altogether.

But language doesn't just go away. Allowing it to get rusty or scrambled results not in unimpeded communication in some other form, but in dangerously ambiguous or erroneous messages. No, the remedy for misuse of words is not to get rid of them, but to get rid of their misuse, for words are the distinguishing characteristics of man's conceptualizing mind. The looming menace of our nuclear-ready rockets will not be lessened by diluting the precision of the meaning of words that bring them orders. Nor will the danger of reducing man to monster be diminished by reducing the precision of the meaning of genes.

So the question is, have we really gotten the message? If words or genes are forced to sudden quixotic changes in their meanings, then it may come to pass that despite the new information we can marshall, McLuhan and we will share only the same risky medium grasp of the message.

7 Life and Death

Background

There was a time when fundamental things in human existence were simple and unvarying. Generations followed one another in predictable, orderly sequence. Life and death were clearly different—almost never was there any mistake about which was which.[1] Both seemed as inevitable as taxes.

But now we linger hesitantly on the threshold of a new time in which even such formerly inflexible guidelines are becoming fuzzy. Whatever tatters of them are left us by the new genetics are likely to be further unraveled by new accomplishments in organ transplantation, creation of artificial organs, life suspension, and retardation of aging. It may become possible for a person to sample a decade in eight or nine different centuries. Can you imagine getting a stern lecture, or even friendly advice, at the age of fifty from your grandfather who is only twenty-five?

The only certainty left us is taxes.

Although science has yet to inform us precisely what life is, man for a long time has been compelled by his culture to decide when it begins and ends. Provision for the spirit and body of the new living child, as well as for those of the person after death, depends on these judgments. Until recently they were not too complicated.

Aristotle believed life begins at the time of "quickening," the first movement of the baby in the womb—and this is the Jewish position today. Catholic doctrine maintains that life begins at conception. One Protestant view concurs. Another holds that while life begins at conception, the person begins only at birth.[2] One could also say that life is present in the sperm and egg and the cells that give rise to them, so that while there may be a moment when a life ends, no life has begun in over three billion years.

When is a person dead? Traditionally the moment of death has been determined by the moment when spontaneous heartbeat and breathing cease. These age-old criteria have become known as the signs of "clinical" death. Throughout history there have been reports of rare individuals who returned to life after such clinical death. And in recent decades we have learned emergency measures to restore breathing and heartbeat that can bring back to life many people who in the past would have been dead permanently.

"Biological death" has been defined as the state of damage and disorganization from which, even with modern medical techniques, the whole person cannot be revived. Various organs die at different rates once heartbeat and breathing have ceased. The brain, highly vulnerable to lack of oxygen, becomes irreversibly damaged after only three to six minutes without freshly oxygenated blood, whereas other organs may survive many hours or even days depending on the conditions of the body, such as temperature and presence or absence of bacteria.

"Cellular death" is an irreversible degeneration or disorganization of the individual cell, and may precede or be delayed long after the death of the rest of the body. For example, throughout life dead skin cells over the entire body surface are constantly shed and replaced from below. On the other hand, cells from a dead person can be kept alive and growing indefinitely in a cell culture. And it is from a preserved sex cell or general body cell that, as we found earlier, a child or identical twin of a person dead for years or centuries might someday be produced.

So it is plain that advances in the various fields of biology are blurring boundaries that used to distinguish clearly between the living and the dead, not to mention those demarcating one person from another. The very meanings of the terms life and death are becoming doubtful. But any redefinitions are portentous for human values, and so should be undertaken only after systematic study and with the most thoughtful caution.

We are all acquainted with general medical progress in prolonging lives of sick individuals, and with resultant psychological, social, moral, legal, and theological conflicts. But these will be bathed in a nineteenth-century nostalgic glow of simplicity as compared with the tangles now being ushered in by an era of rebuilt people, repaired with man-made organs, or natural ones transplanted from other people or even from animals.

While organs transplanted from one person to another "make man ever more literally part of his fellow man,"[3] implanted synthetic organs are erasing the border between man and machine. We now may fit man out with ceramic jawbones, metal thigh bones, silicone rubber lungs and heart valves, dacron arteries, electronic blood pressure regulators and bladder stimulators, and mechanical heart booster pumps. We are also entering a time in which machines independently will perform ever more human mental functions.[4] Perhaps it will help our relations with a clichéic computer of the future to remind it that metal and plastic are also thicker than water.

Death Postponed: Substitute Organs

The best illustration today of the problems raised by controls of life and death is the tragic area of fatal kidney disease, to which every year thousands of people fall victim. It is now possible through periodic use of an artificial kidney machine to keep alive for as long as five years a patient whose own kidney function has been destroyed by disease.[5] However, the machine is cumbersome and the procedure inconvenient. For the first time in history the staggering cost of a new and accepted medical therapy has prevented its widespread use.[6] As a result it has been possible to apply this technique to only a small number of those dying of kidney failure. The choice of who should be the recipient of the limited but lifesaving treatment has fallen on the doctors working in the field.[7] The burden is not deciding who should be helped to live, but rather who should be left to die.

This dilemma has brought into renewed focus the criteria for such decisions. Most people, including doctors, seem agreed that a prolonged life must be meaningful and useful to be worthwhile. But according to which standards and by whom is the assessment to be made? Dr. Gotthard Booth, a psychiatrist, suggested that if the patient is rational his own wishes should be the major criteria.[8] But if he is not rational, or expresses no preference, can we leave the decision to the family? Individual relatives are sure to disagree. What about consulting a colleague? Doctors do not always agree either. The possibility of disagreement with patient, family, and colleagues forces the doctor to be prepared to make and stand by his decision alone on real life situations that don't follow rules.

For example, a previously happy and successful young woman of twenty-one, faced with a life of discomfort and dependency on medical care, told me soberly she would prefer death, and so would refuse another artificial-kidney treatment, although her family and doctor were agreed that her future life seemed meaningful and useful. If he did not insist she continue treatment, could a doctor be found guilty of aiding and abetting a suicide? Another kidney patient, a single man of fifty-seven whom doctors in another city had decided not to treat because of insufficient facilities, had tried to obtain assurances of regular treatment in three medical centers, so urgent was his craving to live.

Commenting on the choices that sometimes must be made between two patients needing the same machine, Rev. Granger E. Westberg has said, "Everyone is willing to turn the machine on, but nobody is willing to turn the machine off." He feels the doctor should have help in making these extraordinary life-and-death decisions.[9] But specific suggestions as to how rules for guidance might be formulated are not frequent for a very good reason. When spelled out they tend to emit a cold totalitarian aura instead of the humane one that comes from an individual doctor's lonely struggle to chart his conscience amid the reefs of the patient's reality.

One of the least ominous suggestions is that of Dr. Leo Shatin, professor of psychiatry at New Jersey College of Medicine. He believes that doctors should be relieved of "such social value decisions that are forced upon them by the unwillingness of society to accept its own responsibilities." He proposes that the choice of patients be determined by the value that society places upon a given person, and suggests that a scale of such values might be worked out through a public-opinion survey.[10] But how many of us are that confident of the public's judgment that we would entrust to it decisions as to our worth relative to that of others, let alone the value to us individually of further life or death?

One might wonder whether these situations are so different from those faced by doctors every day in making life-and-death decisions. They are. In the usual situation the doctor must decide whether to subject a sick patient to a risky treatment in order to benefit him or even save his life. But in the artificial-kidney situation he is sometimes called upon instead to *withhold* from a sick patient a relatively safe treatment that might restore him to reasonable health for several days or weeks. That he may take this course to benefit another patient who can make better use of the extra life only lightens and does not lift the burden. And inevitably there will be instances where this rationalization is denied the doctor, because sometimes he must decide to withhold treatment even when facilities for treatment are adequate for all who need them.

Dr. Paul S. Rhoads has remarked that when there is no chance of the patient being able to lead a full and useful life the doctor must find the strength to say, "No, I'm not going to use the artificial kidney," or other extraordinary procedures to prolong his life. "The obligation of the physician is to do the best he can for the patient. And sometimes the best thing he can do is let the patient die."[11]

A colleague of mine struggled with himself to make just such a tragic decision. His patient was a thirty-nine-year-old woman whose kidneys had been removed surgically because of cancer. Artificial kidney treatments and X-ray therapy had proved successful over an eight-month period. There was talk of giving her a transplanted kidney.

Then the cancer recurred. One eye began to bulge. A rapidly growing lump appeared in her tongue, half of which had to be removed, severely impairing her ability to speak and swallow. The growth invaded the other side of the tongue, filling her mouth and making breathing difficult. Radiation and various medications were ineffective; it was plain she could not live much longer. Admittedly it is often difficult to decide in which situation there is or is not a possibility for the patient to recover. But about this patient there could have been no question.

The family pleaded with the doctor to continue her artificial kidney treatments, and to perform operations on her neck which would allow her to breathe and be fed by stomach tube. The patient expressed no preference whether to give up or go on trying to live. The doctor felt that, since early death was inevitable, to subject the patient to so many uncomfortable procedures and extra days of suffering would go against his ethical obligation to the patient. Even were a cure for cancer to have been found in the next few days, it could not have restored to meaningful and useful life a woman without kidneys. And even were a kidney transplant to have succeeded in so weak a patient, the mutilation of her tongue and throat would have left her unable to speak or swallow. Fortunately, the grieving family finally agreed and the patient died comfortably in the welcome coma of kidney failure.

Dr. Willard Goodwin has pointed out in a lecture on this subject at UCLA that organ transplantation raises still another problem, and a series of unanswered questions. Under what circumstances is it right to make a well person sick to save another from death? How can you be sure a donor is really willing, and not just responding to guilt? It can be expected, as with all major surgical procedures, in time a definite mortality rate will emerge. And even after recovery there will be measurably increased risk to the donor's life through being reduced, for example, to only one kidney. Will the insurance company pay for such risky care? What is the age at which a child should be allowed to decide whether or not to be a donor or recipient? Under what circumstances may the organs of animals be implanted in humans? Under what circumstances may the organs of a dead body be transplanted to a living person?

Where the physician has a direct responsibility to two persons instead of one, the ethical problems are not doubled but multiplied many times. For the donor, the hazards of anesthesia and surgery, the increased risk of living, for example, with one kidney, and the chance that he may be left with a sense of mutilation must be balanced against the real advantages to the recipient, the avoidance of guilt in the case of close relatives, and the satisfaction of spirit in saving a life.

The emotional consequences of organ transplantation from living donors may be as complex as the medical ones. Dr. John P. Kemph in a study through the University of Michigan Medical School found that the new experience of giving and receiving body organs is "rich in human reaction."[12]

Recipients "were ambivalent toward the donors both before and after surgery." They rationalized their indebtedness, saying that in the reverse situation they would have done the same.

Donors before surgery felt "virtuous and morally rewarded," a reaction one might expect to provoke hostility in many a recipient who unconsciously regards his illness as punishment for misdeeds. He can't help but resent that his simple wish to live in this life is made by the donor into an occasion for piling up extra celestial trading stamps with which to outdo him in the next.

Though virtue is supposed to be its own reward, it may be insufficient to compensate for the discomfort and anxiety of sacrificing an organ by surgery. Dr. Kemph reports that after surgery there was often among donors "considerable unconscious resentment toward the recipient and toward hospital personnel who requested or encouraged the transplant." Some donors tended to resent that they received minimal attention as compared with the recipient. As might be expected from the psychodynamics of loss, some developed postsurgical depression.

After operation, some recipients were considerably preoccupied with distortion of "body image," the mental picture each individual has of his own body's size, shape, and components, by the addition of someone else's organ. Others had irrational notions as to organ function, showing confusion and concern, for example, as to future sexual powers.

Autotransplants, such as skin or bone removed from one part to repair another part of the same person's body, are usually readily accepted both by his tissues and his psyche. But homotransplants, which remove tissue from one person and graft it onto another, are a different matter. Even when donor and recipient are identical twins, and when therefore the graft can survive permanently, there is something emotionally unsettling about the idea of one person living the rest of his life using the organ of another. When nonidentical brother and sister or parent and child are involved, the sense of foreignness increases, but not as much as the actual genetic foreignness which will cause destruction of the transplant eventually through formation of antibodies in the blood, despite our present best efforts. Homotransplants between completely unrelated individuals evoke still more intense feelings of strangeness, matched by more rapid rejection of the foreign tissue. And heterotransplants, exchanges between members of different species, ordinarily abruptly withdrawn from emotionally, are rejected by the body most rapidly of all.

If transplanting an internal organ such as the kidney, of which one is never aware, distorts the body image, transplantation of more noticeable organs may prove even more distressing to fragile egos.

How does a vulnerable former cardiac cripple react unconsciously to feeling within him the pulse of a dead man? How will a vulnerable former amputee respond to the stranger's hand that lifts his fork when he is hungry and caresses his wife when he is affectionate?

But as their usefulness enlarges, the psyches of most patients can be expected to accommodate themselves eventually to the organs of other people and even of animals. After all, when it comes to preserving our lives, we all tend to react like Maurice Chevalier who, when asked how he felt about being seventy-one, is said to have replied, "Well, considering the alternatives—"

We have so far been protected to a degree from some problems connected with organ transplantation by the fact that the kidney is a paired organ. On this account it is possible in many cases to obtain living donors from whom one kidney may be transplanted after careful preparation in controlled circumstances.

With other organs, such as the heart we do not have this advantage, and so at present donation of a heart is contingent upon loss of the donor's life. Although the operation itself has proved successful in many cases now, human transplantation of the heart is still in early experimental stages. Complications have frustrated hopes for otherwise likely postoperative good health and normal longevity. Dr. James Hardy recently extended the life of a terminal cardiac victim briefly by transplanting a chimpanzee heart into the patient's chest. Although the operation was surgically successful and the heart functioned, it proved too small for the job.[13] Of course, the patient would have succumbed in time anyway since the body builds up antibodies that sooner or later destroy any foreign tissue, even that coming from a member of the same species. This is the main reason transplanted kidneys fail eventually. But their life has been extended from less than one to more than five years in a few favorable cases by powerful medications which suppress antibody formation.[14] Better methods for preventing this rejection of new organs are in development which have improved the prospects for heart transplants as well.

Although survival so far has been measured only in weeks and months, patients have been given a transplanted human liver. Perhaps eventually it will become possible to transplant the pancreas to cure diabetes, the lungs to eliminate emphysema, or the skin to repair the damage of burns.[15]

Of course someday when they are available, the ideal technique might be to use clonally produced, genetically identical organs, as they will not provoke any rejection reaction in the first place.[16] There is another obvious advantage to clonally produced organs. A well-planned procedure to transplant the heart from one person to another would leave the first one dead unless a substitute were also available for him. Until this technique becomes available, the donor heart must, at least for some time, come from someone who has died. There is no shortage of people who die. But the only ones whose hearts are likely to be serviceable are those who die un-expectedly in accidents. And since in as little time as twenty to thirty minutes without circulation a heart may be damaged irreversibly, it is not very likely that many victims of sudden death will reach specialized facilities in time for heart deterioration to be prevented by establishment of artificial circulation. Then, when a rare usable heart does arrive at a hospital, there may not be a suitable patient prepared to receive it.

Accordingly, methods are now being sought to "bank" organs for later transplantation, as for example by a team of researchers at McGill University in Canada which employs freezing with helium.[17] Eventually a successful technique will be developed. But it will only ameliorate a bit and not eliminate either the shortage or the grisly practice of patients waiting in hospitals hoping for the good luck to be present when a strong-hearted stranger is brought in promptly after losing his life.

These circumstances seem likely to breed a new profession devoted to organ prospecting. Heart hunters would resemble the ambulance chasers of old, except that, instead of offering to sue, they would be prepared to make cold cash payoffs to relatives who promptly sign consent forms for the roadside surgery that would whisk the heart of a departed loved one into a warm hyperoxygenated transfer bath, and thence into the chest of an unknown needy neighbor.

Someday many of us may carry a card that gives permission for such use of all our organs, with or without fee to our families, similar to that which some now carry concerning only their corneas.

As demand increases for hearts and other organs, it will become necessary to reorient the general attitude toward the dead body so that it can come to be regarded not with the reverence once due the person but with the respect appropriate to a kit of replacement parts. Perhaps laws will come making bodies available automatically unless the individual objects before his death. Such a change not only would head off development of black marketeering, but in time would make available fresh supplies to fill the need for all sorts of organs, including the transplantation of a whole upper or lower extremity to replace one destroyed.[18]

We are forced to face conflicts in relation to heart replacement even before the rejection problem has been resolved. Dr. Michael DeBakey of Baylor University College of Medicine and Dr. Adrian Kantrowitz of Maimonides Hospital in Brooklyn have each developed and employed in human patients a mechanical booster pump for aiding a failing heart.[19] It is intended only as a temporary supplemental aid to circulation and is not a complete heart replacement. But other devices to replace the heart completely are now in development, employing compressed air, electricity, or chemical reactions as energy sources. Dr. Willem Kolff has installed a heart device powered by compressed air in the chest of a calf which lived 31 hours, and died only from infection unrelated to the functioning of the heart.[20] The other main difficulty with the artificial heart seems to be clotting.[21] These obstacles may soon be surmounted, making use of such a device feasible in humans.

Shortly before Dr. DeBakey implanted the first artificial booster pump in a patient's chest, he observed that the artificial heart "will entail considerations which will impinge upon the mind and conscience not only of physicians but also of philosophers, theologians, sociologists, jurists and many others."[22] He and his colleagues drew attention to these immediately pressing questions: "Should this lifesaving device be made available to every patient, even the hopeless victim of stroke, cancer or senility? Or should an unbending and restrictive criterion for use be outlined? When and how does one determine death due to other causes? And who decides when to terminate the power flow in such cases?"[23] These questions were only underscored by the death after sixty-five hours of the first patient into whom Dr. Cooley implanted the first total mechanical heart replacement.[24]

To these questions could be added: Upon what basis is a choice made to give one available new heart to a thirty-six-year-old father of four, or a brilliant young woman cancer researcher? Clearly Rev. Westberg's and Dr. DeBakey's thoughts suggest that the workers in this field, as in that of organ transplantation, do not want to be and must not be abandoned to improvise individual answers to questions concerning which the whole community has a responsibility. But as mentioned earlier, up to now more talent has been shown in propounding the questions than in proposing answers.

We have been considering what organ transplants or mechanical substitutes may mean to the individual in extending, enriching, or perhaps imperiling his life. This subject is indivisible from what the new techniques may mean to the individual in extending, impoverishing, or imperiling his death.

Recently at a convocation on medicine and theology at the Mayo Clinic, Rev. Kenneth A. Carlson indicated that a person has the right to die with dignity "and not have the process of death extended agonizingly by artificial means."[25] He told of a woman who had been kept going by a heart and lung apparatus for five years at enormous cost to the family. When the procedure was finally interrupted, autopsy disclosed that "the brain had been destroyed at the onset of the illness." The "person" had died long before, although her body had been kept alive all this time as a sort of organ culture. In this case, since she was unconscious, it would appear that the agony of the artificial extension of her life was not hers but the family's.

But the same techniques, instead of causing agony to anyone, may immeasurably enrich a person's death if he plans to make his organs available to another human being who with their help can go on living.

A doctor of forty-one died several years ago of a slow-growing brain tumor after a long illness. Suppose he had been able to make preparations before his death to donate his healthy heart to the twenty-seven-year-old physicist who lay dying of rheumatic heart disease in a room down the hall. Would not the regret at losing his life have been somewhat tempered by being able to save another's?

In this instance no speculation is required, for he and his wife spoke to me several times of their wish that this could be accomplished. They had read of preliminary research on heart transplantation, but had been unable to find any encouragement from the surgeons, who pointed out that at that time the procedure had never had a full success even in animals. Besides, no one in their area had any experience with it whatever.

The patient resolved to survive as long as possible in hopes that further advances might come soon. He spoke of his idea with the younger man's doctor on the possibility that both patients might be moved elsewhere for the operation. And he wrote to several investigators to ascertain the possibilities before raising the hopes of the other patient. Suddenly his condition became worse and he died.

But there must be many such possibilities. Someday there will be a first bequest of his heart by a living man to a grateful inheritor, and someday a first success in restoring a normal lifespan to a cardiac cripple.

Certainly many people today are impelled by similar feelings, and the chances for mankind's survival would be multiplied many times if they could be shared by the majority.

What would the procedure be? It is already recognized by the Medical Society of New York State that "every human being of adult years and sound mind has a right to determine what shall be done with his own body."[26] The ticklish question is "when does a person become a body?" If we wait for the time-honored criteria of clinical death, cessation of breathing and heartbeat, it is very likely that the heart we are after will be so injured if and when resuscitated that it will be of no use to the recipient. On the other hand, if we do not wait, would removal of the heart from a doomed but "living" patient constitute murder under present laws?

But we no longer believe that the human mind or individuality resides in the heart. Since we now know that the brain is the organ of personality and identity, it has been recommended that we gauge the end of life medically by the cessation of its electrical activity, and that the law be brought into conformity with this newer understanding and practice.[27]

The best indication to date of brain death after loss of consciousness is the gradual cessation of its electrical activity as measured by electroencephalograph (EEG). Although her body continued to live, the woman described by Rev. Carlson had been dead in this sense for years.

Breathing depends on centers in the lower part of the brain, and will stop when that part dies. To maintain the heart in good condition, as the brain dies it will be necessary to use a machine to produce artificial breathing. With such equipment one might be able to wait hours or even days for the rest of the brain to die without greatly jeopardizing the heart. But sometimes months or years will pass before brain death is complete. Leaving aside the enormous economic waste of the procedure, and the lost opportunities to save lives with needed organs, the longer the body is kept in this inactive and dying state the less chance there is that the depleted heart and other organs will survive transplantation and function well.

To avoid these obstacles it seems probable that, as an extension of the recognized right of the individual to die with dignity and to dispose of his body, eventually a procedure will be devised whereby a person will be able to *determine himself* in advance the time of his legal death. Perhaps he would be able to give authorization to his doctors to proceed with transplantation of his organs when his EEG (and other measures as developed) indicates brain damage that is both incompatible with life and irreversible. Had his doctors been armed with such a legal protection as well as a technique for heart transplantation, the physician's death from brain tumor would have been given a meaning and use more in keeping with that of his life, and the young physicist's wife and children might still have had their husband and father.

Life Postponed: Suspended Animation

There already are reports of whole human bodies being preserved by freezing after death.[28] But even aside from the organ damage brought about by the current legal requirement that they die thoroughly beforehand, the methods of freezing now known cause so much cell damage that success in reviving a person so frozen is unlikely.

Formerly it was believed that formation of ice crystals within tissues of itself kills them by mechanical injury. Now it is known that most of the damage from freezing has another cause. When water is removed from solution as ice, the crystals are purified of the various salts and other constituents dissolved in it. In a cell that freezes, it is the injury brought about by the increase in concentration of its salts that seems to prevent full recovery when the tissue is thawed. A "salt buffer" such as glycerol can somewhat protect the cells from these deleterious effects.[29]

This difficulty can be avoided if ice formation can be prevented. If temperature can be lowered fast enough, tissues can enter a noncrystalline solidified state through a process known as "vitrification" in which their water does not separate out as ice. Apparently small vinegar eels can be vitrified by being placed directly into liquid air at 197 degrees below zero centigrade. They will revive without damage if then warmed quickly. These worms are about the thickness of a hair, and so the heat evolved when they enter the solid state can be conducted away instantly by the surrounding liquid air. But apparently larger animals cannot be cooled through their full thickness rapidly enough to ensure vitrification instead of ice crystallization of their body fluids.[30]

In 1886 Turner described how Alaskan blackfish revived after being chopped out of the ice in which they had been stored for weeks. They were eaten and then vomited by dogs. Apparently they came back to life in the warmth of the stomach.[31]

But as long ago as 1766 John Hunter was disappointed by the failure of solidly frozen carp to revive when warmed.[32] Since his time an explanation for these conflicting stories has emerged. Reports of frogs and fish reviving after freezing have been partially confirmed, but always it appears that although part of the fluid in the outer tissues was converted to ice, the deeper organs were not frozen completely. It seems that complete freezing of all the body water kills even cold-blooded animals. For example, goldfish, exposed to liquid air for 15 seconds or less were partially frozen and could be revived. But those exposed for more than 15 seconds never survived.[33]

Because mammals are larger and much warmer to start with, it is more difficult to achieve the needed rapid lowering and raising of temperature. But in recent years it has been shown that various small mammals, such as golden hamsters and newborn ground squirrels, also can be partly frozen and revived. When frozen their breathing and heartbeat ceased completely. Their bodies became rigid and appeared to be solid all the way through, but upon examination it was found that the heart and other deep internal organs were not frozen. Surprisingly, however, considerable amounts of ice had formed in the hamster brain and were no obstacle to revival with complete restoration of normal behavior. Most of the hamsters who were subjected to freezing for 50 to 60 minutes, and whose temperatures did not fall below −1 degree centigrade, recovered fully and lived out normal lives. Under these conditions about half their body water had solidified. Freezing for longer periods of time, or at lower temperatures, markedly reduced revival and survival rates.[34]

If ever it became possible to instantly vitrify instead of freeze a large animal, as can be done with vinegar eels, it would seem that all the problems connected with ice formation could be sidestepped.

But even should this never be achieved, experiments with small mammals suggest that eventually it may become possible to suspend the life of large mammals by freezing. Success would require a technique to distribute an effective protectant throughout its body and then remove it without injury. Also required would be a means to quickly freeze and thaw a body perhaps three hundred times heavier than that of a hamster. When such methods are available it might be possible to bring back to life bodies stored at temperatures as low as −70 degrees centigrade.[35] At that point, revival of man after long periods of preservation could become a reality.

In Swiss newspapers of 1826 there appeared a story of a man whose frozen body was found under a heap of ice. After revival he claimed to be Roger Dodsworth, son of the famous antiquarian of the same name who died in 1654, and said he had been buried by an avalanche in 1660.[36] The fascinating implications of this improbable story are tame compared to those which could be brought about by the new avalanche of cryonic research.

Obviously there is little point in waiting for a young woman to die of exhaustion from a spreading cancer if you hope to freeze and revive her after means of curing cancer have been developed which will allow her to live out her full lifespan. The best chance of success would come from preserving her while she is still in good general health. But would a patient be committing suicide by deliberately entering a frozen state while well? Or would a doctor be committing murder by processing her under these conditions? There would be no way to know in advance whether while frozen she was really in a state of suspended animation or just postponed putrefaction. If she failed to revive when thawed a century later, the question of the doctor's liability by then likely would be moot, unless he too had been frozen successfully and subsequently revived. Suppose no cure had been discovered yet for his ailment, could he be brought back nevertheless ahead of time and made to stand trial? If he were able to show at his trial that the prosecution knew she died from causes unrelated to her suspension, could the prematurely thawed sick doctor then sue for malicious melting?

What about a man's estate? Would his assets be frozen with him until revivification? Or would his will be probated as though he were dead? In the latter case, employing the hindsight furnished by lapse of several frosty decades, could he go back after being revived and disown the wastrel son who was squandering his substance? Would his right to drive a vehicle, vote, and practice a profession remain intact despite a long absence?

We can leave to others more knowledgeable about the unknowable the knotty theological problem of the morality of calling back to the heretofore a soul that may have grown to prefer the hereafter. But we might just consider the unfathomable consequences of reviving two centuries hence a thirty-eight-year-old shipping executive who is suspended today because of a massive coronary thrombosis that must otherwise inevitably cause his death within a few hours. Within two hundred years surely they will have learned how to provide a man with a fine new human or mechanical heart. But what of the rest? Suppose you were he. More poignant than the problems of property, inheritance, and licenses, imagine the shock of waking up in a world that no longer has ships, let alone shipping executives, a world in which you find no familiar face, in which the language and culture have evolved so extensively that you, an average citizen, "suddenly" have become a living museum piece, and find yourself almost unable to communicate in a foreign land.

How can assessment of the adaptive power of an individual be made so that decisions as to the relative humanity or cruelty of a second life can be made wisely? How firmly must a later generation be bound by an earlier generation's decision to try terrestrial life again later?

Long before we have learned all that is needed to preserve a whole human being we are likely to be confronted with the problem of the frozen human brain which, unlike the kidney or heart in the tank nearby, will carry within its icy convolutions the personality of a particular identifiable person. The science fiction horror which depicts a disembodied brain helplessly floating in a nutrient solution while sadistic former relatives and associates force it to perceive agonies impotently through implanted wires is brought to our doorstep by the successes of Dr. Isamu Suda. The Japanese physiologist has succeeded in doing with a cat brain what has been done with a hamster. He first replaced the circulating blood in the brain with nutrient fluid. Next, removing the brain from the animal, he replaced the nutrient fluid with glycerol to keep the vessels open. Then the brain was slowly frozen and placed in solid cold storage at -67 degrees

Fahrenheit. Six months later he thawed it, circulated cat blood through it, and was rewarded by resumption of its normal function, as revealed by tracings of its electrical brain waves.[37]

Of course, it will be some time before such a brain could be transplanted into a cat body, or before even the techniques touched on in Chapter 8 for making contact electronically with the thought of such a disembodied brain have been perfected. But the idea of even cat brains in frozen storage awaiting revival should strengthen our resolve to think all this over before the method is applied to one of us.

Is it justifiable ever to preserve a human brain? Once frozen, would it be justifiable to revive it when we have perfected in animals techniques we think, but do not know, will allow it and us to communicate? Or must we prove their effectiveness on nonfrozen human brains first? To establish a transplanted brain in a new body it will be necessary first to develop ways of inducing its nerves to grow out and hook up with the new organs, or something equivalent. Once this is accomplished, must we consult the preserved brain on the selection of its new abode, or would it be right to make the decision for it on the basis of newer biological information than was available at the time of its suspension?

Reviewing these paragraphs I see how easy it is to slip into speaking of the brain as "it." An impersonal pronoun is all right for a paired kidney or a solitary heart. But we must remind ourselves every time we speak of the living human brain that we are here considering a *human person*. Repeated or sustained lapse of this awareness can trap us in a quicksand of dehumanization as inexorable as our habit of speaking of the people we kill in war as "enemy dead."

Longevity and Values

Despite the efforts man makes periodically to get rid of himself, the human population goes on increasing. And the average length of life goes on increasing.

In remains from the late Stone Age it is rare to find a skeleton that was beyond teen-age at time of death, and the oldest individual was not more than fifty.[38] In Samuel Pepys' time, while the average length of life had reached thirty-three years, it still would have been unusual to encounter a man as old as fifty.[39] One hundred years ago the average lifespan in the United States was forty-one; yet today in the privileged West average longevity is approaching seventy.[40] Perhaps the easiest way to grasp the scope of this change is to ponder the speculation that nearly one-quarter of the people who have ever reached the age of sixty-five are alive today.[41]

But will this figure just go on increasing indefinitely?

Each species seems to have a built-in, genetically controlled clock that runs for about the same number of years in all individuals and establishes the upper limit of lifespan. For the chimpanzee it is about thirty years, for the human being, between eighty and ninety years. Whatever genetic variation there may be is not great. For example, according to Dr. Harry Sobel, a gerontologist at the University of California, Los Angeles, the longest authenticated lifespan is one hundred and twelve years, although there have been unauthenticated reports of up to one hundred and eighty years.[42]

Many of the diseases of aging formerly thought directly related to the calendar are known now to be due to other factors. Arteriosclerosis has been found to begin in infancy and become prominent in some individuals by early childhood, while remaining mild in others who have reached advanced old age.[43] Some of the causes of this kind of damage to the tubes that carry blood to all parts of the body are already understood. Prevention of the death and disability it causes from heart attacks and strokes may not be far off. The symptoms associated with menopause may turn out to be due to a preventable hormone deficiency if current research findings are confirmed and extended.[44] And some of the changes found in muscle, bone, and nerve structure or function may be found to be nutritional rather than temporal.

Many of these deteriorations associated with old age seem not to depend upon changes in the cells of the various organs, but rather upon changes in the connective tissue which hold the cells together. All nourishing substances, including amino acids, carbohydrates, vitamins, minerals, and oxygen must pass from the blood vessels through the connective tissue to reach and penetrate the cells where they are needed. Likewise the wastes given off by the cells, carbon dioxide, urea, and so forth, must pass from the cells through the connective tissue on their way to the blood vessels, which then carry them to the lungs, kidneys, liver, and skin to be eliminated. As the connective tissues age they become less efficient in their ability to transmit nutrients and wastes. It may be that the result is a combination of starvation and poisoning of the cells. Some researchers believe that except for this injurious situation the cells might have an indefinite life, or at least a much longer one.[45]

According to Dr. Sobel, certain chemicals are now being tested for their ability to slow down these age-dependent changes of connective tissue, or even to make aged connective tissue transmit substances more efficiently.[46] Then death generally would result from demise of vital cells whose genetically programmed time had run out, such as brain or heart cells.

Radiation of various kinds is also thought by some investigators to accelerate aging changes. That is one reason it is not wise to expose the skin to excessive amounts of sunlight. For some people especially it will be a difficult adjustment to give up the modern version of sun worship expressed in the high valuation placed today on roasting the naked skin to a deep tan. But there is also a considerable amount of radiation that arises from cosmic waves, nuclear explosions, even the concrete streets and buildings of our cities. Ways to prevent this unavoidable radiation from changing the body's tissues are under exploration.[47] If unsuccessful it may turn out that efforts to disperse large cities and shield smaller ones will be as important for prevention of radiation effect as for any other purpose.

Within the next century we should be able to extend the lifespan of most people to the built-in average of about ninety years. But at present, prospects for doubling or tripling the length of time allotted man by his genes seem more remote. However, we are not able to foresee in detail the consequences of discoveries which may develop in the next few decades. So we might be wise to give some thought to the problems Shaw dealt with in *Back to Methuselah*.

We know that the longevity of animals kept in enriched environments purified of diseases, deficiencies, and traumas can be much increased. And as Dr. Sobel indicated, perhaps 80 percent of our people could achieve in creativity what now only the top 5 percent accomplish.[48] Now, although we prosecute for murder, we do not usually assess responsibility for circumstances which just whittle weeks and months off lifespans and which lop percentages off creativity. But as evidence accumulates that each minor infection, each dietary deficiency, each small accumulation of lead, nickel, mercury, cigarette smoke, or other pollutants in our bodies, each physical or emotional injury that leaves a scar shortens by some fraction our allotted days and stifles our innate inspiration, may we not come round eventually to what Dr. Sobel spoke of as a concept of "partial murder"? Perhaps our sorrow over the loss to individual and community will one day be expressed in a legal mechanism that fixes responsibility for the conditions that make a man die prematurely in body or that stunt his creativity.

Meanwhile, the presently achieved increased longevity characteristic of the industrialized West already is causing great problems familiar to everyone. People are now living longer than their bodies and communities currently can maintain them in health. Some even live longer than their psyches have the appetite or capacity to enjoy. We have emphasized so exclusively and effectively the values of youth, jobs, and of getting ahead that most people have no place to go psychologically when they are old, retired, and slipping behind. And yet we agree that life must be meaningful and useful in order to be worthwhile.

With the coming of abundance, automation-cybernation, organ transplantation, life suspension, the guaranteed annual income, and still greater longevity, people are faced either with whole lives robbed of content, or with a new adventure which ingenuity can fill with substance worthy of the opportunity.

Although recommended by some observers, there is a serious question whether old patterns of several generations living together can be brought back. In the past people have put up with the nuisance because of economic scarcity. Perhaps there was also a need to indoctrinate children in advance by example that they must care for the parents when they too became old.

Now that affluence, population mobility, and social security have so far outdated these motivations, it is unlikely that people will revert to the old family pattern unless some powerful new motivation can be found.

There is a real need to have role models to identify with as we grow older and find our hair turning gray, our waistlines spreading, and our relationships with people changing. But that is not likely to persuade younger people to associate more with older ones, especially until older people are able to do a much better job of making old age appealing than they do at present.

On the other hand, the present pattern of segregating the elderly away from the community in "retirement villages" is apt to become a calamity. It seems likely that more and more people will rebel and refuse it when their time comes. The human waste this pattern embodies must force attention to the psychological, if not the economic, burden of hundreds of millions of castoffs playing shuffleboard and watching TV while waiting to die.

Of course, old age free of disabling illness can be a pleasant last act of life. But for a while at least there will continue to be increasing numbers of us whose as yet incurable ailments render our final months or years of increased longevity an unending misery. This pathetic spectacle, whether permitted to burden the lives of younger relatives at home, or played out in our proliferating old-age homes and "dying hospitals," is one which dehumanizes all concerned. Particularly pitiful is the prolonged agony through which helpless bedridden terminal patients now must sometimes suffer. Often we are medically unable to provide even effective relief from pain and always we are legally forbidden to supply the means of merciful death for which such patients may plead. It may not be long before an outraged public demands injudicious instant elimination of such unnecessary cruelties. Right now is the time for careful exploration and *planning* of a system of voluntary euthanasia which rigorously safeguards the traditional human right to life while permitting those who wish it the new right to a humane death.

Animals age and die, but seem not to pass their lives measuring the amount of time left to them. And they are clear about the difference between life and death. When an animal dies, its fellows no longer treat it as one of them. A chimpanzee mother simply lays her dead baby's body aside somewhere when its behavior makes her no longer recognize it.[49]

Man is the only creature that lives with awareness of his individual mortality. His efforts seem destined first of all to eradicate the simple certainties of the human lifespan. The meaning of life has always been ambiguous. There will not be too much harm done if the meaning of death becomes equally uncertain.

But we had better remain clear in our understanding of the meaning of human personality, lest our quest for Ponce de Leon's fountain of youth turn into Faust's transactions with the Devil.

8 Brain

The brain is an enchanted loom where millions of flashing shuttles weave a dissolving pattern, always a meaningful pattern though never an abiding one.

—Sir Charles Sherrington[1]

Background

As we have seen, the brain of man represents the evolutionary summit to date of all the organ systems of all the creatures who have inhabited the earth and left their descendants upon it today.

When long ago in the warm seas each cell had to perform for itself all the basic functions, no special nerve cells existed. But as the millions of years whirled by, and organisms evolved that had many cells, gradually they became specialized.

Although at first all cells transmitted the messages that coordinated parts of the cluster with the rest, eventually this primitive system was too slow and cumbersome to meet the needs of enlarging creatures for rapid responsiveness. The plants adapted in directions that did not require quick reactions. The animals acquired a nervous system.

At first the nerve cells passed messages through the cluster only about chemical and temperature changes in neighboring cells, or in the water immediately surrounding the small animal. Gradually they developed into many different kinds, some for carrying messages to move muscle cells, some for bringing information from the interior of the body, and eventually some, specialized as receptors for vibrations, sound, or light, for bringing information about conditions at a distance.

The specialized nerve cells slowly became organized into complicated networks, originally arranged in a circle about the opening they regulated in the hollow ball-shaped animal into which food was sucked from the ocean. When the round shape evolved into a long shape with a front and back end and two symmetrical sides, the primitive nervous system became "cephalized," moving into a compact clump in the primitive head. The loose network was transformed into "a great ravelled knot" as Sherrington once called the brain. Long nerve fibers connected each part with the others and with distant parts of the body. If one compares dissected bodies of a fish, a frog, a snake, a rat, a dog, a chimpanzee, and a man, it is evident at once that brain size relative to body size has increased continuously. And it is also plain that the paired cerebral cortices, which are the most recent additions to the primitive brain pattern, comprise progressively larger percentages, until in man they overshadow the other portions. Thought and consciousness are functions of the cerebral cortex.

In man the brain has become an astonishingly complex mechanism of ten billion nerve cells and their fibers, capable of making more different connections than all the telephone systems in the world put together. It has been estimated that between the ages of twenty and eighty, about one-sixth of the nerve cells die, reducing the brain's weight by about 10 percent.[2] Fortunately, we have many more cells than we can use. It is this brain that is capable of handling simultaneously the messages about all of our complicated activities. Think of the details it has to keep track of—the keys, buttons, shoelaces, forks and knives, handshakes, the machinery like typewriters and automobiles—the muscles and glands it must activate and coordinate, the information it must record and recall from decades or minutes ago, the directions it must remember, and all without using more than a fraction of its resources, and while freeing the mind for the important matters we have on it all the time!

And yet as marvelous as the brain is, it is not quite true that by itself man's brain is the pinnacle. For example, the dolphin brain has more nerve cells and more convolutions in its cerebral cortex than ours. Its intelligence is much greater than that of the monkey who requires several hundred trials to learn a task a dolphin can learn in twenty. Moreover, the numerous convolutions are already present in the early embryo which according to Dr. G. Pilleri "underlies the exceptional capacity of the newborn to lead an independent life."[3] Then why are we masters of the earth and not the dolphin?

Almost all animals have pursued the path of adaptation by specializing their body structures. The hoof, fin, and wing better equip their owners for running, swimming, or flying than do man's extremities equip him for these activities. Like all the primates, man has maintained a relatively *generalized* body, including a hand that can perform unaided a vast number of maneuvers, and which when supplemented with tools man's brain invents, enables him to run, swim, and fly better than those with specialized bodies.

The primates and man have specialized instead in *plasticity of social behavior,* for which the unspecialized body is ideal. We saw that early man acquired his hand while his brain was still the size of the brains of contemporary apes. When his skillful hand made a small fumbling brain a liability and a larger, brighter brain an asset, each enlargement of brain that occurred by chance mutation was exploited by dextrous men in finding ways to out-survive and out-reproduce duller contemporaries.

No matter how neatly all this explains the large brain of man, it helps us not at all to account for the dolphin's large brain. His ancestors probably left land and returned to the ocean millions of years before even the relatively awkward early type of primate hand was developed, let alone man's skillful version of it.[4] And the major enlargement of his brain seems to have *followed* return to aquatic life. Because his flippers and entire body are narrowly specialized for swimming, he could not have acquired a bigger brain by the primate (and human) method of specializing in plasticity of behavior.

So as Dr. Stanley M. Garn has said, it appears that man "did not double and nearly redouble his cerebral volume merely to pick up sticks." As a possible alternative he offers the cyberneticists' explanation, using by analogy the electronic terminology of the ratio between "signal," or relevant information, and "noise," or the thousands of bits of information that are irrelevant to survival.

> . . . in a system where "information" is buried, there is need for a further type of circuitry, one that scans incoming signals for *pattern*. In the chaos of exhortations to buy this, do that, or vote for somebody, there are some few bits that are important (like the date for filing income tax), and some patterns that must be recognized (such as repeated failures to get grants). Circuits that discriminate at a low S/N ratio and circuits that are pattern-reading as well tend to be bulky. Is this the meaning of our 50% larger brain . . . ?
>
> . . . it may be that our vaunted intelligence is merely an indirect product of the kind of brain that can discern meaningful signals in a complex social context generating a heavy static of informational or, rather, misinformational noise.[5]

But Dr. Garn's witty description of the human situation could not account for the dolphin's large brain either, because it does not apply. It is only we who must make the successful grant applications, while the dolphin playfully goes on enjoying the simpler social context of his watery world, the only abstruse problems he has being the complexities we introduce by insisting on communicating with him. If Dr. John Lilly or others should be successful in demonstrating that the dolphin can learn both to understand and use human language, perhaps his better brain could be enlisted not only in the effort to obtain grants for its study in the future, but also to resolve the mystery of why his (and our) brain evolved such dimensions in the past.[6]

When he has found us an answer to that question, I suggest that the next item on the agenda of the dolphin's big brain ought to be helping us understand the relationship of brain to mind, which thus far has eluded our smaller brain. In order to maintain the tolerant stance required of a collaborator in this effort, he might keep in mind that even our lesser computer has been working on the problem scientifically for only about one hundred years. And as Lord Russel Brain, a foremost English researcher, has said, ". . . the brain has a complex structure and so has the mind, and we are discovering by degrees what is the relationship between brain structure and mind structure."[7]

The trouble is that once again we are learning to control by even larger degrees structures and relationships we have not yet understood.

But that has been going on in relation to brain in a less ambitious way for millennia. Primitive man devised ways to bring about trances, dreams, and divinings through rhythm, dance, song, feasting and fasting, self-deprivation, and religious ritual. He also found naturally occurring drugs such as alcohol, marijuana, and peyote to make their effects more powerful, which modern man is only extending.

Early efforts at control of brain were often based on ideas that incorrectly located its functions in the heart, gallbladder, or liver.

Greek philosophers were among many who associated man with God, and were the first to consider the brain "the temple of reason." Hippocrates tried to substitute what was for his time the inspired but realistic formulation that "from the brain only arise our pleasures, joys, laughter and jests, as well as our sorrows, pain, grief and tears."

But Aristotle demoted the brain all the way from executory to excretory function, a downgrading trend that unconsciously may have lain behind Robert Fludd's seventeenth-century designation of the head as "seat of the mind."[8] And today, "the head" has become the literal if colloquial word for toilet.

Man's paradoxical ambivalence about his head and its contents was revealed for example by Fludd's adding that mind, intellect, and reason were "a divine light created by the highest heaven."[9] This celestial view was doomed by the gradual recognition that man's brain was not different in kind from the same organ in other animals. And Marx, Darwin, and Freud all helped persuade man that his identity, too, derives from various secular factors. Our continuing tendency today to profane the head may represent in part disappointment that research, such as that on the dolphin, discloses that even in terms of brain capacity man can no longer view himself as top sacred.

And yet we recognize that the brain is linked to "I" so much more closely than are other organs that any tampering with it intuitively evokes in us intense concern. We still have much regard for the secular sanctity of individual personality.

If the dolphin were running things, perhaps he would be casting about for ways to acquire our unspecialized body structure, especially our hand with the opposable thumb, since we owe to it our present level of culture. But we are in control and can ask instead whether we might acquire for ourselves the advantages possessed by the dolphin.

Brain Modification

For example, it takes a long period of development to bring the human infant to a state of independence attained by the dolphin at birth. By accelerating the rate of maturation of the human embryo through genetic or euphenic techniques we might produce a baby who could move about and begin learning to talk at birth. Since increase in brain and head size is limited by the dimensions of the female pelvis, as Dr. Joshua Lederberg has pointed out, delivery of babies with larger brains would be made possible by routine use of Caesarian section.[10] Even more pronounced results might be achieved through lengthening the period of gestation in artificial wombs. The bottles could be built with extra wide necks so that the larger head could be delivered without difficulty following gestation prolonged to perhaps ten, twelve, or even eighteen months. Such techniques might shift pedagogical debates to the merits of starting nursery school at two, three, or four weeks of age. What might the telescoping of physical, psychological, and cultural development mean for our species in the future? One immediately apparent result would be that a child might grow up without having to compensate so much for the long period of dependent helplessness that now conditions the deepest layer of his self image. A lessened tendency toward interpersonal intensity seems another likely result.

Transplantation

What about the other end of life, and the possibility of rescuing the brain and personality from injury through brain disease or disease of other parts of the body? Unlike other cells, brain cells do not ordinarily grow and reproduce throughout life, so they will not heal and "hook up" spontaneously if grafted as healthy spare parts or if transplanted as a whole brain to a healthy body. But this difficulty should be overcome when the techniques for cell regression and growth are perfected. Meanwhile, especially if the donor parts or new body were those of a clone, we already have some reason to believe that there should be no insurmountable surgical problems. Dr. Robert J. White, professor of neurosurgery at Western Reserve University, has succeeded in transplanting a brain from one dog to another.[11] The major blood vessels of the transplanted brain were connected to the recipient's neck vessels. The extra brain functioned almost normally for three days, as indicated by the pattern of its electric brain waves, before failing as a result of blood clotting. Dr. White points out that this method does not join the transplanted brain's nerve cells to the recipient body, which would be necessary before a transplanted brain could use a new body.

But it would be wise for us to consider a host of questions before that final step is achieved. Such as, where would we find donors for the spare parts? In brain banks supplied by deceased humans? And who would the result be if a left cerebral cortex with its connections were grafted onto a man whose speech had been lost from a stroke—the priest donor or the atheist recipient? Or could the brain of a different animal serve for lower structures such as the cerebellum which coordinates and integrates movements, playing no direct part in thought? Or if cerebral parts were used would the surgical hybrid still be human psychologically and legally, or would the admixture of ape disenfranchise him? Would it be completely up to an individual to decide whether, and into whom, and how many times he chose to have his brain transplanted into a healthy new body? For example, could he insist on being relocated only in a series of clonally produced copies of himself? Would he be equally responsible for the children he fathered from the sperm of three unrelated bodies? Would a man be permitted to have his brain transplanted into a female body next time around, or would it be illegal to masquerade in public wearing the body of the opposite sex?

These speculations take on extra pertinence in view of recent success in freezing and reviving animal brains, which seems likely soon to permit preservation of a human brain until the techniques for its successful transplantation are developed.

Electronics

The miniaturized pocket computer, used as an aid to memory or decision making, sounds uninteresting by comparison. But its development will lead to the coupling of human brain tissue directly to electronic units which, sometimes inserted into the skull, will produce a hybrid between machine and man. Such creatures have been named "cyborgs" in advance if not in anticipation of their advent.[12] In addition to supplementing man's memory and problem-solving capacity, such gadgets tuned to the right frequencies could so modify him that mental telepathy would become obsolete before it is even confirmed as a fact. Such radio communication could prove a boon in space exploration by providing the comfort and safety of instant advice in all circumstances. More than that, miniature regulators of all the astronaut's functions would give him the option of going on manual control or tuning in to remote guidance from earth to induce, for example, an instant catnap when he is too tired to sleep and prompt consciousness when too exhausted to awake. Possible abuses on earth range from capture of continents by a few hundred superbly coordinated commandos to inability to escape your wife's heckling at the office by turning off the phone.

These developments are placed on the human agenda by the confirmation about forty years ago of the existence in man's brain of minute electrical currents. The electroencephalograph demonstrated that they are of several types, and that their patterns are changed by various brain diseases and during different normal phases of brain activity.

Dreaming was discovered to be a fundamental physiological process related to other body rhythms and essential to health.[13] Various stages of sleep, alertness, drowsiness, relaxation, and boredom have been distinguished by the EEG.[14] Recognizable patterns have been associated with passive personalities or independent dominant qualities, with those who think visually as contrasted with those who think in sounds, movements, or textures.[15] Although these researches have been unable to discern the pattern of a specific thought, some investigators hope they may not be too far from doing so.

Until some means, whether EEG or other, is evolved for translating directly the thought processes in a brain, it will avail us little to succeed in preserving a living human brain. Even when methods for transplanting it into another body are perfected, certainly the comfort if not the success of the procedure will depend upon being able to communicate with the brain as its nerve fibers gradually grow out to connect with the eyes, tongue, and hands of its new home.

As always, success will not be an unmixed blessing. Those of us who regard the current electronic invasion of privacy as a menace to mind will then have to confront the terrifying possibility that the EEG will have become the super snooper that makes public even the unwhispered thought.

Electrical stimulation of the brain (ESB) increasingly permits us to control brain activity directly before we have learned to decipher its spontaneous electrical currents.[16] Via harmless electrode wires implanted deep in the brain, centers have been identified that when stimulated give rise to activity representing such basic drives as hunger, thirst, sex. Areas or centers of pleasure and pain have been located which an individual will quickly learn to stimulate or avoid stimulating.[17] The story is told of a dolphin who, inadvertently left in a pool with the switches connected, delighted himself to death after an all-night orgy of pleasure.

Behavior in animals that normally live in social groups has been controlled electrically. By stimulating the brain stem of chickens an investigator can evoke almost all forms of activity and vocalization ordinarily observed in them, as well as some composite behaviors which do not occur naturally. A rooster can be made to attack an imaginary enemy, or even a keeper he had always regarded as a friend.[18]

Yale neurophysiologist José M. R. Delgado was able to play with cats and monkeys "like little electronic toys," making them yawn, sleep, fight, or mate at the bidding of the transmitter button.[19]

His major technical contribution to the field is a radio stimulator system which dispenses with cumbersome wires connected to the subject's head. It is this sort of device which creates the possibility of remote control of cyborgs referred to earlier.

Stepping into a corral, Spanish-born Dr. Delgado gives a spectacular demonstration of the power of these new tools. A fighting bull charges at his body. A touch on the transmitter button that sends a signal to the bull's previously implanted electrodes stops him instantly, a few scant feet away from the researcher's body. He presses another button and the bull trots passively away.

The man responsible for these wonders has been working for fifteen years to determine the basis in the brain for thought and behavior. What makes bulls brave or people aggressive, what constitutes human personality, is of intense interest to him as it is to all of us. He hopes to find out, and then control it. He is already well on the way.

A young woman volunteer with epilepsy was implanted with electrodes for treatment of her disease. She is normally of reserved manner, but when Dr. Delgado pushes a button her mood changes immediately. "You are very nice," she says. Taking his hand she adds, "I would like to marry a Spaniard." When another button turns off the current the patient's flirtatiousness suddenly disappears.

Many a man would be happy to invoke such power. And the possibility of its saving some shaky marriages is not to be ignored. Nor is the possibility of its misuse on women by diabolical men. But recent information on the urgent insatiability of female sexuality suggests that we may have more to fear from women if their hands should ever close about the means of electronic seduction.[20]

By stimulating different areas of the brain, Dr. Delgado and others have found that a variety of phenomena can be modified, such as friendliness, pleasure, verbal expression, anxiety, fear, hostility, loneliness, hallucinations, illusions, and memories. Dr. Delgado explains how a simple stimulus can give rise to such intricate responses by making an analogy with the launching of a spaceship. The button in both instances only triggers a programmed series of events. Epileptic attacks that manifest themselves as ungovernable rages have been prevented by pressing a button connected to a stimulator that inhibits a reaction as soon as the patient feels it coming on. The electrodes have been left in place for months and years as therapeutic devices.

So far, the subjects have been voluntary, patients who are investigated in the course of efforts to treat a disease of the brain. But now in several centers the work is being extended carefully to the study of a few patients hospitalized for severe chronic mental illnesses which have not been benefited significantly by known means of treatment. The electrodes are being used initially to determine whether there is any unusual electrical activity deep within the brain that might give us a clue as to the cause or treatment of the disabling condition. But soon electrical stimulation will be put *into* the brain in the hope, for example, of helping a mute patient to talk, a withdrawn apathetic patient to be more sociable and energetic, or a man plagued by hallucinations to get rid of his obscene threatening voices. Not long after, attempts will follow to make results more permanent by destroying tiny areas of brain tissue with electricity or chemicals put in through the electrodes, just as patients have been subjected to surgical lobotomy and topectomy operations for the same purposes. It is likely that some of these efforts will bring results that will relieve or prevent the sufferings of many thousands who today spend wasted lives in hospitals shut away from the world.

Yet we must not overlook aspects of this work that could bring the end of freedom for the individual. The patients on whom such studies are now beginning are not voluntary. Because of the severity of their psychoses they are often unable to make even the most ordinary decision for themselves, such as whether to eat or bathe or have a decayed tooth repaired, and as a consequence have been committed to a hospital by a court. If a permit is required to treat such a patient's pneumonia or appendicitis it must be given by the family. In the same way consent in writing is obtained to implant brain electrodes and the procedures are carried out without the patient's direct assent.

Once brain implant techniques have proved of value in the treatment of severe mental illness we will be urged to extend their benefits to convicted criminals. No one would want to deny medical treatment to a person who is impelled to commit acts that cost him years of imprisonment just because of his refusal of permission. And yet we should have serious qualms about forcing brain implants upon a person who is mentally quite capable of refusing them by our rationalizing that his behavior has been interpreted legally as a forfeiture of his rights. From compelling a chronic offender to submit to electronic policing of his brain, it is only a few short steps to enforcing the implantation of a first offender, for example, a sexual molester of children, whose chances of repeated offenses may be statistically very great. And from there the prospects of involuntary extension by the community to political dissenters or even just to irritating nonconformists are terrifying.

Critics have warned that such wiring of the human brain could destroy the identity and autonomy of the individual, ushering in the nightmare of *Brave New World.* Dr. Delgado acknowledges that it might be possible to regulate the aggressiveness or productivity of an individual, but feels it would be impossible to control an entire population. Because of anatomical and functional differences, it would be difficult to produce the same effect in all people. But more important, as he has shown, electrical stimulation evokes not automatic responses, but reactions that are integrated with the individual's personality and social environment. For example, a monkey stimulated into aggressive behavior will spare his friends and attack only competitive members of his colony. Another aggressive monkey when stimulated goes through a complex routine which includes stopping what he is doing, changing his facial expression, turning his head to the right, climbing up and down a pole, uttering soft noises, threatening subordinate monkeys, and at last resuming his original peaceful posture and activity. The ritual is peculiar to this monkey, and the same stimulation in another would not reproduce it.

But this is feeble reassurance, especially when Dr. Delgado himself has trained monkeys to control one another's behavior by pressing a lever that sends a calming signal to the brain of a hostile member of the group.[21]

While this use suggests a means for preventing human violence, even war, we must realize that the method will appeal strongly also to people fed up with proponents of peace, and unless we can fend off its misuse, it could be employed by them with sufficient effect to make monkeys of us all. Wisdom and foresight are required to allow us to derive the benefit of even today's comparatively primitive equipment without falling into the calamity of electronic tyranny.

Chemistry

The chemical aspect of brain physiology is of equal importance, and cannot be separated from the electrical.[22] Nerve impulses, recorded or initiated by electrical means, are transmitted across each gap or synapse between nerve cells under the control of chemical substances. Fisher and Coury showed that acetycholine injected into a deep central portion of the brain will cause rats to drink enormous amounts of water.[23] Dr. Fisher expected that injection of male hormone into the hypothalamus would arouse a male rat to sexual pursuit of a female. To his disappointment, not to mention the female's, instead of following his script, the male rat maternally picked the female up by the loose skin on her back and deposited her in the corner, as though in a nest. Injection of the same hormone into females at a slightly different spot made them act like sexually aggressive males.[24] Whatever else they disclose, such results show that control of sexual behavior is not simple. These and other intriguing findings are still puzzling, but seem to indicate that, although some investigators disagree, the male and female brain may be identical in character and organization of the nerve cells. Which sort of behavior predominates in adult life apparently depends partly upon which hormone is present and in which precise location, but also upon which hormones influence the immature rat during earliest development.

Although the sexual behavior of higher animals, especially man, is much less under the control of hormones, the possibility is at least raised that subjecting the human brain to injected hormones, particularly during gestation, might affect adult sexual preferences. By these and other means elimination of sexual deviancy, production of harems of hypersexual female concubines, or troops of homosexual males can be envisioned depending on your fantasies. Whether such results are regarded as boon or bane would depend on the observer's values.

Menopausal women are now being given estrogen hormone orally and by injection to maintain their general health and especially their erotic function. In those instances where it fails to maintain libido, perhaps it will be found, as it has been in cats from whom ovaries have been removed, that implantation of estrogen in selected sites of the hypothalamus in five days restores receptivity to the male. But Dr. Fisher cautions that there are definite species differences with regard to chemical brain stimulation. While acetylcholine implanted in certain regions of the rat brain promotes thirst, in the cat it results in anger, fear, or a sleeplike trance.[25] Disgruntlement leading to legal action seems a not unlikely consequence of such a substitution in a human being of insatiable thirst for lust.

Circulation, Nutrition, Drugs

A more accessible approach to the brain is provided by its arteries. In health, by means of an extraordinarily high rate of flow, they bring an organ that comprises only 2 percent of the body's mass more than 25 percent of its blood volume. Interruption of flow for fifteen seconds produces unconsciousness, and for four minutes, irreversible damage to cerebral nerve cells.[26]

Gradual obstructions to the blood flow occur from arteriosclerosis in the neck or in the brain itself, which narrows the passage through which blood must flow. Sometimes clots will form that suddenly interrupt circulation completely, damaging vital functions such as speech and movement. Surgeons are becoming adept not only at removing such clots, but also at splicing in sections of artificial tubing or healthy artery to replace diseased ones, thus preventing or reducing severity of the damage.

Along with oxygen, blood brings amino acids, proteins, enzymes, vitamins, and minerals, the constant supply of which is more critical to the brain than to any other organ. Blood also carries to the brain any drugs administered by mouth or injection. So a means of observing changes in brain vessels and blood circulation directly could be an invaluable way of gauging probable effects of various procedures and substances on brain. Monkeys have been fitted with plastic skull tops which permit such direct vision, a technique which in time should be readily applicable to humans.[27] Then it should be possible to correlate in man the immediate and remote effects on brain and mind of introducing or withholding various nutrients and drugs.

Perhaps our understanding of the cause and treatment of mental retardation, the nutritional defects that result in listless children in areas of famine, or senile brain disease will be improved by use of this method. It might also lead to ways of raising the overall performance of individuals.

But it is clear that this sort of procedure is among many that could potentially threaten our society. We may leave aside the obvious possibility of its unscrupulous misuse for domination of people, but more subtle dangers must be anticipated. Surgeons have long operated and done research on the living human brain, their techniques exposing it to direct view for only a few hours. But what happens to the regard of one person for another whose private organ of personality has become so protractedly visible? Might it be difficult to maintain our special respect for a human being if, as we look him in the eye, we simultaneously see his brain and its most intimate circulatory responses?

Other drugs produce few changes in brain blood circulation but markedly affect behavior. The best known are the sedative drugs, usually barbiturates, which have been employed widely. In selected psychiatric patients, administration of such substances by vein is useful in helping to bring back "forgotten" memories of past, traumatic events, so that the patient can react to them and discharge gradually the anxiety or guilt connected with them. Although this method is not useful even in the majority of psychiatric patients, and certainly does not uniformly result in accurate recollection and recounting of the past, it has acquired an undeserved reputation in criminal investigation.

For example, it has been employed to ascertain guilt or innocence in the mistaken notion that "truth serum," as it is called, can be relied upon to elicit the truth from a suspect. Its reputation is undeserved. Research has shown that normal subjects can stick to invented stories. However, neurotic people will often not only confess more easily, but, because of strong unconscious need for punishment, will confess to fantasied offenses never actually committed. Others, especially with certain types of character neuroses common in criminals, will falsely deny guilt no matter how much drug is administered. So lying in either direction is quite possible, and the story produced cannot be relied upon as conforming with objective fact.[28]

But suppose a drug that is effective in forcing an individual to reveal "truth" is developed. No matter how valuable it might be in assuring that guilt and innocence could be distinguished, we would be wise to prohibit its compulsory use, even in connection with the most heinous crimes, for fear of establishing a precedent that could open floodgates to dictatorship.

As with barbiturates, it appears in general that a drug's effect depends not only on the properties and potency of the substance but also on the characteristics of the subject. These include his basic personality, condition, and mood. Also of great importance is the social and psychological context, particularly the meaning to the person of the drug experience, and his interpretation of the motives of those who supply or administer it. This is well established for alcohol, the most venerable and widely used brain-influencing drug of all, which produces elation or depression, friendliness or fury, agitation or tranquilization, erotic insatiability or disinterest, sleep or even death, depending upon the factors mentioned.[29] The same is true of the minor tranquilizers which are used for control of anxiety, and the major tranquilizers which have prevented or shortened the period of hospitalization required for treatment of so many psychoses.

But especially is it true for the most recent category of drug to tweak the public's fancy, the psychedelics or hallucinogenic agents. The much ridiculed customary caution shown by qualified medical authorities concerning these substances has been justified additionally by the unpredictable finding that LSD, at least, in addition to its other well-known hazards, appears from some but not all studies to be capable of producing damage to the chromosomes with genetic injury to offspring. We generally do not wait to use a new drug until we understand everything there is to know about its nature, action, and effects. If we did we would not now be getting the benefit of the very useful agents mentioned above. But at least we require systematic study of its chemistry, its effects in animals, and its effects in human beings before it is available for widespread use, even under the supervision of physicians. Even so, it is not uncommon for emergency notices to be sent out from a manufacturer calling back a drug that had been approved for general use because further experience has revealed previously unknown undesirable effects.

But the peculiar situation exists that individuals who endorse even stronger controls on other groups of drugs have adopted in relation to the hallucinogens a worshipful permissiveness that views responsible caution on the part of authorities as unwarranted interference with freedom. Admittedly, some therapeutic uses for these agents are suggested by research now under way, and it would seem appropriate that qualified investigators be encouraged to continue their work. Although no reliable evidence exists as yet, there may even be reason to query whether these substances or others may increase the powers of the brain to apprehend broader slices of reality. But to insist as do some evangelists of psychedelia that it is the "right" of any citizen to try these drugs right now without any supervision whatever is like insisting on the right of a one-year-old child to play with a loaded revolver. They are demanding that anyone be permitted to alter his psyche so that, depending upon his personality, his memory may falter, walls may seem to drip, his flesh may seem to fall from the bones, and he may suddenly realize that God wants him to kill the President. To acquiesce would result in less expansion of consciousness than contraction of sanity.

While it is true that hallucinogens are not addictive, they are habit-forming in that individuals who indulge have a tendency to center their lives about the drug experience. The same has been noted for marijuana, often touted as harmless.[30] Although such indulgence undoubtedly has done so in some instances, it does not have to lead to addiction to narcotics such as heroin in order to be destructive. The harm is sufficient if only it makes it unnecessary to satisfy the requirements of reality in order to "feel good." People who wallow in drug-induced euphoria experience little need to master the next step on the human agenda—learning to achieve full individual development amid abundance without the goad and obstacle of scarcity.

Not only does the setting influence the reaction to foreign substances such as LSD, but evidence is accumulating that social environments, including factors such as population density, social group size and composition, social status, and social isolation may have short- and long-term effects upon ordinary brain chemistry. At a recent symposium on Social Environment and Brain Chemistry, evidence was presented indicating that "because the metabolism of substances that transmit and modulate impulses in the central nervous system are affected, the physiology of behavior cannot be fully understood out of context of the social environment."[31] This was borne out by the laboratory finding that the concentration of cholinesterase, an important substance regulating impulse transmission, was higher in the cerebral cortex of rats raised in a stimulating environment. It has also been found to be higher than normal in people suffering from anxiety.[32]

Experience

Even the structural development of the brain is affected by the amount of environmental stimulation. Twelve rats, housed together in a large cage, were supplied with mazes, ladders, and other toys. They could hear and see everything going on in the laboratory, and each rat was allowed to explore new environments out of the cage for thirty minutes each day. As they matured, their play-school schedule was enlarged to include various learning tasks stimulated by reward.

Another group of rats was kept in a dimly lit, quiet room, each rat in a separate cage lined with sheet metal on three sides, and rarely handled or permitted to explore new environments or solve problems.

After eighty days it was found that the rats raised in the stimulating environment had developed significantly heavier cerebral cortices and higher levels of cholinesterase than the deprived group.

Even more interesting, the enriched environment had produced significantly increased problem-solving ability, which could rapidly be reversed by placing the animal in the impoverished situation. Even findings at autopsy were definitely related to the most recent environment in which the animal had been living.[33]

Perhaps the most hopeful result of this research is that the brains of adult rats changed as readily in response to altered environment as those of young rats.

We know that disadvantaged schoolchildren from ghetto areas are intellectually retarded as compared with middle-class youngsters of the same age. Since there is no reason theoretically to doubt that marked and prolonged plasticity also characterizes the human brain, it is likely to become increasingly clear to every legislator that every vote against funds to counter the psychological as well as nutritional deprivations of slum living is a vote for smaller brains and minds. And it may turn out that every vote against funds for enriching the diet and daily lives of the elderly may be a vote for premature senility. Thus do the findings of research underline the bankruptcy of human imagination relative to human resources.

In contrast to their response to intellectual stimulation, subjects kept in a monotonous environment will sink into lethargy. Human volunteers kept experimentally isolated in small rooms or floating in water, with all movement and all perceptions greatly restricted, show various deleterious effects. The brainwave EEG pattern changes. Visual perception becomes distorted, even into hallucinations. And childish emotional responses are exhibited.[34]

The normal function of the brain depends on a continuous "arousal reaction," generated by a part of the brain stem called the reticular formation.[35] Aside from their specific functions of bringing information, sensory stimuli have the general function of maintaining the arousal reaction, and thereby normal brain activity.

These findings have many practical implications. Long-distance truck drivers, frequent victims of monotony, not uncommonly fall asleep. Some have reported hallucinations. In trying to avert these dangers, drivers become addicted to stimulating drugs such as Benzedrine or Dexedrine, and then are exposed to the considerable danger of drug intoxication, including the production of hallucinations. Aviators have reported and astronauts can be expected to experience such phenomena. On a more mundane level, every assembly line of the present, and probably every room where computerized machinery of the future will require an occasional man's supervision, can be expected to be a hothouse for boredom and sensory deprivation. Mechanical stimuli, like background music, which are sometimes employed to relieve it, may only increase the soporific effect. Yet more lively stimuli might dangerously distract the worker. Experience has shown that continual *novelty* of stimuli patterns is a critical factor. In the homogenized and machinelike culture into which we seem to be moving novelty may become as precious for brain health as unpolluted air. The new science of psychological engineering, which has too often been used in dehumanizing ways, has here an opportunity to redeem itself from its traducers.

Inadvertent and dangerous controls of the brain come from various pollutants. For example, it has been found that pesticides impair brain function in various ways. Men working for years in the manufacture of organophosphates were found to be less energetic, and to have more memory difficulties and irritability than persons with minimal exposure. Thirty percent showed abnormal EEGs. DDT and other hydrocarbons present in the tissues of fish and birds may accumulate and be potentially harmful to humans who eat them. Workmen's compensation, or the equivalent for the general consumer, is small recompense for the slow ruination of life by poison in the air and food.[36]

Memory

Perhaps a possibility for the improvement of some of these noisome effects lies in recent experiments with chemicals that improve memory, especially those involved with memory transmission. Before we look at the findings let us review as background for a moment the history of theories of memory.

Democritus in 500 B.C. hypothesized that infinitesimally small "atoms" are continually emanating from everything in the environment, and that these gain entrance to the brain via the sense organs. There they come into contact with the soul, also made up of atoms, whereupon a man perceives whatever had given off the external atoms. The "eidola," as Epicurus subsequently termed the image, is stored in the brain for later reference of the soul as memory. It was essentially this materialist idea that animated the poetry of Lucretius.

Medieval philosophers made the explanation compatible with Christianity by avowing that the material eidola came into contact with an ineffable nonmaterial Christian soul and in some way laid down nonmaterial images that were stored for later recall as memory. As Dr. David Krech of the UCLA Department of Psychology has pointed out, this Christianized version of Democritus persists in the minds of many of us.[37] It is largely on this account that we find the new information on memory transmission so shocking. But I am getting ahead of the story.

In the last hundred years we have learned that it is not atoms from outside but nerve impulses from inside that bring information to the brain, and that there some internal change is wrought that is stored for memory. We cannot help but conceive of it as nonmaterial as a result of our Christian inheritance. People tend to think of memory as a pattern of nerve impulses that can be called up again from "traces" years later, sloughing over the necessity to conceptualize them as in some way inscribed on a material tablet.

But in 1961 at a symposium in San Francisco, Dr. James V. McConnell reported his now classic study of "Memory Transfer Through Cannibalism in Planarians." Those of us who heard him were jolted simultaneously out of any vague nonmaterialism regarding the mechanism of memory, and also out of the unspoken notion that learning is strictly a psychological phenomenon. For his flatworms, normally indifferent to light, acquired a fear of it after eating pieces of other flatworms that had been conditioned to cringe when exposed to light! Sidestepping the arduous work of learning by experience, they had proved they could literally "eat up" learning.[38] As Dr. McConnell pointed out, among other staggering implications is that of a brand-new role for emeritus college professors.

Dr. Holger Hydén of Göteborg, Sweden, suggested there must be a chemical substance in the cytoplasm of nerve cells which could be structurally modified by electrical nerve impulses coming in from the nerve fiber, thus recording and retaining the information. This chemical basis of memory he felt must be RNA, the complex molecule we encountered as the messenger which carries information from DNA and which is the governor of cell metabolism.[39] If correct, this means that RNA can be informed not only by the genes from within, but by experience arising from without. And many investigators believe it is this learned RNA that gives the flatworm its alimentary education.

The memory of goldfish can be enhanced by RNA. And pemoline, a mild central nervous system stimulant known for half a century, has been found to increase RNA synthesis. Rats receiving pemoline learned a jumping trick four to five times faster than untreated animals, and what is more interesting, they remembered what they had learned eight weeks later, whereas the control animals had completely forgotten their lessons.[40] In clinical trials pemoline did improve declining memory in senile and presenile patients. Dr. D. Ewen Cameron reported that in some patients suffering from arteriosclerotic brain disease, senile and presenile psychoses, memory showed unequivocal improvement following RNA treatment. In some the improvement was permanent. In others it disappeared when the drug was withdrawn and reappeared when it was resumed.[41]

Naturally all this raised in the researchers' minds the same question it does in ours. Can one not only stimulate learning and memory in general with RNA, but also transfer specific information in man as in flatworms? Initial experiments at UCLA indicated that, at least for lower mammals, such transfer is possible.[42] When RNA from the brains of trained hamsters was injected into rats, the latter learned the task the hamsters had been taught much faster than rats that had not received injections. Most interesting was that it thus appeared one could transfer memory using the RNA of a different species.[43] But other workers were unable to confirm these findings, leaving the matter in doubt.

However, recently Dr. Georges Ungar of Baylor University College of Medicine reported success in giving untaught mice the benefit of a rat's education. When extracts from the brains of trained and untrained rats were injected into two groups of mice, those given the educated extracts learned a task in less than half the trials required by those receiving the other extracts. Skeptics suggest that these results indicate no transmission of information whatever, but merely that extracts of trained brain have a nonspecific stimulating effect on learning not possessed by extracts of untrained brains. This objection is countered by the results of further experiments. For example, untrained rats show a startle reaction to an unfamiliar sound or to a puff of air. With training, a group of rats can be habituated to either stimulus, so that the startle response disappears. Now, if an extract of sound-habituated rat brains is injected into rats exposed to the same sound, the recipients become habituated faster than rats not receiving extract. But the same extract does *not* speed habituation of rats to a puff of air. Likewise, an extract from the brains of air-puff-habituated animals speeds habituation to air puffs but not to sound. The same sort of specificity is found in relation to extracts of brains of mice trained to turn to the right or to the left. These results suggest, astonishing as it seems, that it is truly *specific information* that is transmitted. Dr. Ungar found that the substances responsible are peptides rather than RNA, but this disagreement does not alter the fact that some agent or other seems capable of transferring memory from one individual to another, even of a different species. As *The Human Agenda* goes to press, more news comes from Dr. Ungar that brings us full circle to our starting place: fear of the dark, which had to be unlearned so painfully. Scotophobin, a peptide extracted from the brains of trained rats, will transmit fear of the dark to untrained rats and mice. Moreover, in his laboratory a closely related chemical that has two-thirds of the activity of injected scotophobin has been *constructed artificially!* Just how it works is unknown, but if such substances prove to be the biochemical basis of memory, they could encode "all the information acquired by the brain in a lifetime."[44]

We have remarked before that results in one species cannot be *assumed* applicable to another without trial. But theoretically in this instance there seems to be no reason to expect a difference in the fundamental reactions of mice and men. Should they be confirmed in man, where might these findings affect our future? In our speculations we should realize that even if they are not confirmed at all these results can be taken as a qualitative model of the sort of advance that can be expected of future research. Education is an obvious area where these findings might be applied to human beings. Perhaps the Head Start program of the future will consist of injections of learned substances. These could be used with more certainty and economy than present methods which rely upon enriching experience. But while they might markedly benefit the underprivileged and even the retarded, it is plain that if distributed unevenly, as are other opportunities now, they could immeasurably widen the existing breach between the privileged and the deprived. And, at least, the generation gap seems destined to increase as a result of such chemical tutoring. How will parents react when their formerly dull or average children outstrip their progenitors?

Presumably there are many differences in the endowment of people other than the kind and amount of RNA and related substances in their brains. And so we would be unlikely to turn out all completely equal when given optimum dosages. But differences in accomplishment might at least be much evened out by such procedures, with results that can be emotionally disastrous in a competitive society. This became clear to me recently when a completely different type of drug, an antidepressant administered by a psychiatrist for depression, unexpectedly produced a phenomenal burst of energy and accomplishment that brought several students to the top of their classes who previously had been failing as a result of their illness. Even though this was a medical procedure, not the human equivalent of doping a healthy horse, it is not hard to understand the displeasure of a classmate (or his parents) at being outdone in this way. But there were also poorly formulated objections from others not directly involved that such drug-facilitated improvement is somehow evil because it distorts the expected normal distribution bell curve! Despite our democratic wish that all have equal *opportunity*, at our present stage of social evolution we do not expect or want to do away with gradations of what are thought to be innate ability and resultant *achievement*. Whether we will or should want to at a future stage involves prediction of facts and values so intricate that we had best start examining the problem now, before student health services receive their first supplies of injectable freshman English or implantable integral calculus.

Famed Canadian neurosurgeon Wilder Penfield found that upon electrical stimulation of the brain during operations patients suddenly recalled with vivid intensity long-forgotten episodes out of the distant past. As long as the electrode continued to activate the same spot they went on recalling more and more about these events.[45] Perhaps future research will make it possible to recover memories of events from early childhood, the period of such great importance to the person's later mental health.

In recent years experience has shown that recapturing memories is not uniformly beneficial in the treatment of mental or emotional illness. But insofar as retrieving lost memories continues to prove of value in future therapy, a physiological recapturing technique would hold much promise.

Perhaps even more valuable will be its other applications, such as reviewing for an exam, or taking a "refresher" course to bring previously learned and forgotten material back to clarity. Its use in the study of history through reviving eyewitness accounts, for example, of President Kennedy's assassination, is especially intriguing.

But the perspective is even broader than might be imagined at first glance. Freud himself found that simple excavation of a memory does not bring a patient the lasting improvement he had hoped. That memory, whether conscious or not, becomes the basis for layer upon layer of experiences and reactions that are built into his character over many years, and are not removed automatically just because at some later time a lost memory and even all the feelings connected with it are recovered. It is similar to the condition of a patient who has a sliver under a fingernail for some weeks. Removing it at last may result in prompt subsidence of the infection, swelling, and pain. But if the abnormal process has reached down through layers of connective tissue to infect the bone, then removal of the splinter may prove of little benefit, and much more treatment will be needed.

But suppose, by some combination of Penfield's electrode eliciting technique and a yet to be discovered RNA-peptide detergent, a method should be developed whereby the emerging memories could be washed away, including not only a crucial traumatic one, but all the subsequent derivatives that have become the web of habit we recognize as unhealthy character traits. Then a man who became homosexual out of terror of competing with his father might not only reread the record of the crushing of his budding sexual interest in women, but expunge it. And replace it with more favorable memories copied from those of other persons or tailored chemically to fit his needs. Perhaps we could administer chemicals to create new memories, say an antiscotophobin to erase fear of the dark or, more important today, a chemical that could quell fear of new ideas or fear of change.

We have always said the past cannot be changed. Memorectomy and replacement is certainly the next best thing. It may be so close to actual change of the past as to require major philosophical reorientation as well as careful assessment in terms of values if we are to negotiate it safely.

It would be redundant at this point to spell out the possible hazards, but we should consider a few more uses that might be made of such transfers.

When a child learns to speak, a center controlling speech is developed on the dominant side of the brain, usually the left. If that center is destroyed in early life, the child will be unable to speak for weeks or months until the previously undeveloped speech area on the other side learns to take over. When the injury occurs in adult life, the recovery of speech is much slower, and may never be complete.

But in recent years patients formerly considered hopeless have been saved and helped to lead full lives by the discovery of new ways to tap the enormous unused potentialities of the brain. This may be why a seven-year-old Philadelphia boy left senseless by an automobile accident could be benefited by "repatterning" passive movements of his limbs that taught his brain to redevelop control. After two years the child was said to be fully recovered.[46] Essentially this is how recovery took place in the Russian physicist Lev Landau, who won the Nobel prize in 1962. Totally unconscious and paralyzed for seven weeks, the patient was able to retrace the stages of his development from infancy through childhood to adulthood under a regime outlined by Dr. Penfield. He had to learn to breathe, hear, speak, walk, and remember even the most basic facts of his life. But within two years, with the help of friends and fellow scientists, his intellect was restored.[47] As we have already noted, instances such as these make more harrowing the decisions of a doctor whether or not to preserve a life. Perhaps the new techniques of memory manipulation will one day help us choose which patient to try to restore, and also reduce the period of lost life in such cases.

Remote Potentials

We saw that it might be possible someday to recreate a genetically identical copy of a living man from a living cell, or a copy of one long dead from the specifications left in his mummified genes. And we remember that these resurrections, like all clones, could not be the same "person" because neither could possess the experiences or knowledge of the original. Now, RNA and other substances are much less stable and preservable than DNA. Furthermore, whereas theoretically one could reconstitute the individual's *genetic* identity from the intact genes of only one cell, in order to reconstitute the *acquired* information in his RNA (and related chemicals), it would be theoretically necessary to have intact and in proper relation to each other all the ten billion nerve cells of his brain so that a computer could analyze each and program the memory-chemicals in a corresponding cell in the clone brain as a duplicate. Naturally, even for the super computer of the future that is a task of formidable complexity. But nevertheless, should a method be found for preserving and analyzing these substances, theoretically it would be possible to equip the genetic copy with the acquired elements of the original's personality as well. Then he would have the same information and memories. He would call himself by the same name. He would have the same indentity. He would be the same person. We could have that chorus of Carusos endowed not only with his genetic predisposition to vocal virtuosity, but also with the original's full emotional as well as musical repertoire. As I write these lines it doesn't escape me that, even esthetically, some people will shudder in horror rather than shiver happily at such a prospect. Perhaps it would be a small comfort to some to be reminded that the same might be done with Chaliapin. Or Rudy Vallee. Or Tom Jones.

If we shift our attention from the vocal to the graphic arts, another interesting prospect appears that resurrects and extends not the artist but just his art.

Dr. Kurt Von Meier, art historian formerly at the University of California, Los Angeles, has suggested that computers, as extraorganismic brains, might be assigned to analyze the paintings of a great artist.[48] For example, from a series of paintings by Mondrian, not only could the computer abstract the characteristics of any individual work, but also the past and future development or evolution of the artist's style, technique, and muse. One might get from a properly programmed and equipped computer a new Mondrian, painted either according to a past phase of the artist's work or according to a future phase that the computer's analysis shows might have occurred had he lived and continued to work.[49]

Furthermore, Dr. Von Meier suggested that it might be possible somehow to couple the computer to a human mind.[50] In theory we could then equip a person with the esthetic attitudes of Mondrian, or of Rembrandt or Leonardo or anyone for whose works a program had been created. Now, he would not look at the world through the unadulterated eyes of Leonardo, for example, unless we blocked out all his twentieth-century experiences and substituted a set faithful to the artist's. But to do that you would need first a program for all Leonardo's experiences. Given sufficient information, in theory again, a computer program could be devised which would accomplish or at least approximate this stupendous achievement.

Now, assuming all this to be possible, how could one enter the information into the mind? Would the brain sorcery of memory transmission be a possible means? Clearly we are not discussing an innovation of the immediate future. But in view of the accelerated rate at which the future seems to be invading the present, it may be worthwhile to cast a thoughtful glance over its approach route. Suppose it became possible for an art student to plug himself into a computer that would program his brain cells with the code of an accomplished artist. Might he then be able not only to see through the artist's eyes but also to produce the new Mondrian with his own hands and out of his "own" mind. Perhaps the next week, working backward, he would connect with the code for Van Gogh, and the week after with that for Vermeer or Rubens. Then he would know from the inside, or rather from having it inside himself, each of these artist's way of perceiving as well as rendering his world.

But if the student's own RNA-peptide memory complex had been replaced completely, would it still be "he" who was producing the new old masterwork? Instead it seems some way would have to be devised of *superimposing* the artist's program on his own. Then the student would be lurking in the shadows observing and learning as the resurrected and internalized mentor guided his novice's hands.

As we have seen, the implications for economy in education are enough to make some elected officials pant. And the implications for possible enforced educational conformity are enough to make the rest of us panic.

But there are also new problems. What would happen to a greedy student who gorges himself simultaneously on Bosch, Rembrandt, El Greco, Van Gogh, Picasso, Mondrian, Keinholz, and Warhol? Beyond that worry, the consequences for esthetics are grave enough to concern an art historian, and the consequences for art historians grave enough to concern a psychiatrist.

We could go on indefinitely. We could explore the interesting possibilities for altering biological rhythms such as the menstrual cycle through the use of brain-controlling chemicals. Particularly fascinating are prospects for reducing the length of time needed for restorative sleep. Or for helping a person sleep faster by dreaming more of the time he is asleep, thereby assuring in few hours a sufficient amount of dreaming to maintain mental health.

But with present techniques of inscribing information onto the brain, the number of details that can be absorbed at one time is limited. Whether dolphin or man, our higher nervous systems will have to await the future before any of us can hope to become painlessly a know-it-all.

9 Mind

Background

The story of mind, as we have seen, is of a trek toward consciousness in the control of behavior. And the peak of consciousness attained so far is the conceptualizing mind of man.[1] The capacity not only to think but to *communicate* in abstractions, to construct and use *symbolic language*, separates us from all other living creatures.

Although the dolphin brain has more convolutions, it is imprisoned in a body narrowly specialized for swimming, lacking in particular the marvelous tool of fingers and thumb. It therefore cannot accumulate the variety of experience and culture which builds man's mind anew each generation. Evolution, which has left the dolphin at sea, truly has had a hand in our mental destiny ashore.[2]

So we are alone.

And the stunning fact is that in addition to all the rest, now the conscious mind of man must assume deliberate control of itself. Like the aforementioned fabled compleat computer, the mind must also undertake the design, manufacture, and repair of itself and its self-reproducing progeny.[3]

Is the mind of man equal to the task of exercising these controls? It must do so. For, ready or not, here comes the future. The adaptations we require must come with it.

Again we are in the predicament, particularly risky in relation to the mind, of being able to start controlling what we have not yet well understood. This is worrisome enough in relation to controlling the brain, which is only the house in which mind lives; the danger mounts when the control exerted by mind is upon its own psychological self. An old

275

medical aphorism warns that "the doctor who treats himself has a fool for a patient." Yet there is no alternative. To deftly control itself at our present stage of knowledge, mind will require the perspicacity of a hungry invisible man plucking an invisible apple from an invisible tree.

Now, while evaluating its resources for the task and some of the controls it might employ, let us explore the challenges confronting mind.

Although they are really inseparable, they can be considered in three groups: demands of daily reality, demands of our own urges, demands of evolution.

Demands of Daily Reality

Things, Consciousness, Habit

Did you ever add up the number of things you must deal with each day? Your morning dream-wish is shredded by the alarm. You push the lever to stop the noise. Your covers must be pulled back, perhaps slippers and robe donned, and two doorknobs turned to reach the bathroom. The ritual there requires manipulating at least two faucets, soap dish, soap, towel, towel rack, comb, toilet cover and handle, and depending on your habits, shower faucets, shower door, toothbrush and holder, toothpaste tube and cap, shaving cream, razor, blade, tweezer, clipper, file, eyebrow pencil, mascara, lipstick, makeup base, perfume, and deodorant. Then turning more knobs on more doors, you make your way to breakfast where you encounter stove, oven, sink, dishwasher and their handles, knife, fork, spoon, plate, cup, saucer, glass, in order to down six edibles. You don nine to fifteen items of clothing and one to five of jewelry. You put six to twelve items in your pockets or purse, including a wallet that contains five to fifty items. Reaching your car, you pull out two to fourteen keys, unlock the door, press the handle, sit on the seat, unlock the ignition, grasp the wheel, and manipulate some of twenty-seven controls, such as parking brakes, gas pedal, gearshift, lights, radio (volume, tone, station, antenna, speaker), air conditioner, ashtray, windshield wiper, turn signal, as well as noting some of six gauges.

You reach your destination and park, lock the car, pocket the keys, enter your place of work or shopping through a door, stairway, or elevator. Then you handle between eight and five hundred items, such as pen, pencil, pencil sharpener, papers, envelopes, stamps, reports, graphs, books, machines such as telephones, recorders, dictators, typewriters, calculators, computers (each of which has ten to seventy-five controls), tools of endless variety, and furniture of at least five kinds. If you go out to lunch, you add ten to one hundred items, such as coat, hat, umbrella, overcoat, automobile controls, restaurant door, menu, foods, paper money, coins, credit cards, toothpick, mint, newspaper (which includes three to thirty separate sheets), and watch. When you return home you encounter many of the same things again, plus thirty to four hundred or so of such items as cocktail glass, lawn mower, dinner (with fifteen to fifty items), television (with two to ten controls), toothbrush and paste, nine to twelve items of clothing, pajamas, pillows, lamp, alarm clock.

Altogether in an ordinary day your mind may be called upon to use and keep track of between five hundred and two thousand things. How does it do it?

Unconsciously, mostly. Through repetition whole sequences of behavior involving hundreds of things gradually become habitual and automatic, thus saving for urgent matters the valuable adaptive tool of conscious attention.[4] For example, you may become so engrossed in thought about a difficult problem that you may suddenly "come to" with no recollection whatever of your forty-five-minute drive through traffic. The scope of such habit behavior is enormous, if not infinite.

Of course, we are considering here the challenges and opportunities of the cultural artifacts encountered by a middle-class person. Naturally, both are reduced for the impoverished or deprived, with evident limiting consequences for adaptability to schools, jobs, and so on.

When you are tired or depressed, you may have noticed a sense of dread when faced with the number of things you must manipulate. You may even have noticed occasionally that actions you perform ordinarily "without thinking" suddenly become a conscious effort. Something is interfering with the automatic processes that usually take over routine tasks to leave your mind free for new circumstances that require attention and concentration.[5]

Disturbed Work, Love, Play: Consumption, Sex, Novelty

A patient who worked efficiently as a teller in a bank had felt just such a strain for several months. He noticed that he was becoming annoyed and snapping angrily at people over irritations that would have been ignored before. Later, he found that he was not able to manipulate various office machines and other things with his ordinary skill.

Several weeks after entering treatment with me, one morning he saw a man with a gun in one hand and a paper bag in the other running out of the bank's front door. He vaulted the counter, sprinted out the door, and helped police catch and subdue the culprit. This was all he remembered having done just before the chase. Later he discovered that he had automatically also closed and locked his cash drawer, pocketed the key, and slipped his pen into his shirt pocket. He even had pulled the emergency switch, a maneuver he had been taught to perform in such a crisis but which obviously could never have become a habit since he had never had to employ it before. For the next week I noticed that his eyes were wider, his spirits cheerier. He too noticed the change. The following week his previous sense of being burdened and slowed by all the things in his life gradually returned.

What had happened to him?

Two years before he had lost a promotion to a fellow employee. Everyone, including himself, was surprised at how little disappointment he experienced.

Time swept by for him quickly and happily as before. Then two months before the holdup he married. The change in his feelings began shortly after. Had he been on the same job too long? It had been five and a half years. He wondered if he were tired.

Of course there is a limit to how physically tired each of us can become without impairing ability. At some point we all begin to lose muscular strength, timing, balance, eye-hand coordination, memory, emotional control, and so forth, including the various habits we have built up that allow us to manipulate many things automatically. But this usually occurs only after prolonged and strenuous effort, such as is encountered in athletics, heavy labor, or war combat. The identifying feature of this type of fatigue is that it is relieved rapidly by rest, so that within a day or so the person is restored to his former level of skill in all deliberate and automatic behaviors.[6]

Assuming that he was just tired, my patient tried getting extra rest on weekends without benefit. He was still overwhelmed by the stress of handling and keeping track of the hundreds of things needed in his usual routine, particularly at work. What was wrong?

A simple illustration of some mental factors in his trouble can be drawn from assembly-line work. Although among the most tedious of tasks, ordinarily it is not exhausting enough physically to cause loss of automatic behavior. Most people can learn the needed operations quickly and then find that, except for making minor adjustments occasionally, which they look forward to doing for obvious reasons, they perform them best by habit without conscious attention. If lucky, they soon learn to focus their thoughts on something private, or if not they spend hours of boredom longing for a transistor radio or a neighbor to talk with. Employers who have tried permitting such distractions even intermittently have been amazed to find that work speed and efficiency have increased.[7] It appears that automatic behavior is oiled by whatever pulls the attention and concentration happily elsewhere.[8]

Moreover, assembly-line workers who find that their efficient automatic habits are breaking down in the presence of boredom may also learn to restore them through an unexpected device: altering one or two elements in their customary procedure.

Once I knew a relatively uncomplicated woman who worked in a cannery for years on a repetitive job in which she placed filled bottles in a machine that capped and labeled them. When she first found that the work was weighing on her, she too tried rest without avail. Even after a Sunday in bed the work now required most of the energy she would have preferred to invest in her "True Romance" fantasies. Having been replayed for decades, these fantasies had become a bit too familiar to command her whole attention. The portion of interest that slipped away while she was working went prospecting for something to explore and fell naturally on the movements of her hands. Under the scrutiny of even this fraction of her attention, the automatic habit became shy and clumsy, just as it may when you self-consciously forget how to do a dance step as you unexpectedly catch sight of your movements in a mirror. Discomfort over the loss of habitual skill on the assembly line or dance floor draws the rest of the conscious attention to the activity, further impairing the automatic behavior. This becomes a vicious circle.

One day the bottling lady accidentally learned that she could regain her ability to work automatically just by changing the hand with which she fed the machine, or the one which operated the open-close lever. Within a few moments the bored and wandering edge of her attention had become absorbed contentedly in the fresh movements, freeing the automatic habit to get on with the job. Simultaneously, the balance of her conscious mind not yet fed up with him was freed to get back to her dog-eared daydreams of Prince Charming. The essential point to keep in mind is that a smidgeon of novelty, for the truant edge of the conscious mind to focus on, paradoxically restores the effectiveness of impaired habit.

Common sense would suggest the contrary, that sticking precisely to an old routine should leave attention and concentration freer than changing some details. How can we understand this peculiar circumstance, and has it any wider significance? For instance, how does it relate to the burdened bank teller? We will see in a few moments that it helps us describe the surface mechanics of the clockwork of his neurosis, although we will need to look more deeply later to find the dynamic forces of the mainspring that powers it.

My patient's initial irritability had soon disappeared without apparent reason, leaving him with the major complaint of increasing tiredness and inability to handle with his usual efficiency mainly the many things encountered at work.

He decided to consult a doctor who sensibly explained that the light routine of his office job could not be producing physical exhaustion, and proceeded to rule out hidden disease with examinations and tests. When all proved negative he told the patient he was well physically, but that an emotional disturbance which he did not feel competent to diagnose or treat could account for such symptoms, and referred him to me.

Before phoning for an appointment the patient tried to think the trouble out reasonably himself. He had for years been wrestling daily with too many hundreds of things, and now it was beginning to catch up with him. The answer was therefore to simplify his life, to cut down on the number of things he had to maneuver. For several weeks he did this, eliminating items of toilet ritual, food, clothing, office materials, and so on.

It worked. His fatigue lifted. His mood brightened. He was sure he had found the answer. He began to tell his friends. Then in two weeks the old symptoms began to recur, and further reduction in the number of things in his life failed to rally him again. Even worse, he began to ruminate about the unfairness of his rival's promotion over him.

Then he came to see me. It was plain to me that his temporary improvement had not been the result of subtracting things but of adding *novelty*.

His general physician had alerted me to the time relationship between his marriage and the slump. Without mentioning the hypothesis to the patient, I looked for possible causal connections between his marriage and his depression.

For years he had spent each weekend going out of town to various hiking, fishing, riding, and skiing resorts. A train timetable had been his frequently consulted constant companion during each workday at his desk. These excursions had stopped when he married. The couple now spent their free time completing and decorating their new house.

We found that he had been able to withstand the stress of being stuck in a boring job because he could look forward to a complete change of scenery, activity, and inner experience every five days. The stimulation, the novelty of vacations has been used by doctors for many generations as treatment for nervous symptoms. The couple began to go away on weekends, keeping his old seasonal schedule.

Their doing so produced a dramatic change. He became much worse.

After the second weekend away they gave it up. He then reported a vivid dream:

> I am very hungry. I go to the refrigerator. It is filled with pineapple doughnuts. I am disappointed but take two. I peel some white sugar off the doughnuts and eat them, without pleasure. I look for something else to eat, but all the cupboards and drawers are filled with pineapple doughnuts. I go next door to my neighbor's house. I look in his garage in a big carton. It is full of nothing but pineapple doughnuts. Discouraged, I drive to the market. As I walk up to the door I see that the shelves are lined only with different size packages of pineapple doughnuts. I feel *trapped* and *doomed* and wake up with my heart pounding.

From his previous dreams we had found that for this patient food usually stood for women. When I asked what pineapple doughnuts brought to mind, he recalled that the previous day on his morning coffee break he had shared an apple turnover with a cute new secretary at work.

"Quite a cupcake?" I asked.

The patient laughed, recognizing my use of the term he had always employed to describe the "delicious" girls he was accustomed to pursuing on his premarital weekend adventures.

"Could all the doughnuts refer to many girls?" I wondered.

He was intrigued by the idea but was puzzled as to why the dream food was a doughnut and not a turnover. I mentioned that in our earlier work we had found that a cupcake meant to him a "good" girl who kept her clothes on despite his best efforts to disrobe her. Suddenly he remembered the white sugar he had peeled off the two doughnuts in the dream.

"When I was a kid, Mom used to tell me to handle a cupcake only by the paper to keep my dirty fingers off it. I guess that to me the white fluted paper on a cupcake is a girl's clothing, meant to fend off a dirty-minded man like me."

Apples reminded him of "some apples!" a disrespectful term from his boyhood days signifying a promiscuous girl's breasts. We then discovered that turnovers to him were "naked," having no coating of paper, or even of sugar like the doughnuts. And they had been "turned over." They referred to girls who had been "rolled naked in the hay" and were not clean and pure.

Our progress came to a halt. He did not ask the next obvious question, so I did.

"That takes care of 'apple' and 'turnover,' but why is it '*pine*apple'?" He said that pineapples come from Hawaii. Then he remembered he had met his wife in Hawaii on a summer vacation during which he had planned to devour a bunch of cupcakes. Instead he had spent ten celibate days courting her, and upon their return home had proposed. He now added the final link in the chain of raw material that led to interpretation of the dream.

"A doughnut has a hole in it, unlike a cupcake. But I had to peel away the sugar to eat it. That reminds me of the frosting on our wedding cake. We had to push it aside before we could cut it."

After a few moments of puzzlement, he found the significance to him of all the frosting that was an obstacle: "That means I had to marry her before having intercourse with her."

He then pointed out that the pineapple doughnuts must stand for his wife. Before their marriage he had regarded her as a luscious cupcake, but now found her "distasteful" like the pineapple doughnuts. He thought the dream meant that he was hungrily looking for other girls wherever he went but was disappointed to find his wife everywhere. And that is when he felt trapped and doomed.

A few minutes of silent digestion followed. Then we tied the dream to his daily life. He had been able to bear the tedium of his workaday routine through the magic of frequent references to his timetable. It had always provided his errant attention the little focus of novelty which the label lady found by changing hands. Although his work was by no means as susceptible to automatic performance as hers, it was usual for him to do most of it by habit. And, like hers, his habit functioned well only when conscious mind got out of the way. At work, triggered by the timetable, his mind kept busy with musings about next weekend's adventures. When he married, the excursions were interrupted and the timetable became meaningless. It could not continue to be the novelty focus for channeling attention because now he was no freer psychologically to fantasize at work than to philander on weekends. The dream also explains why he became worse instead of better when he made the apparently "sensible" decision to resume the trips accompanied by his wife. It was not the outdoor sports, but the indoor spice of his seasonal schedule which had lent these weekly jaunts their absorbing and refreshing powers. Added to his emotional inhibition, naturally the physical presence of his wife, although no interference with swimming or skiing, further curtailed the essential ingredient of his teller's paradise.

His newfound consciousness of the dynamics of his symptoms did not automatically cause them to disappear. That required further work.

Gradually he became aware that he had learned from his mother during childhood to consume food not only as nourishment but as the symbol of love, and as the great solace for everyday tensions. He saw then how at puberty, under his father's chiding, he had shifted to the less fattening and seemingly more grown-up craving to consume girls, as though they were really the cupcakes his teen-age slang suggested.

Slowly he found out how he had created his way of life out of the raw materials his circumstances had made available to him. He had to realize that, in a way, this adaptation was precious to him and that he did not want to give it up. In a sense it was his masterpiece. As a peddler treasures his battered old truck that is carefully held together by his amateur repairs, and that has to be nursed along gently or it will die altogether, he was clinging to his neurosis until certain of something better. Even if the peddler gets a powerful new truck, insecurity about change, about having to learn to negotiate the tricky bends in the road without the guidance of the dented fenders, will create a nostalgia that makes it difficult to let go of the old wreck. And so it was with my patient. Only gradually could he give up his unconscious bakeshop theory of women and frustration tolerance, and achieve through a mature relationship with his wife the comfort which formerly had depended on disguised, infantile guzzling. And before the new adaptation solidified it had to seep down to the deeper layers of mind where it could become automatic. When it did so, he was able once again to keep track comfortably of the great number of things which, during his upset, common sense erroneously had told him was the cause of his difficulty.

This process is something like the way you clear the propeller of an outboard motor of lake weeds. You reach down, grasp the unseen tether, and pull it up into the light so you can follow its strands. Then under direct vision you remove them from the screw, freeing it to resume its automatic activity. Finally you release the whole mass to sink out of sight once again, and proceed on your way. Had it not become an obstruction it would not have seen the light of day at all.

And so we have uncovered a paradox. The story of mind is of a trek *toward* consciousness in the control of behavior. And yet in our daily lives we must guard our efficient unconscious automatic functioning from *interference by* consciousness. So when things go wrong, we must bring that worrisome consciousness to bear intensely on the problem—briefly—and then take it away so that the benefit of its intervention will not be interfered with by an overdose.

My reason for including such detail is to illustrate how complex are the workings of man's mind, even in relation to the seemingly simple realm of "things," and therefore how inappropriate are the oft-proposed simpleminded solutions for the personal or social conflicts supposedly growing out of the complexity of our daily lives. While it may be pleasant or philosophically desirable to reduce the number of things we encounter or to take weekend trips, there is no evidence whatever that such change is necessary or conducive to health. What counts is their *significance* to us.

For my cupcake connoisseur most of the many things in his work life were but nuisances he had to put up with in order to acquire the where-withal to pursue his hobby. In and of themselves very few meant any-thing to him. When his symptoms began he naturally took the language of the unconscious literally and assumed he was tired and depressed about all the things he had to deal with because there were so many of them. But as usual the communication from within really referred to people, although it was phrased in terms of things, because he experienced the people he most needed as *things*. It read, "You cannot go on manipulating the many things in your tedious workaday life because the joy of a variety of edible girl-things has gone out of your weekend life."

Before pulling back to examine the role of things in general, we should cast a still deeper glance at our patient example. How did the disturbance shift from his love life to his work life? We will look into work in detail in Section Two. But here we must notice that beyond the intricacies of neurosis lies the dismal fact that the jobs of many people today are toxic to the human spirit. Assembly-line or clerical work, for instance, often stultifies a person's imaginative spark to a degree not approached even by the endless arduous toil of previous centuries. The craftsman or home-steader may have labored fourteen hours a day, but his efforts included planning, designing, and making the thing from raw material to finished product. Doing the work and maintaining standards of excellence took on the aura of a sacred trust, expressed in institutions such as the medieval guild and in the personal pride of conferring identity upon progeny through names such as Miller, Weaver, or Smithson.[9] A fragmentary at-tempt to restore this vanished relationship to work is found today in the often fruitless struggles of the hippie jeweler or sandal-maker to "do his thing."

My patient really loathed the fragmented, repetitive tasks that eroded his identity while supplying a paycheck. But he was able to submerge his hostility and rebelliousness beneath the torrent of gourmet snacks he consumed on weekends. When his marriage blocked the timetable route for channeling the tension of frustrations at his empty job into gratifying daydreams of the weekend feast, his mounting resentment began to erupt as direct anger against people at work, especially his employer. It was the urgent need to deflect this anger, and the retaliation he feared it would provoke, that led to his fatigue and preoccupation with the number of things at work. His inner character, its roots embedded deeply in child-hood training to manage tension submissively by consuming the things given to good boys, demanded that he remain polite and ingratiating to his boss, the present-day representative of the giving parental authority. Without clear awareness of the process he quickly stifled the budding annoyance at people and transformed it into safer resentment of *things*.

How did all this emerge during treatment? Naturally he was not able to report inner workings of aspects of his mind of which he was unaware. But he was able to demonstrate the difficulty through his behavior toward me, giving me the opportunity first to understand him, and then to help him comprehend and change himself.

When we had worked out the significance of the doughnut dream and its connections, my patient experienced another eruption of anger at his boss. This evaporated in a few days as before, but this time was replaced by only slightly increased on-the-job "thing-symptoms."

The first day he was anger-free at work he missed the freeway turnoff to my office and was fifteen minutes late for his appointment. He complained that the route he had been traveling without a hitch for over a year had suddenly become too much of a burden for him. At the next session he unaccountably knocked a pile of magazines off a table in my waiting room, grimacing piteously to underline his well-intentioned helplessness to handle the many things in my office. After he left I discovered that he had somehow forgotten to raise the toilet seat in my office restroom and had spattered it with urine.

At the next hour I tentatively asked him if he could see any significance in these unaccustomed blunders.

"I must be getting worse despite your help."

By now it was clear to me that his anger, so frightening when experienced in relation to the boss, was being shifted onto me as a safer target. But he was still too scared to feel it consciously and express it directly, so it literally spilled over onto *my* "things." I had made a note in my records to this effect before a striking confirmation began at the next hour.

Describing his depression the patient blurted, "Lately nothing seems to hit the spot!" A few minutes later he morosely ground out his cigarette on the edge of the ashtray in such a way that for the first time he caused live embers to fall onto upholstery and carpet. He scooped them up contritely. Toward the end of the same hour he forgot to tap a cigarette and an inch of ashes fell to the floor. At the next hour he reported being chagrined at his clumsiness while smoking, avowed that it never happened elsewhere, and promptly forgot a lit cigarette propped on the ashtray edge so that when it became shorter it fell while burning onto the tabletop.

A phrase Freud had spoken on a similar occasion, reported to me by my analyst, sprang into my head.

"What have you got against me today?"

Profuse apologies followed. He stopped smoking during sessions completely. But the anger found other means to show itself. We wrestled for weeks with his denials that he was angry with me. Then he began to express resentment of the distance of my office, the difficulty parking there, the complexity of the elevators, and, at last, the "impossibility of getting you to say anything." Continued work showed him that it was the same quality of feeling he had been too afraid to experience toward the boss. Eventually, through a series of dreams we were able to find connections between this feeling and resentment of his father.

At that point he started to feel anger belatedly toward his wife—the anger one would have expected him to have experienced when her entry into his life precipitated his trouble. After months more of effort, he became aware of having felt unloved by mother in childhood, and a resultant admixture of rage in what he had always believed was pure love for her.

At this point we had achieved the following understanding and progress: He had been able to remain unaware of resentment against job and boss so long as his weekends were weekly escapes. His irrational expectation of love and marriage had been that his wife would amplify these rewards as had both his parents. When instead her presence curtailed them, his anger mounted. He tried vainly to get increased satisfactions from his job. Of course, this was impossible, and he grew still angrier. Since he could not permit himself to attack wife or boss directly, the latent resentment of his job was intensified, and in conformity with his usual pattern was transformed into inability to deal with things at the office. Through shifting the anger into the laboratory of treatment in my office, he was able to become aware of these warded-off feelings, and (in brief) find ways to resolve the conflicts without illness. His tiredness and difficulty in managing things disappeared.

Finally, it became plain that he had chosen and stayed with his job because it had been in keeping with his emotional problems. When he resolved these conflicts, he no longer needed to remain on that job. Near the end of therapy he took his wife skiing again. He enjoyed being with her so much this time that the following Monday he found an opening as assistant manager at another branch involving less absorption with "things," but with more possibility for zestful investment of self in work. During two more years of work there is not room even to sketch here, together we arrived with mutual conviction at a coherent picture of his overall maturation and development. What is more important, subtle but far-reaching changes occurred in every part of his functioning. As he slowly changed his way of adapting to life and the structure of his "self," he came to understand how his parents in their striving to give him everything had focused him on *every thing*. He even came to forgive them for having transmitted to him a heavy dose of the thingishness of the society in which he grew up. And gradually his "self-centeredness" decreased, being steadily replaced by an easy concern for the well-being of his wife and others as people.

Meaning of Things

Now we must lift our eyes beyond the dehumanizing nature of many jobs, and the complexities of neurosis, to grasp the changed role of things in our society in general. We must observe first that this man, and all of us, live surrounded by things largely robbed of their enduring significance.

All sorts of products are part of our experience only briefly. Even those that formerly were durable are rapidly outdated by acceleration in the rate of design improvement or planned obsolescence, or the fact that they are manufactured to be disposable. The Kleenex you discard immediately, the ball-point pen you throw away in a week, the threadbare suit you give away in six months, the car you trade in after a year, the house you sell after three years—how can any of these things become significant in the way that a linen hankerchief, a personal fountain pen, a fine gabardine suit, an imperishable Pierce-Arrow, or a family homestead once was? The woodburning locomotive of a hundred years ago, the product of much less rapid engineering progress, was converted to coal after several decades of service, and then was passed appreciatively through more generations of engineers before being retired as a museum piece in the 1920s. Today the average life of a diesel locomotive is eight years.[10] I am not arguing for arrest of technical progress. However, it is important to remember that two hundred years ago a man's psychological identity, although no doubt disturbed by interpersonal stress then as now, was bolstered in ways that have nearly disappeared. One of these was that a large percent of the "things" in his life had lasting meaning! An American might enjoy his homespun clothes for twenty years, sit his favorite horse for fifteen, drive his wagon for fifty. In Daniel Boone's time all his life a man might eat venison taken with his grandfather's rifle, and then pass the same gun on to his grandson. All these durable things carried a supportive significance for your own, your forebears', and your descendants' identities that practically nothing but an occasional book, dish, or pocket watch can have for us today. People today cling to a tattered jacket or perforated shoes yearning to keep touch at least with their own individual past.

When you consider that all things are tools, and that, after words, tools are the most "identifying" features of man's activity,[11] it is plain that the short life of most of our things results in our living in a kind of chronic identity-deficiency state which exists largely outside our awareness. The resultant hunger is what gives the ruins of ancient civilizations and the surviving buildings of medieval Europe a large part of their magnetic appeal. The same need lies behind much of our fascination with antiques. But collecting a flintlock rifle to hang over the fireplace can never supply more than a sliver of the identity support which inheriting and bequeathing that tool provided its several generations of users. Especially when the fine rifle you purchased twenty years ago itself is now looked upon by people as an antique.

Second, when your identity loses the support of things with significance it begins a diffuse searching for them. It then becomes that much more difficult to relate one's "self" to another human being as a person.

The unsatisfied hunger for things with lasting significance becomes distorted into a lasting craving to consume a significant number of things. And the force of such appetite adds to any earlier tendency to treat people as things to be devoured.

Now there is evidence that we can increase considerably the capacity of mind to deal with things. Devices such as teaching machines, sleep-teaching machines, driving simulators, rapid-reading training, drugs, hypnosis, and so on all may have a place in such programs.[12] So we need not necessarily reduce the number of things mind must manage. But it behooves us, contrary to current trends, to improve the *quality* and *durability* of at least some of the things with which that mind must deal directly, and upon which its identity must continue to lean. This means that we must guide production of things in future somewhat according to their significance rather than just their objective use. In relation to things, we must be concerned not only with their worth, but with our values.

Finally, you will notice that here, rather than techniques for increasing mental performance, I have emphasized a potential control for enhancing identity and mental health. Later we will look again at this problem in relation to work, love, and play. But before moving on we should take a moment to gauge the role things, consciousness, and novelty may play in our adaptation to other aspects of the demands of reality.

We all know that a few hours of travel by today's jet has supplanted the several days required by yesterday's train, disrupting our senses of space and time. We understand how superstition and magic withered faster than science filled the gap they left in man's sense of safety, how family and tribe mores crumbled faster than new morality grew, how the range of our choices of occupation, residence, sex partner, and possessions expanded beyond our capacity to prefer. All these have produced such an enormous increase in the rate of change in the demands of the reality to which we must adapt that we have been torn loose from the security of many of our old supports of identity and mental health. As we move into a world of bottle-bred babies, clonal copies of people, transplanted brains, suspended and prolonged lifespans, creative cyborgs, and avalanches of depersonalized things, the mind may whimper a bit for the familiar scarcity of the bad old days. We may yearn to restore their slower pace of change and their illusion of certainty.

To avoid a stampeding escape from new freedom into old tyranny, we need new supports of identity. They will be built best by seeing to it that the joy of novelty is pursued, but not in directions that degrade people into things; that good new things are produced, but not in directions that erase their human significance; that consciousness is sharpened, but not used in directions that interfere with useful habit or prevent understanding of subtle inner human experience.

Demands of Our Own Urges

Consciousness, Wishes, Uncertainty

So it is plainly urgent that consciousness not be allowed to interfere with the smooth functioning of automatic habit where it deals effectively with external reality. But we must recognize also that it is infinitely more important that consciousness not be allowed to *neglect* the process of controlling inner urges.

I am not arguing that consciousness is needed ordinarily to guide the movements required in downing a fancy dessert or making love to a pretty girl, let alone to the process of distinguishing the two enterprises. Once you have decided that the chocolate mousse is good and ready, or the lady is willing and able, that is not the best time for deliberation. But before you get to that point, while you are deciding whether and under what circumstances to satisfy either impulse, and which one first, then consciousness is indispensable. Its role is even more evident in relation to activities with highly lethal potentiality, such as driving a car.

We have glimpsed the universal tendency to adapt to change, and have seen that mind is the most highly developed means for producing adaptation of living creatures. We saw that in contrast to lower animals, the behavior that mind controls in man, although motivated in part by physiologic urges or drives, consists mostly of learned behavior patterns which often become motivations stronger than the physiologic urges themselves.[13]

In general our troubles come from the learned urges. Unlearned urges, such as hunger, erotic need, need for sleep, need for company, and so on, are problems mainly because of the complicated and often conflicting learned behavior we have evolved as ways of satisfying them. We must satisfy hunger, for instance, through a welter of learned urges, to earn money to pay for food, to have it prepared in what we believe to be a hygienic, tasty, and religiously correct manner, and not to become obese from eating too much of it. We have seen how much more complicated the situation is in relation to sex. And we all know, too, that such complexities are part of the warp and woof of the web we prize as civilization. A principal mystery of mind is how any of us remain emotionally well while threading our way through this adaptational tangle.

We traced earlier how man's crucial sense of responsibility for his fate has passed through several stages since the early Stone Age, which today leave us in a better position. The first human minds took the great leap into self-confidence which we described as magic. Its birth meant that man's mind presumed it could control nature! Every rock, tree, animal, plant, and river was alive, and would reward or punish man according to whether his behavior pleased or offended its spirit. All he had to do was learn which behavior produced which reaction, just as he did while growing up with his parents.

Then gods were devised, whose tendency, like man's, to be impulsive, self-indulgent, and cruel allowed for less certainty. But they might sometimes be controlled by sacrifices or good behavior, explanation, persuasion, flattery, or downright trickery.[14]

The mind moved a big step further when monotheists concluded that God was all-knowing and could not be deceived.

To win his approval required the radically different characteristic of sincerity. Increasingly the test this God used was doing justice to God and man. The result was a shift from *chicanery* to *integrity* as the ideal for man's mind. Even so, since God's will remained inscrutable, one could not know with certainty what would be God's notion of justice as he rewarded man's devotion. As it has millions of other men, this problem puzzled Job.

As long as man's terrestrial power to translate wishes into facts remained trivial, it remained necessary for him to invent omnipotent friends. Then science began to arm us to control disease, famines, floods, and other "acts of God." Paradoxically, with new power in his hand, man since then has been finding the courage to recognize and tolerate a little better the fact that uncertainty is his perpetual lot. An example is our current sur-

prised recognition that nowadays our environment is reacting vengefully
to the past century's lack of respect. Hopefully, "neo-animist" conserva-
tionists may yet save us from poisoning ourselves.

Some consequences of this progression for the mind are:

As we are less and less in need of God's approval, we are more and
more in danger from our own multiplying power.

As we feel less and less guilty about transgressing God's laws, we are
more and more aware that we are guilty of transgressing man's rights.

Now that science is rendering obsolete the manipulation, propitiation
of, or submission to deity, the focus of human mind shifts inward to
master the wishing, impulsive brute within us by the reasonable self
that can heed not only inner demands but the requirements of outer
reality.

Understanding and controlling all this requires the most careful and
consistent application of consciousness, one manifestation of which is
rationality.

Rationality, Education, Human Potential

Dr. William Wahl of the Department of Psychiatry, University of California, Los Angeles, believes there is a widespread increase in man's
rationality, as seen in the general decline in religious involvement, whether
formal or secular. He views this as hopeful for man's future because it
indicates he will be less dominated by superstition and less willing to
maim and kill those who disagree with him.[15] I would agree, provided
that we are able to generate as compelling an identification of the individual self with all members of the human species as once existed between
the individual self and God. Only then does the increase in rationality
move to bring about on earth the favorable conditions for human life
which in the past were credible only as a part of one version or another of
the happy hunting ground. And as we all know, there are enormous
forces, such as nationalism, economic privilege, and political power that
exert their influence not only against rationality but against allegiance to
mankind as a whole. Imagine the uproar if suddenly by some peculiar happenstance the federal government, the automobile manufacturers, and
the advertising industry found themselves unable to do anything that
violated rationality and allegiance to mankind!

Come to think of it, as uproars go, it might not be so bad.

As James Harvey Robinson pointed out long ago, intelligence, of
which rationality is one aspect, remains the one hope for meeting the

crisis of civilized society which has not been discredited, because it has not been tried on any large scale outside the realm of science. Rationality leads to free inquiry and honest teaching. And although these are somewhat more respectable than in Robinson's day, what he says about the teaching of our children is still basically correct:

> Think of a teacher in the public schools recounting the more illuminating facts about the municipal government under which he lives, with due attention to graft and jobs! So, courses in government, political economy, sociology, and ethics confine themselves to inoffensive generalizations, harmless details of organization, and the commonplaces of routine morality, for only in that way can they escape being controversial. Teachers are rarely able or inclined to explain our social life and its presuppositions with sufficient insight and honesty to produce any very important results. Even if they are tempted to tell the essential facts they dare not do so, for fear of losing their places, amid the applause of all the righteously minded. . . . We sedulously inculcate in the coming generation exactly the same illusions and the same ill-placed confidence in . . . institutions . . . that have brought the world to the pass in which we find it.[16]

As Bertrand Russell put it, "Should the workingman think freely about property? What then will become of us, the rich? Should young men and women think freely about sex? What then will become of morality? Should soldiers think freely about war? What then will become of military discipline?"[17]

But in the long perpective, free inquiry and honest teaching are leading to just the overthrow of tradition he envisioned. And rationality is increasing. Civilized nations no longer conduct primarily religious wars. In the past, thousands of people died as others tried to obey the biblical injunction "Thou shalt not suffer a witch to live." A witch-hunt today, although as irrational and sometimes as cruel in its long-term effects, at least does not involve ritual murder. The notion of "trial by ordeal," that one could determine guilt or innocence through torture, has been abandoned. We are on the way to relinquishing the idea, tragically promulgated by some organized religions, that one is as guilty for thoughts as for deeds. We no longer draw and quarter a bandit or hang an eight-year-old child for stealing a loaf of bread. Gradually we are modifying the destructive harshness of laws regulating private sexual behavior, abortion, incarceration for mental illness. And so on.

Although millions are still slaughtered in our purges, revolutions, and wars, more millions now recognize, abhor, and strive to end these irrationalities.

On the other hand, our present progress toward fuller and more humane life could be accelerated by our learning to take up the problems on the human agenda in proper sequence. It has been said that there is a time for everything. One of the obstacles to advance of civilization is the addiction to demanding answers to questions too soon.

We today must assign priority to various questions that must be answered before others can be approached, including those we regard as transcendental, so as to bring about safely the revolution that is boiling up under us irresistibly. For instance, we must first determine what are our changed values before we can decide the kind of family structure appropriate for raising people who can live by them.

Education remains the great tool through which mind can both create this revolution and also be controlled. As always, who guides education, and toward what end, will determine which values are promoted and which suppressed. Therefore this remains a hotly contested issue.

Whether or not we choose to unshackle it, there is no doubt that the human psyche is a vast untapped mine whose dimensions we can only surmise at present. The cupcake fancier's dreams and treatment demonstrate a talent for poetic diction and psychological sleuthing that one would not suspect from his mundane exterior. Evidence from hypnosis, dreams, and emergency behavior indicates that there are enormous unused mental powers in all of us exhibited as feats of memory and problem solving sometimes astoundingly beyond the ordinary. Kekule, discoverer of the structure of the benzene ring, reported that the principle came to him in a dream represented by a snake catching its own tail.[18] Individuals as different as Helmholtz, Goethe, Gauss, and Poincaré have reported that inspiration often sprang into their minds after a period of fatiguing effort followed by sleep, a result of unconscious creativity.[19] Some time ago, according to a news story, a man saw that a baby was about to fall from a sixth-floor window, and before he knew his own intention managed to estimate the angle of fall and so position himself as to be able to catch the infant with only minimal injury to either of them. And a few years ago the papers carried a story of a young man confined to a wheelchair by polio disability who somehow managed to hurdle a fence and climb a jungle gym to rescue a strangling child.[20]

Then why do we see the abundant imagination and creativity of charming, spontaneous children give way before our eyes to the stultified, inhibited, rigid, and narrowly conformist tedium of the minds of adults? Allowing for the cooling of the youthful spark that accompanies biological maturation which we can observe even in animals, and for the influence of the home, there is no doubt that much of this transformation results from the way in which we educate our children. And there is no doubt that we could improve their minds by improving the part of their education conducted in schools.

Psychologist Jerome Kagan is among many who emphasize the importance of environmental stimulation in the development of mind, which as we have already seen can even increase brain growth. He says, "The baby is a novelty-digesting machine that devours change,"[21] referring to the sort of novelty that commands full attention rather than the partial sort we discussed earlier. This conclusion is confirmed by the work of Dr. Lewis P. Lipsitt who has shown that even one-day-old infants can discriminate between different sounds and smells.[22] At Yale it has been demonstrated that a three-month-old baby can learn to not only follow but anticipate a pattern of blinking lights. By age four so much learning has already occurred that a twenty point potential IQ gap may show up between slum-raised and middle-class children with good environmental stimulation, especially parents who speak to them easily and well. If properly taught, four-year-olds can learn to deal with factoring, negative numbers, and simple algebra.[23]

As a result of all this new information on the control of development of the mind, the National Education Association has made the revolutionary proposal that all children begin a formal education program at age four.[24] Think what it will mean to the average American child-centered family for mother to be freed (or deprived) of the burden of her little one a whole year or two earlier, and for father to come home to requests that he help little Oedipus with his algebra!

Our Western democratic ideas have been applied to providing for girls the same educational opportunities available to men. Other modern societies such as the Soviet Union have for some time supplemented this idea with extra education that is designed to take into account the biological differences between the sexes.[25] Now it turns out that the innate part of these differences is evident from birth. Male and female babies tend to develop and learn different skills at different rates. And Dr. Nancy Bayley has concluded from a forty-year study that the IQ of grown women is highest in those who as babies began the earliest to use their vocal abilities to express eagerness, pleasure, and delight. But in boys early vocalization is not related to eventual intelligence.[26]

It may prove as difficult to reverse the trend toward unisex in education as it has in hair length, clothing, and behavior. But it may be necessary to do so if the true democratic ideal of providing each human being with the particular opportunities he needs is to be achieved. Unless, of course, hermaphrodites in the future should supplant us poor partial people.

Dr. Nome Baker and others have shown that fourth- through seventh-grade children with superior but not genius-level IQs are capable of learning and understanding the same scientific subject matter as are university graduate students engaged in active research.[27] This may mean that intellectually, at least, we are wasting a full decade of their youthful lives and creativity with our present time-marking school programs.

Then there is the wholly unknown territory of the specially gifted, the children who at age three or five demonstrate astonishing ability in musical composition, mathematics, painting, language, and so on. We know that Bach and Mozart were exposed at home to much musical stimulation, but that other children with the same opportunity did not respond in the same way. There must be some innate factor in such unusual talents, perhaps a genetic one.

Precisely what these special abilities consist of or depend upon, whether they may be mutually incompatible with other desirable qualities, whether they are more widespread than we think, whether they should be sought out or produced deliberately are all uncertain. But it seems likely that methods for exerting control over these mental attributes may confront us not too far in the future with the necessity to make choices made heretofore by chance. Many high school students have contributed excellent new research in medicine, physics, and chemistry which a few decades ago would have been thought impossible. The personality of such accomplished youngsters is no doubt strengthened by such success. But what about emotional stresses of such high-level activity on them and their possibly less gifted age-mates?

Richard Dempsey has found that by reducing the number and extending the length of high school classes, students are enabled to cover more material without deleterious effect on their tested achievement or grade-point averages. This and other modifications in programs designed to reduce pressure on students have had the even more significant result of reducing vandalism, truancy, and strife among cliques, and of cutting in half the tested level of student anxiety.[28]

As Eric Hoffer has pointed out, much of history has been made to happen by juveniles.[29] If these trends toward early learning become generalized as to subject matter and to all children, we may soon be faced with convincing demands from the young, whose education we have so ingeniously enriched, to lower the voting age not just to eighteen but to eight. At first glance the idea may seem as ludicrous to you as it did when it occurred to me. But fantastic as it is, does the notion of the child exercising at least limited political power outdistance the idea of his mastering mathematics, biochemistry, history, anthropology, economics? Suppose the vote applied at first only in municipal elections. The well-being of the community depends largely on the judgment, discretion, and humanity of its voters. From what I know of distorted adults, it might be that these qualities would be at least as prevalent in children. An extra dividend might be that people would learn early in life to wrestle with and master the intricacies of county party committee candidacies, constitutional changes, and bond issues.

Parents concerned about the anxiety under which their children live now might profitably ponder the effects upon their well-being of such increased responsibility. In my view it would be beneficial. There is good evidence from animal and human research that emotional illness is much more likely when the individual feels helpless in the face of threat than if there is something he can do about the danger.[30] However, application of all this new understanding to educational procedures generally could so increase the generation gap that a new profession of "intergeneration arbitrator" will be required. That is, unless the graduates also learn how to understand each successive crop of new and old fogies.

Neurosis, Personality, Sexuality

Helplessness in the face of threat and the generation gap brings us to the subject of neurosis, the result of breakdown in the capacity to reconcile and compromise conflicting urges and necessities. Much of the dismal transfiguration of buoyant childhood into constricted adult personalities I attributed earlier to unfortunate education. A large part of the balance is brought about by neurosis. Dr. Wahl believes that if it were possible to put into action immediately what we now know about the causes of neurosis, we could transform the world in a generation.[31] While I would agree that full application of present knowledge would result in a big decrease in neurotic (and psychotic) suffering, I am more conservative in estimating the efficacy of what we now know relative to the enormous areas yet unknown. Much of human suffering still stems from ignorance, especially in relation to mental illness.

Freud deduced from study of adult neurotics that an enormous part of adult personality depends upon early experience.[32] Other analysts have confirmed his conclusions by direct study and followup of children.[33] Animal behaviorists such as Harry Harlow and Konrad Lorenz have corroborated the cruciality and frequently the irreversibility of the effects of early experience through research with animals.[34] However, recent work with human beings by social scientists as well as clinicians has indicated that large areas of personality functioning remain more flexible into adult life than had been believed previously. Encouraged by these results, substantial human research is now under way.

So crucial a matter as human sexual physiology is only now beginning to receive scientific attention,[35] after thousands of years of uninformed pronouncements by bigots, alarmists, inquisitors, poets, libertines, and psychologists.

As indicated earlier (pp. 149–166) anthropologists have shown that each culture tends to generate a basic personality pattern.[36] As yet not understood, and of crucial importance is precisely *how*. The consequences for human life and health can be enormous when more information creates better possibilities for control.

Application of teams of scientists, armed with computers to analyze the divergent personality patterns that result from growing up on the lower East Side of New York City, on a kibbutz in Israel, in a small town in Chile, in an Eskimo village, and so on, would provide priceless information. So would a comparison of the personalities of children who are swaddled in infancy, such as American Indians and Polish peasants, with those who are not, such as Montanans and Tahitians. So would a comparison of children who are fully clothed from infancy, and almost never allowed to see other children or adults nude, with those who don clothes only when puberty signals sexual maturity, and who are shown in childhood not only adult bodies but techniques of sexual intercourse. So would a comparison of personalities of children for whom money and an allowance are made important incentives with those for whom they are not. There is little doubt that when we understand the impacts of these and other factors we will be able to design environments to develop or suppress whatever human or institutional characteristics are desired, such as the degree of competitiveness or synergy within a society, ultimately reducing the amount of suffering caused by neurosis and other mental illness. And there is no doubt also that the present fabric of society would be ripped apart by the application of such knowledge. Unconscious recognition of this potentiality may be a powerful factor in keeping our scientific minds and machines deflected into such endeavors as "market research" and "simulation saturation bombing."

All these possibilities, whatever their hazards, offer promise of greatly enhanced mental powers. But amid all this positive adventure there are signs in present life of serious interferences with further development of useful controls of mind.

It seems to me on reflection that most of the booby traps are based on one common crucial error: the mistaking of narrow bias for comprehensive truth. Many zealously promoted ideas about man and his impulses fail to take into account enough even of what is currently known about man. As a result of not considering the total picture, solemn recommendations are made which may have hideous consequences. The tragedies brought about by smog accumulation, cigarette smoking, and medical use of thalidomide are obvious instances from other fields of insufficient application of consciousness to the early stages of behavior regulation. In the realm of mind, failure to try consciously to see the whole picture can have equally monstrous results.

Seeing the total picture is difficult when so much of it is invisible. Yet the fact that so much less is known about mind only increases our obligation to proceed thoughtfully.

Pseudo { Certainty / Liberty

We are familiar with the dangerous social conflicts that boil up over separation of church and state, the pressure for full citizenship of minorities, and the teaching of nationalistic allegiances to country versus international allegiance to mankind. Another danger of equal dimension comes from those who pretend to be building on the progress made in recent centuries against superstition and toward rationality, but who in reality propose to substitute their own versions of superstitions and irrationality. The late George Lincoln Rockwell's American Nazi party, L. Ron Hubbard's pseudoscientific Dianetics and Scientology, and Timothy Leary's new religion are examples. The latter is illustrative of many.

Leary's slogan, "Tune in, turn on, drop out," urges everyone to reject as irrelevant practically everything now generally accepted. He and his followers seem not to grasp the simple fact that if the larger community were to join them, they would have nothing to drop out of. Then they include on their list of bourgeois conventions to be disparaged even the use of words for communication. With this one stroke they would prevent any precise tuning in to one another, and also simultaneously deprive themselves of man's most important daily use of symbols, which as we have seen is his crucial advance over animals. They seem not to grasp that LSD itself, their sacramental substance, exists as a hallucinogen a thousand times more potent than those commonly found in nature only because of man's continual diligence expressed in chemistry. Or that their activities are promoted as good business and rewarded by large amounts of the same cash as other "successful" organized human enterprises.

I do not belittle either the engaging irreverence or the moral sense that impels some of Leary's followers. But these assets do not obliterate the fact that their various pronouncements are often mutually contradictory, apparently without their being aware of it. An example is the psychiatric resident doctor who became unable to communicate with the nurses on his ward for the first time following several LSD trips. They could understand his scoldings when his patients missed morning activities because they overslept, but the nurses were bewildered to be berated by him also for awakening the patients on time. This sort of illogicality, this kind of irrationality, is not confined to but increasingly is being recognized as highly characteristic of users of LSD and other psychedelic drugs.

Among the menaces to development of healthy controls of mind are the current zealots of anti-Victorianism. Their theme, variously disguised, goes on always unchanged: prevention of pleasure is the root of all evil; a wish must always be gratified. Fun and happiness are the appropriate human goals.

This group is the heir of the early misinterpreters of Freud who tried to improve education on the basis of their misunderstanding and wound up causing more injury to children than our traditional schools. Stories are still heard of elementary schools they founded upon the erroneous notion that, since neurosis arises in the course of excess and misdirected repression, the best way to raise children is to do away with repression altogether. Accordingly, school days commenced with reenactment of birth by climbing through a cow's pelvis, and proceeded to communal disrobing for a full day of free play, involving putting into action the child's impulses to scream, smear, explore, and destroy, stopping short only of mayhem and murder. There was consternation among parents and faculty when after several years such "nonfrustration" children turned out to be pariahs instead of paragons. Some were not just awful. They were pitifully psychopathic or psychotic, as ought to have been predictable by any sensible observer taking into account the whole human picture.

The first of these would surely have been Freud. He clearly saw that, in addition to consistent parental love, a child must have structure in his outside world in order to have models from which an inner structure of personality may be built.

Parents remain anxious that they will damage their children by exercising their authority in establishing limits for children. They recognize that in a world where realities are changing faster than our ability to adapt to them, it is hazardous to a child to grow up with rigid authoritarian ideas and attitudes taken over from parents. But the solution is certainly not to abandon the child to his own impulses and undeveloped self-control.

I find it helpful to offer parents this notion of what must be conveyed to a child: "I am grown up and you are a child. Until you are old enough to take care of yourself, I am going to take care of you. This means that for now you have to *do* as I say even though you think I am wrong. But you *don't have to think I'm right*. You just have to do what I tell you. When you are grown up you can do as you decide because you will be ready to take care of yourself." As the child matures into rational thought, something like this should be added: "When you think I'm wrong you can tell me so, and I'll think about what you say. I might change my mind. But whether I go along with you or not, I am still the grownup and you have to do as I say."

Parents make two objections. On the one hand, they ask, won't my child be injured by this authoritarian behavior? My answer is that exercise of appropriate authority is not authoritarianism. Then some want to know if children don't need to believe their parents 100 percent right to feel secure. I answer, if they need to at a particular stage, children will believe that no matter what you say to them. What they need even more is help in *getting over* needing to believe their parents are perfect in order to feel secure. In other words, they need to be able to accept that life can still be generally safe and good even though nobody is perfect. Or put still more broadly, as adults we must accept that most things and people are going to be only rough approximations at best of the perfection we all would like, and yet we can find life marvelous.

Most important of all, children need to see that their parents are secure enough to accept their own imperfection and still be unwavering in carrying out the responsibility of taking care of the child. Children in London during the Nazi bombing were able to withstand the terror and destruction if only they had this sort of adult taking care of them. With such parents, children might someday not only come to deserve to vote before puberty but have a better chance of developing the courage and self-control to adapt thereafter as adults to a life of continually accelerating change.

The conviction that urges or wishes should be gratified the moment they appear nowadays permeates all parts of our lives. The coffee break is to me an apt example. I enjoy satisfying a well-developed appetite at lunch. Then I don't eat again until dinner time has restored my zest for food. After the evening meal I don't eat again until breakfast next morning.

I don't recommend this regime for physical health, for some evidence suggests that five or six smaller meals a day provide better nourishment and digestive function for some people. But for me, eating more than three times a day has a most unfavorable effect: I am not hungry at any mealtime. After a few days of never experiencing and gratifying a strong appetite I begin to feel a vague disappointment and depression, and resume my three-meal schedule with relief. If I go to coffee break with friends they are sometimes annoyed if I don't eat with them. One once said to me exasperatedly, "Don't you have any needs!" I tried to explain to him that I had only a little appetite at eleven and enjoyed waiting to eat until I felt really hungry for lunch. He was unable to grasp what I meant, for to him the postponement of any sort of gratification could only be based on puritanical self-denial.

Listening to good music when I am free to give it my attention is a great pleasure for me. The background music we are deluged by forces musical morsels on me all day when they serve only to distract my attention and to spoil my appetite for an evening concert. So I avoid places that play background music.

I used to know an old chef who understood from bitter experience that the price of constant tasting is loss of appetite. He also understood that a delicate balance must be sought between the delight of novelty and the disgust of gluttony. Once I heard him caution a younger colleague about his interest in the pretty young waitresses: "Don't pinch them all, Roscoe, or it will get like with the food."

Psychiatry, and particularly psychoanalysis, are often and unjustly tarred with the brush of the Fun ethic. Both live-it-up exploiters and puritanical critics say that our principle runs, "Explore and understand what your wishes are, and their origins, so that then you can be free to act upon them and feel marvelous." A much more accurate and fair, although also overcondensed articulation, is, "Examine and develop your reasonable self, so that then you can better accord gratification of your wishes with the demands of reality, including the rights of others, regardless of how you feel about it." Leary and his followers, as well as others who reject the reality of reality, are going to be as unhappy with this formulation as the puritans are with the other.

The impairment of the relationship to reality is one reason psychiatrists are so deeply concerned with the uncontrolled use of psychedelic drugs by the general public. No qualified and responsible observer has advanced any convincing evidence of improvement in intellect or creativity brought about by these agents, although individuals often report such effects. Claims have been made that severe alcoholics have stopped drinking after one LSD experience.[37] But even the therapeutic assertions have been negated by more recent studies which showed them to have been "scientifically unjustified."[38] And it should be remembered that the same therapeutic effect has been attributed to seeing a ghost. For most people the best that can be said is that often the drugs cause no impairment.

So the mind is not "expanded," although sometimes the part of it that thinks rationally is severely injured. With others, it seems rather that the parts of the mind which perceive and feel are torn loose from the control of the reasonable part which remains in contact with reality.[39] As a premise for living, this is simply a fancy desexualized version of the Fun ethic in which, instead of Victorian taboos, the bounds of reality in general become the enemy. Consider the consequences of destroying the hard-won victories of mind in freeing itself from ignorance and superstition if the psychedelic experiment became general.

The other reason for psychiatrists' concern is that we are called upon increasingly to pick up and try to repair the wreckage of personality which such drugs induce. In many cases we are not able to prevent the physical mutilation, prolonged psychoses, and suicides that result. Courts might require convicted users or suppliers of these chemicals for unsupervised general use to visit their surviving victims in chronic psychiatric wards.

These enthusiasts crop up in disconcerting guise nowadays. A Catholic nun, complete with regulation beatific countenance, rhapsodized to me at a recent meeting, "Doctor, I just *know* that LSD will bring about the great expansion of the mind we've all been *wishing* for." Startled, I asked mildly whether she had taken the drug or had some other experience with it. "No," she replied, "I just *believe* in it."

The incongruity of this endorsement toppled my ordinary diplomacy in talking with strangers. "Don't you think it would be wise to interpose some evidence between your wishes and your beliefs?" I asked. That must qualify me as some sort of champion of the *faux pas*. The strangest part of it all is that she was so transported by the idea of LSD that she did not notice my megagoof, and only smiled ecstatically and asked, "Oh, do you think so?"

I wonder what the impact on the community would be if organized religion became the purveyor of LSD. Its users have been compared with persecuted early Christians. If the churchmen became LSD promoters, it could set the stage for creation of a new wave of religious martyrs.

There are many other movements in psychology today which do not try to break up the individual psyche, but rather the barriers *between* psyches. They operate on the different premise that the more unrestricted expression of feelings between strangers the better. Some weekend sensitivity training groups, basic encounter groups, body awareness groups, and so on turn into short-term orgies of mutual hostile attack, sexual activity, or crying jags in which everyone's progress is judged according to how completely he has bared himself. These procedures fail to take into account that healthy ego function requires hierarchies of privacy that are broken down only under appropriate special circumstances.[40] In our culture the healthy person does not disrobe psychologically or physically with a group of strangers. He discriminates between various individuals when it comes to intimate confidences or sexual intercourse, expressing hostility, or crying. A psychologically healthy person may permit a stranger to see him completely undressed when in the special situation of a patient visiting a doctor, but removes only footwear while talking to a shoe salesman. Again it is a matter of taking into account the requirements of reality as well as subjective impulse. In a properly conducted psychotherapy group, for example, intimate revelations are not encouraged or forthcoming until the relationships built up among the participants justify them.[41]

Consciousness and Community

Nevertheless, when appropriately employed, the increased openness of communication that is possible nowadays offers promise for enlarging our controls over some forms of disturbed mental functioning. There are hopeful prospects for curing severe personality disorders in the various forms of therapeutic community that are being developed in hospitals and in some prisons.

Another especially impressive new resource for control of mind is the organization called Synanon,* which began in Santa Monica, California, as a modest attempt to help a few drug addicts.[42] The operation has expanded into a social movement with the objective of helping anyone who wants to learn to be more honest and grown-up, whether or not ever addicted to drugs. The essence of the Synanon program is to develop a greater awareness of one's actual day-to-day functioning, so that in time and with the ongoing help of one's fellow participants, he can learn to deal with impulses in a more mature and realistic way. Interested community members may choose to become sponsors or donors. Some people with severe troubles join and become residents of a Synanon house, while others less in need may become Synanon members, but continue to live and work in the larger community. The latter are individuals who get along satisfactorily, but who would like to improve their understanding and control of themselves and enlarge their communication and positive relationships with others.

The Synanon game is a small group interaction which facilitates this process when it works well. It is conducted in a variety of situations over months and years, and so, unlike some quick action "miracle" approaches, it allows for gradual growth and change. Although it includes honest self-revelation and vigorous attack, the game is not intended to promote just the lowering of barriers between people and expression of feelings. Like all other Synanon activities it is meant to develop the mature part of a personality that finds out what it feels, and then does what is necessary regardless.

This does not sound too different from my phrasing of the principle that guides the work of psychiatrists. Both Synanon and my profession emphasize the importance of a person's making a consistent effort to change

*[Third Edition, 1979] The discussion that follows does not reflect changes in the organization subsequent to the first appearance of this book in 1972.

himself in accord with inner and outer realities. In many cases the Synanon program has proved successful where psychiatric treatment has failed.

"Synanon absorbs people into the responsible community," is the slogan of its founder, Charles Dederich, and it must be admitted that it has a most impressive record of doing so, even with the most difficult character neuroses such as those that lead to addiction. This accomplishment has brought about its growth in ten years from nothing to a multi-million dollar nonprofit organization with installations in many cities across the country. Synanon reduces the enormous personal and social burden of addiction, crime, and mental illness. It trains ragged individualists who have never worked or taken the most elementary care of themselves, let alone others, to live together in civilized mutual concern. These people, who have spent miserable years in hospitals and jails, are induced to produce their best for the group and conform to its high standards of responsibility. Synanon members work hard, running not only their own club and residence buildings, but also several profit-making industries which today provide more financial support than all its donors combined.

That is not all it does. Synanon also is an example of many social innovations that threaten some of the values of a large segment of the population. This is why I have thought it worthwhile to go into so much detail. Many of the criticisms of Synanon are based on unconscious anxiety arising from this threat.

Some object that a large percent of the former addicts and criminals "substitute addiction to Synanon for addiction to drugs" by electing to become employees of Synanon after completing the program, rather than "going out and becoming independent." They forget that the world, not notably considerate about offering jobs and other opportunities to rehabilitated criminals, is less in need of their skills than is the ever-increasing population of new addicts entering Synanon, for whose benefit long-term members are urged to stay. They forget also the many graduates who have left and are living and working successfully without drugs in the community. But suppose the indictment were correct, is continued dependence on Synanon so bad, considering the alternative?

The outsider, struggling in a competitive and often heartless world against his own loneliness and wish to be cared for, smugly denounces others for giving in to a temptation he had denied in himself. It is particularly ironic to hear an occasional clergyman make this sort of criticism.

The most outlandish claims are made that members of the community who visit or join Synanon learn to use drugs or become violent. This idea, too, represents an unconscious wish projected as a fear of Synanon. The facts are that use of illegal drugs and physical violence are flatly forbidden by the organization and can result in prompt expulsion. And this within a larger culture that increasingly winks at people smoking marijuana, staggering under regular doses of nonprescribed stimulants or sedatives, and beating up their wives.

The fact that hundreds of men and women live communally in a society without racial discrimination, devoting all their resources to the group while drawing only one to five dollars a week pay, is what really terrifies the cliché 100 percent American, who at least on paper ought not to be so opposed. Again, he projects his own wishes and, ready for a virtuous witch hunt, finds in Synanon a hotbed of illicit sex and communism. What is laughable is that, when a resident is ready and wants to leave, he may do so with the consent, albeit reluctant, of the community, something communist regimes are not noted for. And as for sex, a new resident is not usually permitted even to have dates until the group considers him a reasonable risk for someone's emotional investment, usually about six months after entering the program.

Although Synanon's gas stations could be run efficiently by one third as many employees, many more are assigned deliberately so that they may receive work training and experience most have never had. When you drive in, a swarm of attendants leaves its chores of maintaining sparkling cleanliness and descends on your car as a platoon of gas pumpers, underhood checkers, windshield washers, giving service such as you have never had before. Naturally other stations cannot hire fifteen employees a shift at one to five dollars a week each. And just as naturally, other operators are enraged at this "unfair" competition. It is discouraging to find that so many businessmen do not really believe in private enterprise.

What the devil was to Cotton Mather and other righteous puritans, the source of all evil, most modern scapegoaters desperately seek elsewhere. They find it in those who are socially rejected, such as Jews, Negroes, foreigners, or addicts and criminals, or in organizations such as Synanon, which welcome these individuals as well as anyone else who wants to participate. This behavior represents the familiar need to find an enemy on whom to vent accumulated hate before it can turn inward and poison its unfortunate carrier.

Synanon threatens the scapegoater even more critically by then turning the objects of his "justified" hostility into valuable and valued citizens, thus depriving him of his target. Not uncommonly a slightly more objective critic of this kind reveals this psychological mechanism by readily admitting that Synanon does cure drug addicts and benefits others, and then maintaining that there is something sinister in the very fact that it does so. The same hostility has been directed at me by a family I have deprived of its scapegoat by relieving him of a neurosis.

Some say that Synanon tends to erase individual differences, to force all people into a standard conventional mold. There may be some justice in this claim, since immature addicts need a firm structure on which to rely for support of their shaky resolve to keep away from drugs. But an extra amount of conformity would seem a relatively small price to pay as a transitional step on the way to becoming a person who eventually may be more flexible and reliable.

My own criticism has to do more with the impact of the games on some nonresident players. Remember, these are individuals who are getting along in the larger outside world, and so do not live in and have the support of the Synanon community full time. Several times during the year and a half in which I was a "square game-player"* I saw instances in which the defenses of such participants were subjected to so concentrated and sustained an attack that they developed a degree of anxiety or depression that was temporarily disabling after they left the group to return to their lonely apartments or boring jobs. This sort of effect is comparable to the bad results of starting a regime of physical exercise too vigorously when one is out of condition. It does not mean that the exercise is unhealthy, but only that to enjoy its benefits more caution, careful selection, good judgment, and support are necessary.

Whatever its dynamics in a particular instance, synaphobia may become a widespread disorder unless the majority of our people learn to feel comfortable with the putting into practice of many of the stated ideals of Christianity and American democracy which so often collect dust on the shelf.

Concentration camps, war combat, and polar explorations have produced profound personality changes.[43] The unusual stresses, maintained sometimes for months and years, wear down the person's habits and different behavior appears. A stolid, strong, imperturbable individual may be transformed under such circumstances into a complaining indecisive wretch, whereas a previously fearful and unassertive man will blossom unexpectedly into a dynamic and even heroic leader. Others have been changed deeply by falling in or out of love.

Naturally alterations which depend on such uncommon or unpredictable influences cannot be used as controls of mind, so various attempts are made to regulate more precisely the individual's experience in order to bring about the change desired. The two significant factors are desig-

---

* A nonaddict who participates in the Synanon game.

nated by the words "condition" and "behavior." Synanon is one attempt to manage the conditions of life so that behavior must change. Like psychotherapy, it relies heavily on conscious cooperation in bringing about personality improvement.

Conditioning

Another approach is based on the work of neurophysiologists such as Pavlov and various psychologists who have contributed to what has become today a complex theory of how learning takes place in animals and man. Joseph Wolpe is one of many who are applying this knowledge to treatment of mental disturbances.[44] Their various techniques are known as "behavior therapy," and the fundamental principle employed is to create conditions in which maladaptive behavior is eliminated and more adaptive behavior learned. By consistent repetition of such experience the more adaptive behavior is "reinforced."

In many situations in daily life the opposite occurs. A boy in school may get the teacher's attention, whether stern disapproval or sympathetic concern, only when he strikes another child. As soon as he becomes docile she ignores him. If her responses are changed so that she pays the minimum attention possible to his aggressiveness and consistently gives him approval for peaceful behavior, prompt improvement often follows. He is "conditioned" to behave in a socially acceptable way. It is even possible to change behavior by showing films which associate pleasant and unpleasant consequences with "good" and "bad" behavior.

An essential difference from other methods is that behavior therapy relies less than other methods upon conscious understanding.

Such methods have been applied to a wide range of problems, from the elimination of smoking or alcoholism to amelioration of major mental illness. They have proved useful in teaching autistic children to talk, in curing psychosomatic disturbances and irrational fears, and in motivating severely withdrawn psychotic patients to take care of themselves and participate in the hospital program. No effort is made to understand the psychological meaning of symptoms or to improve personality function in general. But in alleviating the specific symptoms toward which they are directed, these approaches are frequently more successful than older methods.

Psychotherapeutic treatment, for example, depends in large part on developing a good relationship between therapist and patient, and then using it to help the patient gain new understanding of himself and his reality so that his feelings of helplessness are reduced and he can deliberately make the changes needed in his behavior. When this process is successful it often results in lasting personality improvement as well as relief of symptoms. But it is complicated and requires a degree of comprehension, cooperation, and diligence of which some patients are not capable. And even with those who are, unfortunately it is sometimes true that the symptoms are still not eliminated but may thereafter respond to behavior therapy.

Should we then shift all our educational and therapeutic endeavors over to behavior conditioning?

Even in the narrow realm of therapy there have been untoward side effects. Behavior therapy, like so many attempts to understand and alter man without taking into consideration the total picture, is also capable of causing severe imbalances in personality. Even though the experts tell us that the treatment prevents this by inculcating desirable alternative behavior, instances are known in which a painful but stable condition was converted into a catastrophe. I recall a man who underwent conditioning treatment to stop his excessive drinking. It was successful. Except that for the first time in his life he began to expose himself sexually to children, and soon after committed suicide.

We sometimes see patients in whom psychiatric treatment may relieve a depression only to release a paranoid psychosis so severe as to require hospitalization. To the patient and his family, delusions of being poisoned may seem too high a price to pay for relief from feelings of unworthiness. Psychiatrists are not always able to prevent such dangerous side effects either, but understanding of and concern about the dynamics of personality, including the unconscious *meaning* of symptoms, makes it possible to anticipate and prepare for those that do occur. No one whose training or bias equips him to consider only part of the situation is in a good position to do so.

But in the broader perspective beyond therapy of individuals, the controls of mind that behavior conditioning makes possible are both promising and ominous.

Vance Packard, Jules Henry, and others have shown how needs are deliberately generated where none existed previously in order to sell new products.[45] Huge fortunes change hands to assure that in a motion picture one brand of automobile will be featured prominently in association with the leading characters rather than another, thus measurably increasing its sale. And we have been told how subliminal advertising, flashes on the TV screen of commercial messages so brief that we never become conscious of them, can boost sales even higher.[46]

With the proper motivation the technique is available right now to condition our whole nation to favor and finance integration, open housing, slum clearance, higher education, and aid to needy people everywhere. And with equal ease, granting the reverse intentions, the same means could inculcate the exact opposite tendencies.

These methods might assure the election of officials up to and including the President, with a great saving in effort and money as compared with older procedures.

The values which guide the few with the power of decision will decide which programs and individuals will be backed and which opposed, unless some effective barricades against this sort of tiptoe tyranny are promptly erected by the majority to protect themselves.

And so the accomplishments of behavior therapy are haunted by the specter of brainwashing with a detergent of frightening efficacy.

While much has been learned about beneficial control of the individual mind, and some progress has been made in the beneficial control of small groups of minds, we are as yet almost totally ignorant about the beneficial control of the collective mind of great crowds. While not instinctual, as he claims, what Konrad Lorenz calls "militant enthusiasm"[47] can be aroused in support of almost any sort of cause, and once it is mobilized, the restoration of rational control is usually beyond us until its energy is dissipated.

Sex and Violence

This brings me to my last example. We hear frequent vociferous criticism of erotic scenes in motion pictures and on television. Like most psychiatrists, who know that where there is sex there is life (even if new and illegitimate), I am convinced we have much less to fear from filmed sex than from filmed violence.[48]

Obviously there is disagreement. A film producer told me that one of his colleagues, whom he regards as an eminent expert on the psychology of violence, had stated, "Television has brought murder back into the living room where it belongs." Apparently he subscribes to the ancient rationalization that watching violence in a film is generally good for people in that it helps them discharge pent-up aggressive tensions they otherwise would have had to stifle or put into action. Unfortunately some psychiatrists and psychologists have come to the same unsubstantiated conclusions.

Clinical evidence suggests that perhaps for the ordinary person in his ordinary state there may be no harm. But for some people, including some with long-standing mental disturbances or temporary upsets, such exhibitions are directly precipitative of violent behavior. One psychiatrist told a Senate Committee that filmed violence is a preparatory school for delinquency.[49] And in recent years carefully controlled laboratory studies have shown that the preponderant effect on even an ordinary person is to increase the amount of hostile aggression in his subsequent behavior, which in its most extreme form we call violence. There are some extra required conditions. One is that he is first placed in the proper psychological state, say a feeling of justified anger at someone whom he later has opportunity to hurt.[50]

Research to date apparently has disproved the Aristotelian notion of catharsis, which holds that powerful emotions can be discharged by watching spectacles that mobilize them. Even in those rare instances of studies of aggression where this "drainage" theory seems substantiated, it is likely that aggression simply has been turned off rather than reduced in intensity, through an experience which absorbed the attention.[51] After all, many a husband has been spared a wifely tirade by no more significant a distraction than the unexpected ring of a doorbell.

On the contrary, it appears that vicarious experience of violence in motion pictures and television increases the likelihood of hostile aggressive behavior. In one study teenage boys first were angered. Then they were divided into two groups and shown different films of a fist fight. One film focused on the pain cues of the victim, and the other on the aggressor's attack. Some observers would expect the group who had observed the victim in pain to show less intense aggression later out of sympathy. To their surprise, the result was just the reverse. Those who saw the victim's pain showed the most intense aggression later. Any person clinically experienced in the psychodynamics of cruelty and sadistic behavior in our culture might have anticipated the observed result. However, the most significant finding is that *both these groups* displayed much greater intensity of hostile aggression than did a control group which saw a peaceful movie.[52]

After summarizing the growing body of evidence that vicarious participation in it increases hostile aggressive behavior, Albert Bandura concludes:

> It is highly improbable that even advocates of vicarious drive reduction would recommend community programs in which sexually aroused adolescents are shown libidinous movies at drive-in theatres as a means of reducing sexual behavior; famished persons are presented displays of gourmands dining on culinary treats in order to alleviate hunger pangs; and assaultive gangs are regularly shown films of assailants flogging their antagonists in an attempt to diminish aggressive behavior. Such procedures would undoubtedly have strong instigative rather than reductive consequences.[53]

I suspect study might also reveal increased hostile aggression follow-ing such cruel spectacles as bullfights, cockfights, and possibly even prizefights and professional wrestling. In view of all this, it is disturbing to hear the same authorities who inveigh against public entertainments because they inculcate sexual immorality blandly assert that these media provide only "catharsis" when it comes to violence.

In a strange way the Fun ethicists and the few remaining unvanquished Victorians alike, by their constant insistence that what we need is fewer or more restraints on sexuality, are managing to distract attention from our urgent need for greater restraints on violence. And I mean internal restraints as well as external. Our internal ability to control violence would be much greater if people were not constantly assaulted by real violence here and abroad, as well as dramatized provocations to commit it.

"If" is such a small big word. And "consciousness" is such a big small word. Is the consciousness of man equal to the task of exercising safely the controls we have been exploring?

Freud once said that the conscious mind is very little, but it's all we've got.

Demands of Evolution

From here, what can we see of the demands of evolution on mind? As we investigated the demands of external reality and of inner urges, and our mental resources for meeting them, we were forced to consider some aspects of the demands of evolution along the way.

In order to take increased responsibility for directing our own biology, consciousness must be improved steadily, diligently applied to understanding the world and controlling ourselves, but resolutely pre-vented from interfering with activity properly left to automatic behavior.

In order to avoid falling into a dead end of evolution as has our cousin, the dolphin, we must avoid specializations that will narrow rather than broaden the fraction of reality we can come to know.

In order to forestall being swept into an unquenchable thirst to con-sume things endlessly, we must arrange to have some things worth keeping indefinitely.

In order to prevent ourselves from being gently enslaved by a minority, the majority of us must vigorously insist that new controls of mind not be applied by the few without the prior conscious consent of the many, both as to technique and objective.

Sometimes I am asked about the place in man's future evolution of parapsychological and psychic phenomena. At present, passionate advocacy and denunciation often dominates discussion of this field so that it is difficult to collect evidence, or even to formulate the right questions. I suspect that wishes account for conviction here as much as elsewhere, and know of no convincing evidence in support of even the presumed existence of such phenomena, let alone explaining them. Personally, I am dubious that the questions now posed about them will ever attain in the future more status than today is enjoyed by the problem of what number of angels can dance on the head of a pin.

But if we follow the human agenda methodically, it is conceivable that much will become known about areas that today are totally obscured by bias, such as the possibility of extrasensory perception, survival of the personality after death, and so on. Perhaps long after we have departed, the gradual accumulation of information will shed some light on where and how we went. Personally I would be delighted with a world in which resources were diverted from projects to tyrannize, sell, or annihilate minds onto others designed to prove they can surmount distance or survive the grave. That is, provided all minds were permitted and helped to live freely and fully in the interim.

As we cross the threshold from the past era of scarcity to the future era of abundance, the mind is learning the controls required to remain zestfully engaged with life, throughout increased longevity devoid of drudgery and poverty. It must also learn to generate a new sort of man, capable of preserving, amplifying, and passing to our human or posthuman followers the striving for mastery of reality, while preserving its elements of intellect, character, freedom, and joy. Especially joy, for we are entering some of the most joyous of all the moments of man.

SECTION TWO

LOVE, WORK, AND PLAY REVISITED

Introduction

We have compressed absurdly dizzying distances of evolution in order to glimpse them whole. Now we must narrow our perspective in order to pick out some finer details in the development of man. Leafing backward through the pages of the human agenda, we will be concerned mainly with the past few hundred years which have put the stamp we call "modern" on current human life. Our objective is to understand what man has done up to now with his inheritance from earlier forms, and what *specifically* human modifications may be added to it in the future.

With his generalized body, improved hand, and vastly enlarged brain and mind, man already has spun the filaments of animal life into intricate new patterns. We explored how man's mind employs intellect and character to master reality under conditions which will yield the maximum freedom and joy. This process is guided by his constantly heightening level of consciousness.

Of our many new awarenesses, the most critical for human life has been man's unique consciousness of the characteristics of his individual self. These characteristics, and awareness of them, render the range of an individual's possibilities enormous.

When Freud was asked what he thought a normal person should be able to do well, he is reported by Erik Erikson to have answered tersely, "Lieben und arbeiten," "to love and to work."[1]

One might be disappointed that the inspired mind which gave the world psychoanalysis should whittle his answer down to just three little words. But a second thought will replace that reaction with appreciation for the economy of genius. For compressed into this simple formula is

NOTE: A condensed early version of this section was presented at the Fourth World Congress of Psychiatry, Madrid, 1966. See Gorney, "Work and Love Revisited."

the essence of the human experiment. Notice that both love and work are *social* endeavors, depending largely for their existence as well as their significance on *cooperation* between people. Freud, often criticized for treating the individual personality as if it arose independent of society or even entirely in opposition to it, reveals his grasp of the indissociability of the individual human being from the group. His crisp reply shows he understood that society does not simply restrict the human being. It *creates* him. It provides the network of learning experiences wherein his potentials can be realized in a coherent pattern. Without the culture of some society, a baby is not freer, but infinitely impoverished. Not only is there no possiblity of a baby's becoming a human being without cooperative interaction with society, but there is no real possibility of a person's continuing to satisfy his human needs without continued cooperative interaction with society.[2]

As we have seen in Section One, this human pattern of development goes back to the very beginnings of man, and beyond. Experimental work with our closest animal relatives reveals that even to become a satisfactory monkey or ape it is necessary to have a good mother. And it is in that basic mother-child social unit that the baby, human or hominid, learns to be a viable version of whatever its genetic potentialities permit. Monkey, ape, or human, what the baby has learned for millions of years has been how to assure individual and species survival through love and work.

So Freud's dictum has broader significance than he may have realized for man's past evolution as well as application to his current life. But is it equally pertinent to the vastly changed realities we can foresee in his future? After all, Freud studied a world in which very few human beings were burdened with leisure, in which neither complex automation nor simple contraception was available, in which the guaranteed annual income was a crackpot idea instead of an ever more widely distributed reality, in which scarcity seemed certain to be the immutable condition of human life, and universal abundance a naïve utopian wish instead of an emerging fact.

These changes, together with others such as the new biology, constitute the most epochal revolution in man's history. Nevertheless, provided that Freud's formula is enlarged as well as interpreted in terms of the new realities, I believe it will remain the best index of mental health in the future.

The major modification required to make it applicable to the new realities of abundance is addition of a third factor, that of *play,* to love and work. Always of signal importance in the life of animals as well as man, perhaps its significance was obscured to Freud by the more stringent conditions of scarcity then current. At any rate, Freud has been criticized by Reisman, Rieff, and others for his treatment of play.[3] Particularly it appears that he may have focused his attention so largely on the more erotic aspects of play as to have underemphasized those that are related to the development of the ego. Of course it is true that the three fundamental human activities overlap, making sharp demarcations difficult. Yet each is distinct from the other two in its primary function, especially play, which as we will see later, is the only one that arises in the individual as largely *optional* rather than compulsory behavior.

Human activities change profoundly as new techniques are introduced. Our language may or may not change to reflect these changes. Today members of the Teamsters Union have nothing to do with horses, and sailors have nothing to do with sails. A few thousand years ago in all societies the doctor and the priest were one, as they are today among the few remaining nonliterate peoples who retain their "medicine men." But from teamsters and sailors, who still have to do with transportation on land and sea, to doctors and priests who in their separate ways are still concerned with human well-being, the essence of human activities often stays the same despite changes of techniques, words, or roles.

So it is with love, work, and play. To grasp their real meaning we must look past their forms in any particular period and reveal their essence. Because it is so difficult to see through the rapidly shifting smoke screens that envelop these most fundamental human activities today, we must catch glimpses from different vantage points in order to estimate their shape and direction tomorrow.

There are two methods I find useful. One is to look separately at *two main functions* of each of the three basic activities of love, work, and play. The other is to use each of the three activities as a platform for viewing the other two. Of course, the functions of activities as broad as love, work, and play are much too intricate to be reduced to elementary terms, but brief and oversimplified definitions at least provide us with a useful handle with which to grasp the load. Like the hypotheses on which they are based, those that follow are offered in this spirit as tentative formulations, subject to change as need arises.

10 Social and Psychological Functions of Love, Work, and Play

I distinguish between the separate *central social functions* of love, work, and play, and the *crucial psychological function* they share in common.

The central social function of *love* is the creation of workable circumstances for generating and raising children.

The central social function of *work* is the production and distribution of goods and services.

The central social function of *play* is distraction from misery and compensatory domination of others.

In contrast, throughout life the common crucial *psychological* function of love, work, and play is *self-validation*.

Today as in the past, the more dispensable social functions of love, work, and play in many respects overshadow and even eclipse the crucial psychological one. But as human evolutionists interested in the future the latter must be of greater interest to us, because the gradual *withering of the social functions* and *rise to preeminence of the psychological one* are on the next page of the human agenda.

What is "self-validation," this common psychological function of love, work, and play?

By self-validation I mean *confirmation of the existence and worth of the self*.

But self-validation is the outgrowth only of the sort of relationship to love, work, and play which is characterized by *psychic intimacy*.

By psychic intimacy I mean a person's state of *zestful, enduring investment of the self in relation to one of the three basic activities*. The implication of these definitions must await and emerge from the context of the balance of this section.

We noted how "consciousness," present at some level in all forms of life, has been advanced to a new peak by the conceptualizing mind of man. And we reviewed how a prominent factor in the content of this human consciousness has come to be awareness of our own characteristics. As members of a mortal species, we are born, grow old, and die. As persons we observe ourselves developing our unique personalities. We not only attentively and even anxiously assess the degree of our success or failure as a measure of our worth, but we also seek eagerly for almost any evidence that we have an impact on other people and things, and that we in fact *exist*.

What would seem to be "self-evident," that we exist, plainly is not fully so for many people at any time, and for most people at some time. Our language is loaded with hyphenated, negatively charged words that express aspects of the self's sometimes unhealthy effort to achieve solid conviction of its own secure existence, such as "self-centered," "self-absorbed," "selfish," "self-conscious." Even such positively charged words as "selfless," "self-effacing," "self-sacrificing," paradoxically are evidence of the same human concern with the existence of the self.

Descartes was satisfied with his proof, "I think, therefore I am." To many of us, his attempt to base a logically consistent philosophy on an irreducible minimum assumption was puzzling or even irritating. Partly we were avoiding uncomfortable awareness of our own uncertainty. However, in larger measure we were probably also dissatisfied with the idea that something so abstract as thought could prove the existence of what to us is so intensely crucial and personal, the existence of our inner selves. We are much more convinced we exist by evidence that we *affect* somebody or something, and by our *feelings* rather than our thoughts. Perhaps Descartes' idea would be more persuasive if he had said, "I affect and feel, therefore I am."

It is interesting that the English word "affect" in German means "emotional reaction." So I can prove I exist in English by how I affect the world, and in German by the affect the world produces in me.

The sources of self-validation in love, work, and play are therefore important to everyone. What is the condition of *psychic intimacy* in which this confirmation of the existence and worth of the self can be derived from a person's relationship to love, work, and play?

Psychic intimacy in relation to *love* is his zestful, enduring investment of the self in the *specific loved person*. It includes zestful reception of the loved person's reciprocal investment in the self, but it does not include any necessary concern with the central *social* function of love, that of generation and nurture of the young.

Psychic intimacy in relation to *work* is a person's zestful, enduring investment of the self in the *process and product of the work*. It may include concern about the distribution and uses to which the product is put, but no *necessary* concern with the central *social* function of work, that of obtaining a share of goods and services with which to assure survival.

Psychic intimacy in relation to *play* is his zestful, enduring investment of the self in the *specific activity of the play*. It includes the pleasure derived from the senses, particularly the delight of exercising unused physical and mental faculties, but no necessary relation to the central *social* function of distraction from misery or domination of others.

Without psychic intimacy in the relationship, a person may accomplish the central social functions of love, work, or play, but not the crucial *psychological* function, self-validation.

We must recognize that in the present, as in the past, there are a few people who fortunately are able to attain psychic intimacy in their relationship to love, work, and play, although the central social functions of love, work, and play are unquestionably the determining ones in their lives. But it seems to be a sad fact that many millions of people, the large majority, are painfully unable to achieve this relationship to one or more of the three main sources of self-validation.

A colleague and good friend reported that "reading this chapter is like trying to swallow a spoonful of powdered coffee," which reflects a degree of dehydration unusual even for *The Human Agenda*. Perhaps adventurers through these pages will be willing, like other explorers, to add some water of their own.

11 Origins and Development of Love, Work, and Play

Despite the limited expressiveness of lower animals, we were able to trace earlier the origins of the three main self-validative activities in man out of behaviors that arose at various places along the path of animal evolution. There seems to be no doubt that the animal is zestfully involved in what, with some hesitation, we may call its love life, whether it be the courtship of the cichlid fighting fish, the loyalty to mate or friend of grey-lag geese, or the clinging attachment of the chimpanzee baby to its mother. Likewise, it would seem that the animal is zestfully involved in the work of obtaining food, as conducted by a shark, a tiger, or even a chimpanzee.

When it comes to play, things are less clear because, as we observed, it is doubtful that truly playful behavior can be found below birds and mammals. At least among the higher mammals it seems plain that there is a zestful involvement of the animal in play, whether it be the wild chases of otters, the tussling of wolf pups, or the frolicking of monkeys.

What is more, the three different sorts of zestful behavior can be clearly distinguished from one another. But since the "self" never comes to full formation, even in adult animals, their activities can never be fully "self-validating."

The Newborn Human Baby

Now we must trace the outlines and implication of the individual *person's* development during infancy in relation to love, work, and play.

The newborn, like his animal forebears, is "selfless." There can be no psychic intimacy with love, work, or play for him until he acquires a

321

fairly well-developed self to zestfully invest. The new baby's love, there-fore, is confined to its social function. It consists of physiologic tension-reduction and pleasure-seeking directed toward no specific person, but it evokes the needed nurturing response by giving to any passerby the de-light of pleasuring the baby. The new baby's work, for the same reason, is confined to its social function. It assures survival through obtaining in-come: any of a variety of nourishing liquids and other baby care. Play has not yet appeared.

Anyone's capable ministrations, and any suitable supplies, are equally acceptable at this stage. The consequence is that work and love have not yet acquired their later psychological function.

Where does the "self" come from? Even before they can serve to validate a self, the three fundamental activities function, as they do throughout life, as the main *sources* of self and its unique combination of character-istics, or "identity." The self crystallizes gradually out of the infant's love, work, and play *experiences*, although in the absence of psychic intimacy they are conducted at first almost automatically. As the baby becomes capable of focusing his attention and energies, validation of his newfound self can then result from *psychic intimacy* with love, work, and play.

Now, we must look away from the baby as a whole, and consider his basic needs and drives, as well as his love, work, and play, separately.

The baby is forced out into our rather uncomfortable world after only nine months in the uterus. As we saw earlier, after about the same gesta-tion period as the chimpanzee, the new human baby is born in a markedly embryonic or neotenic state, requiring another nine months to reach the level of maturity achieved by our nearest relative at birth.[1]

The baby must immediately find ways to satisfy his basic needs.[2] And if he is to grow up healthy he must early develop confidence that his methods are reliable. This confidence comes from repeated experiences that an impulse, urge, or drive is followed by comforting interactions and cessation of the drive. Before looking at the baby's development in more detail, let us amplify what was presented earlier about the basic needs and drives (pp. 65–66).

In man as well as animals, the basic drives (hunger, thirst, sleep, etc.) are the psychological representatives of the basic needs (food, water, rest, etc.). Both are rooted ultimately in physiological processes. Satisfaction of a basic need, and its associated drive, requires expenditure of energy.

At birth, unlike the relatively mature newborn chimpanzee, the human baby is a collection of tissues and organs only incompletely formed and coordinated with one another. And in bringing about satisfaction of his basic needs he has only a sharply restricted repertoire of reflex responses to inner and outer stimuli. These include the basic physiological reactions such as breathing, crying, sucking, swallowing, urinating, defecating, various random movements, and sleep. All these behaviors occur automatically, that is, without the conscious intent of the baby. At first there is even no participation of the cerebral cortex, since the brain is not yet fully functional physiologically, let alone instructed by experience how to regulate all these activities.

How does this welter of undifferentiated activity bring about satisfaction of vital basic needs? Certain reflex responses in the baby serve his basic needs *indirectly* by controlling the emptying of the gallbladder, the passage of food through the intestine, the rate of heartbeat, the diameter of blood vessels, secretion of adrenalin, and so forth. Because they are regulated automatically throughout our lives, these reflexes do not ordinarily enter our awareness or become of conscious importance in our relationships with others.

But those reflexes that bring about satisfaction of the basic needs *directly* command a great deal of attention. The reflexes that inflate and deflate the lungs satisfy the need for oxygen. Those that produce crying, sucking, and swallowing satisfy the need for water and food. Those that bring about urination and defecation satisfy the need for elimination. Those that result in sleep satisfy the need for rest. Every one of these responses is a communication from the infant which must generate an immediate or delayed reaction from the environment if it is to satisfy a basic need. So that the respiratory reflexes can supply the baby's need for oxygen, not only must adequate air be available, but his nose and mouth must remain unobstructed. Accordingly, a mother sleeping in the same room not uncommonly awakens in response to a slight change in the rate or rhythm of her baby's breathing. She becomes so attuned to its behavior that she often can distinguish tongue and lip movements that indicate desire for food. She may soon be able to recognize the wailing that signals oncoming sleep rather than discomfort. She may soon learn the difference between a cry that indicates a full diaper and that conveying just a need for company. The kind of response she makes to these different signals determines whether or not her baby will survive from moment to moment and day to day.

Much of this is true *briefly* also of other higher animals. But unlike the chimpanzee infant, the human infant will not be able to live without almost constant devoted attention for a long time. Although every mammal depends totally upon its mother for its survival while carried in her womb, only the human baby in its helpless immaturity literally rests its life in her hands for years after birth.

With the internal womb nature invented for the mammal baby came the groundwork of the personal relationship between mother and baby.

With the *external* womb each human mother is forced to devise for her baby (see p. 94) comes the crucial human elaboration of the mammalian psychological innovation, the *inter*personal relationship.

The communication of feeling goes both ways. And love, like all emotions, must be both felt and communicated to have an effect on another person.

Mother does much during infancy to duplicate conditions in the womb. The baby is held, supported against gravity, kept in a warm, quiet environment, and if he is lucky spends many hours in contact with mother's body, rocked by her respiration as in the old days before birth, as well as by her arms. From basic needs tensions build up periodically which are relieved largely through cooperation by mother. The infantile psyche has no limits, and the whole world, including mother and its own tensions and satisfactions, is experienced as one—the "oceanic feeling" described by Freud.[3] In a loving mother's care the baby may encounter brief distress but soon feels safe against all danger, as he learns that distress is shortly followed by relief.

Hunger pain is followed by its cry, and then by the milk-yielding nipple, and relief. This sequence occurs over and over. The baby learns to expect that it will always end the same way. At first he cannot discriminate between events that occur within his own body and those that originate elsewhere. At first it seems to him that his *wish* directly produces the nipple. Then dim awareness arises in him that it usually appears when he cries. Naturally he comes to believe first that the nipple is part of himself, and later that it is at least under his direct control.

But soon he learns how incorrect even this latter theory is. Sometimes the nipple does not come right away, and he is forced to cry louder or in some different special way to summon it. Maybe one day it does not come at all. Instead, after a long wait a strange rubber nipple squirts strange cow milk into his outraged mouth. Then the intestinal cramps of colic instead of peaceful sleep may follow his feeding.

Bit by bit, maturation of his sense organs and more experience draw boundaries separating him from the breast and mother, and outline the increasingly tedious techniques he must employ to please and thereby influence her.

If in learning to control her indirectly his mind is disappointed too often or too severely, either at its dawning or at some time later, his mind will recoil from the painful reality and flee back to its earlier beliefs. And so we see children and adults, too, who fall into the partial regression of believing that their cry (or words) control other people and the world, or into the more complete regression that their simple unexpressed *wish* must do so. Even those of us who do not suffer from such frank disturbances retain in later life a perpetual potential wistful glance over the shoulder at the magic past in which reunion with mother and the world, through erasure of our separateness, beckons seductively.

As the baby grows in its first weeks and months, gradually mother will see two other kinds of activities appear. Between feedings, and with no sign of discomfort, the baby moves his arms and legs about energetically. He may also gurgle and coo or even scream at the same time. Neither the movements nor sounds seem to serve any function, such as the signaling of the discomfort of hunger. In fact, they seem to be accompanied by a pleasant, even joyous, emotion. Furthermore, the baby starts soon after birth to move his tongue between his lips, and learns to suckle vigorously for long periods after the breast is empty, or even on his own finger or thumb. Again the apparent accompanying emotion is contentment. There seems to be no function in these actions except to provide pleasure.

What can we make out of this catalogue of baby behavior? Somewhere amid this collection of rudimentary and undifferentiated activity we must look for the roots of the new person's love, work, and play.

Love

As Freud would agree, it cannot be an accident that he mentioned love first. Love develops immediately following birth, and in its various forms remains of primary importance throughout human life.

My reversal in this section of the order of "work and love" established previously is not just deference to Freud's genius. Rather, it reflects the gradual change in emphasis on the two fundamental activities during the course of evolution, which has brought love to indisputable preeminence in man. In these pages I will try to indicate how love is of signal importance not just for the development and survival of each human being, but also, of course, for our *species*, as well as any others that may be dependent upon or arise from man.

The baby's movements before birth are mainly reflex responses to stimulation arising within itself or its delicately controlled milieu. Aside from a negligible amount of exercise of muscles that are virtually functionless at this stage, they serve no apparent survival purpose. And from the baby's behavior after birth we can surmise that movements of the arms and legs are not sources of pleasure until a month or more has passed. Perhaps the absence of survival or pleasure value to such movements before birth explains why they ordinarily are so brief and spasmodic. (A possible exception is the sustained and apparently pleasurable prenatal thumbsucking that has been noted in babies delivered by caesarian section.)[4]

Suddenly at birth the baby must perform new activities which will bring him the life-sustaining oxygen and nourishment that a little while before flowed automatically into his body through the umbilical cord. And these activities will not succeed in keeping him alive unless they find prompt, devoted cooperation from a mother (or substitute).

During his infancy there are two distinguishable functions served by the baby's love. The first begins urgently at birth and promotes *survival* by evoking the devoted mothering he needs to stay alive. The second begins gradually in his second or third month and helps him lay the foundation of his self-esteem, his feeling that he is "good," that it was worth all his parents' trouble to create and care for him. The first is the earliest form of the *central social function* of love. The second becomes the nucleus of the later *self-validating* function of love. *

We will postpone discussing the self-validating function for awhile, and here consider how the baby's love exercises its central social function by providing workable circumstances for his own nurture.

As we watch a mother respond lovingly to the reflex communications from her baby, we readily understand that her behavior is guided by love. And it is love of the sort we regard as "mature," in that it consists mainly of giving reactions directed to satisfying the baby's needs.

What many of us may not be prepared to learn is that the baby's behavior too is properly regarded as loving. Now obviously I do not mean that the baby who is not yet even able to discriminate between his body and mother's is capable of *deliberately* behaving toward her in a loving way. But that is precisely the point: the baby does not need accurate perception (or voluntary control) to behave lovingly because it is prepared at birth for loving behavior by the three and a half billion years of evolution of life that led up to it, especially the last 200 million years of mammals, and the final two million years of man. In accordance with Ashley Montagu's definition of love as the conferring of developmental and survival benefits upon another in a creatively enlarging manner,[5] it is easy to see how the mother does this for her child. But how does the baby reciprocate?

Immediately after birth the baby is uniquely qualified to do four things for his mother which can simplify the obstetrician's task. Unless the adults officiating find it necessary to interfere with ordinary healthy mammal and primate behavior he will immediately be put to nurse at his mother's

---

* These functions arise during the time described by psychoanalysts as the "early oral" period. My account emphasizes its biological-survival and ego-developmental aspects, as well as its erotic or pleasure-seeking aspects.

breast. Most babies will suck at least a little by reflex soon after their lips are stimulated by the nipple. This sucking sets in motion powerful reflex contractions of the mother's uterus which help deliver the afterbirth, stop bleeding, and begin the process by which the uterus will return to its nonpregnant state. To produce the same contractions a doctor must resort to massage or injections of a powerful uterus-contracting hormone.[6]

The fourth advantage to the mother is primarily psychological. By lying at her side and suckling, the baby becomes real to her. She has an immediate relationship with a living creature who needs her love. This helps to compensate for all her effort, and for the termination of her pregnancy, which to some women is unexpectedly a cause for regret. Equally important, she can experience immediately, although unconsciously, a survival benefit to herself from the baby, and thereby experience the baby as a new *source of love for herself* and not just a sponge absorbing her love. In contrast, the best an obstetrician can do is to convey to the mother in words a pallid forecast of the mutual need satisfactions that await her and the baby when they are finally allowed to get acquainted.

A baby who has a close relationship with mother from birth on shows remarkably little of the emotional upset some suppose to represent instinctual aggression, whereas a baby deprived of this loving interaction shows the distress behavior we identified earlier as the reaction to frustration.[7] We must not forget that this rage is the ultimate plea of which the baby is capable for help in overcoming discomfort which he experiences as a danger to his life.[8]

It is in the course of responding to the baby's communications of his *vital* basic needs that the mother also gratifies what Montagu called his *nonvital* basic needs.[9] These spring from the same sort of physiological states, and must be satisfied if the baby is not only to survive but to develop mental health.

One of these is need for skin contact.[10] All mammal young cuddle against their mothers and siblings in a manner that guarantees skin stimulation.[11] Many must be licked by their mothers in the ano-genital area or they will die from inadequate bladder and bowel function. There is evidence in humans that certain types of childhood asthma are in part due to lack of tactile stimulation. Some asthma attacks may be relieved by putting an arm about the child.[12] Such observations suggest that skin contact (and its psychological reverberations), in its role of stimulating and regulating the nervous system, may actually be a vital basic need. As Montagu shows, there may be more truth than jest in the definition of love as the harmony of two souls and the contact of two epidermes.[13]

Another of the baby's needs thought to be basic but nonvital is the need to feel in social contact with other human beings. This is the need for the companionship of the same species we encountered among the animals.

The need for social companionship, which can be satisfied by many different individuals, must not be confused with the need for *love from a specific consistent mother*. Studies have shown that, after the first month or so, even if all the vital needs are thoroughly satisfied by competent but constantly *changing* nurses, children will fail to grow and develop, become listless, depressed, and susceptible to many diseases. This condition has been called infantile atrophy or marasmus. What is missing, and when present makes other children thrive whose vital basic needs in contrast may not be so lavishly satisfied, is *consistent* mother love. When the mother-deprived child is assigned to *one* nurse for frequent holding, feeding, and fondling, he responds quickly by regaining his zest for life. Although all other conditions remain the same, he begins to grow and develop well and becomes normally resistant to disease (see p. 337).

This brings us to the psychological function of the baby's love. Although for a month or more the baby does not discriminate between others, or even discriminate himself *from* others, he may learn soon after birth to distinguish between ministrations given lovingly and those given with hostility. He may show his grasp of the state of mind of the mother by his comfortable acceptance or fretful crying in response to her care. So beyond bringing about a relationship with mother that assures his biological survival, the baby's love brings about an *emotional reaction in mother*, of which he becomes aware, and which tells him of her affectionate delight or rejecting distaste in caring for him.

From the second month on, the baby's improving abilities to see, hear, and feel help him to form a concept of mother as a person separate from himself, who to varying degrees enjoys or hates what she is doing for him. As he begins to be able to perceive and interpret her smile or frown, her laugh or growl, he begins also to form a concept of himself. He comes to feel that he is "good" or "bad" in proportion to how much pleasure or pain mother experiences in caring for him. If his reflex smile elicits her loving smile and voice and other reactions, a circular conditioning reaction is set up that leads him to expect that his goodness can always be relied upon to evoke love. If it does not, the conditioning lays the groundwork for lifelong depression, suspicion, and fear in response to emotional and physical closeness.

It is conceivable that a clever machine could be devised that would satisfy the baby's vital basic needs, and even his need for skin stimulation. Perhaps one could be designed that would give the baby the feeling of social companionship, even if not of his own kind. Maybe the machine could even show that it "cares" about the baby for himself, delights in tending him, and also that it needs the baby in return. But clearly we are a long way from being able to create a machine that in response to the baby's communications can transmit the huge number of signals that go into acculturating that baby for any human society. Warm relationships with people do not grow out of even warm relationships with machines. We must not forget the implications for man of the psychological disability created in Harlow's monkeys by deprivation of mother or peers.

Now we must examine how the baby's love fits into his daily life. We understand that the baby must receive love in order to develop healthily, and that his mother will experience some of his responses as love he gives in return. But we must distinguish what *motivates* his behavior from how she interprets it. While she benefits from the baby's suckling at birth, his activity is impelled only by an urge to move his lips and tongue in contact with a suitable object. As far as we can tell, this drive, like others, builds up tension gradually. When it reaches a certain level, the baby begins to root for something to suck. The baby's activity seems directed only toward attaining pleasure and reducing the drive-tension.

Pleasurable discharge of drive-tension occurs in the course of one of the three basic human activities, love, work, or play. The *physiological* functions of the discharge, pleasure, and cessation of the drive, are different from the central *social* or *psychological* functions served by the love, work, or play in which that discharge is incorporated.

For example, we all know people who are impelled to have sexual intercourse although at the time they are not driven by sexual tension. Therefore their motivation cannot be the reduction of a physiologically rooted basic need and drive. Instead, they may be impelled by the wish to have children, the central social function of love. Or there may be a sort of reassurance and comfort for them in being needed.

Likewise, we all know people who are impelled to eat although at the time they are not driven by hunger. Therefore their motivation cannot be the reduction of a physiologically rooted basic need and drive. Instead they may be impelled by the wish to remain strong and healthy so they can continue to work at providing the goods and services needed by their family for survival, the central social function of both the work of eating and holding down a job. Or there may be a sort of reassurance and comfort for them in the activities of chewing and swallowing and in the resultant feeling of fullness and heaviness.

And we all know people who are impelled to play although at the time they are not driven by the pressure of any unused capabilities. Some golfers force themselves out onto the links for a second eighteen holes, although physiologically exhausted. Therefore, their motivation cannot be the reduction of a physiologically rooted basic need and drive. Instead they may be impelled by a need for distraction from a vexing problem or for the opportunity to dominate others by beating them at competitive sport. Or there may be a sort of reassurance and comfort for them in not yielding to the need for rest when they are tired.

Freud found that even when drive-tension is present it may be deflected by psychological factors into a drive that superficially appears remote from it. An example would be the clinical observation that if parents disapprove too vigorously of a six-year-old child's masturbation, the drive may completely disappear and be replaced by renewal of the more infantile urge to suck his thumb. Frequent observations of such substitutions bolster Freud's idea that all such rhythmic tension-releasing activities are basically sexual in nature. Freud believed that someday we would find a mechanism in the nervous system through which such a displacement can occur, and in the meantime offered a theory to describe at least the mental aspect of such observations.[14] He suggested that the drives representing bodily tensions in the mind have a certain amount of psychological energy attached to them. This energy, which he called libido, is always of the same kind, no matter what drive it is powering at the moment, and furthermore, can be detached from any particular drive and shifted onto others. In the above example, the libido would be described as having "regressed" to a psychological impulse from an earlier period.[15]

How do we know that these behaviors are not connected with more immediate vital basic needs? For instance, isn't the need to suck really a manifestation of hunger?

The surprising but well-established answer is that it is not. If the baby is not given plenty of time to suck, although his comfort and development may be interfered with, he will not sicken and die as he would if deprived of oxygen or food. That there is an urge for these tension-reducing pleasurable activities completely separate from the vital basic needs is shown most easily in relation to the need for sucking pleasure.[16] If a baby is fed from a nipple that has too large an opening, he will finish his meal and satisfy his hunger before the need to suck has been satisfied. So he will go on sucking for a time after the milk is gone. If a baby is fed from a nipple in which the opening is too small, his sucking need will be satisfied long before his hunger. He will then quit sucking before the milk is gone, and, if this situation goes on long enough, will become severely undernourished.[17]

The important point for our attention here is that at the beginning of life the baby's "love" consists of reflex tension-reducing and pleasure-seeking behavior *directed toward no specific person*. Only after the first month of life does lack of a consistent mother do perceptible damage. Although during his first few weeks the baby will respond in the same way to almost anyone, his limited reflex behavior sustains his life by recruiting devoted adults to his care. And his evident satisfaction at having his needs met makes *them* feel loved!

But however and by whomever the details are arranged, in terms of purpose it is plain that during the first month of life the new baby's rudimentary love is practically devoid of self-validating function and is confined mainly to its central social function. And that is, to repeat, the creation of workable circumstances for generating and raising a child, in this case himself.

Work

Infancy has been described as a period of passive receptivity. This is incorrect. At no other time in his life will a person be as busy. Nearly every moment is filled with active striving to satisfy his basic needs. Those strivings bring about his survival and become organized as the nucleus and forerunner of what we later designate as work.

The baby increases his body weight faster during the first four months of life than at any later time. His rapid rate of growth requires a relatively enormous intake of food, roughly 15 percent or one-sixth of his weight each day. His constantly recurring hunger and thirst push him from within to activity that not only expends a large part of his available energy but constitutes a significant part of the process of replenishing and increasing it. His limited repertoire of reflex responses to discomfort, such as crying and fretful movements, are called into action with regularity and insistence. They function as signals to mother to supply what is needed, and soon she learns to discriminate from others the cry that signals the need to be fed. As in relation to his love needs, at first the baby's lack of clear differentiation between self and outside world prevents him from realizing that satisfaction of his need for food comes from a separate outside person. Consequently anyone's capable ministrations and any supplies of roughly suitable nourishing liquids are equally acceptable at this stage. His rudimentary attention is concentrated only on relieving the uncomfortable inner tension, not on the process or product of the work. Like love at this stage, as mentioned before work has not yet acquired its later self-validating function.

And it is from this elemental relationship to food in infancy that the person's adult relationship to the sort of work that predominates in our present stage of social evolution largely arises. What I have called the central social function of work, guaranteeing survival through obtaining

income, is a *neotenic holdover from the function of work among animals.*
They too work mainly for survival. But animals too, with only the *rudi-ments* of human capacities, will sometimes "work" diligently for a reward
other than satisfaction of a vital basic need. Eider ducks will repeatedly
walk up the banks of streams and launch themselves onto swirling waters
merely for the sensation of shooting the rapids.[18] Better yet is evidence
from the laboratory. Rats will sometimes push a bar for the reward of a
sound or a light flash more doggedly than for food.[19] If given a choice between a bar that yields food and one that yields sensory stimulus, they
will frequently press the bar that yields a sensory sensation even though
quite hungry.[20] Harlow's monkeys will spend hours pressing a button that
yields the reward only of a brief glimpse of another monkey.[21] Admittedly
these fragmentary examples cannot convincingly demonstrate that animals
will work for "self-validation." That would be impossible anyhow, since
in the human sense animals do not have a true "self" to validate. And it
must be acknowledged that these behaviors are difficult to distinguish
from play, the nonutilitarian joy of which we already observed could take
precedence over satisfaction of hunger (p. 192). However, they suffice to
establish the basic premise that "lower" animals descended from those
remotely ancestral to man also exhibit sustained worklike effort for
rewards that are neither productive of subsistence nor particularly joyous,
but instead seem mainly to heighten the vividness of experience or the
sense of having produced an effect on the environment.

As we shall see later, this fragmentary behavior in animals becomes in
man a key feature of his adult relation to work, and the resultant self-
validation is essential to his health throughout life.

Play

The busy newborn baby's love and work seem totally invested during
the first month in securing satisfaction of his vital basic needs, there
being at first no recognizable striving for satisfaction of the nonvital basic
needs, let alone anything resembling "play."

The baby suckles, swallows, cries, eliminates, moves its muscles a bit.
What is missing that we would regard as play?

When we consider an activity "play" we are making a group of judgments about it, the criteria for which remain outside awareness unless we
deliberately try to identify them. We would all agree that a puppy
tussling with a littermate, or later chasing a ball, is playing. Likewise,
we would all agree that a child shaking a rattle or building with blocks is

playing. Or that later on, his run through the woods is play. Our instant diagnosis rests primarily on recognition that the activity, however earnest the concentration or vigorous the effort, is not obligatory but *optional*. It is performed not because it will help *sustain* life, but because it will help *enrich* life. It is performed *for itself*.

An activity we call play also strikes us as in some way *spontaneous* and *free*, perhaps free of the very necessity that in infancy so plainly attaches to love and work. And when the play is genuine there is a quality of *joyousness* to it which in some unmistakable but indefinable ways seems different from the joy attached to over types of activity. OTHER

By the end of the first month the sequence of basic drive, activity, and satisfaction has become fairly well established, leaving the baby a little extra "leisure" and energy for the first fragments of play behavior. Also, by then his nervous system's control of muscles has improved a little, making possible a bit more coordinated movement.

We soon see the beginnings of the smile as a reflex in response to pleasure, and even to the mother's voice which the baby associates with pleasure. Lorenz suggests that this unique innate tribal greeting of man is made over from animal motor patterns of aggression: baring of the teeth as seen in lower mammals.[22] Whether or not this is so, the smile quickly becomes the prized token of acceptance by the baby. So adults practice pleasing the baby in order to be rewarded with his smile.

The next two months bring the beginning of deliberate experimental movements of the arms and hands, integrated following movements of the eyes, and the chortling sounds babies seem to make just for the fun of it.[23] As the baby becomes more alert, he delightedly tries out other dimensions and abilities of his various parts, and incorporates what he learns into his "self," which is slowly emerging from the amorphous newborn haze. As each new capacity is discovered and tested, a short stretch of the blurred psychological line distinguishing him from the outside world is moved outward and inked in more firmly. As he listens ecstatically to his own shriek, thrashes his arms, and eventually pedals the air with his legs, he is also beginning the joyous self-validation which play should bring him from then on throughout his life.

In the childhood years following infancy we see the elements of competition and domination of others gradually superimposed upon play. But insofar as the activity still strikes us as play, they seem subordinate. When we watch the grim determination of the collegiate football player or the grinding rage of the elderly golfer, the impression of play in their activities begins to fade. The sense of optional, spontaneous, free, joyous, self-validating activity engaged in for its own sake is drowned in the riptide of competition and domination.

Correlations

We must try to stand back from these chronological fragments from time to time in order to see each of the three basic activities whole, and also to keep in perspective our view of human life as a whole. Nowhere is this more important than in considering play. For play differs in several important ways from love or work.

The baby's *love,* in addition to providing pleasure and release of tensions, from its very beginning primarily serves the central social function of creating the interpersonal circumstances for nurturing the baby. The baby's *work* primarily serves the central social function of obtaining and processing the goods and services needed for survival.

To underscore what is mentioned above, the baby's *play* is the only one of the three basic activities that from the very beginning is performed "for itself," thus serving primarily the self-validating function. This means that the highest self-validating function of play in later life is the *same* as its initial role in infancy before the self is fully established. Or put another way, whereas the central social functions of love and work predominate at birth, the central social function of play (distraction and domination) is grafted onto it only *later* in life, appearing as a desire to defeat others in games, and *is not present* at the beginning.

The familiar biological dictum, "ontogeny recapitulates phylogeny" (the evolution of the individual repeats the evolution of the group), although rejected elsewhere nowadays, remains at least an apt description of the development of play. "Lower" animals love, thereby generating offspring. Some, like the discus fish, even nurture and feed their young on a secretion from their own bodies.[24] Such animals work, thereby providing themselves with the means of survival. But aside from the stereotyped chases sometimes engaged in by tropical fish, I am unfamiliar with any behavior among animals up through reptiles which we would recognize as play. Only mammals and birds, with their relatively greater emancipation from instinct, seem to engage in the sort of free spontaneous, joyous, improvisational activity we would call play.

The same delayed beginning of play seen in human babies is also found in other mammals. During its first two weeks, the newborn puppy does not even open its eyes or move just for the delight of doing so. Its love and work are encompassed in strivings toward the nipple, whereon it nurses vigorously. At three weeks it begins to explore its bodily capability in what sometimes appears to be solitary play for its own sake. A week or so later it begins the typical tussling play with its siblings.[25]

For a long time in dogs this behavior too remains entirely play, although under wild conditions it shades into the serious struggles that serve to establish their dominance hierarchy. Even in fully grown dogs, wild as well as domestic, the main function of play remains the free enjoyment of unused capabilities, which behavior in man only sometimes becomes elaborated as self-validating play.

Here we must take note of a crucial consequence for man's future of the unexpected difference between play and love or work. In the era of abundance the self-validative function of love, work, and play must take precedence over their central social functions. If we wish love and work to serve mainly the self-validative function, we must help them to *advance beyond* their state in infancy. But if we want play to serve mainly the self-validative function, we must help it *remain in or regress to* its state in infancy. In the case of love and work we must *transcend* our neoteny. In the case of play we must *preserve* it.

During the second, third, and fourth months the normal baby develops the ability to discern differences and to remember. He begins to prefer certain foods, sounds, caresses. Then he begins to discriminate among adults who bring him these experiences. The friendly baby who would welcome anyone's loving attention at one month may cry and fret at the touch of the most solicitous and loving stranger at three months. Although at two months he will smile at the full frontal view of any moving human face (or even a replica), as the months pass he begins to smile selectively only at mother's face, the sound of her voice, the feel of her touch, and the security of the way she holds him.[26] Eventually he may want to be fed and cared for by only this one special person. Now he zestfully invests his crystallizing new self in mother, joyously making his living and loving in the same place.

And now his relationships to love and work, like his initial relationship to play, have belatedly become psychically intimate, and therefore validative of his newly emerging self.

Maturation and Development

As time passes, the new person's abilities expand in a continuous stream. We call the unfolding of the *innate* capacities *maturation.* These include wide variations in physical factors, such as height, muscularity, skin color, and energy level, and psychological factors, such as frustration tolerance, acuity of the senses, and musical aptitude. As we noted earlier, expression of all built-in potentialities depends greatly upon what opportunities the environment provides.

The unfolding of the *acquired* capacities we call *development*. These include the environmentally controlled aspects of physique, as well as skills achieved, such as athletic ability, language proficiency, sociability, and abstract thought. As we noted earlier, expressions of these acquired abilities depend greatly on the innate endowment. Put simply and concretely, both the rickets and musicality of a young Mozart are the outcome of a complicated interaction of inherited maturation factors and environmental development factors. With more vitamin D, his susceptible bones would have grown straight. With no clavichord in the attic, he might never have revealed his genius.

Infancy and Mastery

Now let us turn to the later months of infancy. The studies of Piaget have confirmed Freud's finding that psychological development generally follows the same sequence in all individuals, although some progress faster or slower than others. So we see that the baby learns to turn his head (at about three months) before he can roll over (usually about four months). Then at six months his first tooth begins to push through, and soon he begins to sit up by himself. At about seven months he begins to crawl.[27]

A month later a previously happy, exuberant baby may startle and worry everyone by developing "eight month anxiety." If he has enjoyed a warm, mutually responsive interaction with mother until then, he has developed confidence that when he is in need of anything his signals *automatically* bring the loving care that is followed by relief of tension. He is scarcely aware of the degree to which he has had to learn the subtleties of the kind of cry and other behavior that brings the best results. So he has the impression that his command brings the satisfaction directly just because he wants it.

Then at eight months he seems suddenly to become *fully aware* that he controls mother's reactions only *indirectly*. That is, she must *want* to respond to his demand, or she will not do so. Moreover, he learns she can go away, leaving him with his inadequate resources to deal with painfully mounting tension. The baby now may cry when mother leaves his view, whereas in the past he seemed quite content to let her disappear for a while. It will be a few weeks or months until he develops confidence that he can stand to postpone satisfactions, or can rely on a substitute person until she comes back. If mother disappears for a week or more, the baby is likely to experience such profound helplessness and despair that he will cry for hours, lose weight, become apathetic, and in general enter a state of severe depression.[28]

It is important to realize, as noted earlier, that the urgency of the child's need for a consistent relationship with one mother *declines gradually in the second year.* As walking and talking become better established, his ability to master reality and his confidence in new relationships grow rapidly, so that by the third year he is ready for the modest reduction of interpersonal intensity that may be brought about in American children through nursery school, or the drastic reduction effected in Tahitian children through "cooling."

In a baby's response to experiences during the first year we can see the beginnings of a critical human characteristic. Its various derivatives contribute to the best and worst of man's mental strivings for the rest of his life. For in these early months originates an urgent lifelong craving *to understand, to know with certainty,* and *thereby to become able to control* everything. Particularly urgent is warding off feelings of helplessness and despair. The baby yearns to know exactly where mother has gone and exactly when she will reappear. He yearns to understand the "right" way to bring her back as quickly as possible, and in her most cooperative state of mind.

When it appears later, after much evolution, as intellectual curiosity about how to achieve mastery without mother, this motivation leads to rational study and experiment, and has brought some of the major advances of civilization. When it has been expressed as religious or political dogma, it has brought about crucifixion, the Crusades, the Inquisition, and totalitarian dictatorship.

In raising babies our objective must be to help them become adults who can live without knowing for sure just when "mother" will appear to bring relief, who can relinquish the demand for absolute certainty about what is true and right, and nevertheless resolutely pursue both.

Feeling of Mastery and Sense of Reality

Threading one's way through all these tangles involves working toward a sense of reality. We have been considering the stages through which the sense of reality passes as the baby grows. First comes the dim stage of fusion with the universe, in which the baby perceives his wishes as the cause of everything. Then the baby learns he must do or not do certain things in order to command what has by now become to him the outside world. But for a long time (from two to seven years, according to Piaget) the child's notion of these procedures is magical, anthropocentric, animistic.[29] Gradually in the years that follow, the individual to some extent traces the path of our species' mental development. Little by little he learns to interpret pieces of his experience not in terms of the certainty of irrational magic but in terms of the frequent uncertainties of rational causation.

If a child is asked at age four why the sun sets, he may answer, "Because it is bedtime." He means that his bedtime directly determines when the sun must go to bed. He states this "self" centered explanation without doubt.[30] If he then learns that when he visits northern latitudes the sun does not go to bed at the time he does, his magical certainty may be suddenly and uncomfortably replaced with rational uncertainty. He is likely to yearn for understanding that will bring back his former sense of mastery. If he is given information about the rotation of the earth, when he can grasp the new idea he is able once again to banish doubt with rational certainty. But the security of *control* has been replaced only with the feebler security of *understanding*. Gradually he becomes aware that the true situation is really the reverse of what he had at first believed, that he and all of us go to bed largely *because* the sun sets!

Now not only his original sense of comprehension and control are shaken but also a fundamental value has been called into question. *Should* we go to bed because the sun sets? Perhaps people should determine for themselves when they should go to bed.

He now begins to realize that most of the human behavior he previously had just taken for granted because it seemed to him the natural way to control the universe is in fact a *submission* to the facts of the solar system, biology, or the weight of human tradition. By the time he reaches adolescence, extra hormones only stoke whatever fires of rebellion began years before with the escape of his child's mind from its own earliest magical shackles.

Unless the tyranny of an optional religious or political magic shroud has been forced upon him, these precious flames lead him in maturity to live the adventure of uncertainty with zestful delight. The oil lamp, the candle, and the light bulb, and all they have illuminated through the pages of the human agenda, free him and all of us from the nonhuman or nonrational dictation of not only our bedtime but our fear of the dark and our darkest fears. This precious outcome is the reason we must welcome and not stifle the revolution of mind through which each generation recapitulates our species' liberation from magic.

Origin of the Sense of Reality

In our discussion of the conditions that foster the origin of self-esteem, we have already considered the evolution of the sense of reality from magic to matter-of-fact.

Always we are brought back to self-validation and in particular the importance of psychically intimate love.

And, paradoxically, it is here on the prosaic subject of the sense of reality that we can get special help from poets and their intuitive grasp of psychological truth. Consider the lyrics of the popular song "It's Only a Paper Moon," by E. Y. Harburg, which include these lines:[31]

> I never feel
> A thing is real
> When I'm away from you.
> Out of your embrace,
> The world's a temporary parking place.
>
> Oh it's only a paper moon
> Sailing over a cardboard sea
> But it wouldn't be make-believe
> If you believed in me.
> It's only a canvas sky
> Hanging over a muslin tree
> But it wouldn't be make-believe
> If you believed in me.
>
> Without your smile
> It's a honky-tonk parade,
> Without your love
> It's a melody played
> In a penny arcade.
>
> It's a Barnum and Bailey world
> Just as phony as it can be,
> But it wouldn't be make-believe
> If you believed in me.

Another example is "What is Real?," by Margery Williams.[32]

> What is real?
>   asked the Rabbit one day
> When they were lying
>   side by side
>
> Does it mean having things that buzz inside you
>   and a stick-out handle

Real isn't how you're made
said the Skin Horse

It's a thing that happens to you

When a child loves you for a long long time
not just to play with, but Really loves you,
    then you become real

Does it hurt? asked the Rabbit
    Sometimes said the Skin Horse for he was
      always truthful

When you are Real you don't mind being hurt.
Does it happen all at once, like being wound up,
    or bit by bit.

It doesn't happen all at once. You become. It takes
    a long time. That's why it doesn't often happen
      to people who break easily, or have sharp edges,
        or have to be carefully kept. Generally, by the time
        you are Real, most of your hair has been loved off
        and your eyes drop out and you get loose at the joints
        and very shabby.

But these things don't matter at all because once you are Real
    you can't be ugly, except to people
      who don't understand.

Writing two decades apart, these two artists without too much else in common tell us the same things about the sense of reality—that somehow *love can make fake things real*.

Is that their message? Superficially, yes. But Harburg says in effect that "The fake things *outside* me become real if you love me," while Williams (interpreting her freely) says, "The fake things *inside* me become real if you love me." Or, condensing their messages, "Outside and inside me, *reality is created by your love*."

That is their joint revelation, that the *sense* of reality of both inner and outer worlds originates in the confirmation of the existence and worth of the self through receiving and giving love.

Clinical experience with patients who have impairments of their sense of reality confirms this literary intuition. Such an unfortunate person has suffered severe interference with his earliest love relationships. Somehow he has not been "believed in" enough. Which means he has not been allowed to have enough of the experience of producing a loving effect on and in another person. He has not been loved enough to acquire a sturdy sense of his own goodness, or even the reality of the existence of his own inner self. Thus his work and play have too feeble a foundation on which to add their contributions to his self-validation.

And if, unlike Descartes, you are not convinced of your existence by the fact that you think, if you doubt the existence of your own inner self, how can anything outside you seem real?

Childhood

During the growing up years the child's world expands in all ways. Variations in the direction and degree of expansion are determined by cultural differences. In our culture, by the age of four the child's preoccupation with the triangle between mother, father, and himself is approaching its emotional peak, especially the boy's competition with father for mother's exclusive love, or the girl's with mother for father's exclusive love. In many Western families competition with siblings is also intense.

After nursery school, which helps to dilute this family turmoil, the biggest single change is the one that at age five or six takes the child away from home and to regular school. It is no accident that this is the time when the oedipal conflicts have reached their maximum intensity. Child and family are then most in need of diversion of his energies.

School is the child's work, not play, as some have claimed. His capacity for zestful enduring investment of self in the process and product of the work steadily increases. He also develops new *love* attachments to teachers and classmates, with varying degrees of zestful enduring investment of self in the loved person. The scope of his *play* also enlarges as he learns new mental and physical skills to tap his growing resources for zestful enduring investment of self in various activities.

The decisive element in all this is that in school the child learns not only to work, but subsequently to love, *away from mother*. And he does this mostly for the crucial psychological satisfaction of feeling his "self" to be bigger and stronger, rather than as before, during infancy and early childhood at home, only to assure survival, tension release, and pleasure.

At first, it is not uncommon for the child to keep both his love and work tied to a single person in school just as he did at home. He loves the teacher who also directs his work. But gradually the marriage of work and love is dissolved. The boy or girl may find another child of the opposite sex to love, while remaining attached to teacher in connection with schoolwork. Or later, during the preadolescent years, he may select a chum of the same sex toward whom love is directed. With adolescence, there may come an explosive recurrence of a crush on a teacher of the same or opposite sex, in a regressive attempt to restore the infantile unity of love and work in relation to mother. Eventually there comes a final separation in more or less frenzied absorption in wooing and winning response from an age-mate of the opposite sex.

Meanwhile during these tumultuous years play has ceased to be entirely a "self" developing activity engaged in for its own sake. What had been a zestful, enduring exploration and investment of the self's unused capacities, that functioned simply to expand and enjoy them, has by now been overlaid with other needs. Play has largely become a "recess," the longed-for distraction from the restraints of concentration and immobility in school. It also serves as a permitted direct discharge for the inculcated need to defeat and thus dominate others, the open expression of which was discouraged in the family romance at home, and is not usually welcomed openly in classroom study.

Out of these transitional years and forms will emerge the adult forms of love, work, and play that are most familiar. The self-validating aspects of love, work, and play are established in infancy and become largely predominant during early childhood and school years. But although they persist in adult life, they are pushed once again into the background by the "survival" or central social functions. For as adulthood arrives, we hold out to the young person the reward (or threat) of the adult needs to "make a living" and to "make a home for the kids."

Adulthood

Love and work are primarily social behaviors. Originating in the first interpersonal relationship with mother, throughout life they continue to develop and change always in the course of the later heirs to that relationship. The ways in which a person's love and work operate in human relationships depend upon the particular set of larger realities in which they are embedded.

For want of more graceful language I call the quite stable yet ever-changing patterns "psychosocial constellations." As the person grows older, these complex fabrics progress or regress in both their structures and functions. Here are examples.

The baby's *work* constellation, work-mother-bottle, centering mainly about survival, progresses in childhood to work-teacher-school, centering mainly about self-validation. But its later adult version, work-boss-job, too often becomes reduced again almost completely to survival function in its role as producer of "income."

Meanwhile, the baby's *love* constellation, love-mother-nursery, centering mainly about survival, is succeeded by the predominantly self-validating love-teacher-school, centering mainly about self-validation. Its later adult version, love-mate-home, too often becomes reduced again almost exclusively to survival function in its role as generator and nurturer of children. Notice that then the constellations of both love and work, in fulfilling their adult central social functions, have *regressed to their primary functions in infancy.* Such a dispirited grown person may succeed at tedious work merely in making a living, largely in order to assure the wherewithal to support only a stunted love life at home.

Whereas some identity support derives from being a bored factory worker and apathetic parent, it is plain that little true self-validation can derive from such zestless work and love relations. It is little wonder in such circumstances that love life so readily regresses to infantile tension-reduction and pleasure-seeking under the influence of the Fun ethic considered later.

What about play? Play is the only one of the three basic human activities that has a solitary instead of social origin.[33] It therefore becomes "socialized" only secondarily, and bears a different relationship to psycho-social constellations. Sometimes it remains independent of them. But where play is part of a constellation, it is appended to it rather than built into the structure. As the central social functions of an adult's love and work gradually crowd out their self-validating functions, to make up for the erasing effect of his job and the shadow of love he lives with at home, the psychologically deprived person is forced to drag his blurred identity into the repair shop of play.

By training he has learned to pursue there (1) distraction from constraint, emptiness, and annoyance, and (2) the spurious success of "winning," rather than the joyous exploration and expansion of unused capacities. The result is that he too often emerges with little more confirmation of the existence and worth of his self than is conveyed by generalized fatigue or the ache of a strained muscle.

Having followed the development of love, work, and play in the infant, the child, and the adult, we will now shift our focus from the individual to the species and look at the historical evolution of these activities.

12 *The Eras of Scarcity and Abundance*

We have seen how early man, by the use of fire for cooking, reduced the time he had to spend eating from perhaps five to two hours a day. However, cooking did not prevent most human beings from having to pass the bulk of their lifetimes for nearly two million years just gathering and preparing the foods they could find. Despite this ceaseless toil, virtually every human being lived amid scarcity of food.

In the few hours left over, early man also worked hard to secure his few items of clothing, tools, and shelter. The cave dwellers of more than fifteen thousand years ago somehow found the energy and durable implements to record on stone walls something of their life. While we have no record of their dance, pantomime, music, ceremonies, and so on, the cave paintings and their few surviving ornamented artifacts bring us some idea of their vanished vision.

When he stalked the caribou the hunter carefully cultivated not only his weapons but his relations with the supernatural spirits concerned with the hunt. Considerable psychic intimacy with his work is reflected in those magical trends of thought.

What of his love? Like the pack-hunting wolves, early man left his female behind with the young when he went with his fellows to procure meat.[1] In the rigorous life of this frugal world practical necessity probably required that relationships between men and women be durable. We saw how specialization of social role as well as anatomy contributed to dependence of men and women on one another and to the stability of the family. Nevertheless, development of his love relations beyond the social child-nurture function would have been impeded after childhood by the limitless drain of energies into survival-assuring labor.* So it seems

* There were also other restraints in addition to scarcity. In nonliterate societies, as well as the cultures of the East and West up to the recent past, tightly organized

344

doubtful that his adult love relations achieved full psychic intimacy. And the same seems likely to have been true of play, which in adulthood ordinarily would have been crowded out or turned to utilitarian purposes by the relentless pressure of scarcity. Then twelve to fifteen thousand years ago when the epochal inventions of agriculture and animal husbandry were introduced, a page of the human agenda was reached and acted upon which began suddenly the stampede into abundance now reaching toward its climax. With the grain grown and the cattle corraled just outside the farmer's hearth came the beginning of the end of scarcity. And with it, the end of the beginning of psychic intimacy.

Because parents assured his survival, the prehistoric child, like the child of today, enjoyed a few years after early infancy in which he could focus on the self-validating functions of love, work, and play. Then he too, in turn, became a drudge, on behalf of his own children.

But gradually farming, herding, storing, and other techniques created *surpluses*. And the extra measure of rice or wheat, or the slabs of meat preserved by salting or smoking, made of prehistoric man's storehouse the cradle of leisure.

With surpluses came the first opportunity in two million years for human beings systematically to extend into adult life the childhood preeminence of self-validation over survival. The possibility of this new freedom entered adult human life in proportion to how much the silo and the surplus took over from mother and father. And as these seeds of surplus were propagated around the earth, simultaneously there was entered into a distant page of the human agenda the repeal of the Puritan ethic ten millennia before it was articulated.

True, only a small part of any population benefited in terms of the reduction of drudgery thus made possible. But most were afforded some protection against natural calamities, such as flood, drought, and fire, which produce famine. And from then on all human communities were enriched in their evolution by accelerated division of responsibilities among various specialists, among whom were the thinkers and creators. It was they who first had the leisure to pursue the values of the self-validation that

---

systems of taboos and authority over the individual, including arranged marriage, fostered continuity into adulthood of the limitation on psychic intimacy with love which babies must endure in any society. In such circumstances adults also have no choice of love object, but are required to love as best they can whomever birth, nurture, or custom provides them. In contrast, our current pattern of self-selection of mate, while it permits the freedom needed for a new level of psychic intimacy with love, also creates the conditions for *dis*-continuity with the arranged love life of infancy. Simultaneously it multiplies not only the rewards for success, but the chance of, and punishment for, failure to achieve a satisfactory love relationship.

comes from zestful enduring investment of the self in love, work, and play.

Twenty-five hundred years ago the Greeks had created a society in which a small leisured class lived in abundance, supported by the impoverished and partially enslaved majority. For the privileged few leisure and security brought a revolution of mind. The desperation of magical conjuring in the face of danger could be replaced gradually by the delight and force of rational thought. Because other men cultivated and preserved the products of the earth, these few could regard as their proper work cultivation and preservation of the products of the mind.* With the shift of goal from providing income to achieving intellectual and esthetic excellence came augmentation of the self-validating function of work.

Equally revolutionary were the changes surpluses made possible in the relationships between people. Needing each other for survival less, they were more able to value one another as objects for the zestful enduring investment of self. Thus for the first time love during maturity could be oriented by a few primarily toward psychic intimacy and self-validation. It is on this account that we find in Greek literature an early flowering of love poems.[2] Moreover, it became possible for close relationships to extend beyond the small tribe to encompass the *polis*. Thus the opportunity for self-validating zestful investment of the self in love was enlarged from a community of dozens to one of hundreds and even thousands.

As for play, the Greeks raised to an adult cultural value the exploration and expansion of unused capacities for their own sake. These included the aptitudes for music, painting, and other arts. The fact that they organized their athletic enterprises as competitions must not mislead us. Their goal was not to extol individual domination through defeat of others, but to identify and venerate excellence in the individual as a symbolic self-validation by the community, a communal exaltation of the spiritual aspiration of man.

Even today the mass of humanity still lives in the era of scarcity. And in many areas the prospect of abundance seems to be receding.[3] For example, in our ghettos and in many underdeveloped countries the standard of living of millions of people is declining rather than rising.[4]

---

* Of course the uniqueness of Greek society cannot be traced solely to its economic basis. Other ancient societies, such as those of Crete, Egypt, and Babylonia, had created a small leisure class based on slavery. The Greek experiment had something extra, possibly connected with the democratic social and political closeness of the city and state, which turned the Hellenic mind toward intellectual speculation. Yet, if such speculation did not automatically follow from the leisure of the privileged class, it could not have existed without it.

But at least in large sections of the industrialized West, after ten thousand years of surplus accumulation exclusively through toil, the machine-slave is creating a fundamentally new reality of abundance. For the first time in history *without* human drudgery sufficient abundance can be provided to afford the overwhelming majority of mankind the opportunity for psychic intimacy with love, work, and play. That this potentiality remains unrealized is due not to limitations of productive capacity, but mainly to deficiencies of personality and social organization.

In Sweden progress toward universal abundance far outdistances that achieved elsewhere. Yet many people are bitter rather than pleased about its effects. As a young Swedish social worker told me:

> This is a depressing country. We have no slums, no poverty. We all have a good standard of living, good jobs, pay, medical care, education, unemployment insurance, social security, and retirement plans. But there is no challenge in life. There is nothing to struggle for. We yearn for the bad old days of sweatshops and child labor. Young people are leaving to go someplace where they can *suffer*.

It is this kind of malaise that threatens to become general now throughout the world, far more than that which results from scarcity.

It is fashionable to deny these facts. For some people refusal to acknowledge the new reality serves their need to avoid any possibility of appearing to be naïvely optimistic, a stance that seems to them more embarrassing than cynical pessimism. For others the denial functions to absolve them from the obligation to do anything about distributing abundance to those who need it. Still others are so anxious about having to adapt to a new reality in which everyone has enough that they are desperately trying to maintain the conditions of scarcity even at the risk of blowing up the world in the process.

But whatever their reasons, those who argue that there is nothing fundamentally new in our ability to supply human needs must soon be swamped by contrary evidence. The present dismal conditions of disadvantaged poor in the United States cannot be denied. But they do not justify our ignoring trends and implications of recent improvements.

Ben J. Wattenberg shows that a number of significant advantages have already occurred.[5] Take the proportion of people living in poverty:

YEAR	PEOPLE IN POVERTY (IN MILLIONS)	PERCENT IN POVERTY
1960	40	22.21
1965	33	17.31
1968	25	12.81

Or consider secondary education, however poor or unequal its quality may be:

	PERCENT COMPLETED FOUR YEARS OF HIGH SCHOOL OR MORE	
YEAR	NONWHITE	WHITE
1960	39	64
1965	50	74
1968	58	75

And finally, as miserable as is our waste on means of destruction, consider the apportionment of the federal budget:

	SHARE OF FEDERAL BUDGET, PERCENT	
	DOMESTIC PROGRAMS (HEALTH, LABOR, WELFARE,	
YEAR	HOUSING, EDUCATION)	NATIONAL DEFENSE
1960	23	50
1965	31	44
1968	33	42

As an example of what further improvements might be accomplished, let us look at the peak United States investment in the Vietnam war. There is disagreement over whether our nation could afford both this military expense and the domestic expenditures needed to bring the good life to all our people. But it is clear that, at least in terms of dollar expenditures, we can do one or the other. What are the dimensions of this investment which we *can* afford?

At its peak the war cost: $950 per second
$57,000 per minute
$3.42 million per hour
$82.1 million per day
$2.5 billion per month
$30 billion per year

What is the equivalent power of such resources applied to butter instead of guns? According to Warren Weaver, if that amount were applied to education,

> We could give a 10% raise in salary, over a ten-year period, to every teacher in the United States, from kindergarten through universities, in both public and private institutions (about $9.8 billion); finance seven-year fellowships at $4,000 per person per year for 50,000 new scientists and engineers ($1.4 billion); contribute $200 million each toward the creation of ten new medical schools ($2 billion); build and largely endow complete univer-

sities, with medical, engineering, and agricultural faculties for all 53 of the nations which have been added to the United Nations since its original founding ($13.2 billion); create three more permanent Rockefeller Foundations (1.5 billion); and still have $100 million left over to popularize science.[6]

The hazards of forecasting the future are nowhere more complex than in the realm of economics, where the imponderables of the business cycle and international trade are balanced by the ambiguities of purchasing power and standard of living comparisons. But these difficulties must not dissuade us from at least *attempting* to grasp in greater detail the possibilities on our horizon.

Let us make a further projection of what might be accomplished to improve the daily conditions of life of people now living in misery. The figure of $30 billion annually represents only about 13 percent of our current federal budget (about $225 billion) and only about 3 percent of our present gross national product (about $1 trillion). Furthermore, there is every reason to believe that, given the intention to do so, we could double or triple U.S. industrial productivity within a few years. We could similarly increase at a rapid pace supplies of other components of modern living, including raw materials, communications facilities, and smogless transport, as well as the resources of imagination and skills needed to weave them into wholesome patterns of life. As a conservative estimate, within a few years at least twice the $30 billion we were wasting annually in Vietnam could be generated to supply currently unmet human need. Let us suppose that half of this $60 billion were to be devoted to a renaissance of American life. Surely it is plain that within a decade we could be on our way to raising the income of all Americans to at least the present per capita income level of about $3600 and our land could be well on the way to realizing dreams of a full life for all our people.

Now let us suppose that the remaining $30 billion were to be devoted to helping the rest of the world in need. Herman Kahn has made a projection based on the assumption that world population growth will average about the present level of 2 percent per year.[7] If one trillion dollars ($33 billion yearly) were to be granted in foreign aid between now and the end of the century, there would be enough capital for every nation to attain at least a $300 per capita annual income, and for most to reach $500 per capita (in constant 1965 U.S. dollars).[8] In most underdeveloped areas the equivalent of a U.S. dollar buys much more, up to three times as much.[9] Thus even the lower figure of $300 would provide in terms of *purchasing power* a per capita income of up to $900 per year. If this income were distributed evenly, admittedly only a theoretical possibility, it would mean that a family of four would share in terms of purchasing power about $3600 per year. While in terms of U.S. purchasing power this amount of money would only provide a standard of living in the vicinity of our "poverty line" (about $3500 per year for a family of four), we must remember that in terms of the *standard of living* it could provide people in other countries it is still misleadingly low.

That a comparable standard of living, at least regarding basic necessities (such as food, clothing, and shelter) as well as secondary necessities (such as hygiene, health care, and education) can be attained by two countries with greatly disparate per capita incomes is shown by a comparison of the United States and Ireland:

(1968 FIGURES)		UNITED STATES	IRELAND
Per capita annual income		$3412	$850
Groceries	(equal quantity and	$22.11	$21.46
Clothing	quality, obtained in	$174.80	$83.33
Rent (3-room modern apartment, per month)	Washington, D.C., and Dublin)	$260.00	$48.00
Infant mortality per 1000		21.7	24.4
Life expectancy, years		70	70
Adult literacy, percent		98	99–100

The table discloses not only comparability of *general* indices of national standard of living, but also that (especially in terms of housing) a four-person urban Irish family with $3400 a year can actually enjoy a better basic standard of living in terms of homely consumer goods than such a family in the United States.[10]

Thus, by the year 2000 the United States *alone* could bring the rest of the world up to approximately the standard of living now enjoyed in Ireland, a relatively poor country as compared with its neighbors. If the rest of the developed world just matched our contribution, these projections for the year 2000 would be more than doubled (due to the effect of compound interest), bringing the standard of living of everyone on earth at least close to that now enjoyed by the majority of the population in Western Europe.

Of course all such predictions are fraught with uncertainties, such as the eventual exhaustion of raw materials, the occurrence of natural disasters or man-made wars, or the possible unacceptability to people in other cultures of elements of diet, hygiene, or education we now value. But it is equally true that unexpected future technical breakthroughs might substantially increase the rate and amount of improvement we could effect. For example, already new methods are yielding larger grain crops than were believed possible just a few years ago.

Whether or not this fundamental revision in the universal human condition is brought about in three decades, it is plain that we are moving toward it. Sooner or later, barring only a cataclysm such as nuclear war, or the inauguration of international dictatorship designed to prevent everyone from having enough, the people of the world will see to it that the new power of productivity will bring to fruition the frustrated wishes of two million years.

And before it happens we had best look at the impact of such abundance on the three basic human activities. First, take work.

Since 1874 the average workweek in the United States has declined from approximately seventy hours to less than forty.[11] In 1963, Governor Hatfield of Oregon predicted that by the end of the next decade the average workweek in this country would drop to twenty-five hours.[12]

Whether or not this proves to be so, the facts of our present employment pattern are astonishing, and the probabilities of our *future* employment pattern, truly staggering. For example, in 1965 all our production-oriented activities were carried on by 13¼ percent of our population, and all our service-oriented activities were carried on by 17¾ percent of our population. Comparing these figures with those likely for the year 2000, we find that while the percentage engaged in production-oriented activities seems likely to decline to about 11¾ percent of the total, the proportion engaged in service-oriented activities is likely to increase to over 27 percent of the total.[13] In 1965 about 40 percent of our total population was employed, and by working, on the average, about 2000 hours a year managed to produce a gross national product of 692 billion dollars. Between 1962 and 1967 our annual rate of productivity increase averaged 3.8 percent. By 1968 our gross national product was 861 billion dollars. It seems likely that by the year 2000 we will be able to increase our gross national product to at least 2.2 trillion dollars annually, assuming we maintain our annual rate of productivity increase of 3.8 percent, with each person working only about three-fifths as many hours a year as now.[14] This means that we *could* employ the same proportion of people working only twenty-four hours a week, or three-fifths that number of people working forty hours a week, to produce nearly *three times as much* goods and services!

One corollary is that many of our trade schools are training people in occupations that are certain to disappear during the working lives of their students. So rapid already is the displacement of workers through automation that even some job *re*training programs have been found to be equipping people with skills for occupations that in turn will become obsolete within a short time. The bewilderment and distress soon to be evoked in millions of workers by such upheavals can be foreseen in the misery of a man I treated four years ago for depression, asthma, and insomnia. He had worked at a skilled specialty in the printing industry since age eighteen. He became ill when technological advances eliminated his job. At age thirty-eight he came into treatment and soon after enrolled in a job retraining program. When he was halfway through the five-month curriculum, an industry study revealed that further advances would probably eliminate within seven years the processes he was diligently learning to perform. Nevertheless, he got well again after starting a job in his new field. "See you in seven years," he told me wryly at our last session.

In 1961 President Kennedy said that we would need to create 25,000 new jobs a week to maintain then current levels of employment, and 50,000 a week to make good progress in reaching full employment.[15] Even with the stimulus of the war it has not been possible to achieve this goal.[16] Perhaps an all-out effort to supply the world with what it needs would temporarily help us attain full employment. But it is plain that the contrary trend toward reduction in the number of human beings needed to produce goods and services will eventually drain this job reservoir.

When people do not have jobs they do not have money to buy the things they need. With ever-decreasing levels of employment how will we distribute the ever-increasing abundance? We can expect in this country, at least, a rash of gimmicks such as contests, and "free merchandise" days on which customers will be invited to just come and take whatever they like to keep the walls of stores and warehouses from bursting.

Eventually we will be driven to adopt some such measure as the guaranteed annual income that *separates work from income*. When it was proposed in 1964 by a group of scholars this plan was greeted with widespread derision, hostility, and even suspicious insinuations that its proponents must be tools of the Kremlin. Yet in six years the guaranteed annual income has become, albeit at a very minimal level, the official recommendation of a Presidential commission.[17]

If the link between income and work is severed, then obviously work ceases to be the means of individual survival. With the introduction of other means for generating and nurturing children, love obviously ceases to be the only means of biological reproduction and species survival. With no drudgery to be performed, play largely ceases to be in bondage to escape from misery.

With love, work, and play divorced from their central social functions, their psychological self-validating function can become focal. Whereas the era of scarcity has always forced love, work, and play to remain confined in adult life to their often-crippling survival functions, the era of abundance promises to permit love, work, and play to continue life-long their crucial role in humanizing individual and community.

13 *Values, Technology, Self-Validation*

A value judgment is an appraisal of the worth of a "thing, action, or entity."[1] Because worth must be assessed in terms of a standard of exchange, such as money, a value judgment compares the worth of one thing with that of another. An auto enthusiast may decide that an American Mustang is better or worse than a British MG because it has an automatic transmission. Another person may agree or disagree with his conclusion, but on the entirely different ground that he finds one or the other car more comfortable. A musicologist might estimate the music of Bach as vastly greater than that of Berlin, basing his conclusion on the innate beauty, power, and profundity of the older work. Another, judging on the basis of the number of copies sold per 100,000 population during the first two decades after publication, or even on the percentage of people capable of enjoying the music if they heard it, could reasonably come to the opposite conclusion. Those who favor and oppose capital punishment might disagree on the values they hold most dear: human life or deterrence of crime. Or they might both agree that the supreme value is deterrence of crime and yet disagree as to whether the evidence confirms or refutes the conclusion that capital punishment deters crime.

A series of value judgments concerning important human conflicts are strung together like beads in a necklace into a value "system." Value systems vary enormously with differences in time, geography, and circumstances. They can be quite similar in widely separated societies, and quite dissimilar in societies living near one another.[2] The facts of variations between value systems are so complicated and confusing that it is difficult to make any sense of them. And a man's values are among the most hotly and irrationally defended parts of his life. Perhaps these are the reasons so little attempt has been made to understand the way values become organized into systems and what their relationships are to the rest of man's life.

Whatever the reason, this neglect is risky, for impelled by his values a man may be willing to endure any hardship in life, or bring about his (and everyone else's) death. "Give me liberty or give me death," or "I'd rather die on my feet than live on my knees," are well-known value declarations applying just to the speaker. But today these older individual statements are more often replaced by slogans such as "Better dead than red," or Eichmann's vow, "I would gladly jump into my grave if I knew I had succeeded in my task of taking the Jews with me,"[3] in which others are threatened with sharing the speaker's fate, whether or not they share his values.

We urgently need to understand value judgments and systems in order that we can control them and not vice versa.[4] While we cannot finish the task here, we can at least begin with a grasp on the thread we have been following from clusters of stars to clusters of cells, from masses of mammals to masses of men.

And that thread is the *dynamic of survival*, whether it appears as conservation of energy and matter at the inorganic level, preservation of individual and species at the level of life, or conservation of wisdom at the cultural level. By various devices the cosmos, life, and culture all manage to survive. And *it is as a specifically human survival mechanism that we must view values and value systems*.

Whatever else they may be, value systems are evolved as man's most unique adaptation to a specific set of realities. The deepest layer of those realities is man's basic needs, which are the same for all men everywhere. But the flexibility of human beings above that layer permits great variation in value systems that are compatible with survival. A value system must afford satisfaction of the basic needs within the limitations of outer reality or the people subscribing to it will not survive.

The Scarcity Imperative and the Puritan Ethic

The most powerful molder of value systems has been the nearly universal condition of scarcity. And it is remarkable that in all the temperate zones, where the most vigorous civilizations have arisen, the resultant "scarcity imperative," as it might be called, is recognizable in the constellations of values that have promoted survival.[5]

The scarcity imperative has two components. One is the pressure of needs that are unmet or threaten to become so, because of some sort of shortage. The other is the tendency of well-established need-satisfying devices to persist long after they become outmoded. Both powerfully direct behavior. Examples are the irresistible urge of thirsty travelers in the desert to find water, and the stubborn disease-producing habit of fertilizing food crops with human excrement.

The scarcity imperative expresses itself in two main themes. One is the broad group of efforts to remedy the deprivations of scarcity. The other is the broad group of efforts to remedy the *objections* to the deprivations of scarcity. They are both to be found in varying proportions and patterns in any value system developed out of the scarcity imperative.

Neither scarcity nor long-standing necessity to work hard to survive are sufficient conditions in themselves for the emergence of hard work as a preeminent "value." In addition there must be a facilitating web of philosophical assumptions and social arrangements, such as those that characterized the early American colonists. An example of the opposite circumstances, inhibiting to elevation of the value of hard work, is found in portions of Hindu India which esteem mystic resignation and spiritual advance more than industry and material gain as a reaction to scarcity.

Beyond these factors lie those of utility and reward. No doubt the early Renaissance serf, like the Hindu peasant, worked as hard as anyone ever has. But his primitive farming techniques and his lord's opulent share of the harvest combined to reduce him to penury no matter how faithfully he labored. Aside from a sense of belonging to a deity-sanctioned scheme of things, about all he received in return for his toil was protection from the aggression of rival nobles, whose tyranny from his viewpoint was unlikely to be worse. It is dubious that he developed a "value" of hard work.

In this his master would have agreed, as there was no reward for him in personal drudgery either. Both traditional classes despised labor. To the masters work was for their slaves, and to the slaves, in a more important sense, work was for their masters. For hard work to become a value, there would have to be a possibility of its leading to something one could value.

For complex reasons there arose at this time a *middle* class. Because of various technological and social changes, for them as free men the facts were different. They *could* benefit, and considerably, from hard work. It is not surprising that for them hard work became a "value."

And it is not surprising that hard work became a foremost value for American colonists in their turn. Although the settlers were by no means all middle-class, they were in the main free men, and therefore eligible to benefit from their hard work.

What is the relationship between the scarcity imperative and the list of virtues sometimes designated the "Puritan ethic"? The Puritan ethic became the dominant representative of the scarcity imperative in the United States, and still constitutes the nominal value system of Americans.

It is apparent how hard work, frugality, thrift, humility, respect for elders, chastity, charity, honesty, fraternity, and submission to the will of God, each in concert with the rest, all contributed to survival under conditions of scarcity. Hard work, thrift, and frugality all serve the overriding need of people in such circumstances to provide and conserve the material means of existence. Respect for elders served the double purpose of assuring the young the seasoned wisdom of their parents, as well as affording each generation the security of being cared for when advancing age weakened their powers. Chastity before marriage saved parents from having to provide in middle and old age for grandchildren as well as their own offspring. It also assured the new groom that the precious capacity of the woman to bear him children had not been squandered and perhaps exhausted before purchase of his chattel-bride. And it guaranteed that the 5 percent of women doomed to sterility[6] for a variety of reasons retained their market value before marriage revealed their deficiency.* Charity helped the unfortunate to survive. Honesty allowed you to trust your neighbor not to steal your grain while you were away butchering beef. Fraternity brought enough muscle and will together to raise a barn for mutual food conservation or a militia for mutual defense. And submission to the will of God provided some comfort to those who, having lived all these virtues, were rewarded with the bitter fate of poverty, sickness, and bereavement.

Of course not all Puritans subscribed to the Puritan ethic. Nor was it only the historical Puritans who lived according to its precepts. It is nevertheless true that one of the best distilled and most extreme expressions of this ethical tendency was found among the Puritans.

So in its applicable time, subscription to the Puritan ethic, or its relatives, was of definite survival value. Of more importance for our inquiry is that adherence to its tenets in its applicable time brought about considerable self-validation.

The Heyday of the Puritan Ethic

How could this be so? After all, when the Puritan ethic was most powerful, were not love, work and play anchored firmly to their central social

---

* Since sterile women were spared the test of fecundity constituted by premarital intercourse, they could not be identified and rejected for marriage as infertile women could be among some sexually freer Pacific island peoples who lived in abundance.

functions? Was not love tied to child nurture, work to production of vital goods and services, and what little play people could manage not only desperately needed for distraction from the grimness of life, but viciously attacked as sinful? Where in this dismal web was there a strand of psychic intimacy in the relationship to love, work, and play which would lead to self-validation?

We must look beneath the stifling shroud of scarcity to find the tendrils that manage unexpectedly to survive in its shade. In the first place, we must consider the different outlook of men and women born during the period when the Puritan ethic, at least on paper, was practically uncontested. Most people then tended to demand much less of life. A German proverb of the time ruefully states, "A good soup and a warm bed is already a great deal." No doubt individuals then wished to be happy as much as we. But their *expectations* were much more modest than ours. For clarity let us sketch an admittedly exaggerated caricature of such people.

Their few pleasures, such as the Thanksgiving feast expressing appreciation to God for the humble blessings of the harvest, were usually restrained and pious. Love was looked upon as a capricious madness which, although surrendered to by some people with startling enthusiasm, in general had no necessary relationship to marriage. Marriage usually was arranged by parents on the basis common to all business transactions: mutual material and social advantages. The partners expected one another to fulfill the terms of this survival-promoting contract. Period. If either or both loved the other, or even experienced much happiness in the marriage, that was regarded as an unpredictable extra dividend for which they were most grateful. As a matter of course, a husband was expected to dedicate himself to providing for his wife. Whatever her feelings about him, a woman was expected, and expected herself, to devote her energies first to caring for her husband, conferring survival benefits on him. Because people tend eventually to feel as they behave, in due course they often came to feel love for one another.

No doubt this reaction was fortified for the woman by the consistent meeting of her survival needs by the "good" man selected for her. She and her husband were usually so absorbed in the problem of surviving that they measured their success more in terms of making the food and firewood in the shed last out the winter than in the happiness or unhappiness evoked by the nuances of their spouse's tone of voice or simultaneity of orgasm.

But soon the needier newcomers arrived to command the bulk of their strength and devotion. The wife was usually delivered of her baby at home, and often cared for it and her others without much help. She

tended them through the rigors of the climate, the often brutal neighborhood life, and the ravages of infectious and other diseases that ordinarily
killed five out of ten children before they reached marriageable age.[7]
And she did all this with no disposable tissues, diapers, or cotton balls,
almost no store-bought commodities at all, practically no medical aid, and
little direct help from their overworked father. But this draining regime,
no matter how thoroughly it throttled her other development, called
upon most of her talents and capacities. It therefore made of every day
survived by herself and her brood an anxious delight, and of every child
shepherded safely to maturity a self-validating achievement.

If a man's labor yielded a "good living" he considered himself lucky.
The worker by now was usually a farmer, a craftsman, or a small businessman. It was he himself who prepared the soil, planted the seed, reaped
and disposed of the harvest. Or fashioned the chair from raw material to
finished product. Or purchased, sold, and kept the accounts of the meats
passing through his butcher shop. Thus the range of activities over which
he had direct control was wide. So substantial a proportion of his skills
was called upon at his job as to assure a degree of zestful investment of
the self in the process and product of the work. And although he might
be too exhausted from twelve or more hours a day to do much else, his
endless drudgery often thus yielded the modest self-validation his nomadic forebears had wrung from their more precarious labors.

As for play, the era of scarcity minimized its importance in two main
ways. First, the infant's focus on survival work was often continued into
hours of childhood chores and, sooner or later, into endless adult labor.
This enormous absorption of energies into self-preservation left little over
for self-validation. Second, since love and work demanded of an adult
more variety of activity, he had fewer unused capacities to push for expression in play. The puritanical value judgment denouncing play grew out
of these two factors. We can understand how it promoted survival while
squelching self-validation. If a person engaged in play, other people concluded correctly that he was not pouring his full resources into the "virtuous" central social functions of love and work, and to that extent was
not doing his utmost to wrest from a stingy reality the security his family
needed. By branding play as sinful the community helped the individual
to renounce it. Instead, he was coerced to direct his efforts into assuring
the continued existence of the selves for which he was responsible, although at the expense of depriving them (and himself) of play's contribution to confirmation of their existence and worth.

Of course it was impossible to exterminate the play impulse altogether.
Formal play existed, expressed in games like bowling and chess, but was
officially discouraged. Even among sober New England Puritans there

were some who might informally climb a hill just to watch the sun set, and maybe whittle a stick or saw on a fiddle. After all, amid such harsh realities who would need distraction more than they? But if their indulgences proved too pleasurable they might be forced to rationalize their guilt by carving a kitchen spoon or playing a hymn during "vespers." Thus even play was pressed into service of survival in this world or the next.

Such were and are the grim facts of survival for the vast majority during the era of scarcity. But the tiny leisured minority, spawned during the last two thousand years by the uneven distribution of small surpluses, did not go unnoticed. It was taken as a model by the struggling majority. They pursued the "better life," or at least the material basis of it, which they could glimpse within the aristocrat's castle and emulate at least minimally in their humble homes. The resulting cycle of rising expectations continues today, spurred on by the word and image of abundance brought by electronic media which now reach millions of even the most impoverished people in the world.

The Rise of Technology and Decline of the Puritan Ethic

All around us it is plain that the Puritan ethic no longer has its former unquestioned adherence. And naturally so, for hard work, frugality, thrift, humility, chastity, and charity are not especially adaptive even to current realities. Still less will they prove adaptive to forthcoming abundance, to a world of effective contraception and cradle-to-grave security for all people, regardless of legitimacy. Respect for elders is less and less adaptive to a world in which life-span greatly exceeds the period during which great-grandchildren find senior wisdom of much interest. Submission to supernatural power is not adaptive to a world in which increasingly man himself controls his own future.

But wishes are not riches. How did it happen that the wishes of so many for a share of the riches of abundance have actually been achieved sufficiently to undermine the Puritan ethic?

Until two hundred years ago, man was trapped by a lack of power in his efforts to accumulate surpluses.[8] Perhaps one hundredth of one percent of the energy needed came from wheels turned by wind or water. The rest came from muscle power, eight percent from the muscle of animals, and the rest from the muscle of man. Although other sources of power were known, they were either too paltry or too uncontrollable to be useful. The bent stick known as a bow was capable of hurling an arrow with great accuracy and force. But it could only store for later release energy at first expended by human muscle, and small amounts at that. The same applied to various gravity- and spring-powered devices used in clocks. The Chinese had long since invented gunpowder, but its immoderate reactions made difficult the application of its force to more than ceremonial spectacles or slaughter.

Not that the human mind lacked the concept and technique for producing industrially useful artificial power. The Greeks developed the principles of the steam engine, but because of their reverence for the body and unwillingness to project its function upon a machine, were unwilling to exploit it for productive use.[9] But in fine print somewhere on the human agenda they entered for consideration two thousand years later the possibility that through the expansive power of steam, the energy stored by nature in various fuels could be linked to man's needs. And somehow, perhaps as a result of two millennia of disappointment with muscle-produced surpluses, and because of the intervening development of respect for science and human rights, the possibility was realized.

In 1698 in England a steam engine was used to pump water out of mines.[10] And in the early 1700s inventors created engines that were capable of powering the most complex processes. Suddenly man was released from the prison of having only the power of one or two horses per person, and found himself free to employ hundreds of horsepower per person.

This new strength was systematically linked to machinery for the production of everything from textiles, foods, and chemicals to building materials, tools, and weapons. Enormous surpluses were produced which had to be sold at a profit so that the industries could produce still more. The preexisting apparatus of private enterprise expanded rapidly to handle the task. Gradually improved techniques and competition reduced the prices of goods so that the majority could begin to share in the abundance.

To purchase the wondrous new wares they associated with the better life for which they hungered, people left their old work on farms, in small handcraft shops, and in small businesses for jobs in the mechanized factories. They hoped for more stable and larger income. Often they found only pittance wages, deadly tedium of endlessly repetitive toil, and miserable working and living conditions. But by the time they realized their plight it was frequently impossible to escape. Not only did wealth prove elusive, but now workers were frenzied by the pain of an unexpected decrease in the psychological satisfactions available to them as factory laborers. The technological changes of the Industrial Revolution, rather than expanding the chances for a fulfilling life, actually restricted the possibility of psychic intimacy with work. The limited but reliable self-validation man found in absorption in the full work of farm or shop disappeared in the fragmented work of the factory. A man cannot zestfully invest himself in only a sliver of the process that leads to a finished product.

What happens to his untapped capabilities and his now seriously unmet need for self-validation? Does the tired worker pick up his lunch pail and stride home in happy anticipation of compensation through his love life? Perhaps this has been true of some. But it is unlikely, because a deficiency of self-validation in one area does not lead to optimism about finding it elsewhere.

Even if he is hopeful, further disappointment is probable. We know that it is those individuals who do enjoy a psychically intimate relation with work who are best able to sustain a personal love life. They do not jeopardize love by demanding exaggerated self-validation from it. It is the man who finds his work empty who, by the time he puts his key to the front door lock, is likely to be in a state of bitter hypersusceptibility to any new frustration. It is most often he who must find his wife carefully decorated, smiling tranquilly, and pouring him a precisely mixed martini as he swings open the door, or blow up in hurt anger.

Such hair-trigger sensitivity is improbable in a man whose work offers the self-validation, not to mention physical exhaustion, available to an old style farmer or craftsman. However, in the last few hundred years the technological changes of the Industrial Revolution have not only shortened the workday but have increasingly *depersonalized* work, thereby depriving people of a main source of self-validation. They therefore place correspondingly greater demands upon love life. Inadequately developed personalities in the past, hemmed in in their efforts to master reality by the grim demands of scarcity, settled for modest satisfactions in love. With more and more reality strictures removed by enlarging abundance, more and more such personalities are unable to attain even ordinary success in love, let alone the needed degree of substitutive satisfaction.

These problems are multiplied infinitely by the automation-cybernation revolution now under way. Now it is not only man's muscle that is gradually being made obsolete, but his brain. Whole sequences of manufacture and assembly of parts are carried out by machine under the supervision and control of other machines.[11] The displacement of human minds is proceeding rapidly in business as well as in industry, with jobs of clerical up through middle management levels disappearing faster than they are created. And at this moment a group of scientists is having some success in teaching a computer to practice psychotherapy.[12]

At the same time that a critical source of self-validation is eliminated,

enormous surpluses are produced, inexorably replacing the era of predominant scarcity with the era of predominant abundance. So the individual person becomes unnecessary to the productive process, while
simultaneously his conviction that he ought to live by the values of
scarcity crumbles beneath the floods of goods and aeons of free time. As
the dinosaur in a comic strip remarked ruefully, "What good is an adaptation when the conditions to which it was suited disappear?"

These changes are unraveling the fabric of our daily lives. The processes whereby values are evolved spontaneously seem unable to fill the
values vacuum with a coherent new adaptation in advance of the deluge.
So, material abundance in the outer world threatens to be matched
by character destitution in the inner world. And as even the tedium of
fragmented industrial work disappears, the same old inadequate personalities may be forced to turn in compensation to the love life for a still
more exorbitant amount of self-validation.

Failing to find it in love or work, the starved personality rushes into
play. Here, too, his hopes are too often dashed. For his play becomes
organized into mere distraction or ways to dominate others.

First there is the increasing frantic involvement with defeating someone at games like bowling, handball, tennis, or golf. Then there is the
impassioned identification with a favorite team through which he hopes
to "win" vicariously. Sad to say, I find patients upset consciously more
often by the defeat of a home team than by their own lack of truly self-
validating play. For the adult continues to use play as he has been
taught to do during childhood, as a distraction from the frequently
empty and unrewarding rituals through which he is compelled to suffer
at home and in school. Also early in his life he has been taught to focus
his ambition onto the competitive dimensions of play. He has learned to
"play to win," and thereby achieve dominance over the losers. In this
way we have forced play to be a miniature version of and rehearsal for
the realities of adult life. Or rather, for living out the mistaken notion
that the essence of human social life during a mythical golden past was
"dog-eat-dog" competition, and that therefore we must do our best to
preserve competitive elements and bring them to permanent predominance today.

This view ignores not only all the evidence summarized earlier that the
essence of all survival of all life, particularly man's survival, has always
been cooperation, but also the evidence that the coming era of abundance
makes unnecessary and therefore irrational much of today's competition
among human beings, particularly in the realm of economics. The im-
pertinence of competition is even more clear in relation to play. It is not
self-validation but the competition mystique that pushes children's play

into "organized sports." The delights of batting, running, throwing, and catching are self-validating when engaged in for their own sake, or at least in the course of a fast, spontaneous sandlot game. But self-validation often flies out of the ball park when these activities are organized into uniform fittings, bus trips, pep talks, and other interminable irrelevancies of Little League baseball.

At a somewhat higher level there is the play that requires purchase of a set of power tools, a boat, motorcycle, or plane, or the various do-it-yourself "crazes" that set middle-aged executives to driving a garden tractor in their backyards, wearing engineer's caps and overalls as they build and operate model railways, or applying oil paint to numbered areas on canvas. Then there are the grotesqueries of gambling at Las Vegas, playing pool with Bunnies, or trying to shred quail with buckshot. For most people, these and other play activities do not evolve as ways to engage and enjoy unused capacities. Instead they are suggested to the deprived person directly through advertisements or indirectly through his "crowd." His acceptance of them is a compulsive conformity to its mores rather than a zestful exploration and investment of self. Such play activities thus are sources of distraction and trivial triumph rather than self-validation.

These trends are increasing. If they continue, the only dividend of the era of abundance for many people may be many extra years of "leisure" in which to savor the inescapable bitterness of having satisfied all their wishes without ever having learned how to wish for all their satisfactions.

In our anxiety over change, many of us are clinging absurdly to the most outmoded values of scarcity, while unconcernedly allowing other values to wither which still have adaptive power. For example, under pressure of the advertising seduction to consume on credit, "frugality" and "thrift" are becoming mere catchwords. But not so for work. To the enormous relief of some, "work" (to earn a living) is the one value of scarcity that retains widespread strength because working at a job is still the common pattern of obtaining material goods.

It has become a truism that this is the first moment in history in which there is at last the possibility of freeing man from enslavement to drudgery, permitting him to devote himself to creatively human activity. Ironically it is at this moment that the hidebound try desperately to make permanent the obsolescing connection between work and survival. Even though today a declining percentage of our population works to earn a living, puritanical moralists continue to thunder against welfare programs and the guaranteed annual income with such rusty irrelevances as the Biblical injunction, "If any would not work, neither should he eat."

Even those who recognize some of the problems of modern society do not face the full implications of abundance. For example, Neil W. Chamberlain, Professor of Economics at Yale University, urges us to undertake massive national lifelong educational programs.[13] But to what purpose? So that we can expand continuously our self-validating engagement with life in an era of increasing abundance? On the contrary, the advice aims merely to protect our *employability and earning power*. Such recommendations at one stroke deny the reality of dwindling availability of jobs, and demean education along with work by chaining both to making a living.

Work and Psychic Intimacy

The net result of this frenzied effort is to prevent full psychic intimacy with work by doggedly keeping it tied to its regressively infantile income-producing function. Instead, we should be reacting to abundance by seeking ways to organize work that would elicit zestful investment of the self and reverse psychic alienation from work. This requires us to find ways to increase self-validation by promoting zestful investment of the self in the process and product of work worthy of the attention of a human being.

But how do we accomplish this?

First, we must understand the full significance of work to human identity even when it is organized as jobs performed to make a living. The depression of the 1920s and 1930s was an unintended experiment by our wayward economy well suited to demonstrate the ruinous effects on health of loss of employment. Family relationships are particularly vulnerable to this stress. Following unemployment, parents who formerly got along well with each other and their children often became hostile toward or withdrawn from one another. Especially vulnerable is the self-esteem of the former "breadwinner."[14] According to the Institute for Social Research's study of unemployment,

A considerable proportion of the men exhibited a certain deterioration of personality: loss of emotional stability, breakdown of morale, irritability, new faults such as drinking, unfaithfulness to the wife, and so on . . . in addition to sheer economic anxiety the man suffers from deep humiliation. He experiences a sense of deep frustration because in his own estimation he fails to fulfill what is the central duty of his life, the very touchstone of his manhood—the role of family provider. . . . The feeling of disturbance and humiliation exists irrespective of the intellectual convictions of the man . . . there were some who said "Children's love must be bought"

. . . "children can't help but resent it if he fails in his duty." . . . "I would rather starve than let my wife work." . . . "I would rather turn on the gas and put an end to the whole family than let my wife support me." . . . for most of the men in our culture, work is apparently the sole organizing principle and the only means of self-expression. . . .

The average American has the feeling that . . . no man worthy of his name would be satisfied with growing flowers or painting pictures as the main activity of life unless, indeed, he intended to sell them. . . . The . . . man who made these things the center of his life would be held in some contempt even if he had an independent income. . . . To the question, "What is the most important thing in life?" [the unemployed] are likely to say "work, because with nothing to do you cannot enjoy anything."[15]

Second, we must see that, as Erich Fromm so eloquently puts it, a truly human history begins when "the aim and end of all social life is not work and production, but the unfolding of man's powers as an end in itself."[16]

It appears from Fromm's account of their ideas in "Breaking the Chains of Illusion" that Karl Marx, like Freud, was concerned with man's ability to love and work.[17] He may even have regarded ability to love and work as criteria of what later was to be called mental health, although he concentrated on the sociohistorical roots of the mind and its sickness rather than the biopsychological ones that most interested Freud.

Marx's thought is relevant in several ways to our inquiry into the evolving fate of man. Not only have various versions and interpretations of his writings become the basis for the socioeconomic systems of half the members of our species, but his ideas as to the "nature" of man, like Darwin's and Freud's, have influenced thinkers as well as other men everywhere. It was while preparing this section on work and psychic intimacy that I first found it necessary to explore Marx in detail, particularly his concept of "alienation" as it applies to work.

A glimpse of its background will help clarify his idea. It seems that all cultures everywhere have had the notion that at some golden past time man was at one with his surroundings in a way that is now unknown. We have seen how Freud considered this "oceanic" feeling to be a vague memory of an individual person's state before his mind was developed enough to differentiate his "self" from the outside world. The Bible expresses the feeling in the story of the Fall. Adam and Eve, previously in idyllic harmony with God, were expelled from paradise because a bite of the apple from the tree of knowledge of good and evil had provided information which separated them from God (pure "good").

It was Hegel, however, who first developed the essence of the concept of alienation. He conceived of God as having become estranged from himself in the form of man.[18] He saw history as the process of God's reunion with himself through reincorporating man.

Feuerbach, reversing Hegel, thought of God as man's own powers projected to an outside supernatural being. Thus the more powerful God is, the weaker is man. Thus weakened, man can utilize his own powers only by worship of God. This view has influenced many thinkers, who then have regarded history in one aspect as the process whereby man has become stronger through reclaiming for himself his formerly alienated capabilities that had been surrendered to God.*

Marx was one of these, but he focused instead on man's daily terrestrial life. Following Feuerbach's analysis of man/God, in his early writings Marx also saw man's relationship to the process and product of *work* under conditions of civilized society as an alienation of his powers:

> . . . the more the worker expends himself in work, the more powerful becomes the world of objects which he creates . . . the poorer he becomes in his inner life and the less he belongs to himself; it is just the same as in religion. The more of himself man attributes to God the less he has left in himself. . . . The *alienation* of the worker in his product means not only that his labor becomes an object, assumes an external existence, but that it exists independently, outside himself . . . as an alien and hostile force.[19]

Marx's concept of alienation is sometimes difficult to grasp. Especially confusing and obscure are its relationships to other familiar Marxian ideas, such as those dealing with profit, property, and class. Important as these are to comprehending his thought, unfortunately we must restrict ourselves here only to his view of alienation and work, in relation to which some effort is repaid through the understanding it yields of both the value and limitations of his thinking.

Why does Marx consider the worker's product as not only alien, but *hostile?* On the evidence of his mainly historical studies, he decided that the basic characteristic of the human species is "free conscious activity."[20] However desperate was the struggle to survive amid conditions of scarcity, Marx believed that primitive man's work was not alienated because it constituted "life activity, productive life" through which a person strove by free conscious activity to create what he wanted.[21] His product was needed and belonged to him for his own use.

But with the beginning of civilization (with its great elaboration of division of labor and techniques of exchange of goods), man's more

---

* For comparison, consider the procedure of psychoanalysis, which carries out a related process on an individual level, with the patient slowly reclaiming the powers that previously were alienated from him in unconsciousness.

efficiently produced product became instead a *commodity,* to be used as a means of obtaining the commodities produced by others. No longer was it the outcome of free conscious activity in pursuit of satisfaction of his real needs. The product of his own hands no longer belonged to him directly. For example, there lies the fresh bread he has baked, delicious and tempting, but he may not eat it just because he is hungry. First he must go through a new and alien procedure whereby he *obtains posses-sion of his own product* through barter, purchase, or, if all else fails, theft. The product of his own work, instead of warmly satisfying his need, thus has become transformed into a provocative tease which first whips up his appetite and then sells itself to the highest bidder, surely a hostile relationship to its creator.

Now to capture the hostile product, a man needs money. And in pursuit of it

> Every man speculates upon creating a *new* need in another in order to force him to a new sacrifice, . . . to entice him into a new kind of pleasure. . . . Everyone tries to establish over others an *alien* power in order to find there the satisfaction of his own egoistic need. . . . Every new product is a new *potentiality* of mutual deceit and robbery. . . . Man becomes increasingly poor as man. . . . The need for money is there-fore the real need created by the modern economy, . . . The less you *are,* the less you express your life, the more you *have,* the greater is your *alienated* life. . . .[22]

Marx foresaw in the middle of the nineteenth century that the increasing drives to have and to use more and more things, and to obtain the money needed to acquire them, could eventually cripple man. Since all property, like money, is alienable and can be sold, lost or stolen, that man whose identity lies mainly in his property is in a precariously vulnerable condition.[23]

Through such analyses, Marx supported his postulate that *the way in which man produces determines his way of living,* and this practice of life in turn determines his way of thinking and being.[24] Others had expressed the same idea that "Institutions form men."[25] What Marx added was that the *formative institutions were elements in a given society's system of production.*

Marx shows that "alienation appears not only in the result, but also in the *process* of production . . ."[26] He contrasts the type of production before extensive division and fragmentation of labor with modern production:

> In handicraft . . . the workman makes use of a tool; in the factory the machine makes use of him. There the movements of the instruments of

labor proceed from him; here it is the movement of the machines that he must follow.[27]

What did Marx see in his later works as possibilities for the future? He believed that a necessary precondition for the eventual cure of alienation is reorganization of society, in such a way that the means of production are owned by the public at large, the product being created and distributed solely according to human need. In such a society man consciously would take himself as the subject of history. He would experience himself as the source and control of his powers, and use them to release himself from dependence upon things and external circumstances. He saw the objective as the full development of the individual person's potentialities, stifled now by the techniques employed to make production more efficient.

> Modern Industry, . . . compels society, . . . to replace the detail-worker of today, *crippled* by lifelong repetition of one and the same trivial operation, and thus reduced to the mere *fragment* of a man, by the fully developed individual . . . to whom the different social functions he performs are but so many *modes of giving free scope to his own natural and acquired powers.*[28]

He expected a flowering of freedom in such changed conditions not only for the individual but for the entire human community.

> In fact, the realm of freedom does not commence until the point is passed where labor under the compulsion of necessity and of external utility is required.[29]

How do my ideas about work relate to Marx's? There seems to be no disagreement about the nature of man's relationship to most modern work, which Marx calls "alienated" and I consider lacking in "psychic intimacy." And our ideas appear to correspond well in relation to the expansion of future freedom when work no longer need be tied to survival.

My difference with him has to do with the role of *scarcity* in causing alienation in man's relationship to work, and the distinction I have drawn between the social and psychological functions of work. In my view most human beings have always been so driven by scarcity that they were *never* free to have a psychically intimate relationship to work, and were therefore always alienated from what was experienced as onerous, exhausting toil.

In contrast, it would appear that to Marx scarcity itself did not distort primitive man's relationship to work. Although the gripe of his empty stomach and the shiver of his naked skin were the central stimuli for his activity, he could not be alienated from work because he performed the whole process of production himself and could use his product directly to satisfy his needs. It was only when *civilized conditions of labor* confined him to a fragment of the productive process, and turned his product and his labor itself into commodities, that he became alienated from work. Marx seemingly did not view the brutal necessity that enslaved primitive man even *before* the extensive division of labor as evidence that he had failed to reach "the realm of freedom." This appears to me a contradiction of Marx's own idea quoted above that the realm of freedom commences only when labor is freed from the compulsion of necessity. Why did he make this distinction between the condition for the realm of freedom in past and present?

First of all, Marx's implication that primitive labor was not alienated reaches us via a manuscript not published during his lifetime from which a number of pages have been lost. The discussion breaks off after he has posed but not answered the question, "How is this estrangement rooted in the nature of human development?"[30] Perhaps the apparent disagreement would dissolve if these passages had survived. Second, it is altogether probable that the several decades of thought and experience that separated this paper from his later "realm of freedom" concept changed his ideas. Passage of time has done the same for the ideas of many important thinkers.

Incidentally, both Marx and Freud are said to have had followers who complainingly inquired how their masters could now assert so-and-so when in the past they had written contradictory such-and-such. In exasperation, so the story goes, they replied, "Because unlike you I am not a Marx*ist*," and "Because unlike you I am not a Freud*ian*."

Perhaps it is a result of the lesser imagination possessed generally by followers as compared with that of innovators that the least penetrating parts of Marx's analyses, like Freud's, have so often been seized upon by the implementers of his ideas. Or perhaps this has resulted from the regrettable tendency to find a God in a man, and to be therefore more concerned with establishing an orthodoxy of revealed truth than with testing scientifically the useful ideas of a valued teacher. We have noted before that it requires considerable courage and maturity to live with uncertainty. Lacking both, the unfortunate human tendency is to transform empirically derived conviction into blind faith. It would be well to remember these exchanges today whenever we are tempted to deify the thought or persons of great contributors.

Whether we attribute the responsibility to Marx or to his followers, it seems indisputable that many Marxist views fail to formulate clearly the notion that man must be alienated from work *so long as he is forced to work by scarcity and the necessity to make a living*.

Phrased in my terms, a man must experience a loss of psychic intimacy with work when his efforts are impelled by the central social function of work, or any motive *other than the pressure of his own powers experienced as a desire or wish to do that work.* Although some self-validation derives from hunting for food to ease hunger, or working on an assembly line to earn money to pay for it, full psychic intimacy with work can come about only from zestful, enduring investment of the self in work one does *just because one wants to do it.* By not placing scarcity at the focal point, some Marxists imply that alienation from work would be overcome, despite continued scarcity, simply by restoring to the worker fuller participation in the productive process, as well as control (via social ownership) of the process, its product, and the ends to which it is put.

Whatever other background there may be to such a formulation, an important element is their subscription to a version of the *golden past illusion,* which, as already mentioned, in various forms shapes the thinking of all human groups. Everyone's shadowy recollection of childhood, every culture's mythology, and every religious testament contains an account of paradise, involving unity with all things, from which expulsion was suffered for one reason or another.

. A misreading of human work under such influence would have been easy in Marx's time when not much was known about early human evolution. But in the light of evidence reviewed in earlier chapters, it seems dubious that there ever was a time of unity with work for our species, especially for our most remote forebears. Since scarcity was always their master, we can glimpse over our shoulders no lovely earlier time in which the ordinary man was ordinarily free to do the work he wanted to do just for its own sake.

So we must conclude that only in the *future,* in the brand-new era of abundance, is there a possibility that the majority of human beings will no longer be driven by survival needs and therefore alienated from work. *For they will have reached the "realm of freedom" in which they may select not the activity that sustains biological life, but that which yields the greatest reward of self-validation.*

Another possible cause of misunderstanding of the cure of alienation is inability to grasp the full *magnitude* and *import* of the abundance Marx foresaw. Despite conscious assertions to that effect, I have the impression that *unconsciously* Marxists may not be able to accept, any more than non-Marxists, the idea that elimination of scarcity, and *only* elimination of scarcity, will really permit release of human character altogether from determination by the institutions of production.

Whatever may be one's estimate of the value of socialism as a means of helping people make the transition from scarcity to abundance, it is evident that social ownership of the means, and full participation in the process, of production are neither necessary nor sufficient conditions for the full flowering of man *once general abundance has advanced beyond a certain point.* Providing only that people have security that it will continue, and control over the *uses* to which it is put, at some level or other, abundance will make inconsequential *who* owns or wields the tools that produce it. Or put another way, under such conditions "private" ownership and use of the tools that produce abundance could result in great flowering while under other conditions, social ownership and use of the tools could result merely in social rather than private promotion of alienation. What will count more than the degree of social ownership will be the degree of social synergy.*

Various versions of "Marxism," which have become the ideologies of countries in Eastern Europe and Asia, constitute experiments testing the validity of some of Marx's ideas, or at least those of some of his interpreters.

It is intriguing to speculate what role Marx's early idea that primitive man was not alienated from work may have had indirectly in stimulating such efforts. If one accepts his conclusion, it would be reasonable to suppose that, even without eliminating scarcity, by reducing work fragmentation and increasing control of work process and product to the levels experienced by primitive man, we should be able to eliminate alienation.

One especially interesting experiment is the "decentralized socialism" of Yugoslavia which contrasts with the centralized socialism of the USSR. In the Soviet Union the means of production are owned by the people in general, and managed on their behalf by representatives of a centralized government. As a result, the workers in a particular plant may have little, if any, say concerning their working lives. On the other hand, in Yugoslavia the means of production are both *owned and managed locally by the people who work with them.* This means that the workers of each factory or clothing store or restaurant exercise control over both the process and product of their work. They do this through their representatives who are elected to policy-making bodies called "workers' councils."

The representatives of the assembly-line workers, the salesmen, the designers, and the managers meet to assess the success of last year's prod-

* My account of Marx's ideas may be too psychological and individualistic. I am indebted to Professor John Horton of UCLA for pointing out, for example, that to Marx an important criterion of nonalienated labor is that it must simultaneously serve the needs of the individual and the species. This idea closely parallels Benedict's independently formulated concept of "synergy" reviewed earlier (p. 164).

uct, and to plan the kind and amount of product to be made in the coming year. They make decisions concerning all related matters, such as how to obtain the needed raw materials. The enterprise may be in competition with others and must face the trial of the marketplace in selling its product to the people. At the end of the year, according to a prearranged scheme, profit is distributed to the various categories of workers. A loss might mean wage cuts or, if large enough, financial failure and going out of business.

This system is intended to restore to the worker the control of the process and product of his work lost to him through the division of labor and exchange techniques brought about by civilization. If the assumptions of this version of Marxism are correct, there should be no alienation from work in Yugoslavia. Luckily, relevant information is available.

A Yugoslav social psychologist, Dr. Josip Obradovic, has ascertained in finer detail the circumstances that are associated with alienation from work.[31]

In Yugoslav industry there are today the usual three kinds of production jobs found in modern nations with advancing industrialization, the differences being the sort of technique the worker uses. They are called handicraft, mechanized, and automated. Automated jobs are found mainly in chemical and petroleum industries, which are difficult to discuss because we are not all familiar with their products. For this reason I will discuss the three kinds of jobs *hypothetically,* in relation to shoe manufacturing as a familiar example, although automation is still uncommon today in manufacturing, and may not yet really be available for shoe making.

A handicraft worker performs a considerable sequence of operations with tools he regulates himself, for example, cutting out and shaping the sole and last of a shoe, and then stitching them together. A mechanized worker performs one or a very few operations over and over which are regulated by the speed and rhythm of a moving belt that carries the parts along an assembly line, for example, the pulling of a lever that rivets into place brass eyelets for laces. An automated worker controls an extended process consisting of many mechanized sequences of operations by adjusting buttons and levers according to the overall requirements of the product, often on the basis of readings of the dials of instruments, for example, machinery that would cut soles and lasts, stitch them together, and finally implant the eyelets.

Dr. Obradovic studied a group of workers at each kind of job in various industries with a questionnaire that disclosed two factors: the degree of *alienation from work,* and the degree of *job satisfaction.* Alienation from work was indicated by answers to questions about such feelings as boredom, indifference, apathy, and disinterest in relation to work. Job satisfaction was indicated by answers to questions indicating overall acceptance and pleasure in the total life situation that is determined by the job. Each group of workers was composed half of people who were members of workers' councils and half who were not.

The results showed that *membership in workers' councils made no significant difference* in the degree of either alienation or job satisfaction for workers in any of the three job categories. Apparently this device does not appreciably prevent alienation or restore psychic intimacy with work. This is the result I would expect on the basis of clinical experience. A man's zestful investment of the self in the actual process and product of work he does not want to do for itself is not likely to be influenced by whether or not he participates in collective planning of the work at a time and place remote from the site of the job.[32]

As to the differences between the three groups, the degree of alienation from work was least among handicraft workers, much greater among mechanized assembly-line workers, and highest among automated assembly-line workers. On clinical grounds again, this is the result I would have expected. Zestful investment of the self in the process and product of work is more likely when the attention can be absorbed in the novelty of a variety of operations, each of which must be controlled precisely by the worker who can experience promptly the good or bad outcome of his effort. It is much easier for a shoemaker who can see the consequence of each of his stitches to stick to his last. When a man works on an isolated fragment of a process, it is difficult for him to become *aware of the significance* of minor variations he is causing in the product, let alone emotionally concerned whether the eyelets are located a half inch this way or that. But since he still has some direct contact with materials and tools, he is better off in this respect than the automated worker who may not only have no physical contact whatever with the work, but may see it only through a glass window, or actually perceive nothing of the productive process but its indirect reflection on the faces of his dials. Since for millions of years our brains have been manually oriented, such a worker may yearn to return for an hour even to a grueling assembly line literally out of need to "keep my hand in."

Thus as one might expect, impartial study shows that alienation from work exists in Yugoslavia as it does elsewhere. Evidently, in the continued presence of scarcity the arrangements described are not sufficient to eliminate it entirely. We must of course greet gladly any serious effort to *reduce* alienation from work. But it is important not to confound means of *amelioration,* even should some prove successful, with those of *elimina-*

tion. Elimination of alienation from work, and zestful investment of self in it, can come about only when abolition of scarcity has permitted emancipation of human character and motivations from determination by the institutions of production. (Of course, abolition of scarcity, although a necessary factor, is not by itself *sufficient* to produce this result.)

When it comes to overall satisfaction with the job, the result again ought to have been predictable, but I would not have expected on the basis of clinical evidence that it would be so clear-cut. The greatest job satisfaction was enjoyed by the automated workers, the next highest being that of the handicraft workers, and the least, that of mechanized workers. It appears that the automated workers' more comfortable working conditions and considerably higher incomes are the basis for their ranking first.

Although mechanized workers earn somewhat more than handicraft workers, their job satisfaction is less because the conditions of work on an assembly line are so abysmal that they always tend to produce job dissatisfaction, no matter what income is earned.

Unfortunately Dr. Obradovic was not able to study the loss of psychic intimacy with love in these groups as revealed by the degree of their alienation from family and homelife. But he plans to include this aspect in his future research. What is more, these studies are soon to be expanded by American scientists to include production workers of the three kinds in the United States. It will then be possible to determine with more precision the contributions made to loss of psychic intimacy and alienation by the technical characteristics of the job versus those that are related to the differences between socialist and capitalist economic systems. Endeavors such as these for the depth study of society should be able to absorb usefully a good bit of the resources that eventually will be freed from military budgets, with results that promise to enlarge the prospects for a broader humanity for everyone. It is urgent that they be undertaken promptly before technological disemployment has progressed to the point that there are no longer sizable groups of workers to study in all three categories. However, we must remember that studies can be misused to increase rather than eliminate alienation.

During the 1890s and the first decade of the twentieth century, efficiency experts brought division of labor to its dismal pinnacle through their time and motion studies.[33] In every modern factory could be found at least one such expert, discovering ways to make the production of everything more efficient, including the human misery of loss of psychic intimacy with work.

Then in the 1920s and 1930s the painful consequences of this sort of efficiency became evident. Not only was there marked increase in the pathology of alienation from work, but initially inexplicable breakdowns in the productive process turned out to be attributable to the inability of workers to maintain effective output indefinitely on operations fraction- ated below the minimums the human psyche can bear. In some instances profits actually declined. Accordingly, the experts tried to undo the damage through systematic programs of "job enlargement," in which the objective was to reassemble into somewhat meaningful sequences the fragments that had diligently been put asunder. Although the variety and novelty these measures brought into lives tormented by repetitious as- sembly-line work sometimes brought a little relief and even some im- proved efficiency, in general, job enlargement failed to bring into a worker's life the zestful investment of self in work, of which scarcity, in partnership with excessive division of labor, had deprived him.*

On the basis of general and clinical experience, one must still con- clude that the only way to secure the self-validative benefits of psychic intimacy with work is to work at that which one really wants to do with- out the compulsion of necessity. One often hears that it is unrealistic to expect that the mass of human beings will ever be capable of such work. My response is that, with all the new understanding we are achieving of human potential and means for eliciting it, it is not only unrealistic but unforgivable to do otherwise. I have met many people who one would have no reason to suppose were basically different from their fellows, and yet who possessed remarkable capacity for the sort of involvement with work which in the future must become commonplace.

One example is the bus driver with whom I rode during a visit in Leningrad. He took up a book on interplanetary radio communication dur- ing his break at the end of a run. In response to my expressed curiosity he explained (through an interpreter) that his work was writing a compre- hensive treatise on this subject. Technical library privileges in the USSR are ordinarily limited to those who hold advanced degrees. Although not a university graduate, he had obtained special permission to borrow relevant books from collections all over the country.

"But isn't your work driving a bus?" I asked in puzzlement.

He clarified. "During this transitional period of technical progress it is still necessary to have bus drivers, but driving a bus is only my *job* at which I earn a living. My *work* is the study of interplanetary radio com- munication." Subsequently I found in conversations with Soviet psy- chiatrists that this distinction between "job" and "work" is commonly understood and employed in the USSR. At any rate, I could not doubt the

* The same must be said of minor variations in assembly-line routine, as illustrated on p. 279 in relation to the "labeling lady."

psychic intimacy of that bus driver's relationship to his work, or its intense self-validative significance.

Love and Psychic Intimacy

Sadly we must note that in the course of history not only are we moving away from psychic intimacy with work, but the trend in several ways we will explore later is also away from psychic intimacy with love. By keeping love tied tightly to its regressively infantile functions we are weakening the first of the three main supports of identity.

Probably there have been more conceptions of love than of any other human phenomenon. It could not be otherwise because, at different times and places since the beginnings of records, love has been so often singled out as central in understanding human life, and even the rest of the universe. Here, the widespread unanimity ceases.

Despite significant resemblances, the main rivers of thought about love tend to flow in such different directions as to make their conclusions irreconcilable. Douglas D. Morgan shows that the essence of love is equally of focal importance, for example, as it appears in Plato, in the Bible, and in Freud, but is nevertheless metaphysically and dynamically unrelated.[34] While the Old Testament and Platonic views both accord sexuality a respectable place in human life, their conception of love was critically different. For the Jews, love was the unearned gift of Jehovah for his people, and characterized by such human foibles as possessiveness and jealousy. Jews were enjoined to love and cleave to one another with the same fierce but fruitful fealty as God showed his people. The earthiness of their celestial concerns left no room for a cool three-way division of the universe into Plato's creative force, ideal forms, and imperfect substance.

Despite the oft-remarked parallels between Socrates and Jesus, who were both devoted moral teachers, and who furthermore shared the fate of misunderstanding, persecution, prosecution, and execution for the offense of trying to bring mankind salvation, despite the emphasis of both their teachings upon perfection, and despite many other such parallels, " . . . one cannot possibly be both Platonist and Christian, at pain of outright inconsistency."[35]

Platonist and Christian collide most crucially in their incompatible views of love. Platonic love does not mean what many people think. It regards sex as an acceptable early step in the search for the abstract good which lies behind every imperfect reality. Platonic love is a reaching throughout the universe of the creative force toward the ideal forms, leaving behind the flawed substantial approximations of them we know as the material world. Erotic love in both Old Testament and Platonic versions is a striving to fulfill and validate oneself in response to a sense of inner incompleteness.

As for Christianity, Jesus' personal asceticism was codified in Paul's condemnation of all sexual desire. From then on as someone put it, "Making sex into a problem has been the major negative accomplishment of Christianity."[36]

But the essential contribution of Christianity is *agape*, which in contrast to *eros* is a love of all-encompassing self-sacrifice, a love that gives all without thought of return. As manifested by Jesus' devotion to mankind it included more self-immolation than self-validation. Agapic love may confer survival benefits upon the beloved, but if any accrue to the lover they are likely not to be of this world.

The Freudian conception of love is likewise incompatible with the Platonic and the Biblical (in either testament). To Freud the universe is a complex material mechanism powered without purpose by inexorable forces. He reserves no niche for God or abstract perfection. Whatever happens does so because it is driven blindly from within, not drawn irresistibly toward any ideal perfection.

Freud did restore sexuality to a comprehensible and respectable place in human life, a tenure it already had and kept in Plato. And Freud explored infantile sexuality, of which Plato was aware, and unconscious mental activity, which he implied. Other resemblances, however, such as the triads into which Freud and Plato divided the self, are trivial and misleading. The truth is that just as Marx stood Hegel on his head, so Freud inverted Plato, making us look down, not up, for the source of love.

As compared with accounts of "heroic" deeds, ancient literature gives love scant attention. When represented at all, love between the sexes is often overshadowed by homosexual attachments.[37]

As such literary scholars as Denis De Rougement and C. S. Lewis have shown, our modern conception of love owes much to developments during the middle ages.[38] According to these scholars, love as an abiding passion between the sexes was a song composed, and first sung, by wandering troubadours out of various themes in the culture of eleventh-century Provence. The most important of these influences appear to have been the writings of the Roman poet Ovid, the Albigensian movement, Sufi mysticism, Arab philosophy and mystic poetry, the scarcity of women under conditions of feudal castle living, and other social institutions of the time.[39]

The new religion of love arose in the ambivalences of a Christian context. With its various articles of faith, such as the ennobling power of love, the delectable pain of unconsummated passion, the inescapability of adultery, and the necessity of absolute subservience of the lover to his mistress, it constituted an infantilized caricature of both *eros* and *agape*. But it made converts all over Europe, and ignited artistic sparks that flared in romances such as *Tristan and Isolde*.

The cult of courtly love still has its faithful albeit somewhat reformed devotees today. Translated into less adventurous and adulterous terms, it has supplied the basic idiom for the middle-class customs of courtship and marriage. And perhaps, as De Rougement suggests, the desire to be Lancelot and Guinevere within the bounds of a conventional relationship has ruined many an otherwise viable marriage.

It is important to realize that tales of romantic and often tragic love appear in many cultural traditions, even those in which arranged marriages have long been the custom, indicating that, when strummed, the chord of courtly love evokes sympathetic reverberations in the heart of man generally.

How could such an apparently nonfunctional institution endure and spread so widely? It is difficult to grasp how courtly love conferred any survival benefits upon either partner to its charade. It seems to me that it did so, however, but in a most unexpected way. In a time when scarcity rendered life a bleak prospect for most people, one would expect to find love tied closely, as it was for the majority, to its central social function of nurturance of children, not to mention adults. But for the few able to afford it, courtly love tended to obstruct all but the more abstract (or hurried) intimacies, effectively limiting such practical exchanges while providing *self-validation* of a particularly impractical sort.

This was accomplished in two ways. First, by separating the lovers and subjecting them to the dammed-up tensions of prolonged yearning, it heightened the *sense of self* that is dulled by satiation but sharpened by appetite. Second, by focusing in adolescence the unresolved strivings of the oedipal triangle upon a literal and yet not fully attainable loved one, courtly love preserved, against the grubby realities of most of their adult lives, the zestful hope of childhood that the future could be utterly beautiful, because somewhere waiting to be found was the embodiment of the exquisite perfection of mother or father loved so tenderly and lost long ago.

The catch was that any self-validation achieved in these ways through courtly love (like that of its modern heirs) came through regressive enactment of fantasies rather than mastery of reality, so that in the long run it was likely to shatter when disappointment exposed its emptiness.

If scarcity generally forces love and work to serve survival functions, we would expect that courtly love and romance would blossom in conditions of greater abundance. It is suggestive that the love books of Ovid (whether they were meant seriously or as satires is immaterial) were written during the Pax Augustus, probably the most affluent period of the Roman Empire. And it was following the recovery from the terrible invasions of the Vikings, Saracens, and others, as Europe moved toward the prosperity of the high middle ages, that courtly love was born.

In a fascinating, persuasive, and prescient book, *Eros and Civilization,* written in 1955, Herbert Marcuse challenges Freud's idea that the price of civilization is ever-increasing and crippling repression.[40] He suggests that we distinguish "basic" from "surplus" repression. Basic repression would designate the *inevitable* repression which arises because "any form of the reality principle [i.e., adjustment to reality] demands a considerable degree and scope of repressive control over the instincts."[41] Surplus repression would designate the *avoidable* repression which is in excess of that required for civilization, but has always been exacted by the forces in control of society in order to maintain their domination and exploitation. His premise is that Freud erroneously lumped the two forms of repression together as biological, and thus was driven to his pessimistic conclusions.°

Marcuse shows convincingly that scarcity is now optional, and that with appropriate social reorganization we could reduce the amount of repression civilization exacts to the basic (and tolerable) level.

In a most penetrating review Fingarette shows that in *The Future of an Illusion,* published three years earlier than the pessimistic *Civilization and Its Discontents,* Freud presented more optimistic views on the possibilities of a healthy society that substantially foreshadowed Marcuse's.[42] To me this is one more demonstration of the crucial importance of studying everything that Freud wrote while assiduously following his implied advice to avoid settling down to become a "Freudian" at any juncture.

A more serious criticism of Marcuse is that he ends by recommending not only that we abolish surplus repression but that we also prepare ourselves for and promote as part of the cure for our suffering a kind of regressive pan-eroticism. Such a change, by returning us to the unfocused sexuality of infancy, would both undermine the self and reduce zestful investment of self in the object of love, thereby restricting self-validation. It is just this sort of reaction that seems to be occurring now, around the world, almost as though his book had been a prophecy.

We see today examples of love that range from Quixote's idealization of

---

° Regrettably, however, Marcuse accepts and applies mechanically Freud's theory of biologically spontaneous aggression, including the "death instinct."

Dulcinea at a distance to the passionate and lustful attachments of Sadie Thompson at close quarters; from the celibate devotion of a nun to the Virgin Mary, to the devotion of a boy to his dog. We even designate as love the bizarre fetishistic attractions of some individuals to women's shoes or underclothing, or even to such formless things as pieces of leather, rubber, or fur. Clearly all these behaviors are not the same. Nevertheless there is a thread that runs through them and many others that makes correct their grouping under one general name, however confusing and misleading that categorization may be. That thread is eroticism.

Eroticism, a word derived from Eros, the Greek god of love, has come to refer to pleasurable strivings we associate with sex, including those forerunners in infancy to which Freud drew attention. We explored earlier how these originate in the newborn as drives for pleasure and tension release at first unconnected with any specific person, and how they then become part of the relationship with the mother and others. We also know how they culminate in the heterosexual attachments that today lead most people into marriage, a relationship which is the most frequent, if not always the most deserving, recipient of the appellation "love." While we cannot inquire into all forms of love here, we can learn a good deal of general value about love by investigating what is happening to the thread of eroticism today as we follow its tortuous path from cradle to altar.

Until recent times it was understood that the passionate attachments of most lovers almost never could be consummated in any sort of enduring intimate relationship, least of all marriage. The few exceptions were special people, such as occasional royalty, and usually they too found to their dismay, as do so many people now, that romance is often thwarted by legality. Certainly millions of commoners could enjoy romantic relationships only vicariously.

For most people (even including royalty) the romantic erotic yearnings had to be compressed into tender looks, hurried, risky trysts, and purple prose. Meanwhile the real business of life, which was survival, was carried on around mundane exchanges of property and the tawdry contracts that legitimized them, including marriage. It is difficult for us to realize today that as recently as a century or even a half century ago, most marriages in stable communities were arranged by parents or guardians as aspects of the proper management of property for survival.[43] And in many parts of the world today this is still the prevailing principle.

The unconsummated loves of the past often had the early hallmarks of zestful, enduring investment of the self. Sometimes the passionate infatuation phase was prolonged for years and decades by frustration of its wishes. And of course then the lover's concept of both his beloved and his relationship to her would likely be kept juvenile indefinitely through deprivation of the joys and challenges of reality that sometimes help the thirsty craving of youth to be transformed into the steady cherishing of maturity.

An old friend of Polish origin, now well over seventy, sometimes reminisces with me about his long life. At fifteen, Avrum was betrothed by his parents to a distant cousin. The arrangement was looked upon with satisfaction by everyone involved, including the groom-to-be. His family controlled the town's hides, tallow, and wool, while hers owned the tannery and textile mills. Between them they would have the resources to found and monopolize a third industry, the manufacture of soap. The boy happily embarked upon the study of chemistry and business, as it was to be his privilege to run this new enterprise. Meanwhile he and Tanya began to enjoy friendly chaperoned visits to one another's homes for dinner. One night the aunt who brought the girl took him aside and said that he really ought to kiss his fiancee goodby as he helped her into her droshky. It had never occurred to him before, but that night he pressed his lips against the disappointed girl's cheek as he was used to doing with his sisters when they left for holidays.

About a year later he fell in love with Sophie. The familiar daughter of the local pharmacist, she unaccountably had suddenly become the girl of his dreams. He could not study for writing her love poems. He lost his appetite, developed a sallow, haggard look, took long, solitary walks, sometimes arranging to pass her house twice. One Tuesday he bought some aspirin and handed Sophie a note with his money, declaring his love and imploring her to meet him at the lake Sunday after lunch. He rushed out trembling before she could read it, and took two pills.

She came. And came despite the fact that she had agreed to a "good match," being also very suitably engaged to the son of a local physician. Avrum kissed her on the lips, and nearly fainted. Sophie said she must not come again, but she did. They wrote to one another often, however, and left their missives—get ready—in a hollow tree! Like his, Sophie's often were stained with tears, for she loved Avrum in return.

At eighteen Avrum married. A year later so did Sophie. Their correspondence continued four more years, until Avrum's departure for the United States with his entire family prevented his visits to their secret rustic post office.

Avrum and Tanya settled down to live together. They had three children and financial success. The children and the business got bigger in America. Avrum says, "We have had a good life. Tanya and I are good to one another. We were sensible. Things worked out the way it was planned. Even better after our immigration here. That is more than most people got—on either side of the water. But love? No, we've never been in love with each other. Not like Sophie and me. Love and that kind of happiness I would have had with Sophie, maybe. But Tanya and me, we weren't supposed to be happy. Just to live."

After a silent moment of sad reflection Avrum added, "Tanya bores me. Never reads, has nothing to say, is always cooking. She always says, 'Av, you get too excited about everything.' She never writes a poem. She doesn't even cry a tear! We have been content with life. But happy with *each other* we haven't been. Except maybe for a few minutes every lovely now and then."

This story in its essence represents the lives of millions throughout the world. Sixty years ago young people in love did not as frequently insist on consummating it, let alone marrying because of love. They did not even expect to be happy.

Nowadays the notion that one should marry the person with whom he falls in love predominates in Western societies, and is spreading rapidly through the rest of the world. This is true despite wide promulgation of such sour observations as H. L. Mencken's that "Love is the delusion that one woman differs from another."[44] In 1936 the trend was not so far advanced, and the uniqueness to this country of determination to make passion the center of life was underscored by anthropologist Ralph Linton:

> All societies recognize that there are occasional violent attachments between persons of opposite sex, but our present American culture is practically the only one which has attempted to capitalize these and make them the basis for marriage.[45]

Moreover, nowadays the expectation is that life will be happy, especially married life, since it is now motivated more by cupid than by cupidity. But of course happiness is proving as elusive a quarry as ever. Why?

To begin with, happiness cannot be sought directly as an objective for human life (see also p. 431). In the course of a day together Jan and Alex, a young couple I know, play golf, serve customers in their pastry shop, listen to Mozart recordings, laugh at each other's jokes, and make love. Let us suppose that instead of concentrating on mastering long drives, making a living, savoring musical genius, and thrilling to each other's caresses, they concentrated on being happy. It is doubtful that they would achieve any of these satisfactions, especially happiness. For happiness is always the result of doing something worth doing for some other reason than the happiness it yields. Happiness is the *derivative* of zestful engagement with life.

But both couples would seem to have earned happiness in that way. What is the difference between Avrum-Tanya and Jan-Alex? Both are zestfully engaged with life in general and both enjoy exchanging basic survival benefits with a devoted spouse. But Jan-Alex are blessed with something marvelous beyond fundamentals. It must be admitted that the fuller happiness of love such as theirs depends upon something more, an extra survival benefit, difficult to pin down in words, which imparts a soaring delight to a relationship wherein the partners are both so fortunate as to find in one another the *specific personalities* with whom each can be "in love."

Once it was enough simply to have loved enough to have helped one another survive. But whereas in the past romantic joy was usually considered a luxury, and even if present was recognized as anything but a prerequisite for a successful survival-assuring relationship, now this extra dimension of feeling is regarded as an essential factor in evaluating one's marriage and life as acceptably happy or complete.

The main tragedy is that while nearly everyone tries eagerly to gratify the craving for such love, nearly all are disappointed. Another is that even for the few who find it, often the priorities of their love are strangely inverted, and in a way that readily becomes lethal. Young people now measure the success or failure of their marriage not by how much it helps or hinders their fundamental survival, but *primarily* by whether it provides a constant background of happiness against which they may be willing to put up with no more than a sparse punctuation of sorrows.

Reactions to the Swedish film *Elvira Madigan* illustrate this change.[46] The tempestuous young lovers are so convinced they can live exclusively on love that they make only the most perfunctory efforts to avert starvation, and then when it weakens them in their idyllic meanderings, practically without a struggle they resign themselves to suicide. Many young people are wildly enthusiastic over this film. But it seems that others (and most middle-aged people) are bored and irritated by what they consider the vapid copout of refusal to temper the demand for perpetual happiness with a little life-sustaining attention to metabolism.

How else in the realm of love is this exorbitant demand for happiness expressed? Most eloquently in the increasingly pervasive application to eroticism of what has been called the Fun ethic. This standard places at the top of a person's list, not the worth of a human relationship, marriage or otherwise, but only the "fun" provided by an erotic experience. Through this inversion it contributes substantially to the erosion of a main support of identity, psychic intimacy with love.

To a large extent falling in love depends upon erotic attraction. Therefore, as any purveyor of perfume, tropical cruises, or marriage licenses can testify, circumstances that foster erotic attraction impel toward matrimony. And, naturally, the psychic intimacy (and therefore the stability) of a marriage is intensified in direct proportion to the amount of erotic gratification that can be channeled into the marriage relationship (see p. 168).

In man, instinctually determined releasers of erotic behavior being either absent or relatively weak, culturally determined cues take their place. Take, for example, the varying connection between eroticism and nudity. Among some people it is her donning of clothes at puberty that evokes sexual shyness in a young woman. Doubtless in such a society it also evokes erotic interest in a young man.[47] We all know that in our society the stimulus is the opposite. For us, the unclad (especially female) body is a signal for erotic response.

For several centuries minor variations of fashion in exposure of the female bosom or leg were enough to titillate the erotic appetite. During the same period, total nudity, rendered in every aesthetic convention, from romantic ethereality to lusty pornography, was always a reliable reservoir for sexual arousal. The development of cheap printing methods made nude depictions widely available. And the invention of photography brought a new dimension of vivid reality to the erotic incitement of the nude. Now, rather than being constructed by brush from an impression assembled in the artist's brain, her nearly palpable image could be refracted directly onto the surface untouched by human hands.

Except for the commercial pornographers, the users of this new medium usually diluted the shocking immediacy of their new technique by poeticizing it. The so-called "salon" nudes ordinarily were posed so that recognition of the individual model was impossible, resulting instead in a representation of Woman in general, rather than particular. Sometimes body parts were so arranged, or the shot so composed and cropped, that the result was abstract, not immediately recognizable as a human form. The finished work was often soft-focused or retouched to blur anatomy, and generally included such deliteralizing maneuvers as modification of the surface texture, or manipulation of grain, contrast, or color toning of the print.

Gradually such representations found their way into the popular press. Twenty-five years ago, *Coronet* magazine used to print, among its renowned fine photographs, a few nudes, invariably so designed that the individual identity of the model was concealed. This anonymous figure, like so many of her painted and sculpted predecessors, served to heighten not only generalized esthetic longings, but highly particularized erotic ones. However, *because these urges were aroused by an unidentified, generalized figure, they could be displaced readily in fantasy onto the special loved one, thus intensifying the zestful investment of the self in that love relationship.*

Enter the Fun ethic, for example, the version pioneered by *Playboy* magazine, and now outdistanced by others. In the last decade, dispensed from magazine stands or through home delivery, *Playboy's* millions of copies brought into ordinary living rooms decidedly provocative nudes, often sharp-focused and unretouched, looking full-face into the camera so that they could not help but be recognizable as individuals.

Soon the novelty of this breach of anonymity wore off. But the craving generated for pseudocloseness pyramided and led to the sort of further change one might expect. Nowadays the models in the center spreads are also identified by name, occupation, and city of residence, and may be shown also in additional candid poses with relatives who are also identified.

What is the result? The effect of this technique is to stir up erotic longings for a very fully *identified, specific woman.* Thus, they cannot as easily be displaced in fantasy onto the loved one. Instead, they remain anchored to the literal reality of the specific, provocative model. However zestful this interest may be, it is transitory, casual, and leads nowhere except to the next issue. In this way, the Fun ethic helps divert energies from psychically intimate, enduring love relationships to alienated, transitory, interchangeable pleasure parties. And to the extent that this deflection diminishes psychic intimacy with love, and associated self-validation, identity is weakened.

Where to next? As salt water heightens rather than slakes thirst, pseudo-intimacy only intensifies the craving for true closeness. One might expect that frenzied efforts to obtain gratification in this direction could lead to the general acceptance possibly now under way of frankly pornographic depictions in stills and movies of genitals, sexual activity, and so on.

But from there, where to? Since there are no further obscuring layers of clothing or prudery to be stripped away, the obvious direction is into the body itself. Clearly this boring from without is sadistic perversion. One sort, seriously described to me by a magazine publisher, is a plan to feature in a popular magazine photographs of "the new love." The pictures will reveal simultaneously a woman's facial expression and genital changes during sexual intercourse, the latter being recorded through the sort of transparent penis employed in their research by Masters and Johnson. Of one thing we may be sure, even if penetration of the body is permitted to proceed to the escalating cruelty of sadistic dissection, such depictions will not proceed to satisfying psychic intimacy with love. The long-range outcome of all such grotesque partialisms, including those that transformed human skin into lampshades in Nazi concentration camps, is always maddening insatiability.[48]

Aside from these gruesome extremes, there are some consequences to changing mores concerning nudity which might give us pause. As a woman colleague pointed out to me sadly not long ago, the net result of the increasing acceptance of nudity is that we are rapidly approaching the time when it will no longer constitute an erotic signal. And it is not easy to invent and build into a culture equally effective substitute erotic cues.

In the same direction are the fascination with "toplessness" and "bottomlessness," and the increasing popularity of wife swapping. All of these kindle a brief flash of erotic fire which, like the flare of a burning pinecone, is rapidly exhausted, leaving no lasting warmth, let alone progeny.

Furthermore, all these fragmented frenzies tend to reduce the intensity of psychic intimacy with love to the alienated state to which psychic intimacy with work largely has deteriorated. This question properly follows: What becomes of identity and self-validation if psychic intimacy with both love and work disappear?

Have I exaggerated the gloomy aspects of the current evolution of love and psychic intimacy? After all, isn't it possible that the greater leeway for behavior allowed by the Fun ethic can be incorporated usefully into the zestfully engaged lives of the abundant future? Isn't there reason to believe that fun and psychic intimacy are not necessarily mutually exclusive? Isn't fun only a jeopardy when it becomes the ethical standard by which all else is decided, instead of being welcomed as a by-product of life well lived? Isn't this especially true in the realm of sexuality? Isn't it true, for example, that there is no evidence that "wife lending" among the Eskimos prevented psychic intimacy with love within that culture before it was invaded by whites?

To all these questions I must answer Yes. Lest my concern for the future be regarded as a scientistic puritanism, rather than a well-grounded apprehension about the viability of a society that seems to be moving into the shadow of the *Brave New World,* let us look at the novel.

You will recall that in Huxley's story a young woman might proudly refer to her surgical sterility: "I'm free-martin myself." And that a man might complimentarily refer to her as "wonderfully pneumatic." While art is not proof, it seems to me that here Huxley has shown us a plausible hint of the dehumanization that can result when values become degraded so that self-esteem flows from the edge of a castrating scalpel, and includes the resemblance of a voluptuous female to an inflated inner tube. Erotic openness is too dear at the cost of reducing sex to a mechanical process and human beings to inanimate objects.

My questioners could argue, however, that the full-faced, identifiable nudes of *Playboy* magazine reflect a worthwhile greater acceptance of sexuality. Doesn't the editorial policy of unclothing the late adolescent "girl next door," rather than a love goddess or whore, properly accept as legitimate the sexuality of such everyday, wholesome and appealing females? To this question I would have to answer No. There is no true acceptance of sexuality here either. *Playboy* has simply reduced eroticism to "good clean fun"—to a sorority prank engaged in by fresh young girls who go to bed with the same eager but passionless enthusiasm that they eat pizza, play volleyball, or dance the frug. Everyone with experience must sense that ordinarily such young women are not yet fully awakened sexually, no matter how long ago the alarm went off. In its superficial gaiety the magazine does not attempt to deal with the mature woman's fully developed capacity for erotic involvement. If it did, a full-color centerfold would no doubt prove much less titillating because it would partake less of the spirit of "naughtiness" found at a teen-age pajama party.

Henry Adams found that in the ancient world sexuality was the subject of worship. If the trend *Playboy* represents is the correct measure of this new American worship of eroticism, then we are no closer than the nine-teenth-century society he observed to truly acknowledging "the power of sex."[49]

And it is obvious that much of the athleticism that passes for sexual freedom in our society is merely a transposition of the central social function of play from the tennis court into the boudoir. There, instead of distraction and domination being measured in terms of "love" games, it is assessed in the loveless game of tabulating numbers and simultaneity of orgasms.

Play and Psychic Intimacy

Love and work must mature to be self-validating. In contrast, the situation with respect to play is oddly reversed. By keeping play tied to its more *grown-up* function of distraction and compensatory domination, we prevent it from resuming the unfettered self-validative function with which it began.

The concept of play has changed in various historical epochs. While the ancient Greeks honored play, the Puritans saw it as wickedly inter-twined with the sins of sloth and idleness. We on the threshold of the era of abundance increasingly see play as indispensable to human fulfillment.

The historical record is sparse, perhaps because few historians have made play their work.

Too many thinkers feel uneasy about their play interests or activities, and have to rationalize them in a utilitarian fashion. Thus Aristotle saw play as a kind of emotional escape valve, through which was effected a catharsis of dangerous emotions.[50] Even today we speak of "letting off steam" in play. Similarly, play has been conceived as the discharge of surplus energy, in the theories of Schiller and Herbert Spencer touched on below. The increasingly restless activity of some pent-up animals or school children on rainy days lends credence to the theory that the play drive, or at least the drive for muscular activity, wells up from within spontaneously.

Some of the most frequent attempts to squeeze play into the strait-jacket of useful activity have been those that make it a kind of dress rehearsal for the more "serious" aspects of life. Karl Groos, for example, sees play as an instinctual drive developed by natural selection for utilitarian purposes. Play, according to him, enables the young animal to "pre-exercise" himself in preparation for the critical functions of his later life.[51] In a related way, Jay Nash defines play as "the child's response to the hereditary activity urge and . . . nature's way of guaranteeing that the young organism receives some basic experiences."[52] Such coupling of play with instinct and utility reaches the eerie preserve of Jungian mysticism in G. Stanley Hall's romantic assertion:

> True play never practises what is phyletically new . . . the motor habits and spirit of the past of the race, persisting in the present, as rudimentary functions. In play every mood and movement is instinct with heredity. This is why the heart of youth goes out into play as into nothing else, as if in it man remembered a lost paradise.[53]

In a more helpful manner, Freud related play to the child's attempts to master traumatic experience.[54] And child psychiatrists have followed his lead in regarding play as an essential part of the child's attempts to overcome its helplessness, at least in fantasy, until it is grown.[55] Here Piaget's treatment of play is relevant:

> Far from being preparatory exercises (as according to Groos), most of the games . . . reproduce what has struck the child, evoke what has pleased him or enable him to be more fully part of his environment. . . . they form a vast network of devices which allow the ego to assimilate the whole of reality, i.e., to integate it in order to re-live it, to dominate it or to compensate for it.[56]

And speaking of games, an example of one man's zestful engagement with play is Roger Caillois' treatment of it in *Man, Play and Games*.[57] He achieves mastery over the subject by dividing games into four main categories according to which role is dominant. *Agon*, or competition (sports); *alea*, or chance (gambling); *mimicry*, or simulation (drama); and *ilinx*, or vertigo* (somersault and whirling games). In addition he postulates two subordinate categories: *paidia*, or active, spontaneous, uncontrolled fantasy; and *ludus*, or subordination of play activity to rules. He also formulates a terse rebuttal of Groos which applies equally to many others: " . . . the proper function of play is never to develop capacities. Play is an end in itself."[58]

But however complicated the varieties of play may be, or however obvious their practical value, the essential human function of play as I have attempted to show is self-validation. This is true even of the seemingly puzzling human taste for vertigo and danger. The vertiginous play of children, like the adult's surrender to chance, helps those who fear being weak to enjoy letting the self be swept away, always with the ecstatic fantasy that an invincible guardian angel (Lady Luck) stands watch at the apex of the roller coaster and the elbow of the croupier. Being scared is valued because it heightens awareness of the self, and is followed by the sense of triumph at having emerged from danger unscathed.

However, such heroics and specious invulnerability are unnecessary to normal self-esteem which does not depend on shallow denial of one's real fragility. Deep and abiding self-validation is available through zestful investment of the self in ordinary play activities, without flinging the gauntlet in the face of oblivion.

Play, Eroticism, Creativity, and Culture

There are some additional complications of play that must not be sidestepped even in the present condensed discussion. Perhaps the best way to begin is with some observations made by Franz Alexander:

> Human and animal behavior is traditionally divided into two categories, one serving the survival of the individual, and one serving the preservation of the species through propagation. Freud made this classification the original basis of his theory of instincts. He soon discovered, however, that much of the young animal's or child's behavior does not serve directly either survival or propagation. He called these "pregenital" erotic activities, including among others, thumb-sucking, anal stimulation, the pleasurable excitation of the skin, aimless muscular activity, curiosity for its own sake,—all of which have playful pleasure-seeking connotations

* Dizziness

within the broad category of sexuality. He characterized these activities, which subjectively have erotic connotations, as immature, pregenital derivatives of the instinctual drive which in its mature genital form leads to reproduction. Greek mythology intuitively recognized this affinity between playfulness and sexuality in representing Eros, the god of both love and play, as a child.[59]

Clinical study confirms this association. And upon reflection we must admit that experiences does too. From the lusty thumbsucking of the infant and the delighted masturbation of the child, to the joyous "making out" of teen-agers at a party and the erotic hilarity of their parents on New Year's Eve, the whole spectrum of human sexual behavior has a playful tinge that substantiates the Greek intuition. In fact, adult lovemaking that does not include a playful component not uncommonly becomes boring or even distasteful.

And we must also acknowledge that the seeming nonutilitarian behaviors Freud called pregenital have an unmistakable playful as well as erotic pleasurable quality. Then how can it be, as stated earlier, that the newborn baby's love behavior arises and functions separately from play? Because the playful quality in a baby's well-established pleasure sucking is not evident until the second or third month when play itself can be detected. It is then that the baby's ability to smile, vocalize, and move its arms and legs adds the play element to his erotic behavior. Only then does he have the "leisure" for *optional* activity.

Prior to that time, the baby's love behavior is more soberly conducted, as befits a component of his newborn survival kit, in the service of establishing the relationship with his mother. This relationship, which contributes to the survival of both, becomes also the one upon which his *life* will depend totally for several years, his *love life* partially for over a decade, and his *psychological life* significantly forever. The infusion of playful spice into daily living may later become the *secondary* function of sexuality. But at the beginning of life the child's sexuality has the crucial central social function of assuring the nurture and survival of the new child. During the long darkness of the era of scarcity this also remained its largely unchallenged role in adulthood.

At the time Freud was pioneering, the crucial subtleties of mother-baby relationships in the animal and human worlds were not as well understood. Therefore it was easy erroneously to categorize the "pregenital" erotic strivings as not serving directly the survival of either the individual or species, when in fact they are the first and most critically significant vanguard of all the forces that operate to preserve a new life.

As psychoanalysts have shown, all play activities also have an erotic element. In contrast to the early decisive erotic behavior, those activities we readily call "play" later in childhood and adulthood are truly *optional,* engaged in "just for their own sake." McBride and Hebb give an illustration of the erotic component of play in a male dolphin "which was seen swimming upside down at the top of the tank, towing a feather with its penis erect."[60]

Alexander shows that the realm of play, relatively neglected by authors in this century, received abundant attention in the last. He cites Friedrich Schiller, Herbert Spencer, Jean Paul, Wilhelm Preyer, and Karl Groos as all supporting the theory that play represents the discharge of an animal's surplus energy not needed for activities connected with survival. Spencer added the interesting idea that play is seen only among the higher animals because the lower ones need all their energy for their maintenance. The young of higher animals and man are afforded the surplus energy with which to indulge in play largely through the prolonged period of protective nurture provided by their parents.

Such authors as Freud, Waelder, Erikson, and Lili Peller have shown how play has the utilitarian function of helping the child devise solutions to master inner and outer problems. But Alexander agrees that

> It is important, however, to note that the essential feature of play is that during true playfulness the solution of a problem is not imperative. The young colt playfully romping in a meadow is engaged in pleasurably exercising his mastery of the problem of locomotion. Should he be threatened by an external danger . . . locomotion is subordinated to the serious problem of survival.[61]

So play, with its frequent erotic coloration, which begins as spontaneous self-validative activity, may *later* become organized into those behaviors that serve the central social functions of love and work, and thereby contribute to the survival of individual and species.

In a parallel way it has been asserted that the entire enterprise of civilization depends upon human play. Róheim suggests that agriculture and animal domestication were not devised to begin with for practical purposes, but arose instead from play, from idle hobbies, which later were developed into survival techniques.[62] Alexander and others have pointed out that flying, an example of the startling explosion of recent technologies, was at first but the playful whim of the adventurous in search of mastery, power, and freedom. Only secondarily and gradually was there added to the new practice a payload of passengers and bombs. Thus is raised the paradoxical possibility that while necessity is the mother of invention, its father may be play. Can it be, as he suggests, that

. . . culture is the product of man's leisure and not the sweat of his brow: his productive abilities become liberated when he is relieved from the necessities of the struggle for survival.[?][63]

Long before discovering Alexander's discussion, I had formulated just that conclusion as to the blossoming of man's potential in the future era of abundance. But it well may be that in much smaller scope the same also has been true of his progress in the past era of scarcity.

Such speculations are carried to their furthest extreme by Huizinga, who begins his renowned book, *Homo Ludens,* with the statement, "Play is older than culture, for culture, however adequately defined, always presupposes human society, and animals have not waited for men to teach them their play."[64] He regards contest, quite aside from its economic role, as indispensable to society. As an example he discusses the Potlatch, an institution of Northwest American Indians, the Kwakiutl, in which all manner of precious property was given to others or destroyed to show that the giver could do without it.[65] The express purpose was to win superiority over others who could not outdo his prodigality. He found that this ritual existed in Greek, Roman, old Germanic, Melanesian, and Chinese cultures, and since it is often disastrous, concludes that basically man's relation to material things is nonutilitarian. As Alexander points out,

> That such originally playful contests may, in certain instances, become an integral part of the socioeconomic structure (for instance in the early phase of Western capitalism) and gradually lose their playful characteristics is not noted by Huizinga.[66]

But what Alexander does not point out is that Huizinga's emphasis on play, which leads him to advance play as the fundamental element in human institutions, ranging from lawsuits and science to archaic wars, brings him perilously close to a one-dimensional view of man and history. For example, Huizinga does not even accord to Marx's conceptions a place among the several important contributions to the understanding of human social evolution. Instead he writes of "the shameful misconception of Marxian doctrine that economic forces and material interests determine the course of the world."[67] In this monistic focus on play to the exclusion of love, work, and all other human concerns, I find Huizinga falling into the trap so assiduously avoided by Marx and Freud, among many others, of becoming a worshiper rather than a developer of his own ideas. A measure of the extent of his distortion of man is that he is somewhat consoled about the increasing "rationalization" of current social life, with its often admittedly unnecessary grimness, by his recognition that there are remnants of play to be found in American presidential elections![68]

One final approach to the relation of play to creativity and culture merits attention here. It revolves about the relationships of innovation, language, and communication.

Adaptive behavior may draw upon fruits of play to accomplish a restricted objective in one of only a few effective ways. In contrast, play itself is experimental and free, revealing the player's uniqueness of ability and fantasy. Alexander compares the relation between the two to

> the relation between natural selection and mutation in biology. Mutation can be looked upon as a free and playful experimentation of nature with new, sometimes bizarre, combinations of genes which in themselves are not adaptive but produce individual variations in the species, some of which by chance may have a survival value. These successful experiments are preserved through heredity.[69]

In his last paper, Alexander considered creativity. After reviewing many reports of creative accomplishments during sleep and dreams, he points out that the creative act occurs when the mind is free of the pressure of necessity or emergency, free of the focused sort of activity that goes into conscious effort ordinarily confined to verbal symbols.

He tells us that to be creative we must take temporary leave from the restricting generalizations of the past crystallized into words. However, he is not endorsing the permanent vacation from the assigned meanings of those words recommended by some, which we rejected earlier. He recognizes the value of words in the course of communicating our vision to one another in the rational period after the interlude of creativity.

The creative person is not different from the rest of us in the nature of his conflicts or in his motivation to resolve them. But he transcends us in his capacity to find *novel* solutions which are infused with "some kind of *value* [italics added], be it esthetic, technical or scientific."[70] To these attributes must be added one more. Whether in words or otherwise, the creator has extraordinary capacity to *transmit* his vision to others.

> . . . the pleasure of mastery . . . is what is common in play and creativity. Yet play and creativity are not identical. Play, like dreams, is directed mainly towards self-gratification; in creativity, communication of that which has been discovered in playful activities becomes a basic ingredient.[71]

We must recognize with Alexander that play is "one of the important sources (though not the only one) of man's culture-building faculty . . . "[72] Since learning is the special aptitude underlying man's adaptivity as well as his creativity, we, unlike other species, must preserve the capacity for play throughout our entire life-span in order to retain the self-validating, fresh, joyous experimentalism of youth.

We must, however, keep play in perspective as constituting just one-third of the indispensable humanizing triumvirate of love, work, and play (see also Chapter 19, Creative Frenzy).

14 Self-Validative Love, Work, and Play in the Future of Abundance

As Montagu says, definitions, to be meaningful, should come at the end, rather than the beginning, of an inquiry.[1] Now that we are nearing the end of this exploration, definitions of love, work, and play begin to emerge more clearly in terms of their *functions for the future*. As Malinowski points out, the meaning of all words is derived from bodily experiences.[2] These are actions and reactions. Montagu adds, "The meaning of a word, as the logical and symbolic inheritor of the infant's cry, is the action it produces."[3] The cry or word acquires an assigned meaning in the course of the relationship with a ministering adult who responds to it with a particular action. The function of that word then becomes in one sense the elicitation of a particular behavior from another person.

Man is born as the most educable of all creatures. It has been said of man that he has lost all of his instincts and none of his drives. Thus, in Montagu's words, *human nature is what man learns*.[4] Language is the most characteristic component of his education. And for the future (as the past) the most important words in his language, when defined in terms of their functions, are love, work, and play. For these are the words that designate as well as call forth the actions and experiences that forge individual identity and self-validation.

But does not all this emphasis on "self" signify endorsement of self-centeredness in the sense of immature selfishness? Assuredly not. The individual person is the brick of which the human social edifice is constructed, and anything that can be done to increase his strength, versatility, and adaptiveness contributes to the whole enterprise. Improvement of brick and building are not contradictory but complementary.

Besides, the effectiveness of the entire human structure must be gauged by the degree to which it permits each component person to reach his fullest development and make his fullest contribution. Self-validation leads not to selfish petulance but to the capacity, where appropriate, for devoted "selflessness."

Love

Love *begins* in each human life as part of the innate striving for survival. The baby's warm response evokes the nurturing reaction of grown-ups. But what for millennia has often been called love thereafter actually has been nothing more than the craving experienced by a baby or adult for pleasureable and sustaining ministrations, or at most the presence of the devoted person from whom they are expected.

In the era of scarcity, in actual practice the evanescent infatuations of the adult, which embody his hope of regaining the total devotion of mother for himself, are expressed instead as means for assuring these attentions at least briefly to new infants. In the process, a new generation is more or less haphazardly socialized and acculturated.

We will recall Montagu's definition of love as the conferring of survival benefits upon another in a creatively enlarging manner. In the oncoming era of abundance what must be our definition? If we find satisfactory methods and decide in the future to produce babies outside the female body and raise them outside the family, love need no longer serve to ensnare people into non-self-validating relationships in order to fulfill its former central social function. What survival benefits will there be left to confer?

Freed of its central social function of providing circumstances for generating and nurturing babies, *love will comprise that part of self-validating function which advances the fullest flowering of human potential by bringing individual people into intimate personal caring relationships with one another.*

But no matter how produced and nurtured for basic survival, to the extent that babies are also *humanized,* the process will continue to depend from the beginning on close personal relatedness to some caring, mothering person. Moreover, the sustenance of *adults* in their humanity will continue to depend on personal caring interaction with other human beings throughout life.

These are the specifically *human* nurturing functions which cannot be performed by a machine or any other organism. In their emancipation from indenture to the basic survival of one's own young, they will be free to protectively envelop all people. A major emphasis of life in the future will be the enhancement of the humanizing effectiveness of all human relationships.

As the capacity for love grows, the circle of those a person can embrace with his love widens. In the abundant future, expansion of these circles will strengthen and extend the web of interpersonal allegiances which gives human society a stable, protective framework.

Let us narrow the view from the group to the person. Besides devotion to realization of the beloved's potential, what will psychically intimate love include for the individual in the abundant future? Love of the most binding sort consists of making a zestful enduring investment of self in the full flowering of not just *somebody's* potentialities, but in those of a *particular* person whom, for various irrational and often unfathomable reasons, it *delights* one to foster. A person may behave lovingly to people in general, and take pleasure in fostering their potentials, but only when his behavior and its success evokes in *himself* that *special* subjective delight do we unhesitantly say he loves someone in particular. It is that sort of love that parents often have for their children, and if not may nevertheless be able to give to the children of others. And to be the object of that kind of parental love from someone when you are a child is to acquire a sense of your "all rightness" that no other experience conveys. In fact, experiencing that kind of love even during adult life, if it is returned, makes so vital a contribution to self-validation that finding it becomes the driving force in many personalities. Although such specific love of adults is often requited, it frequently endures in strong people without being returned.

Will or should this kind of love, which carries the aura of the subjective romanticism of the era of scarcity, continue to be cultivated in our abundant future? My answer is Yes. But some people would disagree. They would point to the pretechnologically abundant society of Tahiti in which, as we saw earlier, both the intensity of interpersonal relationships and the level of achievement are relatively low. They would argue that there is a "natural" association between the easing of scarcity pressures and the decline of caring activity of all sorts, and we should accept or even welcome a shift from misery to blandness if that is the price for abundance.

We will not follow their advice, because we will become aware that the only natural thing for us to do, amid and despite abundance, is to foster with our new methods whatever sorts of human relations seem best for people. And even if somewhat reduced interpersonal intensity should become a generally accepted value, it need not bring about rejection of the value of individual love. Also, more of us will become aware that out of the unreasonableness of love *for someone in particular* grow not only the bonds that link human beings most delightfully, but also much of the creativity we prize the most.

Of course we could allow both individual love and its associated creativity to degenerate into the indiscriminate pleasure-seeking style of newborn infancy, but most people eventually will outgrow and reject this alternative, just as they do their taste for penny candy.

Then, aside from our endless love affair with the whole universe, it is difficult from here to see how, when unshackled from the compelling necessities that painted the caves of Lascaux, man's creative impulses could have many more enthralling options to pursue than those that built the Taj Mahal.

Work

Man's work in its simple earlier forms, like that of animals, involves moving mass through distance. Hunting, agriculture, and even manufacture can easily be related to this definition from physics.

But as a result of the evolution and predominance of symbolic communication and action in human beings, while still serving primarily its central social function of providing goods and services for survival, work became transformed for many men into moving nothing heavier than a pen no farther than across a page.

Of course we are not bound to assess human work in the terms applicable to physics. But as it happens, inscribing their thoughts and ideas on papyrus, as did the pharaohs, or on paper, as did General Eisenhower, brought about the moving of more mass a greater distance than had been accomplished hitherto by others. So did the pens that transcribed the words of Jesus and the ideas of Shakespeare, Locke, Paine, Marx, Freud, and Einstein. Man's work changes the world. His written works in many instances have transfigured forever the world of nature as well as man.

Work begins in each human life, as does love, as part of the innate striving of the organism to secure the means of survival. The era of scarcity requires the neotenic institutionalization of this role of work throughout life. When the era of abundance divests it of this necessity, work becomes free to assume centrally its psychological function, self-validation.

Work will comprise that part of self-validating function which embodies a person's major and most sustained encounter with, and means to influence, the phenomena of the universe. Freed of its former central social function of assuring survival, it will serve instead what now are subsidiary social functions which by then will have become central: the orderly mastering of the next step on the human agenda, so that man achieves continuously expanding understanding of himself and the universe, and power to direct the evolution of both.

This is not to say that everyone's work will be in the creative arts or in science, but that each man's contribution of goods or services will move the whole human enterprise in that direction, and be consciously recognized as doing so. And although a man will work at that which provides him the most intense self-validation of which he is capable, the fact that he will be so much more thoroughly a social being than people are today will assure that his contribution will be useful and not destructive.

Perhaps some day every citizen will be able to make such contributions to public life as, to a large extent, each ancient Greek citizen could make. Then the lives of the inheritors of huge American fortunes, such as those of the Kennedys and Rockefellers, will be looked back upon as harbingers of the impact of abundance in fostering rather than stifling zestful engagement with life.

Play

Play, beginning in infancy only after love and work are well established, grows out of a series of reflex actions which gradually become integrated into the joyous exercise of unused capacities for its own sake.

The actions engaged in, and the understanding achieved, are doubtless of practical value later in daily life, especially in work. But their eventual use is not their origin and cause. When later the central social function of distraction and domination is added, unfortunately it often nearly stifles the zestful delight that characterizes play in infancy and constitutes its unique role throughout life.

Play will comprise that part of self-validating function which explores and exercises the person's potentialities for the joy inherent in the activity. In the future it will serve in addition a now subordinate function: impelling celebrations to heighten the joy of living of individuals or groups. Thus play will provide the novelty of expression of faculties idled by the concentration required for work.

Love, Work, and Play: Melded or Discrete?

At first glance many people get the impression that the era of abundance promises not simply to redefine love, work, and play, but to erase the distinctions between them. I believe this is not so, although admittedly it is becoming more difficult all the time to draw their boundaries clearly.

For example, now that abundance is providing us with more effective contraception, protection from venereal disease, and freedom from moral restraint, it might appear that love behavior is already shading off into play. It certainly is true that today in relation to sexual and dating behavior in general a wider range of playful experimentation prevails.

Just as play has erotic aspects, so love contains elements of play. Because love stirs up and evokes expression of many dormant threads in the meshwork of personality, it tends toward joyous exercise of many unused potentialities for their own sake. Thus comes into being the "playful" quality of love at its best. Those who have been fortunate enough to enjoy such lighthearted love know how disappointing it can be if in other relationships Eros is not leavened by a *soupçon* of Pan.

Certainly love at its best includes many playful qualities, but love at its worst is often pursued with all the grim determination of a "sport." A patient told me sadly after pursuing thrills all the way from Tijuana bordellos to nude bathing and wife-swapping parties in Hollywood, "You know, doctor, orgies aren't very *sexy*." He eventually concluded that "If you can't love, at least you can swing."

So much of the frantic search for fun we see everywhere, although often blatantly "erotic," has little if anything to do with sexual pleasure, let alone love. Moreover, the kind of love that summons forth in oneself and the beloved the *full range* of each person's self-validating potentialities, playful and otherwise, is different from and beyond play. "Tennis, anyone?" can turn up an adequate partner for doubles on the weekend but would hardly be expected to disclose a true mate for singles the rest of the week.

In its new role, will work evaporate, or become indistinguishable from play?

Already what is one man's work is another's play. Although it may be increasingly problematic to distinguish between work and play so far as the *activities* they involve are concerned, we can see that there are distinct psychological differences between the two already which the era of abundance will only accentuate. For example, consider the different significances of playing golf.

Let us assume that two men who play golf are millionaires by inheritance, so that neither works "for a living." One has become a professional poet, the other a professional golfer. For the poet, golf has the functions of play. Hopefully this includes some residual self-validative delight in exercising his muscular mastery skills (as in infancy), beyond his needs for distraction and domination. He will look forward to playing golf in a way conditioned by these social and self-validative needs and functions of play.

The professional golfer, on the other hand, will approach the first tee each day with different needs, those connected with self-validative work. The freedom from necessity provided by his fortune should permit him to golf solely for the self-validative satisfactions of work rather than the survival concerns of tournament winnings. But when he wants distraction and the joy of exercising his unused capacities, he will look anywhere but to the links, possibly even to poetry.

As survival needs become less urgent we are seeing more frequently today than ever examples of people who change not only their play but their work even in middle or late life to correspond more fully with their interests and capabilities, and hence their self-validative needs.[5] What counts is the commitment each man makes to the central psychological function, self-validation via zestful, enduring investment in the process and product of work. Generally it is through his work that a man leaves the world different than it was when he entered it. Through his play, which may be more evanescent, he makes an effect mainly on *himself*, so that he can return refreshed to his work on the world. On this account I would guess that failure to qualify for publication in *Poetry* or competition in the Bing Crosby Open would likely be more damaging to the self-validation of the professional in each case than of the amateur.

Curiously, play is the only one of the three basic human activities which for the future era of abundance should be encouraged to remain fixated at (or regressed to) its infantile state. As the causes of aggression are reduced there will be less need to dominate others.[6] And as human life becomes freed from enslavement to survival drudgery there will be less and less need for distraction.

But concomitantly there will be increasing need for exploration and exercise of unused capabilities provided by self-validative play. Whereas work requires focusing of attention and restricting activity to that which is relevant, play requires diffusing attention onto those unused capacities which were pent-up and postponed, and now press for expression.

A word must be said about why the boundaries between play and love, or play and work, seem to be blurring more than the boundary between love and work. On this question I have only the most tentative thoughts.

First, in the era of scarcity it has been play that is most frequently (if disappointingly) associated with *pleasure*, and so it has been into play that those suffering on account of love or work have wanted to escape, blurring the boundaries as they fled. Then, in the world of scarcity, economic pressures sometimes make *work of love*. This leads to prostitution, both literal and figurative, which so often prevents full psychic intimacy with love and, as abundance comes along to liberate people, is understandably resisted. Also resisted is the Puritan ethic's opposite blight, the tendency to make *love of work*, because it has proved self-validative only in the relatively infrequent instances where the work could in fact be loved. More often it led to masochistic submission to suffering and acceptance of one's "lot in life."

Only for the woman was there, in marriage, a relatively accessible combination of love and work which proved satisfactory. For love has always been a woman's work, in the sense of giving loving care to her husband and children. But the price was often becoming practically a slave. Men have usually resisted emulating this trend as "unmanly," but nowadays are learning to welcome it in themselves, although they are no more willing than women to be subjugated and tied to it exclusively. And today women are pressing harder all the time to have their own work outside the home, not so much dissuaded away from domesticity as persuaded toward the outer world by the opportunity to affect it in the ways traditional for men. So it seems that, however willing some men and women may be to exchange roles in relation to love and work, both sexes want to maintain the separateness of love and work. Perhaps this can best be understood at present as a need to keep the intimate and personal distinct from the social and universal, even though one devotedly confers survival benefits on both.

15 Psychic Intimacy as Observed in Psychoanalysis

Perhaps an illustration from one person's life could help clarify how these general ideas relate to the specific familiar emotional disorders called neuroses. Here is an example of the peculiar combinations of difficulty with psychic intimacy that emerge in psychoanalytic treatment of a neurotic patient.

Ned was a talented young architect of thirty who began treatment because of discouragement over inability to stop a self-defeating cycle in his own feelings and behavior. When he came to me he was unaware of most of the connections described below.

The cycle began with his starting a new job, and simultaneously assuming a peculiar unaccustomed defiant attitude toward me, as though somehow he were doing it against my wishes. Becoming completely absorbed in plans for a new building, Ned would work hard at the challenging project and begin to evolve solutions to the design problems it posed. Then, in buoyant spirits, he would seek out and become specially interested in an attractive young woman with whom he would spend evenings and weekends and soon start sexual relations. Riding a crest of energetic optimism, he also would resume playing the rough game of soccer, which he had given up months before.

All would go well for a few weeks as he and his parents rejoiced that at last his fulfillment in life seemed under way. But almost imperceptibly, as he approached success with all its associated rewards, anxiety would begin to overtake Ned. He would first adopt a conciliatory attitude toward me. And then gradually the vague apprehensions crystallized into fears of physical attack and injury by me and other men.

Initially this anxiety would trouble him most at the job. He dreaded success in his work for two main reasons which became clear bit by bit. One, he had unconsciously carried over from early boyhood the combined urge to outdo and fear of competing with his father so common in our society. This arose in the ordinary way, through envy of the father's size and strength, especially his larger genitals. He had concluded that these were the basis for his mother's devotion to father, which he bitterly resented. Accordingly his desire at age four to surpass his father in body and genital size had undergone the usual repression out of fear of retaliation by father. The punishment he feared was castration, both literal and figurative. Now that he was grown the fear had spread to include his urge to best his father, who was a poorly paid commission salesman, in occupational status and income, which for grown-ups acquire central significance in our society as symbols of potency.

Behind that terror lay the other, deeper reason. In growing up he had come to feel that mother's continued love for him was based on his dependence upon her superior skills for every need satisfaction, from making his bed to doing his difficult algebra problems. So he feared success in work would not only alienate father, but would also cost him the magic permanent protection in a dangerous world he felt could come only from the helplessness that guarantees the right to be taken care of by mother forever.

As these apprehensions reached a crescendo he would shrink away from completing the job with a debilitating mixture of regret and relief. His self-esteem would plummet when the boss brought in another man to finish the design, but at least he was compensated by the easing of panicky feelings as success in the world retreated.

Thus deprived of the satisfactions that come from zestful investment in work and its related self-validation, Ned would become depressed and ashamed of his "failure," feeling himself to be weak in character as well as body.

Depleted of energy, under the revived influence of his mother's anxious warnings about physical injury in rough play, he would become unable to enjoy exercise. He would then give up soccer, feeling even more wretched now that he was deprived of the self-validation that derives from zestful investment in play.

At this point, bereft of the satisfaction of both work and play, feeling cowardly and unmanly, he would also begin to lose feeling for his young woman. By then, that relationship too had become a source of anxiety. On the one hand, daring to compete even for a younger woman stirred up his castration dread of father and, on the other, he feared that shifting his dependency away from mother would result in mother's jealous withdrawal of the talisman of her protective love. Repeatedly he found himself identifying with mother by making the same complaints against the younger woman that *mother* had made against *father*, thus rationalizing his withdrawal from the relationship and his zestful investment in love.

Having given up his assertive activity in love, work, and play, the fears subsided completely. He felt safe, but worthless. In despair one day he summed it up, "I have two choices. To be terrified, or to be nothing."

No one can stand to be nothing for long. At this point he always experienced an upwelling of passive homosexual urges. He wanted to be used sexually as a woman by a powerful man. This wish represented his desperate effort to be a successful and loved person without risking the dangers of competing with men. In this way, Ned would try to give up the effort to outdo his father. Instead he would become like his mother and be protected as she was, by a man. But his heterosexual wishes were too firmly grounded to be pushed aside in favor of overt passive homosexuality. Besides, functioning sexually as a woman implies not the larger penis he had wanted as a child, but its replacement by a vagina. Thus homosexual wishes threatened his male identity and anatomy. Therefore, fantasy was as far as he could let himself go in this direction.

Now came a phase of looking for nonfrightening substitutes for what he really wanted. He would try to "settle for less." First he would take a job as a draftsman, or maybe a clerk. Or if he were feeling especially cautious, Ned might even work as a dishwasher or janitor for a while. With the support of the modest self-validation he could extract from such work his self-esteem would increase a little. His transference feelings toward me would take on an abject puppy-like devotion. But covertly Ned would watch me carefully to see if his minor assertion was going to provoke me either to punish or desert him. Soon he would start to toy with the dangerous idea of going back to work as an architect, but would become neurotically so afraid of my reaction that he would hurriedly suppress this urge and turn instead to something safer.

Timidly he would swim for a few minutes each day, an activity he ordinarily disdained as too tame. But it had the advantage of supplying a bit of self-validation, as well as allowing him to meet, without taking any blameworthy initiative, the lonely, unattractive women who lived in his apartment building. At their instigation, for several weeks he would have compulsive sexual affairs with several of them, all the while keeping a hawkeye on me for the slightest indication of disapproval which might send him scurrying back to the security of homosexual fantasy. Not encountering retaliation from me, and feeling the slight boost in self-esteem that comes from being wanted even by someone whose affection he did not reciprocate, he would then contrive to bring about advances from attractive women. With these "appetizing girls" he would have equally compulsive sexual affairs by the dozen, but seek safety in reducing the behavior to its most infantile (and therefore least "punishable") form. With them he experienced intercourse as a magic meal which would protect him from all danger if he pleased his substitute mother through cunnilingus while "eating" her (compare p. 281). But, as he was also careful to let me see, his hostility over being thus compelled to "humiliate" himself barred him from zestfully investing himself in any of these relationships, thus preventing any substantial psychic intimacy with love.

Nevertheless, over the course of several weeks, the fragments of self-validation derived from such unpunished timorous excursions into assertion gradually built up his confidence and courage. As he would begin to search for work in architecture, his alimentary romances would dwindle away. One day Ned would land a job, once more begin feeling truculent toward me, and the agony would start all over again.

During the first year of intensive work Ned gradually became aware of the sequences of his recurrent trouble outlined above. Naturally, a complete picture of the causes of his neurosis and his gradual recovery cannot be conveyed in these few paragraphs. Suffice it to say that after three years of treatment he broke the cycle enough to stick to a good job; after another year he married and terminated analysis; and two years later he is able to sustain psychically intimate relationships with his work (school design) and love (wife and baby girl), but as yet not consistently with play.

This story illustrates how the self-validation derived from psychic intimacy with love, work, and play intertwines with other emotional factors and contributes from day to day to the bolstering or weakening of self-esteem. Of course, as a result of his psychological conflicts, Ned was an especially vulnerable person and responded excessively with elation and depression, but the *kind* of reactions he showed to changes in his relationship to love, work, and play are to some extent characteristic of everyone.

It is also important to realize that it is not always the *current* social reality that denies a person rewarding love, work, and play opportunities. Ned is one of the many who are prevented from enjoying good adult opportunities by a psychoneurosis stemming from childhood.

16 *Psychic Impostor Ethic*

Even more ominous than the Fun ethic is what I call the Psychic Impostor ethic, a rudimentary new value for the era of abundance now promoted by many. Unlike the Fun ethic, which is at least in favor of pleasure while scuttling psychic intimacy, the Psychic Impostor ethic advocates *not* enjoying anything for itself whatsoever. In the guise of "playing it cool," it is against "really meaning it" at any time. Psychic nonintimacy with love and work is not just a by-product of the pursuit of income or fun, *but a central test of success.* What counts is being a popular and persuasive fake. The Psychic Impostor ethic works by completely substituting remuneration for self-validation, and what Jules Henry calls pecuniary truth for real truth.[1] Here are some examples.

Until a few years ago, TV commercials generally were performed by obscure paid actors whose actual identity was usually unknown to the audience. Occasionally a well-known and usually uncomfortable star would endorse a product, filmed in the studio in obviously commercial surroundings, perhaps with other actors playing subsidiary roles. One understood that this was a kind of remunerative dishonesty which is socially permissible, either because the performer's own intimate personal identity was not directly involved, or if it were, because the circumstances were plainly remote from everyday life. But recently, as a writer connected with the project explained to me, a well-known star invited the camera into her own *real* home where she introduced her own *real* daughter to the TV audience. Thereupon she demonstrated a hairspray on the daughter's own *real* hair, meanwhile engaging with her in an obviously *fake* but "realistic" conversation about the merits of the product.

In the old days it was hard enough for an actress to explain why it was all right for Mommy to lie on TV while the child was not allowed to do the same anywhere. But somehow one could stagger past that inconsistency by making clear that it was a lucrative "profession" to tell those clearly anonymous lies. But after the lights and camera are turned off, what do you say to the child whom you have just identified and incorporated into your public lie to help you earn your fee, before an audience of millions who know in their hearts, as do you and your daughter, that neither of you used the product before being handsomely paid for saying you did on TV? Consider what this child has been taught about truth, falsehood, and the Psychic Impostor ethic. For that matter, what is the child *viewing* such a commercial to believe? Either he must force himself to remain impossibly naïve and take the message as real truth, or he must cynically accept the legitimacy of pecuniary truth, and the corruption of self it implies.

Notice that in this illustration of the Psychic Impostor ethic there is revealed the same kind of erosion by our commercial culture of the value of individual identity that was apparent when we explored, in connection with the Fun ethic, the significance of revealing the names of the models in *Playboy*'s center spreads. In their derogation of personal privacy and honesty, both ethics contribute to the lack of self-validation so prevalent in our society.

The gravity of this trend stands out when we compare it with the role of its opposite, the scrupulous protection of one's privacy, pledge, and name in the history of democracy, especially our own. The oaths men have sworn for millennia on the names of various gods have been supplemented, if not supplanted, in everyday life in recent centuries by a human being's own name—the promises made in little signals of humanity which we call words. The fate of John Proctor in *The Crucible*, who chooses death by hanging in preference to setting his name to a proclamation which would falsely acknowledge that he trafficked with the Devil, movingly exemplifies the value placed by American colonists on the honor of a man's word and name. When asked his reason for refusing to save his life, he says, "Because it is my name! Because I cannot have another in my life! Because I lie and sign myself to lies . . ."[2]

As damnable as are the psychological consequences of its handsomely rewarded prevarications, our present system of commercial production and distribution has something even more malignant to offer those who are *poorly* paid for their public lies. I have in mind, as example of others, women who demonstrate and sell hair spray or other such products in retail stores.

Pertinent results have come from experimental tests of what is called the theory of "cognitive dissonance."[3] It asserts that if a person performs an activity on the basis of meager external justification (money), he experiences an uncomfortable disharmony (or dissonance) between two pieces of knowledge (or cognition), one, that he did do the act, and two, that he did not have very much external reason for doing it. Accordingly, he may seek an *internal* justification.

> . . . In one well-known experiment . . . undergraduates who were given $1.00 for telling a fellow student that a dull task they had just performed was really quite interesting, actually seemed to believe that it *had been* more interesting than did undergraduates who told the same lie for $20.00. . . . The finding is clearly predictable from dissonance theory: the cognition that the task had been dull is dissonant with the cognition that I, as a subject, said it was interesting. The more money I receive for lying, the greater the justification, and hence, the less the dissonance. In the $20.00 condition, if I were to ask myself why I said that the task was interesting, I should have a good, sufficient reason—indeed, I should have 20 good reasons. I should be left with knowledge that I had told a lie—but that it has been worth it. In the $1.00 condition, however, I should not have a great deal of justification for having told the lie. In retrospect, the fact that one has sold his soul for $20.00 may seem like a pretty good deal; but it is difficult to justify having sold one's soul for a paltry dollar. Lacking ample monetary justification, I should seek some other kind. . . . One way . . . would be to convince myself that . . . "actually the task wasn't so dull; indeed, if one looks at it in a certain way, it was really quite an interesting or even an exciting task."[4]

So, while the star has sold her soul for thousands of dollars, she retains her own grasp on reality by at least remaining conscious that she lied. On the other extreme, the retail clerk may have sold her psyche for pennies and may not even be able to maintain mental health by preserving her own private judgment of the product, through need to find *internal* justification for having endorsed it.

Some prophets of the doom of abundance inveigh against the corrupting effect of excessively high salaries and wages for an honest day's work. They might profitably ponder the worse degradation that can result from excessively *low* monetary justification for a dishonest evening's mendacity. And the rest of us should demand that he who does a job that debases the spirit must speedily be relieved of it, while in the interim he must be generously overpaid so that at least he can continue loathing it.

Surprisingly, we sometimes hear justification of miserable circumstances in our society from those who suffer from them most, no doubt partially attributable to the fact that it is precisely from those miserable circumstances that the defenders make their living. But I suspect that their puzzling degree of enthusiasm for the status quo may be brought about more by their not making a *good enough* living, that is, by their need to find compensatory internal justification for the lies they are forced to live as well as tell. For example, could underpayment be the reason some assembly-line workers and foot soldiers justify the industrial and military processes that crush their spirits and murder their bodies?

Another poisonous extreme to which the Psychic Impostor ethic can be carried is indicated in this vignette from the therapy of a call-girl patient. The rejected child of an alcoholic mother, she unconsciously loathed herself as not being worthy of love or sexual pleasure, and therefore self-protectively avoided further hurt by firmly renouncing both. She managed to eke out a psychological existence sustained by the crumbs of self-validation extracted from her "work." One day during therapy she indignantly condemned "those filthy chippies who are sleeping around with different fellows every night." It was not the number of their bed partners, or even the potential inroad on her income that upset her. No, it was a problem in identity and self-esteem. She erupted when asked mildly whether they were not doing the same as she. "It's not the same thing at all! I'm a *professional*. I don't *enjoy* it with every man, and they do!"

This poor girl is so hostile that she is completely frigid even in noncommercial intercourse. But she takes great pride in the fact that her customers are all persuaded by her lies that she loves her work and not just the considerable remuneration. Here we see how a desperate defense of the last tatters of shattered self-esteem can prevent precisely that psychic intimacy and self-validation which is needed for repair of self-esteem.

What has this to do with people in general? Surely we cannot judge everyone on the basis of one sick girl. And surely we cannot claim that prostitution and its rationalizations are in any way new.

No, but we can and must see soon how grotesque is the tragedy that, just at the moment when general abundance and human fulfillment could be right around the corner, the Psychic Impostor ethic is eagerly welcomed into so many aspects of our lives. For one does not have to stretch the facts to see the resemblance of my call-girl patient to the righteous woman who for material comfort and social status marries a man she cannot abide.

And we must not forget the man who slaves daily at a job he hates, writing dishonest cigarette ads solely for the paycheck, or the grim golfer who plays only to get away from it all or to triumph over his friends. Then there is the editorial writer who forces his words into the alien philosophy of his publisher, or the lingerie salesman who switches lines from Van Raalte to Maidenform without missing a syllable or losing a customer.

The broader aspects of the Psychic Impostor ethic, of remaining detached and "not really meaning it," must at least be mentioned here in passing. Beyond the rigged quiz shows, the cheaters at the Academy, the dissembling advertisers, are the elected officials solemnly intoning lies, the crowds indifferently watching a murder, the nations methodically escalating a war "in defense of peace." Behind them stands the lonely intimidated individual who, when outraged by injustice, gives in to his fear of retaliation and decides that "it is wrong to make waves." All these are conscious or unconscious supporters of the Psychic Impostor ethic, and at minimum suffer the associated loss of self-validation.

While hard work and frugality are becoming irrelevant, some of the values of scarcity are still viable. Honesty expressed as respect for individual and group forthrightness, charity evidenced as generosity toward the deprived, humility shown in open-mindedness, and fraternity manifested as loving concern for all human beings, are plainly still adaptive. We are all members of professional, business, social, or church organizations. We all have money to donate or to withhold. We are all citizens with a public voice as well as a secret ballot.

We must all be psychically intimate lovers, workers, and players in these dimensions too, or we and our human communities lose identity, integrity, and possibly even our lives.

Summing Up

Psychic Nonintimacy and Regression

For all its pose of cool sophistication, the psychic nonintimacy with love and work which results from tying them to their central social functions has a curiously *infantilizing* effect.

Tying love exclusively to pleasure and tension reduction (Fun ethic) forces the adult to regress to the state of the baby for whom any source of pleasure is the same as any other.

Tying work to survival through obtaining income forces the adult to regress to the state of the baby who must labor indiscriminately many hours a day to keep body and soul together, in an era when automation-cybernation is making drudgery obsolete for adults.

On the other hand, despite its appearance of energetic involvement, the situation with respect to play is the reverse. Tying play to distraction and domination prevents it from *resuming* its primary self-validative function: joyous exercise of the self's unused capacities.

Even worse is the Psychic Impostor ethic which forces the adult to regress to something resembling the state of a *sick* baby for whom, although he is surfeited with food, life in general is devoid of pleasure as well as self-validation.

Prospecting for Values

Even if the tentative shoots of new values which are presently discernible were more encouraging, there is not time to wait for them to mature. Yet we do not know how to devise new values consonant with new realities. But we may be able to learn how if we set ourselves the task.

New value systems can and perhaps must be different from those of the past in many respects. But they must retain and develop further the characteristics of psychic intimacy with love, work, and play in order to be validative of the self, and thereby supportive of identity and mental health.

Résumé

It may be helpful to have a brief recapitulation of main points concerning love, work, and play.

Freud thought abilities to love and work the best indices of mental health. If interpreted in terms of new realities, and supplemented by play, his formula will be applicable to the future.

The coming era of abundance offers the majority of mankind its first opportunity to transform love, work, and play into the distinctively human sources of identity and self-validation which were available during the era of scarcity only to the leisured minority. Yet anxious people struggle to perpetuate the obsolescing compulsion to love merely for pleasure, tension-release, and child nurturing; to work merely for survival; and to play merely for distraction and domination.

Love, work, and play best support mental health when the person's relationship to them is characterized by what I call psychic intimacy, the zestful, enduring investment of the self that crystallizes only gradually during infancy. Such a relationship to love is impelled, beyond pleasure, tension-release, and child-nurturing needs, by zestful enduring investment of the self in the object of the love. Such a relationship to work is impelled, beyond income and subsistence needs, by zestful enduring investment of the self in the process and product of the work. Such a relationship to play is impelled, beyond distraction and domination needs, by zestful enduring investment of the self in the specific activity of the play.

When a person's relationship to them is psychically intimate, love and work validate the self, confirming its existence and worth throughout life. Without psychic intimacy in the relationship, love and work operate as in earliest infancy before differentiation of self, when constant striving was required to meet just the needs for pleasure and subsistence. Work in adulthood then regresses to frustrating depersonalized drudgery while love, in futile compensation, often regresses to disappointing alienated transitory pleasure seeking (Fun ethic). Without psychic intimacy in the relationship, play is prevented from regressing to its original function during infancy of joyous exercise of the self's unused capacities, and so remains degraded throughout life into the compulsive distraction and domination functions it was forced to serve during childhood.

Sometimes further deterioration of personality occurs in which psychic nonintimacy is not recognized as misfortune, but instead becomes a test of success. Then love, work, and play become frauds in which people "play it cool," withhold zestful investment of the self from them; and anxiously collect pecuniary and other rewards in lieu of the self-validation they need but cannot achieve (Psychic Impostor ethic).

We must find new values consonant with new realities. But in doing so we must become psychically intimate lovers, workers, and players in the widest sense, or in the process we will lose identity, integrity, and possibly even our lives.

SECTION THREE

MASTERY OF THE FUTURE

Part I

Ways to Go

Introduction

Now it is our task to discern in which directions we are going, and what evolutionary alternatives we have. New realities are going to require new adaptations. As we have seen, the old realities could be mastered in a number of different ways, one of which, the Puritan ethic, became dominant in the Western world.

Similarly, the world of the future can be adapted to in various ways. The era of abundance and leisure provides many more potentialities than the era of scarcity and drudgery. But as we have seen, there are only a limited number of ways any particular set of realities can be mastered by any particular creature while still maintaining its essential identity. *Combinations* of *different* ways may maintain the creature's essential identity and yet sometimes lead to more complex and effective mastery of its realities. Fish that breathe air, mammals that fly, and men that live in settled agricultural communities remain fish, mammals, and men despite their new talents. But fish that altogether give up gills and fins for lungs and legs, mammals that give up breasts and wombs in exchange for glass bottles, and men who substitute machines for mothers possibly may thereby cease to be fish, mammals, or men.

We are called upon now to make choices about matters that in the past were not within our control, including some fundamentally affecting our identity as human beings. This means we must ask ourselves questions about what is good and bad which we have inadequate experience in deciding. For example, when it was necessary for a man to hunt or farm eighteen hours a day in order to feed himself and family he was under no pressure to decide the virtues of cutting his workday to twelve hours. When the standard workday was twelve hours there was relatively little question in the average man's mind that, reality permitting, it would be better to work only eight hours a day. Now that the standard workday is seven to eight hours, and now that the burden of leisure has begun to weigh oppressively on many people, there *is* increasing question among workers as well as employers whether a further reduction to five or six hours a day—now just around the corner—is desirable. One can only decide such a question on the basis of value judgments, whether conscious and wise, or otherwise.

In reviewing some major trends in the values and life-styles of people we can see all about us, it is essential to keep in mind some characteristics and limitations of this catalogue. First of all, while each of the possibilities itemized below functions in one sense as a way of adapting to and mastering reality, it also functions on the other hand as a way of *controlling anxiety*. In general the ratio between the reality-mastering and anxiety-controlling functions of a trend determines whether we regard it as productive or wasteful. A man who reshingles his roof himself primarily for enjoyment, as well as to stop leaks and to save money for a vacation, is operating in a healthy way. A man who reshingles his own roof despite the fact that it does not leak, that he has no need to economize, that he is up there in the hot sun performing a task he does not enjoy because of unconscious guilt over having a Sunday to himself, and because he is too inhibited to think of or allow himself to do something he *would* enjoy, is behaving in an unhealthy, nonadaptive way, driven primarily by need to control anxiety. In the future our lives must be organized deliberately in such a way as to decrease the amount of wasteful anxiety-controlling behavior, and to increase the amount of our creative productive behavior. Each of the value trends discussed below has a positive and negative aspect. In each instance I have tried to articulate both, but it will be no great trick to determine where my bias lies. The Psychic Impostor ethic described in Chapter 16 could as well have been included here, but it would of course have been no easier here than earlier to set forth its favorable features.

Secondly, I ask you to keep in mind that any diagram or outline of complex conditions is to some degree a misrepresentation. By emphasizing some elements, such an approach may neglect others of equal importance. As we have seen, for clarity the mind finds it necessary to pick out and fix in a spotlight, so that it can be followed easily, one thread running through the intricate tapestry of reality. And in following that thread it will be obvious at certain points that it crosses other threads, merges imperceptibly into them, or possibly even disappears altogether. Such a scheme can never be a final accounting. We must be content if it clarifies our thinking for the time being, and always ready to replace it by a better or more complete one when that becomes possible.

We described the Puritan ethic as a value system composed of a number of subvalues or trends which when put together made a coherent whole. It is immediately evident that diligence fits very nicely with thrift. The two are harmonious with frugality. All three are readily compatible with chastity. Respect for elders, humility, and submissiveness to the will of God form an obvious trio, and neatly supplement the other trends in helping the individual work out an adaptation to a reality characterized by scarcity and drudgery. Even the hostile rejection of pleasure characteristic of the Puritan ethic clearly represented an adaptive safeguard against frittering away much needed energies in a way that did not promote survival.

It is also clear that the value system of Tahiti prior to the white invasion constituted a similarly coherent adaptation to the conditions of universal pretechnological abundance characteristic of that reality. And we can imagine how in less uniform reality circumstances, such as those of revolutionary France, a variety of value adaptations can arise, fitting different individuals to their different circumstances with variable success.

Now we must deal with the most complex life-styles and contradictory value trends in the most varied reality that has ever existed. Western culture, more specifically the culture of the United States, is still nominally dominated by the Puritan ethic. As we have observed, however, in practice it has been markedly eroded and in some areas it has all but crumbled away. Tentatively, I find seven main trends developing within our currently disorganized value system. Unlike those of the Puritan ethic, however, in many combinations they are markedly mutually incompatible. They are:

> Getting Ahead
> Fun Fervor
> Creative Frenzy
> Mystic Withdrawal
> Technique Infatuation
> Big and Little Brother Protection
> Prospectancy

Different parts of our community live according to one or several of these currently operative trends. They are therefore in conflict with other members of the community living according to others of the trends. In fact quite commonly some individuals in the community live according to value trends that are incompatible within themselves. We are all familiar with conflicts that arise on the basis of these incompatible trends in ourselves and in others. Harmonious or not, the various personality patterns we can observe in people we know are always mixtures of several trends in various proportions.

A value system of the future could conceivably be centered about and arise predominantly from any one or a combination of a few of these trends. Therefore I call them "ways to go." Each will be treated in a separate chapter.

Many attempts are made nowadays to predict the future scientifically. The Hudson Institute has given us *The Year 2000;* the American Institute of Arts and Sciences' Commission on the Year 2000 has published *Toward the Year 2000: Work in Progress.*[1] France and the United Kingdom have similar commissions.[2] The First International Future Research Conference met in Oslo in 1967.[3] *The Futurist* is a periodical solely concerned with the future.[4] Now that the future has drawn so close, scientists predominate on the Commission on the Year 2000. There are no artists, politicians, housewives, or writers on the commission. This selection seems to reflect the prevailing attitude toward the future. Apparently impersonal natural and social forces propel us into the future; therefore impersonal social and natural scientists may seem to be those best qualified to investigate where we are and should be headed.[5]

When we study the *past*, however, we look to cultural relics of *all* sorts, to plays, histories, painting, sculpture, clothing, memoirs, not just to the residue of scientists and their work. Just as surely, it seems that hundreds of years from now any who might wish to know what our world was like would include our own literature, painting, movies, and written histories. Admittedly, they could thereby derive as distorted a picture of us as we no doubt have of some extinct societies. Suppose, as suggested by Arthur Clarke, the only surviving artifact of our society were a Donald Duck cartoon! But then, wouldn't their perspective be even more distorted if it were a linear accelerator?

There is just as much to learn about ourselves from our *creations* as from anatomical dissections, biochemical or psychological analyses, sociological investigations, voter profile studies, and census enumerations. After all, the essence of scientific creation is art. The social sciences have performed some of their best work in validating the pronouncements of fiction. For example, political science has discovered that the greatest influence on political party affiliation is parental party membership, as John Marquand and John O'Hara showed so many years before in their "social novels."[6] The irrationality and absurdity of *Catch-22* seems to have previewed the Vietnam war even more accurately than it mirrored World War II.[7] And writers from Sophocles to Shakespeare to Stendhal had been making psychological and sociological analyses long before the words or the validative sciences to which they refer were born.

So, broadly defined, art is the Rosetta stone for translating the past and present. And if, as Marshall McLuhan shows, art is also the vanguard of the future, then futurologists will do well to rearrange their commissions.[8]

In "Ways to Go," then, we will use our seething arts, literature, movies, and television, not as predictions, but as illustrations of existing trends, and their projections into the future.

17 Getting Ahead

Getting ahead is practically synonymous with the American Way of Life. That's why we should consider it first.

Getting ahead has a double meaning. On the one hand it means making progress over one's previous position. But it also means, though a little more secretly, getting ahead of your neighbor. The first significance places the main emphasis on *producing,* while the second places it on *consuming.*

In the days when American life was more thoroughly characterized in practice by the Puritan ethic, as during the settlement of the early colonies, the producing emphasis was predominant. The hearty adventurers who later pioneered the American West climbed out of their Conestoga wagons to make homesteads where they also could get ahead in this sense. To them getting ahead meant acquiring by hard work of their own what they did not have, homes, farms, livestock, food, and other material goods. Their activity was certainly an expression of diligence, thrift, frugality, and so on. Efforts guided by such values produced adaptations pertinent to their realities which were suffused by scarcity.

The modern as well as the pioneer American takes getting ahead as an objective, but there are some subtle significant differences. Although the same kind of effort is still demanded by the realities faced by many of our people, others continue grimly to follow the same values of accumulation now made irrelevant for them by considerable abundance. Getting ahead often has come to mean for them acquiring all the same things *without* hard work by going to the right school, knowing the right people, behaving in the right way. Success in this kind of getting ahead is increasingly gauged according to the consuming emphasis, by the degree to which one is able to assure himself of these comforts without sweat, as well as the degree to which the quality and quantity of one's possessions outstrip those belonging to his friends. Today's American often wants to get ahead only in this second sense, and as a goal in itself. I think that is why so many Americans in their forties are suddenly faced with emotional breakdowns that bring them to marriage counselors and various types of psychotherapists after having achieved a considerable degree of this objective. Once having gotten "ahead" they can see in the next thirty to forty years of their lives only more of the same. In other words, they are not striving to get ahead in the course of accomplishing something else.

The American pioneer, on the other hand, tried to get ahead in circumstances that would guarantee him something more than the material goods and prestige that seem to be the prevalent objectives now. He wanted to establish for himself a kind of *independence and freedom* which it was difficult for him to enjoy in the rapidly urbanizing communities of the East. He wanted to be out in the world of the wilderness and to surmount the challenges it offered. He wanted to raise his children in circumstances he regarded as healthier, freer, and more joyous than they could have had back home. Of course there were many who pursued this new life because of its promise of greater eventual material reward and security, but it is unlikely that even they would have as willingly headed in the opposite direction had more material gain and prestige been offered as the only inducements.

Today material gain and increased prestige are magnetic enough by themselves to drag thousands of American families away from family, friends, and community ties to new homes they dislike in different parts of the country or across the world, even though they already live in comfortable abundance.

The persistence of this shallow trend in American values is ensured by the threat of the continued presence throughout the world of millions of people who still have not acquired sufficient material goods. But our tenacious concentration on material success is fostered even more by failure to grasp emotionally and intellectually the changed realities brought about by our new technology. There can be little freedom for a man who is starving to death. There can be little of the good life for a population unable to afford a clean water supply. But we fortunate few are as often deceived as are the underprivileged about their chances to move up to our standard of living by continued unconscious belief that *scarcity is inescapable.* Failing to take into account the floods of abundance now possible, we and they behave as though they can get ahead materially only by taking away from us what we now enjoy. Those of us in the developed part of the world are thus constantly reinforced in our outdated conviction that we can maintain the good life for ourselves only by depriving others.

We must not be fooled. Our continued affluence depends rather upon comprehending the changed realities, so that *we insist* that peoples of the rest of the world have the opportunity to share as much of it as they wish. Not only such economic factors as our markets and raw materials are at stake, but also the critical matter of mounting animosity and aggression toward us. In a time when nearly any small nation with determination can make or steal nuclear, chemical, or biological weapons of mass destruction, it behooves us to reduce the provocation of poverty to violence. The stability of the social dominance hierarchy of baboons is never threatened under natural conditions by the pressures of starvation because there is enough food to go around and no purpose would be served by denying enough to eat to any member of the troop. Now that we no longer have to do so in getting ahead, why should we subject the human social order to currently unnecessary and therefore "unnatural" stresses? Social stability grows out of social justice, which nowadays means nothing less for everyone than plenty. Anything less amid today's potential abundance can only lead to the sort of social cataclysm that results when inequity is perceived, and correctly, as iniquity.

We must also understand that, while getting ahead in terms of food, shelter, health, and other such necessities is still an essential step in the right direction for underdeveloped countries or underprivileged people in our own country, getting ahead in terms of luxuries, a second car, a third television set, or the latest electric carving knife for privileged people constitutes an emotional dead end. One cannot remain zestfully engaged with a life devoted to pursuit of the trivial no matter how deep and prolonged was his ability to remain zestfully engaged with a life dedicated to acquisition of the truly essential. Loss of psychic intimacy cannot be compensated adequately by acquisition of new gadgets. One's identity cannot be substantially founded on getting ahead in terms of accumulating any "thing," but only upon the basis of continuing psychic intimacy with love, work, and play.

But the very heart of the American profit economy lies in the perpetual stimulation of appetite for new material goods.[1] So successful has it been that our former devotion to diligent production has had little opportunity to energize new possibilities of psychically intimate work because it has become substantially replaced by a mass psychic hunger for ravenous consumption. The Frankenstein monster thus created is tragically spreading its havoc from the realm of human relations to things to that of human relations to human beings. Student-teacher, salesman-buyer, and politician-voter relationships increasingly involve efforts to contrive "images" that will induce one to permit the other in the course of getting ahead to consume and discard him as an empty husk. The "bunny syndrome" is an especially ghastly instance of a turn taken by the consumption craze in the pursuit of pleasure, a phenomenon to which we now turn.

18 *Fun Fervor*

As the hold of the Puritan ethic on our daily life evaporates, one might assume that there would follow an enormous increase in the esteem in which pleasure is held. In a way this is true. At least the average person in the United States today enjoys many more different pleasurable experiences than his forebears did one hundred years ago. So much of our present culture is devoted to just this eliciting of pleasure that it *ought* to be true even if it is not.

Be that as it may, it seems likely that the *amount* of pleasure enjoyed by an individual is not directly related to the number of different supposedly pleasurable experiences he can have. Walter Kerr even concludes that pleasure is declining amid our frenzied and many-faceted pursuit of it.[1]

Strangely enough, it may well be that those in the past who have experienced the most pleasure were just those who were able successfully to integrate their lives according to the Puritan ethic. For pleasure is always a derivative of other activities than *pleasure seeking*.

What today passes for pleasure in most people's lives is often better designated "fun," in the sense that the gayety-frivolity-merriment aspect seems to predominate greatly over the satisfaction-delight-joy element. Fun fervor is a way of designating both the value judgment of the Fun ethic and behavior in its service.

The film *La Dolce Vita* depicted some of the desperate ways fun may be pursued.[2] It also revealed the desperate frustration of life lived according to this objective. Recently a seven-year-old boy found an article his parents had read describing the pleasures of maturity. They included wine drinking, thought-provoking reading, and stimulating conversation. When asked for his comment he whined, "Aw gee, Mom, pleasure just isn't any fun!" And their yield of fun of the sort he would savor seems to be the criterion by which all activities increasingly are being judged, as ours rapidly becomes a "fun culture."

An increasing army of fun partisans is screaming a denunciation of "Victorian" restrictions on impulse. They insist that the solution to all of our problems, and the route to eternal "happiness," lies simply in the unlimbering of previously inhibited impulses so that they may obtain "natural" complete gratification.

Belated anti-Victorians are thus attributing all human psychological suffering to the inhibitions, especially against sex, which have been on the ropes for at least thirty years. So enfeebled have these restrictions become that inexperienced women who two generations ago would have proudly worn their frigidity as a badge of honor today frantically fake orgasms while they enrich the purveyors of graphic sex manuals that purport to teach them how to achieve the real thing.

Various writers create the impression that the amount of fun or pleasure derived from sexuality is its crucial characteristic because fun is supposed to lead to "happiness," without reference to the emotional relationship between the people involved. Since for them fun is connected with variety, the greater his turnover in sex partners the happier an individual will be. By this measure the man who is driven to endless seductions by insatiable need to prove himself lovable is happier than another who is sure of his lovability and comfortable in devoting himself sexually to the woman he loves.

We have already considered *Playboy* magazine in the light of the Fun ethic. Hugh Hefner, originator of this recent and most influential testament of the Fun ethic, is said to have stated candidly, "What we are doing is making a success out of people's dreams." If he meant a financial success his appraisal seems indubitable. But from the psychological viewpoint a more accurate description would be ". . . a success of providing the illusion that gratification of wishes for fun or pleasure by itself assures 'happiness.' " A sampling of people's moods, dreams, and conversation after fun-filled frolics at the Playboy Club has only confirmed my belief that it does not. To paraphrase Oscar Wilde, there is no one so pitiful as a man who didn't get his heart's desire, unless it is one who did.

Enduring happiness, in contrast to either fun or pleasure, derives only from human relationships or human accomplishment. But even if happiness were the result simply of realizing wishes, is happiness by itself an appropriate goal for human behavior? After all, a shot of alcohol or heroin will briefly bring about the state of happiness, sidestepping the difficulties of human relationship and accomplishment that are its only stable source.

But the drug effect is followed by the prompt letdown that so readily leads to the ominous dependence and agony of addiction.

Although it was a great advance that our Declaration of Independence in those puritanical times recognized human happiness as respectable, direct "pursuit of happiness" is bound to lead to disappointment. That is why even those who can afford to devote themselves completely to directly pursuing happiness so often are nevertheless forced to seek psychological treatment.

Even when it grows out of human relationships and accomplishment, happiness is still only their *by-product* (see also p. 383). Pursuit of such a by-product as a *goal* is dehumanizing in that it deflects interest from the human relationships and accomplishment that make life human. Einstein must have noticed that swine seem to have as a goal the dependent craving, swilling, and enjoying of only a by-product, and one which they do not produce at that. I feel sure that it was in this sense that he meant his remark, "Happiness is for pigs."[3]

A while ago I was looking for a used car. When I found a possible good buy, I asked the seller, a private party, why he wanted to sell what seemed to be a very good automobile. He answered, "You see that my office is fitted up with the very best. My clothes are the very finest. I assure you my home is the same. Well, now I'm going to get a Jaguar XKE."

"Why a Jaguar?"

"Because *girls* like them."

This man was a bright young lawyer in his late twenties who had been in practice about a year and was already earning over fifty thousand dollars a year in a plush Beverly Hills practice. His cufflinks, his waiting-room literature, and about three fifths of his self-esteem were clearly lifted from Hugh Hefner's enterprises. Not to be dissuaded by the implication that his old car might be repellent to women, I suggested he consider my offer which was somewhat under his asking price, and handed him my card so that he might reach me if he wished to negotiate further.

As I turned away, his smooth but uncertain manner melted completely. "Psychiatry!" He choked a little as he read my card. "You must think I'm an awful jerk—what I said about girls."

I had to spend a few more minutes doing supportive psychotherapy to rebolster this fellow after the inadvertent trauma I had caused him.

The most interesting aspect of this experience to me is that he was fully aware how pitiful were the criteria on which he was deciding how to make the daily choices of even the "things" he selected for his surroundings. But his system of values, no doubt acquired through a comfortable childhood, high school, college, and professional school career, had equipped him with really nothing more than the fun fervor with its *Playboy* magazine bible as a way of integrating his life. His awareness of the emptiness of his value system, of course, did not automatically remove or change it.

Let us think for a moment about a future filled with an army of these bachelor sophisticates. Fun is the center of their striving. They zealously follow the dictates of their Leader, carefully learning to select and even "like" the products, services, and activities that are "in" in Hefnerdom. Their fragile identities do not allow them to ask themselves the old question, "Am I doing right?" or even the somewhat newer one, "Am I getting ahead?" Instead, in this age of burgeoning abundance and pyramiding leisure their self-query pipes hollowly from an inner voice reduced to a penny whistle, "Am I having fun?"

While we are at it, we must take a look at the position to which the fun fervor relegates women. The enormous youth-centeredness of our culture is brought to a grotesque extreme in the movement best represented by *Playboy*. Twenty-four or five seems to be the upper limit at which a woman may expect to be considered physically desirable. The other quality for which she is valued even below this early obsolescence is curious: a sort of psychological *edibility*. This characteristic is plainly an outgrowth of projection of infantile fantasies, such as those of the cupcake-fancier discussed in Chapter 9.

In the late teens of this century the motion pictures popularized the vamp, personified by Theda Bara, Pola Negri, and a host of now-forgotten imitators. As an ideal of womanhood she possessed some well-developed characteristics, one-dimensional though they might be. She was evil. She was worldly. She was, at least chronologically, likely to be mature. Usually she was scheming to ensnare and destroy the man. And she was wily and clever and capable of carrying out her nefarious wishes. Although such an ideal of womanhood probably never had much survival value in human society, she was at least a formed and recognizable type of creature which one could take a stand "against." Even her predecessor, the "good" girl, sentimentalized, maudlin, and artificial as she was, had a future. She could grow into the loving and devoted silver-haired mother (as represented in *Greed*),[4] and was at least a recognizable type whom one could be emotionally "for."

But what are we to feel about "Bunny?" She is a pretty, youthful, undistinctive, and untouchable creature whose future ends at twenty-five. Apparently what is expected of us is a strange amalgam of clean lust and parental protectiveness which sees to it that sexual impulses must regress to infantile voyeurisms with the usual rapid shifts of interest from one peep show to another.

But beyond this way station lies yet a further frontier of regression. Literally, a bunny is an infantile rabbit which is valued by human beings partly for its "cuteness" and partly because eventually it will be edible. One likes to look at and, if permitted, to pet and cuddle a baby rabbit. Affection and the minor sensuality that go with it are about the extent of the enjoyment available. After the tiny creature develops a bit, it may be able to elicit from us the additional primitive zestful response of wanting to devour it. Any more mature sort of attachment to a bunny is almost unthinkable by definition.

A creature you have to relate to either by petting, protecting, or devouring is not the sort with which a person can be expected to have a mutual human relationship. A bunny does not give back any petting, let alone protection or the other elements that go into the relationship between two mature human beings. In fact it is ludicrous to expect it to do so. A bunny is to be enjoyed for its cuteness until it is ready to be devoured and thus incorporated into one's self and destroyed as a separate creature.

One of the great difficulties we have in trying to help patients have satisfactory relationships with husbands and wives is their infantile inability to regard and treat the other partner as a permanently separate individual. The consequence is that, at least in a psychological sense, one partner devours and thereby destroys the other, and if this arrangement is not possible the two split up and look for other delectable and presumably more digestible tidbits.

Playboy magazine did not invent the expectation that a human being should be an hors d'oeuvre. But the fantasy on which it is building its success comes directly out of the universal oral infantile experience through which all human beings must pass, and from which they must emerge in order to have the developed human relationships that can sustain partners through the inevitable emergencies and disasters of life. Learning how to savor a bunny as a grown man is not a preparation for marriage. It is a perpetuation beyond arm's length of the infantile relationship to mommy and her breast which is based on the urge to devour. As a mature man you cannot regard your beloved woman as you did your mother when you were in the cradle. Psychologically, as an adult you cannot have your wife and eat her too.

The peculiar tragedy of the *Playboy* approach is not that it so thoroughly demeans the woman as an amusement park for a man. Rather it lies in the *reduction of the man to infantile ways of functioning and judging.* He is prevented thereby from developing a lasting relationship with a real person who can act and react upon him and so contribute to his further growth. Instead she is consumed as a brief burst of psychological calories and disappears in the process like a cupcake.

Thus far we have allowed one manifestation of the fun fervor in (chronologically) adult men to stand as an example for all the others. We must at least mention in passing that the scope of this value covers all other parts of our population and the full range of supposedly fun-yielding behaviors from betting, boating, and bowling to movies, TV, gardening, woodworking, knitting and conversing. Obviously it is not the fact that these and infinite numbers of other activities as well as sex can yield fun with which we are concerned. And obviously it is not fun itself which is in any way a threat, but only the *value judgment* that makes fun the central goal of human striving. It should be equally evident that zestful investment of self in a specific play activity results in a delightful exhilaration described as "fun," the desirability of which is proportional to the degree to which it is an embellishment of a life replete with satisfactions from love and work.

Because fun must be sought during time not commandeered by survival activities, increasing abundance makes the fun fervor possible by suffusing our lives with leisure. There is considerable evidence to indicate that leisure time has increased more among American women and American adolescents in the last quarter-century than among adult males. In 1941, the average workweek in manufacturing was 40.6 hours; in 1965, 41.1 hours and increasing.[5] Also, the amount of time consumed in getting to and from work since then has increased to several hours weekly. The American housewife, however, has been inundated with timesaving and laborsaving products in this same period; and a combination of society's increasing affluence and insistence that youth acquire greater education keeps the young in school and out of the labor force longer.

What becomes of this extra leisure? Youth's much-criticized pursuit of fun through wild parties, dancing, and music has sometimes been the least destructive use to which free time has been put. Particularly among the more deprived or disturbed of our youth petty vandalism, gang fights, and even murder have become more malignant substitutes. Faced with such alternatives one could well prefer the fun fervor.

The use of leisure among women is perplexing. Traditionally the most exploited group in society, one might suppose that they would exert every effort to negate forevermore the old adage that woman's work is never done. However, even among women who are not forced to work for income, instead of taking advantage of their new opportunity to engage in activities primarily for self-validation, in larger numbers than ever before women have taken jobs!

That the number of working women should have increased so greatly during this period may be a clue to the failure of the fun fervor to satisfy the need for self-validation. First, leisure activities result in self-validation only if they involve a psychically intimate relation to play, with fun being a *derivative* rather than the central objective. Only zestful investment of the self in the activity of the play, and not just the fun of distraction or domination, yields self-validation. Second, it is not possible to replace with psychically intimate play, let alone with fun, the confirmation of the existence and worth of the self that ought to come out of psychic intimacy with work. Considering the boring nature of many jobs, and the resultant deficiency of the self-validation they can provide, it is remarkable that working so often should be preferred to playing. This fact says very little for, but perhaps a great deal about the state of, leisure activities in general and the fun fervor in particular.

Among the young, part-time jobs often are held principally so that cars, stereos, and clothes can be afforded. Working married women often hold jobs so that the second car, the home in the "nicer" neighborhood, or the trip to Europe may be sooner attained. Earlier we saw that the consumer emphasis has no deadlier enemy than the viewpoint that one should work for no more than is minimally needed, an attitude bitterly resented by the partisan of possession.[6] Now we encounter the peculiar possibility that the pursuit of fun, pleasure, or play is least attractive to those who have the most time to devote to it, an attitude which in our materialistic culture is accepted with revealing unconcern.

Fun fervor also appears in our attitudes toward culture. Mass culture—movies, television, popular novels, and nonfiction—is traditionally seen by some of its critics as material to be consumed and then forgotten, a divertissement for those who seek respite from the harassing competition of getting ahead.

In the first twenty years of their existence, the movies in America were patronized mostly by working people, particularly first- and second-generation immigrants. Until Griffith's *Birth of a Nation* in 1915, at least, movies were looked down upon as vulgar by upper- and upper-middle-class people, and this attitude was reflected in the treatment given movies by newspapers and magazines.[7] After Griffith's triumph, however, movies in America flourished with the expansion of the upwardly mobile population and entered upon an era of rising prestige and enormous popularity.[8] Increasing respect was forthcoming from the other media as well and movie reviews became a regular newspaper feature, while a host of movie magazines appeared. All this was predicated upon the judgment that movies, your best entertainment, were fun.

The concept of the movie as art made slower headway, but in the last decade or so, the idea that motion pictures are a valid art form, and perhaps *the* preeminent art form of this century, has gained widespread acceptance.[9] Concurrently, however, there has developed the idea of movies, and now television, as "educational media," capable of inculcating culture, especially ideas and values, among the masses. But some critics have a storehouse concept of culture. They object that, in order to fill the maw of movies and television, *Hamlet* will be gutted to render it capable of effortless pleasurable consumption, that the great works of Western civilization from Sophocles to Shaw will be exhausted within a few years to satisfy the appetite of the public—and what then? Hannah Arendt has written that

> Entertainment, like labor and sleep, is irrevocably part of the biological life process. And biological life is always, whether laboring or at rest, whether engaged in consumption or in the passive reception of amusement, a metabolism feeding on things by devouring them. . . . [the] danger is that the life processes of society (which like all biological processes insatiably draw everything available into the cycle of its metabolism) will literally consume, by altering, cultural objects.[10]

While this specific theory may seem mystical, the fear on which it is based is well founded. In our attitudes toward culture, and in well-intentioned attempts to promulgate it as a means for filling up increasing leisure time, the fun fervor and consuming emphasis are apparent. My own concern is not so much that great works of art will be debased, but that *people* will be. Shakespeare has withstood Bowdler's censorship, endless squabbling over the accuracy of various folios, and bad movie adaptations well enough. But that the satiated public might lose its capacity and will to discriminate a cultural triumph from a cultural travesty would be a blow from which all of us could never recover.

Arendt notes that bread and circuses belong together. Both are necessary for life, both vanish in the course of the life process, and freshness is the prime criterion for both.[11] For culture of any greater merit, however, the consuming emphasis of demand for newness or novelty in the product is an impossible and therefore fatal standard. Great works of art are those that, instead of themselves being new, constantly refresh *us*. They are those from which something new may be derived each time they are experienced, *albeit with some effort*. If attitudes toward culture generally become dominated by the fun fervor and consumer emphasis, then large numbers of people will substitute a passive, waiting-to-be-filled-up attitude for zestful involvement of self. And when this "culture" fails to foster psychic intimacy and self-validation, what new can be offered a people addicted to the visual nipple of television and movie fun, and now suffering the associated deficiency diseases?

What they are provided is a cascade of trivial new works, and shallow efforts to "modernize" the significant old ones. The total process not only submerges the important classic in a welter of banality, but adds silly innovations of detail to it at the cost of tasteless ruination of its original worth, and without supplying artistic ingredients of culture for which people truly hunger.

Which brings us to "Creative Frenzy."

19 *Creative Frenzy*

Creativity may be described as the capacity to combine familiar elements into new solutions to old problems.[1] This definition encompasses the full range of innovation, from the minor creativity of cooking to the major creativity of mathematics. Although admittedly there are still unknowns about the rare sorts of enormous creativity that proceed from genius, so far as we can tell the talent that underlies it, as well as the creative act itself, is not *qualitatively* different from those involved in ordinary creation. So all true creations, from the homeliest to the highest, represent points on a continuum.

The pouring of virtually all of a person's energy and concentration into realizing his creative capacity can be called "creative frenzy." Depending on the effects of this absorption on him and others, and the value attached to the outcome, his creative frenzy is regarded as good or bad. The insecurities of life in both modern and ancient societies have generally led to such fears of innovation that it is probably correct to say that any manifestation of creative frenzy likely to lead to basic change has been feared and discouraged more often than welcomed. Creative frenzy with such potentiality is most likely to be that invested in either art or science. As J. Bronowski has shown, the creative processes in science and art are closely allied.[2]

Daily work today for most people is much too routine and repetitive to be creative. The dismal fact is that for most people the only creative part of their love lives is the new combinations of genes in their offspring. And play carries such a burden of compensating people for frustrations endured in work and love that it too rarely includes the spontaneous exploration and discovery that lead to creativity.

Nevertheless, we find today as always a minority of people for whom creativity becomes a frenzy. The horticultural heirs to the planters of

438

Greek olive groves are now transforming desert into Eden. The artistic descendants of teams of Renaissance painters include devoted crews who strive to fix the muse on film. And the builders of Roman catapults that launched boulders and fires at the foe are represented today by those who, in developing techniques for the dissemination of bomb radiation and botulinus toxin, put their reliance as well as energy into the creation of annihilation.

The prospects for creative frenzy in the future are of a tidal wave that by comparison will dwarf to a trickle all that went before. Throughout man's two million years, his creativity has germinated in the crevices of leisure conferred by a full belly, the toil of slaves, the largesse of noble patronage, or the modern technique of popular consumption. And despite exceptions, such as businessman-composer Charles Ives or physician-poet William Carlos Williams, today the great bulk of creative activity is done by those whose primary work it is.

There is a large and rapidly growing market for the artistic and technological products of creativity. In the United States, this market is already so diversified that one of the traditional complaints of the artist, that art dependent on public acceptance is stultified due to its economically enforced adherence to middle-class values, is becoming obsolete. Art designed for the American middle class, notably the mass media, is immensely profitable, but avant-garde art, too, can find enough of a middle-class market to enable its creators to make a living, and sometimes, as with Warhol, Lichtenstein and others, a very comfortable living.

The ultimate complete freeing of *work* from its central social function of providing subsistence will nowhere have more impact than in the realm of creativity. Many people will have their first chance to unearth the buried treasure of their unborn sublimations. But some will be too much impeded by anxiety, guilt, or galloping emptiness to do so, and will succumb to psychic backfiring in such forms as depression or authoritarianism. Even worse, at just the time when love and *play* also might be infused with new creativity, it seems likely that they will fall prey to trivialization into diversion by millions of people who are unprepared.

The idea of work will be retained as designating that *central creative self-validative activity* in which one engages on a sustained and dedicated basis to affect the world. Play, in contrast, will refer to those other self-validative activities, only *sometimes* creative, which give one's life balance, novelty, and completeness. I believe that while work and play may come to be even more predominantly the sources of *new* creations, it may be that love may come to function even more than currently as the *conserver* and *transmitter* of the best that has been created.

Whether in the contexts of love, work, and play, or new concepts, we sense that some moments of every life should be consumed in a frenzy of creativity. Only by sometimes reaching these heights can a person be assured that other moments of repose and contemplation attain their full meaning.

In contrast, we all know people whose zestful investment of self, wherever it began, shades off into fanaticism. Examples are the tycoon perpetually driven to add new and unrelated products to his industry's line; the "devoted" housekeeper who empties ashtrays and plumps furniture pillows so constantly as to make everyone miserable, or the Sunday golfer, painter, or stamp collector whose hobby progressively exhausts rather than renews him. For them these behaviors are predominantly futile efforts to control anxiety.

Thus creativity can become a fixed idea, with all the futility of an obsession, delusion, or hallucination. As Koestler suggested in a cautious analogy, just as visual perception may become distorted by prolonged fixation, or a word become meaningless with constant repetition, frenzied direct pursuit of creativity may yield only confusion.[3] The alchemist referred to earlier well illustrated this outcome. As with fun or even happiness, creativity as an end in itself is empty.

Although Freud attempted to characterize the creative process as the "sublimation" of primitive impulses, he ruefully acknowledged that, "Before the problem of the creative artist analysis must, alas, lay down its arms."[4] Koestler sees creativity as stemming largely from those brain elements present in lower mammals, and so regards creation as largely an unconscious process.[5] Hatterer rejects sublimation, stressing the flexibility of the artist's mind that enables him to shift readily between various levels of consciousness from which raw materials can be selected for synthesis into a creative product.[6] All these views agree that the capacity to regress to a lower level while maintaining contact with a higher one seems to be the key to creativity.

Our neoteny and our unique capacity for symbolization are two among many other aspects of the puzzle of creativity. But whatever its components, it is plain that this precious faculty of seeing the old with eyes that are new cannot be brought forth by a direct act of will, although it can be cultivated to some extent in every individual.

One difficulty in understanding this cultivation is that the creative frenzy, which for many people is merely a mask for anxiety, is for others truly the vehicle of accomplishment. This problem is compounded by the tendency to confuse or equate creative frenzy and mental disorder. While it is true that many of our towering figures of science and art were mentally ill, it takes only a passing glance at the productions of thousands of mental patients to realize that mental illness, even when frenzied, does not guarantee creativity. Likewise, creative frenzy, even when severely stress-ful, does not guarantee mental illness. Of course, it is true that in the presence of strong predisposition to mental illness, any stress, even the exhaustion of prolonged creative frenzy, may be risky to mental health. For in a sense the differences between all of us as regards mental illness are only differences in the degree of our predispositions. Under sufficient stress all of us will break down.

Here we must recognize that the individual's plunge from rational con-sciousness into deeper layers of personality during creation is allied in kind to the dive into the depths that occurs during psychosis in that both involve taking leave of conscious rationality. That is why the products of both creativity and mental illness are rich in the archaic form of language we know as metaphors, similes, puns and so on. The difference is that the lifeboat of conscious rationality, which sturdily awaits the mentally healthy artist's or scientist's return from the depths, in psychosis has sprung a leak or foundered altogether, so that for the mental patient little security awaits at the surface. In this connection, it is interesting to recall Salvador Dali's terse self-appraisal, "The only difference between a mad-man and myself is that I am not mad."[7]

The sufferings of the "tortured genius" bear no constant relationship to his achievement. For every isolated and mentally disturbed Leonardo or Newton there is a comfortable well-balanced Einstein. Likewise, for every chaotic and distraught Van Gogh there is a stable Bach. In any event, it would be a mistake to transfer our impression of such exceptions into ex-pectations of ordinary persons. It is crucial to remember that what matters the most to everyone, self-validation, essential for mental health, may be achieved with or without true creativity or creative frenzy.

Koestler has compared the creative process to "drawing back to leap," the fertilization of ideas in the unconscious serving as a springboard into the conscious mind.[8] This is one element of what Ernst Kris called "regres-sion in the service of the ego."[9] The danger is that this regression, like those of the drug cultists and other devotees of fun fervor, may become important as an end in itself. Even everyday habits such as smoking or pacing may become means for clearing the way for creative acts, or they may function only as ways to reduce tension. Sometimes a creator may not realize how dependent he has become on what seemed to him simply a way to facilitate work. Balzac claimed that he had to drink large amounts of black coffee to write, and then found that he could not stop even when the stimulant threatened his health.[10]

Freud described efforts of artists and mystics to recapture the very young child's "oceanic feeling," the sense of limitless extension of the self and oneness with the universe.[11] When this aspect of creative frenzy is prominent, as it often is in mental illness, what frequently seems to result is the evaporation of the discriminating adult part of the personality, with consequent prevention of creation. For as we have seen, the creative process depends not upon abdication of the conscious mind but on keeping open its lines of free communication with lower levels.

Our ambivalence toward the science which both threatens and protects us is reflected in the popular images of scientists. We have "mad" scientists from Frankenstein to Strangelove, and benevolent wizards from Newton to Edison. In view of our similar ambivalence about art, it is odd that popular images of artists, while they include the "mad" artist, do not make room for the benevolent one. The most positive popular image of artists mildly derides them as dreamily ineffectual but attributes no real importance to their contribution.

Yet if we widen the term "art" only as much as we have widened "science," then it is plain that we are now as dependent upon writers, actors, and painters as we have long been upon engineers, physicians, and economists. Besides, in a much more fundamental sense man as a species sometimes seems as dependent upon art as upon science. Farb notes that Eskimos, surviving in an environment that reduces life to its bare essentials, developed a highly sophisticated and intricate art.[12] Art for them is one of the bare essentials. And Norman Mailer allegedly assigns art a similar status in surmising that what keeps modern mass society going is the individual's hope of someday seeing a revitalizing great work of art.

Yet the popular conscious view of the artist and artistic creation in our society tends to be that they are at best impractical and at worst both evil and fascinating. Our preoccupation with a movie star's satin lavender sheets and the succession of a great painter's mistresses betrays the envy and resentment of the inner freedom we attribute to all artists, although it is actually possessed only by some.

The main source of hostility to the artist, nevertheless, is the challenge his view and vision constitute to the established order. A dollar-dominated culture which highly values conformity is always disturbed by the person to whom his creativity is foremost. As Robert Henri said, speaking of the artist within any person, "He disturbs, upsets, enlightens, and he opens ways for a better understanding. While those who are not artists are trying to close the book, he opens it, shows there are still more pages possible."[13]

It has been said that women and men differ in their relationship to creativity. For example, it is alleged that not only is the vast *bulk* of all true creation done mainly by men, but, despite occasional exceptions, the *pinnacle* performances in most fields of original endeavor are those of men.

Such a statement may be dismissed as a chauvinistic slander against women. Or one may retort that in the daily round of home and business life women create more than their share of both the useful and the beautiful. But what about the claim that if one looks over the roster of the *great* creators in any field, even those fields increasingly open to women during the past century, the fact is that for various reasons there is a disproportionately small number of women represented? What about the challenge to us to name a great woman creator in mathematics or musical composition? Without entering into debate on the relative merits of any specific creators, suppose for the sake of discussion we even grant the correctness of these assessments. The questions for us then are, what might be the causes of such conditions, and what implications do the causes and conditions have for creative frenzy and our future?

A multitude of influences springs to mind. We may wonder if the determining ones are biological, sociocultural, or psychological.

The biology of men and women is different. In addition to the distinctions explored earlier are there differences in intellectual ability that would make women less creative? While it is true that women have slightly smaller brains, these are in proportion to the sex difference in total body size, and there seems to be no difference in number of nerve cells or complexity of their connections. And as would be expected from the equality of intelligence in male and female laboratory animals, observations on human beings indicate there are no significant differences in overall intellectual capacity between the sexes. If anything, during grade school years girls seem ahead in some areas.[14]

But there are other differences that extend back to earliest life. In the womb male babies move more vigorously than female babies. At birth males are larger and more active, and remain so throughout life (except for a brief period before and during pubescence when girls grow taller). By the age of two, boys are physically more assertive in getting what they want, whereas girls, being quieter and, in the opinion of many, more winsome, adopt indirect means. And as a wise psychiatric nurse once put it to me, "Perhaps girls learn to do more with charm partly because they are more charming."

Then there is the effect on creativity of the reproductive difference. There may be direct effects on emotional and mental life of cyclic hormonal variations. Except for such phenomena, we then pass beyond the boundary line of biology. It is in this nonbiological realm that different reproductive roles of the sexes become culturally elaborated into different social and psychological roles for men and women.

As Margaret Mead has shown, the *content* of men's and women's behavior is determined almost entirely by the traditions of a particular culture.[15] For example, in East African tribes, including the Chagga and the Kamba, the men stay home to care for children while the women go out and work.[16] However, in every society studied so far, some clear-cut distinction is made between what is considered to be appropriate masculine and feminine behavior.

Any person's identity grows in two clusters, those elements that relate to "being" and those that relate to "doing." In *Western* culture generally, perhaps building on the biologically greater activity of males, men tend toward psychological orientation around the infinitive "to do," whereas women tend to be psychologically oriented much more around the infinitive "to be." What a woman "is" in terms of her social role defines her much more in her own and others' eyes than what she "does." And creative accomplishment depends upon *doing*, whether the activity is frenzied or languid. That is why it is possible to describe a woman acceptably as "being" a wife and mother, but not a man as "being" a husband and father. A man must be described in terms of what he "does": his work, or at least his job. For women, it often suffices in our society to "be" beautiful, sexy (see Quest for Blondness), loving, fertile, and sometimes even witty and intelligent. In addition to some of these, men must "do" well. A basic manifestation of this difference appears in sexual relationships. Provided women "are" all the other desirable things, women (and men) can accept their not having much arousal or an orgasm some of the time without loss of esteem. But no matter how desirable and attractive he "is," a man cannot readily accept even occasional impotence in himself, and often neither can his woman.

Then comes the reproductive difference. While the woman only has to "be" there to receive the product of what the man "does," her automatic inner workings have readied everything for conception, gestation, delivery, and suckling of an infant, all without her having to "do" anything much at all. The woman's creative power is obvious. But while she turns her attention inward to her inner identity, her ability to *re*produce almost entirely by just "being," her man in confirming his identity must turn his attention outward to *pro*duce.

No wonder that *in our culture,* as in many others, so much of a woman's creative capacity for generating, molding, and maintaining culture focuses on her central need for a baby while a man's focuses elsewhere. Notice that the essence of the woman's *identity* thus becomes her accomplishment of motherhood. And that the essence of the man's *identity* comes not from fatherhood but from his productiveness, only part of which is motivated by or devoted to establishing and supporting his reproductive life.

The sexes share their distinctive sorts of central creativity with one another in a similar way. The woman has a child largely as a gift to her husband. But a part of her triumph she reserves to herself. The special closeness to the children is hers alone, the reward for having achieved the status of "mother." Most of what he produces the man gives to the woman and their baby. But it should be no surprise that, in addition to the gratifications he can enjoy from fatherhood, the man may seek to reserve a portion to himself as reward for having acquired the sometimes empty status of a grown man.

Therefore the woman, although by inclination sometimes more of a revolutionary than the man, is compelled to function culturally mainly as a conserver. The man, on the other hand, in many ways more vulnerable, and therefore often more fearful, cannot achieve his central gratifications by gestation within himself, except of ideas. To some degree his whole life becomes a compensation. He must drive himself to surmount his timidity, to become the innovator, the doer, even the revolutionary.

Margaret Mead has pointed out that there is a portentous reversal of the ability of boys and girls to identify with their fathers and mothers as they grow up.[17] As children, boys can readily see the qualitative similarity of their bodies, especially their genitals, to their fathers', whereas girls have difficulty believing that they will one day develop the breasts and other curves their mothers have. But when they are grown, the situation is reversed. Whereas there is no longer any doubt that the girl has become a woman when she bears her child, the boy can never be sure it is he who has become the father and thereby proved he is now a man. Therefore he must go out and build the Empire State Building.

Love secures realization of a woman's inner reproductive creativity. Learning and effort assures realization of a man's outer productive creativity. So a woman's central need is to "be" loved, while a man's is to "do" well or to perform. The woman therefore often spends her main effort in attracting the love that assures realization of her inner reproductive creativity. The man usually spends his main effort on work. This differentiation is also why, in general, men can better stand loss of their looks and even fertility than their other creative powers, and women can often more easily tolerate debility, even invalidism, than loss of their beauty and fertility.

The woman's allure distracts the man—delightfully—from his productive task. At our present stage of development in the West, when a woman's allure becomes deeply split off from her central creative strivings for a child, it can become the distorted and sometimes destructive version of femininity practiced by the prostitute. Contempt for herself and for her client then dominates her attitude toward the man, at least unconsciously. The man is equally contemptuous of this woman, because she has forsaken the creative essence of womanhood for its trappings. But also he shares her contempt for himself, for having allowed himself to become distracted from his central task of productive performance by a mere counterfeit of feminine appeal which, by guaranteeing transcience, excludes not only love but progeny. He settles for physical relief of tension and perhaps the fun of discharge of infantile fantasies, when he has a right to a gratifying current creative reality of family and of love given and received. The man who enjoys the latter may regret the distraction but not begrudge the time and energy taken from his work.

This compressed sketch, if taken literally, justifiably can be regarded as an oversimplification. Obviously, for example, there are many women whose identity is not so stereotyped and does not center in their reproductivity. However, it is not meant as a description of every individual person today, but rather as a composite depiction of how, on the average, various forces have shaped our lives. As indicated earlier, it will be less and less applicable to the changed circumstances of the future when social relationships and distinctions are no longer so tied to biology.

At present, however, our culture still parcels out the fundamental interpersonal rewards of approval and love differentially to boys and girls. Of course both are loved just for "being." But from the first years of life we subtly inform a girl that the largest share of the approval and love she can expect throughout life will continue to depend upon her "being" pretty, nice, warm, cute, cheerful, faithful, friendly, compliant, and so on, whereas only secondarily will she be rewarded for achievement. In contrast, a boy is subtly informed that the largest share of approval and love he can expect will depend upon his "doing" or performing well. While the eyes of mother, father, sister, teacher, sweetheart, and finally spouse bespeak love for the girl just for "being sweet," as they shift their gaze to her brother he can read in their eyes that somehow all suddenly have changed their standards for loving him to his "doing well."

Of course men are expected to "be" always kind, considerate, and loyal, and women are expected to "do" the housekeeping, nursing of the young or ill, and the entertaining, endless tasks that in practice may require them to be busy or on call twenty-four hours a day. Yet an objective appraisal will reveal that while the man is expected "to be" quite good, the woman is not expected "to do" as much that requires a high level of skill, preparation, or excellence. In general, the performance demanded of her is simpler, and is much less variable from woman to woman. The consequence is that, relative to a man, *a woman is loved more unconditionally.*

Is it possible that the sexes' unequal conditions for getting approval and love have an important effect on their differential achievement? Can it be that so many more men accomplish notably simply because so many more are compelled to try? Exceptional achievement in any field is not easy. A man meeting frustrations has little choice but to struggle to overcome them. Mother, wife, friends, and children will diminish their approval and love unless he does. A woman in the same pursuit can shrink back before the obstacle without making the ultimate effort, or do something different or less, and still be approved of and loved. For she still "is" what she was expected all along "to be." It appears possible that creative frenzy is more likely to lead a man to produce a *great* creation simply because he is more likely to produce anything.

We are already in the process of de-emphasizing the behavioral distinctions of the sexes. By the standards of one hundred years ago many modern men would seem effeminate and women masculine. Then, gradually we are removing the socioeconomic barriers which for so long have chained women to menial household duties and barred them from developing their full creative potential. Finally, even the reproductive difference between men and women, the supposed bedrock that causes every culture to find some scheme for differentiating masculine from feminine creativity, is tottering on the brink of possible male gestation, delivery, and suckling of infants. So as we liberate women from the various social restraints that have restricted them from being as externally creative as men, we may be simultaneously opening the door to men to be as internally creative—and externally uncreative—as women were previously.

For every woman who seizes eagerly the opportunities newly available to her for external creative excellence there may be ten men waiting demurely for a chance someday to have a home, child, and a breadwinner to whom to "be" a lovely wife.

It is uncertain whether the combination of all these changes will help intensify the creative frenzy and accomplishment of both sexes, or amid the freedom provided by abundance, will help reduce both men and women to spiritless flaccidity. We may come to yearn for the good old days when men and women divided things unequally, where for want of a world a baby was made, while for want of a womb a world was won.

Our increasing abundance and longevity are adding an unfathomable dimension to the individual's creativity, the chance to express it fully in a succession of different ways. It is true that for centuries a small minority of people could engage effectively in a variety of professions, particularly before the specialization and fragmentation of knowledge required by the Industrial Revolution. A Leonardo da Vinci could be artist, architect, and inventor-designer. A John Locke could be both physician and philosopher. A Franklin or Jefferson could be scientist, inventor, statesman, and philosopher. A Borodin could be chemist and composer. As with most of the several hundred thousand Americans who now "moonlight" on second jobs, these multiple activities usually had to be interleaved with one another during the same period of life. For most people the pressure of scarcity, as well as the value system derived from it, made it unthinkable to abandon a main skill once acquired.

But today many more people are finding themselves with the opportunity to change completely their central work activity several times during their lives. I am not referring to people who simply shift the *setting* or *emphasis* of their major vocational activity, as in my case, for instance, from the private practice of psychiatry to teaching psychiatry in a university. Nor do I refer to the many instances of people who change from one relatively humdrum job to another. Also not included are those who change from what they consider generally unsatisfying drudgery to a more self-validating profession. Rather, I am thinking especially of people I have known well personally or learned of through others who, after achieving considerable success in one field, left a profession they regarded as rewarding to engage and succeed admirably in something creative but entirely different. Politics is perhaps the best-known *consecutively* pursued second career in this country, to which former lawyers, doctors, businessmen, actors, and others devote themselves. Here are other examples.

An architect at forty-two closed his office after nineteen years to complete a musical education and become a conductor. A professional violinist after twenty-five years of teaching and performing with symphony orchestras got a master's degree and became a psychiatric social worker. A puppeteer and a sociologist in their thirties returned to school to become respectively a plastic surgeon and a psychiatrist.[18]

There are even occasional individuals who manage to change creative careers several times. A woman physician retired at thirty to have and raise five children, and twenty years later became a city planner. Another woman who had been a child movie actress, an adult musical-comedy performer, and a repertory theater producer, became a clinical psychologist, and then a criminal lawyer. And finally, a Catholic priest of eighteen years' service quit to marry and become a marine architect, a boat manufacturer, and finally a specialist in sex education for preschool children!

A legitimate question might be raised about the social waste involved in the abandonment by individuals of the fruit of years of arduous study. But that such metamorphoses of career have increasing social import and are pursued with uncommon creative frenzy is indubitable. It has been suggested that today's college graduate may have more than a dozen jobs and several separate "careers" in his lifetime.[19] It is clear that such widened scope of employment and creative endeavor promises great expansion of the self-validation and satisfaction that many lives can yield. The same may be said for the proliferation of "leisure industries," with their schools and facilities for do-it-yourself crafts, painting, writing, adventuring, philosophizing, and so on. But all these concomitants of abundance portend cruel disappointment for those in flight from anxiety or depression who proceed on the assumption that changes of scene or activity by themselves can substitute for integrity of identity, the inner serenity that derives only from years of successful zestful investment of self in love, work, and play.

Yet there can be no doubt that creative achievement gratifies and refreshes us in a way so powerful as to warrant the frenzy with which sometimes it is pursued. We all need an occasional glimpse of Freud's ocean, and a vivifying moment to wade from its beach. For those of us with strong creative ability and urges, more complete plunges and even temporary submergence are in order. Creative giants are psychological amphibians, spending much of their lives in this heady element, and often risking the undertow that crosses Plato's sometimes thin line between poetry and madness.

20 *Mystic Withdrawal*

Though often so depicted, it is not the creative scientist or artist who is usually a solitary, impractical, and eccentric dreamer. Much closer to this description is another ubiquitous figure, the mystic. In all cultures mystics have appeared, to proclaim that the true realities are not related to that which is "known" in the ordinary ways.

The West generally gave birth to more anthropomorphic and therefore more "practical" varieties of mysticism than did the East. One result has been that the faithful of Western religions such as Judaism and Christianity more readily adopted and adapted to the innovations of technology than did, for example, those of the Hindu or Buddhist religions. However, these once sharp differences are blurring as technique and culture in general become more uniform throughout the world. Today Japanese businessmen find no great tension between Zen detachment from temporal concerns and highly competitive business endeavor. And in the United States neighborhood retreats are springing up which permit one to get away from the rat race, and to choose with equal convenience between tennis and meditation. Today, in many places, concern about the human and physical is swallowing up preoccupation with the infinite and the metaphysical, thus returning man to his primordial immediate interests. The results include the declining membership in traditional organized religions and increased subscription to nontraditional movements that promise either more effective magic for grappling wtih current problems, or more blissful surcease of awareness of them.

Regardless of its origins, mysticism serves to induce the individual to stand back for a while and, in honored repose of mind, to contemplate within rather than accomplish in the outer world. Such repose can have the same function as Koestler's "drawing back in order to leap" discussed earlier. Insofar as this process increases a person's awareness of and willingness to excavate and develop hitherto unrealized inner resources, his mystic life may advance him to greater abundance and integrity of personality.

However, all mysticisms to some extent tend to pull the participant away from the current and upcoming steps on the human agenda in favor of absorption in unverifiable eternal verities. Insofar as this process decreases his willingness to master that which is currently knowable it is injurious. And to the extent that it forces him to cope through dogmatic ritual with anxiety it foments about the currently *un*knowable, it stultifies his growth and engenders a crippling disintegration of personality.

When mystic withdrawal is expressed in a clinging to infantile wishfulness, or a retreat to it away from partial maturity once achieved, it constitutes a regression more harmful and commonplace than any disguised as creative frenzy. An example is the petulant, tyrannical young woman who turned her home into a shrine in memory of her over-indulgent dead mother, to whose worship she subjugated the family for a decade. Another is the aging fundamentalist who, during four decades as a municipal official, grew rich on the payoffs from protected brothels, and then decided to make a redemptive swan song through devoting himself piously to "service of the Lord" by harassing teen-agers out of their long hair, miniskirts, and lovers' lanes.

The effects of mystic withdrawal on individual personality are multiplied and ramified in the community in innumerable forms. Some lead to kindly unflagging efforts to promote world peace, and others to callous dedication to preserving the most inhumane aspects of the status quo. A particularly sorry recent instance of the latter was the Protestant clergyman who inveighed righteously against demonstrators as "anti-Christ" when they brought peace placards and black worshipers into his hawkish all-white church. Apparently forgetting that Jesus' execution conformed to the law of the times, and that for centuries Christianity itself was illegal, he added the ironic denunciation, "Those who break the law are enemies of God, for there can be no Christianity without law and order."

Nominally the Christian faith regards conscience as the highest authority over the individual. Yet in practice the individual is often told that this precious human acquisition must in the end be subordinated to mystical authority. Take for example the Pope's recent statement that "conscience needs to be instructed." It should not be "guiltily erroneous," but rather it should conform with "natural law," presumably as interpreted by its Author's proclaimed vicar on earth.[1]

Lately the apocalyptic tradition among fundamentalist Protestant sects has had a new flowering in Southwestern states. Entire congregations are fleeing east to escape divine wrath, which apparently in their view is still distributed with more attention to geography than to sin. And among the less *formally* mystical, the byword is "do your own thing," at once a possible escape from conformity into creativity and also a runaway rationale for the most shallow selfishness and indifference toward others.

Among the more peculiar aspects of our culture are various attempts to alloy mysticism with something else. A combination of the mysticism of salvation with the mystery of the totally sound body may be found in the Christian-Yoga Church, which seems left-handedly to establish respect for the body within a system that vilifies the flesh. Another strange amalgam has combined the unlikely elements of violent personal combat and serene contemplation of the essence of things into a movement called Zen-Karate.

A common and pitiful form of this hybridizing is "seducing Lady Luck," composed in about equal proportions of getting ahead, fun fervor, and mystic withdrawal. We all need awareness that without warning something wonderful may happen, the sun may come out, or we may find a five-dollar bill, or fall in love. In all its guises seducing Lady Luck is to be distinguished from this healthy welcoming of unexpected possibilities by its *demand* that good fortune favor the wooer. Its clamor for special bonanza, for something for nothing, is a peevish rejection of the effort-reward requirement of the Puritan ethic. Such luck, as unfathomable as the maternal care that came at intervals to the baby in the cradle, is conceived of as feminine. It must be courted with superstitious avoidances of the ladder and the black cat, or adherences to the rabbit foot and the holy medallion.

One devotee is the secretly panicky daredevil who must fly his light plane under the Golden Gate bridge in order to deny that he too can die. Another is the military leader risking with barely hidden relish the lives of others in daring exploits, which if successful will bring *him* new luster. Similarly motivated may be the politician of nuclear confrontation who, if he wins, will emerge wtih ominous new dominance over his own and another people. The mechanism of this variant of mysticism is most evident in the compulsive gambler who, because he cannot bear to be ignored as ordinary, insists that Fate at least *frown* if she won't smile upon him. So he risks much, goes through his prayerful rituals, and rolls his number, yearning for a sign that magic mama in the sky loves him best of all, and so will ward off all evil while showering him with the dollar equivalents of milk.

I will not go into extrasensory perception, the occult, or witchcraft, except to observe that modern efforts to validate them scientifically are generally like the interests themselves, based more on fervent wishes than on desire to know the truth however it may lie. An example is the medical clinic wherein an investigation is now under way requiring each new patient to give his name, age—and astrological sign.

Another variant is the crossbreeding of mystic withdrawal with honesty which might be called the "authenticity trip." Leaving aside the mendacity of nations and their wars, from the poisonous menthol cigarette that is touted as a way to partake of the healthful outdoors, to the high school textbook that deliberately distorts the history of black people, so much of our lives is fraudulent that it is both understandable and laudable that a growing percentage of people are rejecting the sham and seeking the substance in all their experiences and relationships. While welcoming the intent, one may regret the direction such quests take. For example, the Psychic Impostor ethic that dominated the life of my call-girl patient is an extreme rejection of fraud in the formative relationships during infancy and childhood, manifested as a grim *embrace* of fraud during adulthood. And because it represents a serious incapacity to experience anything validly, the Psychic Impostor ethic is likely to propagate fraud among others as a kind of psychic epidemic.

In a wholesome effort to escape fraud, many enthusiasts try honesty. But then finding it either ineffectual or too harsh to swallow neat, they dilute it liberally with the mixer of mysticism. Such defeats of self-validation are especially evident in three areas today: the communication of truth, the provision of facilities and programs for enriching human life, and some innovations in the theater.

"Tell it like it is" has become the rallying cry of authenticity trippers. Most of us respond to it positively because it rings with respect for truth, an ancient value dignified by the triumph of both science and democratic revolutions of the eighteenth and subsequent centuries.

The difficulty in applying the maxim is twofold. First, there are many different opinions of how "it is," and the effort to establish one or another as correct or incorrect in the absence of objective proof so often involves recourse to invocation of mystic authority and revelation. For example, recently a patient was much disturbed by a book her parents sent her that asserted in a unique poaching of today's "in" jargon: "To tell it like it is, the principles of psychotherapy are a direct attack upon Christian Ethics." She was comforted by the other authorities she mustered, from a Pope all the way up to her local Pentecostal preacher who asserted on the basis of his knowledge of scripture that there is no conflict. If only authorities would make the slight change of saying "this is my interpretation" instead of "this is the truth"!

Second, the inflated expectations of the power of truth, or at least its prompt effect, result in disappointment. When the walls of Jericho fail to collapse before the cannon of the zealot's candor, the mystic conviction that truth alone will conquer everything drives him to intensify his efforts. For the impassioned truth-sayer it appears that nothing succeeds like failure. For instead of recognizing that, once the truth has been *told*, any improvement will await something effective being done to *implement* it, he redoubles the effort to cure all by telling.

For example, the new left observes that police are often brutal to minorities, and they report as much.[2] When police then fail to be humane, instead of undertaking the vigorous political activity that could result in replacement of responsible officials from the mayor down to the police chief and commissioners, they sometimes merely redouble their efforts to prove that telling it like it is can substitute for making it like it should be. Now the truth is adulterated by hurling the appellation "pig" at the offending cop, and by loud public imprecations that have reference to the officer's supposed proclivity for indulging incestual impulses toward his maternal progenitor. Here we have reached futility. For not only is such accusation a calumny against pigs, who never mace or club one another, but words and subjects are introduced which have no relevance to the problem at hand, and which serve only to further *provoke* the police aggression that led to the complaint in the first place.

A subsidiary but significant additional disadvantage is that in the process a whole generation is encouraged to settle for such imprecise and ineffectual language that their communication abilities become impoverished. Even such words as "man," "baby," and "love" are converted into dreary, empty slogans. Then, in inarticulate desperation over the failure of such irrelevant perversions of meaning to improve things, their users are driven to violence or more malignant varieties of mystic withdrawal.

The trend to further dignify indiscriminate openness and exposure as "therapeutic" has been discussed earlier (page 302). An especially glaring example appeared recently in a newspaper ad soliciting people who seek "complete personal freedom" to live in a new type of apartment building. Rent payers in the "free community" would not only benefit from the finest usual conveniences but would also participate in sensitivity, sensory awareness, and marital enrichment training, as well as the "love feast."

> The love feast is an affirmation and celebration of life . . . a social activity where people gather to enjoy life and one another in . . . complete freedom and vibrant warmth . . . good music . . . candles . . . incense . . . mats and cushions have been spread . . . you enjoy a light, exotic dinner . . . before dinner is over you are clothed only in the warmth and good vibrations of those around you . . . there is gentle laughter and lovemaking . . . and other kinds of parties are never quite the same . . .

The ad goes on to state that "residents will be participating in one of the most far-reaching social experiments of this century. . . . each person will play an integral part in evolving new directions . . . so vital to the future of this society."[3]

Notice that this rather genteel orgy is not just hailed as fun or pleasurable, but that the trappings of pseudoscience are woven into a flat-footed claim that it constitutes not a possible but a *certain* contribution to human progress. In the absence of evidence, such beatific certitude is the hallmark of mystic withdrawal.

Audiences are encouraged to take part in theatrical performances currently hailed as "avant garde," but which are reminiscent of the festival celebrations of many ancient peoples. Again, the theme of these modern presentations seems to be the naïve notion that the maximum removal of restraint is the greatest good, and moreover is the greatest art. What results instead seems to be a chaotic and sometimes horrifying if not boring furor of dehumanization. Julius Novick relates one such event:

> Two customers, evidently unused to being fondled by strange half-naked women, and liberated by the our-thing atmosphere, surrounded one of the women in the company . . . and began fondling back. . . . industriously grabbing, groping and rubbing her, as if she were not a person at all but an inanimate pleasure machine. It was like watching a rape . . . except that the victim did not resist; she just hung in there gamely muttering "Holy love!" . . . though nothing could have been less holy or less loving. Whether the men finished their job I don't know . . . if the woman was not, technically speaking, violated, she was certainly being violated in a more general sense.[4]

Another instance reported in the press carries the implicit sadism to overt levels. At a performance in which the audience was encouraged to take part

> The five—two girls and three young men—went on stage at La Comedie Canadienne carrying a rooster and two doves. After stripping before about 600 patrons, the five killed the birds and drank what appeared to be their blood.[5]

This episode reminds me of the young man I saw in consultation after he had sniped at cars passing on a freeway, killing a teen-age boy. He blandly explained that two years earlier he had impulsively leveled his rifle at a doe standing thirty feet outside his cabin, and as his bullet tore off half her head he had felt a "communion with all past generations of killers." As to shooting unknown human strangers, his attitude was that one had to take some risks in order to fully experience his animal heritage, and he had just had the "bad luck" to get caught. It was his conception, crystallized by writers we discussed earlier, that all large meat-eating animals including man are inveterate instinctual killers. He was shaken and angered by a mild observation that animals ordinarily kill only when hungry, always preying upon a different species, and that thrill killing seemed to be peculiarly an invention of man. He was especially upset by the suggestion that perhaps this sort of killing served him as compensation for slights that made him feel powerless.

Experience during my own adolescence had prepared me for this insight. At seventeen, I was the oldest male working for the summer on a ranch. Sometimes I felt inadequate to my difficult responsibilities. One easy job assigned me was to protect our vegetable garden by shooting daily a few of the rabbits and squirrels that devastated it, thus frightening off the rest. Although this task was emotionally distasteful to me, at least I felt equal to it. Reluctantly I agreed. Within two weeks I was firing over a hundred shells daily at these animals, turning my sights on them at greater and greater distances from the garden, and felling an increasing proportion as my skill improved. As I cleaned the rifle each night I began to have vague fantasies about being the spiritual descendant of Daniel Boone and Davy Crockett.

One day I realized, while walking several miles from the garden and preparing to shoot a squirrel out of a tree, that with such a shot I was in no way protecting our vegetables, but instead was simply looking forward to seeing the animal fall. Until that instant it had not dawned on me that I was just rationalizing that I was only doing my duty, that in fact I was learning to *enjoy* killing because it made me feel powerful. I did not pull the trigger, and from that moment on my shooting was confined to the garden, and except under conditions of clear necessity, I never killed anything again.

It was only years later during my psychoanalysis that I understood fully the compensatory significance of this behavior to an insecure teenager trying to fill the role of a man. And it was only then that I learned the full extent of the obligation of all human beings to resist the tendency to justify their regressive cruelties by mystic withdrawal.

Donald Meyer has traced the rise of a combination of pseudopsychology with pseudotheology in his book, *The Positive Thinkers*.[6] Meyer shows how the American lust for power, wealth, and health has spawned a series of popular semimystics from Mary Baker Eddy to Norman Vincent Peale. Their general trend has been to downgrade and disintegrate the conscious mind. Freud, as well as Lorenz and his followers, blames man's troubles largely on the eruption of unconscious urges too powerful for the conscious mind to manage successfully. For the positive thinkers the stigma lies not in such welling up of animal impulse, but rather in inadequacy of the conscious mind itself, due to dereliction by the subconscious of its duty, the proper programming of the conscious. As a result, "Conscious mind was not equipped for the entry and comprehension of divine Truth or for identity with it."[7] Rather than being overpowered, the conscious mind was *underinstructed* from within. Since the subconscious thus controlled the conscious, the solution is to train the proper attitudes into the subconscious. Repetitive drill would produce an automatized subconscious that in turn would sanitize the conscious mind of all but positive thoughts.[8] (For contrast, see p. 283.)

While its openly religious practitioners have decided that one form or another of rigid control of the conscious is the answer, those who recommend various dropout versions of mystic withdrawal seem to have concluded that the conscious should be *abandoned*. Their implication is that such renunciation will almost automatically be followed by the transcendence of freedom and joy we all desire. This augury is being trumpeted by a quartet of new oracles: Marshall McLuhan, Norman O. Brown, Herbert Marcuse, and Timothy Leary.

McLuhan will be treated more fully under "Technique Infatuation." For now, let us note that his predictions of the end of linear and sequential thinking also strike at the core of logical construction and mastery of reality. McLuhan is also a mystical utopian, whose message is that we need do nothing to be saved, since all problems soon will be solved by electronic technology.[9]

Norman O. Brown hands us the Word as translated into psychoanalytic jargon. Social institutions are stifling us and what is really needed, so that man may overcome his pathological fear of death, is a retreat into infantile "polymorphous perversity." Brown wishes to free us from the "tyranny of the genital impulse,"[10] but it seems that the only way to do so is to tear down not only our social institutions, but the institution of society itself.[11] It seems reasonable to reflect that amid the resultant chaos we might soon notice, in between orgasms of the kneecap and elbow, the even more tenacious tyranny of the stomach.

Herbert Marcuse predicts a new kind of man once "surplus repression" has been abolished along with scarcity. This new man will fear nothing, not even death, and will have every chance to indulge in "polymorphous sexuality."[12] Like Brown's advice, his counsel would seem to be tantamount to regression to the contentment of the infant who has sucked, gurgled, kicked, and been cuddled to the point of satiation. Moreover, Marcuse admits that his critique of society holds out no hope, that he can advocate only a negation, the "Great Refusal," to bridge the gap between present and future. More recently, in lectures he has been advocating "desublimation," and speaking about the need to "revoke the Ninth Symphony" because it is the epitome of man's most sublime achievements.[13] What is pertinent now, he suggests, is not Beethoven but the Beatles. It is difficult to believe, but it appears to be Marcuse's impression that the songs of the Beatles are written and performed without the hard work of transforming primitive impulse into art that we call sublimation.

Timothy Leary is at once the most notorious of the new oracles and at the same time himself one of the most unmistakable victims of mystic withdrawal. From West Point to Millbrook, New York, is a short distance geographically, but in traversing it Leary has gone all the way from plebe to prophet. The use of LSD often results in personality deterioration and even psychotic disintegration, and this he honors as transcendent mystical achievement. Leary can report, as he did in a news interview on November 1, 1968, that he had not met an uptight person since June of that year of ubiquitous continuing hatred, violence, and assassination; that what has happened in the country and the world will get much worse in the next year or two, *but* then get much better. Leary's prophethood is unmistakable: "God commanded me some time ago to do the two things that are required of his messengers—one—not to become a martyr and—two—to do my trade union job: to write a Bible and a theology and prayer book."[14]

One must acknowledge the *possibility* that great new vistas of human life may be opened by the various admixtures of psychedelia and mystic withdrawal. What marks such movements for rejection by the zestful and reasonable person is that they do not examine possibilities for the future but declare the millennium in advance. Their lack of concern for evidence is unmistakable in the fable they circulate about aboriginal usage of drugs. To hear them tell it, the taking of hallucinogenic drugs was as much a part of every person's everyday life as the drinking of water. This seems never to have been the case, such use being confined to those participating in relatively infrequent special rituals and ceremonies. And whenever sudden widespread indulgence has been observed the facts suggest that more than anything else it is symptomatic of despair and withdrawal. Thus the use of peyote became common among Plains Indians only during the last quarter of the nineteenth century as their complete defeat at the hands of the whites became apparent.[15]

Erich Fromm has pointed out that the true ancient prophetic tradition was one of seeing the present reality and expressing the voice of conscience, rather than foreseeing the future: "Prophetic language is always the language of alternatives, of choice, of freedom; it is never that of determinism, for better or worse."[16]

Leary and the others may be new oracles, but they are false prophets. They do not explore the *possibility* of expanding human experience. They *proclaim* it. In true authoritarian fashion, they "know" the truth and are prepared to enlighten others with varying degrees of compulsion. Various psychedelic disciples even spike the punch of unsuspecting guests at parties with LSD.[17] Half-serious plans for dumping LSD in city drinking water have been suggested. Since fluorides have been said to inactivate LSD, one result of such proposals may be that the antifluoride forces may be won over if the choice becomes fluoridation versus hallucination.

In our society, mystic withdrawal is characterized not only by abdications from reality, but by a curious array of attacks upon the self. While the positive thinkers seek to indoctrinate the subconscious, and thereby improve the inadequate conscious mind, the new oracles of regression seek to dissipate the conscious mind in order to transcend the self. The consequence is an elaboration of neoteny into nihilism. In all such mystic withdrawals there beats the heart of dogmatism. Their emphasis is on strategy at the expense of substance. One has but to perform the right *drills*—that is, think the right thoughts, or do nothing, or scuttle the superego, or ingest the proper drugs. The automatic exorcism of evil and death, or materialization of the global village, or attainment of virtue and eclectic ecstasies, or immersion in good vibrations and oneness with the infinite, must unfailingly result.

The spread and acceptance of these forms of mystic withdrawal are linked closely with the growth of conditions encouraging passivity and denigrating the hard-won human capacity for *conscious mastery of reality*. They are particularly forms of malaise of the American middle class, and are symptomatic of a mishandling of the problems of abundance of both material and might. As Meyer says, "Telling legitimately discontented people to find the source of their discontent in themselves was to tell them to shrink further from testing their powers in the society around them."[18] Mystic withdrawal is foredoomed as a tool for resolving individual personal problems, not to mention those of multipersonal society.

He who follows the human agenda and contributes to the understanding of its sequential challenges must have the courage to sustain investigation and to suspend conviction. He must be willing indefinitely to live and progress toward partial understanding despite frankly acknowledged partial ignorance.

21 *Technique Infatuation*

I have learned to love my constant partner on this long journey. Always at my fingertips day or night, selflessly ready to transcribe my thoughts almost before I think them, and asking nothing except an occasional new ribbon, the little portable typewriter on my lap is a marvelous friend and fellow worker. My love is founded not on its specifications—the number of letters it prints per line or the acoustics of its bell that warns me thirty times per page—but rather on performance of its *function*, the tireless rolling out of the leaves of *The Human Agenda*. Through its faithful functioning I am the recipient of the love of its inventors and manufacturer, creatively enlarging my survival benefits. I reciprocate by recommending their product intemperately.

Among our many gadgets, typewriters are some of the most amazingly reliable. One of my friends depends lovingly on a typewriter in service for nearly five decades. Could he imagine himself relying daily on an automobile purchased new by his grandfather in 1921? But then, while typewriters long ago were built for durable function and enduring love, very few cars were ever constructed with more in mind than infatuation.

Technique infatuation means more than our fascinations with and fads involving all sorts of gadgets, from hot rods to home workshops, and more than the crushes on various "things" we are seductively sold. It signifies the general tendency to be interested more in technological method than human purpose. Its hallmark is a chilling preoccupation with *measurements,* whether they be the auto's stroke, bore, and compression ratio, the hi-fi's impedance, resistance, and wattage, the baseball player's lifetime homerun record, batting average, and stolen-bases tally, the Army's reconnaissance range, firepower, and kill ratio, or the beauty contestant's 38, 24, and 37. One can't escape at least a dim awareness when treated to such admirable precision that somehow it misses the main point, the *use* to

460

which these resources are put. Losing sight of the question of what to do with life-enriching mobility, perfect sound, athletic virtuosity, military might, or pulchritude, leads to the sort of grotesquery so eloquently criticized by actress Raquel Welch after entertaining in Vietnam:

> Sending girls like me to Vietnam to entertain the troops is like teasing a caged lion with a piece of raw meat . . . I'm not criticizing our boys' thoughts or feelings one bit, I'm just telling you that I know what is going through their minds . . . they are fighting an aimless war in a foreign land where they aren't wanted . . . Deep down inside, I think it would be best if stars like me stayed home and the Government sent off troupes of prostitutes instead. After all, when you get right down to it, those boys want relief, not more frustration.[1]

Technique infatuation is one consequence of failure to take into account the evolutionary significance of human life. Without that perspective we do not see that our progression through the human agenda depends upon an orchestration of many elements. Foremost among these is the constant heightening of consciousness in the use of intellect and character for the mastery of reality, under the loving conditions of expanding freedom and joy. Unbalanced emphasis on any one or a few elements results in such perverse partialisms as technique infatuation. It also casts over life the cardboard cutout quality so masterfully exemplified in the hackneyed manner, statements, and interpretations of many public "personalities" today.

Before man, living creatures related to "things" as means toward elemental ends. The squirrel stockpiled acorns to guard against winter hunger, not to gloat over with fall's full belly. The firehawk of the Northern Territory of Australia devoured small animals routed with its burning faggots, but did not worship fire. And the chimpanzee fashioned branches into implements or weapons, not swagger sticks.

It took man to symbolize concrete things, or means, into highly abstract ends in themselves, and then to become infatuated with them. It took man's large brain and mind to conceive the scope of life and death, and then to devise the technique infatuation ruse for avoiding the anxiety of grappling with the awesome alternatives thus revealed. Only man can be truly passive because only he has the capacity truly to intervene actively in his own fate. Technique infatuation is a substitution of passive "busyness" for valid adaptive activity.

We all rightfully admire the technique that has brought immeasurable improvements in our well-being. And although some of us have become addicted to the gadgets of everyday life for their own sake, absorption with these aspects of technique is relatively benign. The peril is that this fascination lies on a continuum that can be traversed with imperceptible smoothness, at the extreme end of which lies the technique ethic of Adolf Eichmann and the earlier mentioned lampshades made of human skin. The only safeguard against this dehumanization, as against all others, is unfaltering insistence upon weighing all things in terms of their impact on human values and human beings. As Erich Fromm writes in *Revolution of Hope:* ". . . man, not technique, must become the ultimate source of values; optimal human development, not maximal production, the criterion for all planning."[2]

To move, or even to drift in the other direction, as do such diverse authorities as Herman Kahn, the religiously dogmatic Marxists or Freudians, or the political technocrats, is to risk winding up extinct—or worse, living in something resembling an anthill.

The faith in the inexorability of progress that characterized the nineteenth century has been severely battered by the wars, depressions, and genocides of the twentieth century. Nevertheless, most of us still adhere to the values of progress, however dubious we may be that the chaotic proliferation of technique in any way advances it. Still, as damaging to progress as *dis*organized technique infatuation may be, we may have more to fear in the long run from the total *extermination* of progress, by *organized* technique infatuation, unchecked by Fromm's concern for human values and development. This grim possibility is presented by Roderick Seidenberg in *Post-Historic Man.*[3] There he suggests that human consciousness and freedom, on which Fromm's optimal human development depend, are the product only of a narrow interlude we call "history" between prolonged prehistoric and posthistoric eras.

In the remote prehistoric era instinct so predominated over intelligence that consciousness and freedom had not yet been invented. Among ants there is no room for consciousness, the new idea, or its innovator, the "person," as the perfect adaptation they have achieved among uniform individuals has gone cycling on practically unchanged for some 70 million years under the restrictive tyranny of instinct.

As instinct loosed its hold on man's forebears, intelligence gradually became the predominant but far less fixed social organizing principle. When eventually evolution produced man, intelligence (and the emerging consciousness that guides it) for the first time came to characterize and control centrally a species composed of individual persons with marked variations between them. Optimal development of individual human persons depends upon there being a sizable zone of fluidity of circumstances surrounding each individual. Within that zone, guided by his consciousness, he is free to adapt according to his own potential and inclination. The necessary fluidity of his circumstances is possible only when imbalance of various forces affecting the individual produces constant *changes* in the conditions he must master. These are the processes of history.

As human intelligence gradually attains complete mastery of the environment, as well as complete control of human social and biological adaptation, the constant changes of history may be slowed and eventually brought to a halt. Then the zone of fluidity about the individual would congeal, erasing individual variation, freedom, and consciousness, and leaving man encased in an icy fixity of adaptation rivaling that of ants.

> Consciousness will gradually evaporate and disappear in this posthistoric period, very much as it condensed step by step into ever sharper focus during man's prehistoric era. In the ultimate state of crystallization to which the principle of organization leads, consciousness will have accomplished its task, leaving mankind sealed, as it were, within patterns of frigid and unalterable perfection.[4]

Others, from Lewis Mumford and Reinhold Niebuhr to Arnold Toynbee, do not concur in this overall view. Despite admiration for the lucidity and power of Seidenberg's argument, deserving of fuller consideration than my overcondensation, neither do I. Frozen posthistoric perfection could be the consequence of surrender to technique *infatuation,* but there is no inherent necessity for this outcome in technique *application,* or in the principle of intelligent organization itself. Technique is truly a tool. And foresight, one vital facet of intelligence, can inform us in advance of the various consequences of organizing our lives in this or that direction. When decisions are made on the basis of what is good not for technique but for people, they can create conditions to enhance rather than obliterate variable human beings and human values.

Here we encounter the obstructions of the technological optimists and pessimists, as represented by Marshall McLuhan and Jacques Ellul. Although superficially contradictory, both their arguments run parallel in ignoring the problem of how to preserve and foster human development in favor of promulgating an irrelevant hopeful or gloomy attitude about the effects of technique upon it.

McLuhan's optimism seems as invincible as it is unfounded. The trouble with Western man is that he has broken everything down into its constituent parts, the key dehumanizing basis of *mechanical* technology lying in its fragmentation of perception, particularly into sequential segments. The tyranny of the eye that followed creation of the phonetic alphabet, and was multiplied by the inundation of print after Gutenberg, is being or already has been overthrown by *electronic* technique, restoring the former proper balance of the senses. Motion pictures, radio, television, and related developments are creating a seamless web of communication in which mankind can resume its wholeness by experiencing the world in integrated simultaneity and totality. The medium is the message, which might be translated for the more traditionally minded: God is Gestalt.[5]

Surely our continued reliance on linear communication has not prevented the prophet of the electronic revolution from learning that vision became the predominant sense among monkeys some 25 million years before one of their lines evolved man and his alphabet, let alone McLuhan.[6] One wonders whether he would consider the sensory emphases of monkeys as also unbalanced. In any case, what assistance will electronics provide? Miniaturized boosters for restoring the short-range senses to ratios proper for the shrew? Or supplementation of the movies and talkies with feelies, smellies, and tasties? Somehow one doubts that such maneuvers would offer much to reducing the threats to survival of monkey or man.

The poverty of such implied solutions becomes comprehensible when evaluated in the context of McLuhan's notion of man's condition. Apparently he really believes that to be saved we need do nothing whatever. His indifference to current social crises is astounding, for when he refers to them at all it is likely to be in the past tense: "Tension between black and white in the U.S. *was* solved by . . . [italics added]."[7]

Neil Compton summarizes the utility of these supposedly practical ideas: "McLuhan sees contemporary history as a kind of cosmic *Finnegan's Wake* where some mysterious force is at work to harmonize and reconcile apparent conflicts. Meanwhile, we show signs of lapsing into a technologically sophisticated chaos as he dismisses contemporary problems."[8]

In apparent but deceptive contrast stands the viewpoint of Jacques Ellul, who instead of promoting passivity because all is won, endorses passivity because all is lost.[9] Instead of basking beneath the benign smile of the newfound electronic deity, he crouches submissively before the malignant sneer of the resurrected but electronicized devil. It seems that time has almost run out. Already the human enterprise has been taken over by an autonomous technique-organism, and in any case there is little to be done because the phenomena are so complex that they cannot be apprehended or controlled by the finite human mind. Despite this crushing assessment, Ellul wanly admits that the threat of the "technological society" to humanity might be offset if enough people become aware of it and insist on the primacy of human values.[10]

Ellul's despondency is not warranted by fact. No matter how much the men who conduct diplomacy by overkill behave as though they were computers, the decisions to build biological, chemical, and nuclear weapons are still man-made. Technique is still only an advanced tool that obeys human orders. What we need is not less assertive machinery but more determined men. As to the complexity of the problem, no one has really plumbed the seemingly inexhaustible possibilities of the connections available between the ten billion human brain cells inside each human head. We have no more objective basis for abject surrender to such dismal diabolical reifications as Ellul's than the delightful divine ones of Mc-Luhan. On the contrary, new studies of the brain and mind suggest that their capacities can be expanded as limitlessly as those of electronic technology if the equivalent effort and means are made available for their study and development.[11]

The above, however, is a very large *if*. To accomplish the possible richer life of the future we must loosen the grip upon us of the passivity that obstructs zestful investment of self in mastery of reality. And technique infatuation, precisely because it is so deeply ingrown a source of paradoxical passivity in man, must appear high on the list of hindrances to be uprooted.

We must guard as carefully against technique infatuation with linear language as against technique infatuation with patterned electronics. One good way is to look beyond words at the character patterns revealed in the works of master writers. In assessing technology three literary figures come to mind: Goethe's Faust; Poe's sailor in "Descent into the Maelstrom"; and Twain's Connecticut Yankee. All are creations of the nineteenth century, reflecting that period's increasing doubt about the benefits of technology.

Faust sells his soul to the Devil in exchange for the granting of all his wishes. Limitless knowledge and power are to be his, not just as the means for attaining his gratifications, but as ends in themselves. For he sees knowledge and power, the prime goals of technique, as endlessly worth possessing. Since he cannot envision doing so, Faust specifies that he must grow tired of exercising his powers before the Devil may claim his soul.

> If ever I recline, calmed, on a bed of sloth,
> You may destroy me then and there.[12]

Faust suffers from technique infatuation, for his knowledge and power are to be employed for the immediate delights they yield, without regard to their long-range impact on evolution of consciousness, freedom, and joy. He regains his youth, makes love to Helen of Troy, and, operating with flawless technical efficiency, becomes in effect the uncrowned king of Europe. Since his minions faithfully carry out every command, Faust need not become aware of the details of the dirty work performed in his name.

Similarly, present-day commanders of technique can carry out their will by proxy, without confronting the agonies their bomb runs cause this generation, their medication sales cause the next, or their genetic indulgences cause future generations. As an indifferent tool, technique pays no mind to values.

After a long second lifetime of self-indulgence, Faust embarks upon a master project of building a system of dikes throughout Europe so that nature's energies can be controlled in the service of man. Goethe here seems to imply that even an unsocial immersion in technique will in time lead man to put his powers at the disposal of his fellows. He thus reflects the early nineteenth-century optimism that the burgeoning of technique itself must force human improvement.

When Faust hears that construction of the dikes is under way, he remarks that now he can rest. We infer that until this moment the pursuit of pleasure, or even of knowledge and power divorced from *purpose,* has been empty of real satisfaction. His technique infatuation, which masked a deep passivity, could not provide the sort of gratification that permitted him to rest. That contentment would have to await the zestful investment of self in something larger.

Now Mephistopheles appears to claim his soul, mistaking Faust's repose for the weary boredom of satiation he predicted would overtake him in the end. Goethe, himself enamored of the rosy dividends of technique, here departs from the traditional legend by having God save Faust, cheating the Devil of his due. He thus confirms the modern view that it is not *use* of technique but *domination by it as a central concern* that sells out our souls.

Faust was written when the Industrial Revolution was reaching new peaks in Germany, presaging a brighter age. As the century wore on, the infatuation of intellectuals with technique wore thin. Today it should be plain that, while new abundance will cancel the old reality of scarcity, it will not by itself ordain the millennium.

Poe's sailor saves himself from the maelstrom by idly calculating the relative velocities of pieces of driftwood, thus inadvertently hitting upon a way out of the whirlpool. He was an adequate ideal for the nineteenth century when technical progress made only the modest promise of somewhat ameliorating scarcity by bending natural forces to producing more with less effort. At that time it was a seemingly impossible leap from making a clipper ship run before the wind, to making the wind itself, or from stimulating a failing human heart with a drug to replacing it with a mechanical contrivance.

Today it is no longer necessary for us merely to trickily ride the coat-tails of the whirlpool. Instead we can increasingly command the mael-strom, directing its awesome energies to the task not of alleviating but of completely eliminating scarcity. In the process we are learning that venerable elements of the technique of unequally distributing scarcity are also becoming vestigial. The "market," "supply and demand," and "profit incentive," when floodtide abundance swirls away their foundations, leave their defenders as infatuated champions of outdated technique.

However, the demise of these hangovers amid plenty does *not* auto-matically assure attainment of a new humanity. Instead, new technique infatuation may produce only a transcendence of *things* so overpowering that man barely persists as humanity rapidly fades. Poe's sailor is one of McLuhan's favorite metaphors,[13] but as a technical determinist so rigid as to totter on the precipice of becoming a mystical dropout, McLuhan fails to take into account that electronics notwithstanding, it is only man's *vision-dominated mind* that can save us. Only that mind can frame and adhere to the human values that can prevent man's rescue from the whirl-pool of scarcity from becoming merely a consignment to annihilation in the maelstrom of abundance.

The Connecticut Yankee hoped to bring the benefits of nineteenth-cen-tury technique into King Arthur's Court and the deprived lives of sixth-century England. He was opposed by an entrenched and cruel feudal aristocracy and clergy. To his dismay he found that the modern methods were in danger of being simply taken over and exploited by them accord-ing to the inhumane values of the time. The result was a vast battle which no one "won." Those who survived the carnage died within a few days of a plague induced by mountains of rotting bodies. Twain thus illustrated the pessimism shared by many other observers about the possibility of improving man. We must notice that in doing so he was subscribing gloomily to the same naïve assumption that Goethe had embraced op-timistically a half century earlier, namely, that if there were any way at all to elevate man into true humanity it would of course be simply to place in his hands the enormous technical mastery for which he had always striven.

But the true lesson of the fable is as clear as the lesson of current reality, in which the technique of the twenty-first century and beyond is being introduced explosively to twentieth-century man. As those who know computers best have been telling us for years, while the new powers will open many doors to man, they will *not* automatically carry him through them. To improve himself, man must *apply* his resources. Of foremost consequence among these are the crucial attributes of his mind, his intel-lect, and character operating under conditions of maximum consciousness, freedom, and joy. Yoked to the task of further perfecting themselves, these elements may make us equal to the challenge of grasping our new opportunities.

I must not criticize both the old and new prophets of technique for failing to suggest workable means of reaching the verdant future, and then imitate them. So here, although admittedly incomplete and preliminary, I offer a few thoughts.

First, although they may sometimes seem to us to be mistaken, and often may be disturbing to us and our institutions, we should all honor the efforts of brave individuals to advance through the human agenda against great odds, and at great personal sacrifice. Herbert Marcuse, of whose thinking I have several times been critical, is an example of one who has been stalwart in defending the resolve of young people to throw off the bonds of dehumanizing technique infatuation and focus on the core of humane life. He displays this perceptive and courageous attitude toward not only the traditional Marxist technique of socioeconomic analysis, but also toward unprecedented upcoming phases on the human agenda. He shows that Marxist ideas of socialism can no longer capture the imagination of the young because the techniques it proposes are not radical or utopian enough to fit today's possibilities.[14] An example mentioned earlier is that in the presence of superabundance of "things" what may be critically important is not the *social ownership* of the means of production but the *sociable application* of both means and product, by whomever they are "owned," to the enhancement of people rather than profit.*

The tragedy for human life of trying to maintain the private profit motive was epitomized with grisly clarity recently in a news story concerning the behavior of ambulance crews at the scene of an interstate highway accident. These, like 50 percent of ambulance crews in this country, were employed by morticians.

> . . . an ambulance arrives. The attendants lift one of the bodies into their vehicle, which actually is a hearse owned by a nearby mortician because no real ambulance is available in that community.
>
> Suddenly a second ambulance approaches the scene from the opposite direction and halts near the two fatalities still lying on the highway.
>
> Like predatory animals who see their meal about to be stolen, the first crew jumps from their hearse and, *flailing tire irons,* manages to scare off the invader long enough to get another of the two remaining bodies. The second crew picks up the final body.
>
> Once the dead have been collected, *thus assuring the attendants their bonuses from the morticians,* the crews turn their attention to the injured . . . [italics added].[15]

---

* See pages 371–372.

Sometimes entire counties are left without ambulance service when morticians are forced out of business by spiraling costs.

The irony of such events is that the same communities that provide expensive public fire departments sometimes will not finance ambulance service despite their death rates being up to forty times higher from auto accidents than from fires. The conclusion that our present values emphasize protection of profit and property to the neglect of people is not thereby sufficiently substantiated, and in the land of cigarettes and napalm of course it does not have to be, but it is certainly most poignantly underlined.

So then we must ask ourselves, if the motivating technique of private profit and enterprise held over from the era of scarcity is not effective, what would better provide the protection we want? The first solution that comes to mind is *public* ownership and operation. However, a moment's thought reveals that such a change does not by itself bring the human being into the forefront of consideration either. Anyone acquainted with the red tape of petty officialdom in Western Europe, the discourtesy and slack service in restaurants and department stores in the Soviet Union, or the corruption of some zoning and building inspection authorities in the United States has ample basis for this conviction. If more evidence is required, one has but to recall that the military forces of the world, in the main publicly owned and operated, are notorious not only for the destructive use of their nations' resources against others but also for the most undemocratic and tyrannical mistreatment of their own members. It is not my intention to demean the possible profound effects of elimination of the private profit motivation, but emphatically to affirm that realization of this change will not *by itself* bring the beautiful future into being. To realize a future in which human development will reach its full flowering, we will need techniques that *do* capture the imagination of the young because they *are* radical and utopian enough to fit today's possibilities. And then we have to be intrepid enough to *avoid falling in love with them.* For it is only by firmly and *un*infatuatedly keeping techniques in the category of *means,* from which we will select flexibly what at any moment is needed, that we can move decisively in the direction of optimal human development.

To accomplish this, the throttling grip upon us of the various interlocking ways to go that fortify passivity must be loosened, the dismantling of technique infatuation often being the key to the tangle. But in breaking free we must be sure that it is the *infatuation* we erase and not the technique. It is impractical to the point of absurdity to suggest that the cause of our troubles is the technique itself, or that the cure is to demolish its machinery. The Luddite sect of the early nineteenth century misidentified the enemy in just this way. They tried to destroy physically the weaving machines that put so many Englishmen out of work, rather than to attack the technique infatuation that chained the new methods to escalating profits rather than liberating people. Not only the same long prison terms but the same eventual recognition of having made a sacrifice for an irrelevant gesture awaits those who would try to save us by sabotaging the 7090 computer or the Saturn rocket.

Erich Fromm lists three institutions and methods we must be prepared to live with in a modern society, or risk total disruption: large-scale centralization, large-scale planning which results from this centralization, and cybernation and automation. He suggests a mass movement that is not bureaucratic, and "in its organization and method would be expressive of the aim to which it is devoted: to educate its members for the new kind of society in the process of striving for it."[16] Such a movement of small groups, loosely federated and dedicated to purposeful communal action, would be the ideal means for promoting widespread understanding, for example, of the new biology in time for effective utilization and regulation to be assured.

We must begin now to invent the technique of mobilizing such activity, for the roots of passive resignation are deep and tenacious. The idea of "progress" may well have been devised during the Enlightenment as a bright hope to replace man's lost sense of being the center of the universe. As an ideal, progress has the extra virtue of evoking the activity of *doing*. The fact that an idea was created out of need does not invalidate it. And the constant gloomy pronouncements that progress is not possible in improving the quality of human life are not only erroneous, but moreover are seductions to return to the old passivity, divested of the precious compensatory sense of being important. As a substitute for the tarnished hope for salvation through activity, the infatuated prophets of technique offer us only the morphia of salvation through abdication, in the assumption that time alone will heal all wounds. Such futurolatry is, as Fromm notes, precisely the alienation of hope.[17]

Some doubt the efficacy of organizing people for the new task of running the future. William Burroughs commented that the outcome of our struggle is dependent "not on the people you can mobilize, but the number of people you can disconnect."[18]

The image of disconnection is not as negative as at first it might seem. The electric "juice" upon which so many personalities feed passively is in terms of interpersonal closeness a poor substitute for the milk of human kindness and concern. Although students of the population explosion may cast a jaundiced eye at such changes, certain consequences of the great blackout over the East Coast in 1965 are instructive. All over the area inhabitants reported an unaccustomed close rapport with their fellow victims whether encountered in open fields, subways, elevators, sky-scrapers, or elsewhere. Delayed but concrete evidence of the impact of disconnection on human relatedness came in when the region's birth rate briefly surged upward nine months later.

To survive we must love where we want to go—and each other—more than the machinery that takes us there.

22 Big and Little Brother Protection

Introduction

Ashley Montagu tells the story of a chimpanzee who escaped from a New York zoo. After an exhaustive search he was finally found at the New York Public Library deeply absorbed in two heavy books. In one hand he held the Bible, and in the other Darwin's *Origin of Species*. When questioned by reporters he explained, "I'm trying to decide whether I am my brother's keeper, or my keeper's brother."

He may have been forced to choose. We are not. All men are brothers. And we are all one another's keepers. In this respect history has imitated both scripture and Darwin.

In today's "one world" we are all in shifting relationships of protector and protectee to one another. How we are protected by our big and little brothers, and how we protect them in return, largely determines the quality of our current lives. The same factors will determine not only whether or not our species continues to exist, but whether or not our lives will continue to develop in any way distinctively human.

Fraternal Cooperation and Conflict

In the stages of growth through which we all pass, first come those in which in varying degrees we are preponderantly dependent upon others for survival. Later come stages in which others predominantly depend upon us. Human beings are never totally dependent or independent. In varying proportions of each, always we cooperate. For societies, as for individuals, the central problem of growing up is to adjust our behavior to the inner and outer realities at each stage. The central difficulty is that each advance to new maturity means giving up gratifications enjoyed earlier.

A baby can joyously progress from bottle to cup, despite whatever twinges of nostalgia assail him, provided he is ready for the change and it is presented to him in a way that facilitates cooperative adaptation rather than retards it. Our universal tendency to regress under stress we will consider later.

During infancy and childhood we carry life's broad theme of coopera- tion to a new high point. Then we neotenously retain and weave it throughout our lives into the woof and warp of the most flexible adapta- tion system ever devised, human culture and values. In this way we evolve from ignorant and helpless little brothers into wiser and stronger big brothers. In the beginning we have little to give but freshness of mind and openhearted love. In the process of growing up life writes so closely or scrawls so defilingly upon us that, although we have acquired much more of wisdom and strength to give new little brothers, we sometimes wind up with pathetically little space left in which to receive and record, let alone empathize with, their whispered hopes. So we protectively pass on to them understanding and skill in managing the world as it was and is, but have no will for grasping what *they* want to it *become*. Thus big brothers often jeopardize the young they are trying to protect by forcing them to repeat maladaptively their own often outmoded maneu- vers. Because the message of little brother stirs up the "impractical" idealism which big brother has had to stifle in himself at great cost, big brother is predisposed to react to it with anxiety and anger. If big brothers cannot bear to see how much they have acquiesced in the besmirching of their own slates, so pure when they began as little brothers, they must of course energetically oppose the vision of the young, whether it is com- municated as humble requests or peremptory demands.

Thus Samuel Butler's father tyrannized his son, squelching in the boy the same sparks his father had smothered in him.[1] And thus my genera- tion of parents and school administrators are fighting the same battle with teen-agers today over hotpants and beards which they fought over their own right to continue wearing two-piece bathing suits and Levi's so dirty that "they could stand up by themselves." Attempts to demonstrate this parallel are sadly ineffective, being warded off by the most transparent rationalizations. Sometimes transposing the discussion back to the quaint, and therefore emotionally less charged, struggle of their parents for the right to wear flapper dresses and raccoon coats will establish at least a beachhead of understanding that these issues, in themselves irrelevant, express the urge to grow up. But it is difficult to get embattled adults to recognize that such fashion-fad protests of the young are emblematic of *more* than this effort to become independent. They symbolize and express the inarticulate pressure in man to move in the direction of all evolution, toward higher levels of consciousness, freedom, and joy.

However, when we are in the role of big brother, just *this* much threat to the status quo upon which our security rests may provoke enough anxiety to interfere with our rationality. Then when we notice that some of our little brothers' rebellion also includes explicit contemptuous discarding of *intellect* and *character* in the quest for emancipation, we become even more nervous. And when it becomes plain that for this group the pursuit of utopia also does not seem to involve *mastering reality,* we become frankly angry.

While we can empathize with disdain for war as a means to "peace" or for profit, and possessions as motives, even the most loving big brother may be antagonized by assertions that his efforts to assure little brother's civil rights, freedom from hunger, and safety from pollution are "irrelevant." By a backward sort of logic such provocation leads big brother to absurd denials that his own youthful protests or dissent were in any way whatever akin to those of little brother today. Thus campus democratizers, union reformers, or Czechoslovak libertarians are disowned by some present-day elected public officials, labor leaders, or Soviet rulers, not as dissidents but as faithless to the cause of human justice for which they themselves once had fought.

In the United States this sort of placing of today's rebels beyond the pale is particularly ironic. Not only was this nation born in revolution but its most revered leaders have defended every American's right to rebel. Thomas Jefferson wrote: "I hold it, that a little rebellion, now and then, is a good thing, and as necessary in the political world as storms in the physical."[2] And three-quarters of a century later, Abraham Lincoln said in his first inaugural address: "This country, with its institutions, belongs to the people who inhabit it. Whenever they shall grow weary of the existing government, they can exercise their constitutional right of amending it, or their revolutionary right of overthrowing it."[3] And it should scarcely be necessary to underline for a people whose majority regard him as the incarnation of God that Jesus was himself a kind of revolutionary.

Here let us take a breather to consider the range of meanings of big and little brother protection, as well as the possible relationships of symbolic big and little brothers to one another.

First, big brother is ordinarily experienced as the one who protects little brother. But just as in the life of literal brothers, it may sometimes happen that the roles are reversed. Big brother may need protection himself from a danger he somehow does not see, perhaps because he causes it himself. And when we grow old we are often in the position of being protected by those formerly dependent upon our protection. Protection needed may or may not be either forthcoming or welcome. And it is well to add that peers too may be involved in all these permutations of protection given or received.

Naturally, big brother is inclined to be most protective toward the little brother who, if not docile and submissive, is at least champing at the bit to grow up and join his "side." Thus youth organizations with big-brother orientation, such as Boys' and Girls' States and 4-H Clubs, are more genially regarded than Black Student Unions or W. E. B. DuBois Clubs.

Likewise it is easy to understand the frequent lack of empathy and protectiveness rebellious little brother shows toward the big brother he feels is throttling him. Thus black militants may offer no protection to the university administrator who to them represents only the establishment, although he may have demonstrated clearly that he joins them in opposing the discriminatory policies of his institution. Thus they exert not simply enough pressure to enable him to effect the changes they and he want, but instead let loose a geyser of disruption so diffusely damaging that their ally either resigns in despair or is fired by irate bigger brothers. The result generally is that he is replaced by someone who from little brother's viewpoint is worse, in that he not only opposes the demanded changes in principle but may be prepared to use armed force and criminal prosecution to further delay essential improvements. The new incumbent and the interests he represents may even be delighted to go further, and under the guise of "maintaining law and order" exploit the opportunity to demolish altogether fundamental freedoms of which they were never too fond in the first place. Irreversible totalitarianism, which equally destroys the possibility of optimal human development of both big and little brothers, could be the consequence.

Some little brothers actually desire to be defeated in this kind of confrontation in the hope of bringing the new freedoms closer. They thus betray their misconception that revolution consists of disintegration rather than reintegration. Sad to say, despite the naïve notion that the collapse of order at the price of their martyrdom by itself advances their cause, every indication is that such defeat today is much more likely to assure the triumph tomorrow of reaction rather than revolution, such is the awesome power of big brother. So at this moment big brother, as much as little brother, truly needs the protection of little brother's forbearance as well as idealism. But big brother has seen to it that little brother has precious little restraint left.

And in parallel sorry depletion is the generous protectiveness of big brother toward the young. In view of the present rocketing velocity of evolution toward first possibilities of truly free human life, little brother needs now more than ever the protective support of the wealthy and powerful. But thanks to panic about whether he and his world can survive, injudiciously intensified by the flailings of understandably desperate little brother, big brother is steadily closing his mind to the reality he is best equipped by experience to understand, and therefore closing his fist in terror about the truncheon of punitiveness. Accordingly, when collaboration is required between young and old on proposals for fuller participation of all groups in the future of abundance, we are treated instead to malignant and futile plans for "preventive detention" of the weak protestors by the strong preservers.

"Man may seek to order his life and his relations with others on the basis of love or on the basis of power. The two forces are antithetical . . ."[4]

In these words Ronald Sampson expresses the view many people share, that love and power are incompatible alternatives. Try as I may to follow their often brilliant arguments I cannot be convinced that love and power are antithetical. Perhaps they seem so in the lives of some big and little brothers. But we have only to recall Mohandas Gandhi, that "combination of Jesus Christ, Tammany Hall, and your father," as John Gunther called him,[5] to realize that love and power may be simply different aspects of the same human energy. And what we have learned of evolution confirms that love, as the most intense manifestation of life's predominant cooperativeness, is actually the biologically rooted foundation of all human power.

Of course human beings use what they have. Since big brother has most of the power, it is he who is most often encountered using it. And being less powerful, it is most often little brother who is limited to the less spectacular effects he can achieve through love. Thus there comes about a portentous divergence between big and little brother in their relation to love and power. As big brother gradually accumulates power he becomes less dependent upon love, which then becomes the instrument of fewer and fewer of his actions. Often not only the *proportion* of his behavior consisting of loving assertion declines, but eventually the absolute amount as well. Perhaps he loses the skill through the shift of attention, practice, and satisfaction to the more dramatic effects of power. In any event, little brother, tempted by fewer such alternatives, must rely through more of his life on loving interactions.

Now, property is the main modality of power, while people are both the source and object of most love. The consequence is that while big brother's interest shifts increasingly to the rights of mere property, little brother's tends to remain anchored to the rights of *people*. Of course some poor and powerless individuals subscribe eagerly to the primacy of property, and some other individuals remain centrally oriented to the rights of people despite graduation into big brotherdom's power. But it is plain that the values of most human beings are forced away from people and toward property as they are transformed over one or more generations from little into big brothers. I believe this process underlies the common observation that loving interactions are found so much more frequently among the poor than the rich.

We must take note of the peculiar fact that the biggest little-brother minority in the world is actually the majority of mankind: women. They are born into a state of oppression more widespread and unyielding than any based on color. Leaving the new biology aside, for most women there is even figuratively still no prospect of becoming big brothers. Despite their much-publicized "liberation" in advanced countries, the plain fact is that women are seriously discriminated against by big brother nearly everywhere in terms of education, employment, pay, and especially in terms of the degree of open-minded respect accorded any stranger by average persons, including women. This is particularly ironic since during infancy all of us are dependent for protection upon one woman or another, with the consequence that, like the southern "mammy" of old, she becomes the first model for both our later love objects and the big brothers whom we choose to defy or emulate. Ordinary prudence would seem to require that in the interests of psychological and social health such important persons should be cautiously selected, carefully trained, and abundantly rewarded.

As often alleged by their male ostensible admirers, it is true that women still retain some biological residue of need for protection, and that the quality of soft femininity is one that is not only highly prized by men but one that may be essential to the preservation of a world so heavily tilted in the direction of the supposedly more masculine trait of violent destructiveness. But these are scarcely justifications for injustice. As these same men insist, it may even be that women in general are better fitted to survive in the world of the future by being more love-oriented and less power-oriented than men. This difference would argue for the freeing of women from, rather than freezing them into, the constraints which these spokesmen endorse, and which clearly limit the influence of such reputedly superior creatures.

Regrettably, the countervailing pronouncements of feminist organizations are often cast in such a leatherpants style that they add to big brother's other motivations for keeping women down the not inconsiderable one of keeping the tidal wave of today's humorlessly dogmatic revolutionary propaganda at least out of the bedroom. A related attitude was embodied recently in the slip of a conservative college president. Intending merely to restate the traditional male attitude about the role of women, he inadvertently revealed his unconscious selfish interest in the "alimentary" theory of women discussed earlier (pp. 281–284; 432–434). In the course of an argument with students over the role of higher education for women he irately sputtered, "A woman's place is in the stove!"

At bottom, what we call big brother is in general short for maturity of age, wealth, and power in the service of preserving the status quo. And little brother in general stands for youth, relative poverty and weakness, and boundless energy dedicated to change. While philosophies may vary widely within each group, it is not refined ideology of justice but raw psychology of survival that dictates how each group disposes of its resources. Our only hope of success in recruiting both forces to the service of the future of liberated mankind is to heighten their awareness of the process by which one grows up into the other. To this task little brother can bring only his unflagging wish to live, his imagination, and his devotion, while big brother can call also upon memory.

Big Brother: Government, Business, Labor, Education, Communication

The possibility of life-styles based on getting ahead, fun fervor, creative frenzy, mystic withdrawal, and technique infatuation all depend upon continuation of independence of choice. The main dangers of these ways to go are that their adherents unwittingly might make choices that cancel for everyone the newfound heightened consciousness, mastery of reality, and expanded freedom and joy that are inscribed in the human agenda (p. 312).

Here I must forsake for a little while my concern with the day after tomorrow. For there is a real possibility that *tomorrow* may bring a reversal of man's trek toward freedom. The specter of Orwell's Big Brother has not faded, now that we are more than halfway to 1984. And in the most vigorous little brother movements there lie parallel menaces.

Beyond our national boundaries the upwelling of big brother power is all too obvious. The fanaticism of the Chinese "cultural revolution" that promised to guarantee the future by indiscriminately erasing the past, the clanking military dictatorships sprouting all over South America, Asia, and Africa, the continued snuffing out of dissent by the Soviet Union from Moscow to Prague—all are ominous portents.

Within our borders as well, for those willing and able to see it, there is ample evidence of a burgeoning of autocratic power far removed from control of the theoretically sovereign public. In the sphere of government, even those agencies set up supposedly to serve the public in undramatic domestic matters such as social security, veterans' affairs, welfare, job training, and so on are often found by a respectful applicant to be defensive baronies protected by vassal armies of low-level bureaucrats behind ramparts of quintiplicate paperwork.

Then there are the more glamorous establishments whose avowed purpose, with their computerized dossiers and other equipment, is to "protect" us: the military, the FBI, the CIA, the congressional committees on internal security, the police, and what George Wald has called "the military-industrial-labor-union complex."[6] One has but to glance at them to discern the formidable threats they pose to the expansion of human freedom. Indeed, one may only glance, and not too closely at that. Close scrutiny is usually forbidden the ordinary citizen, unless he is so unfortunate as to have been conscripted or seduced into joining these elite brigades.

Not all the blame may be laid on big government. For the "private enterprise" elements of our society contribute to the stifling of freedom in many ways, quite aside from their partnership with the military. They often bitterly oppose government in exercising functions for which we truly need a big brother to protect us, such as the new one of safeguarding consumer interests. Individuals cannot carry out for themselves the testing of auto safety, the measurements of air and water pollution, or the assessment of the dangers of chemicals in food, medicine, or cigarette smoke. The spectacle of a people sold ABMs and moon rockets being told that its automobile designers and manufacturers are unable to produce a mechanically safe and smogfree car contains a ghastly irony. The placid assurances of the tobacco industry that no causal connection has been demonstrated between cigarette smoking and lung cancer reveal a frightening cynicism. And the defense by publishers on the grounds of economy of the accelerating mergers of rival newspapers that are leaving one major city after another with but one or two daily papers is, from the standpoint of preserving freedom of expression, downright shameful. All these, and multitudinous other travesties in which government is told bluntly to let private enterprise alone, are grim evidence of the degree to which in our society the rights of people are ranked far below the rights of property by our other big brother, big business.

Most of us are scarcely aware of the massive scope and power of big business. For example, if the American Telephone and Telegraph Company and General Motors merged and became an independent country, the new nation would have the seventh-largest national product in the world, exceeded only by those of the United States, the Soviet Union, Japan, West Germany, Britain, and France.[7] Out of 10 million private enterprises in America, the top 500 transact one-third of all business activity.[8] As Robert Heilbroner suggests in his brilliant essay *The Limits of American Capitalism,* there can be little doubt that if the leading 150 companies disappeared, the American economy would be completely shattered.[9] And these mammoths grow cannibalistically. From 1951 to 1962 the 50 largest industrial firms swallowed up 471 smaller firms, with subsequent years speeding the ingestion.[10] As one wag paraphrased Coolidge, "The business of America is conglomeration."

Yet bigness is not the most dangerous aspect of big business. Nor is it, as Lenny Bruce claimed, that the best working definition of monolithic communism is the Bell Telephone monopoly. Rather, it is that while the power of big business is in many respects greater than that of the state in our everyday lives, we ordinary citizens have even less of an effective voice in its activities. Anthony Jay observes that the big business firm resembles the independent or semi-independent European state of the sixteenth and seventeenth centuries. Employees of the firm "live in . . . voteless dependence on the favor of the great," just as did the population of Machiavelli's Florence in the time of the Medicis.[11] The company may juggle men and their families about the nation and globe, uprooting them at will from ties to place and people, precious to identity and self-validation, which are replaced, especially by children and older adults, only with difficulty and at considerable emotional cost. Attendance at joyless company affairs and membership in the "right" clubs may be mandatory. Occasionally, as in the price-fixing scandals of the late fifties, the lumbering giant may run afoul of the law in its obsessive voracity for profit, whereupon it may even select and throw employees as placatory sacrifices to the rather toothless wolves of the antitrust division.

As with big government, big business offers the considerable advantage that a few large firms often are more efficient than many small ones. But we must not deify big brother's efficiency, or we risk the dehumanization and chill entombment that proceeds from technique infatuation.

Modest signs of a "business conscience" are disclosed in the monies now being invested in urban studies, job training, and so on. Such funds as yet usually are but tokens, and where effective often turn out to be but a cruel way of dispossessing the poor from their neighborhoods.

The picture emerging seems to be that of tiny man caught between massive grindstones. Darkening the scene even more is our realization that the supposed countervailing forces of labor unions, education, and the news media all too often are themselves in actuality helping to turn the millstones that bear down upon the fragile human grist of little brother.

Organized labor, thirty years ago a promising force for social reform, has itself become a big business. The "have" unions—teamsters, mine workers, auto workers, carpenters, and so forth—have taken on the character of guilds, jealously protecting their own and sometimes excluding the poor in general and the racial minorities in particular. In the hard decisions faced by unionized teachers around the country, one senses that narrow self-interest and even bigotry might sometimes play as much of a role as they have for so long in the actions of employers and recently in those of blue-collar workers.

Still, there is hope. Some well-established unions are beginning, often in cooperation with government and management, to contribute to efforts to help the disadvantaged achieve a better life. And sometimes we find even a newer union with the vision to place humane cooperation above other considerations. An example comes from the agricultural union which, while literally fighting for its life, gave transportation to non-union laborers who desperately needed the few cents an hour paid strike-breakers.

In education surely lies some of the best help of the present and the great hope of the future. An example of its astonishing power is our totally unprecedented success already in reducing the number of cigarette smokers in the United States, now that at least a halfhearted effort is under way. Since 1966, although the population has increased by eight million, the number of smokers has declined by four and a half million.[12]

Yet we must admit that much of education at all levels is stultifying and in fact operates as an assembly line producing not varied human personalities eager to explore and implement the human agenda, but conformist products that simply perpetuate the past into the future. Students are assiduously discouraged from fundamental examination of the need for adaptive change, and are led to believe that the greatest need lies in fixation of the present. It is perplexing how so many of our high school principals have come to care more about the preservation of traditional barbering than the elimination of traditional barbarism.

Higher education certainly is "big," and perhaps even more deserves the assembly-line label. As an example, we can take the recently abandoned procedure through which young men were fed onto belts preferred by big brother through the Selective Service System. The nation's need for engineers, doctors, economists, or scientists was assessed in terms of so many commodities; and then, through a totalitarianesque process called "channeling" (the selective granting of draft exemptions), the machinery of government guaranteed that the requisite number would be completed annually. Lest anyone doubt that education had thus become the arm of big brother, let us commend to all the explicit pronouncement of former Selective Service Director General Hershey on his view of the partnership between higher education and his agency of military conscription:

> I think a fellow should be compelled to become better and not let him use his own discretion whether he wants to get smarter, more wealthy or more honest . . . I think you should keep a string on them so if you want to use them you can; and you can compel them to stay where you want them because you have a string on them; and if they do not stay where they should, then you put them where you can be sure that you can use them . . .[13]

Thus supported until recently by the draft, and still by business and government-financed grants, higher learning moves in directions which very largely have at least the tacit approval of big brother. The efficacy of withholding such approval is revealed by the experience of the great American sociologist, C. Wright Mills, who found that after *The Power Elite,* his study of who actually rules the United States, appeared he could no longer obtain grants to support his research.[14] Perhaps his experience can help us understand why in the pages of the social science academic journals one cannot find studies of the interlocking connections of law firms, businesses, foundations, and government that make up the nerve center of big brother's power in American life.[15] In striking contrast is the outpouring of papers analyzing in minute detail the anatomy and connections of little brother's much less potent influences, which disparity he understandably finds infuriating. No doubt the same big brother pressures are reflected in the observation of Karl Deutsch, past president of the American Political Science Association, that studies of "mass" outnumber studies of "elite" by one hundred to one.[16]

Fortunately there are growing fractions of the academic world, faculty and administrators as well as students, who are demanding that education not be a transmission belt, and asserting that optimal human development and freedom do not lie in the direction things are moving now. Contrast pronouncements of top academics of even a few years ago with the recent statement of Kenneth Pitzer, former president of Stanford University, on the draft and the war in Vietnam:

> The Ford Motor Company blundered in the Edsel but had the courage to admit the error and stop production. The war in Vietnam is an equally obvious and infinitely greater blunder. . . . [It] is clearly a violation of

human rights to draft a young man to fight a war which he regards as grossly immoral and about which the nation is unsure.[17]

Even the best of education today is constricted by the human character flaw of blindly, and even adamantly, repeating out of habit what is familiar long after it is outdated. And so our educational machinery continues in general to try to instill in students the mistaken conviction that scarcity is an eternal verity, that therefore the only reasonable course for the individual is to strive for the security afforded by money, and that accordingly the proper study of man is business. Very rarely is the student helped to grasp the expanding significance of abundance, that for example, such ideas as working for a living, earning a profit, or saving for retirement are entering obsolescence. So the power orientation of big brother is favored in the values we attempt to inculcate in the young.

At this point the student, unarmed with *understanding* of new reality, senses intuitively that he has been misled and often rejects not just his elders' emphasis on power but their entire world, including regard for any sort of accomplishment, achievement, or excellence whatever. It is then that he may turn in disgust or religious zeal to the caricature of the love-orientation of little brother embodied in hippiedom. Or alternatively, he may attempt to appropriate the instruments of power, and even violence, and turn them against big brother in militant confrontation. In either case his desperation rests upon his miseducation. He has not only been deceived into misapprehension of reality, but is unable to discriminate obsolete adaptations based upon drudgery, hedonism, or violence, from viable ones based upon truly self-validating love, work, and play.

All this is not ameliorated by the incontestable fact that big brother constantly demonstrates his belief in the dictum, often attributed to Lenin, that political power grows out of the barrel of a gun. Nor does it help that even within our own boundaries big brother scarcely hears the pleas of little brother until the justice of his message is underscored by campus rebellion and ghetto revolt. It is a melancholy fact that nothing has been as effective in getting big brother at least to consider ordering his life and relations with others on the basis of love as little brother's expropriation and violent use against him of some of big brother's power.

Finally, we should consider the mass media of communication. Because they are the means for disseminating both information and opinion they are equally crucial to big and little brother. The sheer amount of information new technique supplies can drown the most dedicated observer. Leaving aside the wildly multiplying professional literature, most of us are inundated with published and broadcast material in such quantities that it is a battle to prevent the torrent from driving us out of our homes and offices. McLuhan is correct in attributing to the mass media an important influence in transforming the world into a global village, even if we conclude in opposition to him that their gargantuan message is the message.

A major role of mass media is conveying news. Because things happen rapidly in every corner of the global village, even the most efficient wire services can report only a small fraction of the material reaching them. Our largest newspapers and newscasters can transmit only a small part of what they receive. The news analyst can synthesize and interpret only a little of what he gathers. And you and I cannot always absorb even that much. Thus the trend to condensation, simplification, and distortion, demanded in news magazines and digests for decades, now reaches perilous proportions. Much of the public now accepts placidly the intentional filtration and twisting of news as not only the publisher's right but his *duty*. In totalitarian countries news is tightly controlled by government. We can be grateful that here it is only "managed," leaving most of its deliberate distortion to less efficient competitive private enterprise.*

But as communication increasingly becomes big business monopoly, the views of its owners become more effectively intruded into news reporting. The lessons of advertising and propaganda in pluralistic societies are heeded. The big lie, so effective under totalitarian conditions, ordinarily is carefully avoided so as not to provoke the widespread disbelief engendered outside Germany by Nazi radio broadcasts during World War II. Instead, through easily unnoticed omissions and slantings the desired impression is created. When we realize that this same process equally censors what we receive in the realms of popular philosophy and commentary, as well as drama, comedy, and satire, we cannot be unconcerned. When we squarely confront the fact that a few network executives can thus tailor the profoundly effective educational experience of nineteen million children under six who watch television twenty to thirty hours a week,[18] we must be consternated. The advance of man to new reaches of consciousness and freedom seems unlikely to be thereby facilitated. Nor is the situation improved through clumsy threats by self-seeking officials, who are opposed to free expression of balanced political opinion, to invoke censorship through public denunciations or innuendos about nonrenewal of licenses. It appears rather that the only remedy is somehow quickly to bring this kind of big brother power under the sway of love for people rather than property. Here it should be obvious that we must either give up enormous profit or sustain incalculable loss.

* The newly published *Pentagon Papers* suggest that sometimes this ratio is reversed.

Little Brother: Love, Oppression, Resistance, Rebellion, Restitution, Repression

We have seen how primates were bequeathed life's central propensity for loving cooperation, and how they organized it through elaborate social dominance hierarchies into valuable new tools for survival. We have seen how man honed these dispositions into flexible adaptations transmitted through cultural evolution. And we have observed that thus interwoven love and power are not inherently incompatible. Neither are they always fully compatible, particularly as external danger and internal scarcity gradually cease to be threats to the group. Then habitual assertion of outmoded social dominance defenses often becomes the new menace to both individual and group survival. Functionally obsolete, but still powerful, big brother becomes an obstacle to further adaptive evolution.

A countermovement is rushing up from below. Just as has happened so many times before, those who feel oppressed by big brother are coming together to resist. Whether they blame Truman for Hiroshima, Eichmann for Buchenwald, Brezhnev for Prague, or Daley for Chicago, whether they feel united by skin color, youth, sex, economic exploitation, or unpopular views, and whether or not they identify with one another consciously, in effect these groups and thousands of others around the world are gradually cooperating and collaborating to assert little brother's orientation toward people as opposed to property.

The general effect of their strivings is to elevate *love* as an organizing principle over *power*. But when desperation replaces hope there is apparent everywhere the tendency to grasp and wield the instruments of violent power against big brother, and in the process to trample love underfoot. Then what begins as *the loving wish to survive and grow* becomes debased with "success" into *the power drive to dominate and control*. In this way little brother is all too often short-circuited into the jackboots of big brother, as illustrated by countless examples from Robespierre to Stalin.

But we must not misidentify all little brother protection with guns on campuses, or with burning cities. We must clearly recognize that little brother protection begins with peaceable assertion of demands by excluded minorities for equality, and for the right to jurisdiction over their own lives equal to that exercised by dominant groups. We must see clearly that what ignites the fuse of violent aggression is the fury engendered by the stifling of these legitimate aspirations. If we do not make this distinction, and respond appropriately, we risk escalating into civil war what is only the mark of hope dying and desperation aborning. And we must understand that the outcome of such a struggle here as elsewhere, no matter who prevails, might be a repressive and regressive tyranny that with effective modern means of control could begin the end of our advance toward human liberation.

On the other hand, what we have learned about animal and human aggression offers a practical solution. First, the proper signals must be given by the powerful outsider that the "territory" of the daily lives of the weak will not be further transgressed, and that his hungry frustration will be alleviated. Then, prompt action to implement this message must be undertaken which will satisfy his needs and dissipate his tension to below the point of eruption into violence. Of course this approach, like all others, will not work perfectly in every instance, but it has the virtue of being both rational and in accord with the desires of those in need.

Objection is sometimes made by big brother that experience shows these ideas to be wrong, that little brother was actually less obstreperous when his oppression was unrelenting, that now that things are better, "the more they get, the more they want." This correct observation is used to justify use of repressive force now to bring back those supposedly better times. Unfortunately, it fails to take into account important facts that make today's situation so different as not to be capable of transformation backward into yesterday's, even were that desirable.

To begin with, the reason things are somewhat better for some little brothers is fundamentally that, to an increasingly skilled and automated society, large numbers of illiterate submissive laborers among the young and the minorities are no longer of much economic value. Also, amid growing abundance, it is necessary to dispose of more of the surplus by pricing it low and selling it to the poor. For both these reasons the lot of some of the exploited as to opportunity and material goods has improved a bit in recent years, and of course nothing whets the appetite like a taste of honey. Beyond these obvious factors lies the effect of the mass media in bringing to the *attention* of all people the existence of increasing abundance, and understanding of means whereby more of it can be claimed for the enjoyment of even the formerly most lowly and meek. No amount of nostalgic naïve repression can roll back the mounting drive for liberation against such elevations of consciousness and gusto of little brother for new vistas of freedom and joy.

Little brother is therefore joyously affirming that most people do not need big brother's protection nearly so much as *he* seems to crave acquiescence. The evolutionary record discloses that man's elemental co-operativeness and ingenuity endow him with ability underrated by big brother to solve problems without his intervention. Yet my immediate neighbors and I cannot handle by ourselves the unlimited challenges of current reality. We do need protection from air and water pollution, from deforestation and Strontium-90, from poisoned foods and fatally flawed autos. Much of the animosity toward big brother stems from the fact that he does *not* protect us but rather profits from these dangers he has himself created or expanded, including the specter of communism and the premonition of the anti-antimissile missile gap.

The crucial question seems to be, "How can little brother acquire the *power* needed to control his destiny without losing the *love* needed to assure his survival?" We have reached the point where distinctions between right and left are so often meaningless precisely because in both directions the monotonous transmutation of little into big brother has resulted in the escape of new power from the guidance of old love. This observation has led some to either the cynical conclusion that since someone has to misuse power it had best be themselves, or the hopeless one that the only course is to abdicate from acquiring power altogether.

But we cannot boycott the twentieth century. To parallel Freud's wry appraisal of the conscious mind, it isn't so good, but it's all we've got. In order to reach the twenty-first century, let alone revamp it in advance toward humanistic goals, we simply must master the feat of bringing political, economic, intellectual, and other power under the leadership of love. And in order to learn how to help love grow to luxuriant dominance we must seek to understand it where under harsh circumstances it now grows most tenaciously.

Among the minority communities, deprived of the power that corrupts, the conferring of survival benefits through love is often most prominent because so little else works in the same direction. In the Jewish slum area of lower eastside New York City a half century ago, as in the black and Mexican-American big-city ghettos of today, is where one might find the ubiquitous personal human warmth that seems to evaporate as he searches through progressively higher levels on the social scale. Especially among black people, even those who have never met before, there is an easy light-hearted welcoming of each other as soul-brothers and sisters. Just how to preserve the bond this represents while adding to its owners' power is the challenge, the solution to which no one has yet worked out. Perhaps a useful approach would be to recognize some present obstacles to doing so, and possible ways of avoiding them.

First, of course, is resistance from those who now have the power and do not choose to share it. Beyond that there are less evident but equally obstinate ones. All people tend to develop styles of dress, grooming, and behavior which are the emblems of a particular group, membership in which importantly extends the individual's human identity. Whether they signify distinctions of age, sex, occupation, social standing, race, or religion, such signals as the Boy Scout uniform, the black militant's natural coiffure, and the minister's wife's quietly proper demeanor, all serve to indicate who may be trusted by whom.

Among little brothers, particularly the young, such externals are too often used not as possible clues, but as absolutely reliable *evidence* that the bearer of the accepted signal is to be trusted by them without further question. It is this gullibility upon which narcotics officers depend when they disguise themselves in the unisexual costume of long hair and bell-bottoms in order to entrap teen-agers into marijuana purchases or sales. The obverse mistake occurs when a pregnant hippie girl decides she cannot talk to a decent doctor because he wears a suit and tie, and instead visits an abortion quack sporting beads. Even worse is the mistrust that cuts little brother off from badly needed allies, from warm human relationships across generational and racial lines. By indiscriminately shutting out those with short, gray, or absent hair, those with unacceptable skin pigmentation, or those on the wrong side of thirty, little brother delivers himself into the hands of thieves, academic or sexual exploiters, or even big brothers, all posing as soul-brothers, or at least soul-mates.

Besides, such sociocultural inbreeding makes it all the more unlikely that big brother will be induced to share his power, or that little brother will have the chance to teach his love. The enormous impact of Martin Luther King grew out of his skill at moving back and forth across these barriers so that he carried love out of the ghetto and power back into it. This earned him unjust criticism as an "Uncle Tom." The falsity of this charge, and the proof of his real success, is that unlike Uncle Toms he had to be assassinated.

So little brother would be wise to avoid making group inbreeding into a religion. Particularly authenticity tripping, discussed earlier, must not be taken as the "open sesame" to the fulsome future. Honesty and openness are not sufficient. Also required of those who would improve society is substantial *content,* such as intelligence and information, courage and compassion, hardiness and humor.

An especially difficult challenge to all of us are the campus rebellions observed all over this country. Because they disclose clearly the issues and difficult choices facing us in every sphere of big and little brother interaction they are worth examining closely. For more than a century those in the forefront of liberal humanist leadership have been working to extend equality to everyone.

A noteworthy example is Antioch College. For many decades this small school has honored the ancient tradition of student responsibility and authority which stems from the earliest universities. Among my many good fortunes was the opportunity to study for two quarters at Antioch before being called into service. One of my first memories is of learning as I climbed down from the train that I was expected to serve on the curriculum committee, and should prepare to contribute in a few days to a discussion of new courses that should be offered on Asia. From my experience working on that committee, and participating in other ways in the student-faculty-administration partnership that shares practical community power at the college, I have a sense of the value of charging the student with responsibility for decision making as contrasted with opposing his wish to participate. My all too brief stay at Antioch showed me that the best way to help little brother grow up and contribute to human advance is the simple expedient of *encouraging* him to do so. In particular, the best way to avert unwise expropriation of power by little brother is to insist that he possess and exercise as much power as is appropriate.

Indians, blacks, women, and the young are examples of groups that in general are still shut out of the system, to whom in equity opportunity on the basis of individual merit will have to be extended. As we all know, although some progress has been made, it has been at a pitiably slow pace.

Now the oppressed groups are struggling determinedly, and sometimes forcefully, to achieve more than token advance. And those who have worked long and hard in the same cause cannot help being delighted that it has been joined in force by large numbers of the victims of discrimination themselves. Of course, the allies of little brother in the various echelons of big brotherdom are seriously disturbed about the impact of the violence involved on the university campuses they want to help excluded groups enter. Some who remember Nazi hoodlums on German campuses in the thirties, and how prompt intervention by police spared their lives so that they could emigrate to carry on the fight for democracy here, join those who are insistent upon calling police onto our campuses. Others agree, whose main concern is that force must never be allowed to stifle freedom even in a just cause, or that cause is lost. And then there are those who rightly fear that the majority of Americans are so unsympathetic to the idea of university independence and academic freedom that they will act to destroy universities from the outside if administrators do not "defend" them from within.

However, while juggling these explosive possibilities, all those fundamentally sympathetic to the aspirations of little brother are given pause by the cogent argument that the peaceable methods of the past century have been discredited by failure, and that it is evident that the walls of unjust discrimination which withstood reasoned appeal are finally being breached only by force. In the conflict of judgment and conscience thus created is being hidden a new issue of perhaps even greater cruciality to advance through the human agenda.

The excluded groups are no longer asking that they be admitted equally on the basis of the same criteria applied to others. They now insist that, in reparation for the long deprivation and exploitation to which they have been subjected, what is required in justice is *preferential* admission. And many university authorities, in concert with others, agree with the essential fairness of this idea. Why shouldn't people who have been systematically excluded from higher education before be compensated now by being *included* in disproportionately great numbers? Even the idea of granting them extra financial help and remedial tutoring seems eminently sound in order to prevent belated admission to the university from becoming an empty gesture.

But none of these is in fact the most significant change incorporated in the new program of little brother. For at bottom what is at issue is not whether all should be treated equally on the basis of merit, but whether *merit itself* shall continue to be honored by not only the universities but by the human community in general.

The criteria of merit, even among the dominant white community, have been ability and achievement. Of course they were ignored in favor of occasional obeisance to religion, especially in the case of Jews, and by allowing the power of ethnic group, family, money, and pull to be the deciding factors. The defenders of the system point out that despite losses of talent due to these exceptions, in recent decades of scholarships and other financial assistance, it has operated increasingly to bring to the fore the best endowed and prepared. Now it is proposed not to admit the excluded to equal opportunity in this system, but to *discard the criteria of ability and achievement* as "irrelevant" to merit. Instead, the very basis of previous unfair discrimination against minorities is to be substituted. Race and ethnicity are to be openly considered, except that the groups formerly rejected on these grounds are now to be *favored* for acceptance. Since fitness for education still seems unrelated to race, deliberate "selection of the fittest" on this basis seems on the surface to run contrary to fundamental principles of evolution. But, as we have seen, many factors in our present social order have removed us from "natural" selection, and human as opposed to animal fitness is not an easy matter to discern. For example, while there may be no necessary connection between race and achievement in mathematics, it is possible that in the practice of social work or psychiatry the race of the worker might be a very significant factor in winning the trust of those he serves, without which the worker cannot succeed in helping them.

Therefore those pressing for such changes feel justified in calling upon this nation's tradition of revolution in the cause of justice, and imposing their will by force. Of course, in the process, terms such as "participatory democracy" become a sham, because, however just the cause, by definition violent actions of a minority against a majority cannot be democratic. Worse than this degradation of language into meaningless slogans is the repressive process set in motion, which in his present unpreparedness seems certain to swamp little brother at full tide.

First, deans and college presidents who have struggled for years to bring about the desired advances are cornered between the violent uprising from below and the retaliatory clamor from without. Lacking background as well as machinery for effective negotiation of real conflicts, they are quickly made helpless and eliminated. Then "strong" men are brought in to take their places who invariably represent the most repressive elements of big brother. These leaders in the "defense of democracy" have indicated plainly in some instances that they are resolved as well as prepared to gun down self-professed revolutionaries or even those so labeled by the authorities while demonstrating peacefully. So in playing semantic games with big brother's master charlatans on their own territory, little brother is relying upon a tactic foredoomed to failure, and therefore disapproved by the guerrilla theorists whom he often adulates.

Leaving aside the means, let us consider the ends of such reforms. Friends of mine in the white academic establishment see the fundamental justice in minority insistence that blacks and others must now be admitted in disproportionate numbers to colleges and especially to professional schools. They recognize that merit as disclosed by entrance exams or earlier grades should not be accorded as much weight as the provision of service to groups presently neglected. Others of my friends object that although the theory is sound, most of those so trained do not return to help their own people, but instead after graduation seek and get the same cushy jobs for high pay in government or private business as whites. These faculty are unwilling to give preferential admission to minority students only so that they may go out and use their credentials for their own individual material and social advance. They want any student given such preference to be required to commit himself in advance to return to practice for at least several years with his own people in a deprived ghetto area. This is presently done in the case of some medical students, interns, and residents who receive financial support from states in return for a period of obligatory service where needed after graduation.

So reasonable-sounding a request would not seem to be likely to rouse objection from minority students, but I was shaken recently in a discussion dealing with it by an articulate black student's refusal to make any such commitment. He had first explained that the reason for black insistence on having "relevant black studies under black professors and black control" is only partly to provide blacks a better understanding and image of themselves. The main objective according to him is to assure poorly prepared black students that they can pass a sufficient number of courses to qualify for the diploma, the passport which they believe guarantees escape from pushbroom and ghetto slavery into middle-class freedom. He then went on to assert irately,

> For four centuries you whites taught us by example how to be self-centered, how to exploit us or steal from us for your own benefit. Meanwhile you preached to us from your segregated churches how to do right by your fellow man. Now you want to let us into the colleges to follow not your example but your preaching. Well, we won't do it. We want to be *really* equal to you. We want the right to get into colleges ahead of you, and then turn around and rob you blind if we want, like you did to us.

Such a viewpoint is painful and disheartening. But I must admit that there is much justice in its accusation, and in its insistence that at this time and place true equality includes the right to be unethical. We are hardly in a position to demand of those who have been treated as less than equals in every other way that they must be more than equal to ourselves morally. The predicament for those of us who care about justice and human decency is compounded by the lawsuits now being filed by academically superior white students *who are being excluded on account of race* in order to make room for academically inadequate blacks and others whose preferential admission is not to be made contingent in any way. In such a welter of conflicting claims, which way does conscience lead?

For two minority faculty members conversing at a recent interstate meeting the decision was clear. One was a black professor of music and the other a Mexican American specializing in ceramics. Both had pressed for autonomous Black and Brown Studies Programs. Both were vociferous in demanding that minority students be admitted to half the places in their undergraduate and graduate classes regardless of any qualifications beyond ethnicity and color. I wanted them to know of current progress in my field, and told them with some pride of the increasing numbers of black and brown students admitted to medical school without reference to prior academic achievement or entrance exam scores. There was an uneasy silence during which the two exchanged loaded looks, and both whispered a prayerful "Geez!" Finally the black musician turned to me and chuckled:

> Doc, it's okay about that equality bit when the worst that comes down is an arpeggio with fiddle-scratch or a pot out of round. But Garcia and I, we ain't so sure we'd want one of these numbskull butterfingers taking out our appendix!

Although I recognize the critical difference between the possible consequences of an artistic versus a medical mistake, this sudden forsaking of principle for practicality stunned me. They were reassured by my hasty explanation that while his *past* record would not exclude a minority student, any failure to achieve up to standard *during* medical school would be evaluated carefully, as it is with all students, in deciding whether or not he should be graduated.

This exchange made me understand more fully the warning of another black professional that the production of large numbers of insufficiently skilled minority graduates would in the next few years result in their rejection by their own people, as well as the majority, with resultant further lowering of the self-esteem and prestige of the very groups who can least afford it. Of course, as an accomplished man descended of three generations of professionals, with an international reputation, he does not have to be defensive. It is easy for him to see that, as Roy Wilkins put it in commenting on the pertinence of black studies, what matters the most in advancing in modern society is not knowledge or imitation of one's ancestors and their culture, but knowledge of the modern world. Any little brother already well on his way to power can readily grant that "it's not how a black man wears his hair but what he has in his head" that counts.[19]

How to resolve such dilemmas is clearly a critical challenge to any value system, old or new. The obstinacy of such problems, and the ineffectuality of any current scheme of settlement, impel toward dangerous but disguised withdrawal. Forms of withdrawal vary from the inane "pornopolitics" of the filthy-speech movement to the elevation of withdrawal into moral imperatives of drug-taking, alienation, and abdication. But there is no viable escape. The resolution of such dilemmas must be found if the confrontation of big and little brother is not to reach a calamitous impasse.

It is curious how not only this withdrawal but ambivalence toward one another is revealed in the language and actions of big and little brother. From the podium a rebellious speaker may lead an audience in loud chanting which couples an obscene word for sexual intercourse with the name of a despised public official. This device certainly has the effect of breaking down the Victorian taboo against speaking dirty words "in front of ladies." But little brother does not seem to be aware that to use any term for intercourse as an epithet simultaneously bolsters the most puritanical establishment attitude of rejection of sex, which the self-professed revolutionary insists he embraces as an act of love, or at least as good clean fun. Conversely, big brother, when he undertakes forcible suppression of freedom of speech, is adopting the tactics of the communist adversary with whom he identifies his tormentors.

In the relations of broader groups are instances where the confrontation seems to have been prevented by little brother's joining instead of opposing big brother. Although it minimizes strife, such a course may imperil human survival. Take as example the stands of organized labor. Although it presumably represents little brother, its viewpoint, like that of so many little brothers reaching upward for friendly handclasps, is in transition toward that of big brother. Some spokesmen of organized labor have set themselves against the guaranteed annual income and the upcoming step on the human agenda of freeing work from its archaic social function of providing subsistence. Understandably they do so because unions have developed a vested interest in preserving the tie between work and income. If people get paid without working they will not join labor unions. Workers for income are thus their only source of power. Therefore, to survive, organized labor helps prolong beyond its necessary lifespan the unequal distribution of scarcity in exchange for drudgery. And in so doing it helps big brother delay the transition from work for income to work for self-validative psychic intimacy in the era of abundance.

Even more ironic is organized labor's partnership with big brother in prosecuting the Vietnam war. Labor contents itself with a modest prosperity as its share of the collaboration, instead of opposing the fruitless conflict that builds enormous fortunes for a few investors and executives, and that kills mostly lower and working class American sons. Thus labor helps big brother maintain, largely at its expense, long outdated means for settling human conflict, which operate not only to dominate foreign little brothers but also to teach the principle and premise of violence to everyone at home.

On the still larger scale of international relations we can see bizarre regressions to both the antiquated techniques of reliance on violence and on submissive little brotherism. Just as in long-standing family feuds, among nations it sometimes serves to maintain unchallenged big brother's dominance over his own people to immerse all the little brothers in endless preparations for defense and attack against the other countries.

Thus rival big brothers develop tacit understandings about the sorts of glares, imprecations, and brandishings that are mutually acceptable ways to keep the useful fear and hostility alive. Any departure from this covert covenant is seen as betrayal and evokes strong disapproval. For such a move raises the possibility that the little brother within his own borders will demand reciprocal discarding of his own weapon stockpiles, and liberation from the constraints required by the former threat. Better for two big brothers to be dangerously overarmed against each other than for them to disarm and possibly to find themselves at the mercy of their little brothers. And although the family analogy can scarcely be expected to fully explain international affairs, it is illuminating to notice how certain current international disputes resemble the quarrels of powerful neighbors who could seriously injure one another in a fist fight. Both can safely vent their rage on one another and maintain their authority at home by encouraging their younger and weaker brethren to fight each other while they stand by as seconds.

Conclusions

The big and little brother roles are inherent in both individual and group human development. It is not our task to abolish either, but to assure that their functioning affords everyone the maximum opportunity of realizing his potential. There is loose in the land in both groups the absurd notion that if only all the big or little brothers would unite they could fight a final battle, and history would from then on be set right. But neither group can exterminate the other without putting an end to history. So there can be no battle that is final without its also being a finale.

Instead of readying ourselves for futile battles between big and little brother, we must enter in both roles into loving exchange with one another to foster intrasocial synergy in the never-ending effort to advance man's condition across the next page on the human agenda.

It would help sustain little brother's courage to recall in this connection that even many of the most notorious tyrants—such as Caesar and Napoleon—wound up both deposed and having improved the lot of most of their subjects. Of course, in the twentieth century Orwellian Big Brother is made more malignant by the impersonal wizardry of electronic technique. But this ominous change merely accentuates the truth that it is not the individual exponent but big brother*ism*, a psychic rather than political process, that poses the danger.

When we sleep, or when we are ill, we all regress temporarily to earlier stages of development. Some of us do it when we listen to our advisers, or when we vote. All of us have had parental or other sorts of big brothers. Too many of us are eager to feel safe by blindly imitating them, or by relying upon them or their self-appointed substitutes, long past the time when such dependence is needed.

Today the opportunities to become or to find your own special sort of big brother are vastly enlarged over those of the past. Omniscient big management, big government, big labor, big religion, big news media, big movie stars—all are available to recruit us into telling everyone or being told by someone just what to do. In the past the local mayor, minister, employer, or editor who had to suffice as big brother was of such homely dimension and proximity that the ordinary little brother was able to assess their estimates against his own, and felt more free to accept or reject their pronouncements. Now the relevant realities are often both so panoramic and remote that any latent tendency to regression, encouraged from on high, is activated. Moreover, big rewards are offered for succumbing, and punishments for refusing.

These conditions demand renewed emphasis on the preservation and expansion of counteracting values. To delude ourselves that salvation lies in the direction of imposing or submitting to authoritarian dictation is to cheat ourselves and to cheat our lives of meaning. As Norman Mailer has said, ". . . at the very heart of totalitarianism is the desire to cheat life: to have the sweet taste without putting on the weight."[20]

23 Prospectancy

. . . Chance favors only the prepared minds.
　　　　　　　　　—Pasteur

Three and a half billion human beings sheathe the earth, a thin and discontinuous layer of fumbling wisdom. Among them is a smaller number of people, restlessly stirring in the wide-eyed sleep of current consciousness. Drawn together out of separate slumbers of avarice, ecstasy, mysticism, and power, these few reach to clasp one another. Slowly they are forming a frail network of fresh awareness, a delicate skeleton about which the others lie torpidly drowsing.

More and more people are alerting now. At the cockcrow of a new day for man, we are answering the call of our forward scouts, and closing in on the real dream, the fuller life of freedom and joy in the new era of abundance.

All around us, we see our ancestors, living and dead, frozen in the tracks of their lesser understanding. Now in the vanguard of the long march, it is our task to venture on until new shooting stars of sagacity leap out of us to take the lead, and the parade leaves us too behind.

Meanwhile, we have a compass to show the way, *prospectancy*.

By this neologism I want to convey the core of a new value system that fits the dimensions of reality ahead of us. It consists of a dual attitude toward human life:

Expectancy of new prospects
Prospecting for new expectations

The value systems of the past clustered about assertions that the old prospects and expectations would remain the only ones.

Where value systems of the past in general prepared man for a static reality, ours must be consciously designed for a rapidly shifting reality. Where value systems of the past in general prepared man to adopt the expectations of his parents, ours must teach him to search for new ones that master new facts.

Of course there is still an important place for the distinctions between wishes and facts which the old value systems drew so clearly. We must still help our children to know the difference. When a seven- or eight-year-old child, continuing the fantasies of earlier years, tells us that he flew his bike to Africa and back between lunch and dinner, we still need to help him regard this as a daydream and not reality. But we do not need to tell him this is impossible because "no one will *ever* be able to do that." In fact we must avoid such sweeping pronouncements, not so much to avoid damaging his imagination, the concern of many parents, as to prevent stifling his ability to apprehend onrushing reality.

For the same reason we must forgo the kind of certainty about fundamental or "eternal" truth which the old value systems imparted. In order to find the new expectations and master the new prospects we must accomplish what Bertrand Russell called the central task of man in the twentieth century, learning to live with ambiguity, and accepting that "this is the age of the suspended judgment."[1]

Have we then no guideline by which to steer our prospectant course? Not at all. We simply have no *permanent* guideline. Earlier we have seen how animals and man became organized around the basic activities of love, work, and play in quest for ever-rising levels of consciousness, freedom, and joy. We considered how man advances in this direction by harnessing intellect and character to the challenge of mastering reality. And we explored the significance of oncoming abundance in shifting the emphasis of human love, work, and play from the central social function of assuring physical survival to the central psychological function of providing self-validation. I attempted to show how, despite changes in their roles, all these factors have been characteristics of man since his beginning two million years ago, and will remain so for some time to come during his continued progression through the pages of the human agenda.

So then the question arises, is our *im*permanent guideline nothing more than a finite perpetuation of the past into the future, and can it lead us nowhere but to a replication of previous experience? At the end of this lengthy excursion are we to discover only that we have returned to where we started, to another proof that, as Alphonse Karr put it, "the more things change the more they stay the same?"[2]

Again, not at all. What we are demonstrating is that neither the broad course of life nor the specific identity of man is necessarily disrupted *merely by human acquisition of the means of producing limitless abundance.* However, even within the familiar human framework recapped above, the capacity to produce limitless abundance can in a short time thoroughly transform our lives in endless ways. To begin with, there is the ominous possibility that inadvertent misapplication of the new powers could result in extermination of all life before the new man, or other form, is created to which we in time must pass the torch. The prospectant attitude will guard against such errors by warning us early against dangerous side effects of our innovations. I am thinking here not only of the value to us of prompt recognition of such dangerous potentials of new technique as accumulation in the atmosphere of auto exhaust, or buildup of DDT in marine life. Much more crucial would have been the ability to foresee the subtle emotional disadvantages to people of destroying the psychological supports of familiar intimate neighborhoods in otherwise laudable slum clearance projects. A newer example is the unanticipated ruinous pressures on families and communities resulting from programs to empty state hospitals before provisions have been made to provide special living and working facilities for discharged schizophrenic patients. As I envision it the prospectant attitude does not involve implementing every new possibility uncovered, but rather sifting and weighing each one for the intricate tapestry of its consequences so that those acted upon will not jeopardize but enhance man's adaptation. For the foreseeable future, anyway, it seems plain that putting into action those new possibilities that may diminish zestful investment of self in love, work, and play are serious hazards to continued human life.

But let us consider what byways not incompatible with continued evolution are opened to man by abundance in collaboration with the prospectant attitude.

How many times in our individual and communal lives do we miss a vital chance because we are not expecting new prospects, or are not prepared to seize them when they appear? The ability to do so has long been recognized, although erroneously attributed to the successful seduction of Lady Luck called *serendipity*. The dictionary defines it as "an assumed gift for finding valuable or agreeable things not sought for." Careful evaluation shows that prospectancy, not fortune, is the essential component. In 1937, the Ogburn study of the next thirty years—our immediate past—failed to predict radar, the electronic computer, or the transistor.[3] Yet their separate ingredients existed at the time, awaiting the minds that could and soon did read the recipes on the human agenda.

While some people have the gift and others do not, serendipity is an acquirable trait. The history of medicine provides many illustrations. As a very young man Sigmund Freud studied the properties of cocaine, becoming fascinated with what turned out to be its medically useless and exceedingly dangerous psychological effects. Years later he realized that as a consequence of his "psychedelic" enthusiasm he had fallen a hair's breadth short of making an epochal medical discovery, the powerful local anesthetic effect of cocaine.[4] By then, his own prospectant serendipity had matured and produced out of chance observations the concepts of unconscious mental functioning which were to revolutionize not only medicine but most other aspects of human life. These episodes in Freud's development deserve the thoughtful reflection of today's drug cultists.

When Alexander Fleming looked at a bacterial culture and found suppression of germ growth surrounding a colony of penicillium mold, having been prepared for new prospects by long training, he realized the phenomenon merited investigation. Out of his study of this happenstance came the first clinically effective antibiotic, penicillin. The prospectant attitude helped penicillin's early users recognize that some patients needing the drug to overcome dangerous infections could not tolerate it because of severe allergic reactions. But the prospectant attitude was not sufficiently applied to prediction and prevention of development of penicillin-resistant strains of disease germs. The drug was given to patients who could have done well without it, the unfortunate result being the generation of more such specially dangerous organisms than was unavoidable. Insufficient prospectancy is revealed also in the steady stream of letters that come to physicians concerning prescription drugs. On orders from the Food and Drug Administration, manufacturers write to doctors, coolly withdrawing claims of therapeutic effectiveness or freedom from dangerous side effects. Sometimes they even announce the total discontinuation of sales of a drug touted as a panacea in four-color, double-spread, plastic-overlay, panegyric ads in the medical journals, which at that moment lie on the worried doctor's desk.

A serious part of the problem of use of medicines is the unprospectant insistence of patients that they be given unnecessary drugs. For years many doctors have tried to help patients see the wisdom of selecting a contraceptive other than "the pill," which decades of experience have caused them to suspect might turn out not to be as safe as the assurance of manufacturers and early researchers maintained. It has been their conviction on general medical grounds that the potential risk of using powerful hormone therapy, which acts by disrupting normal pituitary-endocrine cycles, can be justified best where there is either a *medical* need for the drug, or where the social, educational, or other circumstances of the patient make other methods of contraception unsound. For a healthy, mature, intelligent, educated, and economically secure woman and her husband, the decision to use their genitals should be accompanied by the resolve also to use their heads, in this case perhaps by willingness to put up with the admitted one-minute inconvenience of applying the vaginal contraceptives recommended for decades by gynecologists as safe. For a long time it has been disheartening to realize concretely how many such people were unable to call upon the modicum of rational self-control needed to be certain of avoiding unnecessary sickness. Recently, perhaps bolstered by increasingly frequent reports of possible serious side effects, some gynecologists tell me that they are now more successful in enlisting couples' cooperation in the interest of their own safety.

Carefully organized teams of futurologists will be necessary for the predictive and preventive application of the prospectant attitude to the biological revolution on the horizon. If we learn from past successes and mistakes, we ought to be able to extract the flesh from the thorns of the ripe prickly pear constituted by bottle gestation of babies, genetic manipulation, and life-suspension techniques discussed earlier. To do so we will need a change in human emphasis. We must learn to cultivate and respect the generalist's capacity to comprehend broad vistas ahead, as much as the specialist's ability to grasp minute details directly in front of him.

In order to actualize such foresight we may need to find new political forms, new means of nurturing healthy personality and recognizing the specially gifted, and new patterns of family organization.

How might we improve the level of participation of all our poorly informed and harried population in deciding the many issues upon which judgment must be passed? We could facilitate the continuous expression of the citizen's will through a daily poll taken on the fifty most critical local and national matters via a convenient telephone-like instrument installed in each home and connected to a central computer. Would some variety of direct programming of the brain also be valuable, perhaps information-conveying chemicals or permanently implanted electrodes stimulated during sleep? If people neglected their democratic duties, could we arrange that neither front door nor auto ignition locks would open until released by transmission of a signal from their votaphones? What would be our judgment on the proposal that busy citizens be spared nuisance by having the daily referendum taken *automatically* by tapping their permanent brain electrodes for opinion during the final hour of sleep following the nocturnal briefing? That way, assuming we could prevent electronic brainwashing and ballot-box stuffing, both the education of the voter and the recording of his preferences could be made completely independent of his *volition*, liberating him for a life of uninterrupted joy, while assuring society that it will get the best of which his mind is capable, according to the slogan "Free democracy too of drudgery."

One might wonder whether in the process we would be destroying human advance toward heightened consciousness while maintaining only the trappings of regard for the individual. And if so, *where* along this continuum should one put his traditional foot down? These are the sorts of possibilities with which one might get the most help from the prospectant attitude.

Since the individual human being is the ultimate resource of man, means are needed for preventing the dreadful deformations of personality so common at present. At bottom, many of these derive from the unfortunate fact that a baby's perceptions develop so much earlier than his powers. He experiences discomfort from hunger or cold long before he can do anything to relieve them directly, and long before he can even understand that his crying will enlist mother's help. His protracted awareness of dependence for essential food, clothing, and protection during childhood further heightens his anxiety about not being able by himself to master the stresses of life. His inability even to comprehend what his perceptions bring him causes him to spin theories that are intended to give him a feeling of security, but often result instead in generating more anxiety than they relieve. This extra anxiety he then handles by repressing not only the theories but even the perceptions themselves that give rise to it.

Consider an oversimplified illustration. A four-year-old boy who values the urinary and pleasure-giving functions of his penis may explain to himself that a little girl he sees nude has somehow lost the penis she was born with. When later he is punished for masturbating, he may anxiously conclude that this must have been the offense which provoked an adult to *cut off* the girl's penis, and that a female is therefore a castrated male. This whole web of misunderstanding may sometimes be so frightening that the child's mind sweeps it under the rug of unconsciousness, from where it is not accessible and so cannot be corrected by later education. However it nevertheless can go on emitting emergency signals that require more and more effort to repress, and thereby constitute a significant but "irrational" component of a disturbance requiring psychiatric treatment.

We must see that this result is but a miscarriage of a child's *earliest efforts at prospectancy*. If we wish to prevent such unnecessary calamities in this era of "sexual revolution," we must find ways to reshape our folkways where they may count the most, in early childhood. This does not mean adopting the sort of naïve permissiveness discussed earlier (pp. 299–300), but rather a careful revamping of both *what* we teach children and the social *context* in which it is communicated. Even before they can decipher the torrent of violence represented in the mass media, the aura (if not the fact) of violence, tension, and hostility which children feel between adults and toward themselves is the soil in which the ideas of castrating punishment germinate. In contrast, there are societies in which the relations among all people, particularly adults and children, are so arranged that a minimum of tension and hostility is encountered by the child, making it less likely that he will explain female penislessness to himself as the result of any sort of injury.

A prospectant look at our culture in this light might help us find a *sophisticated* application to our complex world of ways to help children grow up with comfortable enjoyment instead of agonizing dread of their feelings and perceptions.

Of course, we must not mistake sexual conflicts and inhibitions as the cause of all our emotional troubles. But, after all, it makes no sense to first create in childhood and then have to dissolve in adulthood the excessive barriers to eroticism which it is now the vogue to try to dismantle through various extravagant ceremonies. However, we should take care that our innovations in childhood experience do not result, as may these adult games, in the overdilution and trivialization of interpersonal relationships. Freeing the child to become a *fully developed* adult depends upon prospectancy being informed by the self-validation that proceeds from psychic intimacy with love. Perhaps one way to this objective might be modification of living arrangements to reduce isolation of families, with the deliberate provision (see pp. 151–154) of additional close parents and age-mates onto whom emotional attachments can be diffused.

We must realize too that our very neoteny, out of which arises so many of our troubles, also makes possible their cure. The long period of childhood dependence and malleability permits us to teach and train children to become almost any sort of grown people they need to be to survive and advance through the human agenda.

Another prospect that grows partly out of such possibilities is reassessment of the institution of marriage. Whereas in the past, as we have seen, people married "for better or for worse" and counted themselves lucky if they encountered occasional happiness, nowadays the expectation is that one should be able to find nearly uninterrupted happiness in a wife or husband who is not only a faithful spouse, but an accomplished helpmate, a scintillating companion, and a matchless lover. With the additional opportunities for more fun, happiness, and creativity in the future's leisured and abundant reality, the demand upon one relationship may become overpowering. Some suggest, as mentioned earlier (p. 168), that therefore marriage is doomed as a social form as its foundations in scarcity evaporate. A different answer might be changes in the *structure* of marriage, for example the various kinds of multiple marriage we hear about within which an extra individual is added to the couple, or in which two or three couples marry in a group to share their fortunes and one another.[5] Maybe several approaches will be compared. Perhaps the many startling unofficial trials going on today, emblazoned in the classified personal ads of the underground press, will become the prospectantly controlled social experiments of tomorrow. Again, the techniques that "work" in facilitating human adaptation will be those that foster self-validative psychic intimacy with love, or zestful investment of the self in the loved persons. Those who expect that multiplication of partners will subtract need for emotional maturity are sure to be disappointed.

A different road to prospectancy, having more to do with work and play, would be to find means of identifying and developing early the specific interests, aptitudes, and needs of each person. Then, instead of glumly conveying to a child that probably he must put aside his preferences in favor of learning to "make a living" at something he does not like, only to be skimpily compensated by play, we would guide him toward doing well what he most enjoys, thereby helping him contribute to an abundant society not only his work and play but the enrichment of his self-validated and satisfied personality.

A different road for finding new adventure in living might be to take advantage of great increases in leisure to expand the system of informal apprenticeships I have experimented with in a small way. For example, always intrigued by fine silver filigree jewelry, once during a vacation I found a skillful silversmith, and proposed that I become his student for a few days. At first he was struck dumb because, "In forty years of questions about metal content, price, and customs regulations no tourist has ever asked me 'How do you make it?' let alone 'Would you teach me?'" Then he accepted, and in several days delightful to both of us, using his tools, materials, and knowledge, I learned his ancient technique well enough to create a design of my own—and to enrich my life ever since. Likewise, I have taken into my practice apprentice physicians from other specialties. Not only have their patients benefited, but the doctors afterward told me that travel, literature, and their families also have proved to be sources of greater satisfaction as a result of the brief but concentrated study of human motivation and conflict.

Also interesting is that I was able to suggest to the silversmith a useful innovation, and of course my physician students had similar new ideas for me. The mutual enrichment might be even greater when the chance comes for me to spend a while with a watch repairman, and to take into my practice gifted people from widely different fields, such as architects, housewives, or farmers.

There was a time when everyone assumed that the four-minute mile was beyond human capability. A few athletes prospected for a new expectation, and found reason to believe that breaking this barrier was just a matter of the right man with the right training and attitude. Roger Bannister broke the ice. Suddenly the expectation became general, and the four-minute mile ceased to be a prospect and became a fact. Leaving aside our potential for deliberate production of genius through genetic controls, suppose we could employ the prospectant attitude only to locate new Mozarts, Einsteins, and Freuds, as well as the frontiers beyond which their gifts might carry us.

Prevention of polio, prevention of cancer, prevention of senile deterioration—these are prospects clearly inscribed on the human agenda which have been, are being, or one day will be realized. A similar sequence is men flying in the atmosphere, men landing on the moon, and men exploring the planets. Another is elimination in civilized societies of individual duels, capital punishment, and international war. Yesterday's wild dream becomes today's possibility and tomorrow's commonplace.

While acknowledging that "improvement" is part of the human past and future, some pessimists sourly maintain that essentially the condition of man's life is no better now than ever as a result of the efforts of previous generations. In response to such assertions I ask their makers to employ a little retrospection to learn whether therefore they would just as soon have lived earlier. It is not necessary to look as far back as the terror of one hundred thousand years ago. One thousand years will do. Would you really just as soon have lived when nowhere in the world was there medical help for your wife threatened by appendicitis, and hardly anywhere was there a soul who would even remonstrate mildly against a king's determination—and right—to roast you alive?

No, there seems solid basis to conclude that, for most of us in the developed nations, things are better, if often only because of the haphazard prospectancy of the past. But now that our powers are multiplying so much more rapidly we can no longer leave to happenstance which possibilities are to become actualities. If we feel it is important to eliminate war, to distribute abundance universally, or to lengthen the human lifespan, *organized* prospectancy will be required both to achieve these goals and generate personalities capable of anticipating, integrating, and mastering their consequences. In the course of such effort, we must blend with care a compound of the various ways to go which will lead to a value system adaptive to new reality. We must not permit ourselves to fall into orgies of material advance, addictions to fun, submergence in creativity for art's sake, ecstasies of the supernatural, romances with gadgets, or suicidal fratricide. The decisions required must be made on the basis of expecting those new prospects and prospecting for those new expectations which strengthen man's intellect, character, and mastery of reality; heighten his consciousness, freedom, and joy; and extend his psychic intimacy with love, work, and play.

Part II

The Quest for Blondness:
AN EXAMPLE EXPLORED

For Anne Gregory

Never shall a young man,
Thrown into despair
By those great honey-coloured
Ramparts at your ear,
Love you for yourself alone
And not your yellow hair.

But I can get a hair-dye
And set such colour there,
Brown, or black, or carrot,
That young men in despair
May love me for myself alone
And not my yellow hair.

I heard an old religious man
But yesternight declare
That he had found a text to prove
That only God, my dear,
Could love you for yourself alone
And not your yellow hair.

—W. B. YEATS

I want to be blond all over.

—Marilyn Monroe

Introduction

We have come through galaxies to suns, from suns to earth, from earth to life, from life to man, from man to love, work, and play in the past and values in the future.

Man is the one creature thus far on whose agenda it is to learn what there is to know about all things. But must we on that account next turn our attention to *the quest for blondness?* Perhaps I can best explain why it comes next on my agenda by recounting the apparently unrelated incidents through which its significance crystallized for me.

Without knowing why, several years ago I began clipping magazine ads for hair-blonding preparations. They accumulated in a file folder on my desk. When my secretary asked where they should be filed I was at a loss. The folder joined an unruly pile marked "to be classified for filing."

One summer afternoon a patient phoned a last-minute cancellation. Bracing myself, I decided to use the free hour to dispose of this collection. But first I made a note in the truant patient's record:

> Patient cancels by phone in favor of beach. "Today I'd rather bask in the sun than my neurosis." As her dream last time suggests, just now she prefers old sol to new solution.

At her last visit this fair-skinned woman had left the label of a skin bleaching cream called Crema Rusa she had brought home from Guadalajara. Mexican women friends used it to lighten their complexions. They told her it would prevent the dark freckles sunbaths always left on her face. She wanted me to find out if it was safe. I had referred her to a dermatologist.

As I replaced her record in its drawer, the label fluttered to the floor. I slipped it into an envelope which contained odds and ends relating to human pigmentation. These included an article about the use of parasols by Negroes in Africa to prevent darkening of skin by sunlight, a dream of acquiring blue eyes by contact lenses, and a reference concerning the widespread association between evil and black. I tossed the envelope onto the pile for filing.

Working through the stack of papers one day I came to the folder of blonding ads, and unaccountably found myself thinking of a professor in another department. About a year before, he had invited me to Sunday brunch and proudly introduced me to his two little girls. "These are my angels." I recalled also meeting his wife, his Swedish housekeeper, and a woman graduate student.

Uneasily I noticed that the memory of my friend and his beautiful "angels" recurred every time the folder of blonding ads came into my hands. Eventually even a hardheaded psychiatrist must listen to such persistent knocking from the netherworld. One day I opened the folder expecting to find a clue in the hair-blonding clippings.

The clue came, but it came from the unexpected appearance in the folder of the Crema Rusa label, and the items about blue eyes, suntanning, and evil/blackness. My secretary swears she did not consolidate the envelope and folder, and so do I. No matter. It is only a question of to whose unconscious the debt is owed. For all these things truly belong together.

Women want to lighten their hair, skin, and eyes in order to resemble my friend's flaxen blonds. These included, I then realized, not only his "angel" daughters, but his housekeeper and graduate student, not to mention his wife. With this realization came release from the unbidden fantasy about my friend's blond harem, and an answer to my secretary's question. All the material formerly in two containers henceforth would be filed under "The Quest for Blondness."

Now I began to wonder why there is such widespread association between lightness and goodness, and between darkness and evil. And why such a dark-complexioned man collected only blonds, and why my patient who strove to be unblemished white also ambivalently roasted herself "black" in the sun. And much more. By then I had begun to write this book and pushed all this material aside.

Years later I found myself again pulling out the "Blondness" material, not knowing why at the moment. Gradually I realized that an astonishing number of themes touched upon earlier intersect in the arena of blondness and feelings about it. Attitudes toward such diverse matters as daytime sunlight and nighttime darkness, biology and the new biology, relationships between the sexes and between the races, the problems of youth and age, deity and demon, good and evil, survival and extinction—all are elucidated in the glow of the quest for blondness.

Also, during days in the library it gradually became clear to me that for clarity the many dimensions of the *evolution of values* needed now to be explored in relation to a concrete example.

Blondness is an aspect of human wishes and conflict which is interesting to everybody, but totally blinding to few. And here is an area in which one can try out ideas that are tentative, ideas that could be disproved without doing serious harm to the prospectant method in whose service they were mustered and related.

So now we will look prospectantly at complexion, especially color of hair, a superficial human phenomenon intrinsically of little consequence, and yet one that emotion loads beyond its depth. Just *because* it matters little in itself, but is familiar and provocative to everyone, it suits our need to find a model topic upon which to practice focusing the pencil of light we kindled from curved outer space to illumine the values of convoluted inner man.

Every human being at one time or another is concerned with physical appearance, and wishes to change his own. Since physical appearance is so much more crucial to women, they are most likely to do something to change it. Everyday experience suggests that the most frequent change undertaken by women, and noticed by men, is an alteration of hair color. By far the most frequent change is to a lighter shade.

A woman's fantasies and dreams may disclose an intricate pattern of conflicts about carrying out her plan. Years of daydreams and scores of tentative tintings to lighter shades often precede a woman's going the whole way and at last becoming—a *blond*.

24 Blondness: First Views

Images

To understand the quest for blondness we must consider the blond image. An image in this sense is a pattern of commonly accepted cliché preconceptions about the characteristics of a person based on limited and often irrelevant information. This collection of biases, prejudices, and facts when seen from a distance is readily assembled into a total "picture" or image of that person.

The image relegates an individual to a recognizable "type." But it has no necessary relationship to his actual characteristics or even those of the group to which he belongs.

It is always difficult to accept the fact that an image in which you believe is invalid. For example, many an educated person would unhesitatingly reject as absurd the ancient Greek image that typed the person with epileptic convulsions as divine, or the medieval Italian image of the turbaned East Indian as possessor of the evil eye, or even the still current Western image that imputes evil to black cats. Yet he will stubbornly defend the accuracy of the image of the black *person* which portrays him as biologically more primitive than the white.

He may cite all sorts of anecdotes about Negro behavior as evidence of biological primitiveness. When you offer proof that this behavior is not universal among or confined to blacks, and therefore must be socially rather than racially acquired, your adversary may condescendingly point out that "you just don't understand the problem," and then try to dignify his superstitions by adding the circular reasoning "after all, where there is so much smoke there must be fire."

Typecasting in the theater and movies is conducted according to these images. Everyone knows that not all ministers' wives are prim and puritanical, not all psychiatrists are bearded and Viennese, not all private detectives are heroic and amorous, and not all blonds are dizzy playmates. Yet there is a market for these readily recognizable stereotypes. Why do people welcome them?

We all know people who use such images to gratify unrealizable wishes —say, to be a dashing hero or a cuddly sex kitten. But equally important is our old acquaintance, the need to know and understand, and therefore be able to predict and control. Since people are so variable and difficult to figure out, it helps an insecure person quell his anxiety about what others are going to do if he feels he can foresee their behavior. The catch is that the image may help him quell anxiety without really informing him about people at all. Thus images share with alchemy, astrology, and many organized religions the comforting but stupefying promise of revealing definite knowledge about the currently unknowable.

Unfortunately, we cannot think without using words based on images. Nouns are words that designate images. How would we manage if one day words such as "automobile" or "physician" or "woman" had no reliable predictive ability? We may soon find out, if industry converts the automobile for use in air and underwater. We may soon find out if the current trend of teaching computers to be doctors develops much further. Your general practitioner, or even your psychiatrist, may come to mean a manufactured collection of electronic equipment rather than a person.

And we will soon find out if the potential of the new biology is exploited to produce human hermaphrodites, thereby melding the meanings of man and woman. Semanticists have shown in detail how essential and yet how risky is our reliance upon such seemingly stable but actually transitory images.[1]

Another dangerous aspect of images is that people use them not only to predict the characteristics and behavior of others but also to mold *themselves* in order to manipulate others, as in the ominous instance of the contrived personalities of some politicians. You can also observe this process in the grave demeanor of the lawyer elevated to the bench, the stalwart posture of the rookie cop, and the prattling emptiness of some very pretty girls. By becoming what their images specify they avoid having to realize the urgency of becoming "themselves."

And so it is with the blond image.

The Blond Image

You can hardly go through a day in any American city without encountering the quest for blondness. Every crop of new movies includes a disproportionate share of astonishingly blond actresses. Airline billboards present a more generous assortment of smiling blond stewardesses than ever become your jetmates. Travel folders for Scandinavia suggest that the genes for dark pigment have migrated south. Your friends spend hours in beauty salons deciding which of dozens of shades of blondness is right, and then being stripped down and toned up to it. Magazine ads assure you that blonds have more fun, and so it would be reasonable to prefer to live your one life as a blond. And the special interest of men in blondness shows as clearly in their behavior while walking down a street as in their associations during psychoanalysis.

It is easy to dismiss such a trend as too frivolous a matter to deserve investigation. But that was not the viewpoint of the inventors of Aphrodite (Venus) and Diana, nor of Helen of Troy and her admirers, nor of their chroniclers in poetry and paint during several thousand years. Yet the literature of history, sociology, and anthropology seems devoid of any comprehensive study of the blond.

From a *clinical* viewpoint, the quest for blondness becomes a severe compulsion for some members of both sexes. Yet my search through the literature of psychology, psychiatry, and psychoanalysis did not disclose a single reference to it. This is a strange omission considering how much effort has been devoted to detailed analyses of impulses much less common, such as the urge to wear the clothes of the opposite sex.

It may be safer to direct inquiry toward interests and behavior that are strange and uncommon than to direct it toward those that are ordinary and involve many people.

Nevertheless, the spreading preoccupation with blondness, backed up by several thousand years of experimentation,[2] so many memorable ladies of Wagner's "Ring Cycle," and five decades of movie heroines, should not be neglected. For here we have one of those fascinating intersections of biology and culture from which we can learn endlessly by watching the traffic in various directions.

The very word "blond" evokes an immediate picture of feminine youth, sexiness, and beauty. Along with these attractions go some secondary features. She is *healthy*, meaning vibrant, energetic, fun-loving, cheerful, and, above all, sweet, unhostile, and uncomplaining. She is *warm*, and is noncompetitive with her man, meaning she admires him, enjoys making love with him, and is inexpressibly delightful to him in bed. She is in some way *unearthly*, her fair skin and golden hair somehow seeming infused with sunlight and blue sky, and therefore evoking the reverence one has for "nature." As an entranced patient put it in describing his blond fiancée, "She's one of our greatest natural resources, like—the Redwoods, or Grand Canyon."

For the unsentimental—and the naturally brunette—I must reiterate: We are considering not the blond *facts,* but the blond *image.*

The blond image is always eloquently erotic. However, it spans a wide spectrum of personality types, from the child-charm of Marie Wilson and Marilyn Monroe on one extreme, passing through the cool aplomb of Grace Kelly in the midzone, to the hard sophistication of Jean Harlow and Mae West on the other. The image is glamorous, plainly not that of a reliable, mature homebody, but is always wholesome in the sense of fresh air, honesty, kindness, or at least something that could be considered "basic decency."

Despite occasional apparent exceptions, the blond image is not mysterious, devious, menacing, or threatening. It depicts the heroine, *not* the heavy. For example, even in Harlow's gun-moll roles you knew that she was really a good girl underneath and that given half a chance she would have done right.

On the other hand, the brunette image, which encompasses the devoted, stable, mature-wife-and-mother aspects of femininity, includes also the "darker" characteristics, exemplified by Theda Bara and the Dragon Lady.[3] International-spy types, arrogant society ladies, and mean stepmothers usually are typed as brunette.

Perhaps you have noticed a peculiar discrepancy in the blond image. It connotes both the innocence and asexuality of childhood and the enthusiastic genital sexual abandon of maturity. We must follow a complicated road before a tentative explanation of this paradox can be offered.

The Vocal Image

The blond image is predominantly visual. There are other images which derive from other senses. Consider the world of opera. It has always been based mainly on a subcategory of auditory image we could call the vocal image. Despite recently increased attention to singers' appearance, opera is a theatrical realm in which the dominant images remain vocal rather than visual. Included in the vocal image, parallel to the blond and brunette images, are a group of subimages we could call coloratura image, tenor image, or bass image, and so on. Are these vocal images used for typecasting in opera in a way parallel to visual images in motion pictures?

What voice usually sings the role of hero and lover? Tenor, of course. And which voice is assigned the role of ingenue heroine and beloved? Soprano, of course. Father and mother, and other older people are usually represented by baritones and basses, mezzo-sopranos and contraltos. When these stereotypes are reversed it usually expresses a dramatic or comic intent. The lyric tenor of the old Faust in Boïto's *Mefistofele* contrasts pathetically with his aged feebleness, and presages his romantic appeal when later he is restored to youth. Or take the comic tenor role in Offenbach's *The Tales of Hoffman,* often sung by an elderly tenor whose wobbly voice contrasts comically with the strong tone of the younger tenor singing the role of Hoffman. Very rarely is the conventional image departed from so far as to make a coloratura soprano the heavy, as is the case in the magnificent characterization of the Queen of the Night in Mozart's *The Magic Flute.* The effect sought, and sometimes achieved, is to present the pyrotechnics of her aria with a menacing ferocity which is heightened by the *incongruity* of the high thin voice we usually associate with an ingenue in love.

Ordinarily the strength of these vocal images is so great as to outweigh visual images completely, so that we usually accept without comment, or even much notice, the round tenor being half a foot shorter than his towering soprano lady, or twenty years older than his bass father. Where does the compelling power of these images arise?

Image and Biological Vocal Maturation

The answer brings us back to the crossroad of man's biological and cultural facets, from which vantage point we should also be able to learn something important about the blond image.

Babies are born with high-pitched voices which deepen and strengthen moderately and slowly during childhood. Then at puberty the voice undergoes a sudden deepening, much more marked in the male. In adulthood, this change may recede somewhat. But ordinarily from then on gradual lowering changes continue which bring the voice to full maturity in the thirties, and usually deepen the tone even further into the fifties and sixties. This developmental process is what singers have referred to for generations as a gradual "darkening in color."[4] This change can be followed easily by listening to a series of recordings made from youth to middle age of singers as dissimilar as Caruso and Crosby. A voice that retains its youthful tone is said to have kept its "light color."

So the very process of physical vocal maturation described causes us to associate higher-pitched voices with youth and deeper ones with age. And it is the force of this elemental biological sequence which is tapped by operatic vocal images so eloquently that we often can ignore grotesque violations of otherwise crucial visual images.

In passing, we might wonder why the romantic hero is usually cast as a tenor, the "lighter" male voice, and therefore, seemingly the least masculine. The obvious first answer is that passionate lovers are usually young. Beyond this, there is something feminine in the young lover which allows him to identify with his beloved. He projects this feminine component of himself onto her and loves it in her. So the tenor voice signifies both the youthful and the feminine aspects of the hero.[5]

But why the association between youthful tone quality and light color? Or between aged tone quality and dark color? On the answer to this question also hinges a deep significance of the blond image. But first we must shift again to our wide-angle lens on human affairs to achieve the perspective with which to grasp the significance of the biological roots of the blond image.

25 *The Blond Image and Light versus Dark*

Beginnings

Modern man, it is said, like primitive man has a universal tendency to fear the darkness of night, with its cold and concealment of dangers. In every culture we can find evidence of a resultant association between nighttime darkness and danger or evil which is elaborated into an attitude toward light and dark in general.

These attitudes go back at least as far as the oldest existing written records, nearly five thousand years. The blond image apparently was crystallized in them as early as 3066 B.C. when Queen Nitocris of Egypt was described as "the noblest and most beautiful woman, fair in colour."[1] In her footsteps came the attitudes, myths, gods, and poets of the Assyrians[2] (whose men powdered their black hair with gold dust),[3] Babylonians, Sumerians, Akkadians, Hebrews, Greeks, Romans (whose custom of dyeing hair long survived their fall),[4] Hindus, Persians, Arabs, Negroes, Japanese (who today are among Clairol's best customers for blonding preparations),[5] Chinese, Polynesians, Turks, American Indians, Norse, English, Germans, and Americans. Despite occasional minor exceptions, as their literatures disclose, all of them associated these characteristics in various combinations: light complexion or hair, sun, light, day, fire, heat, gold, beauty, white, high, heaven, divinity, right, truth, virtue, purity, good, holiness, wisdom, perfume, health, superiority, fertility, and life.[6]

In contrast, these same disparate human groups associated these characteristics in various combinations: dark complexion or hair, night, darkness, black, cold, ugliness, dreariness, low, wrong, falsehood, impurity, bad, filth, noxious odor, evil, ignorance, snake, dragon, witch, fiend, devil, hell, inferiority, left-handedness, disease, pestilence, and death.[7]

Thus many peoples and people have substituted mystically strengthened superstition for judgment about some of their most fundamental concerns. Ironically, even such a demystifier as Feuerbach was under the unconscious sway of the mystic equation of white with good when he wrote the expression, ". . . the unmystified pure, white truth."[8]

It appears that the primordial love of daylight and fear of nighttime darkness almost everywhere may have been elaborated into irrational adulation of light people and disdain of dark people. A particularly striking example of this trend is the myth shared by such widely separated groups as the Aztecs, the Boshongos of the Belgian Congo, and the Magi tribe of the Philippine Islands that predicts the coming to earth of a white-skinned god.[9] One instance is Quetzalcoatl, a sun god of the pre-Aztecs who later became "Lord of the Dawn" and "The Morning Star." He was expected to return to his people in flowing white garb, to lift their oppression, and to bestow arts and culture,[10] while an evil god was believed connected with the evening star. These three cultivated peoples were predisposed to conquest by handfuls of white-skinned European pillagers whom they mistook for gods. The same attitudes persist widely today. For example, a young woman Peace Corps returnee reported being shocked by a self-belittling remark by the mayor of the Philippine village in which she had served. In his welcome to the volunteers he stated: "And I hope your blond young men will improve us by leaving some of their seeds behind."

Growings

The era of scarcity has always placed a premium upon gold, metallic or tonsorial. Whatever other meanings this evaluation has in terms of adulation of light and so on, it must at least in part have been a reaction to the rarity of gold.

Apparently there has never been enough of the precious metal or halo to go around. As a result, counterfeiting of both has often been popular. In fact, blond hair was so much desired that in various cultures it was felt worthwhile to employ powdered gold itself to achieve the effect, both on living heads and on sculptures.[11]

But apparently there also has always been a marked ambivalence toward gold and blonds. Perhaps the scarcity of both has engendered a "sour grapes" attitude. And perhaps horror at the many battles fought over gold and blonds helps account for this widespread ambivalence toward both. Or perhaps the blond image offers better enlightenment, as we will see later. At any rate, in all literatures one can find stories attributing a literal or figurative curse to gold and the urge to accumulate it. Likewise, blond hair and the urge to acquire or become a blond has been "denigrated" throughout the centuries.

Greek women who dyed their hair with saffron and other substances were criticized mercilessly. Menander, a Greek poet of the fourth century B.C., wrote: "Now get out of this house, for no chaste woman ought to make her hair yellow."[12]

At one time Roman prostitutes were required to dye their hair yellow. In the early first century lusty Messalina, third wife of Tiberius Claudius Drusus, capitalized on this licentious association by wearing a provocative blond wig as a disguise while on her nightly adventures. Apparently it worked to stimulate men but not to conceal her identity for it was always gallantly returned the following day. Although she had fooled no one, she had used her political power successfully to bring a measure of respectability—and fashionability—to yellow hair. However, her contemporary, Martial, was not reconciled. Remaining steadfast in his devotion to the pure characteristics of the blond image, he wrote of her: "Her toilet table contained a hundred lies; and while she was in Rome, her hair was blushing by the Rhine. A man was in no condition to say he loved her, for what he loved in her was not herself, and that which was herself was impossible to love."[13] Even then, blonds—at least, genuine blonds—were expected not to lie! True to his position, but less implacably stern, Martial wrote of another "liar":

> The golden hair that Galla wears
> Is hers—who would have thought it?
> She swears 'tis hers, and true she swears,
> For I know where she bought it.[14]

Apparently today's contradictory expectations were implicit in the blond image even then. While being irresistibly attractive because of their delightful sunny coloring, blonds still were expected to be chaste, or at least faithful. Above all they were expected to be honest.

The first blonds in Greece probably were brought as slaves and may have been sold as prostitutes. Women, jealous of their exotic appeal, and men, afraid or unable to enjoy them perhaps because their status as public sex objects conflicted offensively with the cherished blond image, might well have turned against the powerful unconscious trends in themselves that made them admire blonds. They could then have decided that blondness in itself is *bad*, a snare and deceit and therefore should become thereafter the badge of that most despised deceitful group whose practice it is to feign response in every act of "love": the whores. It probably was this tradition of blonding prostitutes that Messalina found useful in her nocturnal misalliances. The irony is that, as is happening today, a quality and behavior that is at first beloved is then scorned, only to be reembraced by the "good" people when one powerful figure readopts it. On such dynamisms are current cosmetic fortunes made.

Crystallizings

Lest anyone dismiss these widespread phenomena as the product only of the narcissism of Nordic people, it must be reiterated that the literatures of peoples of all colors contain many references to the presumed superiority of white skin and blond hair. Especially prominent are such attitudes in the various sacred writings. One substantiating passage from Dr. Eric Berne must suffice:

> . . . In oriental cultures, largely the product of dark-haired, dark-complexioned people, the same condition prevails. Among the ancient Hindus, along with the worship of brightness went the worship of the cow and of milk, the latter equated with semen in the case of golden-haired Agni, the god of fire. To ancient Persia, Mithra with his golden hair and white steed and vestments brought heat, light, fertility, health, wisdom, and holiness. The arch enemy Angra Mainyu was the creator of evil and ugliness, thieves and wild beasts. Even the dark Mohammed in his famous Nocturnal Ascension to Jerusalem saw Jesus and the Angel Gabriel both as blondes.[15]

Descending to the secular, consider this passage from F. Scott Fitzgerald, who has characters say:

> "We took the year-books for the last ten years and looked at the pictures of the senior council. I know you don't think much of that august body, but it does represent success here in a general way. Well, I suppose only about thirty-five per cent of every class here are blonds, are really light—yet *two-thirds* of every senior council are light. We looked at pictures of ten years of them, mind you; that means that out of every *fifteen* light-haired men in the senior class *one* is on the senior council, and of the dark-haired men it's only one in *fifty*."
>
> "It's true," Burne agreed. "The light-haired man *is* a higher type, generally speaking. I worked the thing out with the Presidents of the United States once, and found that way over half of them were light-haired—yet think of the preponderant number of brunettes in the race."
>
> "People unconsciously admit it," said Amory. "You'll notice a blond person is *expected* to talk. If a blond girl doesn't talk we call her a 'doll'; if a

light-haired man is silent he's considered stupid. Yet the world is full of 'dark silent men' and 'languorous brunettes' who haven't a brain in their heads, but somehow are never accused of the dearth."[16]

In the West especially, we still grow up today propagandized by our extensive literatures to connect fairness with goodness and darkness with evil, from the biblical account of the curse of Ham onward.[17] The message relating fairness to truthfulness and beauty, particularly to feminine beauty, was given tongue long ago, and heralded artistically across Europe by singers, writers, and painters. The conventional ideal of the troubadours was "a lady whose skin is white as milk . . . her hair . . . shimmering with a sheen of finest gold." In the most ancient Spanish romances the ideal face is white, the hair of "pure gold." In Germany of the twelfth and thirteenth centuries, the beautiful woman had white cheeks and hair "like gold." In twelfth- and thirteenth-century France, "Nicollete had fair hair . . . so white was she," and another idolized lady had hair so brilliant "the fascinated eye could scarce distinguish the gold of the hair from the gold of the comb." An Irish lass had skin whiter than snow and "glossy golden hair" that reached the calf of her leg. In Italy, Petrarch's Laura and the ladies of other poets, including Boccaccio and Niphus, are white-skinned and golden-haired. Boccaccio's ideal was later visualized in the paintings of Titian. Marie de France, who spent much of her life in twelfth-century England, describes a beautiful woman: ". . . the face white . . . the head curly and blonde; the gleam of gold thread was less bright than her hair beneath the sun." In sixteenth-century France, Gabriel de Minut wrote a sixty-page accolade to the fair-haired beauty of a seventy-year-old woman![18]

The legacy of legend is the art of poets. There is a text one can quote selectively to prove any premise. But the association of light with good and beauty, especially feminine, and darkness with the opposite, is unmistakable.

Ben Jonson sings these love lines about Charis:

> Do but look on her hair, it is bright
> As Love's star when it riseth:
>
> . . . .
>
> O so white! O so soft! O so sweet is she![19]

John Milton tells us his subscription to the age-old association between whiteness and innocent purity in poeticizing a dream of his dear wife: "[She] Came vested all in white, pure as her mind . . ."[20] And he leaves no doubt of his acceptance of the gloomy image of night's darkness in "L'Allegro," where it is associated with depression, loneliness, horror:

Hence, loathed Melancholy,
Of Cerberus and blackest Midnight born,
In Stygian cave forlorn[21]

The case for feminine beauty as whiteness has not been put more eloquently than by Robert Herrick in "To Electra":

More white than whitest Lillies far,
Or Snow, or whitest Swans you are:
More white than are the whitest Creames,
Or Moone-light tinselling the streames:
More white than *Pearls*, or *Juno's* thigh;
Or *Pelops* Arme of Ivorie.
True, I confesse; such Whites as these
May me delight, not fully please:
Till, like *Ixion's* Cloud, you be
White, warme, and soft to lye with me.[22]

Edmund Spenser in *The Faerie Queene* surrounds his fair beauty with good but lesser white creatures and emphasizes the dolorous aspects of black:

A louely Ladie rode him faire beside,
Upon a lowly Asse more white then snow,
Yet she much whiter, but the same did hide
Under a vele, that wimpled was full low,
And ouer all a blacke stole she did throw,
As one that inly mourned . . .[23]

The blondness of the feminine ideal is documented endlessly. Here Milton in *Paradise Lost*, in a rare idealization of Eve, makes her a blond in contrast to a darker Adam:

. . . and Hyacinthine locks
Round from his parted forelock manly hung
Clustering, but not beneath his shoulders broad:
She, as a veil down to the slender waist,
Her unadorned golden tresses wore . . .[24]

And the fair beauty she had in life is present still in dead Lenore's blond hair for Edgar Allan Poe:

The life upon her yellow hair, but not within her eyes—
The life still there, upon her hair, the death
   upon her eyes.[25]

Chaucer describes the Carpenter's young wife as having a glow exceeding that of a newly minted gold coin:

> Fair was this yonge wyf . . .
> Ful brighter was the shynyng of hir hewe
> Than in the Tour the noble yforged newe.[26]

This usage indicates that the reference of fair to complexion was understood, if not crystallized, in the fourteenth century.

Belinda is a white-blond in Alexander Pope's *The Rape of the Lock* and

> Nourished two Locks, which graceful hung behind
> In equal Curls, and well conspir'd to deck
> With shining Ringlets the smooth Iv'ry Neck.
>
> . . . .
>
> Fair Tresses Man's Imperial Race insnare,
> And Beauty draws us with a single Hair . . .[27]

Goethe has Mephistopheles warn Faust of Lillith:

> Beware lest you be caught in her fair tresses,
> The ornament she deems of all most rare.
> If with them a young man should ensnare,
> Not soon will he be freed from her caresses.[28]

One can even find more sentimentalized versions of the same ideas in the nineteenth-century German poets Heine, Scheurlin, Reinick, Gertz, and Hibbel.

Most dolls have blond hair and blue eyes. Most of the good princesses and fairies illustrated in the stories we read are blonds. Popular versions of Mother Goose, the tales of Lang, the Brothers Grimm, and Hans Christian Andersen concur. Even Alice in Wonderland, originally described and illustrated as dark, has been transformed into a blond despite the objections of Tenniel, the original illustrator.[29] Whoever heard of a blond witch?[30] Except in the film *The Wizard of Oz,* where she is a good witch. The wicked witch is dark.[31]

The myths and fairly tales of northern Europe are sprinkled with good blonds and bad brunettes. Bergman's film *The Virgin Spring*[32] depicts a medieval Swedish legend which epitomizes the convention of associating goodness with the fair-haired girl and badness with the dark-haired one.[33]

A glance through today's popular magazines confirms that the blond image is still being trumpeted. I randomly scanned fourteen consecutive ads that used women to promote: a computer introduction service, contact lenses, bathroom fixtures, menstrual tampons, margarine, perfume, deodorant, suntan lotion, embroidered bedspreads, an automobile, electric heat, and pool chemicals. All but the last two were blonds. Electric heat apparently called for a domestic brunette, and at poolside lovely dry chlorine was gracefully poured by a ravishing blond while nasty liquid chlorine was gurgled into the water by a hideous black-clad dark-haired witch.

Yes, there is today an equally widespread *and equally irrational* series of associations with darkness. All the same sources tend to represent evil characters as dark-skinned and dark-haired. Of course, there are also the opposite associations of pallid whiteness with death, and darkness with comforting envelopment in the womb.[34] But especially in the fanatic detergent morality of our culture, evil and dark and bad odor are still associated in the minds of most people.

"Fair"

The English word "fair" has accumulated many meanings over the centuries. In an antecedent of English, in about A.D. 800 it designated beauty in the sense "she was fair to see." About 1200 it took on application to weather as "a fair day." A century later it got the meaning of equitability as in "a fair bargain." In the 1300s it also became a noun denoting a commercial enterprise as in "county fair." Around 1400 it began to signify women as in "fair sex." In the 1600s it was used to express honesty as in "fair play." And finally in the 1700s, what was probably its earliest meaning, no doubt surviving intervening centuries, became crystallized as the appellation for blondness, as in Hull's description: "One is a fair, the other a brunet."[35]

It seems no accident that a word originally standing for physical beauty should pass through so many intermediate meanings, all of which are favorable, only to wind up again representing specially favored physical beauty. Such a progression may be the most recent if not the most rational steps of a theme long ago entered into the human agenda, the forthcoming stages of which we will be forced to take responsibility for since they are increasingly coming under our conscious control.

26 *Pathology*

Community

The dominant white community in the United States even today largely accepts the archaic connections of light and dark, acts on them, and often writes and illustrates its school books and children's books in conformity with them. The blond image's weight in determining attitudes toward racial differences is evident in various examples such as Mighels' revealing nineteenth-century mythologizing of the origin of the "white race":

> She was about three years old and as white as milk. Her hair fell about her like a cloak of spun gold, her eyes were deeply blue and her lips and cheeks of the richest rose color.

> And if there be some accursed villains of the WHITE race amongst us be assured that beneath the white skin there is a heart that belongs to another race.[1]

When social custom ramifies and intensifies an ancient and culturally resonated fear into a "black image," it is little wonder that sometimes unhappy Negro children try desperately to wash the black from their skins.[2]

Among the erroneous images concerning Negroes which are given unwarranted credence today is the one that characterizes them, particularly the men, as being more sexually powerful than the white. The endemic hostility toward Negro men among white southern men often largely represents fear that the image is accurate, while the corresponding fear of Negro men among white women often largely represents hope that it is. When white southern men discuss it at all, they commonly rationalize the alleged sexual superiority of Negro men as being the natural outgrowth of the supposed primitivity of Negroes mentioned earlier. That whites fortify their social and economic dominance with this fiction obviously does nothing to substantiate it.

Clearly, it would be oversimplifying the Nazi preoccupation with blondness to attempt to derive it from primordial fear of darkness, even if we add the more recent cultural inheritances already described as well as other economic, historical, and psychopathological roots of Hitler's "Aryan" delusion. But even after they are included, some part of the significance of Nazi ideology remains obscure. That part stems from the blond image and its emphasis on fairness and youth. This biological connection will be explored later.

It would be intriguing to follow the connections between the blond image and the homosexual elements in purportedly "masculine" Nazi ideology. It would also be revealing to learn how it was possible for a black-haired Bavarian to lead a modern nation into psychic and military ruin on the basis of a blond-superman typology that not only many of them but Hitler himself did not share.

Clinic

What evidence shows up in a psychiatrist's office of these irrationalities that have permeated almost every culture and continent for at least forty-four centuries? Aside from those related to the blond image, there are many derived from its obverse.

As a child grows up we train him carefully to replace his eager pleasure in the dark and "dirty" product of his bowel with socially acceptable abhorrence of dirt.[3]

A six-year-old girl was brought to me suffering from nightmares which began shortly after a Mexican housekeeper joined the household. The parents were especially rigorous in their insistence upon anal cleanliness. But they were otherwise liberal people, and were consternated when during treatment the child's bad dreams were replaced with openly expressed disgust at the housekeeper's "pooh-skin." Fortunately, with help they were able to surmount their own fecal preoccupations, permitting the child in her treatment also to ease the severity of her unconscious fascination-dread conflict involving feces and dirt. In time, the girl brushed aside such irrelevancies and found her way to the reality of affection for a warm, loving, dark-skinned woman.

A young actress came to me complaining of loss of appetite and sleep for a month, during which period she also gradually lost interest in everything, and seemed to be slipping into a depression.

She had always been known as "Sunbeam," her cheery personality being regarded as exactly the right one for a blond. All through school and several work years she had been "luckier than all my brunette friends." Now she was becoming one of the neglected.

All this had followed dyeing her hair dark brown for a film role. "It's alright while I'm working. But I want to die when I see that dreary head in my own bathroom mirror." She insisted there was no alternative till the film was completed. At the second session when her dreams, too, began to intimate suicide, with her permission I phoned the director, inquiring whether she might be allowed to lighten her own hair and finish the role wearing a brunette wig. He agreed and that same day sent her to a beautician.

The next day she felt too well to be troubled with psychotherapy. I had lost the chance to help her achieve a more sturdy emotional balance because a reasonable approximation of her natural hair color had restored precisely her usual buoyant optimism and "health."

A gifted young man in his late twenties came to see me about his "love life." It had consisted since early teens of a series of painful crushes on girls who, although sometimes equally attracted to him, in the end always turned out unsuitable as potential wives. The problem ranged from religious disagreement to irreconcilable attitudes toward other races, with instances of alcoholism, mutual boredom, chronic mental illness, gold-digging, and frigidity in between. This diversity puzzled me because usually one can find some obvious pattern in the repeated failures.

Carlo and his two-years-younger sister had grown up in an intense immigrant Sicilian family in which the sudden explosive rages of father and anguished hand-wringing whimpers of mother had been the background music against which their sensitive thoughtful natures had developed. At puberty, in search of tranquility, the girl decided to become a nun, and later had joined a cloistered order. My patient thought of becoming a monk in the same pursuit, but was deflected as it turns out by having been infatuated with a little girl when he was five.

He brought her up one day almost casually, but my attention was alerted because his affection for her was the only information he had revealed about his early attachments. She was the delicate and demure daughter of a neighborhood drive-in proprietor at whose soda fountain one sultry summer he "fell in love with the girl next door."

Her father and mother were Scandinavian, and over the fence that separated their backyards (for she really was the girl next door) Carlo glimpsed a homelife that seemed to him as serene as his was volcanic. He loved her family and the gentle dignity of their concern for one another as much as he loved Kirsten. But in a few weeks they all moved to Canada and he was heartbroken.

Two years later he fell in love again. It was almost the same story. Except that this time the romance ended for Carlo with a more painful shock. His beloved tied a matchbook to her cat's collar and lit it, laughing gleefully as it dashed away in terror. Much to her disappointment, what she regarded as clever forever destroyed his interest. For she was supposed to be as "sweet and angelic" as Kirsten.

Twice more he loved briefly, the second time at a distance and vainly all through his twelfth and thirteenth years, for the girl did not respond. Then at seventeen came the romance he had initially reported to me as his first, and which ended on the shoals of religious difference.

He brought me pictures of his most recent amour, and while looking at the conventionally pretty face, I asked if his family had a photo album. This in itself is not unusual for me, as often a series of snapshots has proven helpful in therapy. But it was not clear to me why the idea occurred just then.

A box of unmounted photos gave us glimpses of eight of his loves, although none of Kirsten. From looking at the others I was able to describe her myself, for quite without his awareness Carlo had selected all her successors, including the one whose photo he had shown me first, on the basis of their concordance with the blond image. Here was the warp and woof of the pattern that had escaped me. Until I called it to his attention, he had been unaware of the unrelenting blondness of his loves, because in his Sicilian family loving outside of the ethnic group had been profoundly taboo.

Kirsten had been first in his heart, and in his life so short a time that it had been easy to overlook or ignore her defects. She had incarnated for him the blond image which our culture's five millennia and his five years of strife had taught him to crave.

This is not the place to detail his further treatment. But it must be mentioned that he is contentedly married to a medium-dark-haired woman, although a reproduction of his favorite painting, Botticelli's "Birth of Venus," still hangs in his study, and for a long time his hobby was collecting illustrations of Harriet Beecher Stowe's Little Eva.

27 Blondness: Further Views

The association between darkness and masculinity is a bridge back to the biological root of the blond image with which we began.

The same myths and fairy tales that cast the heroine as a blond usually specify that the hero is dark. Similarly, most of the leading men in motion pictures are dark.

Masculinity is associated not just with darkness but with tallness. The hero is tall and dark. The heroine often is correspondingly small and light. It is this size aspect of image that we must sometimes overlook in opera in favor of the vocal image.

Why is masculinity so firmly associated with tallness and femininity with smallness? After all, while it is true that on the average men are taller than women, there is normally great range of height in both sexes, so that it is commonplace to see masculine men who are smaller than feminine women. And why is masculinity associated with darkness and femininity with lightness? After all, there is a great range of pigment in both sexes, and many highly feminine women are dark while many masculine men are light.

We all know of the sufferings in high school of the short boy who feels unmasculine and the tall girl who feels unfeminine. But not everyone has seen, as I have, a towheaded adolescent boy who startles his family by darkening his hair to get rid of his "feminine" appearance. Incidentally, you will grasp immediately, as I did, why another family whose boy *bleaches* his hair was not startled but dismayed. Intuitively we all recognize that, however unexpected it may be, the appearance of darker hair on a boy brings him closer to the masculine image, whereas the appearance of blond hair on a boy moves him toward the feminine image.

Since it shows up more, a man whose head, face, and body hair are black seems to have *more* hair, and therefore to be more masculine. "The

Hairy Ape"[1] epitomizes masculinity. And Samson's strength dwelt in his hair. In view of this, why don't adults welcome young men wearing their hair long? Provided it were dark, long hair would seem to fit well with the masculine image. Is rejection of it simply a result of the fashion that associates long hair with the feminine image?

Probably not. Notice the subtle difference in the quality of hostility toward the idea of a man's bleaching his hair versus wearing it long. The male reaction toward a man questing to be blond is more likely to be derision, whereas male long hair elicits forthright anger. It is the length rather than the color of male hair that is most likely to provoke the high school principal's prohibition. This difference is one indicator that blonding is interpreted as a partial *retreat* from masculinity, whereas growing long hair is interpreted as *assertion* of masculinity, and in a Samsonesque form school administrators find particularly challenging as they try to prevent their temples from being demolished. And remember that when the rebellious Three Musketeers were sporting their long hair, peasant humility was expressed by modestly shorn locks.

While man's ancient legends, traditions, and fear of the dark afford us some understanding of gender images, here too they do not seem adequate to explain the widespread *force* of the images. Our inquiry leads us again back to biology. The *process of maturation,* as it has in our exploration of vocal images, will give us the clue we need.

Image and Biological Pigment Maturation

Many babies of all races are born with lighter skins than they will have as adults. More babies are born with light eyes and blond hair than ever reach maturity as blonds.[2] Some babies' eyes will turn brown in the first months of life, while their hair may gradually darken over the first one to five years of childhood. Others who reach adolescence with light brown hair will have dark brown hair by middle life. A much smaller group remain light all their lives. On the other hand, no normal babies are born with dark skin, eyes, or hair and then gradually lighten as they grow up.[3] Therefore, we associate blondness with youth and darkness with maturity. In a group of siblings the blondest one is often automatically thought to be the youngest. Beauticians explain that blond hair softens a face and thereby makes it look younger.

Ordinarily the mature voice of a man differs from the voice of a child more than does that of a woman. On the average a mature man has grown more in height than has a woman. The social role of a man traditionally

differs from that of a child more than does that of a woman, since usually
the man must go out and deal with the wider world while often the woman can elect to remain engrossed with home and childhood things, albeit
in a different relationship. For these reasons a grown man must give up, or
at least disguise, his childhood passive dependency more than a woman,
who is accepted as normal if she continues to exhibit quite a bit of it relatively unchanged. (The same is true for the minor expressions of latent
homosexual attachment. Women are freer in our culture than men to hug
and kiss each other.)

For all these reasons the masculine *image* is further removed from the
childhood state than is the feminine *image*. Therefore, when a woman
lightens the color of her hair she is changing herself toward the images
of both femininity and childhood.

Blondness and Neoteny

By now the reader may have heard the faint psychological overtones of an
ancient theme, the general tendency of some organisms to preserve primitive, nonspecialized characteristics, which is called neoteny. We glimpsed
earlier how it is always the neotenic form that gives rise to the next big
change on the agenda of evolution. For example, it was the descendants of
less specialized reptiles who leaped into the sky as feathered birds, and
into the personal relationship as wombed mammals.

And man is the most neotenic of primates, both as a species and
throughout individual life. We saw how man owes to his neoteny the
enormous scope of his adaptive capacity. Now we must notice that,
nevertheless, during his lifetime the individual human being too goes
through a process of specialization which gradually narrows the range
of choices his basic neoteny allows him. If a person in childhood spends
his developing years on the ski slopes he is forever forsaking the piano-
forte at Carnegie Hall in favor of a shot at an Olympic medal, and vice
versa. The processes of maturation, development, and education thus
progressively confine us to zones of achievement smaller than the range
not only of our lifelong wishful fantasies, but also of our actual original
endowment. Hence, the more specialized we become in maturity, the
more we miss the omnipotentiality of our youth.

Since men in general are usually rewarded in our world for their increasing specialization of "doing" in the larger world, while women in
general are not rewarded equally for their increasing specialization of
"being" homemakers, it is presently inevitable that women will yearn

more than men for restoration of the seemingly endless vistas open to them in childhood. In the absence of a true elixir, perhaps women content themselves with ways to "be" blonder and thereby create at least the illusion of rejuvenation of opportunity as well as body in accordance with the blond image.

Can it be that the quest for blondness is at this root but a faint cultural echo of a biological imperative, a disguised and distorted transformation of a survival value of species twisted into a psychological value of persons?

Image: Good Feminine and Evil Masculine

But what about the qualities of good and evil we considered at the beginning? Isn't it true that the feminine image is associated with good, while the masculine image is associated with evil? To some extent, yes. It is just this aspect of the images that became a basis for the Victorian enshrinement of women by men as "virtuous," by which was meant not only general gentleness and goodness, but also a specific incapacity for fully enjoying genital sexuality. Although increasingly disdained today as a manifestation of immaturity or emotional disorder, at that time frigidity was widely regarded as superior to the "bestial" lustiness of men. The large, dark "hairy ape" was contrasted to the smaller, smooth-skinned, pure white ideal woman chronicled by the poets.

Traditionally children are romanticized as "sweet and good." In addition to being often more fair in color than adults, they lack facial and body hair, as well as capacity for full genital response. So here are other cords of neoteny which bind the feminine image to the characteristics of childhood, a connection that has long been used destructively to keep women in socioeconomic bondage.

The assumption is made on the basis of such facts that in toto the *fully developed and mature woman* is innately and naturally less differentiated from the child than is the mature man. The error of such a judgment is best illustrated by reversing it. Infants and young children have lower limbs that are much shorter than their torsos. Adult men have lower limbs about equal in length to their torsos, whereas women's lower limbs grow considerably *longer* than their torsos, a fact that gives them their much-admired long-stemmed look. But should we conclude from this happy circumstance that a grown woman is therefore in *all* ways *more highly* differentiated from a child than is a grown man?

Thus we have here disclosed again our ambivalence about growing up versus remaining infantile. We idealize in women the "childlike" qualities of being small, fair, good, and relatively less responsive genitally, while appreciating their paradoxically more differentiated longer legs. On the other hand, it is to the tall, dark, relatively shorter-legged but presumably more genitally responsive, more evil, and more dangerous man that we mainly entrust the fate of the world.

Parenthetically, images of course evolve too over time under the influence of reality changes, or even in our conception of reality. For example, the work of Masters and Johnson has already dented the masculine and feminine images by providing evidence that women in general may turn out to be more genitally responsive than the most powerful men.[4]

The associations of light and dark considered above are reversed in the Oriental tradition. *I Ching* ("Book of Changes") records symbolism that may be four thousand years old in which *yang*, the male or positive aspect of nature, is connected with light, and *yin*, the female or negative aspect, with darkness. While the male principle is identified with the light of the sun, the female principle is connected with the light of the moon. In characteristic Oriental terms, the *yin* and *yang* are mutually complementary and necessary aspects of the whole rather than eternally opposed to one another. As Watts says: "Though called male and female they are never personified as god and goddess progenitors of the world, nor is there the slightest hint of their being engaged in a cosmic war of light against darkness or good against evil."[5]

The Western tradition also identified the sun with the male principle, but *did* personify it as God. It remained for this tradition to dualize good and evil and conceive of them as engaged in eternal battle, one against the other, rather than as inseparable parts of an indivisible unity. To this tradition was coupled, in Mithraic cults and in Christianity, the additional theme of the virgin birth of God and veneration of feminine "purity." Perhaps this combination helped bring about the opposite associations of light with female and dark with male. A contribution to this switch no doubt was made by the proximity of light-skinned blond people to the centers of the origins of Western traditions.

Or perhaps we must look to the later centuries during which Western Europeans came to dominate the world. Possibly the Western gender associations of light and dark arose mainly in the time of chivalry when it became fashionable for the men who represented the ideal of masculinity to go off on suntanning quests on behalf of pale women who stayed at home. This arrangement accentuated the contrast between male force and aggressiveness, always associated with the sun, and female softness and dependence, often associated with the moon. When in succeeding centuries Western European men went questing to spread their dominion around the world, mainly over dark people, their mental picture of women and children at home by the hearth might well have been blanched by their human need to see them as very different from the darker-skinned people they were called upon in their hideous day-to-day work to subdue and slaughter.

In any event, by the succession of Queen Victoria, the fair-skinned, blond-haired good girl had become firmly established as the ideal who stayed at home having the vapors while her man was off on what inwardly both felt was his more brutal, if not more dark and evil, work.

Meaning of the Blond Image

When a woman turns herself into a blond, she is moving closer to the feminine and childhood (and therefore "good") images. If she then has more fun it will be one of the dividends of the greater proximity to the image of childhood, which especially includes fun.

But she is likely to find that she is expected not so much to *have* more fun as to *be* more fun, particularly by men who want to exploit her for their own real, although more covert, adventures in regression to the Fun ethic of childhood. A man will want her to have the "innocent sweetness" of childhood, combined with a mature genital sexuality of which no child is capable.

The meaning of this fantasy, and the interpretation of the paradox of the blond image, is that a man wishes himself into believing he has now discovered the *grown-up* version of the delightful little girl who at five may have been as eager as he to play doctor in the attic with no strings attached. Hefner's bunnies, although of all shades, if only in fantasy fulfill the same role. The trouble is that, even if a bunny has become genitally responsive by now, in reality there can be no such immature creature who also is capable of the enduring love and reliability which a man is going to want from her in addition, once he has fallen in love with this recreated and enlarged version of his childhood playmate. And this is probably a good part of the tragedy of women like Marilyn Monroe, who once said ruefully, "I guess I'm a fantasy." They try to build a "self" based upon the blond image only to find that they have become successful in fulfilling the fantasies of millions without being successful in filling the reality needs of anyone.

A natural blond who *has* developed her own identity may wonder if Yeats was right, that only God can love her for herself alone. She may have difficulties because of the blond image in professional as well as personal life. She may be refused responsible employment or advancement because the image erroneously leads employers to conclude that she is too young, too frivolous. For example, a middle-aged plumbing contractor had three women working in his office. When the office manager retired he decided to promote one of his other employees to her job. The two younger women were both petite and youthful, but one was an olive-skinned brunette while the other was a corn-silk blond. He automatically selected the brunette and left her a note informing her of the promotion with her paycheck. That evening he received a phone call from a tearful young woman whimpering something garbled about the appointment to the office manager's job. Out of his many years of experience he expected the *blond* would call to protest, so he used his best comforting fatherly voice.

"Now Alice, I know you're disappointed. But we just have to recognize that Ethel is older and has more experience."

"But this *is* Ethel," the voice wailed, "and this is my first job. I just can't be office manager!" Before he could readjust his paternalism she went on.

"Anyway, what do you *mean* I'm older! Can't you see I'm seven years younger? Besides, Alice has worked at three more jobs."

His discomfiture at the hands of the blond image was complete when later Alice did call to complain.

On the other hand, several naturally blond young women looking for husbands have told me that the stable, marriageable sort of man avoids them while they are besieged by playboys with offers of weekend vacations. I know a number who dyed their hair dark on this account, and apparently have had some success in escaping the image.

It is interesting and impressive, however, that despite complaining of these difficulties blond women are much more inclined to tell you wistfully how much fairer they used to be, and to use artificial means to lighten their hair rather than to escape the troubles by moving toward the darker realms. As Lawrence Gelb, the founder of Clairol said, "Nine out of ten women would choose to be blonds if they could do it by pressing a button. Nothing has ever induced women to favor darker hair."[6]

What about the large group of brunettes whom men prefer to blonds? We do not have to assume that such men are masochistically interested in the Theda Bara image. Because most people tend to grow toward emotional maturity despite their neuroses, it is understandable that many men seek out a brunette who matches the image most associated with the role of mature wife and mother. We should add in haste that the brunette *image* may have no more to do with the real characteristics of a particular individual than does the blond image. I recall here the petulant brunette patient who complained to me bitterly that she had a "blond soul" but was never treated the right way by men because of her dark complexion.

Of course not everyone whose hair is lightened or whose eye is turned by it must be concerned with the extreme degrees of the blond image and what it signifies. But might it not be of benefit to have thought about all this when we are faced with the avalanche of blonding fantasies, ads, chemicals, teen-agers, grandmas, and political manipulations among future possibilities on the human agenda?

Biology, Experience, and Values

After chasing this tangle of separate strands through the mesh, we might rest a moment, look over and assess the terrain traversed, the direction the road takes from here, and the difficulties of the climb ahead.

To assess something means to evaluate it, to estimate its value. In doing so we employ our previously established values. We are likely to assess the value of an automobile or piece of real estate in dollars, since dollars are the usual standard employed to evaluate "things" in our society.

But we may also assess the values implicit in the way the automobile has been designed or the land improved. We may note that style features have been ranked ahead of utility and safety, and say that this automobile or house emphasizes esthetic over functional values. We may also discover that the builders rank the value of profitability higher than service, and so on.

Now we must assess the truth or falsity, the social utility or injury, the enrichment or stultification of the individual which attach to the blond image.

We began with the primal fear of night and darkness. Now that man understands the daily march of the sun across our skies, now that we know its light and warmth are always "there" for the half of our world beyond the horizon's bend, and now that we are sure that in a few hours our turn to wheel beneath its benediction will come again without our least effort, why does this ancient dread persist?

Despite the evidence against existence of instincts in man (pp. 64–66), many will answer, "It must be instinctual." Even if we assume that so ubiquitous a fear has biological roots, we saw in Chapters 5 through 10 how potent are the newer possibilities for direct biological controls of all behavior.

For the purpose of the present discussion let us deal only with the *experiential* controls of behavior. Any "instinctual" predisposing factor in man could reach overt expression only through experience.

For example, even with Lorenz's ducklings, it was *experience* that taught them he was their mother.[7] We all know that the "instinctual" enmity between dogs and cats evaporates under the experience of growing up together. Occasionally a grown cat violates its instincts sufficiently to adopt a squab or a chick, whereupon the two live happily together thereafter. We have seen that in man, aside from a few reflexes, and with the exception of tool-using, language, and social organization, which depend on learning, there are no universal patterns of behavior (see Chapters 3 and 4).

Therefore in man the persistence of so primitive a reaction as fear of the dark and all its derivatives must depend largely upon experience (compare p. 269). The correctness of this conclusion is immediately apparent from a study of the people we all know. Children in the same family vary enormously in their fear of the dark. Even identical twins may differ, an especially striking indication of the role of experience. What can we do about these experiences?

Fear of the dark itself ordinarily is relatively mild in those who grow up in emotionally secure homes. In the few cases where it has become disabling, treatment must include detoxification of the past and present circumstances intensifying the fear. So this is one more example of the urgency of improving the quality of childhood experience.

But things are not so plain when it comes to the attitudes and fears remotely derivative of the central fear of darkness. We live in a world of diversity and variation, the increasing complexity of which generates anxiety which both mobilizes and undercuts our old value adaptations. Human beings adapt mainly through cultural evolution, and so they come to overvalue hard-won and venerable truths long after they have become shibboleths. A prejudice is not abandoned until some new adaptational tool is developed, even though the objective circumstances make the old one lethal. Witness the Sioux Indians and their outmoded but tenacious disinterest in private property.[8] Remember the adherence of certain fanatics to sabbath observance in the face of catastrophe. Or visualize the tranquility of the refugee a patient told me about who stepped from his sinking ship into the ocean while clutching two fifty-pound suitcases of jewels and watches.

Primordial fear of the dark has less and less survival value in a world increasingly tamed by man. But the blond image is one of its derivative crystallizations that nevertheless is woven tightly into the fabric of adaptations on which an enormous part of day-to-day interpersonal security rests.

Consider racial distinctions. Friends of mine have a mixed marriage, the wife Negro and the husband Caucasian. One day the wife was industriously washing the windows of the expensive new house they had just bought. The white lady of an even more elegant house across the street watched her in silence for a time from her front porch. Then she summoned up courage to walk by idly and whisper, "If you ever want a better job come and see me!" When she discovered that her poaching efforts actually had been directed to her new neighbor rather than a "maid," her cordial attitude gave way at once to arctic hostility. She had a welcome place in her mental cupboard for the Negro servant but not for the black neighbor.

Such a woman likely would find no difficulty in seeking treatment for fear of night darkness, nor in accepting help designed to minimize her children's outmoded fear of darkness, but she may bristle angrily and defend herself viciously against any effort to help her or the children shed the absurd image that is the basis for automatically consigning every dark skin to domestic servitude.

First of all, her self-validation is founded in a system of feelings of superiority. She must fight any inroads on that precious structure until her self-esteem can be planted more reliably on psychically intimate love, work, and play.

Second, there is the help shortage. As people have for millennia, she abhors dull repetitious labor. So she looks for someone else to do it. Every time a dark skin turns before her eyes from a maid into a neighbor her problem of finding someone else to do the nonvalidative drudgery is compounded.

So we have the paradox that her very effort to escape from drudgery into a more abundant life mires her more deeply in the prejudices of the Negro image. In a grossly oversimplified way this vicious circle may represent a model of the conflict we face on the broader horizons of industrial work, international relations, and general intellectual growth.

But as we have seen earlier, we need not remain caught in this ancient paradox because *it is becoming truly unnecessary to relegate anybody to stultifying drudgery.* The machine servants are ready and able—and so far even willing—to do it for us. But that will leave us with the practical problem of drudgery resolved, while for many people the psychological problem of shaky self-esteem is intensified. Application of automation and cybernation can be accomplished without disorganizing society only by a coordinated successful effort to replace obsolete value judgments with new ones that are adaptive to the new reality.

When we ask how this is to be done we confront the complex realm of education, and the web of platitudes related to improving it. If we expect to forge and embrace new values based upon better understanding, this education must by-pass the hackneyed and include factors ordinarily outside awareness, or it will never seep down to the "gut level" where new conviction can give birth to changed action. This is the level that must be reached if we are to use our understanding of the quest for blondness to help resolve that most crucial conflict between black and white—"race relations."[9]

We cannot erase the invidious elements in the Negro black image by outlawing it, although we can weaken its effects by outlawing destructive behavior based upon it, such as segregation in housing or transportation. Black is beautiful, but the only fundamental antidote for negative associations of an image is overwhelming positive ones.

Since the positive associations of the Caucasian white image derive partly from the power of the sun, it is reasonable to assume that positive associations of the black image must find equally powerful roots. In the past the power of black has been associated with the Devil and evil. Intellectually we have left behind those truly benighted times. It should be plain that the sun, as the source of energy of all life on earth, is related with equal closeness to men of all shades. Now that the processes of evolution are understood, it should be possible to generate equally positive associations to the dark skin of people who have managed to become adapted to the sun's damaging rays, as to the light skin of people who have remained vulnerable.

Although almost all power on earth derives from the sun, white power on earth does not spring directly from the heavens but from white appropriation of the derivative sources of earthly power. And the advocates of black power, however belatedly they may have seen "the light," and however injudicious may be some of their language and tactics, are correct when they insist that the status and image of Negroes will become equal only when they have acquired their share of earthly power.

There has been much public discussion of racial mixing and, depending upon your biases and proclivities, its "obvious" advantages and drawbacks. The genetic aspects and the esthetic ones have been dealt with elsewhere. But here I want to reconsider some of them in terms of unconscious roots of the blond image.

Primitivity

It appears that there are no significant sense organ or brain volume differences between races.[10] Whether or not we can base practical decisions in tomorrow's world upon such factors, it is demonstrable that in other ways, contrary to common bias, it is the Caucasian group of mankind that is biologically the most primitive.

The one exception may be the general evolutionary trend in man toward smaller jaws, teeth, and facial bones which, with its somewhat negative survival value, is apparently better developed in whites.[11]

With respect to evolution of skeletal and muscular dimensions, particularly the relative reduction of pelvic/shoulder width, black people are more advanced than white.[12] Hairlessness is in the direction of man's specialization for rapid heat loss during exercise and artificial insulation by clothes, and both Orientals and blacks have much less face and body hair than whites.[13] Black skin is of obvious advantage in areas near the equator where sunlight is the most intense. There deep skin pigmentation protects not only against sunburn, but against the serious toxicity caused by excess Vitamin D production in the skin, which may develop readily in whites exposed to too much sunlight. On the other hand, white skin appears to have evolved as an adaptation to the feebler sunlight, and lessened Vitamin D production, encountered as man migrated north. Now that rickets can readily be prevented in all people by supplemental Vitamin D in the early years, dark skin is of no great disadvantage anywhere, whereas white skin still predisposes to sunburn, skin cancer, and other skin disturbances.[14] The general increase in human height may be especially pronounced among certain Negro groups. Perhaps some of these are among many and more obscure factors that bring about the disproportionate number of outstanding Negro athletes now that some of them get adequate nutrition and opportunity.

This catalogue, of course, omits any references to such factors as emotional characteristics, special talents, warmth in child nurture and so on. For now, it will be useful to confine our attention to the physical factors. With this perspective we are faced objectively with a different question relative to race mixture than has been considered most commonly by those concerned with it.[15]

Objective study indicates that rather than finding ways to maintain the purity of the supposedly superior white group, the pertinent question may be whether it is possible to benefit Caucasians by alloying their genes with others that may improve their musculoskeletal proportions and give them the protection from radiant energy of which they are deprived by their presently maladaptive whiteness. Naturally, dark-skinned people may give some thought to the possibility of injury to their progeny which might result from adding white genes. Especially so if it becomes widely understood that light pigment is not only a retained infantile human condition, but may be actually a neotenic holdover of a primitive characteristic of remote nonhuman forebears. As British anthropologist Sir Arthur Keith put it:

> Fair hair is a foetal character of primates which has become permanent in Northern Europeans, and is found distributed sporadically in North Africa and Central Asia. Here again we see characters which were marked out in foetal months passing on to become characters of adult life.[16]

"Black Is Beautiful" Revisited

Black supremacist ideas are often regarded by both whites and blacks only as defensive reactions against white oppression. While they have this defensive significance, we must not ignore the possibility of a deeper and healthier meaning in them.

Until lately, the social status of the lighter-skinned mulatto in this country tended automatically to be higher than that of his darker-skinned fellows, reflecting acceptance of the predominant white man's valuation of youthful immaturity as well as race. But like paler people, darker people are often born lighter too, and darken gradually as they grow older. And more recently, blackness has become associated with pride and strength. These facts suggest that much of the new regard for blackness is not defensive, but is rather a symbolic assertion of an aspect of *maturity* so far only dimly perceived as crucial for human safety. Let me explain.

Of course it is most unlikely that there is any widespread understanding of the ways in which the Negro group is more highly evolved biologically than the Caucasian. And of course it is most unlikely, however widespread may be its unconscious recognition, that many blacks or whites ever think consciously even about the physical association in the individual person between blackness and maturity.

However, both blacks and whites are increasingly aware of some specific ways in which black *culture* outdistances white. I do not have in mind here the well-known and much appreciated contributions of blacks to music, theater, literature, and so on, but rather the general psychological characteristics of black personality and social relationships. As compared with whites, blacks display toward one another a greater warmth, spontaneity, gayety, humor, exuberance, kindness to strangers, "brotherhood," and willingness to nurture the young. These characteristics have been belittled in the past by whites in their stereotypes of the "mammy" and the "happy nigger." Although ostensibly admired, both were looked down upon as "childish," or lacking in the sober and sour evidences of maturity valued in puritanical white society. But now ridicule is turning into respect.

Can it be that the greater warmth of black people, far from reflecting arrest of development or immaturity, indicates an advanced degree of the quality that has been most important to the evolution of all life and man in particular, *cooperativeness within a species?* And is it possible that "black is beautiful," for example, refers in the main neither to esthetics nor to the connection between skin darkness and physical maturation, but rather to unconscious recognition of how especially abundant black culture is in this vital contribution to man's survival?

If, as I believe, our answers must be Yes, then we are led to a paradoxical conclusion. The indispensable element of black culture is the neotenic preservation and expansion of loving playfulness, one of our most fundamental species characteristics, into viable truly human individual maturity.

The root of mature interpersonal warmth lies in the womb, before the baby ever knows anything but physical warmth. Only when he lies chilly evaporating amniotic fluid after birth does he learn the meaning of cold. Only then can he learn to associate physical warmth with other human beings who give him nurturing care. And only gradually does he learn later to conceptualize interpersonal relations characterized by readiness to nurture as "warm."

What is the relation between attitudes toward people and attitudes toward the light and warmth of day or the dark and cold of night? At first, all primitive people were dependent upon the sun for light and warmth. Then mastery of fire, clothing, and shelter brought them some freedom from need for the heavenly source of both. Better equipped, they were able to begin to value instead of fear darkness and cold. But as happens so often with outmoded bodily structures, new functions were found for their old belief and value-system adaptations. Many were retained as fearful folkways built into dogmas of religions, myths, legends, totems, castes, and political structures. Some were elaborated into the social and economic distinctions that allowed skin color to determine not just personal relationships but whether a man was to be encouraged or enslaved.

Just as man has emancipated himself from abject dependence upon the sun, and as every child must free himself from dependence upon parents, so both whites and blacks must separate primordial dependence upon solar or parental light and warmth from our values now and in the future. Particularly as regards skin color, some day we should be able to decide what shade to be entirely on esthetic grounds, and without

being influenced by overtones of ancient biological necessities or prejudices derived from them. Then a man could decide whether to be ebony
or ivory or azure as might suit his taste and not his terror.

But just as blacks have long struggled to be included in what they erroneously thought of as the promised land of white society, whites today,
sensing the cardboard emptiness of their ethos, sometimes clutch at blackness of skin, association, or mannerism to find their souls. They too must
escape the prejudice that, without reference to reality, elevates an archaic
color response into a value. As the revamping of white and black personalities within a generation under changed conditions has proved, *the
evil or the good* is not genetic whiteness or blackness, but rather *human
coldness and withdrawal versus warmth and cooperation*, wherever and
under whatever skins they are found.

28 Image and Sex Object Selection

Deliberate eugenic admixture of races would entail extensive and heated contest among people holding incompatible values. But leaving aside any organized plan, just the intermingling of populations and the loosening of social structures around the world are increasing the previously unlikely sexual possibilities upon which the individual may act or refuse to act. Some of these situations involve relationships between individuals who really know each other as individuals. The rest represent the usual blind acting out of various tensions, including those arising out of the pressure of images.

When adequate contraception eliminates the particularly conflictual problem of racial mixing, it is easier to focus on the less dramatic but actually more interesting and important factor of the unconscious influence of images on choosing a sex partner.

As an illustration of the myriad possibilities let us consider the compulsion of some white men to have sexual relations indiscriminately with dark or black women. Dreams and associations of two such patients in psychoanalysis showed the unconscious equation "darkness equals masculine." Both were struggling unconsciously to ward off homosexual urges. Both discharged these impulses according to the unconscious irrational formula, "I can't allow myself to have sexual relations with a man . . . but a black woman is almost the same as a man."

It is important to recognize that I am not attributing latent homosexual significance to the sexual interest of every white man in a black woman. For example, if a white man has been raised by a black woman, or develops an attachment to a specific black woman, analysis reveals the usual predominantly heterosexual elements. There are also powerful nonvisual factors that become stereotypes with varying validity and produce attraction to a group other than one's own, such as the comparative informality of far-western Americans, the gentle tranquility of the Japanese, or the warmth and good humor of black Americans.

Then there is the opposite situation of the very fair young woman who indiscriminately pursues affairs only with black men. Such behavior usually signifies both the woman's prejudice against Negroes and her own low self-esteem along the unconscious line "this is all I deserve" or "this serves me right," based upon the supposed inferiority of blacks. Also clear to everyone in such behavior are the elements of defiance of parents or society.

What has not been emphasized is the meaning to a blond woman of sexual relations with a black man in terms of the fantasies connected with the blond image. In teen-age vernacular a blond is sometimes called a "flashlight." This means she is easily seen at night, shines as a good beacon in the dread darkness. It is a term obviously related to the blond image, and is welcomed by the girl because it plainly reflects admiration and approval. Having built her identity around the blond image, she naturally seeks opportunity to heighten her experience of her "self" as an incarnation of the image by using a very dark man as background or frame. A lovely fragile young blond girl whom I saw in consultation revealed this mechanism very plainly in her fantasies. She was the fairest in all ways. No man she knew was right for her. She was particularly disinterested in the "clean-cut" young men whom her cold and distant parents favored. She preferred the dirtier and to her more masculine hippies, long hair and all. But still something was missing. She was a flashlight. But no stygian gloom worthy of her beams had yet appeared.

While studying *Othello* in high school, she found a picture of Paul Robeson in the title role. Suddenly everything was clear. She was Desdemona reborn. She must find her Moor.

And she did. In a local bowling alley. Tall, muscular, Negro, and brown —he was the perfect setting for her desdemonomania. She fell in love. They were together constantly. But a few weeks later her ardor shifted. Her fancy was taken by another Negro young man of similar proportions but better color. He was blacker. She fell in love with herself all over again, replacing her first Othello with the second whom she herself described as "more the type."

It was astonishing how utterly indifferent this usually considerate girl was to the pain of her rejected first Moor. Assuming she had left him for a white rival, he was doubly crestfallen to discover one day that his replacement was darker than he. But she was too completely absorbed in trying to squeeze a few drops of self-validation from her pursuit of images to notice any of this.

Of course, there was no real closeness to the second Moor either and so he gave way to a third, and then a fourth. Each thirsty attempt to bolster her sense of self by color contrast ended, as it must, in the desert of anonymous interchangeability. She had no relationship to the man behind the skin, so developed no psychic intimacy, and derived no self-validation from the relationship.

In less extreme forms, pursuit of the blond image dominates the fantasy and often the behavior of many people. Take the married man who told me he seeks out a parade of "sunny twits" to drain off a craving tension that periodically makes him irritable with his family. Thus he maintains an otherwise happy marriage. His wife, a charming and accomplished brunette, is no more concerned about these flings than other women are about their husbands' periodic workouts on the squash court. The danger for this generally happy couple, aside from the trouble that could be caused them by a resentful ex-sunny twit, is that the adaptation is highly unstable and vulnerable to the changes that time brings in attractiveness, money, and potency. If someday the man can no longer siphon off disruptive psychological pressures in this way, he may be unable to prevent them from overflowing as hostility onto his wife and children.

Then there are the people who carry pursuit of the image into a succession of marriages, leaving little nests of children here and there with more or less bewildered successive former spouses. The ex-mates are sometimes aware of their physical similarities but do not know how to interpret the ever-lengthening chain of petite blonds or tall-dark-and-handsomes.

Queen Nitocris, Helen of Troy, Cleopatra, and their admirers long ago assured that the quest for blondness would come up on the human agenda with increasing insistence in the dawning era of abundance. Now we must ask ourselves, what are we to *do* about the blond image or those who exploit it?

29 *Blondness and Decision*

Image and Action

Shall we rush out and quell the "be-a-blond" advertisers? Or, remembering that today's chemicals for blonding the hair may soon be supplemented by tomorrow's agents for bleaching the genes, shall we go the other way? Shall we change the slogan to "Be *Born* Blond" and thus democratically give everyone equally the advantage of facing the era of abundance as a symbolic incarnation of man's ancient preference for daylight and regressive urge to return to "carefree" childhood?

What about the monotony of uniformity?

We earlier considered whether or not the right to decide her child's pigmentation in advance is a power the community should leave to the individual mother. We know now that exposure to sunlight is injurious to all skin, especially very fair skin. Suppose a girl vindictively blames her mother for making her so fair that beaches are off-limits because throughout her life the main dividends of sunbathing will be burns, rapid aging, and skin cancers.[1] What might be the mother's legal liability? Already a suit has been filed on behalf of a thalidomide-damaged child against the mother who took the injurious pill.

Besides, do we really want to ratify by action the flimsy fabric of magic and myth we have called the blond image at a time when greater understanding and control of all elements of life is giving us the tools for emancipating ourselves from the tyranny of illusions?

In that case perhaps we should go completely in the opposite direction and dye everyone's genes black. This would have several advantages. In addition to protecting everyone from damaging sunlight, we would be simultaneously rejecting the primordial fear of the dark, and its irrational connection with ideas of evil and dirt. Also we would be aiding everyone to renounce fantasies of regressing to (Caucasian) childhood, helping everyone to develop adult identity, and encouraging all to make the continuing sober appraisal of reality hitherto expected mainly of the mature man.

Just such an approach can well squeeze the joy out of life, if the leaden foot of the technician displaces the firm handclasp of the humanist in the guidance of man's future. It will take our best minds and warmest hearts to avoid the dead ends that could be ferreted out by the humorless application of mechanistic thought to changing values.

Image and Education

Prohibition does not work as a device to prevent abuse of alcohol, LSD, or sexuality. But, as long and varied experience indicates, compulsion may play a useful role in learning. Compulsory public schooling, compulsory integration of public schools and transportation, or compulsory vaccination—all create the circumstances wherein not only is some reality changed but some opportunity is created for information to reach the nucleus of personality in which experience is crystallized into habits and values. For some time it may remain necessary to retain compulsion in public education, until delight of increasing one's knowledge and mastery has become strong and widespread enough to constitute replacement motivation. In the meanwhile, it is essential that the compulsory factor be restricted carefully so that it does not narrow the scope and content of the ideas the student may investigate. Particularly is this true when the objective is to provide the information and stimulus that can lead to changes in the values connected to a set of such largely unconscious attitudes as the blond image. Only by encouraging the widest range of adventurous inquiry concerning such an image can we perfect human life without taking the flavor out of it. To continue for a moment more the comfort of such regressively oral terminology—only by confining compulsion in education to the expansion of freedom can we make life more delicious without thereby rendering it less digestible. If our electric circuitry can be hooked up to such objectives, including elucidation of the blond image, computers and teaching machines pose no threat to a full life and plainly enhance our chances.

What harm is there in a woman enjoying the playful regression of becoming a blond? What if a man enjoys her doing so, or for that matter, does the same himself? The diminished demand for subsistence drudgery, the guaranteed annual income, and so on, just like the new jet airliners which make it quite possible now to go from Los Angeles to Paris for the weekend, will make possible, and even necessary for emotional health, development of ability to engage in such rompish explorations of personal possibilities not feasible in the past.

Besides, isn't the neotenic preservation of immature nonspecialization one of man's most precious resources? Of course. But the safeguarding of the true flexible potential that allowed a primitive fish to evolve into an amphibian which can breathe air throughout life, or a primitive ape to evolve into a man who can play joyously all his days, is one thing. Resort to imitation of the *visible surface characteristics* of infancy is quite another. When they become serious preoccupations, pretended youth or fictional purity are ignominious retreats from the adaptive power of reason, and *literal* regressions to the pitiable magic of childhood.

So in all this education for experimentation it is essential for personality integrity that the self-validation of psychically intimate love, work, and play be relied upon as the basis of identity, and not the trivial modification of externals.

A man or woman may have fun (and profit) with the quest for blondness, but not much more. With the courage to experiment and enjoy creating illusions must go the nerve to disbelieve nirvana.

SECTION FOUR

CONCLUSIONS

Conclusions

In this most marvelous moment of man, our future holds more than distraction of the leisured few from the pain of the many they enslave, more than an endless flood of goods and services, more than increasing liberation from drudgery and disease. It pledges the joyous delight of ever-expanding horizons, and the brand new assurance that freedom to range over them need be denied to none. To redeem that pledge requires only the difficult but entirely possible feat of recruiting the mass of human beings to its promise.

We have seen how all unfolds from what went before, how nothing happens independently, how each galaxy, star, planet, species, individual, organ, cell, molecule, atom, and particle is linked in a chain of mutual command. We know, beyond John Donne, that no *matter* is an island, that the bell of any in the universe, however faintly, tolls for all.

Whether to have stability or revolution is a choice we humans are not offered. Nothing in the universe is static, everything evolves, and—measured on the relevant time scale—evolution *is* revolution.

Although many people find it comforting to believe they can cause or prevent revolution, even within the subsidiary of the cosmic enterprise we have called the human agenda, they are mistaken. The simple truth is that revolution is continuous. Our only options are to regulate the velocity and guide the direction of its changes. But within these options, our choices are many and momentous in their results for man. Every day more so, our fate is becoming our own artifact.

The most remote past or future pages of the human agenda we cannot read clearly. But we can analyze the more recent past pages and foresee a few of those to come. The task of each generation is to devise, through heightening of its consciousness, appropriate adaptations to the items on not only the next page, but also to those on the page after next. If we are faithful to this trust, the future of man can be secure amid the endless revolutions of evolution.

But change has become so rapid that our society can no longer leave speculation only to the science fiction writers. Captain Nemo's underwater diving equipment became available only ninety years following publication of *Twenty Thousand Leagues Under the Sea*. Buck Rogers is coming true today, only twenty-five years later, instead of in the twenty-fifth century A.D. And an unreasonable facsimile of the biology of *Brave New World* is being realized now, instead of six hundred years "after Ford," as Aldous Huxley originally predicted.[1]

A pivotal purpose of education long has been to force the young to renounce or confine their imaginative fantasies within the bounds of mundane old reality. Today the challenge of education is increasingly to teach adults, as well as children, judiciously to call upon the fullest range of imaginative fantasy in order that the fantastic new reality can be apprehended and mastered in time. This challenge is being met. An indication is Professor P. B. Medawar's conclusion that "almost everything one can imagine possible will in fact be done, if it is thought desirable."[2]

The central fact of this human revolution is that today we are leaving the old era of scarcity for a new era of abundance, which can terminate two million years of submission to the cruelties imposed by seemingly uncontrollable fate. Although abundance is not yet evenly distributed, word of it is reaching people everywhere. The poorest peasant scratching the world's most undeveloped land with his wooden plow can be found receiving the news of forthcoming abundance via the transistor button in his ear.

He is becoming aware that scientific and technical advances have emancipated many in wealthier lands from famine, pestilence, barriers of time and distance—and have introduced surpluses, pollution, overcrowding, and nuclear war. He is learning, as we are, that ineffective magical efforts to woo supernatural forces are being replaced by definite acts of control, placing increasing power in our once helpless hands, and reposing increasing responsibility on our once benighted minds.

All over the world upheavals boil up as aspirants to the new life strain to shake off adaptations they experience as creaking shackles, and replace them with pertinent new ones. The central change we all strive to master is not just the innovation of abundance, but also the outmoding of the entire fabric of values based on scarcity.

And that outmoded fabric includes those judgments that until recently allowed us, in our efforts to elude scarcity, blindly to exhaust the earth's finite resources and endanger the environment. But now that these problems are beginning to be recognized, already there are indications of ways in which they also may be overcome.

The sad irony is that even at this magnificent moment of advance so many are inclined to give up the struggle. Terrified by a future in which delight in the widest possible distribution of opportunity must supplant greedy personal accumulation, they are tempted to impose upon all of us the pseudosolution of hydrogenocide.

But except for a fanatic blunder or tragic accident that halts the parade, they cannot win. The past cannot be preserved indefinitely by forcing the present into its mold. Man's circles of cooperation soon will girdle the globe. For the central current of cooperation that guides all life, and was raised to new potency by higher primates, will not long be deflected by the temporary imbalance of development that allowed man to become his only real enemy. We have only to survive the next three decades. Thereafter the likelihood of man's self-extermination will have been eliminated.

True, shortcomings of the human mind left us for the last few thousand years in a complexifying world without either sufficient wisdom to fulfill our needs peaceably or effective inhibitions against doing so violently. But we are at this instant being rescued from the cul-de-sac of shrewishly ravenous acquisitiveness by the very adaptational agency whose deficiency exposed us to the danger in the first place. Through its *neoteny* man's mind is now repairing its own defect. The instruments of repair are *dilating imagination* and *loving playfulness*, qualities of young mammals taken over, preserved, and expanded by the neotenic human mind.

By way of these characteristics man is coming to appreciate and value the unity of universe, life, and man, as well as to understand and reject the absurdities that pit subdivisions of man against each other and rationalize their mutual violence as natural.

Although not in the form of rigid and foredooming inherited "instincts," our biological ancestry runs within us as a strong stream of interdependency. Like all creatures that clung reflexively before us for security, we do the same, both physically and psychologically.

Our more recent primate forebears innovated something momentous for man in specializing their clinging hands also for *grasp*. Paradoxically, in the human species and individual just as in our clambering ancestors, it is the emergence of grasp that permits a creature to cling a bit less desperately. For it is *manual* grasp that brings the palpable unknown close to the eyes for understanding. And it is the human elaboration of *mental* grasp that brings the impalpable unknown close to the heart for comprehension. With our dextrous manipulative hands and imaginative symbolizing minds we learned to protect ourselves from most external dangers, created much of our own reality, and earned the leisure to review the vast trek the universe, life, and we have made to reach our present state.

That is all very well. But what are we offered in exchange for the comforting security of clinging to abject dependence upon parents and gods, the faiths of our individual and species childhoods? Only the simple dignity of self-reliance in confronting the truth of our time.

But that is quite enough. To ease our clinging for security to the fixed familiarity of perfect certainty, our manual and mental grasp at any instant need not fully unravel the unknown. All it need do is show us that we are the natural-born but maturing children of change, and how sufficient for man are the satisfactions of constantly growing into greater mastery.

One example is the findings of research in many fields that converge on the conclusion that human beings need not surrender themselves to a mythical instinct of inexorable violent aggression. Although we have never tapped fully the enormous resources for educating people to live together peaceably, we have nevertheless achieved fantastic success in teaching the overwhelming majority to live at peace. And the plain fact is that we can choose whether to *cling* to behavioral malformations only poorly adaptive to the past reality of scarcity or to *grasp* the new opportunity of abundance to weld our wisdom into a life of universal human freedom and joy.

We hardly ever stop to think of the truly astounding amount of human kindness shown us, or the geysers within us of kind feeling toward others. Most of our daily experience is conditioned by the values of commerce which focus our attention on individual indulgences such as carnivorous automobiles, outdoor cigarettes, and busy vacations. Except for an hour on Sundays we are rarely reminded explicitly of the joys of joining with others to extend the range of the social cooperativeness which is more characteristic of us than of any other species. So disdained is behavior and satisfaction grounded in social cooperation that the term "do-gooder" ranks not far below "subversive" in our lexicon of opprobrium.

It is often said that adversity inevitably brings out the grisly viciousness of human beings. And yet on the contrary it seems that adversity more often brings out the most sociable aspects of man's behavior. From the barn raisings in colonial America to replace burned structures, through the ubiquitous friendly helpfulness toward strangers in London during the Blitz, to the striking concern of foreigners for flooded Florence, the responsive upwelling in human beings of generous protectiveness is unmistakable. Only when calamity becomes extreme does one see the gradual hideous constriction of the circle to which concern is extended,

disgrace · for outrageous Conduct

until finally only the immediate family or self is included. It is notable that indications of ultimate deterioration in the ties within a culture are observed only after the ravages of protracted exhaustion and despair. And soon all people will live, and will know they live, within subdivisions of just one human—and humane—culture.

In view of our emphasis on the preeminence of the individual, the constant barrage of frustrations and anxieties to which we subject him, and the endless examples of and provocations toward violence with which we surround him, the wonder is that we live in social orders of peaceful hundreds of millions with deaths from assaults, riots, automobile accidents, and other violence measured only in the tens of thousands.

Of course, we must not ignore such grisly exceptions as those in which groups of people remain detached while a fellow human being is injured by impersonal forces, or even beaten to death before their eyes by another person. No doubt the habit of passivity while watching actual and staged killings on TV, the "I don't want to get involved" ethic promulgated by part of our society, and the inculcation over millennia of widespread but often concealed *delight* in violence are some of the causative factors. But far more relevant is the lack of careful preparation and training of our people in both the method and the necessity for prompt lifesaving intervention in such crises. Only the foresighted and practiced person is capable of efficient response. One powerful influence in bringing about such preparation is law.

Attitudes toward the citizen's obligation to safeguard his fellow's life are revealed poignantly in the law of this and other countries. Our citizens may or may not feel themselves bound ethically to rescue an endangered fellow human being. But they are not required by law to do so. Thus the fault of callous *omission* of humane action is not defined as a crime or even a civil offense. Those who do not intervene to prevent a murder or even notify authorities are not liable under our law even though they could safely have done so.[3] And what is even worse, until recently the law made the rescuer responsible for any bad consequences to the person helped. But since the courts decide liability on the issue of whether or not he acted in good faith and did what a reasonable ordinary man would do in such circumstances, for the average citizen there was little danger that his humane act would jeopardize him legally. However, until recently in most places, if the rescuer happened to be a physician who stopped to render aid to an accident victim he could be held liable if the outcome of his freely given assistance did not reflect his practice of the level of knowledge and skill that ordinarily would be employed by a physician of his training and experience in the area wherein the help was rendered.[4] Hence, many physicians were afraid to stop to help those injured in automobile crashes. Now many states have enacted "Good Samaritan" laws which specify that so long as the assistance is rendered reasonably and in good faith the medical helper too cannot be held liable for bad results.[5]

Our sort of statute is at best *permissive*. In contrast, beginning as early as the middle of the nineteenth century, those of fifteen of the sixteen nations of Western and Eastern Europe have become *obligatory*. In France, for example, the legally defined "duty to rescue" obliges any person who sees another struggling in the Seine to give help. If he is a good swimmer, he is liable legally if he does *not* dive in to the rescue. Similarly, even if he is a nonswimmer, if he fails to use an available boat, rope, or life preserver, or to alert others who could help, he is liable.[6]

Another example is illuminating. Most nations subscribe to international law and also have signed various agreements on human rights, conduct of warfare, and so on, which designate certain acts as forbidden even to military forces during armed conflict.[7] Signatories vary in the respect paid this commitment both in the spirit and letter of their laws and rules of military discipline. While the United States Army Field Manual, *The Law of Land Warfare*, clearly states ". . . members of the armed forces are bound to obey only lawful orders," certainly the main emphasis in all relevant publications and training procedures is on unquestioning obedience to authority.[8] Recent events have suggested that troops are not only frequently given orders of dubious legality, but also that in practice they are often completely untrained to distinguish one kind of order from another.

For comparison one may consider the laws of many European nations, such as France and Italy. In addition to rejecting "passive obedience" as a justification for an illegal action, they establish a positive "duty to *disobey*" an illegal order, violation of which is a punishable crime. And their instructors are reputed to be diligent in teaching military personnel the difference between legal and illegal orders.[9]

West Germany, of all nations, has gone even farther in assuring that its forces never again will become the uncritical mechanical expediters of genocidal or other atrocious programs. Its army has established an "Inner Leadership" school in which thousands of commissioned and noncommissioned men are taught that a military person is still a citizen, and that as such he is obligated to refuse to obey an order that violates his *conscience*.[10]

Certainly we must recognize that law does not automatically change people. But it is sadly ironic that in the United States, where they have played so critical a role historically, individual responsibility and conscience may be less firmly supported by the educative and moral strength of law than elsewhere.* The discrepancy between our theory and practice in such respects reflects a lag in evolution of values that ill-equips us for the future in which our survival must rest on unambiguous devotion to safeguarding human life. Young people increasingly are rejecting as inauthentic and hypocritical institutions which they perceive as currently following obsolete values instead of those pertinent to present reality. Just as archaic injurious sexual taboos are being swept aside, including their elaborations in the form of the "double standard" and the subjugation of women, so too must be jettisoned obsolete racial, political, and economic ideas held over as vestigial remnants of the era of scarcity. To the extent to which such formerly unchallenged doctrines as "white man's burden," "national sovereignty," or "private enterprise" have become empty fictions without correspondence to today's reality, continued demands for their blind acceptance as guidelines into the era of abundance become prescriptions of disaster.

While winnowing out the irrelevant and destructive formulations of the past in the service of future human fulfillment, we will need a judicious prospectancy to preserve and increase our capacity for zestful investment of self in love, work, and play. And the resultant self-validation of individuals is essential if man as a species is to attain the devoted collaboration required for coalescing about the geosphere and biosphere as an enduring homosphere.

Detailed decisions as to which tools and techniques to invent and employ are made by men according to the value system of their group. Value systems of the past have been relatively simple adaptations to relatively simple sets of realities. Satisfactions of the survival needs of the Eskimo for warm clothing, shelter, high caloric food, mutual cooperation, and unsentimental disposition of the elderly were ranked high in his value system. A man who rejected these adaptive values probably would soon be forced to choose between death and migration southward. Stability of Eskimo adaptive methods was assured by the very slow rate of change in both external reality and the modest scientific and technical knowledge of the group.

Elsewhere neither of these factors has been so unchanging. We are now at the threshold of the qualitatively new phase of human evolution in which man has begun creating deliberately, in addition to much of

* As *The Human Agenda* goes to press, according to the *Los Angeles Times* of April 26, 1971, American servicemen are being shown films enjoining them to adhere to the provisions of law of the Geneva Conventions and "not to obey any 'clearly illegal' orders . . ."

external reality, also his own biological and psychosocial self. In such circumstances, values tend toward rapid obsolescence, and must be consciously and continuously revised to remain adaptive.

The fragility of value systems must be appreciated, as disclosed by the disintegration of nonliterate societies under the impact of minor changes introduced from industrialized civilizations. The value system of Australian aborigines, including intertribal, monetary, and man-woman relationships, has been nearly destroyed by the importation of one European tool: the steel axe.[11]

On the other hand, we must also confront the durability of certain outmoded values to which we cling tenaciously at the peril of stifling our Western societies, such as the recklessness with which we encourage not only unlimited reproduction numerically, but also multiplication of genetic defect and disability.

In the oncoming era of abundance it is plain that hard work, frugality, thrift, chastity, respect for elders, and submission to supernatural power are of decreasing adaptive relevance. What will take the place of the Puritan ethic which has long since begun to fail?

The broad outlines of a value system adaptive to the era of abundance are clear. They sketch a way of life that permits people to satisfy their individual needs and those of the group by the same acts, one characterized in general by *high synergy*. But of course specifically which values in detail will be woven into the social fabric cannot now be foreseen fully. Because we do not understand completely the finer processes by which values evolve, let alone how to control them, we need careful research into their connections with the origins of personality differences. We need to study carefully individuals who have psychically intimate enduring love relationships versus those whose loves are brief and transient, with special attention to differences in self-esteem, adaptability, and values of the two groups. We need also comparable study of those who do and do not have psychically intimate relationships with work and play. We need further research into the impact on human life and values of technological disemployment, job retraining, guaranteed income, as well as explorations of processes by which preferences for life styles, people, and things arise as both manifestations of and crystallizations into values.

In particular, we need careful consideration of the impact of biological innovations such as, for example, producing babies who are born in a state of advanced maturity. The probable benefits of elimination of 2:00 A.M. feedings must be weighed against the possible curtailment of interpersonal intensity. The probable advantages of reducing anxieties associated with prolonged dependency must be weighed against the possible difficulties of socializing a child who on his own can reach the crassness loosed by TV knobs before he has been reached by the nuances of mother's voice.

In doing all this we must be careful not to repeat the mistake of the alchemists who confidently began their fruitless search for the philosopher's stone with the prior assumption that it was possible to create a specific, highly valued, scarce substance using only means and material then available somewhere. We must remember that it was only as a by-product of going through the proximate steps on the human agenda, without advance certainty of ultimate success, that lead ever was transmuted into gold.

Such rigid erroneous presuppositions are found in everyday practice with psychiatric patients who experience overwhelming anxiety about, and therefore impenetrable resistance to, giving up their hard-won but agonizing adaptive masterpieces. Take for example the painful condition of chronic dread of death. Sufferers may try openly to convince others that anyone who is *not* tormented by death anxiety is sick. On the other hand, they may struggle long and hard in treatment to get rid of the panic, and also unconsciously to hang onto it as a rationalization for not becoming maturely involved with life. After recovery, a young woman patient said of her previous state, "It was a foot-stamping copout. The world isn't fair. I was a sorehead about grown-up problems here-and-now which mommy can't fix. Because I couldn't face that, I quaked instead about hereafter. . . . That way I could avoid living as a responsible adult now. I could also believe that precious me wouldn't ever disappear, and by yelling hard enough maybe arrange to be a dead baby, well cared-for by mommy forever! . . . nowadays I get on with what is necessary now, even if it is disagreeable. And somehow I don't worry about what may come later." Thus the pathological fear of death includes a projection of the combined wish for and fear of return to the infantile helplessness which shapes us.

Among people who do not consider themselves in need of treatment, the prospect of having to abandon their entire sets of a priori assumptions, including values, is so catastrophic that sometimes they come to prefer extinction. We must learn to recognize and circumvent en masse this obstacle to survival on pain of not making it into the era of abundance.

We are menaced in this country and elsewhere by an ominous hardening of conflict into two opposed camps, both of which insist on pursuing, on the basis of fixed assumptions, obsolete and therefore foredoomed courses. Young, self-declared, virtually unarmed revolutionaries proclaim their dedication to living in the era of abundance, but seem determined to die romantically on whatever flimsy barricades their empty hands can throw up against an increasingly panicky, and therefore stubbornly resistant, establishment. A thoughtful review of the situation could bene-ficially enlighten both sides. In this unmoderated confrontation between idealistic sacrifice to progress and grim resolve to hang onto control, mas-sacre hovers just over the horizon and the outcome seems obvious. While we cannot predict which side will be victorious with certainty, of two points we may be sure. *It will not be the powerful who succumb. And, nevertheless, making their regime secure will not be what the survivors have won.* Even if history should surprise us, the pace of change is now so rapid that any new order instituted will shortly become tomorrow's despised establishment.

That we are still faced with such an archaic threat at this time, when the significance of the evolutionary error of modern human violence is within our grasp, is due to an ancient reversal of human mental priorities. Long ago, when man was most vulnerable, we acquired the habit of exerting our main efforts to *control* external reality first and *understand* it later. Now that our powers are so enlarged we must reverse this emphasis, as much for satisfaction as for safety.

As Freud clearly indicated, in addition to earning an adequate living the primary satisfaction a psychoanalyst can legitimately expect from his work is that of *understanding* human motivation and behavior, his own included. After that comes opportunity to help his patient change, the sense of contributing to the psychological improvement of future gen-erations, and so on. But, as I try to show young doctors studying psy-chiatry, if the physician does not derive his primary satisfaction from his understanding, there is danger he may ignore or override the needs of patients. In his craving to be powerful he may push the patient in unwise directions, even precipitating a more severe illness, or he may develop an inordinate demand for "things" that are hallmarks of success in our so-ciety, and therefore set his fees at an exorbitant level.

So it is with therapists for ills of the *community*. Insistence that one has magic answers, or demand for exorbitant rewards in exchange for unveiling them, will lead only to side effects worse than the original symp-toms, or to compounding the fury of the deprived by the misuse of funds meant to help them. It is in these ways that some "poverty" programs, for example, can be turned into thoroughly profitable total losses.

I am usually on the side of chiding those who make no effort to improve reality conditions. But here I must argue instead for the primacy of under-standing. Too often even people who do make the effort to improve reality jump prematurely into trying to bring about what should or ought to be. Always, understanding must be our main motive and tool. Always, we must try to *com*prehend before using what we have learned to *pre*hend. Always we must try to fathom before we fix.

Once having grasped what is known about present reality, where can we turn for guidance on desirable changes? In the remote past both the nature of what exists and what man had best do about it were left to religions. The scientific revolution resulted in leaving the description of reality mostly to science, and in the withdrawal of religious authority largely to the realm of "shoulds and oughts." Although the claim has not been pressed effectively in the past, it is essential today that science also be consulted about the shoulds and oughts.[12]

Demythification is one of the main satisfactions on the human agenda. The central position of the earth in the universe, the special creation of man, the association of goodness with light and darkness with evil, the asexuality of childhood, the instinctuality of human aggressive violence—all these and many more are high on the list of shackles already or soon to be cast off by man's mind. There are those who insist sourly that this delight is specious since man has no choice but to replace the crutches of myths debunked with new ones wrapped in the current scripture of science. It is difficult to know how to respond to anyone who ignores the distinction between the dogmatic propounding of eternal verities and the prospectant proposing of tentative hypotheses. Perhaps the best way to put it is that representatives of these two spirits of inquiry are in most fundamental disagreement.

We cannot deny that man has a yearning for certainty of belief beyond the scope of what at any time it is possible for him to know. But acknowledgment of the widespread existence of this neotenic demand for perfect security should be followed by efforts to understand and renounce it rather than insistence upon satisfying it. Our advance must pursue the course of judicious prospectancy, not fervent wish. To those who would "expand" our minds by dissolving their attainments so that we may perpetually feel marvelous we must reply that maturity requires us to accord gratification of our wishes with the demands of reality, regardless of how we feel about it.

Occasionally I wonder whether my vigorous defense of rational maturity constitutes only an "uptight" defensiveness, as claimed by the new mystics, and therefore ought to be abandoned. However, when it comes to maintaining the courage to confront the unknown with objective open-mindedness, I cannot persuade myself that it is any improvement to shift from being uptight to downloose.

But after all, aren't there truths not accessible to our five senses, aren't there as many realities as people describing their perceptions, isn't experiencing life fully just as important as understanding, and isn't the universe absurd? Of course there are truths not yet known, but there is no basis for assuming that they are not all part of the same single reality, of which only parts can be grasped by any or all of us. Of course experiencing life fully is as important as understanding, but can a man who neglects to develop his understanding be said to be experiencing life fully? No, the universe is not absurd, but the man who expects it contritely to yield its mysteries in response to his reproof, and henceforth meekly conform to his human formulations or hopeful fictions is not only absurd, but in present perspective a bit ridiculous. There is, for example, no "justice" in the universe. It is our job to learn to control its behavior in accordance with our preferences by discerning *its* principles, not to indulge in outraged tantrums or ludicrous seductions until it agrees abjectly to be guided by ours.

The universe seems to be winding down, its energies constantly declining to lower levels as they are transformed from one system to another. The particles of matter which the energies drive fall into disorder as their motive energies degenerate. It is this deterioration of energy and order, called increasing entropy, that characterizes the death and dissolution of an organism, and that seems to portend the death of the entire universe ten to thirty billion years hence.

The most captivating phenomenon in the universe that reverses the entropic process is self-reproducing biological life. The energy of the sun, filtered by the particles of the atmosphere, falls upon the erodings of mountains, which are swept downhill by water and deposited as soil. The solar light presses also upon a seed, the molecules of which are organized in an order of fantastic complexity. At twice the efficiency of any man-made contrivance, the seed sprouts green leaves which transform the sun's energy into food for animals. Animals transform the energies of plants into food for man. And man transforms the energies of their flesh, all with startling efficiency, into comprehension of and eventually control over all these systems. For better or worse, man will decrease entropy, at least temporarily, by controlling rain, hurling pieces of earth to the moon and other planets, and transforming his genes to guide his brain and mind.

Not all our science can fully account for life as yet. But when confronted by such unknowns, and there are many others, we have two choices. We can either assume that the phenomena imply an unbridgeable disjuncture from the rest of the universe and demand a supernatural interpretation, or we can compose ourselves and work persistently until science can deliver new understanding. The most persuasive reason for making the latter choice is of course the past success of science in unraveling other tangles. But a close second is provided by the failure of revelation to do so. Of course, since health is on the same side, it is also compatible with the mature personality to side with patience rather than with petulance.

Barbara Ward has eloquently sketched our perspectives and prospects in these lines:

> The most rational way of considering the whole human race today is to see it as the ship's crew of a single spaceship on which all of us, with a remarkable combination of security and vulnerability, are making our pilgrimage through infinity. Our planet is not much more than the capsule within which we have to live as human beings if we are to survive the vast space voyage upon which we have been engaged for hundreds of millennia—but without yet noticing our condition. This space voyage is totally precarious. We depend upon a little envelope of soil and a rather larger envelope of atmosphere for life itself. And both can be contaminated and destroyed.[13]

It is fair to say that in all men there is a bit of absurdity. But it is difficult to specify in just what it consists. Perhaps it is connected somehow with our uncorroborated conviction that on the largest scale it "matters" whether or not we go on comprehending a widening slice of reality. Or maybe it is related to the naïve curious trust that allows some of us to go on peering out at the universe inquisitively with tragicomic optimism that we can seize the unknown future while capering deliberately backward toward the brink that overtook our predecessors even without their collaboration.

Or can it lie instead in the unconscious hope that by composing thoughts into sequences of words with sufficient euphony one can substantially advance movement through the human agenda?

In any event, that we sometimes have the detachment to laugh at our neotenic shortcomings I would call—if the word had different overtones—our salvation. For grasp of the texture and consistency of our absurdity, whatever its source, gives us the chance to quit clinging to the leaden anchor of pomposity. The scientific mode of knowing goes wrong only when the leaven of humility and humor is omitted from its loaf. Kierkegaard, entwined in transcendental convolutions and suspicious of scientific objectivity, at least agreed on the indispensability of the lighter touch:

> I ask nothing better than to be pointed out as the only one in our serious age who is not serious.[14]

And we might well agree with Finian, the Irish immigrant father of *Finian's Rainbow* who, surveying the calamities about him, decides realistically, ". . . things are indeed hopeless, hopeless—but they're not serious!"[15]

At the end, we are left with the small comfort that certain principles emerge from the study of the universe which appear repeatedly in later phases of evolution of earth, of life, and of man. The universality of fundamental particles and forces, the ubiquity of order, change, interdependence, conservation, predictability—all within an area of uncertainty—impress us over and over as implicit in each series of phenomena we have examined so far.

While it is not everything, we should recall that for man, as the German proverb has it, "a good soup and a warm bed is already quite a lot." Comprehension of this modest recurrent skeleton of knowledge can give us a sufficient security of the familiar in confronting that which is currently unknowable. It allows us to approach the next few steps on the human agenda with the confidence that resolution of their challenges will, as in the past, open vistas that in turn eventually will answer our premature questions, or show them to have been improperly framed. It makes of life without a finished cosmology an on-going adventure instead of an agony of apprehensive doubt.

That is, it does so for the new sort of man who is adapted to live in the era of abundance. His outlines are emerging. Willing to live perpetually with uncertainty, he abhors fixed dogmatic schemes which decide rigidly in advance about unpredictable inner or outer potentialities. Next, you will see in him a pervasive willingness to concentrate and attend, to experience and register, and to delightedly invest himself in the new life. And finally, he insists on controlling and transforming his inner self to bring it into harmony with its total internal capacities as well as current external needs and possibilities. Habit, the automatic application to the present of past judgments, he allows only the subsidiary role of copilot.

This new man will engage himself in substituting for values evolved unconsciously others developed consciously to better equip our human survival kit.

For a long time there have been a few such people—Goethe, Freud, Shaw, Einstein, Picasso, Russell—who are known to everyone because of other attainments, but who are also extraordinary in having ordered their lives according to prospectancy, as do increasing numbers of less accomplished men and women.

These lives illuminate in flashes what human lives in general must become, as we quest into the abundant future of man.

Epilogue

The apes, after two and a half million generations, lived their lives much the same as did their earliest ancestors. They remained stooped, languageless, cultureless, static. But they were loving and generally peaceful.

Then a remarkable thing happened. Out of one of their lines, man was born. And though basically loving, he has become the only known creature massively destructive of his own kind. By contrast with the apes, men have accumulated all that our distinctive minds have learned in three percent as many generations. For man was born only eighty thousand generations ago.

Almost everything known as civilization has been devised by the most recent one half percent of man's generations.

For example, agriculture and the possibility of living in settled communities were invented only five hundred generations ago.

Recorded history is only two hundred generations old.

The Golden Age of Greece lived but one hundred generations ago.

The entire span of the scientific era is encompassed by the last twenty generations.

The mind of man has been subjected to his scientific study for only the last three generations.

The era of nuclear power is only a little more than one generation old.

The awareness of the possibility of universal abundance is less than one generation old.

That we have come so far in the human agenda in so few reproductive cycles, particularly in the last twenty, and especially in the last three, makes the only emotional posture appropriate to a human being one of considered confidence.

Yes, we can rightfully take heart from the incredible speed at which our innovations have brought us to the edge of doom.

Another way to grasp the dimension of man's achievement is to imagine its two million years compressed into a single lifetime of, say, fifty years. In constructing this perspective, I have borrowed and amplified from *Mind in the Making* by James Harvey Robinson, which marvelous half-century-old book on its scale was written only a few hours ago.[1] Here is the chronicle of all human lifetimes condensed into one.

After shivering through darkness into middle-aged adulthood, at the age of thirty-seven, men fully tamed fire.

Only after forty-nine and three-quarters years of wandering as hunters did they settle down to till the ground, harvest crops, domesticate animals, weave rough cloth.

Six weeks ago some men invented writing. Three weeks ago the Greeks carried literature, art, philosophy to a pinnacle that set standards for the succeeding weeks. They also devised political democracy for the minority who were free citizens. And Hippocrates laid the foundation for the ethical practice of clinical medicine.

Eighteen days ago Jesus was born and died, and the people of what is now Vietnam began their continuing struggle against invaders. Five days ago the printing press was invented, and Vesalius did his pioneering human dissections. A day and a half later Shakespeare sent his winged words across linguistic and temporal boundaries, and Harvey discovered the circulation of the blood. Thirty-six hours ago Jenner introduced vaccination for smallpox, and the United States became an independent nation dedicated to the extension of democracy, whose people were expected to understand and express their judgment about all matters affecting their mutual future. On the same day the steam engine was invented, Pinel unchained the mental patients, and for the most part men stopped eviscerating in public those who had new ideas of government or hanging old women accused of traffic with the Devil.

Late yesterday afternoon steamships and railroad trains began hastening about the globe, and Lister introduced antisepsis. This morning Freud launched his daring expedition to the lost inner continent of the unconscious, and the magic of electricity was tamed. At noon today men learned to sail beneath the waves and in the air.

Also around lunchtime a great war was fought to make the world safe for democracy. Six hours ago Fleming discovered penicillin, and another great war was fought, this one to save democracy for the world. Shortly thereafter, the atom and hydrogen bombs were born. Five hours ago the television industry was born, three and one-half hours ago the war in Korea ended, Americans began to replace the French in Vietnam, and Salk introduced immunization against polio. Less than ninety minutes ago the Nuclear Test Ban Treaty was signed, and President Kennedy was murdered.

Half an hour ago, two astronauts from opposite sides of earth took astonishing walks in space. We had been reminded how tenuous is our mastery of even commonplace technology when half an hour earlier the lights mysteriously went out over the eastern end of the country. And less than a quarter of an hour ago, before most of us watching at home had become aware that our pollutions might destroy our life on earth, two of us celebrated our fifty-first birthday on the moon.

All of civilization spans only one-half of one percent of man's existence. Is this flicker of time a fair trial of so brave an effort?

❖   ❖   ❖

At birth a baby is programmed for a loving interaction with others. If he is lucky, he and his mother are allowed to satisfy one another's needs immediately. He is permitted to nurse at her breast right away, drinking the colostrum which brings him antibodies, vitamins, and minerals, while he stimulates, by his sucking, reflexive womb contractions that deliver the afterbirth, stop bleeding, and prevent afterpains. And in this mutual giving is born synergically the bond of affection that ties the new baby to others for the rest of his life.

We all need each other. We are biologically predisposed to loving interdependence on one another. We become destructive only when our love needs are severely frustrated. And from birth to death, they so often are.

Few of us have had the chance to grow up as fully loving people. But we all know a few fortunate individuals whose needs have been met so consistently that they have learned to live in loving peace with others all their lives. When they are met with aggression they usually are able to turn it off by behavior that satisfies some of the need whose frustration evoked the aggression. Compassion, a smile, the handshake, and the helping hand can often quell violence.

The same happens in the animal world, where mutually understood behavior prevents or shortens combat. In a fight, when one wolf gets the advantage the other rolls on his back. The winner ordinarily accepts this sign of submission and stops his attack. You see, a wolf can roll on his back without losing face.

Above all, animals do not fight to destroy one another. What lower animals do individually partly by instinct, we must learn to do through loving learning in masses of men called nations, thereby outmoding social control through threat, tyranny, and combat with our invention of justice.

There is much more that we must do in order to bring the benefits of loving interdependence to people everywhere. As we follow the human agenda, let us keep in mind that because man has substituted learning for instinct, *"human nature is what man learns."*[2] What we have learned is that in the transition from the brutish past to the beautiful future, modern man must be the loving vehicle, or he will become the missing link.

❋   ❋   ❋

J. Bronowski reminds us that in 1580 Philip Sidney defended poets and all unconventional thinkers from Puritan charges that they are liars: "A maker must imagine things that are not." And that William Blake two centuries later added, "What is now proved was once only imagined." Bronowski concludes, "The human gift is the gift of imagination."[3]

Out of imagination come foresight, empathy, and the precious spice of humor. All human beings share this gift, especially scientists and poets.

The poet dreams of new reality. The scientist realizes old dreams.

Whether or not we think about it, the future goes right on arriving day by day. Yet those who wish to look ahead at the future in imagination, and to find the best way, are often scorned as impractical utopians.

Because we human beings soon must choose which poetic dreams should and should not be scientifically realized, we soon must learn that the rainbows of one good utopian are worth more than the mudpuddles of a thousand cynics.

In resolutely and prospectantly turning the pages of the human agenda as we enter upon the conscious mastery of our evolution, let us honor the human imagination.

Only thus will we heed the message that has been passed to us through eighty thousand generations, the deathless whispered hope of the promise of man.

Précis

The Human Agenda is an exploration of the evolution of human values, man's specific tool for adaptation and survival.

The book examines the processes that have produced the universe. It traces man's quest for understanding of them. And it conveys a glimpse of one person's struggle to synthesize from a rational view of evolution a concept of the direction in which human values must be guided to assure man's survival. So complex a problem cannot be reduced to a simplified linear explanation. The question of which values will promote human survival, now that we are acquiring the capacity and responsibility to select them deliberately, is examined from as many viewpoints as possible.

Vulnerable early man sought *safety* through the magic of revealed truth, which would give him power and control over the unknowable. Preoccupation with the supernatural and submission to fixed doctrine are traceable to man's frantic urge to escape his primordial helplessness, recapitulated at each new baby's birth. Increasing natural power of the human individual and species reduces need for supernatural power. For example, with the invention of artificial sources of heat and light the need to propitiate and control the sun by worshiping it declined. But the ancient compulsion to submit to omnipotent friends in the sky has left fearsome residues in man's adaptive values here on earth. We continue to be terrified of the unknown and to demand the tranquilizing magic of definitive answers to prematurely or irrelevantly formulated questions. And we continue to be weighed down by resultant dogmas about race, economic systems, life after death, and so on.

But now we have grasped the ubiquity in the known universe of order, interdependence, conservation, change, and the prospect of constant expansion of human understanding within an area of uncertainty. And by now we have learned enough of the continuum of "causation" that generated our universe, earth, and man to achieve a sense of contented belongingness in the cosmos without the crippling shackles of mystical pseudounderstanding.

The above-listed organizing principles of evolutionary change in the inorganic universe are found on the agenda of life in the form of its crucial axis: cooperation. Appearing first as the tendency of individual cells to thrive in clusters, and later to revitalize one another by exchanging genetic material, cooperation has been elaborated by higher species into the mutual conveying of survival benefits which we call love.

Competition and aggression are far less significant in all living creatures than cooperation and love. Especially is this true for primates and man, whose *inventions* (combinations of upright posture, bipedal gait, prehensile hands, binocular vision, big brains, and substitution of learning for instinct in the control of behavior) freed them from the restrictions imposed by such adaptations as claw, hoof, and wing, as well as completed the process of emancipation from innately generated combative aggression. Particularly is this true for man, who in addition evolved the mind that can symbolize imaginatively, thereby learning to adapt to the widest variety of conditions through modification of his tools rather than limiting specializations of his body, and simultaneously becoming potentially free from all outworn dogma. New controls of biology must not be allowed to destroy this precious "neotenic" generalized primitivity.

Man is now in the midst of his most momentous evolutionary leap, the transition from the era of scarcity to the era of abundance. For the first time the love, work, and play of all human beings can shift from their central social functions of assuring survival to their crucial psychological function of promoting optimum growth of human personality. It is ironic but comprehensible that there should arise at this instant from those with a vested interest in the past powerful support for the erroneous rationalization that man's violent aggressiveness—even including the evolutionary mistake called war—is instinctual and therefore immutable. Promoted coincidentally by others as inevitable and desirable is the triumph of various inane versions of the Fun ethic.

Values adaptive to the era of abundance must rest on fact rather than fancy, whether dismal or hilarious. For the full flowering of human life we need demythification, including for example emancipation from the residue of sun worship embodied in our almost automatic association of good and evil respectively with light and dark. We need forthright recognition that man's health derives from zestful involvement of self in resolute efforts to surmount successive obstacles to human understanding and mastery, not from panicky or petulant demands for immediate satisfaction. And we need to foster the kind of personality which prospectantly surveys its page of the human agenda, and lovingly sets about raising human life to new levels of consciousness and joy while maintaining the grace and courage to live without final certainty.

Notes

These notes include elaborations on the text and customary references to source materials. Although the latter are offered as substantiation, more often (especially in the instance of ephemeral popular periodicals) they are included to help the reader decide the weight a particular recent or uncertain point deserves. They may also suggest a way to tie the divergent threads of daily experience into a coherent strand which has excitement and utility.

PROLOGUE

1. In Whyte, *The Next Development in Man*, p. 1.
2. In Einstein, *Albert Einstein: Philosopher-Scientist*, p. 23.
3. Muggeridge, personal communication.
4. Toffler, *Future Shock*, p. 2.
5. Bartlett, *Familiar Quotations*, 14th ed., p. 925.

CHAPTER 1
UNIVERSE AND GOD

1. Documentation for most of Chapter 1 may be found in the following readily accessible sources: George Abetti, *The History of Astronomy;* Isaac Asimov, *The Intelligent Man's Guide to Science;* David Bergamini, *The Universe;* John Langdon Davies, *Man and His Universe;* George Gamow, *The Creation of the Universe;* Fred Hoyle, *Astronomy;* Gwyn Jones, *Atoms and the Universe;* Arthur Koestler, *The Sleepwalkers;* Willy Ley, *Watchers of the Skies;* Homer Smith, *Man and His Gods;* Allan Winspear, *The Genesis of Plato's Thought.*
2. See the *New York Times,* July 2, 1968, p. 1; July 3, 1968, p. 34; July 5, 1968, p. 23.

CHAPTER 2
EARTH AND LIFE

1. Documentation for most of Chapter 2 may be found in the following readily accessible sources: Isaac Asimov, *The Intelligent Man's Guide to Science;* Arthur Beiser, *The Earth;* David Bergamini, *The Universe;* Elof Carlson, ed., *Modern Biology,* and *The Gene: A Critical History;* Richard Carrington, *The Mammals;* Winterton Curtis and Mary Guthrie, *Textbook of General Zoology;* Charles Darwin, *The Origin of Species;* Theodosius Dobzhansky, *Evolution, Genetics, and Man;* René Dubos, *The Torch of Life;* Loren Eiseley, *The Immense Journey;* George Gamow, *The Moon;* Robert Hegner and Karl Stiles, *College Biology;* Lorus and Margery Milne, *Patterns of Survival;* Ashley Montagu, *The Direction of Human Development,* and *The Human Revolution;* Ruth Moore, *Evolution;* John Pfeiffer, *The Cell;* Carl Sagan and Jonathan Leonard, *The Planets;* George G. Simpson *et al., Life: An Introduction*

to Biology; Homer Smith, *Man and His Gods;* Tracy Storer, *General Zoology.*

2. Muller, "Artificial Transmutation of the Gene"; "The Production of Mutations by X-Rays."

3. Nitrogen containing animal wastes can be eliminated most simply in the form of highly poisonous ammonia, but this requires the unlimited quantities of water available continuously only to fish, tadpoles, and other aquatic animals. When the crossopterygians became amphibians, the reduced amount of water available to them necessitated a change to a waste form of nitrogen sufficiently less toxic that it could be concentrated in the blood and urine and excreted in a comparatively small volume of water. Accordingly, to this day when a tadpole exchanges gills for lungs and becomes a frog it also begins to eliminate nitrogen as urea in the solution called urine.

But elimination of urea in urine still requires substantial amounts of water daily. Since reptile eggs are laid ashore and can enclose only a very limited supply of water, another biochemical change was necessary to prevent the embryo from being killed by toxic concentrations of its own wastes. Nitrogen could also be removed from solution by conversion into a nonsoluble crystalline form instead of urea, a bill filled by uric acid. Precipitated as crystals which cannot enter the cells, uric acid is excreted by reptiles throughout life in a semisolid state through the "cloaca," the single opening which also emits feces.

This pattern is retained by birds and even the egg-laying mammals. But in placental mammals the embryos are not encased in a shell but connected to the mother's bloodstream through which they can readily be washed free of urea. For them insoluble uric acid would present a disposition problem during a long gestation. Placental mammals have therefore gone back to excreting most of their waste nitrogen as urea which after birth they eliminate, as did their amphibian ancestors, dissolved in urine. Accordingly, placental mammals have developed two separate excretory openings, one for solid feces and the other for liquid urine.

This long-accepted theory of uric acid has recently been challenged. See the article by Folk; see also the exchange of letters in *Science* (October 2, 1970), pp. 98–99.

CHAPTER 3
ANIMAL AND MAN

1. Eimerl and De Vore, *The Primates,* p. 10.

2. Berrill, *Man's Emerging Mind,* p. 33.

3. *Ibid.,* pp. 33–34, 36–37.

4. Eimerl and De Vore, *op. cit.,* pp. 10–11.

5. *Ibid.,* p. 13.

6. The preceding three paragraphs are based on Berrill, *op. cit.,* pp. 36–38, and Eimerl and De Vore, *op. cit.,* pp. 10–14, 61.

7. *Ibid.,* p. 13.

8. Tinbergen, *Animal Behavior,* pp. 127–136.

9. *Ibid.,* p. 134.

10. *Ibid.,* pp. 66, 155.

11. *Ibid.,* p. 129.

12. See William Etkin, "Social Behavioral Factors in the Emergence of Man," in Garn, ed., *Culture and the Direction of Human Evolution,* p. 81.

13. Langlois' discussion of the small-mouth bass, in his "Sociological

Succession," pp. 458–461; cited in Montagu, *The Direction of Human Development*, p. 43.

The latter work and personal communications from the author constitute the general basis for my discussion of instinct, as well as for the subsequent treatment of basic needs and urges.

14. This follows the distinction made in Etkin, *op. cit.*, p. 86.

15. It is true that in Part III of *Moses and Monotheism*, written in his last years, Freud expressed the view that in some way acquired memory-traces are transmitted genetically, and that here he used the German word *Instinkt* and not *Triebe* (*Moses and Monotheism*, pp. 99–102). However, no matter what interpretation or credence one might give this Lamarckian speculation, it is still true that in all his earlier work the word *Triebe*, though often mistranslated as "instinct," referred only to the impulse, urge, or drive component of behavior.

16. Farb, *Man's Rise to Civilization as Shown by the Indians of North America from Primeval Times to the Coming of the Industrial State*, pp. 119–124.

17. Harry and Margaret Harlow, "A Study of Animal Affection," pp. 48–55; Harry and Margaret Harlow, "Social Deprivation in Monkeys," pp. 136–146.

18. Ford and Beach, *Patterns of Sexual Behavior*, pp. 199–249.

19. See Dunlap, "Are There Any Instincts?" pp. 307–311; Bernard, *Instinct: A Study in Social Psychology*.

20. Dunlap, *op. cit.*, pp. 307–311; Bernard, *op. cit.*

21. The preceding three paragraphs are based on information found in Berrill, *op. cit.*, p. 44, and Montagu, *The Human Revolution*, pp. 4, 141–143.

22. Berrill, *op. cit.*, p. 57; Eimerl and De Vore, *op. cit.*, pp. 18–19.

23. See Howell, *Early Man, passim;* Ruth Moore, *Evolution, passim.*

24. Berrill, *op. cit.*, pp. 49–50.

25. Montagu, *op. cit.*, pp. 2, 4. (The Arnhem land hawk referred to in this source is more properly known as the "firehawk.") See Lockwood, *I, the Aboriginal*, p. 93; personal communication from Montagu.

26. Eimerl and De Vore, *op. cit.*, p. 153.

27. Howell, *op. cit.*, p. 50.

28. Montagu, *op. cit.*, pp. 11–12; Howell, *op. cit.*, pp. 36–37.

29. Montagu, *op. cit.*, pp. 14–15.

30. *Ibid.*, p. 16.

31. *Ibid.*

32. *Time*, August 29, 1969, p. 50.

33. Howell, *op. cit.*, p. 83.

34. *Ibid.*, p. 55.

35. Montagu, *The Human Revolution*, pp. 80–82.

36. Howell, *op. cit.*, pp. 48–52.

37. *Ibid.*

38. *Ibid.*, pp. 53–54.

39. Montagu, *The Human Revolution*, p. 34.

40. Berrill, *op. cit.*, p. 54.

41. Montagu, *The Human Revolution*, p. 33.

42. Howell, *op. cit.*, pp. 79–80, 83.

43. *Ibid.*, p. 83. The higher figure represents new African finds and was presented in a lecture by Richard Leakey on January 17, 1971, at UCLA.

44. *The Marshall Cavendish Encyclopedia*, p. 122.

45. Cassirer, *An Essay on Man*, p. 26.

46. Montagu, *The Direction of Human Development*, pp. 49–58.

47. Eimerl and De Vore, *op. cit.*, *passim.*

48. Bronowski and Bellugi, "Language, Name, and Concept"; Gardner and Gardner, "Teaching Language to a Chimpanzee"; Eimerl and De Vore, *op. cit.*

49. Imaniski, cited in Garn, *op. cit.*, p. 89; Eimerl and De Vore, *op. cit.*, p. 89.

50. Bronowski and Bellugi, *op. cit.*

51. Kanzer, "Acting Out, Sublimation, and Reality Testing," p. 663.

52. Eimerl and De Vore, *op. cit.*, pp. 20–21.

53. Collias, "Aggressive Behavior Among Vertebrate Animals," pp. 84, 89–90. Professor George Bartholomew of the UCLA Department of Zoology concurs, in a personal communication.

54. Ardrey, *The Territorial Imperative*, pp. 107, 156–158.

55. Montagu, *The Human Revolution*, pp. 116–117.

56. Eimerl and De Vore, *op. cit.*, pp. 21, 38.

57. For a more thorough discussion, see Montagu, *Anthropology and Human Nature*, pp. 341–345.

58. Eimerl and De Vore, *op. cit.*, p. 108.

59. *Ibid.*, p. 38.

60. *Ibid.*, pp. 152, 37.

61. *Ibid.*, p. 142.

62. According to the personally communicated estimate of A. Acosta, curator of mammals at the Los Angeles Zoo, the forebears of baboons became terrestrial about ten million years before the apelike early forebears of man.

63. Eimerl and De Vore, *op. cit.*, p. 113.

64. Reynolds, *The Apes*, pp. 121, 130, 148; Clarke, *Man Is the Prey*, pp. 26–27, 29–30, 135, 203.

65. Eimerl and De Vore, *op. cit.*, p. 130.

66. *Ibid.*, pp. 130–132.

67. *Ibid.*, pp. 118–119.

68. Ardrey, *op. cit.*, p. 3.

69. Eimerl and De Vore, *op. cit.*, pp. 130–131.

70. The following account is drawn from Harry and Margaret Harlow, "A Study of Animal Affection," and "Social Deprivation in Monkeys."

71. Eimerl and De Vore, *op. cit.*, p. 112.

72. *Ibid.*, p. 132.

73. Again, the following account derives from Harry and Margaret Harlow, "A Study of Animal Affection," and "Social Deprivation in Monkeys."

74. This table was constructed using data from the following sources: Asdell, "Gestation Period," p. 372; Eimerl and De Vore, *op. cit.*, p. 86; Harry and Margaret Harlow, *op. cit.*; Lawick-Goodall, "New Discoveries Among Africa's Chimpanzees," p. 10; Montagu, *The Human Revolution*, p. 84; Ruth Moore, *Evolution*, p. 142; Spector, *Handbook of Biological Data*, p. 182; *1970 New York Times Encyclopedic Almanac*, p. 492.

75. Montagu, *The Human Revolution*, p. 86.

76. *Ibid.*, pp. 83–87.

77. Carter, *A General Zoology of the Invertebrates*, pp. 384–389, and *Animal Evolution*, pp. 311–326.

78. Hecht, "Amphibia," p. 816.

79. *Ibid.*

80. Montagu, *The Human Revolution*, pp. 127–128.

81. *Ibid.*

82. *Ibid.*, p. 136.

83. *Ibid.*

84. *Ibid.*, p. 131.

85. *Ibid.*, pp. 130, 87; Schultz, *The*

Primates, p. 167; Hooten, *Man's Poor Relations*, pp. 26–27, 87–88, 130.

86. This table was constructed using data from the following sources: Asdell, "Gestation Period," p. 372; Eimerl and De Vore, *op. cit.*, p. 86; Harry and Margaret Harlow, "A Study of Animal Affection," and "Social Deprivation in Monkeys"; Lawick-Goodall, "New Discoveries Among Africa's Chimpanzees," p. 10; Montagu, *The Human Revolution*, p. 84; Ruth Moore, *Evolution*, p. 142; Spector, *Handbook of Biological Data*, p. 182; *1970 New York Times Encyclopedic Almanac*, p. 492.

87. Montagu, *The Direction of Human Development*, pp. 22–23.

88. *Ibid.*, p. 23.

89. Tinbergen, *op. cit.*, p. 153.

90. Kropotkin, *Mutual Aid: A Factor of Evolution, passim*.

91. Carrighar, *Wild Heritage*, p. 139.

92. Kropotkin, *op. cit.*, p. 25.

93. *Ibid.*, p. 51.

94. Carrighar, *op. cit.*, p. 102.

95. Eimerl and De Vore, *op. cit.*, pp. 140–141.

96. Montagu, *The Direction of Human Development*, p. 36.

97. Kropotkin, *op cit.*, p. 15.

98. *Ibid.*, pp. 58 ff.

99. Eimerl and De Vore, *op. cit.*, p. 135.

100. *Ibid.*, pp. 37, 39, 94.

101. *Ibid.*, p. 134.

102. *Ibid.*, pp. 108–109.

103. *Ibid.*, p. 110.

104. *Ibid.*

105. *Ibid.*

106. *Ibid.*, pp. 138–139.

107. *Ibid.*, p. 144.

108. *Ibid.*, pp. 122–125.

109. *Ibid.*, pp. 112–113.

110. *Ibid.*, p. 107.

111. *Ibid.*

112. Farb, *op. cit.*, p. 122.

113. Eimerl and De Vore, *op. cit.*, p. 111.

114. Lorenz, *On Aggression, passim*.

115. *Ibid.*, p. 22.

116. *Ibid.*, p. ix.

117. Personal communication from Judd Marmor.

118. Lorenz, *op. cit.*, pp. 271–283.

119. Montagu, *Man and Aggression, passim*.

120. Scott, "Biology and Human Aggression," p. 572.

121. Montagu, *The Human Revolution*, p. 117.

122. Ardrey, *African Genesis*, and *The Territorial Imperative*.

123. Dart, "The Predatory Transition from Ape to Man," pp. 201–208.

124. Montagu, *The Human Revolution*, p. 110.

125. *Ibid.*

126. *Ibid.*, p. 113.

127. Lorenz, *On Aggression*, p. 231.

128. For example, see Berndt, *Excess and Restraint*, pp. 269–290.

129. Montagu, *The Human Revolution*, p. 121.

130. Wright, *A Study of War*, pp. 65–67.

131. *Ibid.*, pp. 38–41.

132. Farb, *op. cit.*, pp. 126, 43–46, 92.

133. *Ibid.*, pp. 97, 168–179.

134. *Ibid.*, pp. 43–46.

135. Montagu, "The New Litany of 'Innate Depravity,' or Original Sin Revisited," in Montagu, *Man and Aggression*.

136. "A Talk with Konrad Lorenz," p. 29.

137. *Ibid.*, p. 21.

138. Lorenz, *Studies in Animal and Human Behavior*, Vol. I, pp. xii–xiii.

139. Ruth Moore, *Evolution*, p. 37.

140. Berrill, *op. cit.*, pp. 74–75.

141. *Ibid.*

142. See Carrighar, *op. cit.*, pp. 125–130; Eimerl and De Vore, *op. cit.*, p. 18.

143. Eimerl and De Vore, *op. cit.*, pp. 92–93.

144. *Ibid.*, p. 94.

145. Ruesch, *Top of the World*, p. 104.

146. Farb, *op. cit.*

147. Montagu, *The Human Revolution*, pp. 111, 121.

148. Sigmund Freud, *Totem and Taboo*, pp. 13–14.

149. Eimerl and De Vore, *op. cit.*, p. 124.

150. E. T. Hall, *The Silent Language*, p. 164.

151. Zuckerman, *The Social Life of Monkeys and Apes*, *passim*; Calhoun, "Population Density and Social Pathology," *passim*.

CHAPTER 4
ADAPTATION AND THE HUMAN AGENDA

1. Homer Smith, *Man and His Gods*, p. 369.

2. *Ibid.*, p. 371.

3. *Ibid.*, pp. 372–373.

4. See editorial in the *Los Angeles Times*, October 14, 1969, Part II, p. 7.

5. Cited in David Starr Jordan, *War and the Breed*, p. 92.

6. Hobhouse, *Social Evolution and Political Theory*, p. 24.

7. See Martindale, *The Nature and Types of Sociological Theory*, p. 163.

8. Darwin, *The Descent of Man*, p. 134.

9. *Ibid.*, cited in Jordan, *op. cit.*, pp. 1–2.

10. Cited in Kuhn, *The Structure of Scientific Revolutions*, p. 150.

11. See Hofstadter, *Social Darwinism in American Thought*, *passim*.

12. For a brief summary of Scott's work, see Rushler, "Of Mice and Man." Also see Scott, *Aggression*.

13. Zuckerman, *The Social Life of Monkeys and Apes*, *passim*.

14. Eimerl and De Vore, *passim*.

15. *Ibid.*, pp. 108–109.

16. Freud, *Civilization and Its Discontents*, *passim*.

17. Bigelow, *The Dawn Warriors*, *passim*.

18. Morris, *The Naked Ape*.

19. Montagu, *The Direction of Human Development*, pp. 245–247.

20. Montagu, *The Human Revolution*, pp. 143 ff.

21. Morris, *op. cit.*, pp. 72–78; see also Montagu, "The Buttocks and Natural Selection."

22. Ford and Beach, *Patterns of Sexual Behavior*, pp. 85–90.

23. *Ibid.*

24. Montagu, *The Human Revolution*, p. 92.

25. One version of this widely held view: Montagu, *The Direction of Human Development*, pp. 167 ff.

26. Morris, *op. cit.*, p. 241.

27. Storr, *Human Aggression*.

28. *Ibid.*, p. 18.

29. *Ibid.*, p. 14.

30. *Ibid.*, p. 15.

31. *Ibid.*

32. *Ibid.*

33. *Ibid.*, p. 16.

34. *Ibid.*, p. 18.

35. *Ibid.*, pp. 25–27.

36. For instance, see Zuckerman.

37. Storr, *op. cit.*, p. 62.

38. *Ibid.*

39. *Ibid.*, p. 67.

40. Suttie, *The Origins of Love and Hate.*

41. From the context it is plain that in this sentence the author uses the term "instinct" to designate what in the previous chapter have been termed basic urges. In later sentences he appears sometimes to intend by it other psychological or biological meanings.

42. Suttie, *op. cit.*, p. 12.

43. *Ibid.*, p. 18.

44. *Ibid.*, p. 207.

45. Tielhard de Chardin, *The Future of Man*, p. 64, and *The Phenomenon of Man*, pp. 88, 90, 121.

46. Lorenz, *On Aggression*, pp. 208–209.

47. *Ibid.*, pp. 163–170.

48. *Ibid.*, p. 142.

49. This quoted expression is used by Lorenz to designate his position; Lorenz, *Studies in Animal and Human Behavior*, p. xii.

50. Lorenz, *On Aggression*, pp. 74, 208–211, 289.

51. This table was compiled using data from the same sources as given in note 74, Chapter 3, and adding material found in Eimerl and De Vore, pp. 89 and 121.

52. Freud, *The Ego and the Id*, pp. 13–66.

53. Freud, *The Psychology of Love*, p. 172.

54. See Srole and others, *Mental Health in the Metropolis: The Midtown Manhattan Study, passim.*

55. The following paragraph draws mostly from personal and published communications of Dr. Levy.

56. Robert Levy, "Tahitian Adoption as a Psychological Message," in Carroll, ed., *Adoption in Eastern Oceania*, pp. 71–87.

57. *Ibid.*

58. *Ibid.*

59. *Ibid.*

60. *Ibid.*

61. *Ibid.*

62. *Ibid.*

63. Andrews, *Dictionary of the Hawaiian Language*, pp. 375–376.

64. Moorehead, *The Fatal Impact*, pp. 6, 32. For comparison of a related Cook Island culture, Mangaia, see Marshall, "Sexuality—Two Anthropological Studies: Too Much in Mangaia," pp. 43–44 and 70–75.

65. On written language: Danielsson, *Love in the South Seas*, p. 41; anonymous personal informant; Robert Levy, "Personality Studies in Polynesia and Micronesia: Stability and Change."

66. Quotes from Morrison, Forster, and Forster from Robert Levy, "Tahiti Observed," pp. 35–36.

67. *Ibid.*

68. *Ibid.*

69. Robert Levy, "On Getting Angry in the Society Islands," in Caudill and Lin, ed., *Mental Health Research in Asia and the Pacific*, pp. 358–380.

70. Tyree, "A Study of Status, Conflict, and Suicide in Hawaii."

71. Personal communication from Robert Levy.

72. Robert Levy, "Tahitian Folk Psychotherapy," p. 12.

73. Franz J. Kallmann, "The Genetics of Mental Illness," in Arieti, *American Handbook of Psychiatry*, Vol. I, p. 190.

74. Personal communication from Judd Marmor.

75. Kardiner, *The Individual and His Society: The Psychodynamics of Primitive Social Organizations*, pp. 111–117 and 121–126.

76. *Ibid.* For observations on Tahiti, see pp. 148–158 in this chapter.

77. Linton, *The Study of Man*, pp. 348–355 and *passim;* Linton, *The Tanala: A Hill Tribe of Madagascar*, *passim;* Marmor, "Some Observations on Superstition in Contemporary life."

78. Kardiner, *op. cit.*, p. 284.

79. Marmor, *op. cit.*, p. 127.

80. Kardiner, *op. cit.*, pp. 287, 292–297.

81. *Ibid.*, pp. 282–283.

82. *Ibid.*, pp. 286–290; Marmor, *op. cit.*, p. 128; Linton, *The Tanala: A Hill Tribe of Madagascar*, p. 285.

83. Personal communication from Judd Marmor.

84. See Maslow, "Synergy in the Society and in the Individual"; Maslow and Honigmann, "Synergy: Some Notes of Ruth Benedict." For a general discussion of synergy in sociology see Slater, "Social Bases of Personality," in Smelser, ed., *Sociology: An Introduction*, pp. 566–570.

85. Maslow, *op. cit.*, p. 154.

86. *Ibid.*

87. *Ibid.*, pp. 154–155.

88. *Ibid.*, pp. 155–156.

89. *Ibid.*, p. 156.

90. Maslow and Honigmann, *op. cit.*, p. 329.

91. *Ibid.*, pp. 330, 327.

92. Spiro, *Children of the Kibbutz*, *passim;* Bettelheim, *Children of the Dream*, pp. 326–340.

93. See, for instance, Mead's interview, p. 31. Agnes Heller suggests that monogamy will cease to become the predominant pattern in the relations between the sexes, but warns that this change in itself guarantees neither greater humanization of male-female relations nor greater liberation for women. See Heller, "On the Future of Relations Between the Sexes."

94. Barrett, *The Universe and Dr. Einstein*, p. 52.

95. Berrill, *Man's Emerging Mind*, p. 130. For a discussion of the effects and consequences of this and similar language constructs, see Farb, *Man's Rise to Civilization as Shown by the Indians of North America from Primeval Times to the Coming of the Industrial State*, pp. 235–239.

96. Berrill, *op. cit.*, p. 126.

97. Barrett, *op. cit.*, pp. 41–42.

98. Belazs, "Relativity," p. 97.

99. Schollander, Irving, and Grinnell, "On the Temperature and Metabolism of the Seal During Diving," pp. 67–78.

100. DiCara, "Learning in the Autonomic Nervous System," pp. 37–39.

101. P. J. Schollander, "Animals in Aquatic Environments: Diving Mammals and Birds," in Dill, ed., *Adaptation to the Environment, Handbook of Physiology*, p. 730.

102. See Robinson, Abele, and Robinson, "Attack Autotomy: A Defense Against Predators," pp. 300–301; Ferenczi, *Thalassa: A Theory of Genitality*, p. 29.

103. Carrighar, *Wild Heritage*, pp. 123–124; Berrill, *op. cit.*, p. 29.

104. Freud, *Beyond the Pleasure Principle*, pp. 7, 9.

105. *Ibid.*, pp. 57–58.

106. For a fuller description of such experiments see Lilly and Miller, "Operant Conditioning of the Bottlenose Dolphin with Electrical Stimulation of the Brain," p. 73; and Bishop, Elder, and Heath, "Attempted Control of Operant Behavior in Man with Intracranial Self-Stimulation," in Heath, *The Role of Pleasure in Behavior*, p. 55.

CHAPTER 5
GESTATION

1. Lorenz, *On Aggression*, pp. 159–211.

2. Goro, "Control of Life: Exploration of Prenativity," p. 62.

3. Nadler, "Prenatal Detection of Genetic Defects," pp. 132–143; Rorvik with Shettles, "You Can Choose Your Baby's Sex," pp. 88–98.

4. Amarose, Wallingford, and Plotz, "Prediction of Fetal Sex from Cytologic Examination of Amniotic Fluid," p. 715; Goro, *op. cit.*, pp. 59–79; Rorvik, "The Brave New World of the Unborn."

5. *Los Angeles Times*, November 1, 1969, Part II, p. 1.

6. Janowsky, Gorney, and Kelly, "The 'Curse'—Vicissitudes and Variations of the Female Fertility Cycle," p. 242; Janowsky, Gorney, and Mandell, "Psychiatric and Ovarian-Adrenocortical Hormone Correlates of the Menstrual Cycle," p. 459; Janowsky, Gorney, and Davis, "Premenstrual-Menstrual Emotional Upsets in Nursing Students," *passim;* Janowsky, Gorney, Castelnuovo-Tedesco, and Stone, "Premenstrual-Menstrual Increases in Psychiatric Hospital Admission Rates," pp. 189–191.

7. Gouldner, "Children of the Laboratory," p. 13.

8. Grad, "Legislative Responses to the New Biology: Limits and Possibilities," p. 503.

9. Rosenfeld, "Control of Life: The New Man—What Will He Be Like?" p. 96.

10. Gouldner, *op. cit.*, p. 14.

11. *Ibid.*

12. Grad, *op. cit.*, p. 487; see also page 215 of this book.

13. "Human Ova Fertilized After Frozen Storage," p. 34.

14. *Ibid.*

15. *Ibid.*

16. Rosenfeld, *op. cit.*

17. "Human Ova Fertilized After Frozen Storage," p. 35.

18. Address by N. Corwin in "The Human Agenda: Biological Prospects and Human Values," UCLA Faculty Lecture Series, May 23, 1966.

19. Goro, *op. cit.*, p. 75.

20. See Waddington, *Principles of Embryology, passim;* Willier, Weiss, and Hamburger, *Analysis of Development, passim.*

21. Pincus and Shapiro, "The Comparative Behavior of Mammalian Eggs in Vivo and in Vitro," p. 631.

22. Pincus and Shapiro, "Further Studies on the Parthenogenetic Activation of Rabbit Eggs," pp. 163–165.

23. "Curtain Rises Early on Antibody Activity," p. 60.

24. See, for instance, Wieland, Folk, Taylor, and Hanwi, "Studies of Male Hypogonadism," p. 763.

25. See Cabanes, *The Erotikon.*

26. Goro, *op. cit.*, p. 60.

27. SenGupta, Taylor, and Kolff, "An Artificial Placenta Designed to Maintain Life During Cardiorespiratory Distress," p. 63; Taylor, Kolff, Sindelar, and Cahill, "Attempts to Make an 'Artificial Uterus,'" p. 1295.

28. Baker, Boolootian, and Dutton, "An Experience in Conducting Seminars and Laboratory Seminars in Biochemistry, Zoology, and Physiology for Gifted Children," p. 24.

29. Mangel, "Bobby Joins His World: Five Million Brain-Damaged Children Can Be Helped," pp. 84–88; "Hope for the Brain Damaged," pp. 31–34.

CHAPTER 6
GENETICS

1. Stanley M. Garn, "Culture and the Direction of Human Evolution," in Garn, *Culture and the Direction of Human Evolution*, p. 15.

2. Golding, "Ethical Issues in Biological Engineering," pp. 444, 453, 474.

3. Carlson, "The Inevitability of Genetic Control for Human Survival."

4. Dobzhansky, *Evolution, Genetics, and Man*, p. 378.

5. George and Muriel Beadle, *The Language of Life, passim.*

6. Elof Carlson, "When Man Seeks to Control Heredity," *Providence Sunday Journal*, June 5, 1966, Sec. N, p. 44.

7. Beadle, *op. cit.*, p. 221.

8. Golding, *op. cit.*

9. Personal communication from Elof Carlson.

10. Carlson, "The Inevitability of Genetic Control for Human Survival," p. 7.

11. *Ibid.*

12. Personal communication from Elof Carlson.

13. Grad, "Legislative Responses to the New Biology: Limits and Possibilities," p. 486.

14. Personal communication from Elof Carlson.

15. "Human Ova Fertilized After Frozen Storage," p. 34.

16. Batt, "They Shoot Horses, Don't They?: An Essay on the Scotoma of One-Eyed Kings," p. 529; Golding, "Ethical Issues in Biological Engineering," p. 463; Grad, *op. cit.*, pp. 486, 491.

17. Herman J. Muller, "Means and Aims in Human Genetic Betterment," in Sonneborn, ed., *The Control of Human Heredity and Evolution*, p. 116.

18. *Ibid.*

19. "The Unfit: Denmark's Solution," p. 74.

20. Personal communication from Elof Carlson.

21. Landauer, "Aristogenics," p. 816.

22. *Los Angeles Times*, October 17, 1968, Part I, p. 1.

23. Grad, *op. cit.*, p. 489; see also p. 273 of this book.

24. Irving Benglesdorf, *Los Angeles Times*, May 11, 1969, Sec. B, p. 1.

25. Muller, *op. cit.*, p. 102.

26. "DNA and a Mouse of a Different Color," p. 24.

27. *Los Angeles Times*, June 3, 1970. Part I, p. 1; *ibid.*, November 12, 1970, Part I, p. 8; *ibid.*, November 16, 1970, Part I, p. 3.

28. "Rhythmic Cells Set Beats for Human Bioclock—Scientists See RNA as Conductor of Unexplained Physiologic Patterns," p. 176.

29. Rollin D. Hotchkiss, "The Nature of the Revolutionary New Biology—Discussion," in Sonneborn, *op. cit.*, p. 38.

30. Batt, *op. cit.*, p. 530.

31. Dobzhansky, *op. cit.*, p. 267.

32. Lederberg, "Experimental Genetics and Human Evolution," p. 519.

33. Grad, *op. cit.*, p. 494.

34. Hans Sperman, "Embryonic Development and Induction," in Carlson, ed., *Modern Biology*, pp. 114–127.

35. Gurdon and Vehlinger, "'Fertile' Intestine Nuclei," p. 1240.

36. Lederberg, *op. cit.*, p. 525; Grad, *op. cit.*, p. 494.

37. Grad, *op. cit.*, p. 494.

38. "Curtain Rises Early on Antibody Activity," p. 60.

39. For a discussion of the constitu-

tional implications of resurrection, see Grad, *op. cit.*, p. 486. For a discussion of positive eugenics, see *ibid.*, p. 491. Generally see Batt, *op. cit.*, p. 529; Golding, *op. cit.*, p. 443.

40. Carlson, "Inevitability of Genetic Control for Human Survival," p. 11.

41. Kimball Atwood, "The Nature of the Revolutionary New Biology—Discussion," in Sonneborn, *op. cit.*

42. Lederberg, *op. cit.*, p. 527.

43. Loomis, "Skin Pigment Regulation of Vitamin-D Biosynthesis in Man," *Science* (August 4, 1967), pp. 501–506.

44. Arthur J. Snider, "A Geneticist Would Mold Man of Future," *New York Post*, August 24, 1966, p. 32.

45. Golding, *op. cit.*, pp. 444, 473.

46. Beadle, *op. cit.*, p. 233.

47. Golding, *op. cit.*, p. 475; Grad, *op. cit.*, p. 492.

48. John W. Crenshaw, Jr., "Direction of Human Evolution: A Zoologist's View," in Garn, ed., *Culture and the Direction of Human Evolution*.

CHAPTER 7
LIFE AND DEATH

1. Sanders and Dukeminier, "Medical Advance and Legal Lag: Hemodialysis and Kidney Transplantation," p. 407.

2. Dan L. Thrapp, "All Men Entitled Held to a Dignified Death," *Los Angeles Times*, April 23, 1967, Sec. H, p. 6.

3. "Control of Life," Part III, "Rebuilt People," p. 66.

4. *Ibid.*

5. Sanders and Dukeminier, *op. cit.*, p. 357.

6. George Getze, "Kidney Machines Force Doctors to Choose Patients Who Will Live," *Los Angeles Times*, July 5, 1965, Sec. I, p. 6.

7. Sanders and Dukeminier, *op. cit.*, p. 366; Grad, "Legislative Responses to the New Biology: Limits and Possibilities," p. 497.

8. "M.D.s, Clergy Discuss Prolonging Life," p. 9.

9. *Ibid.*

10. "Medical Ethics in a Changing World," p. 66.

11. "M.D.s, Clergy Discuss Prolonging Life," p. 9.

12. "Some Psychologic Effects of Medical and Surgical Advances," p. 1.

13. "Medical Achievements of the Year—Transplants and Immunity," p. 38.

14. "Curtain Rises Early on Antibody Activity," p. 60.

15. See generally Francis Moore, *Give and Take: The Development of Tissue Transplants*.

16. See Grad, *op. cit.*, p. 494; and pp. 222–223 of this book.

17. "Internal Helium Freezing, Warming 'Promising' for Organ Preservation," p. 33.

18. "Restoring Severed Limbs," p. 34.

19. "The Pump Worked Beautifully," p. 37.

20. Kolff and others, "An Artificial Heart Inside the Chest," p. 792.

21. Kolff, "Today the Calf, Tomorrow the Man," pp. 23–24.

22. "Medical Ethics in a Changing World," p. 63.

23. *Ibid.*

24. *Los Angeles Times*, April 5, 1969, April 6, 1969, April 7, 1969, Part I, p. 1; "Weighing Plastic Heart Against Clinical Rules," pp. 6–7.

25. Thrapp, *op. cit.*, p. 6.

26. "Medical Ethics in a Changing World," p. 68.

27. Harry Nelson, "Death: Deciding When It Comes May Save Others," *Los Angeles Times*, March 24, 1967, Part II, p. 6; Cohn, "Transplantation in Animals," p. 10.

28. Henderson and Ettinger, "Cryonic Suspension and the Law," p. 414; "Cryo-Burial Raises Scientific Heat," p. 34; Ettinger, "Lasting Indefinitely," p. 64.

29. Meryman, *Cryobiology, passim;* Whitelock, "Freezing and Drying of Biological Materials," pp. 501–734; Audrey Smith, "Hamsters Cooled below 0° Centigrade," p. 392.

30. Audrey Smith, *Biological Effects of Freezing and Supercooling,* pp. 270–275.

31. *Ibid.*

32. *Ibid.*

33. Audrey Smith, "Hamsters Cooled below 0° Centigrade," p. 392.

34. Audrey Smith, *Biological Effects of Freezing and Supercooling;* Popovic, "Survival of Newborn Ground Squirrels After Supercooling or Freezing," p. 949.

35. Audrey Smith, *Biological Effects of Freezing . . . ,* pp. 270–275.

36. *Ibid.*

37. "Frozen Cat Brain Revived After Six Months," p. 37.

38. Comfort, *The Process of Aging,* p. 35.

39. Dublin and Lotha, *Length of Life,* p. 34.

40. "Progress in Longevity Since 1850," p. 1.

41. *California Medical Association News,* p. 2.

42. Address by Harry Sobel in "The Human Agenda: Biological Prospects and Human Values," UCLA Faculty Lecture Series, April 25, 1966.

43. "Programming the Body for a Ripe Old Age," p. 63.

44. "Is the Menopause Necessary?" p. 63.

45. Sobel address.

46. *Ibid.*

47. "Chemical Enables Animals to Survive Lethal Radiation," p. 31; "Making Rats Grow Old Before Their Time," p. 55.

48. Sobel address.

49. Lawick-Goodall, "New Discoveries Among African Chimpanzees," p. 802.

CHAPTER 8
BRAIN

1. "The Brain," p. 113.

2. *Ibid.*, p. 115.

3. Pilleri, "It's Man's Hands Not His Brain That Make Him More Advanced Than Dolphins," p. 25.

4. Romer, *Vertebrate Paleontology;* Kellogg, "The History of Whales— Their Adaptation to Life in the Water," p. 29.

5. Garn, *Culture and the Direction of Human Evolution,* p. 14.

6. "Dolphin Gets Message, Sends One of Its Own," p. 9.

7. "The Brain," p. 119.

8. *Ibid.*, 113.

9. *Ibid.*

10. Lederberg, "Experimental Genetics and Human Evolution," p. 519.

11. "Brain Transplant in Dog Works for Three Days," p. 30.

12. Wilson, *The Mind,* p. 176.

13. Kleitman, "Patterns of Dreaming," p. 82.

14. Wilson, *op. cit.*, p. 174.

15. "The Brain," p. 116.

16. Batt, "They Shoot Horses, Don't They?: An Essay on the Scotoma of One-Eyed Kings," p. 523.

17. Olds, "Pleasure Centers in the Brain," p. 105.

18. Von Holst and Von St. Paul, "Electrically Controlled Behavior," p. 50.

19. "Radio Signals Trigger Off Mixed Emotions," p. 32; see also Delgado, *Physical Control of the Mind: Toward a Psychocivilized Society, passim.*

20. Sherfey, "The Evolution and Nature of Female Sexuality in Relation to Psychoanalytic Theory," p. 99.

21. "Radio Signals Trigger Off Mixed Emotions."

22. See generally Ruch and Fulton.

23. Wilson, *op. cit.*, p. 178.

24. Fisher, "Chemical Stimulation of the Brain," p. 60.

25. *Ibid.*

26. "The Brain," p. 114.

27. Wilson, *op. cit.*, p. 186.

28. Freedman, "Truth Drugs," p. 145.

29. Barron, Jarvik, and Bunnell, "The Hallucinogenic Drugs," pp. 29–37.

30. Ungerleider and Fisher, "Problems of LSD^{25} and Emotional Disorder," *passim.*

31. "Social Environment and Brain Chemistry."

32. "The Brain," p. 117.

33. Krech, "In Search of the Engram," p. 20; "Study Verifies Relation Between Brain Traits and Intelligence," p. 1.

34. Herron, "The Pathology of Boredom," p. 52.

35. French, "The Reticular Formation," p. 54.

36. "Can Pesticides Cloud the Brain?" p. 118.

37. Krech, *op. cit.*, p. 20.

38. McConnell, "Memory Transfer Through Cannibalism in Planarians," pp. 542–548.

39. *Ibid.*

40. "Drug's Effects Raise Hope for a 'Memory Pill,' " p. 24.

41. "Brain Extract Educates Mice by Proxy," p. 32.

42. Jacobson, Babich, Bubash, and Jacobson, "Differential Approach Tendencies Produced by Injection of Ribonucleic Acid from Trained Rats," pp. 656–657.

43. "RNA May Play an Important Role," p. 15.

44. Essman and Lehrer, "Facilitation of Maze Performances by 'RNA Extracts' from Maze-Trained Mice," p. 263; Ungar, "Chemical Transfer of Learning: Its Stimulus Specificity," p. 207; "Memory Transfer by a Protein Achieved," p. 1.

45. See generally W. Penfield and L. Roberts.

46. Mangel, "Bobby Joins His World: Five Million Brain-Damaged Children Can Be Helped," p. 84.

47. Cutler, "The Persistent Russian," p. 66.

48. Address by Kurt Von Meier in "The Human Agenda: Biological Prospects and Human Values," UCLA Lecture Series, May 9, 1966.

49. For additional discussion of the role of computers, see p. 217 in this book and Grad, "Legislative Responses to the New Biology: Limits and Possibilities," p. 489.

50. Von Meier address.

CHAPTER 9
MIND

1. Harrison Brown, *The Challenge of Man's Future*, p. 4.

2. Pilleri, "It's Man's Hands Not His Brain That Make Him More Advanced Than Dolphins," pp. 25–27.

3. Stanley M. Garn, "Culture and the Direction of Human Evolution,"

in Garn, ed., *Culture and the Direction of Human Evolution*, p. 15.

4. Alexander, "A Contribution to the Theory of Play," p. 180.

5. For a general discussion of the interference by unconscious mental activity in voluntary behavior, see: Sigmund Freud, *The Psychopathology of Everyday Life;* Hartmann, *Ego Psychology and the Problem of Adaptation.*

6. Bills, "Fatigue," in *Encyclopaedia Britannica*, p. 112. For a general text see Bartley, *Fatigue and Impairment in Man.*

7. Maier, *Psychology in Industry*, pp. 536–537.

8. Hartmann, "On Rational and Irrational Action," in *Ego Psychology and the Problem of Adaptation*, pp. 379–380.

9. Cole, *Guild Socialism Restated*, pp. 42 ff.

10. Personal communication, superintendent, mechanical division, Southern Pacific Railway, February, 1968, indicates that the horsepower of diesel locomotives is increased by the manufacturer about every three years, and that railroad operators may maintain their locomotives up to fifteen years through periodic overhauls, at which time they are usually retired in favor of later models.

11. Montagu, *The Human Revolution*, p. 1.

12. Lumsdaine and Glaser, *Teaching Machines and Programmed Learning.* For a brief report on teaching through hypnosis, see "Teaching Through Trance," pp. 106–107.

13. Etkin, "Social Behavioral Factors in the Emergence of Man," in Garn, *op. cit.*, p. 86.

14. Three references among many which convey this general impression are: Frazer, *The Golden Bough;* Graves, *The Greek Myths;* Homer Smith, *Man and His Gods.*

15. William Wahl, remarks included in UCLA Faculty Lecture Series, "The Human Agenda: Biological Prospects and Human Values," UCLA Lecture Series, May 2, 1966.

16. James Harvey Robinson, *The Mind in The Making*, pp. 21–22.

17. Quoted in Robinson, *op. cit.*, p. 28.

18. Richard Anschutz, "August Kekule," in Farber, ed., *Great Chemists*, p. 700.

19. Alexander, "Neurosis and Creativity," pp. 116–130; Wordsworth and Schlosburg, *Experimental Psychology*, pp. 838–841; Ghiselin, *The Creative Process.*

20. "Cripple Rescues Strangling Boy," *Los Angeles Herald-Examiner*, October 7, 1967.

21. "Unlocking Early Learning's Secret."

22. *Ibid.*

23. *Ibid.*

24. *Ibid.*

25. Personal communication from a Soviet psychiatrist, a Soviet schoolteacher, and several parents of schoolchildren in Leningrad, Summer, 1963.

26. Bayley, Livson, and Cameron, "Infant Vocalizations and Their Relationship to Mature Intelligence," pp. 331–333.

27. Baker, Boolootian, and Dutton, "An Experience in Conducting Seminars and Laboratory Seminars in Biochemistry, Zoology, and Physiology for Gifted Children," pp. 24–27; Lehman, "College Math for 11-Year-Olds," p. 367; *New Developments in High School Science Teaching.*

28. Dempsey, "Reducing Educational Pressures," p. 117.

29. Hoffer, "A Time of Juveniles," pp. 15–24.

30. Bettelheim, *The Informed Heart;* Eitinger, *Concentration Camp Survivors in Norway and Israel,* pp. 69 ff.; Strassman, Thaler, and Schein, "A Prisoner of War Syndrome," pp. 998–1003. For an illustration involving animals see Munn, *Handbook of Psychological Research on the Rat,* p. 422, with reference to Humphreys and Marcuse.

31. Wahl, *op. cit.*

32. Sigmund Freud, *A General Introduction to Psychoanalysis.* For example, see the discussion of the classic case of "little Hans" in "Analysis of a Phobia in a Five-Year-Old Boy."

33. Anna Freud, *Ego and Mechanisms of Defense;* Anna Freud, *Normality and Pathology in Childhood: Assessments of Developments;* Erikson, *Childhood and Society.*

34. Harlow and Woolsey, *Basis of Behavior;* Lorenz, *On Aggression.*

35. Kinsey, Pomeroy, Martin, and Gebhard, *Sexual Behavior in the Human Male;* Kinsey, Pomeroy, Martin, and Gebhard, *Sexual Behavior in the Human Female;* Masters and Johnson, *Human Sexual Response;* Masters and Johnson, *Human Sexual Inadequacy.*

36. Kardiner, *The Individual and His Society: The Psychodynamics of Primitive Social Organizations.*

37. Abramson, *The Use of LSD in Psychotherapy and Alcoholism.*

38. Ludwig, Levine, Stark, and Lazar, "A Clinical Study of LSD Treatment in Alcoholism," pp. 59–69.

39. Ungerleider and Fisher, "The Problems of LSD[25] and Emotional Disorder," p. 50.

40. The concept of "ego boundaries" in relation to maintaining the sense of reality is elaborated in Federn, *Ego Psychology and the Psychoses.* (See especially the introduction by Eduardo Weiss.)

41. This principle has long been recognized in psychoanalytic writing as applicable to psychotherapy in general. See, for example, Piers, *Shame and Guilt,* p. 34.

42. Yablonski, *The Tunnel Back.*

43. Elizabeth Rosenberg, "A Clinical Contribution to the Psychopathology of the War Neuroses," pp. 32–41; Peary, *Secrets of Polar Travel,* p. 52; Sigmund Freud, "Memorandum on the Electrical Treatment of War Neurotics," 211–215; see also: Bettelheim, *op. cit.;* Eitinger, *op. cit.*

44. Wolpe and Lazarus, *Behavior Therapy Techniques: A Guide to the Treatment of Neuroses;* Hunt, "A Neurosis Is Just a Bad Habit," pp. 38–47.

45. Packard, *The Waste Makers;* J. Henry, *Culture Against Man,* pp. 19–20; Lynes, *The Tastemakers.*

46. Packard, *The Hidden Persuaders,* pp. 42–43.

47. Lorenz, *op. cit.,* p. 250.

48. See *Los Angeles Times,* August 7, 1970, Part I, p. 1.

49. Skornia, *Television and Society,* p. 168.

50. Berkowitz, *Advances in Experimental Social Psychology,* Vol. II, pp. 35–41.

51. Albert Bandura, "Vicarious Processes: A Case of No-Trial Learning," in Berkowitz, ed., *Advances in Experimental Social Psychology,* Vol. II, p. 28.

52. *Ibid.,* pp. 23–25.

53. *Ibid.,* pp. 21–28. For supplemental reading see: Schramm, Lyle, and Parker, *Television in the Lives of Our Children;* Bandura, Ross, and Ross, "Imitation of Film-Mediated Ag-

gressive Models," pp. 3–11; Albert Bandura and Richard Walters, "Aggression," in Stevenson, ed., *Child Psychology*, pp. 364–415, in particular, an excellent and comprehensive bibliography.

LOVE, WORK, AND PLAY REVISITED—INTRODUCTION

1. Erikson, *Childhood and Society*, p. 229.
2. Montagu, *The Direction of Human Development*.
3. See David Riesman, "The Themes of Work and Play in the Structure of Freud's Thought," in Riesman, *Individualism Reconsidered and Other Essays*, pp. 365–387.

CHAPTER 10
No Notes......

CHAPTER 11
ORIGINS AND DEVELOPMENT OF LOVE, WORK, AND PLAY

1. Montagu, *The Human Revolution*, pp. 82–89.
2. The following five paragraphs owe much to Montagu's *The Direction of Human Development*, Chapter 6.
3. Freud, *Civilization and Its Discontents*, p. 64.
4. See David Levy, "Fingersucking and Accessory Movements in Early Infancy," p. 882; also see *The Marshall Cavendish Encyclopedia of the Human Mind and Body*, p. 69.
5. Montagu, *The Direction of Human Development*, pp. 176, 295; Montagu, *The Human Revolution*, p. 90.
6. Montagu, *The Direction of Human Development*, pp. 167–168.
7. *Ibid.*, p. 120; citing Suttie, *The Origins of Love and Hate*, p. 35.

8. *Ibid.*
9. Montagu, *The Human Revolution*, pp. 118–121, 150.
10. *Ibid.*, pp. 121 ff.; also see Montagu, *Touching: The Human Function of the Skin*.
11. Montagu, "The Sensory Influence of the Skin," pp. 291–301.
12. Montagu, *The Direction of Human Development*, pp. 364 ff.
13. *Ibid.*, p. 121.
14. Scattered throughout Freud's writings are numerous indications of his lifelong conviction that someday progress in biological science would explain, complement, or supplant psychoanalytic formulations, and provide control over the psychological phenomena with which they deal. For example: ". . . we must recollect that all our provisional ideas in psychology will presumably some day be based on an organic substructure" (*On Narcissism: An Introduction*, p. 78); "The deficiencies in our description would probably vanish if we were already in a position to replace the psychological terms by physiological or chemical ones . . ." (*Beyond the Pleasure Principle*, p. 60); "It is here, indeed, that hope for the future lies: the possibility that our knowledge of the operation of the hormones . . . may give us the means of successfully combating the quantitative factors of the illnesses . . ." (*New Introductory Lectures on Psychoanalysis*, p. 154).
15. Freud, *Three Essays on Sexuality*, p. 170.
16. David Levy, "Fingersucking and Accessory Movements in Early Infancy," pp. 881–918. Levy also cites G. Compayré, *Intellectual and Moral Development of a Child*, p. 81.
17. David Levy, "Thumb or Fin-

gersucking From the Psychiatric Angle," pp. 99–101.

18. Thorpe, *Learning and Instinct in Animals*, p. 362.

19. Olds, "Pleasure Centers in the Brain," pp. 105–117.

20. *Ibid.*, pp. 110, 114.

21. Harry Harlow, "Basic Social Capacity of Primates," p. 51.

22. Lorenz, *On Aggression*, pp. 171–172.

23. Gesell, *The First Five Years of Life*, pp. 19, 21.

24. Wolfsheimer, "The Discus Fish Yields a Secret," pp. 679–681.

25. Scott, "Critical Periods in the Development of Social Behavior in Puppies," pp. 42–54.

26. Spitz, *The First Year of Life*, pp. 87–88. Personal pediatric informants indicate an earlier onset in some instances than given by Spitz (2 months, 6 months) of the smile and specific-nurse preference.

27. Gesell, *op. cit.*, pp. 21, 22, 24.

28. Spitz, *op. cit.*, pp. 151–160; Montagu, *The Direction of Human Development*, pp. 200, 258.

29. "The Emergence of Jean Piaget," p. 2.

30. *Ibid.*

31. "It's Only a Paper Moon," E. Y. Harburg and Billy Rose, music by Harold Arlen.

32. Margery Williams, *The Velveteen Rabbit*, pp. 16–17.

33. Gesell, *op. cit.*, p. 251.

CHAPTER 12
THE ERAS OF SCARCITY AND ABUNDANCE

1. Montagu, *The Human Revolution*, pp. 62 ff.

2. Hunt, *The Natural History of Love*, p. 16.

3. See Charles Williams, "Scientists Review Their Forecast for 'The Next Hundred Years.'"

4. Indeed, for the period from early 1965 to late 1969 the average workingman in manufacturing in the United States saw his purchasing power decrease slightly as higher taxes and inflation stemming from the Vietnam war more than canceled out wage increases. See "The Dollar Squeeze," *Life* (August 15, 1969), pp. 20–25.

For conclusions on standards of living in underdeveloped countries, see Piel, *Science in the Cause of Man*, p. 213.

5. Ben J. Wattenburg, *Los Angeles Times*, December 28, 1969, Section H, p. 1.

6. Weaver, "What a Moon Ticket Will Buy," p. 38. Herein Dr. Weaver illustrates the magnitude of the cost of putting men on the moon, a figure that by chance approximates our former annual expenditure in Vietnam.

7. Kahn and Weiner, *The Year 2000*, pp. 140–141.

8. *Ibid.*, pp. 252–255.

9. Usher, *Rich and Poor Countries*, pp. 35–39.

10. Not all of the discrepancy between per capita income and actual standard of living is to be accounted for, of course, by the evident differences in dollar purchasing power. Part of it results from the fact that at this income level such an item as a car, needed and possessed by some poor Americans, is not only out of reach of the poor in Ireland but is unnecessary because of shorter distances and excellent *public* transportation. A further factor is that because the Irish spend only 4 percent of their national budget for defense, in contrast to our 44 percent, a much larger proportion

of their resources can go into other enhancements of the standard of living, such as health care, education, etc.

Data on national defense expenditures from *The Statesman's Yearbook 1969–1970,* pp. 545, 1065; on poverty-level income from *Statistical Abstract of the United States, 1970,* p. 327. Data for the table in the text are for 1968 and are taken from the *1970 New York Times Encyclopedic Almanac,* pp. 179, 492, 806; data for groceries, clothing, and rent from the London *Financial Times,* December 5, 1968, courtesy of Benjamin Aaron, Ph.D., Professor of Law and Director of the Institute of Industrial Relations, UCLA. Professor Aaron and Professor Frederic Meyers (Professor of Industrial Relations and Research Economist, Institute of Industrial Relations, UCLA) are also due my thanks for critical review of the material dealing with international economic comparisons.

11. U.S. Bureau of the Census, pp. 91–92.

12. *Los Angeles Herald-Examiner,* October 23, 1963, p. A–7.

13. "Production-oriented" includes mining, manufacturing, construction, transportation, and utilities. "Service-oriented" includes trade, finance, real estate, services, and government. *U.S. Statistical Abstract, 1966,* as cited in Kahn and Weiner, *op. cit.,* p. 176.

14. Kahn and Weiner, *op. cit.,* p. 126, Figure 5.

15. This estimate, in fact, proved to be low. At about the same time the United Auto Workers' research staff estimated for the ten years of the 1960s we would need 80,000 new jobs every week—41 million in all. Of course, this need was not met. See Kirstein, "The Manpower Revolution," pp. 140–141.

16. Theodore White wrote in 1969 that from 1960 to 1968 ten million new jobs were created, or about 21,500 per week. White, *The Making of the President, 1968,* p. 496.

17. *Los Angeles Times,* November 13, 1969, Part I, p. 5.

CHAPTER 13
VALUES, TECHNOLOGY, SELF-VALIDATION

1. *Webster's Third New International Dictionary,* Vol. III, p. 2531.

2. Thus, for instance, technology tends to impose similar values in industrial societies, even those with officially opposed ideologies such as the United States and the Soviet Union. On the other hand, the close geographical proximity of Beverly Hills and Watts belies the often quite different value systems operating in those communities.

3. There are several versions of this statement, the one cited in the text having appeared in a periodical now unavailable to me. One version appears in Hausner, *Justice in Jerusalem:* "I will jump with joy into my grave in the knowledge that I drag with me millions of Jews" (p. 267). Another version, quoted in Pearlman, *The Capture and Trial of Adolf Eichmann,* reads: "And, toward the end of the war, Eichmann had told him that he would 'leap laughing into the grave' with extraordinary satisfaction 'at the knowledge that he had helped to exterminate five million Jews'" (p. 17).

4. For fuller discussions of values published after these passages were written, see Baier, "What Is Value?" in Baier and Rescher, *Values and the*

Future; Taviss, "Futurology and the Problem of Values."

5. Toynbee, "The Virtues of Adversity," in Vol. I of *A Study of History.*

6. Buxton and Southam, *Human Infertility,* p. 7.

7. Charles F. Westoff, "The Fertility of the American Population," in Freeman, ed., *Population, The Vital Revolution.*

8. Piel, *Science in the Cause of Man, passim.*

9. Grotjahn, "The New Technology and Our Ageless Unconscious," pp. 8–18.

10. Langer, *An Encyclopedia of World History,* p. 458.

11. Piel, *op. cit.,* pp. 150–151.

12. Colby, Gilbert, and Watt, "A Computer Method of Psychotherapy: Preliminary Communication," pp. 148–152.

13. Chamberlain, "Retooling the Mind."

14. The Institute for Social Research, *The Effect of Unemployment upon the Status of the Man in 59 Families, passim.*

15. *Ibid.,* pp. 66–82.

16. Fromm, *Beyond the Chains of Illusion,* p. 36.

17. The following account is drawn from *ibid.,* pp. 36–179.

18. *Ibid.,* p. 44.

19. *Ibid.,* p. 45. Fromm cites Marx, *The Economic and Philosophical Manuscripts of 1844.*

20. *Ibid.,* p. 46.

21. *Ibid.*

22. *Ibid.,* p. 50.

23. *Ibid.,* p. 84.

24. *Ibid.,* pp. 40–41.

25. *Ibid.,* p. 40. Fromm cites Montesquieu here.

26. *Ibid.,* p. 45. Fromm cites Marx, *The Economic and Philosophical Manuscripts of 1844.*

27. *Ibid.,* p. 47. Fromm cites Marx, *Capital.*

28. *Ibid.,* p. 48. Fromm cites Marx, *Capital.*

29. *Ibid.* For a different interpretation of the same problem see Marcuse, "The End of Utopia," in *Five Lectures,* Chapter 4.

30. Marx, *The Economic and Philosophical Manuscripts of 1844,* p. 118.

31. Obradovic, *Participacije i motivaticije u radničkon samoprauljanju obzirom na technolološki nivo proizvodnje.*

32. A later study showed that *job satisfaction* was increased for handicraft and mechanized workers, but *alienation also* was increased for *all three levels* by participation in workers' councils. See Obradovic, "Participation and Work Attitudes in Yugoslavia," pp. 161–169.

33. See, for instance, Frederick Taylor, *The Principles of Scientific Management.*

34. Morgan, *Love: Plato, the Bible, and Freud.*

35. *Ibid.,* p. 115.

36. This opinion is shared by Dr. W. H. Masters, who would broaden it to include "individual interpretations of orthodox religious tenets, regardless of which of the three major faiths is involved" (personal communication from Dr. W. H. Masters).

37. Hunt, *The Natural History of Love,* pp. 42–48; see also, for example, Petronius, *The Satyricon.*

38. Hunt, *op. cit.,* pp. 131–172.

39. *Ibid.*

40. Marcuse, *Eros and Civilization.*

41. *Ibid.,* p. 34.

42. Fingarette, "Eros and Utopia," pp. 660–665.

43. Landis, "Marriage," *Encyclopaedia Britannica*, Vol. XIV, pp. 928–929.

44. Mencken, *A Mencken Chrestomathy*, p. 619.

45. Linton, *The Study of Man*, p. 175.

46. Directed by Bo Widenberg (1967).

47. Flugel, *The Psychology of Clothes*, pp. 58–59.

48. See, for instance, Krafft-Ebbing, *Psychopathia Sexualis, passim;* and Sigmund Freud, *Three Essays on Sexuality, passim.*

49. Adams, *The Education of Henry Adams*, pp. 384–385.

50. Aristotle, *On Poetry and Style*, p. 12.

51. For a fuller account of Groos's views on play, see Piaget, *Play, Dreams and Imitation in Childhood*, pp. 150–156.

52. Nash, *Philosophy of Recreation and Leisure*, p. 82.

53. G. Stanley Hall, *Youth*, pp. 73–74.

54. Sigmund Freud, *Beyond the Pleasure Principle*, p. 15.

55. Piaget, *op. cit.*, p. 154.

56. *Ibid.*

57. Caillois, *Man, Play, and Games.*

58. *Ibid.*, pp. 12–26.

59. Alexander, "A Contribution to the Theory of Play," p. 175.

60. *Ibid., passim;* McBride and Hebb cited in *ibid.*, p. 178.

61. Alexander, *op. cit.*, p. 186.

62. Róheim, cited in Alexander, *op. cit.*, p. 187.

63. Alexander, *op. cit.*, p. 188.

64. Huizinga, *Homo Ludens*, p. 1.

65. *Ibid.*, pp. 23, 58.

66. Alexander, *op. cit.*, p. 189.

67. Huizinga, *op. cit.*, p. 192.

68. *Ibid.*, p. 207.

69. Alexander, *op. cit.*, p. 192.

70. Alexander, "Neurosis and Creativity," p. 122.

71. *Ibid.*, p. 125.

72. *Ibid.*, p. 126.

CHAPTER 14
SELF-VALIDATIVE LOVE, WORK, AND PLAY IN THE FUTURE OF ABUNDANCE

1. Montagu, *The Direction of Human Development*, p. 2.

2. Malinowski cited in Montagu, *op. cit.*, p. 56.

3. *Ibid.*, pp. 52, 56.

4. The cited phrase, "Human nature is what man learns," was enunciated by Dr. Montagu in a lecture. For similar formulations of this idea, see Montagu, ed., *Man and Aggression*, p. xii; Montagu, *The Biosocial Nature of Man*, p. 80; Montagu, *The Human Revolution*, p. 118.

5. See Chapter 19 of this book.

6. Suttie, *The Origins of Love and Hate, passim.*

CHAPTER 15
No Notes......

CHAPTER 16
PSYCHIC IMPOSTOR ETHIC

1. Henry, *Culture Against Man*, pp. 49–52.

2. Arthur Miller, *The Crucible*, p. 138.

3. Feldman, *Cognitive Consistency, Motivational Antecedents, passim.*

4. *Ibid.*, pp. 104–110.

WAYS TO GO: INTRODUCTION

1. Kahn and Weiner, *The Year 2000;* Bell, Daniel, ed., *Toward the Year 2000: Work in Progress.*

2. See Heilbroner, "Futurology," for a brief but thoughtful critique of developments in studying the future.

3. *Ibid.*

4. *The Futurist,* published by the World Future Society, Washington, D.C.

5. Heilbroner, *op. cit.*

6. Brodbeck and Burdick, *American Voting Patterns, passim,* contains a good summary of parental influence on party membership and voting patterns. See also Marquand, *The Late George Apley;* O'Hara, *Ten North Frederick.*

7. Joseph Heller, *Catch-22.*

8. McLuhan, *Understanding Media,* p. x.

CHAPTER 17
GETTING AHEAD

1. See, for instance, Galbraith, *The Affluent Society,* and *The New Industrial State.*

CHAPTER 18
FUN FERVOR

1. Kerr, *The Decline of Pleasure.*

2. Directed by Federico Fellini (1960).

3. The correctness of this quote, and my interpretation of it, have been confirmed in a personal communication from Professor Ernst Straus of the University of California, Los Angeles, former assistant to Professor Einstein at the Institute of Advanced Studies in Princeton.

4. Directed by Erich von Stroheim (1924).

5. Galbraith, *The New Industrial State,* p. 371.

6. *Ibid.,* p. 279.

7. Jacobs, *The Rise of the American Film,* p. 168.

8. Ramsaye, *A Million and One Nights,* p. 641.

9. For a representative comment on this idea, see *Esquire,* August, 1969, p. 6.

10. Hannah Arendt, "The Crisis in Culture," in Arendt, *Between Past and Future,* pp. 205, 207.

11. *Ibid.,* p. 206.

CHAPTER 19
CREATIVE FRENZY

1. Koestler, *The Act of Creation,* p. 120.

2. Bronowski, *Science and Human Values, passim.*

3. Koestler, *op. cit.,* p. 158.

4. Sigmund Freud, "Dostoevsky and Parricide," p. 177.

5. Koestler, *The Ghost in the Machine,* pp. 180–181, 295.

6. Hatterer, *The Artist in Society,* p. 24.

7. Dali, *Diary of a Genius,* p. 7.

8. Koestler, *The Ghost in the Machine,* p. 167.

9. Kris, *Psychoanalytic Explorations in Art,* p. 177.

10. Koestler, *The Act of Creation,* p. 318.

11. Freud, *Civilization and Its Discontents,* p. 64. For further related thoughts, see Gorney, "Of Divers Things: Preliminary Note on the Dynamics of Scuba Diving."

12. Farb, *Man's Rise to Civilization as Shown by the Indians of North America from Primeval Times to the Coming of the Industrial State,* p. 36.

13. Henri, *The Art Spirit,* p. 5.

14. Grace Rubin-Rabson, "A Warning to the Feminists," *Los Angeles*

Times, March 15, 1970, opinion section.

15. Mead, *Male and Female, passim.*

16. Personal communication from Thomas Eggleston.

17. Mead, *op. cit.,* pp. 80–89.

18. For more examples, see Bayer, "Beginning Again in the Middle," pp. 50–57.

19. In the mid-1960s, even the U.S. Department of Labor estimated that the average 20-year-old *then* during his working life would have six or seven jobs. Toffler foresees an emerging dominant pattern of segmented careers in the American job market (Toffler, *Future Shock,* p. 95).

CHAPTER 20
MYSTIC WITHDRAWAL

1. *Los Angeles Times,* February 13, 1969, Part I, p. 12.

2. See almost any issue of any "underground" newspaper.

3. *Los Angeles Free Press,* March 14, 1969.

4. Novick, "The Fallacy of the Living Theatre," p. 27.

5. *Los Angeles Times,* February 18, 1969, Part IV, p. 10.

6. Meyer, *The Positive Thinkers.*

7. *Ibid.,* p. 72.

8. *Ibid.,* pp. 72–75.

9. See Benjamin DeMott, "Against McLuhan," in Stearn, ed., *McLuhan Hot and Cool,* pp. 250–251.

10. Norman O. Brown, *Life Against Death,* pp. 27–32 and 110–134.

11. *Ibid.,* pp. 10–19.

12. Marcuse, *Eros and Civilization,* pp. 183–184.

13. Marcuse, *One-Dimensional Man,* p. 257; Herbert Marcuse, Hans

Meyeroff Memorial Lecture, UCLA, October 31, 1968.

14. Timothy Leary, Interview in *East Village Other,* November 1, 1968, p. 3.

15. Farb, *Man's Rise to Civilization as Shown by the Indians of North America from Primeval Times to the Coming of the Industrial State,* pp. 285–289.

16. Fromm, *The Revolution of Hope,* p. 18.

17. Wolfe, *The Electric Kool-Aid Acid Test,* p. 244.

18. Meyer, *The Positive Thinkers,* p. 292.

CHAPTER 21
TECHNIQUE INFATUATION

1. Quoted in *Atlas* magazine, February, 1969, p. 16.

2. Fromm, *The Revolution of Hope,* p. 100.

3. Seidenberg, *Post-Historic Man.*

4. *Ibid.,* p. 180.

5. See McLuhan, *Understanding Media,* and *The Gutenberg Galaxy, passim.*

6. In addition, experiments in human perception have shown McLuhan to be wrong in many of his basic assumptions. See Mayberry, "McLuhan's Physiology."

7. Cited in Stearn, *McLuhan Hot and Cool,* p. 247.

8. Neil Compton, "The Paradox of Marshall McLuhan," in Rosenthal, ed., *McLuhan: Pro and Con,* p. 122.

9. Ellul, *The Technological Society, passim.*

10. *Ibid.,* p. xxx.

11. See "Prospects for Control: Mind," Chapter 9 of this book.

12. Goethe, *Faust,* trans. by Walter Kaufman, p. 187, ll. 1693–1694.

13. Compton, *op. cit.*, p. 111.

14. See Marcuse, *An Essay on Liberation, passim.*

15. *Los Angeles Times*, April 13, 1969. Section C, pp. 1, 6.

16. Fromm, *op. cit.*, pp. 97, 157.

17. *Ibid.*, p. 3.

18. Interview in *Los Angeles Free Press*, November 15, 1968.

16. *Ibid.*, p. 42.

17. *Stanford Campus Report*, April 10, 1969.

18. *Los Angeles Times*, May 8, 1969, Part IV, p. 22.

19. Roy Wilkins, quoted in *Los Angeles Times*, May 13, 1969, Part I, p. 15.

20. Alvarez, *Under Pressure*, p. 133.

CHAPTER 22
BIG AND LITTLE BROTHER PROTECTION

1. Sampson, *The Psychology of Power*, p. 102.

2. Jefferson, *The Writings of Thomas Jefferson*, Vol. VI, p. 65.

3. Lincoln, *Abraham Lincoln: His Speeches and Writings*, pp. 586–587.

4. Sampson, *op. cit.*, p. 1.

5. Gunther, *Procession*, p. 166.

6. George Wald, "A Generation in Search of a Future," speech at Massachusetts Institute of Technology, March 4, 1969.

7. This was true in the mid-sixties. Today a few more nations may have caught up—Italy, China, and India, for instance. Personal communication from José Acosta, International Economic Analysis Division, Ampex, Inc.

8. Heilbroner, *The Limits of American Capitalism*, p. 10.

9. *Ibid.*, pp. 11–13.

10. *Ibid.*, p. 19.

11. Jay, *Management and Machiavelli*, p. 17.

12. *Los Angeles Times*, September 10, 1970, Part I, p. 1.

13. Lewis Hershey, testimony before House Armed Services Committee, June, 1968.

14. Horowitz, "Billion Dollar Brains," p. 43.

15. *Ibid.*, p. 44.

CHAPTER 23
PROSPECTANCY

1. Cited in McLuhan, *Understanding Media*, p. 62.

2. Karr, *En Fumant*, p. 54.

3. Ogburn, *Technological Trends and National Policy, Including the Social Implications of New Inventions.*

4. Ernest Jones, *Freud*, Vol. I, pp. 78–97.

5. For some speculation on group marriage, see Constantine, "Where Is Marriage Going?"; Rimmer, *The Harrad Experiment, The Harrad Letters,* and *Proposition 31.*

CHAPTER 24
BLONDNESS: FIRST VIEWS

1. Hayakawa, *Language in Action, passim;* Korzybski, *Science and Sanity, passim.*

2. *A Dip Into History*, p. 2; Corson, *Fashions in Hair, passim;* Frank, "Brunette Today, Blonde Tomorrow," *passim.*

3. "Theda was heartless, cruel, mercenary . . . she despised those whom she relieved of honor, wealth, fame and fortune, before permitting them to expire after the most glorious of little deaths. They were fools who thought they heard the heavenly music of the spheres in the rustles of bedsheets,

fools to be kissed during the course of a thousand and one secret delights known only to Theda. . . . Destroyed beyond redemption, each of these ruined demigods gloried in his fall, accomplished in chambers reminiscent of Poe's *Ligeia*—a swan-boat bed with silken sheets so perfumed they made laundresses lovesick, a cloth-of-gold tent in the garden of Scheherazade, a barge whose poop was beaten gold, with sails of purple filled with scented winds—ah!—these were the heavenly, sensual hells viewed by the sighing, itching man in the ten-cent seat, for whom Theda and hell for a dime was more of a bargain than the best five-cent cigar" (Shulman, *Harlow*, p. 95).

4. Another meaning of the term "darkening" is the change to a more resonant tone quality produced by the singer at will.

5. Weiss, "Uber einen noch nicht beschriebene Phase der Entwicklung zur heterosexueller Liebe."

CHAPTER 25
THE BLOND IMAGE AND LIGHT VERSUS DARK

1. Brugsch-bey, *Egypt Under the Pharaohs*, p. 50.

2. Hastings, *Encyclopedia of Religion and Ethics*, p. 50; H. Langdon, trans., "Ishtar and Izdubar," and Talbot, trans., "Assyrian Talismans and Exorcism," in *World's Great Classics*, Vol. XXI, pp. 3–154, 202–205.

3. Wilcox, *The Mode in Costume*, p. 8.

4. *Ibid.*, p. 20.

5. Frank, "Brunette Today, Blonde Tomorrow," p. 46.

6. Berne, "The Mythology of Dark and Fair: Psychiatric Use of Folklore," p. 2.

7. *Ibid., passim.*

8. Feuerbach, cited in Marx, *The Economic and Philosophic Manuscripts of 1844*, p. 39.

9. Caso, *The Aztecs, passim;* Prescott, *History of the Conquest of Mexico, passim;* Hilton-Simpson, *Land and People of the Kasai, passim;* Leach, *The Beginning: Creation Myths Around the World, passim;* Diaz del Castillo, *The Discovery and Conquest of Mexico, 1517–1521, passim.*

10. This myth may have been based upon an actual pre-Columbian white visitor, but is significant nevertheless.

11. Ellis, *Sexual Selection in Man*, p. 188.

12. Corson, *Fashions in Hair*, p. 57.

13. *Ibid.*, p. 73.

14. *Ibid.*, p. 74.

15. Berne, *op. cit.*, pp. 4, 11–12.

16. Fitzgerald, *This Side of Paradise*, pp. 128–129.

17. Jordan, *White Over Black*, pp. 17–19, 35–36.

18. Ellis, *op. cit.*, pp. 146–152.

19. Quiller-Couch, *Oxford Book of English Verse*, pp. 199–200.

20. *Ibid.*, p. 353.

21. *Ibid.*, p. 329.

22. Martin, *The Poetical Works of Robert Herrick*, p. 34.

23. J. C. Smith and E. De Selincourt, *Spenser: Poetical Works*, p. 4.

24. Milton, *The Poetical Works of John Milton*, p. 108.

25. Campbell, *The Poems of Edgar Allan Poe*, p. 70.

26. F. N. Robinson, *The Works of Geoffrey Chaucer*, p. 49.

27. Tillotson, *The Poems of Alexander Pope*, p. 128.

28. Goethe, *Faust*, p. 209.

29. Lennon, *Victoria Through the Looking-Glass*. Cf. Hubbell, "Triple Alice," pp. 174–196; Collingwood, *The Life and Letters of Lewis Carroll*, photographs on pp. 81, 94, 358, 366: as cited in Berne, "The Mythology of Dark and Fair: Psychiatric Use of Folklore."

30. Margaret Murray, *The Witch Cult in Western Europe;* Kittredge, *Witchcraft in Old and New England;* Ernest Jones, *Nightmares, Witches, and Devils:* as cited in Berne, *op. cit.*

31. Directed by Victor Fleming (1939).

32. Directed by Ingmar Bergman (1960).

33. Les Malmstrom and David Kushner, trans., "The Daughter of Tore in Vange," in Hallmundsson, ed., *An Anthology of Scandinavian Literature*, pp. 275–277.

34. Robert Graves' *The White Goddess* has an informative discussion of whiteness in regard to leprosy. "The Rime of the Ancient Mariner" by Samuel Coleridge is only one of many examples that could be cited, wherein whiteness is equated with death (see lines 180–199).

As Eric Berne shows, extremes of pigmentation have associations opposite to the usual ones. Extreme lightness has ghostly and ghastly overtones, while extreme darkness has reassuring ones. White hair of advanced age, like albinism and the pallor of leprosy or death, has negative connotations, whereas extreme darkness partakes of the comfort connected with envelopment in the womb or in mother earth.

35. Sir James Murray, *The Oxford English Dictionary: A New English Dictionary on Historical Principles*, Vol. IV, pp. 25–28.

CHAPTER 26
PATHOLOGY

1. Mighels, *Fairy Tale of the White Man Told From the Gates of Sunset*, pp. 13–14, and introduction (unpaged).

2. Bovell, "Psychological Considerations of Color Conflicts among Negroes," pp. 447–459.

3. Freud and other analysts reported this process in many papers dealing with anality, reaction formation, and character development.

CHAPTER 27
BLONDNESS: FURTHER VIEWS

1. O'Neill, *The Hairy Ape*.

2. It is not uncommon that parents who are dark, and who naturally expect their child to be dark, nevertheless anxiously watch week after week in hopes that the blue eyes of the baby will not darken. Obviously the desire for blue eyes includes elements similar to those expressed in the desire for light-colored hair. This interesting aspect will not be dealt with here for several reasons: Eyes and their coloring do not represent as prominent a feature as hair and its coloring. You can verify this by inquiring of your friends about the hair and eye colors of mutual acquaintances. In most cases you will not find a good recollection of eye coloring. Moreover, hair coloring can be changed without regard to eye coloring. Finally, the state of cosmetic technique, despite frequent inaccurate references to tinted contact lenses, does not provide ready methods for making dark eyes blue—at the moment!

3. The one exception is the occasional baby who is born with dark hair

which is lost in the first few months after birth and later replaced by lighter hair. Perhaps the skin darkening reflects an evolutionary adaptation to the lessened need for Vitamin D in adults once the period of growth is completed and rickets is no longer a threat.

4. Masters and Johnson, *Human Sexual Response, passim.*

5. Watts, *Psychotherapy East and West,* p. 56.

6. Frank, "Brunette Today, Blonde Tomorrow," p. 46.

7. Hess, " 'Imprinting' in Animals," *passim.*

8. Erikson, *Childhood and Society, passim.*

9. Bovell, "Psychological Considerations of Color Conflicts among Negroes," pp. 447–459.

10. Montagu, *Man's Most Dangerous Myth: The Fallacy of Race,* pp. 60–67.

11. *Ibid.,* p. 228.

12. *Ibid.,* pp. 232–234.

13. *Ibid.,* pp. 236–237.

14. Loomis, "Skin Pigment Regulation of Vitamin-D Biosynthesis in Man"; Sunderman and Boerner, *Normal Values in Clinical Medicine,* pp. 716–717.

15. Montagu, *op. cit.,* pp. 52–67.

16. Keith, *Concerning Man's Origin,* p. 46.

CHAPTER 28
No Notes ......

CHAPTER 29
BLONDNESS AND DECISION

1. One of the major ironies of the blond image is the subdivision of it which requires that, once located, the fair white blond be dangerously sunroasted to a more ordinary brown color.

CONCLUSIONS

1. Huxley, *Brave New World,* p. xiii.

2. Wolstenholme, *Man and His Future,* p. 362.

3. Prosser, *Law of Torts,* p. 339.

4. *California Business and Professions Code* (San Francisco, Bancroft-Whitney Co., 1944, with rev., n.d.), pp. 241–242, §2144.

5. "Good Samaritans and Liability for Medical Malpractice," p. 1301.

6. André Tunc, "The Volunteer and the Good Samaritan," in Ratcliffe, ed., *The Good Samaritan and the Law,* pp. 43–56; Alexsander Rudzinski, "The Duty to Rescue: A Comparative Analysis," in Ratcliffe, *op cit.,* pp. 91–99; Hans Zeisel, "An International Experiment on the Effects of a Good Samaritan Law," in Ratcliffe, *op. cit.,* pp. 209–212.

7. Morse, "Why Doesn't the U.S. Outlaw Genocide?" p. 40.

8. U.S. Department of the Army, *The Law of Land Warfare,* Manual No. 27–10, pp. i–iii, 3–7, 17–19, 176–183.

9. See Henri Meyrowitz, "Le Nouveau Règlement de Discipline Générale de l'Armée Française," in *Annuaire Français de Droit International XII–1966,* pp. 822–831; Paoli, pp. 301–302.

10. *Los Angeles Times,* June 21, 1969, Part I, p. 1.

11. McLuhan, *Understanding Media,* p. 24. McLuhan cites Robert Theobald, *The Rich and the Poor.*

12. See Fred Polak, "Towards the

Goal of Goals," in Jungk and Galtung, eds., *Mankind 2000*, pp. 307–329.

13. Ward, *Spaceship Earth*, p. 15.

14. Kierkegaard, *Concluding Unscientific Postscript*, p. 251. I am greatly indebted to Dr. Howard V. Hong, St. Olaf College, Northfield, Minnesota, for locating this passage in Kierkegaard's voluminous writings.

15. Harburg and Saidy, *Finian's Rainbow*, p. 141.

EPILOGUE

1. James Harvey Robinson, *The Mind in the Making*, pp. 83–85.

2. See Chapter 14, note 4.

3. Bronowski, "The Reach of Imagination," pp. 34–35.

Bibliography

I. BOOKS

Abetti, George, *The History of Astronomy*, trans. by Betty Abetti. New York, Henry Schuman, 1952.

Abramson, Harold, ed., *The Use of LSD in Psychotherapy and Alcoholism*. Indianapolis, The Bobbs-Merrill Company, Inc., 1967.

Adams, Henry, *The Education of Henry Adams*. New York, Modern Library, 1931.

Adorno, Theodore, and others, *The Authoritarian Personality*. New York, Harper & Brothers, 1950.

Alvarez, A., *Under Pressure*. Baltimore, Penguin Books, Inc., 1965.

Andrews, Lorrin, *Dictionary of the Hawaiian Language*. Honolulu, Henry M. Whitney, 1865.

Annuaire Français de Droit International XII–1966. Centre National de la Recherche Scientifique, Paris.

Ardrey, Robert, *African Genesis*. New York, Dell Books, 1967.

————, *The Territorial Imperative*. New York, Atheneum Publishers, 1966.

Arendt, Hannah, *Between Past and Future*. Cleveland, The World Publishing Company, 1963.

————, *The Origins of Totalitarianism*. New York, Harcourt, Brace & Company, 1951.

Arieti, Silvano, ed., *American Handbook of Psychiatry*, Vol. I. New York, Basic Books, Inc., 1959.

Aristotle, *On Poetry and Style*, G. M. A. Grube, ed. New York, Liberal Arts Press, 1958.

Asimov, Isaac, *The Intelligent Man's Guide to Science*. 2 vols. New York, Basic Books, Inc., 1960.

Baier, Kurt, and Rescher, Nicholas, *Values and the Future*. New York and London, The Free Press and Collier-Macmillan, Ltd., 1969.

Barrett, Lincoln, *The Universe and Dr. Einstein*. New York, William Sloane Associates, 1950.

Bartlett, John, *Familiar Quotations,* 14th ed. Boston, Little, Brown and Company, 1968.

Bartley, Samuel, *Fatigue and Impairment in Man.* New York, McGraw-Hill, Inc., 1947.

Beadle, George and Muriel, *The Language of Life.* Garden City, N.Y., Doubleday & Company, Inc., 1966.

Beiser, Arthur, *The Earth,* rev. ed. New York, Time-Life, 1968.

Bell, Daniel, ed., *Toward the Year 2000: Work in Progress.* Boston, Houghton Mifflin Co., 1968.

Bergamini, David, *The Universe,* rev. ed. New York, Time-Life, 1968.

Berkowitz, Leonard, ed., *Advances in Experimental Social Psychology,* Vol. II. New York, Academic Press, Inc., 1965.

Bernard, L. L., *Instinct: A Study in Social Psychology.* New York, Holt, 1924.

Berndt, R. N., *Excess and Restraint.* Chicago, University of Chicago Press, 1962.

Berrill, N. J., *Man's Emerging Mind.* Greenwich, Conn., Fawcett Premier Books, 1965.

Bettelheim, Bruno, *The Children of the Dream.* New York, Avon, 1970.

———, *The Informed Heart.* Glencoe, Ill., The Free Press, 1963.

Bigelow, Robert, *The Dawn Warriors.* New York, Little, Brown and Company, 1969.

Brodbeck, Arthur, and Burdick, Eugene, *American Voting Patterns.* Glencoe, Ill., The Free Press, 1959.

Bronowski, J., *Science and Human Values.* New York, Harper & Row, 1965.

Brown, Harrison, *The Challenge of Man's Future.* New York, The Viking Press, Inc., 1954.

Brown, Norman O., *Life Against Death.* New York, Anchor, 1959.

Brugsch-Bey, Heinrich, *Egypt Under the Pharaohs,* trans. by Philip Smith. New York, n.p., 1891.

Buxton, Charles, and Southam, Anna, *Human Infertility.* New York, Paul Hoeber, Inc., 1958.

Cabanes, Augustin, *The Erotikon,* trans. by Robert Meadows. New York, Anthropological Press, 1933.

Caillois, Roger, *Man, Play, and Games,* trans. by Meyer Barash. New York and Glencoe, Ill., The Free Press, 1961.

Campbell, Killis, ed., *The Poems of Edgar Allan Poe.* New York, Russell and Russell, Inc., 1962.

Carlson, Elof, *The Gene: A Critical History.* Philadelphia and London, W. B. Saunders Company, 1966.

———, ed., *Modern Biology.* New York, George Braziller, 1967.

Caron, M., and Hutin, S., *The Alchemists.* New York, Grove Press, Inc., 1961.

Carrighar, Sally, *Wild Heritage.* Boston, Houghton Mifflin Company, 1965.

Carrington, Richard, *The Mammals.* New York, Time-Life, 1963.

Carroll, Vern, ed., *Adoption in Eastern Oceania.* Honolulu, University of Hawaii Press, 1969.

Carter, G. S., *Animal Evolution,* rev. ed. London, Sidgwick and Jackson, Ltd., 1954.

————, *A General Zoology of the Invertebrates*, 4th ed. rev. London, Sidgwick and Jackson, Ltd., 1961.

Caso, Alfonso, *The Aztecs*. Norman, Oklahoma, The University of Oklahoma Press, 1958.

Cassirer, Ernst, *An Essay on Man*. New Haven and London, Yale University Press, 1944.

Caudill, William, and Lin, Tsung-yi, eds., *Mental Health Research in Asia and the Pacific*. Honolulu, East-West Center Press, 1969.

Clarke, James, *Man Is the Prey*. London, André Deutsch, Ltd., 1969.

Cole, G. D. H., *Guild Socialism Restated*. London, L. Parsons, 1921.

Collingwood, Stuart, *The Life and Letters of Lewis Carroll*. New York, Century, 1898.

Comfort, Alex, *The Process of Aging*. London, George Weidenfeld and Nicolson, Ltd., 1964.

Compayré, G., *Intellectual and Moral Development of a Child*. New York, Appleton and Co., 1896.

Corson, Richard, *Fashions in Hair*. London, Peter Owen, Ltd., 1965.

Curtis, Winterton, and Guthrie, Mary, *Textbook of General Zoology*. New York, John Wiley and Sons, Inc., 1938.

Dali, Salvador, *Diary of a Genius*, trans. by Richard Howard. New York, Doubleday & Company, Inc., 1965.

Danielsson, Bengt, *Love in the South Seas*, trans. by F. H. Lyon. New York, Reynal & Company, Inc., 1956.

Darwin, Charles, *The Descent of Man*, 2d ed. London, John Murray (Publishers), Ltd., 1875.

————, *On the Origin of Species by Means of Natural Selection*. New York, The Modern Library, Inc., 1948.

Davies, John Langdon, *Man and His Universe*. New York and London, Harper & Brothers, 1930.

Delgado, José M. R., *Physical Control of the Mind: Toward a Psychocivilized Society*. New York, Harper & Row, 1969.

Diaz del Castillo, Bernal, *The Discovery and Conquest of Mexico, 1517–1521*, Genaro Garcia, ed., trans. by A. P. Mandslay. New York, Farrar, Straus & Cudahy, 1956.

Dill, D. B., ed., *Adaptation to the Environment, Handbook of Physiology*, Section 4. Washington, D.C., American Psychological Society, 1964.

Dobzhansky, Theodosius, *The Biological Basis of Human Freedom*. New York, Columbia University Press, 1956.

————, *Evolution, Genetics, and Man*. New York, John Wiley & Sons, Inc., 1955.

Dublin, Louis, and Lotha, Alfred, *Length of Life*. New York, The Ronald Press Company, 1949.

Dubos, René, *The Torch of Life*. New York, Pocket Books, 1962.

Eimerl, Sarel, and De Vore, Irven, *The Primates*. New York, Time-Life, 1965.

Einstein, Albert, *Albert Einstein: Philosopher-Scientist*, 2d ed., Paul Schlipp, ed. New York, Tudor Press, 1951.

Eiseley, Loren, *The Immense Journey*. New York, Random House, Inc., 1946.

Eitinger, Leo, *Concentration Camp Survivors in Norway and Israel*. London, Allen and Unwin, 1964.

Ellis, Havelock, *Sexual Selection in Man*. Philadelphia, F. A. Davis Co., 1921.

Ellul, Jacques, *The Technological Society*. New York, Alfred A. Knopf, Inc., 1964.

Erikson, Erik H., *Childhood and Society*. New York, W. W. Norton & Company, Inc., 1950.

Farb, Peter, *Man's Rise to Civilization as Shown by the Indians of North America from Primeval Times to the Coming of the Industrial State*. New York, E. P. Dutton & Co., Inc., 1968.

Farber, Eduard, ed., *Great Chemists*. New York, Interscience Publishers, Inc., 1961.

Federn, Paul, *Ego Psychology and the Psychoses*. New York, Basic Books, Inc., 1952.

Feldman, Shel, ed., *Cognitive Consistency, Motivational Antecedents, and Behavioral Consequence*. New York and London, Academic Press, Inc., 1966.

Ferenczi, Sandor, *Thalassa: A Theory of Genitality*, trans. by Henry A. Bunker. New York, The Psychoanalytic Quarterly, Inc., 1938.

Ferkiss, Victor, *Technological Man*. New York, George Braziller, 1969.

Feuerbach, Ludwig, *Vorläufige Thesen, Werke*, 2d ed. F. Jodl, 1904.

Finkelstein, Sidney, *Sense and Nonsense of Marshall McLuhan*. New York, International Publishers, 1968.

Fitzgerald, F. Scott, *The Great Gatsby*. New York, Charles Scribner's Sons, 1962.

————, *This Side of Paradise*. New York, Charles Scribner's Sons, 1962.

Flugel, J. C., *The Psychology of Clothes*. London, The Hogarth Press, 1950.

Ford, Clellan, and Beach, Frank, *Patterns of Sexual Behavior*. New York, Harper & Brothers, 1951.

Frazer, James, *The Golden Bough*. New York, The Macmillan Company, 1922.

Freeman, Ronald, ed., *Population, The Vital Revolution*. Garden City, N.Y., Doubleday & Company, Inc., 1964.

Freud, Anna, *Ego and Mechanisms of Defense*. London, The Hogarth Press, 1937.

————, *Normality and Pathology in Childhood: Assessments of Development*. New York, International Universities Press, Inc., 1965.

Freud, Sigmund, *Beyond the Pleasure Principle*, in *Complete Psychological Works*, standard ed. (London, The Hogarth Press, 1966), Vol. XVIII.

————, *Civilization and Its Discontents*, in *Complete Psychological Works*, standard ed. (London, The Hogarth Press, 1966), Vol. XXI.

————; *The Ego and the Id*, in *Complete Psychological Works*, standard ed. (London, The Hogarth Press, 1966), Vol. XIX.

————, *A General Introduction to Psychoanalysis*. New York, Liveright Publishing Corporation, 1935.

————, *Moses and Monotheism*, in *Complete Psychological Works*, standard ed. (London, The Hogarth Press, 1966). Vol. XXIII.

————, *New Introductory Lectures on Psychoanalysis*, in *Complete Psychological Works*, standard ed. (London, The Hogarth Press, 1966), Vol. XXII.

————, *On Narcissism: An Introduction*, in *Complete Psychological Works*, standard ed. (London, The Hogarth Press, 1966), Vol. XIV.

————, *The Psychology of Love*, in *Complete Psychological Works*, standard ed. (London, The Hogarth Press, 1966), Vol. XI.

————, *The Psychopathology of Everyday Life*, in *Complete Psychological Works*, standard ed. (London, The Hogarth Press, 1966), Vol. VI.

————, *Three Essays on Sexuality*, in *Complete Psychological Works*, standard ed. (London, The Hogarth Press, 1966), Vol. VII.

————, *Totem and Taboo*, in *Complete Psychological Works*, standard ed. (London, The Hogarth Press, 1966), Vol. XIII.

Fromm, Erich, *Beyond the Chains of Illusion*. New York, Simon and Schuster, Inc., 1962.

————, *Escape From Freedom*. New York, Avon, 1965.

————, *The Revolution of Hope*. New York, Bantam Books, Inc., 1968.

Fuller, R. Buckminster, *Ideas and Integrities*. Toronto, Collier, 1969.

————, *Utopia Versus Oblivion*. New York, Bantam Books, Inc., 1969.

Galbraith, John K., *The Affluent Society*. Boston, Houghton, 1958.

————, *The New Industrial State*. New York, Signet, 1968.

Gamow, George, *The Creation of the Universe*. New York, Compass, 1960.

————, *The Moon*. New York, H. Schuman, 1953.

Garn, Stanley, ed., *Culture and the Direction of Human Evolution*. Detroit, Wayne State Press, 1964.

Gesell, Arnold, *The First Five Years of Life*. New York and London, Harper & Brothers, 1940.

Ghiselin, Brewster, ed., *The Creative Process*. Berkeley and Los Angeles, University of California Press, 1954.

Goethe, Johann Wolfgang von, *Faust*, trans. by Walter Kaufman. Garden City, N.Y., Doubleday & Company, Inc., 1961.

————, *Faust*, trans. by J. F. L. Raschen. Ithaca, N.Y., The Thrift Press, 1949.

Graves, Robert, *The Greek Myths*. Baltimore, Penguin Books, Inc., 1955.

————, *The White Goddess*. New York, Vintage, 1958.

Gunther, John, *Procession*. New York, Harper & Row, 1965.

Hall, E. T., *The Silent Language*. New York, Fawcett, 1969.

Hall, G. Stanley, *Youth*. New York, D. Appleton and Co., 1909.

Hallmundsson, Hallberg, ed., *An Anthology of Scandinavian Literature*. New York, Collier Books, 1965.

Harburg, E. Y., and Saidy, Fred, *Finian's Rainbow*. New York, Random House, Inc., 1947.

Harlow, Harry F., and Woolsey, Clinton N., eds., *Basis of Behavior*. Madison, University of Wisconsin Press, 1958.

Hartmann, Heinz, *Ego Psychology and the Problem of Adaptation*. New York, International Universities Press, Inc., 1958.

Hastings, James, ed., *Encyclopedia of Religion and Ethics*. New York, Charles Scribner's Sons, 1926.

Hatterer, Lawrence, *The Artist in Society*. New York, Grove Press, Inc., 1965.

Hausner, Gideon, *Justice in Jerusalem*. New York, Harper and Row, 1966.

Hayakawa, Samuel I., *Language in Action*, 2d ed. New York, Harcourt, Brace, & World, Inc., 1964.

Heath, R. G., ed., *The Role of Pleasure in Behavior*. New York and Evanston, Ill., Harper & Row, 1964.

Hegner, Robert, and Stiles, Karl, *College Biology*, 7th ed. New York, The Macmillan Company, 1959.

Heilbroner, Robert, *The Future as History*. New York, Grove Press, Inc., 1961.

———, *The Limits of American Capitalism*. New York, Harper Torchbooks, 1966.

Heller, Joseph, *Catch-22*. New York, The Modern Library, Inc., 1966.

Henri, Robert, *The Art Spirit*, 5th ed. Philadelphia, G. B. Lippincott, 1930.

Henry, Jules, *Culture Against Man*. New York, Grosset & Dunlap, Inc., 1954.

Hilton-Simpson, Melville, *Land and People of the Kasai*. London, Constable and Company, Ltd., 1911.

Hobhouse, Leonard, *Social Evolution and Political Theory*. New York, Columbia University Press, 1922.

Hofstadter, Richard, *Social Darwinism in American Thought*. Boston, Beacon, 1955.

Hooten, Earnest, *Man's Poor Relations*. Garden City, N.Y., Doubleday, Doran & Co., Inc., 1942.

Howell, F. Clark, *Early Man*. New York, Time-Life, 1965. Rev. ed., 1968.

Hoyle, Fred, *Astronomy*. New York, Doubleday & Company, Inc., 1962.

Huizinga, Johann, *Homo Ludens*. Boston, Beacon, 1955.

Hunt, Morton, *The Natural History of Love*. New York, Minerva Press, 1967.

Huxley, Aldous, *Brave New World*. New York, Bantam Books, Inc., 1958.

The Institute for Social Research, *The Effect of Unemployment upon the Status of the Man in 59 Families*. New York, Dryden Press, n.d.

Jacobs, Lewis, *The Rise of the American Film*. New York, Columbia Teacher's College Press, 1968.

Jay, Anthony, *Management and Machiavelli*. New York, Bantam Books, Inc., 1969.

Jefferson, Thomas, *The Writings of Thomas Jefferson*, Andrew Lipscomb, ed. Washington, D.C., The Thomas Jefferson Memorial Association, 1905.

Jones, Ernest, *Freud*. 3 vols. New York, Basic Books, Inc., 1953.

———, *Nightmares, Witches, and Devils*. New York, W. W. Norton & Company, Inc., 1931.

Jones, Gwyn, *Atoms and the Universe*. London, Eyre and Spottiswoode, 1956.

Jordan, David Starr, *War and the Breed*. Boston, Beacon, 1915.

Jordan, Winthrop, *White Over Black*. Chapel Hill, N.C., University of North Carolina Press, 1968.

Josephson, Matthew, *The Robber Barons*. New York, Harcourt, Brace & World, Inc., 1962.

Jungk, Robert, and Galtung, Johan, eds., *Mankind 2000*. Oslo and London, Universitetsforlaget and Allen and Unwin, 1969.

Kahn, Herman, and Weiner, Anthony J., *The Year 2000*. New York, The Macmillan Company, 1967.

Kardiner, Abraham, *The Individual and His Society: The Psychodynamics of Primitive Social Organizations*. New York, Columbia University Press, 1939.

Karr, Alphonse, *En Fumant*. Paris, Lévy, 1861.

Keith, Sir Arthur, *Concerning Man's Origin*. New York, G. P. Putnam's Sons, 1928.

Kerr, Walter, *The Decline of Pleasure*. New York, Simon and Schuster, Inc., 1962.

Kierkegaard, Søren, *Concluding Unscientific Postscript*, trans. by David Swenson and Walter Lowrie. Princeton, Princeton University Press, 1941.

Kinsey, A. C., Pomeroy, W. B., Martin, C. E., and Gebhard, P. H., *Sexual Behavior in the Human Female*. Philadelphia, W. B. Saunders Company, 1953.

——, *Sexual Behavior in the Human Male*. Philadelphia, W. B. Saunders Company, 1948.

Kittredge, George, *Witchcraft in Old and New England*. Cambridge, Mass., Harvard University Press, 1929.

Koestler, Arthur, *The Act of Creation*. New York, Dell Books, 1967.

——, *Darkness at Noon*. New York, Signet, 1959.

——, *The Ghost in the Machine*. London, Hutchinson & Co. (Publishers) Ltd., 1967.

——, *The Sleepwalkers*. New York, Grosset & Dunlap, Inc., 1963.

Kornhauser, William, *The Politics of Mass Society*, New York, The Free Press, 1959.

Korzybski, Alfred, *Science and Sanity*. Lakeville, Conn., International Non-Aristotelian Library Publishing Co., 1962.

Krafft-Ebbing, Richard von, *Psychopathia Sexualis*. Evanston, Ill., Greenleaf, 1965.

Kris, Ernst, *Psychoanalytic Explorations in Art*. New York, Schocken Brothers, 1952.

Kropotkin, Petr, *Mutual Aid: A Factor of Evolution*. Boston, Extending Horizons Books, 1955.

Kuhn, Thomas S., *The Structure of Scientific Revolutions*. Chicago, University of Chicago Press, 1962.

Langer, William, *An Encyclopedia of World History*. Boston, Houghton Mifflin Company, 1968.

Lapp, Ralph, *The Weapons Culture*. New York, W. W. Norton & Company, Inc., 1968.

Lawick-Goodall, Jane, *My Friends the Wild Chimpanzees*. Washington, D.C., The National Geographic Society, 1967.

Leach, Marie, *The Beginning: Creation Myths Around the World*. New York, Funk & Wagnalls Company, Inc., 1956.

Leary, Timothy, *The Politics of Ecstasy.* New York, G. P. Putnam's Sons, 1968.

Lennon, Florence, *Victoria Through the Looking-Glass.* New York, Simon and Schuster, Inc., 1945.

Levy, Robert, *The Organization of Tahitian Experience.* In preparation.

Lewis, J., and Powers, B., *Naked Ape or Homo Sapiens.* New York, Humanities Press, 1969.

Ley, Willy, *Watchers of the Skies.* New York, The Viking Press, Inc., 1963.

Lincoln, Abraham, *Abraham Lincoln: His Speeches and Writings,* Roy Basler, ed. Cleveland and New York, The World Publishing Company, 1946.

Linton, Ralph, *The Study of Man.* New York, Appleton-Century-Crofts, 1936.

Lockwood, Douglas, *I, the Aboriginal.* Adelaide, Australia, Rigby, Ltd., 1962.

Lorenz, Konrad, *On Aggression,* trans. by Marjorie Kerr Wilson. New York, Bantam Books, Inc., 1967.

———, *Studies in Animal and Human Behavior,* Vol. I, trans. by Robert Martin. London, Methuen & Co., Ltd., 1970.

Lumsdaine, A. A., and Glaser, R., eds., *Teaching Machines and Programmed Learning.* Washington, D.C., Department of Audio-Visual Instruction, National Education Association, 1960.

Lundberg, Ferdinand, *The Rich and the Super-Rich.* New York, Lyle Stuart, Inc., 1968.

Lynes, Russell, *The Tastemakers.* New York, Grosset & Dunlap, Inc., 1964.

McClellan, David, *The Achieving Society.* New York, The Free Press, 1967.

McLuhan, H. Marshall, *The Gutenberg Galaxy.* Toronto, University of Toronto Press, 1965.

———, *The Medium Is the Massage.* New York, Bantam Books, Inc., 1967.

———, *Understanding Media.* New York, McGraw-Hill, Inc., 1965.

Maier, Norman, *Psychology in Industry,* 3d ed. Boston, Houghton Mifflin Company, 1965.

Marcuse, Herbert, *Eros and Civilization.* New York, Vintage, 1955.

———, *An Essay on Liberation.* Boston, Beacon, 1969.

———, *Five Lectures.* Boston, Beacon, 1970.

———, *One-Dimensional Man.* Boston, Beacon, 1964.

Marquand, John P., *The Late George Apley.* New York, The Modern Library, Inc., 1940.

The Marshall Cavendish Encyclopedia of the Human Mind and Body. London, Marshall Cavendish, 1969.

Martin, L. C., ed., *The Poetical Works of Robert Herrick.* Oxford, The Clarendon Press, 1956.

Martindale, Don, *The Nature and Types of Sociological Theory.* Boston, Houghton Mifflin Company, 1960.

Marx, Karl, *Capital.* 3 vols. Chicago, Charles H. Kerr Co., 1906.

———, *The Economic and Philosophical Manuscripts of 1844,* Dirk Struik, ed. New York, International Publishers, 1964.

Masters, William H., and Johnson, Virginia, *Human Sexual Inadequacy.* Boston, Little, Brown and Company, 1970.

————, *Human Sexual Response*. Boston, Little, Brown and Company, 1966.

Mead, Margaret, *Male and Female*. New York, William Morrow and Company, Inc., 1949.

Mencken, H. L., ed., *A Mencken Chrestomathy*. New York, Alfred A. Knopf, Inc., 1949.

Mendel, Werner, ed., *A Celebration of Laughter*. Los Angeles, Mara Books, 1970.

Meryman, Harold, *Cryobiology*. New York, Academic Press, Inc., 1966.

Meyer, Donald, *The Positive Thinkers*. New York, Anchor, 1966.

Mighels, Ella, *Fairy Tale of the White Man Told From the Gates of Sunset*. San Francisco, Pacific Publication Co., 1915.

Miller, Arthur, *The Crucible*. New York, Bantam Books, Inc., 1959.

Mills, C. Wright, *The Power Elite*. New York, Oxford University Press, Inc., 1959.

————, *The Sociological Imagination*. New York, Oxford University Press, Inc., 1959.

Milne, Lorus and Margery, *Patterns of Survival*. Englewood Cliffs, N.J., Prentice-Hall, Inc., 1967.

Milton, John, *The Poetical Works of John Milton,* with introductions by David Masson. London, Macmillan and Company, Ltd., 1929.

Montagu, Ashley, *Anthropology and Human Nature*. New York, McGraw-Hill, Inc., 1957.

————, *The Biosocial Nature of Man*. New York, Grove Press, Inc., 1956.

————, *The Direction of Human Development,* rev. ed. New York, Hawthorn Books, Inc., 1970.

————, *The Human Revolution*. New York, Bantam Books, Inc., 1967.

————, ed., *Man and Aggression*. New York, Oxford University Press, Inc., 1968.

————, *Man's Most Dangerous Myth: The Fallacy of Race,* 3rd ed., rev. and enlgd. New York, Harper & Brothers, 1952.

————, *Touching: The Human Function of the Skin*. New York, Columbia University Press, 1971.

Moore, Francis, *Give and Take: The Development of Tissue Transplants*. Philadelphia, W. B. Saunders Company, 1964.

Moore, Ruth, *Evolution*. New York, Time-Life, 1962. Rev. ed., 1968.

Moorehead, Alan, *The Fatal Impact*. New York, Harper & Row, 1966.

Morgan, Douglas, *Love: Plato, the Bible, and Freud*. Englewood Cliffs, N.J., Prentice-Hall, Inc., 1964.

Morris, Desmond, *The Naked Ape*. New York, McGraw-Hill, Inc., 1967.

Mumford, Lewis, *The Myth of the Machine*. New York, Harcourt, Brace & World, Inc., 1967.

Munn, Norman, *Handbook of Psychological Research on the Rat*. Boston, Houghton Mifflin Company, 1950.

Munsterberg, W., and Esman, Aaron, eds., *New Psychoanalytic Study of Society*. New York, International Universities Press. In press.

Murray, Sir James, *The Oxford English Dictionary: A New English Dictionary on Historical Principles.* Oxford, Clarendon Press, 1933.

Murray, Margaret, *The Witch Cult in Western Europe.* Oxford, Clarendon Press, 1921.

Myers, Gustavus, *History of the Great American Fortunes.* New York, The Modern Library, Inc., 1936.

Nash, Jay, *Philosophy of Recreation and Leisure.* St. Louis, C. V. Mosby, 1953.

National Academy of Sciences, *Weather and Control Modification.* Washington, D.C., National Research Council, 1966.

New Developments in High School Science Teaching. Washington, D.C., National Science Teachers Association, 1960.

1970 New York Times Encyclopedic Almanac. New York, New York Times, 1969.

Obradovic, Josip, *Participacije i motivaticije u radničkon samoprauljanju obzirom na technološki nivo proizvodnje.* Zagreb, n.p., 1967.

O'Hara, John, *Ten North Frederick.* New York, Random House, Inc., 1955.

O'Neill, Eugene, *The Hairy Ape,* in *Plays* (New York, Random House, Inc., 1955), Vol. III.

Orwell, George, *Animal Farm.* New York, Signet, 1956.

———, *1984.* New York, Signet, 1961.

Packard, Vance, *The Hidden Persuaders.* New York, David McKay Co., 1957.

———, *The Waste Makers.* New York, David McKay Co., 1960.

Pearlman, Moshe, *The Capture and Trial of Adolf Eichmann.* London, George Weidenfeld and Nicolson, Ltd., 1963.

Peary, Robert, *Secrets of Polar Travel.* New York, The Century Co., 1917.

Penfield, Wilder, and Roberts, Lamar, *Speech and Brain-Mechanisms.* Princeton, Princeton University Press, 1959.

Petronius Arbiter, *The Satyricon,* trans. by William Arrowsmith. Ann Arbor, University of Michigan Press, 1959.

Pfeiffer, John, *The Cell.* New York, Time-Life, 1964.

Piaget, Jean, *Play, Dreams and Imitation in Childhood,* trans. by C. Gattegno and F. M. Hodgson. New York, W. W. Norton & Company, Inc., 1962.

Piel, Gerald, *Science in the Cause of Man.* New York, Alfred A. Knopf, Inc., 1962.

Piers, Gerhardt, *Shame and Guilt.* Springfield, Ill., Charles C Thomas, 1953.

Polanyi, Karl, *The Great Transformation.* Boston, Beacon, 1957.

Prescott, William, *History of the Conquest of Mexico.* New York, The Modern Library, Inc., 1936.

Prosser, W. L., *Law of Torts,* 3d ed. St. Paul, Minn., West, 1964.

Quiller-Couch, Sir Arthur, ed., *The Oxford Book of English Verse.* Oxford, The Clarendon Press, 1939.

Ramsaye, Terry, *A Million and One Nights.* New York, Simon and Schuster, Inc., 1964.

Ratcliffe, James, ed., *The Good Samaritan and the Law.* New York, Doubleday & Company, Inc., 1966.

Reynolds, Vernon, *The Apes.* New York, E. P. Dutton & Co., Inc., 1967.

Reisman, David, *Individualism Reconsidered and Other Essays*. Glencoe, Ill., The Free Press, 1954.

Rimmer, Robert, *The Harrad Experiment*. New York, Bantam Books, Inc., 1967.

———, *The Harrad Letters*. New York, Signet, 1969.

———, *Proposition 31*. New York, Signet, 1969.

Robinson, F. N., ed., *The Works of Geoffrey Chaucer*, 2d ed. Boston, Houghton Mifflin Company, 1961.

Robinson, James Harvey, *The Mind in the Making*. New York, Harper & Row, 1950.

Róheim, Géza, *The Origin and Function of Culture*. New York, Nervous and Mental Monographs, 1943.

———, ed., *Psychoanalysis and the Social Sciences*, Vol. I. New York, International Universities Press, Inc., 1947.

Romer, Alfred, *Vertebrate Paleontology*, 2d ed. Chicago, University of Chicago Press, 1945.

Rosenthal, Raymond, ed., *McLuhan: Pro and Con*. New York, Funk and Wagnalls, 1968. Pp. 106–124.

Ruch, Theodore, and Fulton, John, eds., *Howell's Medical Physiology and Biophysics*, 18th ed. Philadelphia, W. B. Saunders Company, 1960.

Ruesch, Hans, *Top of the World*. New York, Harper & Brothers, 1944.

Sagan, Carl, and Leonard, Jonathan, *The Planets*, rev. ed. New York, Time-Life, 1968.

Sampson, Ronald, *The Psychology of Power*. New York, Vintage, 1968.

Schramm, Wilbur, Lyle, Jack, and Parker, Edwin, *Television in the Lives of Our Children*. Palo Alto, Stanford University Press, 1961.

Schultz, Adolph, *The Primates.* New York, Universe Press, 1969.

Scott, J. P., *Aggression*. Chicago, University of Chicago Press, 1958.

Seidenberg, Roderick, *Post-Historic Man*. Boston, Beacon, 1957.

Shulman, Irving, *Harlow*. New York, Dell Books, 1964.

Simpson, George Gaylord, Pitterdreigh, Colin, and Tiffany, Lewis, *Life: An Introduction to Biology*. New York, Harcourt, Brace, and World, Inc., 1957.

Skornia, Harry, *Television and Society.* New York, McGraw-Hill, Inc., 1965.

Smelser, Neil, ed., *Sociology: An Introduction*. New York and London, John Wiley & Sons, Inc., 1967.

Smith, Homer, *Man and His Gods*. New York, Grosset & Dunlap, Inc., 1957.

Smith, J. C., and De Selincourt, E., eds., *Spenser: Poetical Works*. London, Oxford University Press, 1965.

Sonneborn, T. M., ed., *The Control of Human Heredity and Evolution*. New York, The Macmillan Company, 1965.

Spector, William, ed., *Handbook of Biological Data*. Philadelphia, W. B. Saunders Company, 1956.

Spiro, Melford, *Children of the Kibbutz*. Cambridge, Mass., Harvard University Press, 1958.

Spitz, René, *The First Year of Life*. New York, International Universities Press, Inc., 1965.

Srole, Leo, and others, *Mental Health in the Metropolis: The Midtown Manhattan Study.* New York, McGraw-Hill, Inc., 1962.

Stearn, Gerald, ed., *McLuhan Hot and Cool.* New York, Dial Press, 1967.

Steinberg, S. H., and Paxton, John, eds., *The Statesman's Yearbook 1969–1970.* London, Macmillan and Co., Ltd., 1969.

Stephenson, William, *The Play Theory of Mass Communication.* Chicago, University of Chicago Press, 1967.

Stevenson, Harold, ed., *Child Psychology.* Chicago, University of Chicago Press, 1963.

Storer, Tracy, *General Zoology.* New York and London, McGraw-Hill, Inc., 1943.

Storr, Anthony, *Human Aggression.* New York, Atheneum Publishers, 1968.

Sunderman, F. W., and Boerner, Frederick, *Normal Values in Clinical Medicine.* Philadelphia, W. B. Saunders Company, 1949.

Suttie, Ian, *The Origins of Love and Hate.* London, Penguin, 1960.

Taylor, Frederick, *The Principles of Scientific Management.* New York and London, Harper & Brothers, 1919.

Teilhard de Chardin, Pierre, *The Future of Man.* New York and Evanston, Ill., Harper & Row, 1964.

———, *The Phenomenon of Man.* New York, Harper & Row, 1961.

Theobald, Robert, ed., *The Guaranteed Income.* Garden City, New York, Doubleday & Company, Inc., 1966.

———, *The Rich and the Poor.* New York, C. N. Potter, 1960.

Thorpe, W. H., *Learning and Instinct in Animals,* 2d ed. London, Hazell Watson and Ulney, Ltd., 1963.

Tillotson, Geoffrey, ed., *The Poems of Alexander Pope,* Vol. II. London, Methuen & Co., Ltd., 1954.

Tinbergen, Niko, *Animal Behavior.* New York, Time-Life, 1965.

Toffler, Alvin, *Future Shock.* New York, Random House, 1970.

Toynbee, Arnold, *A Study of History,* D. C. Summerville, ed. 2 vols. New York, Dell Books, 1965.

U.S. Bureau of the Census, *Historical Statistics of the U.S. From Colonial Times.* Washington, D.C., 1960.

———, *Statistical Abstract of the United States, 1970.* Washington, D.C., 1970.

U.S. Department of the Army, *The Law of Land Warfare.* Manual No. 27–10, Washington, D.C., July 18, 1956.

Vogel, Ezra, and Bell, Norman, eds., *A Modern Introduction to the Family.* New York, Free Press, 1968.

Waddington, C. W., *Principles of Embryology.* London, Allen and Unwin, 1956.

Ward, Barbara, *Spaceship Earth.* New York, Columbia University Press, 1966.

Watts, Alan, *Psychotherapy East and West.* New York, Pantheon, 1961.

———, *The Two Hands of God.* New York, George Braziller, 1963.

Webster's Third New International Dictionary. 3 vols. Chicago, Encyclopaedia Britannica, 1966.

Weiner, Norbert, *The Human Uses of Human Beings.* New York, Avon, 1967.

Wells, H. G., *The Outline of History*. Garden City, N.Y., Garden City Books, 1961.

White, Theodore, *The Making of the President 1968*. New York, Atheneum Publishers, 1969.

Whyte, Lancelot Law, *The Next Development in Man*. New York, Henry Holt and Co., 1948.

Wilcox, Ruth, *The Mode in Costume*. New York, Charles Scribner's Sons, 1942.

Williams, Margery, *The Velveteen Rabbit*. New York, Doubleday & Company, Inc., 1958.

Willier, Benjamin, Weiss, Paul, and Hamburger, Viktor, eds., *Analysis of Development*. Philadelphia, W. B. Saunders Company, 1955.

Wilson, John, *The Mind*. New York, Time-Life, 1964.

Winspear, Allan, *The Genesis of Plato's Thought*, 2d ed., rev. New York, S. A. Russell, 1956.

Wolfe, Tom, *The Electric Kool-Aid Acid Test*. New York, Bantam Books, Inc., 1969.

Wolfenstein, E. Victor, *The Revolutionary Personality*. Princeton, Princeton University Press, 1967.

Wolpe, Joseph, and Lazarus, Arnold, *Behavior Therapy Techniques: A Guide to the Treatment of Neuroses*. New York, Pergamon Press, Inc., 1966.

Wolstenholme, Gordon, ed., *Man and His Future*. Boston, Little, Brown and Company, 1963.

Wordsworth, Robert, and Schlosburg, Harold, *Experimental Psychology*. New York, Henry Holt, 1960.

World's Great Classics. London and New York, The Colonial Press, 1901.

Wright, Quincy, *A Study of War*, 2d ed. Chicago, University of Chicago Press, 1964.

Yablonski, Lewis, *The Tunnel Back*. New York, The Macmillan Company, 1965.

Zuckerman, Solly, *The Social Life of Monkeys and Apes*. New York, Harcourt, Brace & Company, 1932.

II. ARTICLES, MONOGRAPHS, FILMS, ETC.

Alexander, Franz, "A Contribution to the Theory of Play," *Psychoanalytic Quarterly* (1958), pp. 175–193.

———, "Neurosis and Creativity," *American Journal of Psychoanalysis* (1964), pp. 116–130.

Amarose, Anthony, Wallingford, Arthur, and Plotz, E. Jurgen, "Prediction of Fetal Sex from Cytologic Examination of Amniotic Fluid," *New England Journal of Medicine* (September 29, 1966), pp. 715–717.

Asdell, S. A., "Gestation Period," *Encyclopaedia Britannica* (Chicago, William Benton, 1967), Vol. 10, pp. 372–373.

Baker, Nome, Boolootian, Richard, and Dutton, Wilbur, "An Experience in Conducting Seminars and Laboratory Seminars in Biochemistry, Zoology, and Physiology for Gifted Children," *Bioscience* (March, 1964), pp. 24–27.

Bandura, Albert, Ross, Dorothea, and Ross, Sheila, "Imitation of Film-Mediated Aggressive Models," *Journal of Abnormal and Social Psychology* (January, 1963), pp. 3–11.

Barron, Frank, Jarvik, Murray, and Bunnell, Sterling, "The Hallucinogenic Drugs," *Scientific American* (April, 1964), pp. 29–37.

Batt, John, "They Shoot Horses, Don't They?: An Essay on the Scotoma of One-Eyed Kings," *UCLA Law Review* (February, 1968), pp. 510–550.

Bayer, Ann, "Beginning Again in the Middle," *Life* (June 12, 1970), pp. 50–57.

Bayley, Nancy, Livson, Norman, and Cameron, James, "Infant Vocalizations and Their Relationship to Mature Intelligence," *Science* (July 21, 1967), pp. 331–333.

Belazs, Nandor, "Relativity," *Encyclopaedia Britannica* (Chicago, William Benton, 1967), Vol. 19, pp. 95–102.

Bergman, Ingmar, director, *The Virgin Spring*. Film, Sweden, 1960.

Berkowitz, Leonard, "The Effects of Learning Violence," *Scientific American* (February, 1964), pp. 35–41.

Berne, Eric, "The Mythology of Dark and Fair: Psychiatric Use of Folklore," *Journal of American Folklore* (January, 1959), pp. 1–13.

Bills, Arthur, "Fatigue," *Encyclopaedia Britannica* (Chicago, William Benton, 1967), Vol. 9, pp. 112–113.

Bovell, Gilbert Balfour, "Psychological Considerations of Color Conflicts among Negroes," *Psychoanalytic Review* (October, 1943), pp. 447–459.

Bronowski, J., "The Reach of Imagination," *Annual Proceedings of the American Academy of Arts and Letters and the National Institute of Arts and Letters* (1967), 2d ser., No. 17, pp. 31–42.

Bronowski, J., and Bellugi, Ursula, "Language, Name, and Concept," *Science* (May 8, 1970), pp. 669–673.

Calhoun, John B., "Population Density and Social Pathology," *Scientific American* (February, 1962), pp. 139–148.

Carlson, Elof, "The Inevitability of Genetic Control for Human Survival." Unpublished paper, Department of Zoology, University of California, Los Angeles, 1966.

Chamberlain, Neil, "Retooling the Mind," Leaflet No. 14, American Alumni Council, n.d.

Chaplin, Charles, director, *Modern Times*. Film, United States, 1936.

Cohn, Roy, "Transplantation in Animals," *Stanford Today* (Winter, 1967), p. 10.

Colby, Kenneth, Gilbert, John P., and Watt, James, "A Computer Method of Psychotherapy: Preliminary Communication," *Journal of Nervous and Mental Disease* (1966), pp. 148–152.

Collais, Nicholas, "Aggressive Behavior Among Vertebrate Animals," *Physiological Zoology* (January, 1944), pp. 83–123.

Constantine, Larry and Jean, "Where Is Marriage Going?" *The Futurist* (April, 1970), pp. 44–46.

Cutler, Ann, "The Persistent Russian," *Esquire* (May, 1965), pp. 66–67 and 150–153.

Dart, Raymond, "The Predatory Transition from Ape to Man," *International Anthropological and Linguistic Review* (1953), pp. 201–208.

Dempsey, Richard, "Reducing Educational Pressures," *Science* (September 8, 1967), p. 117.

DiCara, Leo, "Learning in the Autonomic Nervous System," *Scientific American* (January, 1970), pp. 31–39.

Dunlap, Knight, "Are There Any Instincts?" *Journal of Abnormal and Social Psychology* (December, 1919), pp. 307–311.

Essman, W. B., and Lehrer, G. M., "Facilitation of Maze Performances by 'RNA Extracts' from Maze-Trained Mice," *Federation Proceedings*, Federation of American Societies for Experimental Biology, Physiology Sessions (March-April, 1967), p. 263.

Ettinger, Robert C. W., "Lasting Indefinitely," *Esquire* (May, 1965), pp. 64–65.

Fellini, Federico, director, *La Dolce Vita*. Film, Italy, 1960.

Fingarette, Herbert, "Eros and Utopia," *Review of Metaphysics* (June, 1957), pp. 660–665.

Fisher, Alan, "Chemical Stimulation of the Brain," *Scientific American* (June, 1964), pp. 60–68.

Fleming, Victor, director, *The Wizard of Oz*. Film, United States, 1939.

Folk, Robert, "Spherical Urine in Birds: Petrography," *Science* (December 19, 1969), pp. 1516–1518.

Frank, Stanley, "Brunette Today, Blonde Tomorrow," *Saturday Evening Post* (September 9, 1961), pp. 20–21.

Freedman, Lawrence, "Truth Drugs," *Scientific American* (March, 1960), pp. 145–155.

French, J. D., "The Reticular Formation," *Scientific American* (May, 1957), pp. 54–60.

Freud, Sigmund, "Analysis of a Phobia in a Five-Year-Old Boy," in *Complete Psychological Works*, standard ed. (London, The Hogarth Press, 1966), Vol. X, pp. 3–149.

———, "Dostoevsky and Parricide," in *Complete Psychological Works*, standard ed. (London, The Hogarth Press, 1966), Vol. XXI, pp. 177–194.

———, "Memorandum on the Electrical Treatment of War Neurotics," in *Complete Psychological Works*, standard ed. (London, The Hogarth Press, 1966), Vol. XVII, pp. 211–215.

Gardner, A. R. and B. T., "Teaching Language to a Chimpanzee," *Science* (August 15, 1969), pp. 664–672.

Golding, Martin, "Ethical Issues in Biological Engineering," *UCLA Law Review* (February, 1968), pp. 443–479.

Gorney, Roderic, "Interpersonal Intensity, Competition, and Synergy: Determinants of Achievement, Aggression, and Mental Illness," *The American Journal of Psychiatry* (October, 1971), pp. 436–445.

———, "The New Biology and the Future of Man," *UCLA Law Review* (February, 1968), pp. 273–356.

———, "Of Divers Things: Preliminary Note on the Dynamics of Scuba Diving," *Psychoanalytic Forum* (1966), pp. 266–269.

———, "Work and Love Revisited," *Proceedings of the Fourth World Congress of Psychiatry* (1966), pp. 1439–1441.

Gorney, Roderic, Janowsky, David, and Kelley, Bret, "The Curse—Vicissitudes and Variations of the Female Fertility Cycle" (Part II), *Psychosomatics* (September–October, 1966), pp. 283–287.

Goro, Fritz, photographer, "Control of Life: Exploration of Prenativity," *Life* (September 10, 1965), pp. 59–79.

Gouldner, Helen, "Children of the Laboratory," *Transaction* (April, 1967), pp. 13–19.

Grad, Frank P., "Legislative Responses to the New Biology: Limits and Possibilities," *UCLA Law Review* (February, 1968), pp. 480–509.

Grotjahn, Martin, "The New Technology and Our Ageless Unconscious," *Psychoanalytic Forum* (1966), pp. 8–18.

Gurdon, J. B., and Vehlinger, V., " 'Fertile' Intestine Nuclei," *Nature* (June 18, 1966), pp. 1240–1241.

Harburg, E. Y. (Yip), and Rose, Billy, "It's Only a Paper Moon," music by Harold Arlen. © Copyright Anne-Rachel Music Corporation, Harms, Inc., 1933.

Harlow, Harry, "Basic Social Capacity of Primates," *Human Biology* (February, 1959), pp. 40–53.

Harlow, Harry and Margaret, "Social Deprivation in Monkeys," *Scientific American* (November, 1962), pp. 136–146.

———, "A Study of Animal Affection," *Natural History* (December, 1961), pp. 48–55.

Hecht, Max K., "Amphibia," *Encyclopaedia Britannica* (Chicago, William Benton, 1967), Vol. 1, pp. 813–820.

Heilbroner, Robert, "Futurology," *New York Review of Books* (September 26, 1968), pp. 53–56.

Heller, Agnes, "On the Future of Relations Between the Sexes," *International Social Science Journal*, UNESCO, No. 4 (1969), pp. 535–544.

Henderson, Curtis, and Ettinger, Robert C. W., "Cryonic Suspension and the Law," *UCLA Law Review* (February, 1968), pp. 414–419.

Herron, Woodburn, "The Pathology of Boredom," *Scientific American* (January, 1957), pp. 52–56.

Hess, Eckhard, " 'Imprinting' in Animals," *Scientific American* (March, 1958), pp. 81–91.

Hoffer, Eric, "A Time of Juveniles," *Harpers* (June, 1965), pp. 15–24.

Horowitz, David, "Billion-Dollar Brains," *Ramparts* (May, 1969), pp. 36–44.

Hubbell, George, "Triple Alice," *Sewanee Review* (1940), pp. 174–196.

Humphreys, L. G., and Marcuse, F., "Factors Influencing the Susceptibility of Albino Rats to Convulsive Attacks Under Intense Auditory Stimulation," *Journal of Comparative Psychology* (1941), pp. 285–306.

Hunt, Morton, "A Neurosis Is Just a Bad Habit," *The New York Times Magazine* (June 4, 1967), pp. 38–47.

Imanishi, Kinji, "Social Behavior in Japanese Monkeys," *Psychologia* (1957), pp. 47–54.

Jacobson, Allan, Babich, Frank, Bubash, Suzanne, and Jacobson, Ann, "Differential Approach Tendencies Produced by Injection of Ribonucleic Acid from Trained Rats," *Science* (August 6, 1965), pp. 656–657.

Janowsky, David, Gorney, Roderic, Castelnuovo-Tedesco, Pietro, and Stone, Charles, "Premenstrual–Menstrual Increases in Psychiatric Hospital Admission Rates," *American Journal of Obstetrics and Gynecology* (January 15, 1968), pp. 189–191.

Janowsky, David, Gorney, Roderic, and Davis, J. M., "Premenstrual–Menstrual Emotional Upsets in Nursing Students," in preparation.

Janowsky, David, Gorney, Roderic, and Kelley, Bret, "The 'Curse'—Vicissitudes and Variations of the Female Fertility Cycle" (Part I), *Psychosomatics* (July–August, 1966), pp. 242–247.

Janowsky, David, Gorney, Roderic, and Mandell, Arnold, "Psychiatric and Ovarian-Adrenocortical Hormone Correlates of the Menstrual Cycle," *Archives of General Psychiatry* (October, 1967), pp. 459–469.

Kanzer, Mark, "Acting Out, Sublimation, and Reality Testing," *American Psychoanalytic Association Journal* (October, 1957), pp. 663–684.

Kellogg, Remington, "The History of Whales—Their Adaptation to Life in the Water, *The Quarterly Review of Biology* (March, 1928), pp. 29–76; (June, 1928), pp. 174–208.

Kirstein, George, "The Manpower Revolution," *The Nation* (February 10, 1964), pp. 140–144.

Kleitman, Nathaniel, "Patterns of Dreaming," *Scientific American* (November, 1960), pp. 82–88.

Kolff, Willem, "Today the Calf, Tomorrow the Man," *Journal of the American Medical Association* (September 28, 1963), pp. 23–24.

———, and others, "An Artificial Heart Inside the Chest," *The Journal of Thoracic and Cardiovascular Surgery* (December, 1965), pp. 792–799.

Krech, David, "In Search of the Engram," *Medical Opinion and Review* (August, 1966), pp. 20–24.

Landauer, Walter, "Aristogenics," *Science* (August 20, 1965), p. 816.

Landis, Judson T., "Marriage," *Encyclopaedia Britannica* (Chicago, William Benton, 1967), Vol. 14, pp. 926–931.

Langlois, T. H., "Sociological Succession," *Ecology* (1937), pp. 458–461.

———, "A Study of the Small-Mouth Bass, *Micropterus dolomieu* (lacepede) in Rearing Ponds in Ohio," Ohio Biological Survey, *Ohio State University Studies*, Bulletin No. 33, Vol. 6 (1936).

Lawick-Goodall, Jane, "New Discoveries Among Africa's Chimpanzees," *National Geographic* (December, 1965), pp. 802–831.

Lederberg, Joshua, "Experimental Genetics and Human Evolution," *American Naturalist* (September-October, 1966), pp. 519–531.

Lehman, Eugene, "College Math for 11-Year-Olds," *Science* (July 28, 1967), p. 367.

Levy, David, "Fingersucking and Accessory Movements in Early Infancy," *American Journal of Psychiatry* (1928), pp. 881–918.

———, "Thumb or Fingersucking From the Psychiatric Angle," *Child Development* (1937), pp. 99–101.

Levy, Robert, "Community Function of Tahitian Male Transvestitism," *Anthropological Quarterly* (1971).

———, "Ma'chi Drinking Patterns in the Society Islands," *The Journal of the Polynesian Society* (September, 1966), pp. 304–320.

———, "Personality Studies in Polynesia and Micronesia: Stability and Change," Working Paper No. 8, Honolulu, University of Hawaii Social Science Research Institute, 1969.

———, "Tahiti Observed," *The Journal of the Polynesian Society* (March, 1968), pp. 33–42.

———, "Tahitian Folk Psychotherapy," *International Mental Health Research Newsletter* 9 (Winter, 1967), pp. 12–15.

———, "Tahitian Protestantism: Personal Forms and Meanings," *Journal de la Société des Océanistes* (1969), pp. 125–136.

Lilly, J. C., and Miller, A. M., "Operant Conditioning of the Bottlenose Dolphin with Electrical Stimulation of the Brain," *Journal of Comparative Physiology and Psychology* (February, 1962), pp. 73–79.

Loomis, W. Faunsworth, "Skin Pigment Regulation of Vitamin-D Biosynthesis in Man," *Science* (August 4, 1967), pp. 501–506.

Ludwig, Arnold, Levine, Jerome, Stark, Louis, and Lazar, Robert, "A Clinical Study of LSD Treatment in Alcoholism," *American Journal of Psychiatry* (July, 1969), pp. 59–69.

Mangel, Charles, "Bobby Joins His World: Five Million Brain-Damaged Children Can Be Helped," *Look* (November 15, 1966), pp. 84–88.

Marmor, Judd, "Some Observations on Superstition in Contemporary Life," *American Journal of Orthopsychiatry* (January, 1956), pp. 119–130.

Marshall, Donald S., "Sexuality—Two Anthropological Studies: Too Much in Mangaia," *Psychology Today* (February, 1971), pp. 43–44 and 70–75.

Maslow, Abraham, "Synergy in the Society and in the Individual," *Journal of Individual Psychology* (1964), pp. 153–164.

Maslow, Abraham, and Honigmann, John, "Synergy: Some Notes of Ruth Benedict," *American Anthropologist* (April, 1970), pp. 320–333.

Mayberry, Milton, "McLuhan's Physiology." Unpublished paper prepared for the UCLA Psychology Department, March, 1969.

McConnell, James, "Memory Transfer Through Cannibalism in Planarians," *Journal of Neuropsychiatry* (August, 1962), pp. S42–S48.

Mead, Margaret, interview in the *UCLA Alumni Magazine* (Summer, 1969), p. 31.

Montagu, Ashley, "The Buttocks and Natural Selection," *Journal of the American Medical Association* (October 3, 1966), p. 51.

————, "The Sensory Influence of the Skin," *Texas Reports of Biology and Medicine* (1953), pp. 291–301.

Morse, Arthur, "Why Doesn't the U.S. Outlaw Genocide?" *Look* (March 10, 1970), p. 40.

Muller, H. J., "Artificial Transmutation of the Gene," *Science* (1927), pp. 84–87.

————, "The Production of Mutations by X-Rays," *Proceedings of the National Academy of Science* (1928), pp. 714–726.

Nadler, Henry L., "Prenatal Detection of Genetic Defects," *Journal of Pediatrics* (January, 1969), pp. 132–143.

Neumann, H. M., and Perlman, I., "Isotopic Assignments of Bismuth Isotopes Produced with High Energy Particles," *Physical Review* (May, 1950), pp. 191–198.

Novick, Julius, "The Fallacy of the Living Theatre," *The Humanist* (March-April, 1969), pp. 26–27.

Obradovic, Josip, "Participation and Work Attitudes in Yugoslavia," *Industrial Relations* (February, 1970), pp. 161–169.

Ogburn, William, *Technological Trends and National Policy, Including the Social Implications of New Inventions*. Report of the Subcommittee on Technology to the National Resources Committee. Washington, D.C., Government Printing Office, June, 1937.

Olds, James, "Pleasure Centers in the Brain," *Scientific American* (October, 1956), pp. 105–117.

Paoli, Gennaro delli, "L' adempimento di un dovere come causa di esclusione della punibilita'nel sistema penale militare," *The Military Law and Law of War Review* (Brussels, 1966), pp. 301–302.

Pilleri, G., "It's Man's Hands Not His Brain That Make Him More Advanced Than Dolphins," *Physician's Panorama* (June, 1965), pp. 25–27.

Pincus, Gregory, and Shapiro, Herbert, "The Comparative Behavior of Mammalian Eggs in Vivo and in Vitro," *Proceedings of the American Philosophical Society* (1940), pp. 631–647.

————, "Further Studies on the Parthenogenic Activation of Rabbit Eggs," *Proceedings of the National Academy of Sciences* (March, 1940), pp. 163–165.

Popovic, Pava and Vojin, "Survival of Newborn Ground Squirrels After Supercooling or Freezing," *American Journal of Physiology* (May, 1963), pp. 949–952.

Robinson, Michael, Abele, Lawrence, and Robinson, Barbara, "Attack Autotomy: A Defense Against Predators," *Science* (July 17, 1970), pp. 300–301.

Rorvik, David, "The Brave New World of the Unborn," *Look* (November 4, 1969), pp. 74–83.

Rorvik, David, with Shettles, Landrum, "You Can Choose Your Baby's Sex," *Look* (April 21, 1970), pp. 88–98.

Rosenberg, Elizabeth, "A Clinical Contribution to the Psychopathology of the

War Neuroses," *The International Journal of Psychoanalysis* (1943), pp. 32–41.

Rosenfeld, Albert, "Control of Life: The New Man—What Will He Be Like?," *Life* (October 1, 1965), pp. 94–96.

Rushler, Katherine, "Of Mice and Man," *S.K. & F. Psychiatric Reporter* (November-December, 1963), pp. 3–6.

Sanders, David, and Dukeminier, Jesse, Jr., "Medical Advance and Legal Lag: Hemodialysis and Kidney Transplantation," *UCLA Law Review* (February, 1968), pp. 357–413.

Scholander, P. F., Irving, Laurence, and Grinnell, S. W., "On the Temperature and Metabolism of the Seal During Diving," *Journal of Cellular and Comparative Physiology* (1942), pp. 67–78.

Scott, J. P., "Biology and Human Aggression," *Journal of Orthopsychiatry* (July, 1970), pp. 568–576.

————, "Critical Periods in the Development of Social Behavior in Puppies," *Psychosomatic Medicine* (1958), pp. 42–54.

SenGupta, Amarenda, Taylor, Howard, and Kolff, Willem, "An Artificial Placenta Designed to Maintain Life During Cardiorespiratory Distress," *Transactions of the American Society of Artificial Internal Organs* (1964), pp. 53–65.

Sherfey, Mary Jane, "The Evolution and Nature of Female Sexuality in Relation to Psychoanalytic Theory," *Journal of the American Psychoanalytic Association* (January, 1966), pp. 28–128.

Singer, Charles, and others, "Science, History of," *Encyclopaedia Britannica* (Chicago, William Benton, 1967), Vol. 20, pp. 7–17.

Smith, Audrey, *Biological Effects of Freezing and Supercooling.* Monograph of the Physiological Society. London, Edward Arnold, Ltd., 1961.

————, "Hamsters Cooled Below 0° Centigrade," *Proceedings of the Royal Society*, Series B, Biological Sciences (July 24, 1956), pp. 391–426.

Spitz, René, "The Smiling Response," *Genetic Psychological Monographs*, Vol. 34 (1946).

Strassman, Harvey, Thaler, Margaret, and Schein, Edgar, "A Prisoner of War Syndrome: Apathy as a Reaction to Severe Stress," *American Journal of Psychiatry* (1956), pp. 998–1003.

Stroheim, Erich von, director, *Greed.* Film, United States, 1924.

Taviss, Irene, "Futurology and the Problem of Values," *International Social Science Journal*, UNESCO, No. 4 (1969), pp. 574–584.

Taylor, Howard, Kolff, Willem, Sindelar, Paul, and Cahill, John, "Attempts to Make an 'Artificial Uterus,'" *American Journal of Obstetrics and Gynecology* (1959), pp. 1295–1300.

Tyree, Andrea, "A Study of Status, Conflict, and Suicide in Hawaii." Unpublished M. A. thesis, University of Hawaii, 1964.

Ungar, Georges, "Chemical Transfer of Learning: Its Stimulus Specificity," *Federation Proceedings*, Federation of American Societies for Experimental Biology, Physiology Sessions (March-April, 1966), p. 207.

Ungerleider, Thomas, and Fisher, Duke, "Problems of LSD[25] and Emotional Disorder," *California Medicine* (January, 1967), pp. 49–55.

Usher, Dan, *Rich and Poor Countries*. London, Institute of Economic Affairs, Eaton Paper No. 9, n.d.

Von Holst, Erich, and Von St. Paul, Ursula, "Electrically Controlled Behavior," *Scientific American* (March, 1962), pp. 50–59.

Weaver, Warren, "What a Moon Ticket Will Buy," *Saturday Review* (August 4, 1962), pp. 38–39.

Weiland, Ralph, Folk, Robert, Taylor, Jack, and Hanwi, George, "Studies of Male Hypogonadism," *Journal of Clinical Endocrinology and Metabolism* (1967), pp. 763–767.

Weiss, Eduardo, "Uber einen noch nicht beschriebene Phase der Entwicklung zur heterosexueller Liebe" ("On a Not Heretofore Described Development Towards Heterosexual Love"), *International Zeitschrift für Psychoanalyse* (1925).

Welles, Orson, director, *Citizen Kane*. Film, United States, 1941.

Whitelock, Otto V. St., editor in chief, "Freezing and Drying of Biological Materials," *Annals of the New York Academy of Sciences* (April 13, 1960), pp. 501–734.

Widenberg, Bo, director, *Elvira Madigan*. Film, Sweden, 1967.

Williams, Charles W., "Scientists Review Their Forecast for 'The Next Hundred Years,'" *The Futurist* (June, 1968), pp. 44–45.

Wolfsheimer, Gene, "The Discus Fish Yields a Secret," *National Geographic* (May, 1960), pp. 675–681.

III. UNSIGNED ARTICLES

"The Age of Man," *Time* (August 29, 1969), p. 50.

"The Brain," *MD* (July, 1963), pp. 113–119.

"Brain Extract Educates Mice by Proxy," *Medical World News* (September 8, 1967), p. 32.

"Brain Transplant in Dog Works for Three Days," *Medical World News* (April 7, 1967), p. 30.

[No title], *California Medical Association News* (February, 1966), p. 2.

"Can Pesticides Cloud the Brain?" *Medical World News* (June 2, 1967), p. 118.

"Chemical Enables Animals to Survive Lethal Radiation," *Medical World News* (September 30, 1966), p. 31.

"Control of Life," Part III, "Rebuilt People," *Life* (September 2-x, 1965), pp. 66–84A.

"Cryo-Burial Raises Scientific Heat," *Medical World News* (February 24, 1970), p. 34.

"Curtain Rises Early on Antibody Activity," *Medical World News* (April 28, 1967), p. 60.

A Dip into History, a "How To Do Better Haircoloring" pamphlet, Clairol, Inc., 1962.

"DNA and a Mouse of a Different Color," *Medical World News* (February 6, 1970), p. 24.

"The Dollar Squeeze," *Life* (August 15, 1969), pp. 20–25.

"Dolphin Gets Message, Sends One of Its Own," *Medical World News* (February 12, 1965), p. 9.

"Drug's Effects Raise Hope for a 'Memory Pill,'" *Medical World News* (January 14, 1966), pp. 24–25.

"The Emergence of Jean Piaget," *Roche Report—Frontiers of Hospital Psychiatry* (October 1, 1967), pp. 1–4.

"An Empire Built on Sex," *Life* (October 29, 1965), pp. 68–73.

"Frozen Cat Brain Revived After Six Months," *Medical World News* (December 9, 1966), p. 37.

"Good Samaritans and Liability for Medical Malpractice," *Columbia Law Review* (November, 1964), p. 1301.

"Hope for the Brain Damaged," *Roche Medical Image* (August, 1966), pp. 31–34.

"Human Ova Fertilized After Frozen Storage," *Medical World News* (March 5, 1965), p. 34.

"Internal Helium Freezing, Warming 'Promising' for Organ Preservation," *Medical World News* (January 16, 1967), p. 33.

"Is the Menopause Necessary?" *Medical World News* (June 23, 1967), p. 63.

"Making Rats Grow Old Before Their Time," *Medical World News* (May 5, 1967), p. 55.

"M.D.s, Clergy Discuss Prolonging Life," *American Medical Association News* (May 9, 1966), p. 9.

"Medical Achievements of the Year—Transplants and Immunity," *Medical World News* (January 15, 1968), p. 38.

"Medical Ethics in a Changing World," *Medical World News* (May 20, 1966), p. 66.

"Memory Transfer by a Protein Achieved," *Hospital Tribune* (January 25, 1971), p. 1.

"Programming the Body for a Ripe Old Age," *Medical World News* (February 25, 1966), p. 63.

"Progress in Longevity Since 1850," *Statistical Bulletin*, Metropolitan Life Insurance Company, July, 1963.

"The Pump Worked Beautifully," *Medical World News* (May 6, 1966), p. 37.

"Radio Signals Trigger Off Mixed Emotions," *Medical World News* (June 11, 1965), p. 32.

"Restoring Severed Limbs," *Medical World News* (March 26, 1965), p. 34.

"Rhythmic Cells Set Beats for Human Bioclock—Scientists See RNA as Conductor of Unexplained Physiologic Patterns," *Medical World News* (November 26, 1965), p. 176.

"RNA May Play an Important Role," *Medical World News* (January 21, 1966), p. 15.

"Social Environment and Brain Chemistry," *American Association for the Advancement of Science Bulletin* (November, 1966), unpaged.

"Some Psychologic Effects of Medical and Surgical Advances," *Roche Report—Frontiers of Hospital Psychiatry* (June 15, 1966), p. 1.

"Study Verifies Relation Between Brain Traits and Intelligence," *Roche Report—Frontiers of Hospital Psychiatry* (August 1, 1967), p. 1.

"A Talk With Konrad Lorenz," *New York Times Magazine* (July 25, 1970), pp. 27–30.

"Teaching Through Trance," *MD* (September, 1963), pp. 106–107.

"The Unfit: Denmark's Solution," *U.S. News and World Report* (March 7, 1966), p. 74.

"Unlocking Early Learning's Secret," *Life* (March 31, 1967), pp. 40–47.

"Weighing Plastic Heart Against Clinical Rules," *Medical World News* (April 25, 1969), pp. 6–7.

Expanded Contents

SECTION TWO: LOVE, WORK, AND PLAY REVISITED

SECTION THREE: MASTERY OF THE FUTURE

Part I. Ways to Go

Part II. The Quest for Blondness: An Example Explored

INDEX

Child raising, 300
  human cultures as natural experiments in, 148
  in Israel, 166–167
  responsibility and, 300
  in Soviet Union, 166–167
  synergy and, 166–167
  in Tahiti, 151–152, 156
  techniques, 148–149, 166–167
  values and, 149
Children
  authority versus authoritarianism and, 299–300
  belief in perfection and, 300
  creativity in, 293, 295
  imagination in, 293
  intellectual retardation in, 266
  "nonfrustration" and, 299
  raising of, 300
  security and, 300
Chimeras, 224–225
  Atwood on, 224–225
  defined, 224
  medical ethics and, 225
Chimpanzees
  clinging and, 321
  dependency in, 145
  gestation period of, 93
  infant, 323
  language and, 78, 80
  lifespan of, 93, 145
  love and, 321
  maturation of, 93
  play and, 99
  sexual maturity in, 93, 99
  weapons and, 461
  work and, 321
Chlorophyll, 40–41
Choice
  human mind and, 177
  technology and, 177
Cholinesterase, 265
Chordates, 48–49
Christianity
  agape and, 378
  law and order and, 451
  love and, 377–378
  sexual desire and, 378
Christian-Yoga Church, 452
Chromosomes, 210, 212
  damaged, 216

Chromosomes (*cont.*)
  extra, 213
  Mongoloid idiocy and, 213
Chuckchee
  ambitious striving, 159
  Benedict and, 164
  personality structure, 159–160
Cichlid fish, aggression in, 131, 144
Circulation, brain and, 262
Circulatory system, 211
Circumstances, fluidity of, 462–463
Civilization
  commodity and, 370
  division of labor and, 370
  human generations and, 569
  product as "hostile" and, 367–368
  recency of, 569, 571
  work and, 367–369
Clarke, Arthur, 424
Clinging, 91–93, 321
  to group, 89
  and identity, 89–91
  to mother, 92–93
Clones, 220–224, 272–273
  cell preservation and, 223–224
  defined, 221
  frog, 221–222
  generation gap and, 222
  genetic potential of, 224
  human, 222–224
    consequences of, 222–224
    identity and, 223
    as "organ farms," 222–223, 239, 256
Cloning, delayed, 224
Clothing, sexual temptations and, 118
Cocaine
  Freud and, 499–500
  psychological versus local anesthetic effect, 499–500
  serendipity and, 499–500
Cognitive dissonance, theory of, 409–410
  Psychic Impostor ethic and, 409–411
Color blindness, 218
Combativeness, *see* Aggression *and* Competition
Common sense, Einstein on, 173
Communication
  animal, 102

Prospectant attitude
  abundance and, 498–499
  serendipity and, 499–500
Prostitution, 402–403, 411
  blondness and, 522–523
  distorted femininity and, 445
Protection
  mutual, by big and little brother, 474–475
"Protection" agencies
  CIA, 479
  expanding human freedom and, 479
  FBI, 479
  police, 479
Protections
  cooperation with economy, 30
  submission to theology, 30
Proteus salamander, 95, 97
Pseudocloseness
  insatiability and, 386
  sadism and, 386
Psychedelic drugs
  future possibilities and, 458
  personality and, 302
  reality and, 301
Psychiatrists, work of, 303–304
Psychic alienation, from work, 365
Psychic Impostor ethic, 408–412, 415, 422
  cognitive dissonance and, 409–411
  defined, 408
  fraud and, 453
  identity erosion and, 409
  mental health and, 410
  nations and, 412
  pecuniary truth and, 408
  regression and, 413
  self-validation and, 409, 412
  television commercials and, 408–409
Psychic intimacy
  alienation and, 369, 370–371
  defined, 318
  early man and, 344–345
  Fun ethic and, 386
  gestation and, 199
  Industrial Revolution and, 362
  infant, 321–322
  loss of, 428

Psychic intimacy (*cont.*)
  love and, 199, 319, 377–388, 402–403, 414
  marriage and, 384–385
  need for study of, 562
  observed in psychoanalysis, 404–407
  play and, 199, 320, 388–390, 414
  self-esteem and, 411
  self-validation and, 319–320
  work and, 199, 319–320, 335, 362, 365–377, 414, 435, 494
  zestful self-investment and, 414, 437
Psychic nonintimacy
  infantilization and, 413
  personality deterioration and, 415
  regression and, 413
Psychoanalysis, 367n
  psychic intimacy observed in, 404–407
Psychological development, sequence of, 336–337
Psychological edibility
  infantile orality and, 433
  Playboy magazine and, 432–434
Psychological engineering, 267
Psychological identity, durable things and, 287
Psychoneurosis, self-validation, illustrated, 404–407
Psychosis, creativity and, 441
Psychosocial constellations
  love and, 342
  play and, 342
  work and, 343
Psychotherapy group, intimate revelations and, 303
Psychotic disintegration, LSD and, 458
Ptolemy, 27
Public ownership and operation, 469
Punitiveness, big brother and, 476
Puritan ethic, 150, 154, 423, 429
  abundance and, 360–364
  as adaptation, 423
  compatibility of subvalues included, 423
  component values of, 357
  decline of, 360–365
  effort-rewarded requirement of, 452

About the Author

Born in 1924, Dr. Roderic Gorney grew up in New York City and Los Angeles. After attending Antioch College and Yale University, he graduated from Stanford University, Stanford University School of Medicine, and the Southern California Psychoanalytic Institute.

After nine years of private practice of psychiatry in San Francisco, the author joined the faculty of the Department of Psychiatry at the UCLA School of Medicine. He is the director of the department's new Program on Psychosocial Adaptation and the Future. In 1971 he was a recipient of the Essay Prize of the American Psychiatric Association for essays on the theme of Aggression and Alternatives to Violence.